Norman Naval Operations in the Mediterranean

T0341477

WARFARE IN HISTORY

ISSN 1358–779X

Series editors
Matthew Bennett, Royal Military Academy, Sandhurst, UK
Anne Curry, University of Southampton, UK
Stephen Morillo, Wabash College, Crawfordsville, USA

This series aims to provide a wide-ranging and scholarly approach to military history, offering both individual studies of topics or wars, and volumes giving a selection of contemporary and later accounts of particular battles; its scope ranges from the early medieval to the early modern period.

New proposals for the series are welcomed; they should be sent to the publisher at the address below.

Boydell and Brewer Limited, PO Box 9, Woodbridge, Suffolk, IP12 3DF

Previously published titles in this series are listed at the back of this volume

Norman Naval Operations in the Mediterranean

Charles D. Stanton

THE BOYDELL PRESS

First published 2011
The Boydell Press, Woodbridge
Paperback edition 2016

ISBN 978 1 84383 624 7 hardback
ISBN 978 1 78327 138 2 paperback

The Boydell Press is an imprint of Boydell & Brewer Ltd
PO Box 9, Woodbridge, Suffolk IP12 3DF, UK
and of Boydell & Brewer Inc.
668 Mt Hope Avenue, Rochester, NY 14620–2731, USA
website: www.boydellandbrewer.com

A CIP catalogue record for this book is available
from the British Library

The publisher has no responsibility for the continued existence or accuracy of
URLs for external or third-party internet websites referred to in this book,
and does not guarantee that any content on such websites is,
or will remain, accurate or appropriate

This publication is printed on acid-free paper

Contents

Illustrations

Figures

Maps

To Kristy Suz
My Love, My Inspiration
'Face to the Wind'

Acknowledgments

The portrayal of Norman naval operations in the Mediterranean to the end of the Hauteville Dynasty has been a daunting but extremely rewarding undertaking. I owe my mentor, David Abulafia, a great debt of gratitude not only for encouraging this old navy man to take up the challenge, but also for inspiring me with the body of his work. The one overarching concept I have gleaned from him is that the Mediterranean Sea is a stage upon which no act occurs in isolation. The ripples caused by social, economic and political events on one shore wash up on another at some point in time. Two of Abulafia's works, in particular, prompted me to investigate the rise of Norman sea power in the central Mediterranean: an article entitled 'The Norman Kingdom of Africa and the Norman Expeditions to Majorca and the Muslim Mediterranean'[1] and the book *The Two Italies*.[2] Both works are seminal and neither has been superseded. This current effort is merely an extension of an exploration initiated by these two contributions more than twenty years ago.

John Pryor's research on medieval maritime technology in the Mediterranean has also proven invaluable to this study. His notion that control of the land meant control of the sea due to the limitations of galley fleets is fundamental to my thesis that the conquest of Sicily enabled the Normans to control the central Mediterranean. I am also grateful for the many suggestions he offered to improve the book. I took some but not all, thus he cannot be held accountable for any perceived errors/omissions or, indeed, any of my conclusions. For those I accept full responsibility. I am beholden to Liesbeth van Houts for her insights on Norman feudal obligations, drawing my attention to the details of Norman historiography and imbuing me with her intellectual curiosity concerning the principal personalities of the era. And no one can study the Normans of southern Italy without consulting the extensive contributions of Graham Loud on the subject. His thorough critique of my research and all-encompassing erudition on the subject of the Normans in the South helped me correct several critical misconceptions concerning Norman administrative practices. Moreover, his unpublished translations of Falco of Benevento and the charters of King William II of Sicily, which he so generously shared with me, proved invaluable. I also must offer heartfelt appreciation on behalf of all linguistically challenged

---

[1] D. Abulafia, 'The Norman Kingdom of Africa and the Norman Expeditions to Majorca and the Muslim Mediterranean', *Anglo-Norman Studies*, VII (1985), pp. 26–49.
[2] D. Abulafia, *The Two Italies: Economic Relations between the Norman Kingdom of Sicily and the Northern Communes* (Cambridge, 1977).

students of medieval history to those gifted academics like Elizabeth Jeffreys, Liesbeth Van Houts and Graham Loud who perform the meticulous translations that enable more plebeian scholars to process a larger volume of primary source material in a shorter period of time.

The Faculty of History at the University of Cambridge has my earnest thanks for generously funding a period of field research in Italy and France. Along those same lines, the Master and Fellows of my own Fitzwilliam College also deserve a share of the credit for having contributed both moral and monetary support to the endeavor. I would be remiss if I did not also praise the American Academy in Rome, which hosted me for a goodly portion of my field research in Italy and helped this neophyte researcher pry open the doors of the Biblioteca Apostolica Vaticana. Were it not for the cartographic skills of Phillip Judge, my maps would have been a confusing series of squiggly lines. The assistance of Stella Panayotova at the Fitzwilliam Museum of Cambridge and Gillian Grant of the Bodleian Library of Oxford was also invaluable.

Special thanks is owed to Boydell & Brewer for allowing me to reuse, in a reworked form, excerpts from my 2007 article in Vol. 19 of the *Haskins Society Journal* (pp. 120–136) entitled 'The Use of Naval Power in the Norman Conquest of Southern Italy and Sicily'. This paper, first presented at the annual Haskins Society Conference at Georgetown University in 2006, was the germinating seed for Chapter 1: The Conquest (827 to 1101). I am particularly grateful for the permission to reprint the map of the twelfth-century Mediterranean on page 122 of the *Journal* and my concept of a Norman-Italian warship of the eleventh century on page 128.

And, of course, I owe a great measure of gratitude to Caroline Palmer and Rohais Haughton, my editors at Boydell & Brewer, for helping me turn the manuscript into something someone may actually wish to read. Lastly but most importantly, I must recognize the encouragement provided by my long-suffering soul mate, Kristy, who was not only my muse and intellectual sounding board, but my primary emotional and financial backer for this endeavor.

Preface

A few notes about the scope of this exploration and the methodology used to conduct it may be helpful to the reader. First of all, this is not an in-depth examination of Norman naval organization and infrastructure in the Mediterranean. The sources to permit such an investigation simply do not exist. Instead, I have focused on what the sources can tell us about Norman naval operations and expansion under the House of Hauteville. What little information that can be inferred from the sources on the nature of the Norman fleets themselves, I have provided in Appendix A.

Secondly, I have adopted an essentially narrative approach to convey the results of my research, because I hold the strong conviction that the facts found can only be appreciated within the context of the wider Norman narrative. Again, this conviction is inspired by the belief that nothing happens in isolation on the great arena that is the Mediterranean. Every occurrence must be related to the events that it affects and that are affected by it. Therefore, my analysis of the facets of Norman naval power has been interwoven into a chronological history of the Normans in the Mediterranean. Accordingly, the study concentrates on political and military aspects.

Thirdly, in order to make the work more appealing to a wider audience, I have quoted from established English translations (duly documented), known for their readability. Where I believed a more precise translation was necessary, I have provided my own. For those who wish to translate Latin and Old French passages themselves, I have furnished the original text in the footnotes.

Readers will note that I have included the theories of a number of venerable researchers who are now considered out of date on the personal theory that some observations from even the most antediluvian of academics remain valid. The hope is that the readers may be able to review and critique these academic assessments themselves using the evidence provided. Finally, in regard to the spelling of Arabic and Greek names and places, I have followed the lead of such distinguished Arabists as D. S. Richards, Jeremy Johns and Alex Metcalfe as well as such noted Byzantine scholars as R. J. H. Jenkins and Elizabeth Jeffreys, while eliminating most diacritical markings, particularly those for Arabic, for the sake of clarity. I hold dear to the notion that our mission as scholars is ultimately to teach and foster thought, not merely to expound to one another.

Abbreviations

AIBL	Academie des Inscriptions et Bélles Lettres
BAS	*Biblioteca Arabo-Sicula*
BEFAR	Bibliothèque des Écoles Françaises d'Athènes et de Rome
CAPIR	Constitutiones et Acta Publica Imperatorum et Regum
CCCM	Corpus Christianorum, Continuatio mediaevalis
CDG	*Codice Diplomatico della Repubblica di Genova*
CDRS	Codex diplomaticus regni Siciliae
CHMBL	*Catalogue of the Hebrew Manuscripts of the Bodleian Library*
DRIG	Diplomata Regum et Imperatorem Germaniae
Dromōn	*The Age of ΔΡΟΜΩΝ (Dromōn), The Byzantine Navy ca 500–1204*
DSS	Documenti per servire alla storia di Sicilia
EP	Epistolae
FSI	Fonti per la storia d'Italia
MGH	Monumenta Germaniae Historica
OMT	Oxford Medieval Texts
RHC, Occ	*Recueil des historiens des croisades, Historiens occidentaux*
RIS	Rerum Italicarum Scriptores
RRH	*Regesta regni Hierosolymitani*
RS	Rolls Series, Rerum Britannicarum Medii Aevi Scriptores
SRG	Scriptores Rerum Germanicarum
SRLI	Scriptores rerum Langobardicarum et Italicarum
SS	Scriptores
TSC-ULC	Taylor-Schechter Collection, University Library of Cambridge

Introduction

Control of the Mediterranean had been the key to wealth and power in the Western world of antiquity. It was the core of the Roman Empire, which made it into the 'mare nostrum' ('our sea'). Upon the fall of Rome, the Eastern Empire under Byzantium inherited sway over the sea and struggled for centuries to maintain it against barbarian incursions and the onslaught of Islam. In *Mohammed and Charlemagne*, the Belgian historian Henri Pirenne identified a dramatic shift in the balance of power in the Mediterranean in the last half of the first millennium. He called it 'the end of Mediterranean unity' and he blamed the change on 'the rapid and unexpected advance of Islam'.[1] While his conclusions have been called into question by later historians, his description of a pronounced power swing toward the East remains indisputable. At the beginning of the second millennium, Islam and Byzantium still dominated the Mediterranean. However, according to the maritime historian A. R. Lewis, that Eastern hegemony was effectively brought to an end in the last half of the eleventh century and a new era of Western maritime ascendancy took its place.[2] The rise of Norman sea power was the primary reason for that profound change.

The seminal event in this seismic shift on the medieval 'middle sea' was the seizure of Sicily by the Normans. Sicily, in the center of the Mediterranean astride the east–west shipping channels, had long been the cornerstone to its dominance. The island's loss to the Aghlabids of North Africa in the ninth century terminated the Byzantine thalassocracy forever and established what Lewis termed 'the Islamic Imperium'.[3] The Byzantine Empire, the German Empire and the papacy all made attempts to recover it, but failed. Muslim pirates from North Africa took root in Calabria and Apulia, prompting the Arab historian Ibn Khaldun to claim that 'the Muslims had gained control over the whole of the Mediterranean'.[4] The Norman conquest of Sicily in the eleventh century under the relentless Hautevilles brutally halted that Muslim suzerainty. The Norman knight chiefly responsible for that feat was Roger de Hauteville, who with some initial help from his more famous brother, Robert Guiscard, managed to subdue

---

[1]   H. Pirenne, *Mohammed and Charlemagne*, trans. B. Miall (New York, 1992; original publication Paris, 1937), p. 284.
[2]   A. Lewis, *Naval Power and Trade in the Mediterranean A.D. 500 to 1100* (Princeton, 1951), p. 225.
[3]   Lewis, *Naval Power and Trade*, p. 132. The Aghlabids were Arabs from the tribe of the Banu Tamim.
[4]   Ibn Khaldun, *The Muqaddimah, An Introduction to History*, trans. F. Rosenthal (Princeton, 1967), p. 210.

the island after a dogged thirty-year campaign. It was his son, Roger II, however, who subsequently turned the island into a bastion of unrivaled strategic importance, which would help make Western naval power pre-eminent in the region throughout the remainder of the Middle Ages. The establishment of an aggressive naval presence in the central Mediterranean by the Normans thus wrested control of the sea from Eastern dominance, thereby allowing West Italian sea power, particularly that of Genoa and Pisa, to expand eastward in conjunction with the Crusades. It was a development from which neither Islam nor Byzantium would ever recover. With the possible exception of the Ottomans in the fifteenth and sixteenth centuries, the East would remain on the defensive against Western intrusions for the balance of the Middle Ages and beyond. At the same time, Norman naval power under Roger II and his brilliant admiral, George of Antioch, would grow to have a profound impact not only on the shifting balance of power in the Mediterranean, but also on burgeoning Western commerce.

Sicily's strategic significance

The reason why the Norman conquest was so pivotal to Mediterranean history resides in the strategic significance of the conquest's crown jewel: Sicily. A solid understanding of this principle is necessary to put the current examination in proper perspective. From the moment that the Hautevilles seized Sicily and made it the core of their kingdom, it was the object of heated competition among the reigning powers of Christendom. Throughout the twelfth century, a primary desideratum of imperial foreign policy, both Byzantine and German, was to wrest control of the Kingdom of Sicily from the Normans. A succession of Eastern and Western emperors, occasionally in collaboration with the papacy, attempted by all available means, military and diplomatic, to claim the crown for themselves. This was ostensibly because, as David Abulafia states in *The Two Italies*, 'The German and Byzantine emperors refused to recognize it as a kingdom at all, and regarded Roger II's coronation as the first King of Sicily in 1130 as an impudent usurpation of their own sovereign rights.'[5] A more fundamental reason was the kingdom's dominance of the central Mediterranean, which brought it enormous wealth and power.

To fully grasp why Sicily was of such profound strategic significance, one must have an understanding of the naval technology of the era. Until the twelfth century, the predominant warship of the medieval Mediterranean was the Byzantine *dromōn*. Variations of it were used by virtually all contemporary fleets, including those of Sicily which was, until the Arab conquest, a major Byzantine naval *thema* (district administrative unit). Additionally, marine archaeology has determined that ship architecture improved little from the end of the Roman

[5] Abulafia, *Two Italies*, p. 32.

Empire to the early fourteenth century.[6] Roughly 115 feet long and about 14 feet abeam,[7] the *dromōn* carried an *ousia* (crew complement) of 108 men plus 30 to 40 marines and officers.[8] Because the oars had to be close to the waterline in order to enter the water at an efficient angle (10 to 15 degrees), the craft had a low freeboard (the distance from the waterline to the deck amidships), perhaps less than a meter (around three feet).[9] It also had a shallow keel so that it could approach close to shore and be easily beached. All of this meant that it was susceptible to being swamped in foul weather. John Pryor, an authority on the *dromōn*, observes that 'a heel under sail of a mere ten degrees or so would put the under edges of the lower oar ports at the flat water line.'[10] Contemporary chronicles are rife with tales of fleets decimated by storms. Thus, the *dromōn* needed easy access to safe havens and had to avoid the stormy winter months. Moreover, primitive navigation at the time required these vessels to go under way only during daylight hours and to hug the shorelines.[11]

Whenever they could get under way, they made achingly slow progress. Even though they possessed two lateen sails, their low freeboard and shallow keel meant they could rarely use them, and tacking directly into the wind was all but impossible. As a result, their normal cruising speed was less than four knots.[12] 'A galley could maintain its maximum speed under oars of some seven knots for no more than twenty minutes,' observes John Guilmartin, an expert on sixteenth-century warships, 'and the best sustained speed which it could manage was only about three knots or a little more.'[13] After examining dozens of recorded journeys of oared vessels from the twelfth to the sixteenth century, Pryor determined that over the course of a long passage (several days or more) galley fleets averaged only two to three knots per hour.[14] In fact, based upon a similar study of ancient and early medieval voyages, the classicist and maritime scholar Lionel Casson

---

[6] F. Hocker, 'Late Roman, Byzantine, and Islamic Galleys and Fleets', in *The Age of the Galley, Mediterranean Oared Vessels since Pre-Classical Times*, eds R. Gardiner and J. Morrison (London, 1995), pp. 86–100, especially 94–7.

[7] Hocker, 'Late Roman, Byzantine, and Islamic Galleys and Fleets', pp. 94–7.

[8] J. Pryor and E. Jeffreys, *The Age of ΔΡΟΜΩΝ (Dromōn), The Byzantine Navy ca 500–1204* (Leiden, 2006), pp. 255–6.

[9] J. Pryor, *Geography, Technology, and War: Studies in the maritime history of the Mediterranean, 649–1571* (Cambridge, 1988), p. 65 (fig. 24) and p. 72.

[10] J. Pryor, 'Types of ships and their performance capabilities', in *Travel in the Byzantine World*, ed. R. Macrides (Aldershot, 2002), pp. 33–58, especially 45.

[11] J. Pryor, 'From Dromōn to Galea: Mediterranean bireme galleys AD 500–1300', in *Age of the Galley*, pp. 101–16.

[12] Pryor and Jeffreys, *Dromōn*, pp. 255, 343.

[13] J. Guilmartin, *Gunpowder & Galleys: Changing Technology & Mediterranean Warfare at Sea in the 16th Century* (Cambridge, 1974, revised 2003), p. 77.

[14] Pryor, *Geography, Technology, and War*, pp. 73–5.

Fig. 1. Piscina Mirabilis. Carved out of the tufa cliffs at Bacoli around 25 BC to supply the Roman fleet at Misenum, the Piscina Mirabilis is one of the largest cisterns the Romans ever built. (Credit: C. Stanton)

concluded, 'With unfavorable or very light winds, a fleet usually could do no better than 1 to 1½ knots.'[15]

The limitations on galley crews were even more severe than on the ships themselves. Rowing was grueling work under the best of conditions. During prime sailing season, the summer months, when temperatures hovered around 35°C (about 100°F), dehydration was an ever-present problem. Galley crews required enormous amounts of water. The sea trials of the *Olympias*, an exact replica of an Athenian trireme, revealed that each man required at least one liter per hour.[16] On top of that, their victuals consisted primarily of ship's biscuit, an awful, desiccated concoction that required an abundance of water to digest.[17] The *Liber secreta fidelium crucis* ('Book of the secrets of the faithful of the cross') of the fourteenth-century Venetian nobleman Marino Sanudo, called Torsello, indicates that this *panis biscocti* ('twice baked bread') was made from grain (most probably wheat).[18] Alternatively, the curators of the Galata Museo del Mare of Genoa contend they also could have contained broad beans or chestnuts. Regardless of their precise ingredients, these sea biscuits had to be ground up and stewed in a soup in order to be rendered palatable. Based upon examinations of the Angevin registers and the *Liber secreta fidelium crucis*, John Pryor estimated that each mariner required at least 750 grams of biscuit per day, along with 40 grams of cheese, 50 of salted meat or fish and 100 grams of dried legumes.[19] Ample quantities of water were essential in the consumption of all these foodstuffs. Accordingly, each crewman must have consumed around eight liters per day, meaning the average *dromōn* crew required at least 1,000 liters or one metric ton of water per day.[20]

The need of galley fleets for colossal quantities of water is underscored by one of the great engineering feats of the Roman era: the *Piscina Mirabilis* in the Campi Flegrei west of Naples (see Figure 1). Carved out of the tufa cliffs at Bacoli around 25 BC to supply the Roman fleet at Misenum, this cistern is the largest the Romans ever built. It measures 72 meters (220 feet) in length, 25 meters

[15] L. Casson, *Ships and Seamanship in the Ancient World* (Princeton, 1971, reprinted Baltimore, 1995), p. 296.

[16] J. Coates and J. Morrison, 'The Sea Trials of the Reconstructed Athenian Trireme *Olympias*', *The Mariner's Mirror*, LXXIX (1993), pp. 131–41.

[17] Guilmartin, *Gunpowder and Galleys*, p. 54, note 26.

[18] Marino Sanudo Torsello, *Liber secretorum fidelium crucis super Terrae Sanctae recuperatione et conservatione* ..., ed. J. Bongars (1611, reprinted Jerusalem, 1972), pp. 60–4. (This book was Marino Sanudo's comprehensive plan for the recovery of the Holy Land in the aftermath of the fall of Acre in 1291.)

[19] Pryor, 'Modelling Bohemond's march to Thessalonikē', in *Logistics of Warfare in the Age of the Crusades*, ed. J. Pryor (Aldershot, 2006), pp. 1–24, especially 9–15.

[20] Coates and Morrison, 'The Sea Trials of the Reconstructed Athenian Trireme *Olympias*', pp. 131–41; J. Coates, J. Morrison and N. Rankov, *The Athenian Trireme: The History and Reconstruction of an Ancient Greek Warship* (2nd edn, Cambridge, 2000), p. 238; Pryor and Jeffreys, *Dromōn*, p. 357.

(75 feet) in width and 15 meters (45 feet) in depth. Lined with pounded terra-cotta and supported by 48 massive square pilasters, it has a capacity of over 12,000 cubic meters or 424,000 cubic feet. It was fed by the *Aqua Augustus* (also known as the Serino Aqueduct), a 96-kilometer-long aqueduct capable of producing 48,000 cubic meters of flow per day from its source near Santa Lucia di Serino. Water was, indeed, the fuel upon which all galley fleets ran, yet restricted cargo capacity limited onboard supplies to no more than four days' worth.[21] This meant that galley crews had to replenish their water reserves often, which, in turn, meant that they were heavily dependent upon admission to friendly shores. Pryor explains why: 'Moving into waters off enemy-controlled coasts deprived fleets of fresh water unless they could take it by compulsion, which would not normally be easy since most coastal water sources lay under the walls of fortified habitations.'[22]

Consequently, galleys needed three things: (1) access to shelter from storms, (2) large quantities of fresh water and (3) food, not to mention an occasional rest from exhausting labor. Accordingly, galleys put into shore almost daily. John Pryor said it nicely: 'Control of the land meant control of the sea, because control of the land carried with it both control of the refuges to which all galley fleets had to have recourse in inclement weather and also control of the water supplies, without which no naval forces could operate for more than a few days.'[23]

Moreover, the unique meteorological and physical characteristics of the Mediterranean favored sea travel along the northern shores. First of all, the prevailing northerly winds made the south littoral the lee shore, fraught with the potential danger of being forced aground. Secondly, the relatively higher profile of the northern shores made for easier visibility and navigation. Thirdly, the greater water depth along the north coast made for safer sailing. Fourthly, the higher number of bays and inlets of the north littoral provided many more havens from inclement weather than that of the south. Finally, numerous reefs and shifting shoals made the coast of North Africa a good deal more treacherous for maritime traffic.[24]

From the forgoing it can be deduced that the ultimate strategic advantage would be to control a platform with an unlimited supply of water and an abundance of food, located towards the north shores of the Mediterranean at approximately the center, astride the west–east shipping lanes. Sicily, by virtue of its fortuitous location, was the strategic linchpin of the Mediterranean. Whoso-

---

[21] J. Pryor, 'A view from a masthead: the First Crusade from the Sea', *Crusades*, VII (2008), pp. 87–152, especially 104.

[22] Pryor, 'View from a masthead', p. 90.

[23] J. Pryor, 'Byzantium and the Sea: Byzantine Fleets and the History of the Empire in the Age of the Macedonian Emperors, C. 900–1025 CE', in *War at Sea in the Middle Ages and the Renaissance*, eds J. Hattendorf and R. Unger (Woodbridge, 2003), pp. 83–104, especially 99.

[24] Pryor, *Geography, Technology, and War*, pp. 20–2.

ever held it held the key to east-west movement on the sea. Moreover, its proximity to the Italian Peninsula and the Maghrib (essentially the coastal plain of Morocco, Algeria, Tunisia and western Libya) enabled it to control the sea passages between the western Mediterranean/Tyrrhenian Sea and the eastern Mediterranean/Ionian Sea. The Sicilian Channel between Mazara del Vallo in southwestern Sicily and Cape Bon of Tunisia, for instance, is barely one hundred miles wide. In his paper, 'Henry Count of Malta and his Mediterranean Activities, 1203–1230', Abulafia clearly describes Norman naval strategy with respect to the Sicilian Channel:

> The Norman conquest of Malta was part of a wider plan to gain security for the south and east of Sicily and, ultimately, to control the entire straits between Sicily and Africa. Pantelleria and Lampedusa were also of value, but they remained largely unpopulated and lacked Malta's excellent harbors. When the Normans attempted to install themselves in the North African towns they relied on the intermediate islands as bases for their swoops on the Tunisian and Barbary coasts.[25]

While it was, indeed, possible for unsanctioned ships to transit the channel unchallenged, control of the landmasses on either side by a hostile power meant this was a somewhat risky adventure, especially given the need for frequent water replenishment. This was exponentially true of the Strait of Messina, which is a mere three miles wide.[26] Traversing the strait undetected would have been very nearly impossible. Furthermore, in *Geography, Technology and War*, Pryor notes the natural conditions that tended to force maritime traffic through the Strait of Messina. Indeed, pilots were often needed to usher traffic through the strait.[27]

It must be emphasized at this juncture that the Normans did not control these passages with their fleets. Pryor, and Guilmartin before him, have proven that patrolling sea passages with flotillas of galleys was simply not technologically possible. Maximum visibility from the tops of mastheads (no more than 12 miles) and closing speeds (less than 10 knots) made interdiction at sea improbable.[28] The Normans gained some measure of control over the sea lanes through the central Mediterranean by virtue of their control of the lands adjacent to these waterways, because transiting vessels needed access to those lands in order to replenish their supplies, especially water. The Normans used their fleets primarily to help conquer and defend the lands bordering the Sicilian Channel and the Strait of Messina, most vitally Sicily.

John Pryor's recent research on the naval logistics of the Crusades has revealed that the Genoese, the Pisans and even northern European naval contingents were

---

[25] D. Abulafia, 'Henry Count of Malta and his Mediterranean Activities, 1203–1230', in *Medieval Malta: Studies on Malta before the Knights*, ed. A. T. Lutrell (Supplementary Monograph of the British School at Rome, London, 1975) pp. 104–25, especially 106.

[26] Pryor, *Geography, Technology, and War*, pp. 6–7, 12–25, 92–3.

[27] Pryor, *Geography, Technology, and War*, pp. 90–3.

[28] Coates, Morrison and Rankov, *Athenian Trireme*, pp. 262–5; Pryor and Jeffreys, *Dromōn*, pp. 388–9.

greatly reliant upon Sicily and Calabria for their participation in the Crusades because of the need for resupply.[29] Furthermore, anecdotal evidence from the Cairo Geniza indicates that Norman control of the central Mediterranean may well have induced lasting changes in trading patterns across the sea.[30] Thus, it is no accident that the rise of West Italian sea power coincided with the Norman conquest of Sicily and that the Norman Kingdom of Roger II became rich and powerful. And, no wonder why all the other powers of the Mediterranean sought at one time or another to wrest control of that island from the Normans.

[29] Pryor, *Geography, Technology, and War*, pp. 100–15.
[30] S. Goitein, *A Mediterranean Society*, Vol. I, *Economic Foundations* (6 vols, Berkeley, 1967), pp. 32–40.

1

The Conquest (827 to 1101)

Before the arrival of the Normans, the central Mediterranean belonged to the Muslims of North Africa. The Aghlabid conquest of Sicily and the subsequent establishment of pirate bases on the south Italian peninsula in the ninth century gave the Muslims control of both the north and south shores of the central Mediterranean as well as the islands in-between. This enabled them to effectively regulate maritime traffic through the Sicilian Channel and the Strait of Messina and harry Christian commerce at will. For all intents and purposes, such a stranglehold essentially bisected the 'middle sea' and denied east–west movement to all except Aghlabid allies like Amalfi and Naples. It is precisely this dominance of the north and south shores and the islands in-between that the Normans would eventually supplant, returning control of the central Mediterranean to the Christian West for the first time since the fall of Rome.

The Muslim conquest and the coming of the Normans

The seeds of 'Saracen' suzerainty over the central Mediterranean germinated in Ifriqiyah, the old Roman province of Africa, which consisted of the coastal regions of western Libya, Tunisia and eastern Algeria.[1] Here, in this region just south of Sicily in 800, the Abbasid caliph of Bagdad, Harun al-Rashid, appointed Ibrahim ibn al-Aghlab as emir for an annual tribute of 40,000 *dinars*.[2] Thus began the Aghlabid dynasty, which would eventually conquer Sicily. It was Ibrahim ibn al-Aghlab's son and successor, Abu-l-Abbas Abd-Allah I, who built the powerful navy that his successor, Ziyadat Allah I,[3] would wield against the Byzantine province of Sicily. Ziyadat Allah used his formidable fleet tentatively at first. In 816–17,[4] he sent it on an expedition to Sardinia and in 819 he dispatched

---

[1]   Abulafia, 'Norman Kingdom of Africa', p. 26.
[2]   J. Abun-Nasr, *A History of the Maghrib in the Islamic period* (Cambridge, 1987), pp. 53–4. According to the numismatist, Philip Grierson, the Arabic gold *dinar* was a coin containing 4.25 grams of gold. P. Grierson and L. Travaini, *Medieval European Coinage, 14, Italy (III) (South Italy, Sicily, Sardinia)* (Cambridge, 1998), p. 3.
[3]   A. Ahmad, *A History of Islamic Sicily* (Edinburgh, 1975), p. 5.
[4]   Ibn al-Athir, *Biblioteca Arabo-Sicula*, ed. M. Amari (2 vols, Turin, 1880–1), I, p. 364.

it on a brief raid of Sicily.[5] A falling-out between Constantine, the Byzantine *strategos* (governor) of Sicily, and Euphemios, the *tourmarches* (commander) of the Sicilian naval *thema*, gave Ziyadat Allah the opportunity for which he had been waiting. Euphemios offered the Aghlabid emir his help in conquering the island on the condition he would be made governor.[6] In response, Ziyadat Allah mounted a massive expedition under the command of Asad ibn al-Furat, which numbered 70 vessels,[7] carrying some 700 cavalry and 10,000 infantry.[8] This force of Arabs, Berbers and Spanish Muslims stormed ashore in June 827 at Mazara and defeated the Byzantine commander known to Arab sources as 'Balatah'; then, drove on to Syracuse, which it besieged by land and sea.[9] Sufficiently alarmed, the Byzantine Emperor Michael II dispatched a sizable relief fleet. Its arrival in 829, along with an outbreak of pestilence in the Muslim camp, which killed Asad Ibn al-Furat, caused the Muslims to burn their ships and retreat inland. They successfully took the fortress of Mineo, about 40 miles west of Catania, and sacked the key port city of Girgenti (present-day Agrigento) on the south coast of the island, but ultimately the Muslim army was defeated while besieging nearly impregnable Castrogiovanni (present-day Enna) in the center of the island. Both Euphemios and Asad's replacement, Muhammad ibn abi al-Gawari, were killed.[10] The remnants then retreated to Mineo and Mazara, the only two possessions still in Muslim hands, but the process had begun and it was irreversible. 'The Agarenes,'[11] from this moment, are not only masters of Sicily, but also Calabria and most of Italy,' wrote the Byzantine historian John Skylitzes. 'Everywhere they make raids and ravage everything.'[12]

In 830, a combined armada of nearly three hundred ships landed a huge army of Aghlabids and Spanish Muslims, which swiftly relieved their besieged brethren at Mineo; then marched on Palermo. The Byzantine governor of the city capitulated after a withering siege of nearly a year, which vanquished all but a handful of the Greek garrison.[13] The capture of Palermo (September/August 831) was crucial to the Muslim advance. It gave them a superb port facility on the north shore of Sicily, which enabled them to easily assault Messina and, thus, gain control of the strait by the same name. It also permitted them to conduct

---

[5]   *Annales Cavenses*, ed. G. Pertz (MGH, SS, III, Hanover, 1839), anno 819, p. 188. See also Ahmad, *History of Islamic Sicily*, p. 5.

[6]   Ibn al-Athir, BAS, I, pp. 364–5; John Skylitzes, *Empereurs de Constantinople (Synopsis historiōn)*, trans. B. Flusin (Paris, 2003), pp. 44–5.

[7]   Ibn Adari, BAS, II, p. 5.

[8]   Al-Nuwayri, BAS, II, p. 116.

[9]   Ibn al-Athir, BAS, I, pp. 365–7.

[10]   Ibn al-Athir, BAS, I, pp. 367–8; Al-Nuwayri, BAS, II, pp. 117–19.

[11]   The contemporary Christian term used to designate Muslims from North Africa and Sicily. B. Kreutz, *Before the Normans: Southern Italy in the Ninth and Tenth Centuries* (Philadelphia, 1991), p. 49.

[12]   John Skylitzes, *Synopsis historiōn*, p. 45.

[13]   *Cambridge Chronicle*, BAS, I, p. 278; Ibn al-Athir, BAS, I, pp. 368–9.

lucrative raids on Italy's Tyrrhenian coast. A. R. Lewis noted the significance: 'From that time on it was to be the most important base and center of Islamic power on Sicily.' He added, 'All but autonomous, though nominally subject to North African rule, it was the port par excellence from which the Muslim fleets put out to harry the coasts and commerce of Italy and the Byzantine parts of the island.'[14]

This is not to imply that the conquest of the remainder of Byzantine Sicily was a simple, swift affair. It was not. Repeated attempts by Constantinople to recover its profitable province, stiff resistance by the indigenous Greek population and internecine warfare among the various Muslim ethnic groups slowed the process considerably. From the first landing at Mazara in 827 to the reduction in 902 of Taormina, the last Byzantine bastion, the conquest took three-quarters of a century to complete. Messina was not taken until 843 and, even then, the Aghlabids required subterfuge and the aid of some Neapolitan allies to finish the undertaking.[15] The fortress of Cefalu finally fell to the Sicilian emir al-Abbas ibn al-Fadl in 857–8 followed, at last, by Castrogiovanni in January 859.[16] The fall of Castrogiovanni was a particularly severe blow to Byzantine hopes of maintaining a toehold on the island, for Constantinople had just transferred the administration of the province from Syracuse to this seemingly invincible citadel.[17] Syracuse itself was subject to several serious assaults, notably in 866 and 868 by Muhammad ibn Khafaja, the then Aghlabid emir of Sicily.[18] By the time the emir Ja'far ibn Muhammad encircled the city in 877 by land and sea, the unremitting pressure had already substantially degraded Syracuse's ability to resist. Constantinople had attempted to succor its western jewel, but its relief fleet was ineffectual.[19] Syracuse was forced to endure a strangling, nine-month siege during which a monk named Theodosius claims the inhabitants resorted to cannibalism.[20] When the Muslims entered the city, at last, on 21 May 878, John Skylitzes, a late eleventh-century historian at the court of Constantinople, records that they 'made a great massacre of its inhabitants and took the rest into captivity: the city was destroyed from top to bottom, its holy churches burnt and this city up until that day so celebrated and so brilliant, which had repulsed so often the assaults of the barbarians, lost in a blink of an eye all that made its glory.'[21] Taormina and the overwhelmingly Greek Val Demone region in the mountainous northeastern corner of the island lingered on until 902, when

---

[14]   Lewis, *Naval Power and Trade*, p. 133.
[15]   Ibn al-Athir, *BAS*, I, p. 374.
[16]   Ibn Idari, *BAS*, II, p. 12.
[17]   Ibn al-Athir, *BAS*, I, p. 379.
[18]   Ibn al-Athir, *BAS*, I, p. 388; Ibn Khaldun, *BAS*, II, pp. 183–4.
[19]   *Cambridge Chronicle*, *BAS*, I, p. 278; Ibn al-Athir, *BAS*, I, p. 396; Ibn Idari, *BAS*, II, p. 12.
[20]   A. Vasiliev, *Byzance et les Arabs* (3 vols, Brussels, 1935–68), II, pp. 70–9.
[21]   John Skylitzes, *Synopsis historiōn*, pp. 132–3.

it suffered a similar fate at the hands of the cruel Ibrahim II ibn Ahmad, the Aghlabid emir.[22] The 'Saracen' seizure of Sicily was complete.

The development could hardly have been more disastrous for the western Byzantine Empire. The loss of Sicily to the Aghlabids was accompanied by the capture of the islands of Pantelleria (834–5) and Malta (870).[23] This assured the Muslims of crucial control of the Sicilian Channel between Sicily and Ifriqiyah. Moreover, Constantinople's possessions on the Italian peninsula were now threatened. Even before the Muslims had mopped up the last Greek resistance on Sicily, Byzantine Calabria and Apulia were subject to raids, increasing in violence and frequency. In short, the conquest of Sicily had made Byzantium's standing in the West tenuous to the point of being untenable, yet the Byzantine navy had been powerless to prevent it. To be fair, the Eastern Empire had dispatched fleets on several occasions in hopes of salvaging the island. Some simply failed. A huge, 300-ship flotilla of *chelandia* (a version of the *dromōn*)[24] dispatched by the Emperor Michael III under the command of Constantine Kondomytes in 859 was waylaid by an Aghlabid fleet west of Messina and destroyed.[25] The Byzantine navy lost 100 ships in one of the worst defeats in its history. Other expeditions were only able to achieve temporary success. The Kurdish historian, Ibn al-Athir (1160–1233), reports that the arrival of 'large naval forces of the Rum' in 837–8 broke up a long Muslim siege of Cefalu,[26] but no such relief force was there to prevent al-Abbas ibn al-Fadl from forcing the same garrison's surrender in 857–8.[27] Similarly, a 'powerful force' sent from Constantinople may have helped lift a serious siege of Syracuse in 868,[28] even though it was eventually defeated. Another relief fleet, however, apparently could not even reach Sicily in time to save the city in 878, owing to adverse winds.[29] The problem was essentially the inability of Constantinople to maintain a permanent maritime presence in the area. As a result, once a Byzantine fleet either succumbed to defeat or simply departed, the Muslims resumed raiding and conquering. Accordingly, the fourteenth-century Muslim scholar from Tunis, Ibn Khaldun, was inspired to make the following overblown boast:

---

[22] Ibn al-Athir, *BAS*, I, pp. 393–4; Al-Nuwayri, *BAS*, II, pp. 151–2; John Skylitzes, *Synopsis historiōn*, p. 152.

[23] Ibn al-Athir, *BAS*, I, pp. 370–1, 387; *Cambridge Chronicle*, *BAS*, I, p. 279.

[24] Gardiner and Morrison (*Age of the Galley*, p. 248) define a *chelandion* as 'a Byzantine warship, first mentioned around the beginning of the ninth century AD, possibly derived from *keles*, a fast merchant galley of classical Greek times; the term later had the specific meaning of a transport galley, especially for horses'.

[25] Ibn al-Athir, *BAS*, I, pp. 380–1. See also Ahmad, *History of Islamic Sicily*, p. 13.

[26] Ibn al-Athir, *BAS*, I, p. 372. ('Rum' in this context refers to the Byzantines.)

[27] Ibn Idari, *BAS*, II, p. 12.

[28] Ibn al-Athir, *BAS*, I, p. 385. See also Lewis, *Naval Power and Trade*, p. 137.

[29] John Skylitzes, *Synopsis historiōn*, pp. 132–3.

During all that time, the Muslims were gaining control over the largest part of the high sea. Their fleets kept coming and going, and the Muslim armies crossed the sea in ships from Sicily to the great mainland opposite Sicily, on the northern shore. They fell upon the European Christian rulers and made massacres in their realms. This happened in the days of the Banu Abi l-Husayn,[30] the rulers of Sicily, who supported the 'Ubaydid [Fatimid] propaganda there. The Christian nations withdrew their fleets to the northeastern side of the Mediterranean, to the coastal regions inhabited by the European Christians and the Slavs, and to the Aegean islands, and did not go beyond them. The Muslim fleet had pounced upon them as eagerly as lions upon their prey. They covered most of the surface of the Mediterranean with their equipment and numbers and traveled its lanes [on missions both] peaceful and warlike. Not a single Christian board floated on it.[31]

With the conquest of Sicily and the islands of the Sicilian Channel, the Muslims of North Africa had only to secure control of the north shore, that is, southern Italy, in order to close their grip on the central Mediterranean. The process was well underway long before Ibrahim II ibn Ahmad obliterated Taormina in 902 and immediately crossed the Strait of Messina to Calabria. Muslim raids had begun ravaging the southern Italian peninsula from the moment the Aghlabids became entrenched on Sicily. In 838, only seven years after the Muslim acquisition of Palermo, the *Chronicon Salernitanum* reports that a Muslim fleet (probably Aghlabid) passed through the Strait of Otranto and briefly captured Brindisi before returning to Sicily.[32] From that time on, the raiding was very nearly incessant. In 839–40, Ibn al-Athir records that a Muslim fleet crossed to Calabria and waged war at will until it encountered a Byzantine flotilla, which it put to flight.[33] In 840, it was Apulia's turn again. The *Chronicon Salernitanum* documents the seizure of Taranto by an 'Agarene' fleet captained by a certain Saba.[34] Nor was Campania spared. John the Deacon, a contemporary Neapolitan cleric, tells of 'Saracens' ensconcing themselves on the island of Ponza in 842 with the apparent intention of setting up a pirate base – that is, before a coalition of Neapolitans, Amalfitans, Gaetans and Sorrentines chased them off.[35] Moreover, these raids were often brutal, deadly affairs. Around 842 the Cassinese monk Erchempert reports raiding in Apulia where the 'Saracens' penetrated urban places in secret, and slaughtered some innocent people by the sword, and

---

[30] The Kalbite governors of Sicily in the latter part of the tenth and the beginning of the eleventh centuries.

[31] Ibn Khaldun, *Muqaddimah*, p. 210.

[32] *Chronicon Salernitanum*, ed. U. Westerbergh (Stockholm, 1956), ch. 72, p. 70. See also G. Musca, *L'Emirato di Bari, 847–871* (Bari, 1964), pp. 15–16.

[33] Ibn al-Athir, *BAS*, I, p. 373.

[34] *Chronicon Salernitanum*, ch. 81, p. 79. See also Musca, *Emirato di Bari*, pp. 17–18.

[35] John the Deacon, *Gesta Episcoporum Neapolitanorum*, ed. G. Waitz (MGH, SRLI, VI–IX, Hanover, 1878), ch. 60, p. 432.

placed others in captivity.'[36] The same source later recounts, 'During that time [851–2] the Agarenes dwelling in Bari began to devastate the land, plundering all of Apulia and Calabria, and also started step-by-step to depopulate Salerno as well as Benevento.'[37] The word '*depopulor*', referring as much to the gathering of slaves as to the perpetration of wanton slaughter, would appear over and over again in the Latin chronicles of the region over the next two centuries.

Not even Rome was sacrosanct. The Eternal City itself was assaulted in 846. According to John the Deacon, a huge force arrived from Palermo and captured the castle at Misenum (the old Roman naval base). He indicated its ultimate objective was Rome.[38] An eyewitness cited in the *Liber Pontificalis* ('Book of the Popes', a biographical compendium of the popes up to the fifteenth century) estimated that the force that eventually landed at Ostia numbered 73 ships, 11,000 men and 500 horses.[39] It easily massacred a motley militia, hastily recruited from the ranks of Saxon, Frisian and Frankish pilgrims; and then rushed on to Rome, even bringing some of their ships up the Tiber.[40] The Aurelian wall apparently kept them from entering the city, but they were able to loot the basilica of St Peter and possibly that of St Paul before heading back to Campania. Another Muslim force threatened Rome three years later, but this time it was met by a combined Amalfitan–Neapolitan fleet under the command of Caesar, son of Duke Sergius of Naples, which defeated it in what came to be known as the Battle of Ostia.[41] Barbara Kreutz assessed the situation as follows:

> In sum, Arab raiders were a threat along both coasts of southern Italy, as indeed they now were virtually everywhere in the Mediterranean. They had sacked and even briefly held some of the region's key ports, cities well-known since Roman days. And worst of all, the Arabs were not only pillaging the monasteries and churches of southern Italy and showing no mercy to monks or other peaceful indi-

---

[36] Erchempert, *Historia Langobardorum Beneventanorum*, ed. G. Waitz (MGH, SRLI, VI–IX, Hanover, 1878), ch. 16, p. 240. '*Hii autem, ut sunt natura callidi et prudentiores aliis in malum, subtilius contemplantes munitionem loci, intempesta noctis, christicolis quiescentibus, per abdita loca penetrant urbem, populumque insontem partim gladiis trucidarunt, partim captivitati indiderunt.*'

[37] Erchempert, *Historia Langobardorum Beneventanorum*, ch. 20, p. 242. '*Per idem tempus Agareni Varim incolentes coeperunt devastantes stirpitus depredare totam Apuliam Calabriamque ac pedetentim Salernum ac Beneventum depopulare initiarunt.*'

[38] John the Deacon, *Gesta Episcoporum Neapolitanorum*, ch. 60, p. 432. '*Propterea magnus exercitus Panormitanorum adveniens, castellum Misenatium comprehendit. Ac inde Africani in forti brachio omnem hanc regionem divastare cupientes, Romam supervenerunt…*'

[39] *Le Liber Pontificalis*, ed. L. Duchesne (3 vols, BEFAR 2, série 3, Paris, 1886–1957), II, *Vita Sergius II*, p. 99.

[40] *Liber Pontificalis*, II, *Vita Sergius II*, p. 100. '*In Crastina autem feria IIII, cum securi essent praefati custodes et sedentes ut cibum sumerent, irruerunt repente super eos Sarraceni et circumdantes occiderunt eos, ut pauci ex eis remansissent. Et insecuti sunt eos qui evaserant usque Galeriam. Et iter assumentes navigio et pedestres simul et equestres coeperunt Romam festinare.*'

[41] John the Deacon, *Gesta Episcoporum Neapolitanorum*, ch. 60, pp. 432–3; *Liber Pontificalis*, II, *Vita Leo IV*, p. 118.

viduals, but they dared to penetrate the holiest shrines of Rome itself, plundering and destroying.[42]

It would get far worse. In addition to the recurrent raids dispatched from Sicily or even Africa, the Muslim marauders began to establish a permanent presence on the mainland. Some of these enclaves were either pirate nests (like Tropea, Santa Severina and Amantea in Calabria)[43] or advance bases for pillaging the interior (like Venafro near Montecassino and Sepino in the area of Benevento),[44] but others bore all the earmarks of colonization. The most troubling of these would be on the coast of Apulia. In 847, a certain Kalfun, reported to be a freed Berber slave of the Aghlabid emir Muhammad I Abul-Abbas ibn al-Aghlab, seized Bari from the Byzantines; then, according to the ninth-century Arab historian Ahmad ibn Yahya al-Baladhuri, Kalfun requested the official sanction of the Abbasid caliph, al-Mutawakkil ala Allah. Al-Baladhuri, a familiar figure at the court of Baghdad and in a position to know, attests that formal recognition was subsequently granted to one of Kalfun's successors, known in Christian chronicles as 'Sawdan', the third and last Muslim ruler of Bari.[45] Hence the Emirate of Bari was born. It would endure for a quarter of a century. It was the Muslims of Bari (probably Berbers) that Erchempert reports as having 'depopulated' Apulia and Calabria all the way up to Benevento in the early 850s.[46] And in 862 it was the dreaded Sawdan who established the advance base at Venafro from which his raiders despoiled the revered abbeys of San Vincenzo and Montecassino, extorting 3,000 gold pieces from each in return for not razing their buildings to the ground.[47] Moreover, Sawdan evidently had advance bases not just at Venafro, but possibly also at Telese, Alife, Sepino, Boiano and Isernia (all in the Benevento region).[48]

In the same timeframe, Taranto was also absorbed into the 'Saracen' sphere. Following its capture by the Aghlabid leader, Saba (Sahib al-Ustul), in 839–40,[49] Ibn al-Athir indicates that the Muslim occupation took on a perpetuity: 'In the same year [846–7], Muslims came to the city of Taranto in Lombardia and settled there.'[50] Jules Gay, an early twentieth-century specialist on Byzantine Italy,

[42] Kreutz, *Before the Normans*, p. 28.

[43] John Skylitzes, *Synopsis historiōn*, pp. 133–4. See also J. Gay, *L'Italie méridionale et l'empire byzantine depuis l'avènement de Basile I jusqu'à la prise de Bari par les Normands (867–1071)* (Paris, 1904), pp. 132–3.

[44] Erchempert, *Historia Langobardorum Beneventanorum*, ch. 29, p. 245; ch. 79, pp. 263–4.

[45] Al-Baladhuri, *BAS*, I, pp. 269–70.

[46] Erchempert, *Historia Langobardorum Beneventanorum*, ch. 20, p. 242. 'Per idem tempus Agareni Varim incolentes coeperunt devastantes stirpitus depredare totam Apuliam Calabriamque ac pedetentim Salernum ac Beneventum depopulare initiarunt.'

[47] *Chronicon Vulturnense*, ed. V. Federici (3 vols, Rome, 1925), I, pp. 360–1; Erchempert, *Historia Langobardorum Beneventanorum*, ch. 29, p. 245.

[48] *Chronicon Vulturnense*, I, p. 360.

[49] *Chronicon Salernitanum*, ch. 81, p. 79. See also Musca, *Emirato di Bari*, pp. 20–1.

[50] Ibn al-Athir, *BAS*, I, p. 376.

1. Muslim incursions in southern Italy, 827–1016.
(Credit: C. Stanton with P. Judge)

summed up the state of affairs this way: 'Before the middle of the ninth century, all the coasts of southern Italy, from Siponto in the east up to the mouth of the Tiber in the west were overrun by bands of Saracens come from all points of the Mediterranean.'[51] Most of the pressure, however, was clearly originating from North Africa and Sicily. It is no wonder that Gay went on to insist that 'toward 860, Muslim power was as strong and formidable in southern Italy as it was in Sicily.'[52] While this may seem something of an overstatement, there can be no doubt that, at this point in time, the Muslims had gained a measure of control over the northern shores of the 'middle sea'. The central Mediterranean was essentially ensconced in Dar al-Islam (the House of Islam) (see Map 1).

The economic impact of this development must have been harsh. The Mediterranean was now effectively divided in half. While there is ample evidence to suggest that trade between the Latin West and the East persisted, commercial traffic moved west to east upon the sea mostly at the pleasure of the Muslims of North Africa. Only Muslim merchants from Spain and the Maghrib along with a few Muslim allies from among the Christian cities like Amalfi were welcome to transport their merchandise (probably for a fee) through the Sicilian Channel or the Strait of Messina to the markets of the East and vice versa. Most others were confined to trade on the Tyrrhenian Sea – trade subject to constant harassment by Muslim raiders. As a result, Christian commercial activity on the northeast Tyrrhenian coast remained severely depressed as long as the Muslims maintained a stranglehold on the central chokepoint of the Mediterranean.[53]

The Christian powers of both the East and West would make several concerted efforts to wrench it from their grasp, but would achieve little lasting success. Shortly after the fall of Taranto in 840, the Emperor Theophilos dispatched the *Patrikios* (Patrician) Theodosius to Venice to enlist the aid of the Doge Pietro Tradonico in taking it back. The doge responded by sending 60 vessels to Taranto in the spring of 841, but the fleet of the pirate leader Saba intercepted them in the Ionian Sea and vanquished the Venetians. The triumph immediately prompted Saba's 'Saracens' to surge up the Adriatic and wreak havoc as far north as the peninsula of Istria, torching Ancona in the process and enslaving its citizenry. A similar fate befell another Venetian fleet the following year off the island of Susak (Croatia).[54] For decades afterwards, the Muslims of Taranto terrorized the seas around them and despoiled the Apulian countryside with apparent impunity.[55] They were not evicted from Taranto until 880.[56] Even then, the city

---

[51] Gay, *Italie méridionale et l'empire byzantine*, p. 49.

[52] Gay, *Italie méridionale et l'empire byzantine*, p. 49.

[53] Lewis, *Naval Power and Trade*, p. 177.

[54] *Chronicon Venetum*, *Cronache veneziane antichissime*, ed. G. Monticolo (FSI, XIX, Rome, 1890), pp. 113–14. See also Musca, *Emirato di Bari*, pp. 18–19.

[55] *Chronicon Salernitanum*, ch. 81, p. 79; Erchempert, *Historia Langobardorum Beneventanorum*, ch. 38, p. 249.

[56] Lupus Protospatarius, *Annales*, ed. G. Pertz (MGH, SS, V, Hanover, 1844), anno 880, p. 53.

continued to be harried by Muslim marauders. In 927, Lupus Protospatarius, a Byzantine civil servant who wrote a set of annals for the *thema* of Longobardia (Apulia) from 855 to 1102, reports, 'The destruction of Taranto was accomplished, and all the men were killed fighting; the rest were then carried off to Africa.'[57] Various other Latin annals substantiate the event.[58] According to Ibn al-Athir, the city was demolished once more in 976–7, this time on the orders of the Kalbite emir of Sicily, Abu l-Qasim al-Kalbi, who subjugated Sant'Agata in Calabria and Gravina in Apulia on the same expedition.[59]

The Emirate of Bari would prove equally obdurate. It had bedeviled the region for twenty years by the time the German Emperor Louis II finally launched his campaign to eradicate it in 867. It was a long and difficult process. Marching from Benevento, he first attacked and set fire to Matera, which had become a forward base for inland raids; then, he pitched camp at Venosa and sent a garrison to occupy Canosa. He ultimately took Oria as well in an effort to isolate Taranto and Bari from one another.[60] He was unable, however, to effectively besiege Bari, largely because he lacked any sort of naval power. The *Chronicon Salernitanum* indicates Louis sought naval support from the Byzantine emperor, Basil I, as early as 868.[61] Both Constantine VII Porphyrogenitus and John Skylitzes attest that he finally got it along with ships from Ragusa and the Slavic regions of the northern Dalmatian coast.[62] This enabled him to ultimately take Bari in February 871.[63] It is clear from a letter that Louis dispatched to Basil that his intention was to seize Taranto at the same time,[64] and, indeed, Erchempert states that he ordered it besieged, but there is no evidence that this was actually done.[65]

In any event, the removal of the Bari emirate did not solve the 'Saracen' problem in southern Italy. Sawdan had barely been dragged back to Benevento in

---

[57] Lupus Protospatarius, *Annales*, anno 927, p. 54. '*Fuit excidium Tarenti patratum, et perempti sunt omnes viriliter pugnando; reliqui vero deportati sunt in Africam.*'

[58] *Annales Barenses*, ed. G. Pertz (MGH, SS, V, Hanover, 1844), anno 929, p. 52; *Anonymi Barensis chronicon*, ed. L. Muratori (RIS, V, Milan, 1726), anno 926, p. 148.

[59] Ibn al-Athir, *BAS*, I, p. 432.

[60] Erchempert, *Historia Langobardorum Beneventanorum*, ch. 33, p. 247.

[61] *Chronicon Salernitanum*, ch. 107, p. 107. '*Expulsi ut diximus Agareni ex Italia, tantum Varim ubi ipse Sagdan preerat, et aliquante alie civitates illorum omnimodis resistebant propter Agarenorum metum. Sed ut cognovisset ille imperator, ut minime Varim expugnare valeret, eo quod non haberet marinos hostes, statim Constantinopolim Basilio imperatori legacionem misit, quatenus sine mora navalis exercitus micteret, ut Varim una cum ipso posset attribuere.*'

[62] Constantine VII Porphyrogenitus, *De Administrando Imperio*, ed. G. Moravcsik, trans. R. Jenkins (Budapest, 1949; 2nd edn, Washington, DC, 1967), ch. 29, pp. 126–9; John Skylitzes, *Synopsis historiōn*, p. 125.

[63] *Annales Beneventani*, ed. G. Pertz (MGH, SS, III, Hanover, 1839), anno 871, p. 174; *Chronicon Salernitanum*, ch. 108, p. 121; *Chronicon Vulturnense*, I, p. 361.

[64] *Chronicon Salernitanum*, ch. 107, pp. 119–20.

[65] Erchempert, *Historia Langobardorum Beneventanorum*, ch. 33, p. 247.

chains when an enormous Aghlabid force laid siege to Salerno in the fall of 871.[66] Estimates vary. Erchempert says there were 30,000 'Saracen' troops,[67] but the author of the *Chronicon Salernitanum* asserts, 'Abdila, the king of the Agarenes of whom we have spoken before came to Salerno through Calabria with sixty-two thousand fighters, and seized several Calabrian towns.'[68] Whatever the exact figure, the Muslims were sufficient in number so that, in the course of a year-long siege, the lands of 'Naples, Benevento and Capua were partly depopulated.'[69] Louis, though temporarily held captive at Benevento, eventually freed himself and amassed an army that succeeded in chasing the invaders away. Even so, the retreating Aghlabid army left a path of devastation in Calabria so horrendous that the land became 'deserted as if the result of a deluge.'[70]

Nonetheless, the problem not only persisted, but it morphed into a much more virulent and protracted one. Internecine squabbling among the Lombard principalities of Campania soon invited other Muslim warriors in as mercenaries. They stayed as marauders, ravaging the entire region for decades. Erchempert testifies that around 880 Athanasius II, the prince-bishop of Naples, 'entered peace with the Saracens and established them between the harbor and the walls of the city, from where they laid ruin to all of Benevento as well as even Roman territory and the lands of Spoleto.'[71] Concurrently, another group of Aghlabids was permitted to settle at Cetara, just north of Salerno, with an equally delete-rious impact on that community. Within a couple of years the two city-states were compelled to join forces in order to expel the raiders from their midst.[72] The Muslim marauders simply migrated elsewhere. Many turned up at Agropoli near Paestum, just a few miles further south, but by 884 the bulk of them had established a permanent pirate base at the mouth of Garigliano River, welcomed by their allies, the Gaetans.[73] According to the chronicles of San Vincenzo al Vulturno and Montecassino, these bands of entrenched Aghlabid raiders were

[66] *Chronicon Salernitanum*, ch. 111–18, pp. 124–32; *Chronicon Vulturnense*, I, pp. 361–2; Erchempert, *Historia Langobardorum Beneventanorum*, ch. 35, pp. 247–8.

[67] Erchempert, *Historia Langobardorum Beneventanorum*, ch. 35, p. 247.

[68] *Chronicon Salernitanum*, ch. 111, p. 124. 'Agarenorum rex de quo prediximus Abdila cum sexaginta duo milia pugnatorum per Calabriam Salernum venit, et nonnulla oppida Calabrita-norum cepit.'

[69] Erchempert, *Historia Langobardorum Beneventanorum*, ch. 35, p. 248. '... depopulati sunt ex parte Neapolim, Beneventum et Capuam.'

[70] Erchempert, *Historia Langobardorum Beneventanorum*, ch. 35, p. 248. 'Cuius advento cognito, Saraceni Salernum relinquentes, Calabriam adeunt eamque intra se divisam repperientes, funditus depopularunt, ita ut deserta sit veluti in diluvio.'

[71] Erchempert, *Historia Langobardorum Beneventanorum*, ch. 44, p. 251. 'Per idem tempus Athanasius presul Neapolim militum magister preerat ... cum Saracenis pacem iniens ac primum infra portum aequoreum et urbis murum collocans, omnem terram Beneventanam simulque Romanam necnon et partem Spoletii dirruentes.'

[72] *Chronicon Salernitanum*, ch. 126, p. 139.

[73] Erchempert, *Historia Langobardorum Beneventanorum*, ch. 49 and 51, pp. 255–6; Liudprand of Cremona, *Antapodosis: The Works of Liudprand of Cremona*, trans. F. Wright (London,

responsible for the worst desecrations of the era. On 10 October 881, they fell upon the monastery of San Vincenzo on the Vulturno River. After slaughtering most of the monks, they set fire to the abbey and purloined its treasures.[74] Two years later, on 22 October 883, the same cruel fate was meted out to the monastery of Montecassino. The very edifice that housed the revered remains of Saint Benedict was put to the flame and Abbot Bertherius was run through at the altar.[75] The surviving Cassinese monks fled the area, first to Teano, then to Capua, and did not return until 949.[76] Finally outraged by the incessant depredations, the Neapolitans, Amalfitans and Capuans formed an alliance in 903 to root out the Garigliano pirate nest. They were thwarted, however, by the Gaetans.[77] It was not until August 915 that the colony was finally eradicated in a massive undertaking. Pope John X managed to cobble together an even larger coalition, which included not only the Capuans and Beneventans, but also men from Salerno and Spoleto. In order to ensure its success, he even purchased the neutrality of Gaeta with papal land and beseeched the Byzantine *strategos* of Longobardia, Nikolas Picingli, to use his fleet to blockade the mouth of the river. The Garigliano Muslims were wiped out after a three-month siege.[78]

Even then, there was no end to it. Muslim raiding of the *Mezzogiorno* (southern Italy and Sicily) continued unabated. The various relevant chronicles (Latin, Arab and Greek) list 34 Muslim incursions into Apulia or Calabria in the tenth century alone, a rate of about one every three years. In reality the frequency was probably much higher. Surely not every foray was noted. Many must have occurred beyond the knowledge of the few clerics capable of committing them to a chronicle. The ubiquitous use of the word '*depopularunt*' in the annals to describe the actions of the marauders indicates that the latter often left few witnesses for the sake of posterity. In point of fact, the raiding was likely unremitting. Ibn al-Athir made the following comment in regard to the death of al-Abbas ibn al-Fadl, the Aghlabid emir of Sicily, in 861: 'Al-Abbas had governed a good eleven years; having always continued the holy war winter and summer; having infested the [perfidious] territories of Calabria and Longobardia, and

1930), Bk II, ch. XLIV, pp. 90–1; *Die Werke Liudprands von Cremona*, ed. J. Becker (MGH, SRG, 3rd edn, XLI, Hanover, 1915), Bk II, ch. XLIV, p. 57.

74 *Chronicon Vulturnense*, I, pp. 362–5.

75 *Chronica Monasterii Casinensis*, ed. H. Hoffmann (MGH, SS, XXXIV, Hanover, 1980), Bk I, ch. 44, pp. 11–15.

76 *Chronica Monasterii Casinensis*, Bk I, ch. 59, pp. 147–8. See also G. A. Loud, 'Southern Italy in the tenth century', in *New Cambridge Medieval History, Volume III, c.900–c.1024*, ed. T. Reuter (Cambridge, 1999), pp. 624–45, especially 639–40.

77 *Chronica Monasterii Casinensis*, Bk I, ch. 50, pp. 130–1.

78 *Annales Beneventani*, anno 916, p. 175; *Chronica Monasterii Casinensis*, Bk I, ch. 52, pp. 133–4; Liudprand of Cremona, *Antapodosis: Works of Liudprand of Cremona*, Bk II, ch. LI–LIV, pp. 9–6; *Die Werke Liudprands von Cremona*, Bk II, ch. LI–LIV, pp. 61–2; Lupus Protospatarius, *Annales*, anno 916, p. 53.

having had Muslims settle in those provinces.'[79] Indeed, all evidence indicates that prosecution of an aggressive and continual 'jihad' against the 'Infidels' of southern Italy was considered a moral obligation of the emir of Sicily, that is, part of the unspoken job description, so to speak. Accordingly, most emirs, who were in a position to do so, dispatched raids as often as they could. Ibn al-Athir describes a 925–6 campaign into Longobardia and Calabria generated by Salim ibn Rasid, the Fatimid governor of Sicily, in coordination with Ubayd-Allah al-Mahdi, the first Fatimid caliph: 'They did not then cease to make raids upon all the towns of the island itself and of Calabria, which were held by the Rum, nor from the sacking and ravaging of those lands.'[80] Some of these campaigns were on an ominous scale. The Fatimid caliph al-Mansur bi-Allah reportedly launched an armada against Calabria in 951–2 that comprised 7,000 cavalry, 3,500 infantry and 'sailors beyond count', which ended up butchering the forces of Malachianos, the Byzantine governor of Bari.[81]

Moreover, whatever pirate nests or advance bases continued to exist had only one purpose: plunder. It was their *raison d'être*. They would hardly have taken a year or two off to plant crops. The only real solution was to evict them from the peninsula altogether in such a manner as to discourage further raiding. According to Thietmar (975–1018), bishop of Merseburg and chronicler of the Ottonian era, this is exactly what the German Emperor Otto II had in mind when he brought a huge army into southern Italy in the fall of 981.[82] On several occasions in the preceding half-dozen years Abu l-Qasim al-Kalbi, the emir of Sicily, had crossed over from Messina to wreak havoc in Calabria and exact tribute from its towns. Cosenza, Taranto, Gravina, Oria and Otranto were all attacked.[83] Consequently, when Abu l-Qasim came ashore in Calabria again in the summer of 982, Otto rushed to meet him. The battle took place at either Capo Colonna near Crotone or possibly Stilo, further down the east side of the toe (the exact site remains unclear). The result was a disastrous Christian defeat. Otto's magnificent army was decimated along with the flower of German nobility and such leading Lombards as Landulf of Capua and Pandulf of Salerno. Otto himself just barely managed to escape on a Byzantine *chelandion*.[84] Calabria and Apulia were, once

[79] Ibn al-Athir, *BAS*, I, p. 382.

[80] Ibn al-Athir, *BAS*, I, pp. 411–12.

[81] Ibn al-Athir, *BAS*, I, pp. 419–21; *Cambridge Chronicle*, *BAS*, I, pp. 289–90; Lupus Protospatarius, *Annales*, anno 951, p. 54.

[82] Thietmar of Merseburg, *Ottonian Germany: The Chronicon of Thietmar of Merseburg*, trans. D. Warner (Manchester, 2001), Bk 3, ch. 20, p. 143; *Die Chronik von Bischofs Thietmar von Merseburg*, ed. R. Holtzmann (MGH, SRG, IX, Berlin, 1935), Bk III, ch. 20, pp. 122–3. 'Calabriam a crebra Grecorum incursione et Saracenorum depredatione magnam vim perpeti cesar comperiens, ad supplementum exercitus sui Bawarios ac fortes in armis Alemannos vocavit.'

[83] Ibn al-Athir, *BAS*, I, pp. 431–2; Lupus Protospatarius, *Annales*, anno 976–7, p. 55.

[84] *Chronica Monasterii Casinensis*, Bk II, ch. 9, pp. 186–7; *Annales Beneventani*, anno 982, p. 176; Ibn al-Athir, *BAS*, I, pp. 433–4; Thietmar of Merseburg, *Ottonian Germany*, Bk 3, ch.

again, helpless to ward off the ravages of the Muslim raiders. In the last few years of the tenth century Lupus Protospatarius alone records four serious incursions in which Calabria was repeatedly devastated and the Apulian environs of both Taranto and Bari were attacked. In the final episode (994), Matera was burned.[85]

There were, of course, several reasons why the raids persisted. First of all, dissension reigned among the ranks of the polyglot Christian communities of southern Italy. The various Lombard princes were happy to hire bands of Muslim mercenaries in their aspiration to aggrandize their holdings at the expense of each other. Then there was the complicity of the Campanian city-states. Amalfi, Gaeta and Naples often fostered the favor of the Muslims, because, to be fair, they had little choice. If the mercantile communities, of which Amalfi was the most prominent, wanted continued access to the lucrative markets of the East, such as Alexandria and Constantinople, they had to maintain friendly relations with the Muslims. The latter held the central Mediterranean. In his ground-breaking 1967 article in *Speculum*, 'The Relations of Amalfi with the Arab World before the Crusades', Armand Citarella encapsulates the situation nicely:

> The conquest of Sicily placed under Arab control not only the colonies of Palermo and Messina but, vastly more important, the vital route to Egypt and the East Mediterranean via the Strait of Messina. A state war, or even unfriendly relations with the Arabs, would have inflicted unbearable losses on the shipping of the republic [Amalfi] and the commercial ventures of her citizens. All of these reasons made coexistence and even collaboration with the Arabs an absolute necessity from which no deviation was possible.[86]

No wonder Pope John VIII's offers of huge payoffs and trade concessions combined with threats of excommunication in the 880s failed to induce the Amalfitans to break ranks with their Muslim partners.[87] But an even more glaring explanation for the failure to curtail Muslim raiding in southern Italy was the inability of the two great Christian powers of the era, the Byzantine Empire and the German Empire, to maintain a permanent military presence in the region. In regard to the German Empire, the problem was compounded by the fact that it possessed no maritime assets at all. The proximity of the Muslims in Sicily and North Africa meant that they would always be able to have their way in Apulia and Calabria once imperial forces from either the East or the West were withdrawn.

Regardless of the reasons for the raiding, the eleventh century began no better than the tenth ended. The *Annales Beneventani* reports that Bari was attacked in

---

20–1, pp. 143–4; *Die Chronik*, Bk III, ch. 20–1, pp. 122–5. *Anonymi Barensis*, p. 148, and Lupus Protospatarius, *Annales*, p. 55, implausibly call it a victory for Otto and note it in 981.

[85] Lupus Protospatarius, *Annales*, anno 994, p. 56.

[86] A. Citarella, 'The Relations of Amalfi with the Arab World before the Crusades', *Speculum*, XLII (1967), pp. 299–312, especially 303.

[87] Pope John VIII, *Papae Registrum*, ed. E. Caspar (MGH, EP, VII, Berlin, 1928), no. 246, pp. 214–15; no. 250, pp. 218–19.

1002, as were Naples, Benevento and Capua. Ascoli was actually taken.[88] A year later, the *Annales Barenses* records that a certain *caid* (Muslim military leader) named Saphi laid siege to Bari from May until October, at which time the blockade was forcibly lifted by a Venetian fleet under the command of the Doge Peter Orseolo II.[89] Montescaglioso was besieged in 1003 as well[90] and Capua was assaulted once again in 1007.[91] Bitonto and Cosenza were both captured in 1009.[92] And several of the pertinent Latin annals report a 'Saracen' siege of Salerno in 1016.[93]

The failure of this latter siege would mark a dramatic turning point. After 1016, there were no further recorded incursions by the Muslims of North Africa or Sicily in Campania whatsoever. In fact, in all of southern Italy there would only be one final spate of Muslim raiding for almost half a century. Lupus Protospatarius documents four attacks on Calabria and Apulia between 1020 and 1031: the capture of Bisignano in 1020, a brief siege of Bari in 1023 followed by the seizure of Palagiano near Taranto, the siege of the Castello Obbiano (Uggiano) at Otranto in 1029, and the taking of Cassano in 1031 accompanied by the defeat of the Greek *catepan* (provincial governor), Pothos.[94] The great nineteenth-century Italian Orientalist Michele Amari attributes all of these raids to a certain Apulian (presumably a Muslim) named Rayca and one of the last Kalbite emirs of Sicily, Ahmad al-Akhal.[95] Ibn al-Athir describes the latter as follows: 'Al-Akhal started out in government with virtue and zeal for the holy war: he called the warriors to arms; he sent the *gualdane* [legions] into the land of the Infidels, where the Muslims burned, plundered, led [the inhabitants] into captivity and brought disorder.'[96] He would be the last emir of Sicily to do so. Between 827, when the Aghlabid conquest of Sicily was begun, and 1031 there were well over sixty 'Saracen' raids of southern Italy recorded by the relevant contemporary sources. After 1031 Muslim raiding of the Italian mainland all but ceased.

There are probably a multitude of reasons for this, such as open discord among the 'Saracens' of Sicily, but one glaring fact stands out: by 1016–17 the Normans had arrived. While we can never be certain, the Normans may even have been

---

[88] *Annales Beneventani*, anno 1002, p. 177; *Annales Cavenses*, anno 1002, p. 189; *Annales Ceccanenses*, ed. G. Pertz (MGH, SS, XIX, Hanover, 1866), anno 1002, p. 281; *Annales Casinenses*, ed. G. Pertz (MGH, SS, XIX, Hanover, 1866), anno 1001, p. 305.

[89] *Annales Barenses*, anno 1003, p. 53.

[90] Lupus Protospatarius, *Annales*, anno 1003, p. 56.

[91] *Annales Beneventani*, anno 1007, p. 177.

[92] *Annales Beneventani*, anno 1009, p. 177; Lupus Protospatarius, *Annales*, anno 1009, p. 56.

[93] *Annales Beneventani*, anno 1016, p. 177; *Anonymi Barensis*, anno 1016, p. 148; Lupus Protospatarius, *Annales*, anno 1016, p. 57.

[94] Lupus Protospatarius, *Annales*, anni 1020, 1023, 1029 and 1031, p. 57.

[95] Amari, *Storia dei Musulmani di Sicilia*, ed. C. Nallino (3 vols, 2nd edn, Catania, 1935–9), II, pp. 401–2.

[96] Ibn al-Athir, *BAS*, I, p. 444.

involved in the failed 'Saracen' siege of Salerno. There is a pervasive tradition among several of the Latin chroniclers that a small group of Normans led the lifting of the siege. This account, among other competing narratives, has been mired in controversy and exhaustively investigated by a host of modern scholars, most prominently Einar Joranson and John France.[97] The most dispassionate and reasonable discussion, however, is provided by Graham Loud, who sees plausibility in some elements of each of the various versions of the story.[98] Amatus, a Benedictine monk of Montecassino and Italo-Norman chronicler, relates the tale of 40 Norman pilgrims returning from Jerusalem who, around the turn of the millennium, found Salerno under siege by 'Saracens' demanding tribute. Outraged, they convinced the prince of the city to give them arms and horses with which they drove the raiders into the sea. The grateful prince then richly rewarded them and begged them to return with some of their warlike compatriots.[99] This story was later repeated almost verbatim in the second redaction of Leo Marsicanus's *Chronica monasterii Casinensis*.[100] Conversely, neither William of Apulia nor Geoffrey Malaterra, the other two primary chroniclers of the Normans in the south, mentions the Salerno story. William focuses, instead, on a chance meeting between Melus, an anti-Byzantine Lombard patriot, and some Norman pilgrims at Saint Michael's sanctuary on Monte Gargano (northeastern Apulia) in 1016.[101] Malaterra addresses neither tradition, but Orderic Vitalis (born 1075), perhaps the best-known Norman historian, not only recounts the Salerno story, but adds a few more lurid details. He tells of a hundred Norman knights riding down some 20,000 hapless Muslim marauders on the shoreline.[102] Orderic's description is typically fanciful, but it contains some elements of plausibility and may have, in fact, not been far from the mark. The beach before Salerno is and, judging from late medieval maps of the city, has always been quite narrow. It would require no great stretch of imagination to envision a small but audacious band of Norman cavalry, backed by an aroused citizenry, charging into the midst of a large group of Muslim marauders dining on Campanian bread and cheese while waiting patiently for the delivery of their demanded tribute. It would have been a very nasty shock indeed, doubtless engendering a general

97   E. Joranson, 'The inception of the career of the Normans in Italy – legend and history', *Speculum*, XXIII (1948), pp. 353–96; J. France, 'The occasion of the coming of the Normans to Italy', *Journal of Medieval History*, XVII (1991), pp. 185–205.

98   G.A. Loud, *The Age of Robert Guiscard: Southern Italy and the Norman Conquest* (Harlow, 2000), pp. 60–6.

99   Amatus of Montecassino, *The History of the Normans*, trans. P. Dunbar (Woodbridge, 2004), Bk I, ch. 17–19, pp. 49–50; *Storia de' Normanni*, ed. V. de Bartholomaeis (FSI, Rome, 1935), Bk I, ch. XVII–XIX, pp. 21–4.

100 *Chronica Monasterii Casinensis*, Bk II, ch. 37, pp. 236–7.

101 William of Apulia, *La Geste de Robert Guiscard*, trans. M. Mathieu (Palermo, 1961), Bk I, lines 11–27, pp. 98–101.

102 Orderic Vitalis, *The Ecclesiastical History of Orderic Vitalis*, ed. and trans. M. Chibnall (6 vols, OMT, Oxford, 1968–80), II, Bk III, pp. 56–9.

panic and rout. While none is recorded, there certainly could have been a siege of Salerno around 1000, given the frequency of Muslim raiding at that time. The story could also have actually referred to the 1016 siege as Ferdinand Chalandon surmised in his magisterial two-volume study of the Normans in the South.[103] And it is assuredly not beyond the realm of possibility that the Normans were present as pilgrims or more likely, soldiers of fortune. 'The story of Amatus that there was a Muslim attack on Salerno c. 999/1000 is therefore perfectly credible,' observes Loud, who adds, 'One need not dismiss it as legend, nor does one have to redate it to c. 1016, on the eve of Melus's second attack on Apulia, as Chalandon and others have done.'[104] Nonetheless, it is entirely plausible that Norman knights contributed to the failure of the 'Saracen' siege of Salerno in 1016.

Whatever actually occurred, one thing is indisputable: as of 1017, the Normans were present in southern Italy. Nearly all the Latin chronicles agree that this was when a small contingent of them had joined the Lombard noble Melus for the invasion of Byzantine Apulia.[105] They began the campaign from Capua in Campania, gaining some initial successes. Amatus later recounts, 'When it became known at Salerno how the Normans had fought to aid Melus and how they died, the Normans of Salerno came with a great army and filled the country with brave knights.'[106] When ultimately Melus's comrades were defeated by the Byzantine *catepan*, Basil Boiannes, at Cannae in 1018, it was to Campania that the Normans returned.[107] Subsequently, the Norman adventurers took up employment with the various Lombard princes of Campania, eventually earning a stronghold for themselves at Aversa in 1031 under their leader, Rainulf.[108] Thus, it was, in all probability, no coincidence that Campania was the first region of southern Italy to free itself from Muslim raiding.

---

[103] F. Chalandon, *Histoire de la Domination Normande en Italie et en Sicile* (2 vols, Paris, 1907), I, p. 49.

[104] Loud, *Age of Robert Guiscard*, p. 64.

[105] Amatus, *History of the Normans*, Bk I, ch. 21, p. 51; *Storia de' Normanni*, Bk I, ch. XXI, pp. 27–8; *Annales Beneventani*, anno 1017 p. 178; *Annales Cavenses*, anno 1017, p. 189; *Annales Casinenses*, anno 1016–17, p. 305; *Annales Ceccanenses*, anno 1017, p. 281; *Anonymi Barensis*, anno 1017, p. 148; *Chronica Monasterii Casinensis*, Bk II, ch. 37, pp. 236–40; Lupus Protospatarius, *Annales*, anno 1017, p. 57; William of Apulia, *La Geste de Robert Guiscard*, Bk I, lines 52–6, pp. 102–3.

[106] Amatus, *History of the Normans*, Bk I, ch. 23, p. 52; *Storia de' Normanni*, Bk I, ch. XXIII, p. 30. 'Mès, quant fu seü a Salerne que ensi avoient combatu li Normant por aidier à Melo et estoient mort, vindrent cil Normant de Salerne. De li Normant vint grant exercit, et emplirent la contrée de fortissimes chevaliers.'

[107] Amatus, *History of the Normans*, Bk I, ch. 20–3, pp. 51–2; *Storia de' Normanni*, Bk I, ch. XX–XXIII, pp. 27–38; *Anonymi Barensis*, anni 1018–19, pp. 148–9; *Chronica Monasterii Casinensis*, Bk II, ch. 37, pp. 236–40; Lupus Protospatarius, *Annales*, anno 1019, p. 57; William of Apulia, *La Geste de Robert Guiscard*, Bk I, lines 52–94, pp. 102–5.

[108] Amatus, *History of the Normans*, Bk I, ch. 42, p. 60; *Storia de' Normanni*, Bk I, ch. XLII, pp. 53–4; William of Apulia, *La Geste de Robert Guiscard*, Bk I, lines 170–4, pp. 108–9.

Soon, the Normans would spread to Apulia and Calabria. By 1041, following participation in the ill-fated Byzantine invasion of Sicily in 1038 under the Byzantine general Giorgios Maniakes, a band of Normans from Salerno had established themselves at Melfi in the Basilicata near the Apulian frontier under the leadership of a north Italian mercenary named Arduin.[109] And in the mid-1040s a Norman presence was initiated in the Val di Crati area of Calabria, first at Scribla then later at San Marco d'Argentano, under none other than Robert Guiscard, the most notorious Hauteville of them all.[110] In other words, for whatever the reasons, the cessation of Muslim raiding in the *Mezzogiorno* coincided almost perfectly with the arrival of the Normans under arms. After 1031, there are only two more recorded raids on the *Mezzogiorno* for the entire remainder of the eleventh century. Both were on Nicotera on the west coast of Calabria, one in 1074 and the other in 1084; and both were met with brutal, swift responses by the Norman lord who led the conquest of Sicily, Robert's brother Roger. In the first incident, the North African pirates who raided Nicotera returned the following year to try their luck at Mazara, Sicily. This time Roger rushed to Mazara, broke the siege and drove the marauders into the sea.[111] The second raid was committed by Ibn el-Werd (Benarvet in the Latin chronicles), the 'Saracen' emir of Syracuse. It, too, was answered the very next year, but the response was massive. Roger fanned the flames of religious fervor, giving the enterprise a crusade-like aura. He spent the winter building a whole fleet at Messina; then sailed into Syracuse harbor the following spring and personally engaged Ibn el-Werd's flagship. The Muslim emir ended up at the bottom of the harbor and Syracuse became the latest Norman conquest.[112] There were no other recorded Muslim raids on southern Italy or Sicily until well into the twelfth century.

Thus, as the Normans moved southward and down from the hinterlands into the coastal areas, the Muslims retreated into a defensive posture until they no longer represented a threat to the southern Italian peninsula. To be sure, internal strife within Kalbite Sicily was the primary reason for the reversal Muslim fortunes on the peninsula. More or less constant civil warfare predominated on the island following the 1037 assassination of Emir Ahmad

---

[109] Amatus, *History of the Normans*, Bk II, ch. 19, p. 70; *Storia de' Normanni*, Bk II, ch. XIX, pp. 77–8; Geoffrey Malaterra, *Deeds of Count Roger of Calabria and Sicily and of his brother Duke Robert Guiscard*, trans. K. Wolf (Ann Arbor, 2005), Bk 1, ch. 8–9, pp. 56–7; *De rebus gestis Rogerii Calabriae et Siciliae comitis et Roberti Guiscardi ducis fratris eius*, ed. E. Pontieri (RIS, 2nd edn, Bologna, 1927–8), Bk I, ch. VIII–IX, pp. 11–12; William of Apulia, *La Geste de Robert Guiscard*, Bk I, lines 216–47, pp. 110–13.

[110] Amatus, *History of the Normans*, Bk III, ch. 7, p. 88; *Storia de' Normanni*, Bk III, ch. VII, pp. 120–1; Malaterra, *Deeds of Count Roger*, Bk 1, ch. 12, p. 60; *De rebus gestis Rogerii*, Bk I, ch. XII, p. 14.

[111] Malaterra, *Deeds of Count Roger*, Bk 3, ch. 8–9, pp. 138–9; *De rebus gestis Rogerii*, Bk III, ch. VIII–IX, p. 61.

[112] Malaterra, *Deeds of Count Roger*, Bk 4, ch. 1–2, pp. 177–9; *De rebus gestis Rogerii*, Bk IV, ch. I–II, pp. 85–6.

al-Akhal. By the time the last Kalbite emir, Hasan as-Samsam, was deposed in 1053, Muslim rule on Sicily had degenerated into a handful of petty principalities whose violent rivalries irrevocably weakened the position of the Muslims in southern Italy.[113] Nonetheless, the arrival of the Normans almost certainly exacerbated the process. They had horses, they had hauberks, and they were there to stay. Moreover, they were mercenaries bent on conquest, just like their Muslim predecessors in the region; only they brooked no competition. Therefore, given the geography of the region, it was only a matter of time before they also had ships and the will to use them. Phase one of the Norman conquest of the central Mediterranean had begun; the Muslim grip on the north shore had been broken.

Brothers in battle: joint naval operations by the Hautevilles

In truth, there was no Norman conquest in the sense of a concerted effort to subjugate southern Italy by a unified front of Norman knights. What occurred could more aptly be characterized as a hostile takeover by the House of Hauteville. When these pilgrims-turned-mercenaries first appeared in Apulia, Calabria and Campania in the early eleventh century, they operated in small bands as soldiers-for-hire to the highest bidder. They changed allegiances whenever it seemed advantageous and fought with one another as much as they did with the Byzantine and Lombard princes who competed for their services. The Normans eventually appropriated petty lordships for themselves at places such as Aversa more by serendipitous opportunity than by any cohesive strategy.[114] That all changed when the first of Tancred de Hauteville's twelve sons appeared on the scene in the late 1030s.[115]

Portentously, the brothers William, Drogo and Humphrey arrived in Campania on the eve of the great amphibious assault on Sicily mounted in 1038 at the behest of the Byzantine Emperor Michael IV, the Paphlagonian (the Epileptic). There had been at least two previous attempts by Constantinople to recover the island. Both failed miserably. In 965, the Emperor Nikephoros II Phocas sent the *Patrikios* Manuel with an army of some 40,000 combatants and 'a considerable fleet' against the 'Saracens' of Sicily.[116] The campaign began well enough with the capture of Messina, but then the young, impetuous noble allowed his army to be ambushed and annihilated in the rugged terrain near Rametta northwest of Mount Etna. Shortly afterwards, the accompanying armada was

---

[113] Ibn al-Athir, *BAS*, I, pp. 444–7. See also Ahmad, *Islamic Sicily*, pp. 35–6; Loud, *Age of Robert Guiscard*, pp. 147–8.

[114] Amatus, *History of the Normans*, Bk I, ch. 42, p. 60; *Storia de' Normanni*, Bk I, ch. XLII, pp. 53–4; William of Apulia, *La Geste de Robert Guiscard*, Bk I, lines 169–74, pp. 108–9.

[115] Malaterra, *Deeds of Count Roger*, Bk I, ch. 4–5, pp. 53–4; *De rebus gestis Rogerii*, Bk I, ch. IV–V, p. 9.

[116] Ibn al-Athir, *BAS*, I, p. 425; John Skylitzes, *Synopsis historiōn*, p. 220.

destroyed by a Fatimid fleet in a fierce naval engagement near Messina, known in Muslim sources as the 'Battle of the Strait'. Its *drungarios* (admiral of the fleet), the eunuch Niketas, was hauled off to Africa in chains.[117] The second expedition was organized by the Emperor Basil II Bulgaroctonus (Bulgar-slayer) in 1025 to take advantage of the chaos occurring in Kalbite Sicily at the time. He had gathered a massive force of Macedonians, Russians, Vlachs, Bulgars, Turks and Varangians under the trusted eunuch Orestes Kytonitos and sent it ahead to Calabria. The Kalbite emir of Palermo, Ahmad al-Akhal, was so alarmed that he sought salvation from the Zirid prince of Ifriqiyah, al-Mu'izz ibn Badis. Al-Mu'izz responded by dispatching a 400-ship armada, but it was waylaid by a storm off the island of Pantelleria and shredded. In the end, the invasion fell apart when Basil II passed away a few days before Christmas of 1025.[118]

The 1038 enterprise would achieve much greater success. This was, in part, because it was commanded by the highly competent general, Giorgios Maniakes, who had won several notable victories in Asia Minor. His forces included the vaunted Varangian guard with the celebrated Harald Hardrada at its head.[119] But, if the Norman chroniclers Amatus of Montecassino and Geoffrey Malaterra can be believed, the success of the campaign was, in large measure, due to the 300-knight contingent of Normans led by the brothers Hauteville: William, Drogo and Humphrey.[120] They were provided by their employer at the time, Guaimar IV of Salerno, who was apparently trying to get rid of the troublesome trio.[121] Once again, the operation began promisingly with the swift capture of Messina, followed by the massacre of a Muslim army at Troina. Even strategically vital Syracuse soon became a Byzantine possession once again.[122] Ultimately, however, the effort foundered when squabbling erupted over booty and Maniakes was recalled to Constantinople owing to court intrigue.[123] Apparently, the hot-tempered Maniakes had publicly rebuked the incompetent but well-connected

[117] *Cambridge Chronicle*, BAS, I, p. 293; Ibn al-Athir, *BAS*, I, pp. 425–9; John Skylitzes, *Synopsis historiōn*, pp. 224–5; Leo the Deacon, *The History of Leo the Deacon*, trans. A. Talbot and D. Sullivan (Washington, DC, 2005), Bk V, ch. 7–8, pp. 115–17.

[118] *Annales Barenses*, anno 1027, p. 53; *Anonymi Barensis*, anno 1025, p. 149; Ibn al-Athir, *BAS*, I, p. 440; John Skylitzes, *Synopsis historiōn*, p. 306.

[119] Lupus Protospatarius, *Annales*, anno 1038, p. 58; John Skylitzes, *Synopsis historiōn*, pp. 316–17, 320–1, 330. Hardrada was Harald Sigurdsson, later King Harald III of Norway, defeated at Stamford Bridge in 1066.

[120] Amatus, *History of the Normans*, Bk II, ch. 8, p. 66; *Storia de' Normanni*, Bk II, ch. VIII, p. 68; Malaterra, *Deeds of Count Roger*, Bk I, ch. 7, pp. 55–6; *De rebus gestis Roger*, Bk I, ch. VII, pp. 10–11.

[121] Malaterra, *Deeds of Count Roger*, Bk I, ch. 7, p. 55; *De rebus gestis Rogerii*, Bk I, ch. VII, p. 10.

[122] Amatus, *History of the Normans*, Bk II, ch. 8–9, p. 66; *Storia de' Normanni*, Bk II, ch. VIII–IX, pp. 68–70; Malaterra, *Deeds of Count Roger*, Bk I, ch. 7, pp. 55–6; *De rebus gestis Rogerii*, Bk I, ch. VII, pp. 10–11.

[123] Amatus, *History of the Normans*, Bk II, ch. 9, pp. 66–7; *Storia de' Normanni*, Bk II, ch. IX, pp. 69–70; Malaterra, *Deeds of Count Roger*, Bk I, ch. 8, pp. 56–7; *De rebus gestis Rogerii*,

admiral of the fleet, Stephen, the Emperor Michael's brother-in-law.[124] Nonetheless, the experience may well have provided the spark that would engender Norman naval power in the Mediterranean. It most certainly provided the three Hauteville brothers with an object lesson in amphibious operations, one that must have included the over-water transportation of horses. William of Apulia indicated that a large cavalry component was present and, of course, the chief value of the Normans would have been as mounted warriors who normally rode their own specially trained *destriers* (warhorses).[125] Indeed, the eleventh-century Madrid manuscript of John Skylitzes' *Synopsis historiōn*, the so-called *Skylitzes Matritensis* (Codex Vitr. 26–2) of the Biblioteca Nacional, contains a miniature that depicts Maniakes' army defeating the Muslims at the Battle of Troina with a massive cavalry charge.[126] It was during this very engagement that Geoffrey Malaterra insists that William de Hauteville was in the vanguard, 'engaging the enemy with no more than his own knights',[127] presumably the Normans, all of whom must have been mounted. They would have paid keen attention to the means by which the Byzantines had conveyed those battle-winning mounts to the island. They would also have had a good look at a highly desirable land, which must have instilled in their minds some very attractive possibilities. Whatever the Hautevilles gleaned from the experience they would certainly have passed it on to their younger brothers, who arrived in the years following.

Another significant benefit of their participation in the Sicilian campaign of 1038 was that it enabled the Hautevilles to establish a reputation as formidable fighters. William, who had killed the *caid* (military governor) of Syracuse in single combat, would forever be known as 'Iron-Arm'.[128] This notoriety helped them acquire positions of leadership among the Norman cadres of southern Italy. Apparently dissatisfied with the division of booty, the Normans under William deserted the Greeks in Sicily and returned to the mainland in 1041. They soon established themselves at Melfi (in the Basilicata) under the loose command of Arduin of Milan, another disgruntled condottiere.[129] After the

Bk I, ch. VIII, pp. 11–12; William of Apulia, *La Geste de Robert Guiscard*, Bk I, lines 206–21, pp. 110–11.

[124] John Skylitzes, *Synopsis historiōn*, pp. 330, 336.

[125] William of Apulia, *La Geste de Robert Guiscard*, Bk I, lines 196–206, pp. 108–11. See also R. Davis, *The Medieval Warhorse* (London, 1989), pp. 55–61.

[126] V. Tsamakda, *The Illustrated Chronicle of Ioannes Skylitzes in Madrid* (Leiden, 2002), p. 239, miniature 504, fol. 213r.

[127] Malaterra, *Deeds of Count Roger*, Bk 1, ch. 7, p. 56; *De rebus gestis Rogerii*, Bk I, ch. VII, p. 11. '... *cum suae gentis tantum militibus cum hoste congreditur.*'

[128] Malaterra, *Deeds of Count Roger*, Bk 1, ch. 7, p. 56; *De rebus gestis Rogerii*, Bk I, ch. VII, p. 11.

[129] Amatus, *History of the Normans*, Bk II, ch. 14–19, pp. 68–70; *Storia de' Normanni*, Bk II, ch. XIV–XIX, pp. 72–8; Malaterra, *Deeds of Count Roger*, Bk I, ch. 8–9, pp. 56–7; *De rebus gestis Rogerii*, Bk I, ch. VIII–IX, pp. 11–12; William of Apulia, *La Geste de Robert Guiscard*, Bk I, lines 206–47, pp. 110–13.

latter disappeared from the scene, they briefly took up with Argyrus, the son of Melus, but when Argyrus switched sides and joined the Byzantine cause, the Normans of Melfi elected William Iron-Arm as their leader.[130] Under William they waged a war of petty conquest against the Byzantines of Apulia, which, despite some notable victories, was ultimately ineffective, achieving only ephemeral results. The Normans convincingly defeated the *Catepan* Michael Dokeianos twice in 1041: at the River Olivento in March and at Cannae in May.[131] But their subsequent efforts against Trani, Bari and other coastal communities came to naught.[132] The siege of Trani in 1042 fell apart when their unreliable ally, Argyrus, abruptly defected to the Greeks,[133] while the 1043 siege of Bari in alliance with the Guaimar IV of Salerno was scuttled after a mere five days.[134] This led Graham Loud to observe, 'The Byzantines retained possession of most of the larger towns: Bari itself, Trani, Brindisi, Taranto, Matera and Otranto.' Tellingly, he adds, 'It was only the smaller settlements, most of them inland, which had fallen to the invaders.'[135] Loud ascribes this to their small numbers, but the lack of naval assets and the ability to use them effectively must also have been a factor. Moreover, there appeared to be no master plan or overarching goal. The Normans operated basically as gangs of mounted thugs, preying on whomever they could.

When William died around 1046, Drogo took his place.[136] A year later the latter was confirmed as lord of the Apulian Normans by the Western Emperor,

---

[130]   Amatus, *History of the Normans*, Bk II, ch. 28–9, pp. 75–6; *Storia de' Normanni*, Bk II, ch. XXVIII–XXIX, pp. 91–5; Lupus Protospatarius, *Annales*, anno 1042, p. 58; Malaterra, *Deeds of Count Roger*, Bk I, ch. 9–10, pp. 58–9; *De rebus gestis Rogerii*, Bk I, ch. IX–X, pp. 12–13.

[131]   Amatus, *History of the Normans*, Bk II, ch. 21–3, pp. 71–3; *Storia de' Normanni*, Bk II, ch. XXI–XXIII, pp. 79–83; *Annales Barenses*, anno 1041, pp. 53–4; *Anonymi Barensis*, anno 1041, p. 149; Lupus Protospatarius, *Annales*, anno 1041, p. 58; Malaterra, *Deeds of Count Roger*, Bk I, ch. 9–10, pp. 57–9; *De rebus gestis Rogerii*, Bk I, ch. IX–X, pp. 11–12; William of Apulia, *La Geste de Robert Guiscard*, Bk I, lines 254–304, pp. 112–15; John Skylitzes, *Synopsis historiōn*, pp. 354–5.

[132]   John Skylitzes, *Synopsis historiōn*, pp. 354–5. 'And thus, the Franks occupied Italy as a conquered land and the indigenous populations, willingly or under duress, rallied to them, with the exception of Brindisi, Hidrous, Taranto and Bari. These four cities in fact remained loyal to the Romans.'

[133]   Amatus, *History of the Normans*, Bk II, ch. 28, p. 75; *Storia de' Normanni*, Bk II, ch. XXVIII, pp. 93–5; *Annales Barenses*, anno 1042, p. 56; *Anonymi Barensis*, anno 1042, p. 151; Lupus Protospatarius, *Annales*, anno 1042, p. 58; William of Apulia, *La Geste de Robert Guiscard*, Bk I, lines 478–85, pp. 124–5.

[134]   *Anonymi Barensis*, anno 1043, p. 151; William of Apulia, *La Geste de Robert Guiscard*, Bk II, lines 5–7, pp. 132–3.

[135]   Loud, *Age of Guiscard*, p. 100.

[136]   Amatus, *History of the Normans*, Bk II, ch. 35, p. 79; *Storia de' Normanni*, Bk II, ch. XXXV, pp. 101–3; Lupus Protospatarius, *Annales*, anno 1046, p. 59; Malaterra, *Deeds of Count Roger*, Bk I, ch. 12, p. 60; *De rebus gestis Rogerii*, Bk I, ch. XII, p. 14; William of Apulia, *La Geste de Robert Guiscard*, Bk II, lines 20–37, pp. 132–5.

Henry III.[137] The veneer of legitimacy did not change the Norman *modus oper-andi*, however. They ruthlessly ransacked the countryside until they became reviled. Continued Norman excesses in the region resulted in Drogo's murder in 1051 at Montillaro, near Bovino in northern Apulia.[138] Humphrey assumed the reins from him, but his leadership was as aimless as that of his predecessors. The plunder of Beneventan lands that were under papal protection at the time eventually caused the Normans to run afoul of Pope Leo IX. Outraged to the point of action, the pontiff gathered a sizable army of recruits from the local populace, along with 'innumerable Swabians and Germans'[139] who, according to Malaterra, were supposedly supplied by the German Emperor Henry III.[140] He even struck an alliance with the Byzantine *catepan*, Argyrus, to rid the land of the Normans once and for all.[141]

With a huge papal army marching from the north and a Greek–Lombard army under their erstwhile ally, Argyrus, moving up from the south, the position of the grossly outnumbered Normans looked untenable. A little-touted engagement at Siponto, just south of the Gargano Peninsula, prior to the arrival of papal forces, however, set the stage for what would become one of the greatest ever Norman battlefield triumphs. Humphrey's knights apparently controlled the interior of Apulia to such an extent that Argyrus felt compelled to transport his troops from Bari to Siponto by sea. Humphrey and Peter Amicus, a powerful Norman count of northern Apulia, must have learned of the move, because they were there at Siponto waiting for him. The *Anonymi Barensis* reports that Argyrus's men were slaughtered and he himself just barely managed to escape to Vieste on the Gargano Peninsula.[142] Thus, the papal forces ended up meeting the Normans at Civitate without the support of Argyrus's army.

Though still outnumbered, the Norman heavy cavalry proved decisive at Civitate in the summer of 1053. The Norman knights ran the Italians/Lombards from the field and annihilated the Swabian–German contingent to the last man.[143]

---

[137] Amatus, *History of the Normans*, Bk III, ch. 1–2, 7, pp. 87–8; *Storia de' Normanni*, Bk III, ch. I–II, VII, pp. 116–17, 120–1; Malaterra, *Deeds of Count Roger*, Bk I, ch. 12, p. 60; *De rebus gestis Rogerii*, Bk I, ch. XII, p. 14.

[138] Amatus, *History of the Normans*, Bk III, ch. 22, pp. 93–4; *Storia de' Normanni*, Bk III, ch. XXII, pp. 135–8; *Annales Beneventani*, anno 1051, p. 179; *Anonymi Barensis*, anno 1051, p. 151; Lupus Protospatarius, *Annales*, anno 1051, p. 59; Malaterra, *Deeds of Count Roger*, Bk I, ch. 13, pp. 60–1; *De rebus gestis Rogerii*, Bk I, ch. XIII, pp. 14–15; William of Apulia, *La Geste de Robert Guiscard*, Bk II, lines 75–80, pp. 136–7.

[139] William of Apulia, *La Geste de Robert Guiscard*, Bk II, lines 80–4, pp. 136–7. '… Alemannis innumeris et Teutonicis…'

[140] Malaterra, *Deeds of Count Roger*, Bk I, ch. 14, p. 61; *De rebus gestis Rogerii*, Bk I, ch. XIV, p. 15.

[141] Amatus, *History of the Normans*, Bk III, ch. 18, 23, 24, 37, pp. 92, 94–5, 99; *Storia de' Normanni*, Bk III, ch. XVIII, XXIII, XXIV, XXXVII, pp. 133, 138–40, 150–1.

[142] *Anonymi Barensis*, anno 1052, p. 152.

[143] Amatus, *History of the Normans*, Bk III, ch. 39–40, pp. 100–1; *Storia de' Normanni*, Bk III, ch. XXXIX–XL, pp. 152–6; *Annales Beneventani*, anno 1053, p. 179; *Anonymi Barensis*,

The Italo-Normans had won so devastating a victory that the ultimate conquest of southern Italy was virtually inevitable. In fact, Malaterra goes so far as to profess that, in the aftermath, the pontiff 'conceded to them all the land that they had conquered – as well as any they might acquire in the future in the regions of Calabria and Sicily – as a hereditary fief from St Peter to be held by Humphrey and his heirs'.[144] Such a papal proclamation, even if true, was obviously derived under duress and was, perhaps, a bit premature, but it was certainly predictive. After all, Civitate gave the Normans military supremacy over the lower Italian peninsula. More importantly, it brought to prominence the man who would lead the final stage of the conquest and make it a reality: Robert de Hauteville.

At first, Robert operated as chief of a band of mounted brigands in the hard-scrabble Scribla area of Calabria in the service of his older brother, Drogo. The latter suppressed Robert's ambitions by keeping him in poverty.[145] Following Drogo's assassination, his brother Humphrey, typical of the Hauteville clan, treated his penurious younger brother no better. Nonetheless, Robert's wits as a soldier of fortune soon earned him a following as well as the sobriquet *Guiscard*, meaning 'the cunning' in old French.[146] He increased his stature immeasurably by his courageous leadership of one of the three Norman wings at Civitate.[147] William of Apulia, Guiscard's principal biographer, likened Robert's heroics to that of an enraged 'lion'.[148] It was not, however, until the death of Humphrey and the arrival of Roger in 1057 that a path towards empowerment began to take shape.[149] From that point on, a pattern can be discerned in the chronology and

anno 1052, p. 152; *Annales Casinenses*, anno 1053, p. 306; *Annales Cavenses*, anno 1054, p. 189; Lupus Protospatarius, *Annales*, anno 1053, p. 59; Malaterra, *Deeds of Count Roger*, Bk I, ch. 14, pp. 61–2; *De rebus gestis Rogerii*, Bk I, ch. XIV, p. 15; William of Apulia, *La Geste de Robert Guiscard*, Bk II, lines 80–286, pp. 136–49.

[144] Malaterra, *Deeds of Count Roger*, Bk I, ch. 14, p. 62; *De rebus gestis Rogerii*, Bk I, ch. XIV, p. 15. '... omnem terram, quam pervaserant et quam ulterius versus Calabriam et Siciliam lucrari possent, de sancti Petri haereditali feudo sibi et haeredibus suis possidendam concessit circa annos MLII[I].'

[145] Amatus, *History of the Normans*, Bk III, ch. 7–9, pp. 88–9; *Storia de' Normanni*, Bk III, ch. VII–IX, pp. 120–2; Malaterra, *Deeds of Count Roger*, Bk I, ch. 12, p. 60; *De rebus gestis Rogerii*, Bk I, ch. XII, p. 14.

[146] Amatus, *History of the Normans*, Bk III, ch. 11, p. 89; *Storia de' Normanni*, Bk III, ch. XI, pp. 125–6; Malaterra, *Deeds of Count Roger*, Bk I, ch. 16–17, pp. 62–5; *De rebus gestis Rogerii*, Bk I, ch. XVI–XVII, pp. 16–18; William of Apulia, *La Geste de Robert Guiscard*, Bk II, lines 127–30, pp. 138–9.

[147] Amatus, *History of the Normans*, Bk III, ch. 39–40, p. 100; *Storia de' Normanni*, Bk III, ch. XXXIX–XL, pp. 152–6; Malaterra, *Deeds of Count Roger*, Bk I, ch. 14, pp. 61–2; *De rebus gestis Rogerii*, Bk I, ch. XIV, p. 15; William of Apulia, *La Geste de Robert Guiscard*, Bk II, lines 82–257, pp. 136–47.

[148] William of Apulia, *La Geste de Robert Guiscard*, Bk II, lines 228–31, pp. 144–5. 'Ut leo, cum frendens animalia forte minora acriter invadit ... insanit, magis et maioribus ira accensa stimulat...'

[149] Amatus, *History of the Normans*, Bk III, ch. 43, p. 100; Bk IV, ch. 2, p. 111; *Storia de' Normanni*, Bk III, ch. XLIII, p. 159; Bk IV, ch. II, pp. 181–2; Malaterra, *Deeds of Count Roger*,

geography of Robert and Roger's actions that bespeak an evolving master plan – one that, of necessity, had to include the use of naval forces.

On his death bed, Humphrey apparently made Robert caretaker of his Apulian lordship until his son, Abelard, could come of age. Robert seized it in perpetuity instead and immediately gave flight to his plan.[150] Roger appeared at his side at almost the same moment.[151] Together, they embarked upon the conquest of Calabria. Robert quickly subdued Nicastro, Maida and Canalea in the north while Roger pacified the Saline Valley.[152] Robert was at the siege of Cariati in 1059 when he learned of Pope Nicholas II's presence at the synod of Melfi.[153] The pontiff, in contention with competing papal claimant Benedict X and at odds with the German emperor, badly needed a champion. Robert seized the opportunity.[154] We know nothing of the negotiations that subsequently took place at Melfi. We only know the result. In August 1059, the Norman knight swore fealty to the Holy See with an oath that began with these words: 'I, Robert, by the grace of God and St Peter, Duke of Apulia and Calabria, and in the future with the help of both of Sicily...'[155] Leo Marsicanus corroborates this in the chronicle of Montecassino: 'In these days there, the pope confirmed the principality of Capua to Richard and to Robert the duchy of Apulia and Calabria and of Sicily.'[156] Sicily was almost certainly Robert's idea. The pope had no choice but to acquiesce because of his desperate need for military support. Thus, from this moment on, it was clear that the Hautevilles' ultimate goal was the conquest of an island. Robert must have known then that he was going to require the use of maritime assets.

In any event, Robert wasted no time in capitalizing on his newly won legitimacy. He completed the siege of Cariati; and then subjugated Rossano,

---

Bk 1, ch. 18–19, p. 66; *De rebus gestis Rogerii*, Bk I, ch. XVIII–XIX, p. 18; William of Apulia, *La Geste de Robert Guiscard*, Bk II, lines 358–80, pp. 150–3.

[150] Amatus, *History of the Normans*, Bk IV, ch. 2, p. 111; *Storia de' Normanni*, Bk IV, ch. 2, p. 111; Lupus Protospatarius, *Annales*, anno 1056, p. 59; Malaterra, *Deeds of Count Roger*, Bk 1, ch. 18, p. 66; *De rebus gestis Rogerii*, Bk I, ch. XVIII, p. 18; William of Apulia, *La Geste de Robert Guiscard*, Bk II, lines 364–7, pp. 152–3.

[151] Amatus, *History of the Normans*, Bk III, ch. 43, p. 101; *Storia de' Normanni*, Bk III, ch. XLIII, p. 159; Malaterra, *Deeds of Count Roger*, Bk 1, ch. 19, pp. 66–7; *De rebus gestis Rogerii*, Bk I, ch. XIX, pp. 18–19; William of Apulia, *La Geste de Robert Guiscard*, Bk II, lines 360–4, pp. 152–3.

[152] Malaterra, *Deeds of Count Roger*, Bk 1, ch. 18–19, pp. 66–7; *De rebus gestis Rogerii*, Bk I, ch. XVIII–XIX, pp. 18–19.

[153] William of Apulia, *La Geste de Robert Guiscard*, Bk II, lines 389–406, pp. 152–3.

[154] H. Cowdrey, *The Age of Abbot Desiderius: Montecassino, the Papacy, and the Normans in the Eleventh and Early Twelfth Centuries* (Oxford, 1983), pp. 112–13.

[155] *Le Liber Censuum de l'Eglise Romaine*, eds P. Fabre and L. Duchesne (3 vols, BEFAR 2, série 6, Paris, 1889–1952), I, pp. 421–2. See also Loud, *Age of Guiscard*, p. 130. 'Ego Robertus Dei gratia et sancti Petri dux Apulie et Calabrie et utroque subveniente futurus Sicilie...'

[156] *Chronica Monasterii Casinensis*, Bk III, ch. 15, p. 377. 'Hisdem quoque diebus et Richardo principatum Capuanum et Robberto ducatum Apulie et Calabrie atque Sicilie confirmavit.'

Cosenza and Gerace in rapid succession as he worked his way down the toe of Calabria towards Reggio.[157] Finally, in late autumn 1059, he and Roger laid siege to Reggio, the last bastion of the Byzantine Empire in Calabria and springboard for the invasion of Sicily.[158] Chalandon asserts that the duke then left his younger brother in charge of the siege while he returned to Apulia and rapidly reduced Brindisi and Taranto.[159] The *Chronicon Breve Nortmannicum* supports this contention, but unfortunately this source is suspect and no other chronicle records these actions,[160] save perhaps Lupus Protospatarius who mentions that Robert 'again seized Brindisi' in 1062.[161] If he in fact did so, it may have been because he wanted to shore up his rear and keep the Byzantines off guard so that they could not easily relieve Reggio. In any event, Robert rejoined Roger before the walls of Reggio and soon gained the city's submission.[162] Thus, in the space of a mere four years, beginning with assumption of Humphrey's domains in 1057, Robert had gone from bandit to master of most of Apulia and all of Calabria. By early 1060, he and Roger now sat poised in Reggio, ready to launch their long-anticipated invasion of Sicily.

They did not wait long. Roger made a reconnaissance raid across the strait with 60 knights later that year. They landed near Messina and were promptly attacked by the city's Muslim garrison. Malaterra, Roger's biographer, tells us that the young Norman knight and his men got the best of it, but the fact is that they were forced to withdraw.[163] Robert sent his brother on another such mission the following year, this time under the guidance of Geoffrey Ridel, an experienced soldier.[164] Malaterra says there were 160 knights, but Ibn Khaldun insists

---

[157]   William of Apulia, *La Geste de Robert Guiscard*, Bk II, lines 407–15, pp. 154–5. See also Chalandon, *Histoire de la Domination Normande*, I, p. 173.

[158]   Amatus, *History of the Normans*, Bk IV, ch. 3, p. 112; *Storia de' Normanni*, Bk IV, ch. III, pp. 182–5; Malaterra, *Deeds of Count Roger*, Bk 1, ch. 34, p. 74; *De rebus gestis Rogerii*, Bk I, ch. XXXIV, p. 23.

[159]   Chalandon, *Histoire de la Domination Normande*, I, p. 174.

[160]   *Chronicon Breve Nortmannicum*, ed. L. Muratori (RIS, V, Milan, 1726), anno 1060, p. 278(V). This source should be viewed with great skepticism in any event. Among others, André Jacob, 'Le Breve Chronicon Nortmannicum: a veritable faux de Pietro Polidori', *Quellen und forschungen aus Italienischen Archiven und Bibliotheken*, LXVI (1986), pp. 378–92, regards this source as a forgery by the seventeenth-century historian, Pietro Polidori. Nonetheless, some scholars like Ferdinand Chalandon contend it may have been based on some lost annals of Bari or Otranto and is included here for the sake of completeness.

[161]   Lupus Protospatarius, *Annales*, anno 1062, p. 59. '*Et in hoc anno intravit Robertus dux in civitatem Oriem, et iterum apprehendit Brundusium et ipsum miriarcham.*'

[162]   Amatus, *History of the Normans*, Bk IV, ch. 3, p. 112; *Storia de' Normanni*, Bk IV, ch. III, pp. 182–5; Malaterra, *Deeds of Count Roger*, Bk 1, ch. 34–5, p. 74; *De rebus gestis Rogerii*, Bk I, ch. XXXIV–XXXV, p. 23.

[163]   Malaterra, *Deeds of Count Roger*, Bk 2, ch. 1, p. 86; *De rebus gestis Rogerii*, Bk II, ch. I, pp. 29–30.

[164]   Amatus, *History of the Normans*, Bk V, ch. 9–11, p. 136; *Storia de' Normanni*, Bk V, ch. IX–XI, pp. 231–4.

that 600 participated in the raid.[165] The latter figure is probably accurate, because it likely includes squires and attendant infantry.[166] So, already the Normans were transporting hundreds of combatants with horses across the treacherous strait, even though the ways of the sea were yet unfamiliar to them. They landed near Milazzo on this occasion, but once again the garrison of Messina reacted and the Normans found themselves besieged on the shores of the strait, waiting for the weather to clear.[167] They were able to make the return crossing only after three days of constant fighting. Even then, according to Amatus, they were hotly pursued by 'Saracen' ships, which apparently bested a small, makeshift flotilla sent out from Reggio to cover the retreat.[168]

   With the exception of some booty, neither mission had amounted to much. Nevertheless, the Hautevilles were learning and they were learning quickly. They knew at this point they were going to have to cross in greater force, which meant they were going to need more ships – many more. Until then, they had probably used whatever vessels could be found in the harbor at Reggio – merchant vessels, doubtless – but the minor naval skirmish that occurred upon the return of the last raid assuredly told the Hautevilles that they would eventually need ships of war as well.[169] The storm that delayed the return of that same expedition taught them that they must also take into account the strait's capricious weather.[170] Furthermore, the excursion revealed to them that they would have to become more expert at transporting horses. After the storm passed, Amatus notes, 'They then began to slaughter or abandon the animals, because they feared that if they took them they [the horses] would delay them or cause their death at sea.'[171] Nor could the need for sound intelligence have escaped the two brothers. They needed to know where they could disembark an expeditionary force undetected. Most of all, they came to understand the vital importance of gaining a beachhead on the island. They had to capture Messina.[172]

[165] Ibn Khaldun, *BAS*, II, p. 202.
[166] Chalandon, *Histoire de la Domination Normande*, I, p. 194.
[167] Malaterra, *Deeds of Count Roger*, Bk 2, ch. 4–7, pp. 87–9; *De rebus gestis Rogerii*, Bk II, ch. IV–VII, pp. 30–1.
[168] Amatus, *History of the Normans*, Bk V, ch. 10–11, p. 137; *Storia de' Normanni*, Bk V, ch. X–XI, pp. 232–4.
[169] C. Manfroni, *Storia della Marina italiana dalle invasioni barbariche al trattato di Ninfeo, anni di C. 400–1261* (3 vols, Livorno, 1899), I, p. 111.
[170] Amatus, *History of the Normans*, Bk V, ch. 10, p.137; *Storia de' Normanni*, Bk V, ch. X, pp. 232–3; Malaterra, *Deeds of Count Roger*, Bk 2, ch. 6, pp. 88–9; *De rebus gestis Rogerii*, Bk II, ch. VI, p. 31.
[171] Amatus, *History of the Normans*, Bk V, ch. 10, p. 137; *Storia de' Normanni*, Bk V, ch. X, pp. 232–3. 'Et adont comencerent à occire lo bestiame, et lo laisserent; quar avoient paor, s'il lor portoient ou se tardoient, ne lor fust occasion de morir en mer.'
[172] Chalandon, *Histoire de la Domination Normande*, I, 194; Manfroni, *Storia della Marina italiana*, I, 112.

By the spring of 1061, the two brothers felt ready to launch a full-fledged invasion to do just that.[173] Ibn al-Thumnah, the emir of Syracuse and Catania, had previously come to Roger at Mileto seeking aid in his struggle against his rival, Ibn al-Hawwas, the emir of Girgenti and Castrogiovanni.[174] Their new-found ally clearly must have furnished the Hautevilles with all the intelligence they needed. This proved essential from the start, because the emir of Palermo had sent a fleet of 24 ships to prevent their crossing.[175] The chroniclers indicate that the vessels that the Normans had gathered – probably transports and light galleys – were no match for the larger, more specialized Muslim warships.[176] 'For although our fleet was greater in number, theirs was more abundant in bigger and stronger ships,' testifies Malaterra. 'We had only *germundi* and *galeas* while the Sicilians had not only *catti* and *golafri*, but also *dromundi* and ships of various other constructions.'[177] Subterfuge was their only chance for success. Amatus says that Robert and Roger took 'two fast, maneuverable galleys' (*'II galeez subtilissime et molt velocissime'*) on a scouting excursion; then decided that Roger should make a surreptitious night crossing.[178]

Malaterra notes that Roger initially proposed taking 150 knights (*'centum quinquaginta militibus'*) and ended up taking 300 men altogether.[179] Amatus says the number was 270 and that they used 13 vessels, which landed at Tremes-tieri (a few miles south of Messina). The Hautevilles' restricted naval capability at the time is underlined by the fact that Roger was compelled to return the ships to Robert so that the latter could send reinforcements.[180] Amatus says that Robert embarked 170 knights (*'cent et septante chevaliers'*) for the return

---

[173]   *Anonymi Barensis*, anno 1061, p. 152.

[174]   Ibn Al-Athir, *BAS*, I, pp. 445–7.

[175]   Amatus, *History of the Normans*, Bk V, ch. 13, p. 138; *Storia de' Normanni*, Bk V, ch. XIII, pp. 234–5.

[176]   Malaterra, *Deeds of Count Roger*, Bk 2, ch. 8, pp. 89–90; *De rebus gestis Rogerii*, Bk II, ch. VIII, p. 31.

[177]   Malaterra, *Deeds of Count Roger*, Bk 2, ch. 8, p. 90; *De rebus gestis Rogerii*, Bk II, ch. VIII, p. 32. '*Nam, quamvis noster navalis exercitus plurimus esset, eorum tamen amplior et fortioribus navibus abundantior erat. Nostri denique tantummodo germundos et galeas, Sicilienses vero cattos et golafros, sed et dromundos et diversae fabricae naves habebunt.*' Speculation on the ship types to which these terms may refer is discussed in greater detail in Appendix A, but the following explanations are offered in brief. Amari, *Storia dei Musulmani*, III, p. 68, considers 'germundos' a Latinized distortion of the Arabic word *dermudos* for dromōns. Gardiner and Morrison, *Age of the Galley*, p. 249, define 'galea' as a 'light, fast single banked scouting vessel' in late Roman times, but said the term later referred to 'any oared vessel'. They identify 'cattos' (p. 248) as large Muslim galleys, perhaps *triremes* with castles. John Pryor (*Dromōn*, p. XLI) surmises that 'golafros' was a Western term for galleys derived from the Arabic *ghurāb*, 'war galley'.

[178]   Amatus, *History of the Normans*, Bk V, ch.14, p.138; *Storia de' Normanni*, Bk V, ch. XIV, p. 235.

[179]   Malaterra, *Deeds of Count Roger*, Bk 2, ch. 10, pp. 90–1; *De rebus gestis Rogerii*, Bk II, ch. X, p. 31.

[180]   Amatus, *History of the Normans*, Bk V, ch.15, p.138; *Storia de' Normanni*, Bk V, ch. XV, pp. 235–6.

journey.[181] Why only 170? The reason is probably the same reason why Roger originally suggested only 150 knights: it was the maximum number of steeds that they could load onto the 13 ships available to them. This was because they were probably using transport vessels in much the way the Byzantines used the *chelandion*, a variation of the *dromōn*. The eighth-century Byzantine chronicler, Theophanes the Confessor, specified that each *chelandion* of the fleet that the Emperor Constantine V sent against the Bulgars carried twelve horses.[182] Furthermore, John Pryor's research on medieval horse transports confirms that twelve was approximately the number of horses that a modified *chelandion* could have, in fact, accommodated along the keel.[183] Dividing 150–170 by thirteen yields a number around twelve. Thus, the Normans were using whatever transport galleys, perhaps even *chelandia*, that they could find – thirteen in this case – and were, therefore, limited to 150–170 mounts. Accordingly, the men in excess of those numbers on the initial transit of the strait that night with Roger were most likely not mounted. Clearly then, the Normans were initially compelled to improvise in order to overcome limitations in naval assets. The lesson would not be lost on them. In any event, even with his small mounted cadre, Roger was able to surprise Messina the next day and capture it.[184] Chalandon surmises that the Muslim garrison was absent from the city, either engaged in coastal watch or aboard the Muslim flotilla cruising the strait.[185] All evidence indicates that Messina remained overwhelmingly Greek Christian, so the inhabitants likely greeted Roger with open arms.

As for the Muslim fleet, robbed of its safe harbor, it had little choice but to return to Palermo.[186] Norman ownership of both sides of the Strait of Messina denied the Muslim ships any opportunity for replenishment of their water supplies. Besides, lingering in the strait was no option. Its waters were notoriously treacherous. 'The Straits of Messina, with their whirlpools and tidal rips, *tagli*, gave rise in antiquity to the legend of Scylla and Charybdis,' points out Pryor.[187] Ibn Jubayr, who nearly perished during his passage through the narrows, was far more expressive: 'The sea in this strait, which runs between the mainland and

---

[181]   Amatus, *History of the Normans*, Bk V, ch.17, p.139; *Storia de' Normanni*, Bk V, ch. XVII, pp. 236–7.

[182]   Theophanes the Confessor, *The Chronicle of TheophanesConfessor, Byzantine and Near Eastern History, AD 284–813*, ed. and trans. C. Mango and R. Scott (Oxford, 1997), *annus mundi* 6254, p. 599.

[183]   Pryor and Jeffreys, *Dromōn*, pp. 322–3.

[184]   Amatus, *History of the Normans*, Bk V, ch. 15–18, pp.138–9; *Storia de' Normanni*, Bk V, ch. XV–XVIII, pp. 235–7; Malaterra, *Deeds of Count Roger*, Bk 2, ch. 10, p. 91; *De rebus gestis Rogerii*, Bk II, ch. X, p. 32.

[185]   Chalandon, *Histoire de la Domination Normande*, I, p. 195.

[186]   Amatus, *History of the Normans*, Bk V, ch. 18, p. 139; *Storia de' Normanni*, Bk V, ch. XVIII, p. 237; Malaterra, *Deeds of Count Roger*, Bk 2, ch. 12, p. 91; *De rebus gestis Rogerii*, Bk II, ch. XII, p. 33.

[187]   Pryor, *Geography, Technology, and War*, pp. 13–15.

the island of Sicily, pours through like the "bursting of the dam" and, from the intensity of the contraction and the pressure boils like a cauldron."[188] Thus, the taking of Messina had effectively removed the naval threat to further Norman cross-channel operations.

Amatus relates that Robert then joined Roger with the rest of the army in whatever ships ('*diverse maniere de navie*') he could commandeer, 'especially the [big] ships' (*nez: naves* in Latin).[189] The two made a brief foray into the interior as far as Castrogiovanni, but were eventually obligated to return to Messina.[190] At that time, Robert was compelled to cross back to the mainland in order to deal with his ever-contentious Apulian nobles. He left his younger brother a small contingent of knights to carry on the struggle. Fortuitously for the Normans, a sizable relief armada sent from Mahdiyah by the Zirid emir, al-Mu'izz Ibn Badis, was decimated off Pantelleria by an awful autumn storm.[191] But that was not the end of Zirid attempts to succor their coreligionists on the island. After all, much was at stake for the Zirid dynasty. The Hilali invasions of the early 1050s prompted by the Fatimid caliph of Cairo had caused such agri-cultural devastation to Zirid Ifriqiyah that Sicily had become its primary source of wheat.[192] Soon after al-Mu'izz passed away in 1062, Ibn al-Athir purports that his successor, Tamim, sent his sons, Ayub and Ali, with an armada and an army to Sicily. Ayub disembarked the army at Palermo while Ali proceeded with the fleet to Girgenti.[193] Ali's ships, however, never came into play. No attempt was made to assert control over the Strait of Messina and, thus, cut off Roger's supply lines. Graham Loud feels limited water supplies, the treacherous currents of the strait and the lack of a nearby safe harbor may have been factors.[194] What-ever the reasons, the Normans were apparently allowed to cross with impunity. If Ali had been able to interrupt this vital link, there is little the Normans could have done to prevent it. They lacked the naval assets at the time, and besides, Roger was occupied with his war of attrition in the interior.

As it was, the Norman campaign was then interrupted by a number of events. Roger returned to Calabria to marry Judith of Évreux whom Malaterra says he

---

[188] Ibn Jubayr, *The Travels of Ibn Jubayr*, trans. R. Broadhurst (London, 1952), pp. 336–7.

[189] Amatus, *History of the Normans*, Bk V, ch. 19, pp. 139–40; *Storia de' Normanni*, Bk V, ch. XIX, pp. 237–8. 'Adont comanda que *diverse maniere de navie et de mariniers venissent devant la soë presence, et particulerement devissent aler les nez*.' (Dunbar translation: "Then he ordered that various kinds of ships and mariners be brought before him, especially the [big] ships.' *Nez* or *naves* literally means 'ships', but the word is often used by chroniclers to signify larger ships, perhaps even transports.)

[190] Amatus, *History of the Normans*, Bk V, ch. 20–3, pp.140–1; *Storia de' Normanni*, Bk V, ch. XX–XXIII, pp. 238–43; Malaterra, *Deeds of Count Roger*, Bk 2, ch. 13–17, pp. 92–4; *De rebus gestis Rogerii*, Bk II, ch. XIII–XVII, pp. 33–4.

[191] Ibn Al-Athir, *BAS*, I, p. 448.

[192] Abulafia, 'Norman Kingdom of Africa', pp. 27–8.

[193] Ibn Al-Athir, *BAS*, I, p. 448.

[194] Loud, *Age of Robert Guiscard*, p. 150.

'had desired for a long time'.[195] Soon afterwards, a nasty spat broke out between the two brothers over the partition of conquered Calabrian properties.[196] Meanwhile, Roger's Muslim ally, Ibn al-Thumnah, was ambushed and killed at Entella, 25 miles southwest of Palermo.[197] Once the fraternal altercation was amicably resolved, Roger returned to Sicily with his bride only to be faced with a serious revolt of local Greeks at his mountain redoubt of Troina.[198] He eventually managed to quash it, however, and win a lopsided victory in 1063 at Cerami (near Castrogiovanni) over an enormous Muslim army, which Malaterra says included 'Africans' (i.e., Ayub's troops).[199] Later that same year Malaterra attests that 'the Africans and Arabs wanted revenge for the victory that had been taken from them at Cerami', so they attempted to ambush Roger and a couple of hundred of his knights returning from a raid on Girgenti.[200] The result was apparently another rout of Ayub's men.

The best opportunity Ali would have had to engage the 'Infidel' invaders with his fleet would have been the 1063 Pisan attack on Palermo. According to Malaterra, the Pisans invited the participation of Roger's cavalry in an all-out assault on the Muslim capital, but the Norman knight declined, saying he was otherwise occupied.[201] In any event, the raid came to nothing. Without support of land forces, the Pisans could do little but cut the chain closing the harbor, cull out six large, fully loaded merchant vessels and return home.[202] Ali's ships apparently remained in Girgenti and were not involved in the action. Ibn al-Athir claims Ayub and Ali returned to Mahdiyah with the fleet in 1068 following a falling out with Ibn al-Hawwas, the emir of Castrogiovanni and Girgenti, which resulted in the latter's death.[203] In all probability, however, the real reason was the disastrous defeat that the two brothers suffered at the hands of Roger's cavalry at Misilmeri

---

[195] Malaterra, *Deeds of Count Roger*, Bk 2, ch. 19, p. 95; *De rebus gestis Rogerii*, Bk II, ch. XIX, p. 35. '*Denique ex multo tempore eam cupiens…*' (Judith was the half-sister of Robert de Grandmesnil, the Norman abbot of St Eufemia in Calabria.)

[196] Malaterra, *Deeds of Count Roger*, Bk 2, ch. 21–8, pp. 96–102; *De rebus gestis Rogerii*, Bk II, ch. XXI–XXVIII, pp. 35–9.

[197] Malaterra, *Deeds of Count Roger*, Bk 2, ch. 22, pp. 96–7; *De rebus gestis Rogerii*, Bk II, ch. XXII, p. 36.

[198] Malaterra, *Deeds of Count Roger*, Bk 2, ch. 29–30, pp. 102–5; *De rebus gestis Rogerii*, Bk II, ch. XXIX–XXX, pp. 39–41.

[199] Malaterra, *Deeds of Count Roger*, Bk 2, ch. 33, pp. 107–11; *De rebus gestis Rogerii*, Bk II, ch. XXXIII, pp. 42–5.

[200] Malaterra, *Deeds of Count Roger*, Bk 2, ch. 35, pp. 112–14; *De rebus gestis Rogerii*, Bk II, ch. XXXV, pp. 45–6. '*Porro Africani et Arabici, cum essent cupientes ulcisci de victoria in Ceramensi proelio sibi oblata …*'

[201] Malaterra, *Deeds of Count Roger*, Bk 2, ch. 34, pp. 111–12; *De rebus gestis Rogerii*, Bk II, ch. XXXIV, p. 45.

[202] Bernardo Maragone, *Gli annales Pisani di Bernardo Maragone*, ed. M. Gentile (RIS, vol. VI, pt II, Bologna, 1936), pp. 5–6. See also W. Heywood, *A History of Pisa, Eleventh and Twelfth Centuries* (Cambridge, 1921), pp. 26–9.

[203] Ibn Al-Athir, *BAS*, I, p. 449.

(six miles southeast of Palermo) in early 1068.[204] After the withdrawal of Zirid forces, the Muslims of Sicily were on their own. The only thing that spared them for the time being was that Roger had too few forces to follow up his victories.

During all this, Robert had managed to suppress the petty insurrections in his duchy long enough to unite with Roger for a combined assault on Palermo in 1064.[205] Malaterra reports that the Hauteville brothers brought 500 knights with them this time, which meant they were becoming expert at moving their mounted forces across the strait by boat. Nonetheless, the subsequent siege of Palermo was to no avail, because they did not have naval forces to effect a blockade of the port, through which the city received provisions from Africa. Life for the besieged, in this case, was far more pleasant than for the besiegers, whom Malaterra describes as having had the misfortune of bivouacking on a tarantula-infested hill.[206] According to Amatus, it was a lesson that Robert would not forget: 'When the most wise duke saw the disposition of Palermo and how provisions were being brought there from neighboring lands, which would be carried there by sea if anyone denied access by land, he prepared himself to seize other cities in order to gather another fleet of ships with which to encircle Palermo and prevent any aid from reaching it by land or sea.'[207] There would be no further attempt on Palermo until the Hautevilles could amass the necessary maritime muscle to close off the port completely. Robert became determined to take Bari first. This would remove the last Byzantine outpost in Italy and theo-retically intimidate his fractious Apulian nobles into submission. More impor-tantly, it would provide him with the ships and sailors he needed. Unfortunately, he first had to deal with yet another revolt, this one led, in part, by Abelard, Humphrey's son whose county Robert had usurped.[208] Roger, of course, lacked the manpower to do much in Robert's absence other than prosecute a guerrilla war in the interior of the island.

Robert finally quelled this latest revolt in Apulia by September 1068 so that he could begin the siege of Bari. This action represents something of a turning point in Norman naval warfare and, thus, demands closer examination. If the

---

[204] Malaterra, *Deeds of Count Roger*, Bk 2, ch. 41, p. 119; *De rebus gestis Rogerii*, Bk II, ch. XLI, pp. 49–50.
[205] Lupus Protospatarius, *Annales*, anno 1065, p. 59; Malaterra, *Deeds of Count Roger*, Bk 2, ch. 36, p. 114; *De rebus gestis Rogerii*, Bk II, ch. XXXVI, p. 46.
[206] Malaterra, *Deeds of Count Roger*, Bk 2, ch. 36, p. 114; *De rebus gestis Rogerii*, Bk II, ch. XXXVI, pp. 46–7.
[207] Amatus, *History of the Normans*, Bk V, ch. 26, p. 143; *Storia de' Normanni*, Bk V, ch. XXVI, pp. 246–8. '*Et quant lo Duc sapientissime vit la disposition et lo siege de Palerme, et que des terres voisines estoit aportée à la marchandise; et, se alcuns negassent la grace par terre, lui seroit portée par mer, appareilla soi à prendre altre cité, à ce que assemblast autre multitude de navie pour restreindre Palerme, que né par terre né par mer puisse avoir ajutoire.*'
[208] *Chronicon Breve Nortmannicum*, anno 1068, p. 278(VI); Lupus Protospatarius, *Annales*, anno 1068, p. 59; William of Apulia, *La Geste de Robert Guiscard*, Bk II, lines 445–78, pp 156–9.

first siege of Palermo in 1064 convinced Robert of the need to master maritime blockade operations, Bari was to be the learning experience. It would be an arduous one. The sources say that this time Robert was determined to cut off his prey completely. Malaterra's account is the most detailed:

> Because the city of Bari was situated on a certain angle of land that extended out into the sea, Robert used his cavalry to close off, from one shore to the other, that part of the city which opened toward the land. At the same time, he used his ships, spread out over the sea and firmly joined to one another with iron chains like a fence, to close off the city from the sea, so that there was no opening anywhere through which anyone could leave the city. He also constructed two jetties ['*pontes*' – 'bridges'], one from each side of the city, which reached out from the shore on both sides far into the sea and to which the line of ships was attached at each end. He did this so that if by chance the people of Bari tried to attack his ships, there would be a path connecting the knights on the shore with the ships, thus expediting their defense.[209]

Amatus, Lupus Protospatarius and William of Apulia all support this description to a varying degree, the last two mentioning a cordon of ships and some sort of bridge apparatus.[210] This had to have been a daunting enterprise. The city of Bari was established on a stubby peninsula that extends nearly half a mile out into the Adriatic. Encircling the city in such a manner would have necessitated a military engineering feat on a scale commensurate with the construction of the Roman ramp and circumvallations at Masada by Flavius Silva in AD 73.[211] The cordon required to accomplish it would had to have been a combination of ships and jetties about a mile and a half long. If the ships were lashed together gunnel-to-gunnel abreast in the crescent-shaped formation recommended by the tactical manuals of the Emperor Leo VI and Nikephoros Ouranos for both stability and defense,[212] that would have meant something in the order of 400 vessels the size of fifteenth-century Venetian 'great galleys' (i.e., seventeen feet of beam – probably much larger than eleventh-century merchant galleys)[213] as well as

---

[209] Malaterra, *Deeds of Count Roger*, Bk 2, ch. 40, p. 117; *De rebus gestis Rogerii*, Bk II, ch. XL, pp. 48–9. '*Et quia ipsa civitas, quasi in quodam angulo sita, in mare porrigitur, ipse cum equestri exercitu ipsam partem qua civitas versus terram patebat, quasi ab uno mari in aliud claudens, navibus per mare extensis, una ad alteram firmiter ferreis catenis, ac si sepem faciendo, compaginatis, ita totam urbem cinxit, ut nullo latere exitus ab urbe progrediendi pateret. Duos quoque pontes, unum videlicet ab unaquaque ripa constituens, qui longius in mare usque quo navium funes ab utraque parte attingebant, porrexit,ut, si forte Barenses aliquem incursum versus naves attentarent, directo cursu a militibus navibus expeditius subveniret.'*

[210] Amatus, *History of the Normans*, Bk V, ch. 27, p. 143; *Storia de' Normanni*, Bk V, ch. XXVII, pp. 248–55; Lupus Protospatarius, *Annales*, anno 1071, p. 60; William of Apulia, *La Geste de Robert Guiscard*, Bk II, lines 479–528, pp 158–61.

[211] A. Goldsworthy, *The Complete Roman Army* (London, 2003), pp. 190–1.

[212] Leo VI, *The naval warfare of the Emperor Leo* (*Taktika*, Constitution XIX), trans. Jeffreys, *Dromōn*, Appendix Two, par. 1–2, pp. 516–17; Nikephoros Ouranos, *On fighting at sea*, trans. Jeffreys, *Dromōn*, Appendix Five, par. 71, p. 603.

[213] L. Casson, 'Merchant Galleys', in *Age of the Galley*, pp. 117–26, especially 124.

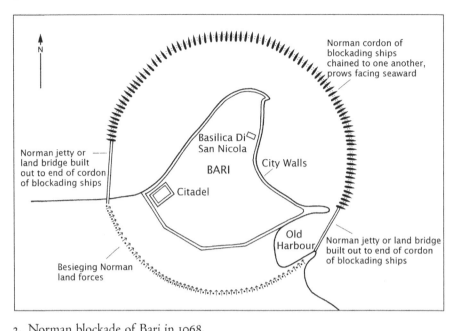

2. Norman blockade of Bari in 1068.
(Credit: C. Stanton with P. Judge)

two 500-foot bridges or jetties (see Map 2). Such a mind-boggling effort reveals the low state of Norman knowledge in maritime operations at the time. Robert was obviously attempting to replicate land-based battle conditions by extending terrestrial siege procedures out onto the water. William of Apulia indicates he even went so far as to build a siege tower on a bridge.[214] Whatever rudimentary blockade interdiction techniques may have existed at the time, Robert was either ignorant of them or he had little confidence in his commandeered Calabrian crews to carry them out. The vessels that Robert was using were probably Calabrian merchant ships manned by ordinary seamen.[215] Moreover, it would have been nearly impossible to maintain the integrity of such a cordon in inclement weather for a prolonged period of time, not to mention tying up that many merchant vessels. The maintenance problems alone would have been horrendous.

Robert may have initially employed this sort of blockade, but it is highly doubtful he was able to sustain it. This would explain why the blockade was broken several times, once by a relief fleet. In fact, the performance of Robert's ship captains in these incidents could not have inspired much faith in their abilities. Amatus recounts that Bizantius, the leader of the pro-Byzantine faction of Bari, not only penetrated the blockade in an effort to seek relief from Constanti-

---

[214] William of Apulia, *La Geste de Robert Guiscard*, Bk II, lines 525–8, pp 160–1.
[215] *Anonymi Barensis*, anno 1064, p. 152; William of Apulia, *La Geste de Robert Guiscard*, Bk II, lines 485–6, pp. 158–9.

nople, but his small flotilla beat off 'the four swift galleys' (*'quatre galéez legeres'*) that Robert had sent in pursuit, sinking two and damaging the others. Worse still, when Bizantius returned with provisions, he captured two of the three galleys Robert dispatched to intercept him.[216] There were evidently some successes, however. The *Anonymi Barensis* records that the Normans intercepted a Greek relief squadron captained by Stephen Pateranos, the newly appointed Byzantine *catepan*, at Monopoli in 1069 and destroyed twelve vessels, mutilating and killing their crews.[217] But for the most part, the Normans continued to demonstrate a pronounced ineptitude at sea.

Consequently, the siege lasted nearly three years.[218] During that time, a further demonstration of Norman inexperience with land–sea sieges of port cities came with Robert's attempt to reduce Brindisi while still engaged at Bari. Lupus Protospatarius tells of an assault on Brindisi in 1070, which ended with the heads of 40 Norman knights and their 43 attendants being sent back to Constantinople.[219] According to the disputed *Chronicon Breve Nortmannicum*, a Greek fleet under a certain 'Mabrica' was responsible.[220] Pryor identifies 'Mabrica' as Michael Maurēx, a naval commander from Paphlagonia (an ancient Greek province north of Anatolia on the Black Sea), who had assembled his own fleet.[221] The same man had thwarted the raid of Geoffrey of Taranto on the Dalmatian coast in 1066[222] and had brought Varangian reinforcements to Bari that same year.[223] The setback at Brindisi signifies that either Robert could spare insufficient naval assets from the siege of Bari or those he was able to muster were no match for the Greek admiral. In fact, it may have been this catastrophic failure at Brindisi that induced Robert to enlist the aid of his brother Roger, who by now may have become more experienced in naval operations by virtue of having to transit the Strait of Messina on a continuing basis.

Indeed, what finally ended the siege was the introduction of Sicilian naval assets and expertise under Roger's command. Roger's seamanship apparently enabled him to intercept a large relief flotilla from Byzantium. Twenty vessels bringing supplies and reinforcements, commanded by the Norman renegade,

---

[216] Amatus, *History of the Normans*, Bk V, ch. 27, pp. 143–4; *Storia de' Normanni*, Bk V, ch. XXVII, pp. 248–55.

[217] *Anonymi Barensis*, anno 1069, p. 153.

[218] Amatus, *History of the Normans*, Bk V, ch. 27, pp. 143–6; *Storia de' Normanni*, Bk V, ch. XXVII, pp. 248–55; Malaterra, *Deeds of Count Roger*, Bk 2, ch. 43, pp. 120–2; *De rebus gestis Rogerii*, Bk II, ch. XLIII, pp. 50–1; William of Apulia, *La Geste de Robert Guiscard*, Bk III, lines 112–63, pp. 170–3.

[219] Lupus Protospatarius, *Annales*, anno 1070, p. 60.

[220] *Chronicon Breve Nortmannicum*, anno 1070, p. 278(VI). See also Chalandon, *Histoire de la Domination Normande*, I, p. 188.

[221] Pryor, 'View from a masthead', pp. 117–18.

[222] Lupus Protospatarius, *Annales*, anno 1066, p. 59.

[223] *Anonymi Barensis*, anno 1066, p. 153.

Jocelyn of Molfetta, attempted to run the blockade in the spring of 1071.[224] Roger had known enough to set a night watch, which spotted the approaching Byzantine flotilla and recognized Jocelyn's flagship, according to Malaterra, by the two lanterns it carried. Roger dashed right for it and engaged it. His men, showing they were still unseasoned in battle at sea, rushed to one side, causing their ship to roll and dump 150 of them in full armor into the Adriatic.[225] Nonetheless, the onslaught sent the enemy squadron into disarray. Roger captured Jocelyn and nine of his ships.[226] The mere fact that Roger had been willing to risk a night engagement against a flotilla that must have included warships was a measure of how confident the Normans were becoming on the water. The fact that they had actually won the encounter, their first naval victory, must have buoyed their confidence even more. William of Apulia observes that because of this triumph, Robert 'foresaw the Normans, henceforth, engaging in naval combat with greater assurance.'[227]

Secure in their rear and reinforced with naval contingents from Bari, the two Hauteville brothers immediately redirected their focus on Palermo. 'The conqueror,' reports William of Apulia, 'ordered the inhabitants of Bari to prepare arms and supplies and follow him wherever they see him go.'[228] Sending Roger ahead to mobilize an army, Robert then proceeded to Otranto where he amassed a significant number of vessels, many of which must have been from Bari, along with their crews.[229] Lupus Protospatarius puts the figure at 58,[230] while Amatus confirmed in his account that there were at least 51 (Robert's flagships plus 'ten catti and forty other ships').[231] At this point, it is clear that the Normans were still appropriating whatever vessels they could get their hands on. Malaterra tells of Guiscard 'making his men level a hill so as to render the descent to the sea

[224] Amatus, History of the Normans, Bk V, ch. 27, p. 145; Storia de' Normanni, Bk V, ch. XXVII, pp. 248–5; Malaterra, Deeds of Count Roger, Bk 2, ch. 43, pp. 120–2; De rebus gestis Rogerii, Bk II, ch. XLIII, pp. 50–1; William of Apulia, La Geste de Robert Guiscard, Bk III, lines 112–31, pp. 170–1.

[225] Anonymi Barensis, anno 1071, p. 153; Malaterra, Deeds of Count Roger, Bk 2, ch. 43, pp. 121–2; De rebus gestis Rogerii, Bk II, ch. XLIII, p. 51.

[226] Amatus, History of the Normans, Bk V, ch. 27, p. 145; Storia de' Normanni, Bk V, ch. XXVII, pp. 248–55.

[227] William of Apulia, La Geste de Robert Guiscard, Bk III, lines 137–8, p. 17. '... securius unde subire iam cum Normannis navalia proelia sperat.'

[228] William of Apulia, La Geste de Robert Guiscard, Bk III, lines 163–5, p. 172. 'Perque dies aliquot hac victor in urbe moratus, mandat cum sumptu Barensibus arma parari, ut properent secum, quo se properare videbunt.' (English translation by G. A. Loud at www.leeds.ac.uk/history/weblearning/ MedievalHistoryTextCentre/medievalTexts/html.)

[229] Malaterra, Deeds of Count Roger, Bk 2, ch. 43, p. 122; De rebus gestis Rogerii, Bk II, ch. XLIII, p. 51.

[230] Lupus Protospatarius, Annales, anno 1071, p. 60.

[231] Amatus, History of the Normans, Bk VI, ch. 14, p. 156; Storia de' Normanni, Bk VI, ch. XIV, pp. 276–7. '... X gat et XL autres nez.'

easier for getting horses onto ships.'[232] In other words, he had to 'make do' with existing merchant vessels rather than employing ships built for the purpose.

At least some of these vessels, however, must have been warships, including perhaps the Byzantine vessels captured during the defeat of Jocelyn's relief flotilla at Bari. And the Normans were evidently learning how to use them. As Robert's fleet approached Palermo, William of Apulia reports how Robert's men prepared for combat against a combined Sicilian–African armada: 'They arranged their ships according to all the rules of naval warfare, and covered them entirely with red felt to repel the blows of the stones and javelins.'[233] Their efforts must have paid off, because the Normans prevailed. They pursued the surviving Muslim vessels into the harbor, breaking the chain that sealed the entrance and setting fire to many of the ships.[234]

Having vanquished all opposition at sea, Robert was then able to totally enclose the city. In fact, it is not inconceivable that Robert replicated the naval blockade strategy that he had employed at Bari by simply replacing the harbor chain of Palermo with a cordon of linked ships. Only this task must have been a much simpler operation. The tenth-century Arabic geographer, Mohammed Abul-Kassem ibn Hawqal, describes the naval arsenal of Palermo as being located in the Al Halisah quarter, which was on the southeastern side of the old harbor or La Cala.[235] According to Vincenzo di Giovanni's planimetric reconstruction of Muslim Palermo in the tenth and eleventh centuries, the mouth of La Cala was barely 200 meters or approximately 660 feet wide (see Map 3).[236] The Normans would have only needed some forty ships abreast to seal off the entrance. A blockade of this nature would have been preferred to a full-scale assault on the port, even though the Al Halisah contained the sultan's palace and the royal *diwān* (fiscal administration) as well as the arsenal.[237] La Cala was a confined area, no wider than 200 meters at any point, flanked on the southeast side by the walled Al Halisah quarter and on the northwest by the heavily fortified Castellammare.[238] Had Robert's ships lingered long in there, they would have been subjected to a withering crossfire of machine-launched projectiles.

In any case, the method employed must have been sufficient. The city fell after only a few months. In January 1072, Robert and Roger marched triumphant into

---

[232] Malaterra, *Deeds of Count Roger*, Bk 2, ch. 43, p. 122; *De rebus gestis Rogerii*, Bk II, ch. XLIII, p. 51. 'Toto junio et julio mense apud Ydrontum moratus, montem, quo facilius descensus ad mare – equos navibus introducens – fieret, rescindere facit.'

[233] William of Apulia, *La Geste de Robert Guiscard*, Bk III, lines 229–33, pp 176–7. 'Instructis ergo carinis exigit ut belli navalis rite paratus, proque repellendis saxorum vel iaculorum ictibus obtectis rubicundis undique filtris...'

[234] William of Apulia, *La Geste de Robert Guiscard*, Bk III, lines 225–54, pp 176–9.

[235] Ibn Hawqal, *BAS*, I, pp. 11–12.

[236] V. di Giovanni, *La topografia antica di Palermo dal secolo X al XV* (Palermo, 1890), 'Pianta Etnografia di Palermo dal sec. X al XII'.

[237] Ibn Hawqal, *BAS*, I, pp. 11–12.

[238] Di Giovanni, 'Pianta Etnografia di Palermo'.

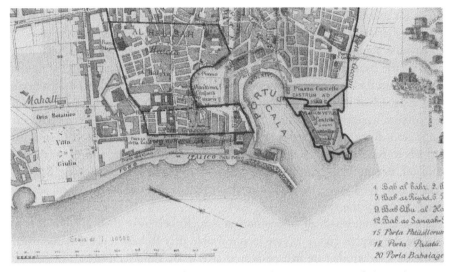

3. Port of Palermo in the eleventh century. This planimetric map of eleventh-century Palermo shows the Al Halisah quarter, which contained the sultan's palace and Arab arsenal, just south of the Cala.
(Credit: Vincenzo di Giovanni in *La Topografia Antica di Palermo dal secolo X al XV*, published in Palermo, 1890)

Palermo.[239] As a harbinger of things to come, William of Apulia records, 'After having taken hostages and prepared some castles, Robert returned victorious to the city of Reggio, leaving in Palermo a knight of his same name, who was given to the Sicilians as *amiratus*.'[240] Guiscard had, of course, intended for his representative to serve purely as a military governor. His use of the word 'amiratus', meaning 'emir', was done merely as a palliative for his new Muslim subjects. Nonetheless, the term would eventually develop much more of a maritime connotation in the future. For the time being, however, factoring out the events that neither brother could have foreseen – the quarrels with one another and the various baronial revolts – the Hautevilles had stuck tenaciously to their purpose. The grand strategy put in motion not fifteen years previously at Humphrey's death had achieved its goal and naval power had played an integral part.

---

[239] Amatus, *History of the Normans*, Bk VI, ch. 13–19, pp. 155–8; *Storia de' Normanni*, Bk VI, ch. XIII–XIX, pp. 275–82; *Annales Beneventani*, anno 1072, p. 181; *Anonymi Barensis*, anno 1072, p. 153; Malaterra, *Deeds of Count Roger*, Bk 2, ch. 45, pp. 124–5; *De rebus gestis Rogerii*, Bk II, ch. XLV, pp. 52–3; William of Apulia, *La Geste de Robert Guiscard*, Bk III, lines 187–337, pp 174–83.

[240] William of Apulia, *La Geste de Robert Guiscard*, Bk III, lines 340–3, pp. 182–3. 'Obsidibus sumptis aliquot castrisque paratis, Reginam remeat Robertus victor ad urbem, nominis eiusdem quodam remanente Panormi milite, qui Siculis datur amiratus haberi.'

Guiscard's amphibious assaults on Byzantium

Following the capture of Palermo, the two brothers pursued separate goals, but sea power remained vital to the efforts of each. Robert first occupied himself with consolidating his hold on Apulia and Calabria while extending his authority into Campania. His first prize was the thriving port of Trani in Apulia, which he captured by a land and sea siege in January or February of 1073.[241] His second was Amalfi, a glittering maritime trophy in Campania, which fell to him fortuitously later that same year. Robert's brother-in-law, Gisulf, the prince of Salerno, had been harassing Amalfitan shipping for some time in an apparent effort to curtail commercial competition. When Gisulf seized three castles in 1073 belonging to the maritime republic, the city fathers sought Robert's protection. The duke gladly gave it in return for the city's submission.[242] As a result, Guiscard gained the allegiance of one of the most prosperous port cities on the Tyrrhenian Sea along with all its ships and seamen. Moreover, Gisulf's continued depredations would eventually give Robert the pretext to seize another great Campanian maritime power, Salerno itself. In May 1076, Guiscard invested the city by land and sea, assisted by Amalfi's ships, no doubt. This time there were no breaks in the blockade.[243] William of Apulia describes the gruesome effects: 'After four months of siege, such a famine pressed the unfortunate inhabitants of the city that the mob could scarcely sustain themselves on dogs, horses, rats and cadavers of asses.'[244] By now, Robert had become grimly expert at besieging port cities. Salerno capitulated in December.[245] As an epilogue to this episode it is worth mentioning that Robert, in return for Richard of Capua's support during the siege, sent the Norman prince ships from Amalfi and Calabria to aid in the latter's unsuccessful investment of Naples.[246] The implication here is that the Hautevilles now controlled nearly all the maritime assets of Norman Italy.

---

[241] *Anonymi Barensis*, anno 1073, p. 153; Lupus Protospatarius, *Annales*, anno 1073, p. 60.

[242] Amatus, *History of the Normans*, Bk VIII, ch. 6–7, p. 191; *Storia de' Normanni*, Bk VIII, ch. VI–VII, pp. 347–8; William of Apulia, *La Geste de Robert Guiscard*, Bk III, lines 413–19, pp. 186–7.

[243] Amatus, *History of the Normans*, Bk VIII, ch. 14, p. 194; *Storia de' Normanni*, Bk VIII, ch. XIV, pp. 354–6; William of Apulia, *La Geste de Robert Guiscard*, Bk III, lines 424–45, pp. 186–9.

[244] William of Apulia, *La Geste de Robert Guiscard*, Bk III, lines 427–30, p. 186. '*Quartus erat mensis completus ab obsidione; tanta fames miserae cives invaserat urbis, ut canibus vel equis vel muribus aut asinorum turba cadaveribus vix vivere posset edendo.*'

[245] Amatus, *History of the Normans*, Bk VIII, ch. 24, pp. 199–200; *Storia de' Normanni*, Bk VIII, ch. XXIV, pp. 364–6; *Annales Beneventani*, anno 1075, p. 181; *Annales Casinenses*, anno 1075, p. 306; *Annales Cavenses*, anno 1076, p. 190; Lupus Protospatarius, *Annales*, anno 1077, p. 60; William of Apulia, *La Geste de Robert Guiscard*, Bk III, lines 442–6, pp. 188–9.

[246] Amatus, *History of the Normans*, Bk VIII, ch. 25, p. 200; *Storia de' Normanni*, Bk VIII, ch. XXV, pp. 366–7.

Ever the warrior, Guiscard then turned his attention toward the Byzantine Empire. Aside from a seemingly insatiable appetite for power, Robert must have borne Byzantium a great enmity for fomenting disaffection among his nobles in Apulia. Chalandon maintains that the *Catepan* Aboulchare and Perenos, the Greek governor of Durazzo, were responsible for much of the unrest of the 1060s.[247] Moreover, both Maurēx and Jocelyn had launched their Greek fleets from Durazzo during Robert's siege of Bari.[248] Therefore, Robert must have longed for an opportunity to rid himself of Byzantine interference. The overthrow of the Emperor Michael VII Doukas in 1078 by Nikephorous III Botaniates provided Guiscard with the desired pretext.[249] Four years earlier, in 1074, Robert had concluded a highly advantageous marriage agreement with Michael VII to unite the latter's son Constantine with Guiscard's daughter, later christened Helena by the Byzantine court. The resultant *chrysobull* (golden bull or imperial decree), penned by the noted Byzantine scholar and court advisor Michael Psellus, had promised to bestow on Robert the high court dignity of '*nobilissimus*' ('most noble one') plus 43 other imperial titles, all with hefty annual stipends, to dispense as he saw fit.[250] Michael VII's ouster meant the abrogation of the agreement and the incarceration of Helena in a convent. Consequently, Robert soon began preparations for an invasion, ostensibly to free his daughter and restore Michael (or at least his imposter) to the throne.[251]

This unfortunately put him into direct conflict with one of the great maritime powers of the age: Venice. The Venetians rued Robert's growing sea power for two very understandable reasons. First, the duke was the protector of Amalfi, one of their major competitors. Secondly and far more compelling, they feared that if Robert gained control of both shores of the southern Adriatic, Venice could, to some extent, become bottled up in the north. Robert would certainly be in a position to harass Venetian vessels exiting the sea. Consequently, when Alexios Komnenos, who had by now assumed the purple robes of the Byzantine *basileus*,[252] approached the Venetians in regard to an alliance against the Normans, he found a willing audience. In 1081 the Venetians entered into a pact with Byzantium, which promised naval support against Robert in return for

---

[247] Chalandon, *Histoire de la Domination Normande*, I, pp. 179–82.

[248] Malaterra, *Deeds of Count Roger*, Bk 2, ch. 43, p. 121; *De rebus gestis Rogerii*, Bk II, ch. XLIII, p. 51. See also Chalandon, *Histoire de la Domination Normande*, I, p. 188.

[249] Anna Comnena, *The Alexiad of Anna Comnena*, trans. E. Sewter (London, 1969), pp. 57–8; *Alexiade (Règne de l'Empereur Alexis I Comnène 1081–1118)*, ed. and trans. B. Leib (3 vols, Paris, 1937), I, Bk I, ch. XII, pp. 42–7.

[250] H. Bibicou, 'Une page d'histoire diplomatique de Byzance au XIe siècle: Robert Guiscard et la pension des dignitaires', *Byzantion*, XXIX–XXX (1959–60), pp. 43–75.

[251] Malaterra, *Deeds of Count Roger*, Bk 3, ch. 13, pp. 143–5; *De rebus gestis Rogerii*, Bk III, ch. XIII, pp. 64–5; William of Apulia, *La Geste de Robert Guiscard*, Bk IV, lines 1–5, pp. 204–5.

[252] *Basileus* simply meant 'monarch' or 'sovereign', but it was often used as a title for the Eastern Emperor.

commercial concessions. It was these privileges that would enable *La Serenissima* to dominate trade in the eastern Mediterranean for centuries.[253]

The Venetians' concerns were not unfounded. While they and Alexios were negotiating their agreement, Guiscard was gathering a huge fleet at Otranto, barely fifty miles across the strait from the Albanian coast. At the same time, he was making a conscious effort to shore up his maritime base in Apulia. Both Lupus Protospatarius and the *Anonymi Barensis* report that Robert reasserted his authority over the key port cities of Bari and Taranto in 1080, coming to new agreements with each. The *Anonymi Barensis* adds Trani to the list.[254] Moreover, Robert had persuaded the Dalmatians, supposedly under Venetian suzerainty at the time, to provide his fleet with transport vessels. Some of these may, in fact, have been Byzantine-style horse transports, probably modified *chelandia*, since William of Apulia says Robert embarked horses on them.[255] This is also a sign that Robert was now actively seeking to constitute a fleet of ships specially designed for the task, rather than simply adapting whatever was available. In fact, Malaterra breaks out into lyrical verse to confirm that the whole fleet was purpose-built:

Cut timber is ordered from the very best at this craft;
Everywhere the art of plank-making is practiced.
Oak trees are felled and dried, craftsmen shaping the severed pieces of timber.
The smith places the iron in the fire.
An anchor is forged, a mold for nails prepared.
These very nails are used to fasten the joints of a ship.
Other craftsmen cover the cracks with down,
And hasten to add some liquid pitch.
Some prepare the sails; others dedicate themselves to the ropes.
Not a single ship but an entire fleet is fitted out.[256]

The exact size of the force mustered by Robert is not known. The estimates of the chroniclers vary wildly. Anna Comnena, Alexios' daughter and biographer,

---

[253] Manfroni, *Storia della Marina italiana*, I, pp. 121–5. *La Serenissima* is a diminutive of the formal title *La Serenissima Repubblica di Venezia*, meaning 'Most Serene Republic of Venice'.
[254] *Anonymi Barensis*, anno 1080, p. 153; Lupus Protospatarius, *Annales*, anno 1080, p. 60.
[255] William of Apulia, *La Geste de Robert Guiscard*, Bk IV, lines 123–36, pp. 210–11.
[256] Malaterra, *Deeds of Count Roger*, Bk 3, ch. 14, p. 145; *De rebus gestis Rogerii*, Bk III, ch. XIV, pp. 65–6:
Ligni caesores mandantur in arte priores;
Undique terrarum conducitur ars tabularum.
Robora caesa cadunt; resecantur; sectaque radunt
Artifices ligni. Ferrum faber applicat igni.
Anchora conflatur, clavorum forma paratur.
Compago navis texitur superaddita clavis.
Obducunt imas alii lanugine rimas,
Atque picem liquidam properant superaddere quidam.
Vela sinunt isti, studium dant funibus isti.
Classis adaptatur, non navis sola paratur.

Fig. 2. Byzantine siege vessel of the eleventh century. This waterborne siege engine depicted in an eleventh-century manuscript of the *Poliorketika* of Philon of Byzantium may represent the sort of siege technology Robert Guiscard envisioned using at Durazzo in 1081.
(Credit: Ms Vat. Gr. 1164, fol. 100r of the eleventh century, reproduced here by permission of the Biblioteca Apostolica Vaticana ©, with all rights reserved)

says there were 150 ships, carrying 30,000 men with horses and armor – a clearly unrealistic figure.[257] William of Apulia notes 50 ships[258] while the *Chronicon Breve Nortmannicum* gives no number for the ships, but reports there were 15,000 men, as does the *Chronica monasterii Casinensis*.[259] Geoffrey Malaterra probably comes the closest by insisting that the core of Robert's army was composed of 'no more than 1,300 knights'.[260] It was, in any case, very likely the largest Norman force transported by sea since William the Conqueror's invasion of England. In fact,

[257] Anna Comnena, *Alexiad*, p. 69; *Alexiade*, I, Bk I, ch. XVI, pp. 56–7.
[258] William of Apulia, *La Geste de Robert Guiscard*, Bk IV, lines 200–1, pp. 214–15.
[259] *Chronicon Breve Nortmannicum*, anno 1081, p. 278 (VI); *Chronica Monasterii Casinensis*, Bk III, ch. 49, p. 429.
[260] Malaterra, *Deeds of Count Roger*, Bk 3, ch. 24, p. 154; *De rebus gestis Rogerii*, Bk III, ch. XXIV, p. 71.

Bernard Bachrach has theorized that the Normans of the south transmitted to Normandy some of the nautical technology and procedures that William used to ferry his force to England, particularly with respect to horse transports,[261] but the chronology of the respective conquests and the gradual adoption of Mediterranean maritime practices by the Normans of southern Italy make this improbable. If anything, the reverse may well be true. William's 1066 transit of the English Channel with an invasion fleet may have been the model for Robert's 1081 enterprise across the Strait of Otranto. The distances are roughly comparable: between fifty and seventy miles, presenting similar challenges. Surely Robert would have known something of William's cross-channel operations, given the southward migration of clerics from abbeys like St Évroul in Normandy to St Eufemia in Calabria.[262] Nonetheless, Anna attests that Robert employed a few tricks of his own: '... wooden towers were constructed in the larger vessels and covered with leather hides; everything essential for a siege was hastily put on board the ships; horses and armed knights embarked on the *dromōns*.'[263] Indeed, an eleventh-century Greek manuscript in the Biblioteca Apostolica Vaticana (Ms Vat. Gr. 1164, the *Poliorketika* of Philon of Byzantium, fol. 100r) depicts some sort of siege structure affixed to the deck of a ship (see Figure 2).

Robert sent his son Bohemond ahead with 15 ships to capture Corfu. The two failed raids across the Strait of Messina twenty years prior must have impressed upon Guiscard the need to establish a secure beachhead in enemy territory. Bohemond captured Butrinto on the mainland opposite Corfu, but was not able to take the island itself until Robert joined him with the rest of the fleet. The combined forces quickly secured the island by capturing Kassiopi (northeastern Corfu) and Kerkyra (the port of Corfu). Afterwards they moved up the coast of the mainland where they seized Avlona (modern-day Vlorë).[264] From Avlona, Bohemond proceeded north with part of the army while Guiscard sailed the fleet out of the Gulf of Avlona (today's Gulf of Vlorë) with the intention of turning north to Durazzo (modern Durrës). But a nasty storm waylaid the fleet off Glossa Point (present-day Kepi i Gjuhëzës, which encloses the Gulf of Vlorë) and many of the supply ships were lost. Once again, Norman inexperience at sea was highlighted by calamity. Anna Comnena describes how the blunder of having the siege machines prebuilt and placed aboard ship came back to haunt Guiscard: 'The hides that covered the towers were slackened by rain, so that the nails fell out and the hides naturally became heavier; their weight

---

[261] B. Bachrach, 'On the Origins of William the Conqueror's Horse Transports', *Technology and Culture*, XXVI (1985), pp. 505–31.

[262] Orderic Vitalis, *Ecclesiastical History*, II, Bk III, pp. 100–3.

[263] Anna Comnena, *Alexiad*, p. 131; *Alexiade*, I, Bk III, ch. XII, p. 139.

[264] *Anonymi Barensis*, anno 1081, p. 153; Lupus Protospatarius, *Annales*, anno 1081, p. 60; Malaterra, *Deeds of Count Roger*, Bk 3, ch. 24, pp. 153–4; *De rebus gestis Rogerii*, Bk III, ch. XXIV, p. 71.

caused the wooden towers to collapse. They fell in ruins and sank the ships.'[265] Robert sought refuge with the remnants of his fleet up the Aoos River (just north of Avlona) at a place Anna Comnena called Glabinitza. There, he licked his wounds and gathered reinforcements. Undaunted, Robert soon continued north to Durazzo where he laid siege to the city and first encountered the Venetian fleet.[266]

The details of the initial clash differ according to who is telling the story, but the consensus is that the Normans were badly beaten. While the Latin chroniclers are understandably sketchy, Anna Comnena's account is the fullest and most credible. In July 1081, the Venetian fleet under the personal command of the Doge Domenico Selvo arrived at Pallia, a spit of land a few miles north of Durazzo, and anchored. According to the Italian maritime historian Camillo Manfroni (though he does not specify his source), it consisted of 14 light galleys, nine large vessels, which he termed either *uscieri* (horse transports) or *carracks* (an anachronistic reference to large sailing transports), and '36 other ships'.[267] Robert apparently sent Bohemond out to them with a squadron of light galleys in an attempt to convince the Venetians to switch sides. They were waiting. The previous night Selvo had had his men lash the larger vessels together to form a waterborne bulwark – what Anna Comnena called a 'sea harbor'.[268] Manfroni believes that they had arranged themselves in a semicircle with their bows facing outward, protecting the smaller vessels within the concavity.[269] This would have been the classic crescent fighting formation advocated in the Emperor Leo VI's *Taktika*.[270] On the mastheads of these tall ships they had constructed wooden platforms (or more likely hauled up the skiffs) and placed upon them men with weighty projectiles, such as stones and blocks of wood. When Bohemond realized that battle was inevitable, he ignored the smaller Venetian galleys and rashly charged this floating fortress with predictably disastrous results. His ship, a light galley with low freeboard, was holed with heavy objects dropped from the mastheads of the Venetian ships and sank. Worse yet, several more Norman vessels probably suffered the same fate, since Anna Comnena reports 'others followed him', possibly stacking up behind him as he attempted to ram the sea fort. Bohemond managed to escape on one of the remaining Norman galleys, which the Venetians hotly pursued to the beach.[271] Malaterra claims that they even resorted to Greek fire: 'The Venetians, craftily using that substance which they call "Greek

---

[265] Anna Comnena, *Alexiad*, p. 132; *Alexiade*, I, Bk III, ch. XII, p. 140.

[266] Anna Comnena, *Alexiad*, pp. 131–5; *Alexiade*, I, Bk III, ch. XII, pp. 140–2; *Anonymi Barensis*, anno 1081, pp. 153–4; Lupus Protospatarius, *Annales*, anno 1081, pp. 60–1; William of Apulia, *La Geste de Robert Guiscard*, Bk IV, lines 200–34, pp. 214–17.

[267] Manfroni, *Storia della Marina italiana*, I, p. 125.

[268] Anna Comnena, *Alexiad*, p. 138; *Alexiade*, I, Bk IV, ch. II, pp. 147–8.

[269] Manfroni, *Storia della Marina italiana*, I, pp. 126–7.

[270] Leo VI, *The naval warfare of the Emperor Leo* (*Taktika*, Constitution XIX), *Dromōn*, Appendix Two, par. 50, p. 505.

[271] Anna Comnena, *Alexiad*, p. 138; *Alexiade*, I, Bk IV, ch. II, p. 148.

fire" – which cannot be extinguished by water – blew it through tubes under the water and burned one of our ships – known as a *cattus* – right there on the sea.'[272] While the account demonstrates Malaterra's poor grasp of how 'Greek fire' was deployed, it is apparent that the Normans were clearly out of their element and at a huge disadvantage. Having observed all this, the besieged Greek garrison of Durazzo sortied out into the midst of the confusion. The result was very nearly a Norman rout.

Thanks in part to some Ragusan archers,[273] Robert managed to recover and eventually resume the siege, but the Venetians made sure that the Normans could expect no reinforcements.[274] They and the Greek fleet under Maurēx patrolled the coast continuously. Robert had, in fact, conceded the sea to the Greeks and Venetians.[275] Anna Comnena says he went so far as to have all of his vessels beached. Later, both she and Malaterra note that prior to the fateful land engagement with the Emperor Alexios, the duke even had them all burned, lest the courage of his troops be corrupted by hope of escape. What was worse, Anna Comnena relates that 'the inhabitants of the little places along the coast of the mainland, and all the others who were paying tribute to Robert, becoming courageous at his misfortunes and hearing about his defeat on the sea, were not so ready to meet the heavy obligations he laid on them'.[276] Essentially, all of the gains that the Normans had made in their endeavor to control the lower Adriatic were slipping away. If Guiscard still harbored any reservations concerning the critical importance of sea power, they had now been jettisoned.

Robert won the subsequent land confrontation with Alexios before the walls of Durazzo on 18 October 1081;[277] and, after a long siege, he finally succeeded in taking the city by suborning one of its leading citizens, ironically a Venetian.[278] The *Anonymi Barensis* records that, in the process, Guiscard managed to capture the commander of the Venetian fleet along with his ships and many of his men.[279] William of Apulia corroborates this to an extent, saying that Robert,

[272] Malaterra, *Deeds of Count Roger*, Bk 3, ch. 26, p. 156; *De rebus gestis Rogerii*, Bk III, ch. XXVI, p. 73. 'Sed illi artificiose ignem, quem graecum appellant, qui nec aqua extinguitur, occultis fistularum meatibus sub undis perflantes, quandam navem de nostris, quam cattum nominant, dolose inter ipsas liquidi aequoris undas comburunt.'

[273] William of Apulia, *La Geste de Robert Guiscard*, Bk IV, lines 300–6, pp. 220–1.

[274] Lupus Protospatarius, *Annales*, anno 1081, pp. 60–1.

[275] Anna Comnena, *Alexiad*, pp. 138–9; *Alexiade*, I, Bk IV, ch. III, p. 148. See also A. Ducellier, *La Façade Maritime de l'Albanie au Moyen Age: Durazzo et Valona du XIe au XVe siècle* (Thessaloniki, 1981), p. 102.

[276] Anna Comnena, *Alexiad*, p. 139; *Alexiade*, I, Bk IV, ch. III, pp. 148–9.

[277] Anna Comnena, *Alexiad*, pp. 146–8; *Alexiade*, I, Bk IV, ch. VI, pp. 157–63; Malaterra, *Deeds of Count Roger*, Bk 3, ch. 27, pp. 157–8; *De rebus gestis Rogerii*, Bk III, ch. XXVII, pp. 73–4; William of Apulia, *La Geste de Robert Guiscard*, Bk IV, lines 367–424, pp. 224–7.

[278] Lupus Protospatarius, *Annales*, anno 1082, p. 61; Malaterra, *Deeds of Count Roger*, Bk 3, ch. 28, pp. 158–9; *De rebus gestis Rogerii*, Bk III, ch. XXVIII, pp. 74–5; William of Apulia, *La Geste de Robert Guiscard*, Bk IV, lines 450–504, pp. 229–31.

[279] *Anonymi Barensis*, anno 1082, p. 154.

indeed, seized the doge's son, but notes that the fleet succeeded in sailing away.[280] In any case, the Byzantine Empire's primary port on the Adriatic was now in Norman hands. What Alexios lost on the battlefield, however, he won back in the council chamber. His behind-the-scenes intrigues began to pay off. He had previously inveigled Robert's disaffected nephew, Abelard, to 'stir up trouble in Robert's rear', and had promised King Henry IV of Germany a total of 360,000 pieces of gold to descend into Italy in Guiscard's absence.[281] Consequently, on the cusp of his march on Constantinople itself, Robert received urgent news from home that baronial revolts had once again erupted in Apulia and that Henry IV was marching on Rome in a direct threat to Pope Gregory VII, technically Robert's liege lord.[282] Alexios' machinations had all worked brilliantly. Robert had no choice but to return to Italy, leaving prosecution of the Greek campaign to his son Bohemond.[283] While Guiscard was gone, his Balkan conquests withered away, not only because he could spare little support for Bohemond, but also because the Venetian fleet ensured that the Norman expeditionary force remained isolated and harassed. A combined Greco-Venetian armada under Maurēx retook all of Corfu except the citadel at Kassiopi and even briefly besieged the Norman garrison at Durazzo.[284]

It took better than two and a half years, but Guiscard succeeded in putting his house in order. With the help of his brother, Roger, and other loyal vassals, he finally crushed the rebellion led by the usual suspects: his nephew Abelard, the latter's half-brother, Herman, and Geoffrey of Conversano, another nephew. He confronted them at Cannae, which he seized and utterly demolished.[285] Then, he amassed the largest army he had ever recruited and marched on Rome. He chased Henry back north and rescued Gregory from the Castel Sant'Angelo, setting fire to the Eternal City in the process.[286]

With the pope safely ensconced in Salerno, Robert resumed the task he had undertaken nearly four years before. In the fall of 1084, he set about mobilizing

---

[280] William of Apulia, *La Geste de Robert Guiscard*, Bk IV, lines 494–501, pp. 230–1.

[281] Anna Comnena, *Alexiad*, pp. 126–8; *Alexiade*, I, Bk III, ch. X, pp. 132–5.

[282] *Annales Beneventani*, anno 1083, p. 182; *Annales Casinenses*, anno 1082, p. 306; *Annales Cavenses*, anno 1083, p. 190; Malaterra, *Deeds of Count Roger*, Bk 3, ch. 33, p. 163; *De rebus gestis Rogerii*, Bk III, ch. XXXIII, p. 77.

[283] Anna Comnena, *Alexiad*, pp. 161–2; *Alexiade*, II, Bk V, ch. III, pp. 14–17; Malaterra, *Deeds of Count Roger*, Bk 3, ch. 33–4, pp. 163–4; *De rebus gestis Rogerii*, Bk III, ch. XXXIII–XXXIV, pp. 77–8; William of Apulia, *La Geste de Robert Guiscard*, Bk IV, lines 506–45, pp. 231–5.

[284] William of Apulia, *La Geste de Robert Guiscard*, Bk V, lines 80–105, pp. 240–3.

[285] *Anonymi Barensis*, anno 1083, p. 154; Lupus Protospatarius, *Annales*, anno 1083, p. 61; William of Apulia, *La Geste de Robert Guiscard*, Bk IV, lines 528–31, pp. 232–3.

[286] *Annales Beneventani*, anno 1084, p. 182; *Annales Casinenses*, anno 1083, p. 306; *Annales Cavenses*, anno 1084, p. 190; *Annales Ceccanenses*, anno 1083, p. 281; *Anonymi Barensis*, anno 1084, p. 154; Lupus Protospatarius, *Annales*, anno 1084, p. 61; Malaterra, *Deeds of Count Roger*, Bk 3, ch. 34–7, pp. 164–8; *De rebus gestis Rogerii*, Bk III, ch. XXXIV–XXXVII, pp. 77–80; William of Apulia, *La Geste de Robert Guiscard*, Bk IV, lines 524–71, pp. 233–5.

what Lupus Protospatarius calls 'a huge gathering of ships and an innumerable army of men'.[287] William of Apulia reports that the fleet consisted of 120 armed ships ('*armatis centum viginti navibus*') along with an unnamed number of 'transport vessels filled with horses, provisions and arms'.[288] This is probably an inflated figure, but there can be no doubt that Robert assembled a very large fleet, given his prior experience with the Venetians. According to Malaterra, the staging point was once again Otranto, mostly likely because Robert's main Adriatic shipyard was there.[289] Be that as it may, both William of Apulia and Lupus Protospatarius indicate Robert moved the fleet to Brindisi for the crossing, because he thought it would provide better shelter from storms, as it was already autumn – late in the sailing season.[290] Obviously, the horrific meteorology lesson of Glossa Point four years before still resonated with him.

Just as he did in 1081, Robert sent a contingent ahead to seize Avlona, this time under the orders of his sons Roger Borsa and Guy. They succeeded. Commanding the main fleet, Robert rendezvoused with his sons at Butrinto, which was also captured.[291] There, they were compelled to wait out bad weather for two months. Once it finally broke in November, they moved to reclaim Corfu.[292] Robert anchored his entire fleet at Kassiopi, on the northeastern shore of the island with the idea of relieving his garrison there. A combined Venetian–Greek fleet was moored a few miles south at Passaron (the harbor of modern-day Kerkyra, judging from Anna's description). Once its commanders learned of Robert's arrival, they proceeded north to engage him.[293] The encounter took place in the channel between northeastern Corfu and the mainland and, once again, according to William of Apulia, 'The Venetians put their trust in nine tall triremes which they knew were excellent in combat'.[294] As before, they rained heavy projectiles down upon the low-riding Norman galleys and, yet again, the Normans suffered defeat. Robert's galleys managed to disengage, but were beaten a second time three days later. After this last thrashing, the Venetians and Greeks assumed Robert was finished and returned to Passaron for the winter.

[287] Lupus Protospatarius, *Annales*, anno 1085, p. 61. '… *grandem apparatum navium multitudinemque hominum innumerabili exercitu …*'

[288] William of Apulia, *La Geste de Robert Guiscard*, Bk V, lines 146–50, pp. 244–5. '… *naves oneraria quarum lex erat, has et equis sumtuque replevit et armis …*'

[289] Malaterra, *Deeds of Count Roger*, Bk 3, ch. 40, p. 170; *De rebus gestis Rogerii*, Bk III, ch. XL, pp. 81–2. William of Apulia, *La Geste de Robert Guiscard*, Bk V, lines 140–5, pp. 242–3, also identifies Taranto as a major muster point for Robert's forces.

[290] Lupus Protospatarius, *Annales*, anno 1085, p. 61; William of Apulia, *La Geste de Robert Guiscard*, Bk V, lines 130–40, pp. 242–3.

[291] Anna Comnena, *Alexiad*, p. 189; *Alexiade*, II, Bk VI, ch. V, p. 51.

[292] William of Apulia, *La Geste de Robert Guiscard*, Bk V, lines 153–6, pp. 244–5.

[293] Anna Comnena, *Alexiad*, p. 189; *Alexiade*, II, Bk VI, ch. V, p. 52.

[294] William of Apulia, *La Geste de Robert Guiscard*, Bk V, lines 161–2, p. 244. '*Altera turba, novem confisa triremibus altis, quas habiles bello magis esse Venetia novit.*' (The anachronistic reference to *triremes* here seems to be William's way of emphasizing the size of the vessels.)

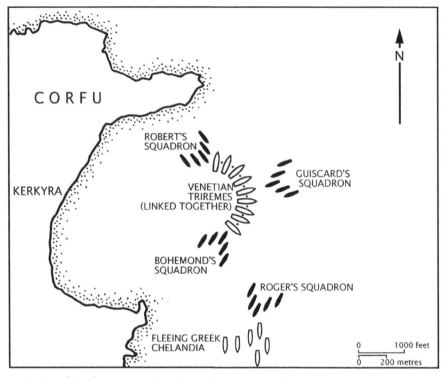

4. Battle of Corfu in 1084. (Credit: C. Stanton with P. Judge)

Concerned about the onset of stormy winter weather, the Venetians apparently sent their light galleys back to Venice, confident they would no longer need them.[295] In doing so, they violated a major tenet of war: know one's enemy. Because if they had, they would have known that Guiscard was nothing if not utterly relentless. It proved to be a terrible mistake. Robert, learning that the Venetians had reduced their forces through overconfidence, gathered his for one more try. He gave command of five ships to his son Roger Borsa, another five to the latter's brother Robert and five more to Bohemond, keeping five for himself.[296] The four squadrons then made their way to Passaron where they surprised the Venetians. In Anna Comnena's words: 'The latter were astounded by the unexpectedness of it, but lost no time in linking their bigger vessels with iron chains in the port of Corfu [Kerkyra], with the smaller ships inside this compact circle [the so-called 'sea harbor'].'[297] Robert ordered Roger Borsa to assail the accompanying Greek *chelandia* and separate them from the rest of the fleet. He did so, scattering them.

[295] Anna Comnena, *Alexiad*, pp. 188–9; *Alexiade*, II, Bk VI, ch. V, pp. 52–3.
[296] William of Apulia, *La Geste de Robert Guiscard*, Bk V, lines 157–60, pp. 244–5.
[297] Anna Comnena, *Alexiad*, p. 190; *Alexiade*, II, Bk VI, ch. V, p. 53; William of Apulia, *La Geste de Robert Guiscard*, Bk V, lines 162–73, pp. 244–5.

Robert then attacked the Venetian 'sea harbor' with the other three squadrons.[298] If the 'sea harbor' was, in fact, a semicircle or a crescent formation, as Manfroni suggests,[299] and not a circle, logic dictates that two of the five-ship squadrons would have attacked the flanks while the third slammed into the center. This was precisely the tactic recommended by both Emperor Leo VI and Nikephoros Ouranos for combating the classic crescent fighting formation (see Map 4).[300] The Venetian floating fortress was particularly vulnerable to this kind of assault, according to Anna Comnena, because the ships, having exhausted much of their cargo of provisions, 'floated on the surface as if buoyed up by the waves.'[301] In other words, the Venetian vessels were dangerously top-heavy and susceptible to being capsized. Conjecture has it that when the Normans smashed into the flanks of the semicircular 'sea harbor', those vessels on the ends overturned and sank, quite possibly dragging down the vessels chained to them, one after the other. William of Apulia reports seven Venetian ships were lost and two more were knocked out of commission.[302] This would account for the appalling loss of life suffered by the Venetians as a result. It was late November and the water must have been quite cold. Hypothermia alone would have claimed many. Anna Comnena says, 'Up to thirteen thousand were drowned.'[303] Lupus Protospatarius claims a more modest 5,000, but it is clear that the defeat was one of the worst ever endured by *La Serenissima*.[304] William of Apulia also notes that 2,500 prisoners were taken.[305] The Venetian chroniclers hardly speak of the battle; though Andrea Dandolo, the fourteenth-century doge and historian of the Republic, notes that the Doge Domenico Selvo was replaced shortly afterwards.[306]

As for Robert, he would not live to capitalize on his victory. According to both William of Apulia and Anna Comnena, he made the fateful decision to winter his fleet on the River Glykys in the Thesaprotia region of northern Epirus, opposite Corfu. Ironically, the Glykys is more commonly known as the Acheron, which means 'river of woes' after the river of the same name that passed through mythical Hades. There, the water subsided during the winter months so that all of Robert's ships became marooned. Disease soon set in, decimating his army. Guiscard managed to refloat his fleet in the spring by cleverly shoring up the banks of the river to constrict and thus deepen its flow, but

---

[298] William of Apulia, *La Geste de Robert Guiscard*, Bk V, lines 174–88, pp. 244–7.

[299] Manfroni, *Storia della Marina italiana*, I, p. 130.

[300] Leo VI, *The naval warfare of the Emperor Leo* (*Taktika*, Constitution XIX), *Dromōn*, Appendix Two, par. 52, p. 505; Nikephoros Ouranos, *On fighting at sea*, *Dromōn*, Appendix Five, par. 50, p. 593.

[301] Anna Comnena, *Alexiad*, p. 190; *Alexiade*, II, Bk VI, ch. V, p. 53.

[302] William of Apulia, *La Geste de Robert Guiscard*, Bk V, lines 187–98, pp. 246–7.

[303] Anna Comnena, *Alexiad*, p. 190; *Alexiade*, II, Bk VI, ch. V, p. 53.

[304] Lupus Protospatarius, *Annales*, anno 1085, p. 61.

[305] William of Apulia, *La Geste de Robert Guiscard*, Bk V, lines 198–201, pp. 246–7.

[306] Andrea Dandolo, *Chronica Per Extensum Descripta*, ed. E. Pastorello (RIS, vol. XII, Bologna, 1938–42), p. 217 and note 1.

by that time he, too, had contracted the 'flux'.[307] He died of fever a few weeks later while attempting to take Cephalonia with his son Roger Borsa.[308] And so, a few virulent microbes accomplished what the German emperor, the papacy, Islam, Byzantium, rebellious barons and the Venetians could not. Nonetheless, before he succumbed, Robert Guiscard had fashioned a fleet that managed to vanquish what was to become the greatest Mediterranean maritime power of the age. And, in an ominous sign of how confident the Normans had become in naval warfare, Lupus Protospatarius professes that, at the time of his death, Guiscard was 'preparing himself, with the equipping of a great naval force and an innumerable multitude of knights, so that he might direct himself to the royal city [Constantinople] by ship'.[309]

Roger's use of sea power to complete the conquest of Sicily

While Robert was strengthening his grip on his mainland domains and pros-ecuting his wars against the Byzantine Empire, Roger was left to complete the conquest of Sicily essentially on his own. After the fall of Palermo in 1072, Guiscard never returned to the island. Not only could Roger expect little support from his older brother, he frequently had to use what scarce manpower he possessed to help Robert suppress a seemingly unending series of baronial revolts in Apulia. As a consequence, it took the count twenty more years to subjugate all of Sicily. He soon learned that naval power was a necessary tool for defending and expanding his new lordship. His first experience with piracy came in June 1074, when raiders reportedly sponsored by Tamim (the Zirid ruler of Mahdiyah) plundered Nicotera, not ten miles from Mileto, Roger's Calabrian capital.[310] The next year, the same group of marauders from Mahdiyah attacked Mazara in western Sicily with 150 ships and besieged the Norman fortress there. This time, however, Roger reacted quickly. He rushed to relieve the city, driving the raiders into the sea and capturing Tamim's nephew.[311] Two years later, the

307 Anna Comnena, *Alexiad*, pp. 139–40; *Alexiade*, I, Bk III, ch. XII, p. 149; William of Apulia, *La Geste de Robert Guiscard*, Bk V, lines 202–54, pp. 248–51. Anna erroneously places the stranding of the fleet on the Glykys before the capture of Durazzo in 1081, but William more plausibly describes the episode as having happened after the defeat of the Greco-Vene-tian fleet at Corfu in 1084.

308 Anna Comnena, *Alexiad*, pp. 191–2; *Alexiade*, II, Bk VI, ch. VI, p. 55; *Annales Beneven-tani*, anno 1085, p. 182; *Annales Cavenses*, anno 1085, p. 190; *Annales Ceccanenses*, anno 1085, p. 281; *Anonymi Barensis*, anno 1085, p. 154; Lupus Protospatarius, *Annales*, anno 1085, pp. 61–2; William of Apulia, *La Geste de Robert Guiscard*, Bk V, lines 292–338, pp. 252–5.

309 Lupus Protospatarius, *Annales*, anno 1085, p. 62. '... *praeparans se, qualiter cum grandi apparatu navium et militum innumera multitudine ad regiam tenderet navigio urbem.*'

310 Malaterra, *Deeds of Count Roger*, Bk 3, ch. 8, p. 138; *De rebus gestis Rogerii*, Bk III, ch. VIII, p. 61.

311 Lupus Protospatarius, *Annales*, anno 1076, p. 60; Malaterra, *Deeds of Count Roger*, Bk 3, ch. 9, pp. 138–9; *De rebus gestis Rogerii*, Bk III, ch. IX, p. 61.

count decided to shore up his presence on the western end of the island, doubt-less to discourage such activity. He assembled an armada, which Malaterra effu-sively professes was the equal of 'the fleet of Alexander the Great';[312] then sailed to invest Trapani.[313] The fleet was probably commanded by Roger's son Jordan in this case, since Malaterra relates, 'The count with a warrior's visage, leading his cavalry, makes his way through the mountain peaks and valleys, however arduous, supported by a multitude of war-minded youths.'[314] Thus, it was Jordan who must have directed the fleet to Trapani and to whom credit must go for bringing the siege to a successful conclusion. He used a few of the ships to seize the city's livestock from a narrow spit that jutted out from the city walls into the sea, thereby depriving the inhabitants of vital victuals and breaking their will.[315] In 1079, Roger employed the fleet again to blockade Taormina by land and sea. It was effective. 'Finally, their bread exhausted, the hungry people [of Taormina] are overcome,' recounts Malaterra. 'The count is summoned and he becomes master of the fortress to do with as he wishes.'[316] It is worth noting that during the siege, an amicable exchange occurred between Roger and the commanders of a fleet of 14 Muslim ships called *golafri* (warships). When queried, they report-edly responded 'that the ships had been sent by order of Tamim to chase pirates from the sea if they could find any, and were prepared to assist the count if necessary'.[317] The clear implication here is that the count had precluded further pirate raids originating from Mahdiyah by coming to an agreement of some sort with its ruler.

For several years afterwards Roger embarked upon no major undertak-ings with or without the use of naval power – perhaps because, as Manfroni theorizes, he was obligated to support Robert's adventures against the Greek

---

[312] Malaterra, *Deeds of Count Roger*, Bk 3, ch. 11, p. 140; *De rebus gestis Rogerii*, Bk III, ch. XI, p. 62. '*Classis magni Alexandri non fuit hac pulchrior*'.

[313] W. Cohn, *Die Geschichte der normannisch-sicilischen Flotte unter der Regierung Rogers I. und Rogers II. (1060–1154)* (Breslau, 1910), p. 93, believes that Malaterra indicated that the fleet was composed of *galeas*, but he is in error. He mistranslated the phrase, '*Clipeos, auro fulgentes, et splendentes galeas…*' in *De rebus gestis Rogerii*, Bk 3, ch. XI, p. 62. Given the context of the whole sentence, '*Clipeos, auro fulgentes, et splendentes galeas sol cum tangit, intuentum aciem reverberat*', the word '*galeas*' means 'helmets' here. Malaterra, in actuality, never identified the ship types on this expedition.

[314] Malaterra, *Deeds of Count Roger*, Bk 3, ch. 11, p. 141; *De rebus gestis Rogerii*, Bk III, ch. XI, p. 62. '*Sed transcendit equitatu comes, fronte bellica, montium scopulosorum ima, sive ardua, bellicosae juventutis multa fultus copia.*'

[315] Malaterra, *Deeds of Count Roger*, Bk 3, ch. 11, pp. 140–2; *De rebus gestis Rogerii*, Bk III, ch. XI, pp. 62–4.

[316] Malaterra, *Deeds of Count Roger*, Bk 3, ch. 15–18, pp. 146–9; *De rebus gestis Rogerii*, Bk III, ch. XV–XVIII, pp. 66–7. '*Deficit ut panis, populus superatur inanis. Sic comes accitur, castro pro velle potitur.*'

[317] Malaterra, *Deeds of Count Roger*, Bk 3, ch. 17, pp. 147–9; *De rebus gestis Rogerii*, Bk III, ch. XVII, pp. 66–7. '*Sed potius ex edicto regis Thimini, ut infestos piratas a mari, si invenirentur, propellerent, missos, eius famulatui et, si necesse foret, inservire paratos …*'

Empire.[318] Malaterra does, however, note that in 1081 the count took on an ambitious building project in Messina. Roger had a church, a fortress and a tower constructed there because, as Malaterra put it, 'He valued this city over the rest of the cities that he held, as if it were the key to Sicily.'[319] It would then seem logical that Roger would also have had an arsenal built there. One can only speculate, although Manfroni is convinced that this was the case.[320] At any rate, in two years' time Roger would be brutally reminded of its apparent necessity. Nicotera was attacked again – this time by the fleet of Benarvet or more correctly Ibn el-Werd,[321] the emir of Syracuse. The Muslim invaders utterly devastated the town, carrying off many captives. They desecrated the churches of St Nicholas and St George near Reggio too, then laid waste to the convent of the Virgin Mary at Rocca Asini near Squillace.[322]

Ibn el-Werd had been an irritation to Roger for a long while. In 1075 he had engineered an ambush near Catania, which cost the life of Hugh de Gircé, one of Roger's sons-in-law, and nearly ended that of his son, Jordan. This latest provocation had finally exceeded the count's patience. According to Malaterra, he virtually declared a holy war on the Muslim leader: 'In response to this, the count, divinely inspired with an unusually intense anger, ardently rose up to avenge the tremendous injury that had been inflicted on God.'[323] Roger immediately directed the outfitting of a fleet. Six months later, in the spring of 1085, it was ready. The ships almost certainly were prepared at Messina, because Malaterra says the fleet moored the first night out at Taormina, a few hours down the east coast from Messina in the direction of Syracuse. On the third night Roger rendezvoused with Jordan, who was leading the cavalry, just north of Syracuse.[324] From there, he sent a certain Philip, son of a patrician, on 'the speediest ship' ('velocissima sagacia' – probably a sagitta, a light, fast vessel often used for scouting) crewed by Arab and Greek speakers to reconnoiter the 'Saracen' fleet at Syracuse.[325] The next day, armed with the resultant intelligence, Roger led the Norman fleet into Syracuse harbor. He was confronted by the belligerent Ibn el-Werd, primed for combat. A battle of the flagships apparently ensued and a wounded Ibn el-Werd

---

318   Manfroni, *Storia della Marina italiana*, I, p. 133.

319   Malaterra, *Deeds of Count Roger*, Bk 3, ch. 32, pp. 162–3; *De rebus gestis Rogerii*, Bk III, ch. XXXII, p. 77. '*Et, quia hanc, quasi clavem Siciliae, aestimabat prae caeteris urbibus quas habebat.*'

320   Manfroni, *Storia della Marina italiana*, I, p. 134.

321   Amari identified Benarvet as Ibn el-Werd in *Storia Dei Musulmani*, III, p. 151, note 1.

322   Malaterra, *Deeds of Count Roger*, Bk 4, ch. 1, p. 177; *De rebus gestis Rogerii*, Bk IV, ch. I, p. 85.

323   Malaterra, *Deeds of Count Roger*, Bk 4, ch. 2, p. 177; *De rebus gestis Rogerii*, Bk IV, ch. II, p. 85. '*Qua de re comes, divinitus ira plus solito inspiratus, in ultionem tantae Deo illatae injuriae ardentissime insurgit.*'

324   Malaterra, *Deeds of Count Roger*, Bk 4, ch. 2, pp. 177–8; *De rebus gestis Rogerii*, Bk IV, ch. II, pp. 85–6.

325   Malaterra, *Deeds of Count Roger*, Bk 4, ch. 2, p. 178; *De rebus gestis Rogerii*, Bk IV, ch. II, p. 86.

ended up tumbling, armor and all, into the sea, never to be a vexation to Roger again. Dispirited, the remaining 'Saracen' ships were easily defeated and Syracuse itself eventually surrendered.[326] This would be the last great naval battle the count would ever fight and the final skirmish in the struggle to seize Sicily. The conquest ended with the unsolicited capitulation of Noto in 1091.[327]

At this point, Roger evidently faced little serious opposition at sea. Only the fleet of Tamim remained as a potential rival, and its fate was sealed in 1087 when the Pisans and Genoese combined forces for an assault on Mahdiyah.[328] They invited Roger to join the enterprise, but he declined, indicating that he had a treaty and a flourishing trade relationship with its Muslim ruler: 'Tamim will say to me: "You betrayed me; broke our agreement," and the friendship and commerce between us and Africa will come to an end.'[329] Nevertheless, Roger almost certainly benefited from the subsequent campaign, because, according to the contemporary *Carmen in victoriam Pisanorum* ('Poem of the Pisans in victory'), the West Italians effectively eradicated Tamin's fleet in the process of taking Mahdiyah: 'What is more, they [the raiders] ruin the wonderfully built port; similarly destroy the arsenals and all the towers; thence drag onto shore a thousand ships which are burned.'[330] The poem's author is assuredly guilty of exaggeration, but one outcome of the episode is indisputable: any credible competition to Norman control of the central Mediterranean had been eliminated for some time to come.

The 'Great Count' exercised his newfound naval supremacy by mounting an amphibious expedition against Malta in 1091. It turned out to be a nearly bloodless affair. The armada he amassed at Capo Scalambri (southwestern Sicily) was so intimidating that it cowed the *caid* of the island's principal city into submitting with hardly a struggle.[331] Malaterra gives no estimate of the fleet's size, but says it was large enough to carry 'a great army gathered from all over Sicily and Calabria in the month of July'.[332] Moreover, the chronicler gives evidence that

---

[326] Lupus Protospatarius, *Annales*, anno 1088, p. 62; Malaterra, *Deeds of Count Roger*, Bk 4, ch. 2, pp. 178–9; *De rebus gestis Rogerii*, Bk IV, ch. II, p. 86.

[327] Malaterra, *Deeds of Count Roger*, Bk 4, ch. 15, p. 190; *De rebus gestis Rogerii*, Bk IV, ch. XV, p. 93.

[328] *Annales Beneventani*, anno 1089, p. 182; *Annales Casinenses*, anno 1087, p. 306; *Annales Cavenses*, anno 1087, p. 190; *Annales Ceccanenses*, anno 1087, p. 281; *Carmen in victoriam Pisanorum*, ed. H. Cowdrey in 'The Mahdia campaign of 1087', *The English Historical Review*, CCCLXII (1977), pp. 1–29, especially 9, 24–9; Ibn al-Athir, *BAS*, I, pp. 440–2.

[329] Ibn al-Athir, *BAS*, I, p. 451 (English translation by David Abulafia in 'Norman Kingdom of Africa', p. 29); Malaterra, *Deeds of Count Roger*, Bk 4, ch. 3, pp. 193–4; *De rebus gestis Rogerii*, Bk IV, ch. III, p. 179.

[330] *Carmen in victoriam Pisanorum*, p. 27, par. 53: 'Alii confundunt portum factum mirabiliter; darsanas et omnes turres perfundunt similiter; mille naves trahunt inde que cremantur litore.'

[331] Malaterra, *Deeds of Count Roger*, Bk 4, ch. 16, p. 193; *De rebus gestis Rogerii*, Bk IV, ch. XVI, p. 95.

[332] Malaterra, *Deeds of Count Roger*, Bk 4, ch. 16, p. 192; *De rebus gestis Rogerii*, Bk IV, ch. XVI, p. 94. '... ab omni Sicilia et Calabria plurimo exercitu julio mense conflato.'

it even transported horses. Roger's flagship alone had at least fourteen: 'The count's ship, which sailed ahead of the rest thanks to its speed, was the first to make landfall. The count left the ship with only thirteen knights. They mounted their horses and attacked the great multitude of inhabitants who had come to meet them at the shore to prevent them from advancing.'[333] Even though his ships must have carried a sizable force, Malaterra notes that Roger had room to board all the Christian slaves of Malta for the return journey and still plunder the island of Gozo along the way.[334] Maltese scholar Charles Dalli notes that, rightly or wrongly, Roger is still regarded as the 'Christian liberator' of the island: 'Numerous legends connected to Roger's stay on the island were fashioned to distinguish the Maltese as a Christian people who had suffered the yoke of their Muslim overlords until the Norman leader liberated them from their captivity.'[335]

After the submission of Malta, it seems Roger's involvement in military operations of any kind was limited to assisting his nephew, Roger Borsa, in maintaining the latter's ducal domains on the mainland. The 'Great Count' was now the real power in the region. Malaterra put it in stark terms: 'For, as we have said, the duke used the count as if he were a scourge against all his adversaries in an effort to frighten them.'[336] Roger employed his military might at Cosenza in 1088 to force Borsa's brother, Bohemond, to make peace.[337] The count was back at Cosenza again in 1091 to help Borsa suppress the city's rebellious citizenry.[338] He was also at the siege of Castrovillari in 1094 to bend William Grandmesnil to the duke's will.[339] Amalfi's attempt to rid itself of Duke Roger's rule in 1096 gave Count Roger one last opportunity to employ his fleet in siege operations, though this campaign foundered when Bohemond chose to join the First Crusade, taking a great many knights with him.[340] And finally there was the subjugation of Capua in 1098 on behalf of Richard, son of Prince Jordan of

---

[333]   Malaterra, *Deeds of Count Roger*, Bk 4, ch. 16, p. 193; *De rebus gestis Rogerii*, Bk IV, ch. XVI, p. 95. 'Navis vero comitis, caeteras velocitate praecedens, ut primum terram attigit, comes, navi digressus, cum tredecim tantum militibus equos ascendens, plurimam incolarum multitudinem, quae, ut impediret, ad ripam obviam fuerat, aggrediens...'

[334]   Malaterra, *Deeds of Count Roger*, Bk 4, ch. 16, pp. 193–4; *De rebus gestis Rogerii*, Bk IV, ch. XVI, p. 95.

[335]   C. Dalli, *The Medieval Millennium* (Malta, 2006), p. 70.

[336]   Malaterra, *Deeds of Count Roger*, Bk 4, ch. 10, p. 186; *De rebus gestis Rogerii*, Bk IV, ch. X, p. 91. 'Nam, ut diximus, contra omnes sibi adversantes, illo quasi pro flagello, ad terrendum alios, utebatur.'

[337]   Malaterra, *Deeds of Count Roger*, Bk 4, ch. 10, pp. 186–7; *De rebus gestis Rogerii*, Bk IV, ch. X, p. 91.

[338]   Malaterra, *Deeds of Count Roger*, Bk 4, ch. 17, pp. 194–6; *De rebus gestis Rogerii*, Bk IV, ch. XVII, pp. 96–7.

[339]   Malaterra, *Deeds of Count Roger*, Bk 4, ch. 22, pp. 199–202; *De rebus gestis Rogerii*, Bk IV, ch. XXII, pp. 99–101.

[340]   *Annales Cavenses*, anno 1096, p. 190; Lupus Protospatarius, *Annales*, anno 1096, p. 62; Malaterra, *Deeds of Count Roger*, Bk 4, ch. 24, pp. 203–5; *De rebus gestis Rogerii*, Bk IV, ch. XXIV, p. 102.

Aversa.[341] Roger willingly played the role of loyal vassal to his brother's son and successor, but he was not entirely motivated by altruism. He made Borsa pay dearly for any support rendered.[342] Malaterra reports, for example, that Roger's very first intervention on behalf of the young duke cost his nephew all of the fortresses of Calabria, which the count had previously shared with Guiscard, the duke's father.[343] The successful siege of Cosenza in 1091 won the count half of that city.[344] And on it went, each service bringing yet another concession until the dominion of the count eventually dwarfed that of the duke. This meant that he controlled not only Sicily, but also Calabria and the crucial Strait of Messina in-between.

The strait's strategic significance could not have been lost on Roger. There is strong evidence that both he and his brother, Guiscard, made a conscious effort to protect the western approaches to it. A charter of Count Roger in 1088 confirms the establishment of the monastery of St Bartholomew on the island of Lipari, the largest of the Aeolian Islands, just to the west of the Strait of Messina.[345] A subsequent diploma of his son, Roger II, in 1134 confirmed all the donations to the abbey previously made by Count Roger and Duke Robert, including all seven islands of the group: Alicudi, Filicudi, Salina, Lipari, Vulcano, Panarea and Stromboli.[346] There are even indications that Count Roger wanted the abbey made the seat of a bishopric, though Pope Urban II did not accede to this wish.[347] Nonetheless, Roger insured that the monastery was extremely well-endowed. He issued a charter in 1094, which not only confirmed the generous donations of his barons, but added several substantial offerings of his own. They included the castles of Fitalia, Panagia, San Salvatore and Naso scattered along the northeastern coast of Sicily. At the same time, he founded the abbey of Patti on Sicily just south of Lipari and placed it under the auspices of the abbot of St Bartholomew's.[348] Subsequently, in 1095, Abbot Ambrose, who was appointed by Roger, decreed very liberal land-holding policies for Latin-speaking newcomers to Lipari in order to encourage the island's colonization.[349] All of this caused

---

[341] *Annales Cavenses*, anno 1097, p. 190; Malaterra, *Deeds of Count Roger*, Bk, 4, ch. 26–8, pp. 207–12; *De rebus gestis Rogerii*, Bk IV, ch. XXVI–XXVIII, pp. 104–6.

[342] Chalandon, *Histoire de la Domination Normande*, I, pp. 337–8.

[343] Malaterra, *Deeds of Count Roger*, Bk 3, ch. 42, p. 172; *De rebus gestis Rogerii*, Bk III, ch. XLII, p. 82.

[344] Malaterra, *Deeds of Count Roger*, Bk 4, ch. 17, pp. 195–6; *De rebus gestis Rogerii*, Bk IV, ch. XVII, pp. 96–7, note 1.

[345] R. Pirro, *Sicilia sacra*, ed. A. Mongitore (2 vols, 3rd edn, Palermo, 1733), II, p. 952.

[346] *Rogerii II. Regis Diplomata Latina*, ed. C. Brühl (CDRS, Ser. I, II, 1, Cologne 1987), no. 36, pp. 101–3.

[347] *Regesta pontificum Romanorum ab condita ecclesia ad annum post Christum natum MCXC-VIII*, eds P. Jaffé, S. Loewenfeld, F. Kaltenbrunner and P. Ewald (2 vols, 2nd edn, Leipzig, 1885–8), no. 5448, p. 668; Pirro, *Sicilia sacra*, II, p. 952.

[348] Pirro, *Sicilia sacra*, II, p. 771.

[349] L. White, *Latin Monasticism in Norman Sicily* (Cambridge, MA, 1938), p. 85.

ecclesiastical historian Lynn Townsend White to observe, 'We must conclude that, insofar as practical motives were mixed with spiritual in Roger's mind, the object of St Bartholomew's was not to establish a bishopric, but to make a desert bloom.'[350] His most compelling motivation to do so is inherent in the geography of the Aeolian islands: the chain extends about 50 miles from west to east (Alicudi to Stromboli) and 33 miles south to north (Vulcano to Stromboli) and lies less than 40 miles to the west of the strait. Patti on the north coast of Sicily is less than 15 miles from Vulcano. When the visibility is good, the south-west coast of Calabria, the northeast coast of Sicily and the Strait of Messina in-between can easily be seen from the four easternmost islands in the Aeolian chain. In other words, it would have been nearly impossible to approach the strait from the west in mild weather without being observed. Thus, the proper-ties of the ecclesiastical complex of Lipari–Patti effectively guarded the western approach to the Strait of Messina and, although the abbey was not required to maintain a watch since it owned its lands allodially (free and clear of encum-brances), it would have been in its best interest to do so. Roger had, in effect, established a coastal watch.

Aside from supporting his nephew, Roger's principal use for his fleet in the waning years of his rule was to serve as a ceremonial escort for his betrothed daughters. Around 1086, he sent his daughter Emma, by Judith, with a flotilla laden with treasure to St Gilles in Provence to wed Philip of France. The betrothal turned out to be a ruse by Philip, who was already married, in order to purloin the opulent dowry; so Emma ended up marrying William III of Clermont instead.[351] Before that, Roger had presided over the nuptials of his eldest daughter, Matilda, to Raymond, Count of Toulouse; then sent the newlyweds back to Provence with a fleet of specially outfitted ships.[352] In 1095, Roger's daughter Constance became betrothed, through the intercession of Pope Urban II, to Conrad, the eldest son of the German Emperor, Henry IV. 'After making the appropriate preparations,' reports Malaterra, 'Roger sent his daughter, enriched with many treasures, along with the bishop of Troina and others from among his barons, to Pisa accompanied by a great fleet.'[353] The process was repeated in 1097 when daughter Busilla became engaged to Coloman, king of the Hungarians; only this time the matrimonial flotilla went from Palermo to a place called 'Alba', probably

350 White, *Latin Monasticism in Norman Sicily*, p. 80.
351 Malaterra, *Deeds of Count Roger*, Bk 4, ch. 8, pp. 184–5; *De rebus gestis Rogerii*, Bk IV, ch. VIII, p. 90. See also Chalandon, *Histoire de la Domination Normande*, I, pp. 350–1.
352 Malaterra, *Deeds of Count Roger*, Bk 3, ch. 22, pp. 151–2; *De rebus gestis Rogerii*, Bk III, ch. XXII, p. 70.
353 Malaterra, *Deeds of Count Roger*, Bk 4, ch. 23, pp. 202–3; *De rebus gestis Rogerii*, Bk IV, ch. XXIII, p. 101. '*Porro comes Rogerius, apparatis iis quae ad id officii congruebant, plurima classe per episcopum Traynensem et alios barones suos filiam, multis thesaurorum exeniis ditatam, Pisam usque conducere fecit.*'

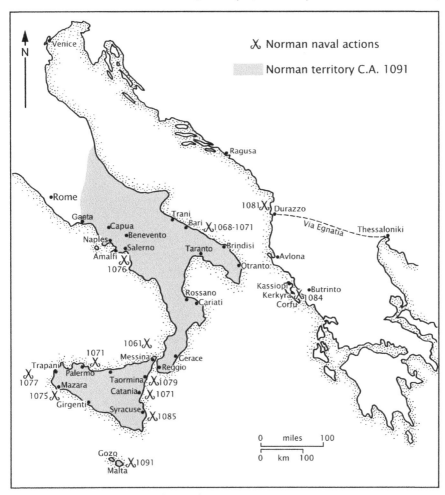

N

X Norman naval actions

Norman territory C.A. 1091

Venice

Ragusa

Rome

1081 X Durazzo

Gaeta
Trani
Bari X 1068-1071
Via Egnatia — — Thessaloniki

Capua
Naples
Benevento
Salerno
Amalfi X
1076

Taranto
Brindisi
Otranto

Avlona

Rossano
Cariati

Kassiopi
Kerkyra X 1084
Corfu
Butrinto

1061 X

1071
Messina
Trapani
X
1077
Palermo
Mazara
1075 X
Girgenti

Taormina X 1079
Catania X 1071
Syracuse X 1085

Gerace
Reggio

0   miles   100
0   km   100

Gozo
Malta X 1091

5. Norman naval activity in the Mediterranean, 1061–1091.
(Credit: C. Stanton with P. Judge)

somewhere on the Dalmatian coast.[354] The grand ceremonial fleet was almost certainly Roger's way of projecting his power to the greater nobility of Europe while at the same time discouraging any designs on his dominion.

As Roger settled comfortably into his role as the elder statesman of Norman Italy, he could be justly proud of his accomplishments. After all, he had helped his brother Robert complete phase one of the Norman takeover of the central Mediterranean: the conquest of the north shore. Now he, himself, had concluded phase two: the seizure of Sicily and Malta (see Map 5). Though he was unaware of it at the time, in 1095 Roger's third wife, Adelaide del Vasto from Savona,

---

354 Malaterra, *Deeds of Count Roger*, Bk 4, ch. 25, pp. 205–6; *De rebus gestis Rogerii*, Bk IV, ch. XXV, pp. 102–3.

made the greatest contribution to the final phase of the conquest and the future of the realm. She became pregnant with his son, Roger II.[355] When Roger senior finally passed away at Mileto in 1101,[356] he had bequeathed to his heir the ideal tool for ensuring the prosperity and security of what would become the Norman Kingdom of Sicily: a strong naval capability.

---

[355] Romuald of Salerno, *Romualdi Salernitani Chronicon*, ed. C. Garufi (RIS, 2nd edn, vol. VII, Citta di Castello, 1935), p. 236, states Roger II was fifty-eight years, two months and five days old when he died on 27 February 1154, making his birth date 22 December 1095.

[356] *Annales Beneventani*, anno 1101, p. 183; *Annales Cavenses*, anno 1101, p. 191; Al-Idrisi, *BAS*, I, p. 57; *La première géographie de l'Occident*, trans. P. Jaubert, eds H. Bresc and A. Nef (Paris, 1999), IV, 2, p. 306; Lupus Protospatarius, *Annales*, anno 1101, p. 63.

2

The Apogee (1101 to 1154)

Norman expansion under the Hautevilles was far from over. As David Abulafia aptly observes, 'Those that conquered Sicily and southern Italy so easily and so rapidly, came to think that they had breached the gates of the whole Mediterranean, and that a limitless empire lay prone before them.'[1] While credit for the conquest of Sicily must go chiefly to Roger de Hauteville, the 'Great Count', it was his son, Roger II, who subsequently elevated his father's county to the kingdom that would become the envy of the western world. Both Byzantine and German emperors sought incessantly to seize it. The basic reason, of course, was the kingdom's contemporary reputation for great wealth. Its centerpiece was its namesake, Sicily, which King Roger's geographer al-Idrisi called 'the pearl of the age for its abundance and beauty',[2] and which inspired the twelfth-century Andalusian pilgrim Ibn Jubayr to insist, 'The prosperity of the island surpassed description.'[3] Roger II achieved this wealth and attendant power by pursuing three overarching and overlapping objectives: (1) the consolidation of his reign on the mainland in the face of a rebellious nobility operating in alliance with the papacy and the German Empire, (2) the defense of the realm against Byzantine designs and (3) the expansion of Norman power on the Maghrib coast of North Africa. He and his brilliant admiral, George of Antioch, accomplished these objectives through the implementation of a comprehensive naval strategy. The key to this strategy was Sicily, which, through the blessing of geography, effectively controlled the central Mediterranean. Roger manifestly understood this, for he used every available asset, including his splendid fleet, to enhance the island's natural advantage. As a result, he was able to regulate maritime traffic transiting the 'middle sea' to alter the regional balance of power in his favor. Thus, by virtue of this simple stratagem, Roger II established a maritime empire that would endure to the end of the twelfth century, ushering in an era of western naval supremacy.

---

[1] Abulafia, 'Norman Kingdom of Africa', p. 47.
[2] Al-Idrisi, *BAS*, I, p. 55; *La première géographie de l'Occident*, IV, 2, p. 305.
[3] Ibn Jubayr, *BAS*, I, p. 145; *Travels of Ibn Jubayr*, p. 339.

Naval policy in Roger II's early years

When Roger I, the feared and respected 'Great Count of Sicily', died in 1101,[4] his son, Roger II, was not even six years old.[5] Little is known about the regency of his mother, Adelaide, except that she was almost certainly responsible for his survival. She did the one thing that would enable him to mature and establish his power base in relative peace. She moved the comital household from Roger I's castle at Mileto in Calabria to Sicily, first to Messina then to Palermo. A series of diplomas noted by both Erich Caspar and Ferdinand Chalandon indicate that Adelaide had transferred the official residence to Messina shortly after the death of her older son, Simon, in September 1105.[6] By June 1112, they were firmly ensconced in Palermo.[7] This served to insulate Roger from the fractious and dangerous Norman barony and taught him to rely on the Greek and Muslim advisors who would become the heart of his administration. More importantly, it gave him a bastion from which he was able to nurture his strategy of dominating the central Mediterranean.

Roger's upbringing among Greek and Muslim statesmen on Sicily insured that his intellectual and political orientation was from the south and east. For instance, the man German medievalist Hubert Houben believes was responsible for Roger's education was the *amiratus* Christodoulos,[8] Roger I's 'first minister', a Greek thought to be from Rossano. The Byzantine Emperor Alexios I regarded him so highly that he conferred upon him the high court dignity of *protonobilissimos* ('first most noble one').[9] Christodoulos, whose name means 'servant of Christ',[10] was also apparently known among the Muslims of North Africa. Abu Muhammad Abd Allah ibn Ahmad at-Tijani, the fourteenth-century author of the *Rihla* ('Travelers' Tales') from Tunis, referred to him as Abd al-Rahman ('servant of Allah') or Abd Allah al-Nasrani ('servant of the Merciful God').[11] Very probably then, the *amiratus* tutored the young count in the Arab culture

---

[4] *Annales Beneventani*, anno 1101, p. 183; *Annales Casinenses*, anno 1101, p. 308; *Annales Cavenses*, anno 1101, p. 191; Al-Idrisi, *BAS*, I, p. 57; *La première géographie de l'Occident*, IV, 2, p. 306; Lupus Protospatarius, *Annales*, anno 1101, p. 63; Romuald of Salerno, *Romualdi Salernitani Chronicon*, pp. 202–3.

[5] Romuald of Salerno, *Romualdi Salernitani Chronicon*, p. 236.

[6] *Anonymi Vaticani Historia Sicula*, ed. L. Muratori (RIS, VIII, Milan, 1726), p. 777; E. Caspar, *Roger II. (1101–1154) und die Gründung der Normannisch-sicilischen Monarchie* (Innsbruck, 1904), Reg. nos 4–19, pp. 483–7. See also Chalandon, *Histoire de la Domination Normande*, I, pp. 357–9; H. Houben, *Roger II of Sicily, A Ruler between East and West*, trans. G. A. Loud and D. Milburn (Cambridge, 1992), pp. 26–7.

[7] Caspar, *Roger II*, Reg. nos 20–2, pp. 487–8.

[8] Houben, *Roger II*, p. 25.

[9] L.-R. Ménager, *Amiratus-Ἀμηρᾶς, L'Émirat et les Origines de l'Amirauté (XI–XIII siècle)* (Paris, 1960), pp. 28–9, 36, Appendix II, no. 5, pp. 171–2; H. Takayama, *The Administration of the Norman Kingdom of Sicily* (Leiden, 1993), pp. 44–5.

[10] Ménager, *Amiratus*, p. 29.

[11] At-Tijani, *BAS*, II, p. 66.

as well as the Greek. This meant that Roger was probably conversant in both languages and schooled in Oriental diplomacy and statecraft. He would not be the normal Norman knight who achieves his ends by brute force alone.

Perhaps even more significantly Christodoulos may have, in fact, been responsible for supplying his princely protégé with the single most important asset of his future royal administration: a Greek Melkite by the name of George of Antioch.[12] Fluent in Arabic as well as Greek, George and his father Michael were serving Byzantine financial interests in Syria when the emir Tamim ibn al-Mu'izz ibn Badis recruited him for the Zirid court of Mahdiyah. He performed exceptionally well, overseeing the emir's revenues and expenditures, even rising to the position of governor of Susa for a time. Tamim's death in 1108 and the enmity of his son and successor, Yahya ibn Tamim, prompted George to seek employment elsewhere. He contacted the Norman court in Palermo by letter to offer his services, which were gladly accepted.[13] According to at-Tijani, George slipped out of Mahdiyah during Friday prayers on a Sicilian galley with his family and followers, all dressed as sailors.[14] Leon-Robert Ménager, a French scholar specializing in Italo-Norman prosopography, contends that this could not have occurred in 1108 since Roger II was only around twelve then,[15] but an obscure biography of the great *amiratus* by the fifteenth-century Egyptian historian, Taqi ad-Din al-Maqrizi, explains how it may well have happened at that time.[16] Recently brought to light by English Arabist Jeremy Johns, al-Maqrizi's passage on George in the biographical dictionary called the *Kitab al-tarikh al-kabir al-muqaffa li-Misr* clearly states that it was Christodoulos to whom George had written: 'So he wrote to the sultan Abd al-Rahman [Christodoulos], the vizier of King Roger, son of Roger, king of the Franks, known as Abu Tillis ['Old Wheatsack'], lord of the island of Sicily, ordering him to send a raiding-galley so that he could escape in it.'[17] Al-Maqrizi goes on to specifically note the year: 'The galley arrived at al-Mahdiyah in the year 502 [11 August 1108 – 30 July 1109], with an ambassador to the sultan Yahya ibn Tamim.'[18] And it was to Christodoulos that George and his family reported upon arrival in Sicily: 'When they came before [Abd al-Rahman], he treated them well, and put them in charge of the *dawawin*

---

[12] A Melkite is a Christian who abides by Greek Orthodox liturgy but recognizes the authority of the pope.

[13] Al-Maqrizi, translated by Jeremy Johns in *Arabic Administration in Norman Sicily: The royal dīwān* (Cambridge, 2002), pp. 80–2; At-Tijani, *BAS*, II, pp. 65–6; Ibn Khaldun, *BAS*, II, p. 206.

[14] At-Tijani, *BAS*, II, p. 66.

[15] Ménager, *Amiratus*, p. 45.

[16] Al-Maqrizi, translated by Johns in *Arabic Administration in Norman Sicily*, pp. 80–2.

[17] Al-Maqrizi, translated by Johns in *Arabic Administration in Norman Sicily*, p. 81. According to Johns (Appendix 3, pp. 326–8), the sobriquet 'Old Wheatsack' ascribed to Roger I was most likely a reference to the profitable wheat trade that the count of Sicily maintained with Ifriqiyah in the late eleventh century.

[18] Al-Maqrizi, translated by Johns in *Arabic Administration in Norman Sicily*, p. 81.

[plural of *diwan* – administrative bureau] of Sicily.'[19] This account is highly cred-ible, even though neither at-Tijani nor al-Maqrizi were contemporaneous with the events in question. Johns has convincingly argued that the source for both authors was Abu l-Salt Umayya ibn Abd al-Aziz, the official historian of the Zirid court up to 1123.[20]

Therefore, George of Antioch was not simply the man destined to become the young sovereign's closest and most trusted advisor, but he also must have helped Christodoulos mentor the future monarch in the final four formative years of his minority. Clearly, both men had key roles in shaping Roger's view of the world and his place in it. Their ideas must have become part of his poli-cies and strategies. Al-Maqrizi substantiates this: 'They [George and his family] expounded good counsel and acquired standing with him [Roger]. [When] King Roger came of age, he [George] shared absolute authority with the vizier Abd al-Rahman.'[21] And, given their respective backgrounds, these two sagacious coun-selors surely imparted to their young lord a unique knowledge of Byzantine and Arab methods of government. Al-Maqrizi even describes how George influenced Roger's dress and manner, imbuing it with a distinctly Muslim flavor.[22] More-over, they must have impressed upon him the potential significance of Ifriqiyah and the Maghrib coast to his nascent realm. The *amiratus* Christodoulos had clearly taken George under his wing and made certain that he would be a part of the ruler's inner circle for the foreseeable future. He even convinced Roger to send George on a crucial trade embassy to Egypt. The success of that endeavor won Roger's favor and, from that moment on, George never relinquished his privileged position at the sovereign's side.[23] This shrewd advisor undoubtedly apprised his new lord of the lucrative opportunities offered by North Africa.

A diploma of 12 June 1112 to Archbishop Walter of Palermo, confirming all the privileges granted by the 'Great Count', officially designated Adelaide's son '*Rogerius jam miles jam comes*' ('Roger, now knight, now count').[24] He had achieved majority at the age of sixteen and Adelaide's regency was at an end. The countess was free to fulfill her own aspirations. In so doing, she demonstrated that something of Roger I's formidable fleet remained. Desperate for funds, Baldwin I, King of Jerusalem, had sought the hand of the wealthy countess and she had accepted. In 1113, an impressive flotilla was assembled to transport her to the Latin Kingdom in a manner befitting a queen. Albert of Aachen, a chronicler of the First Crusade, describes it in sumptuous detail:

[19] Al-Maqrizi, translated by Johns in *Arabic Administration in Norman Sicily*, p. 81.
[20] Johns, *Arabic Administration in Norman Sicily*, pp. 84–90.
[21] Al-Maqrizi, translated by Johns in *Arabic Administration in Norman Sicily*, p. 81.
[22] Al-Maqrizi, translated by Johns in *Arabic Administration in Norman Sicily*, p. 82.
[23] At-Tijani, *BAS*, II, p. 66.
[24] *Rogerii II. Regis Diplomata Latina*, no. 3, pp. 6–8.

She had two trireme dromons, each with five hundred men very experienced in warfare, with seven ships laden with gold, silver, purple, and an abundance of jewels and precious garments, besides weapons, hauberks, helmets and shields resplendent with gold, and besides all the other weaponry which powerful men are accustomed to carry for the defense of ships.[25]

Clearly, Albert has embellished the account with fanciful features: there was no known variant of the *dromōn* capable of carrying five hundred men. Nonetheless, it is certain that Adelaide engaged a flotilla suitable for transporting and protecting the immense dowry expected by Baldwin. William of Tyre, a Levantine prelate and perhaps the best-known chronicler of the Latin Kingdom, confirms the event, but is less effusive in his description, saying only, 'The ships were loaded with grain, wine, oil, and salt meat, and equipped with armed men and splendidly mounted knights.'[26] He includes, however, details of a prenuptial agreement, which stipulated that if Baldwin 'should die without an heir by that union, Count Roger, her son, should be the heir and should succeed him in the realm as king, without trouble or gainsaying.'[27] Thus, when the duplicitous Baldwin, in a fit of illness-induced remorse, sent her back to Sicily four years later on the grounds that he was already married, the blow struck both the mother and the son hard. In William's words, Roger 'conceived a mortal hatred against the kingdom and its people.'[28] This would explain why Roger never aided the Latin Kingdom of Jerusalem in any substantial way during his reign. Ironically, it was also a factor in the development of his subsequent and highly successful policy of concentrating on the central Mediterranean.

Soon afterwards, Roger got his first opportunity to capitalize on the counsel George must have imparted to him regarding the strategic potential of Ifriqiyah and the Maghrib coast. In 1118 Rafi ibn Makkan al-Dahmani, governor of Gabes, ran afoul of Yahya's successor as emir of Mahdiyah, Ali ibn Yahya ibn Tamim, who took exception to Rafi's attempt to construct a commercial vessel in competi-

---

[25] Albert of Aachen, *Historia Ierosolimitana*, ed. and trans. S. Edgington (OMT, Oxford, 2007), Bk XII, ch. 13, pp. 842–3. *'Fuerunt ei duo dromones triremes, singuli cum quingentis uiris bello doctissimis, cum nauibus septem auro, argento, ostro, gemmarum uestiumque preciosarum multitudine onustis, preter arma, loricas, galeas, clipeos auro fulgidissimos, et preter omnem aliam armaturam quam ad defensionem nauium solent uiri potentissimi comportare.'*

[26] William of Tyre, *A History of Deeds Done beyond the Sea*, trans. E. Babcock and A. Krey (2 vols, New York, 1943), I, Bk 11, ch. 21, p. 497; *Willelmi Tyrensis Archiepiscopi chronicon*, ed. R. Huygens, H. Mayer and R. Gerhard (2 vols, CCCM, nos 63–63A, Turnholt, 1986), Bk 11, ch. 21, p. 526. *'… oneratis navibus frumento, vino et oleo et salsis carnibus, armis preterea et equitaturis egregiis…'*

[27] William of Tyre, *History of Deeds Done beyond the Sea*, I, Bk 11, ch. 21, p. 496; *Willelmi Tyrensis Chronicon*, Bk 11, ch. 21, p. 526. *'… quod si absque herede ex eadem comitissa suscepto defungeretur, comes Rogerus, filius eius, heres existeret et in regno sine contradictione et molestia rex futurus succederet.'*

[28] William of Tyre, *History of Deeds Done beyond the Sea*, I, Bk 11, ch. 29, p. 514; *Willelmi Tyrensis Chronicon*, Bk 11, ch. 29, p. 542. *'Qua redeunte ad propria turbatus est supra modum filius et apud se odium concepit adversus regnum et eius habitatores immortale.'*

tion with his own.[29] The thirteenth-century Egyptian scholar al-Nuwayri records that the Zirid emir dispatched six *harbiah* (men-of-war) and four other galleys to blockade the harbor at Gabes. Rafi was dumfounded since Ali's father had not only approved the project, he had supposedly even supplied the wood and iron. Rafi petitioned Roger for help. The young count responded by sending southward his first expedition, a fleet of 24 vessels.[30] The affair became a fiasco. At-Tijani, whose account appears to be the most complete, reports that the Sicilian fleet was spotted passing Mahdiyah. Outraged, Ali ordered the remainder of the Zirid fleet to trail the Norman ships to Gabes where they surprised them and sent them scurrying home. At-Tijani insists that there was a battle in which the Zirids 'killed a great number of Rum', but he is the only Muslim chronicler to do so.[31] Ibn al-Athir attests only that 'the Frankish fleet withdrew'.[32] Nonetheless, it was a humiliating stumble, which did not sit well with Roger.

Until that episode, the Normans had enjoyed friendly relations with the Muslims of North Africa. The peace treaty that Roger's father had established with Tamim of Mahdiyah was still technically in place.[33] In addition, Roger himself had interceded with the Hammadid emir of Bejaïa (Bougie) on behalf of some monks of Montecassino captured by pirates in 1114, implying a pact with that ruler as well.[34] Roger had even attempted to renew the treaty of friendship with Mahdiyah. Ibn Idari, a late thirteenth-century Moroccan historian, reports in the *Kitab al-Bayan* that the Norman prince dispatched an ambassador to the Zirid court for that purpose in 1118/19, but relations had been too strained by the Gabes affair. Contacts quickly deteriorated into a petty, tit-for-tat exchange of invectives. Ali had apparently detained some Sicilian commercial agents in Mahdiyah and Roger had demanded their return in immoderate language.[35] The Zirid ruler complied, but he must have seen what was coming. Al-Nuwayri reports, 'Ali had his fleet renovated; he prepared ten *harbiah* ships and thirty *aghriba* [warships, probably galleys], and filled them with men, munitions, naphtha [petroleum-based incendiary] and as much else as was needed.'[36] Worse still, the Zirid prince had sought the aid of the powerful Almoravid emir of Marrakech, Ali ibn Yusuf ibn Tashfin. Even though Ali suddenly died in 1121 and was succeeded by his twelve-year-old son, al-Hasan ibn Ali ibn Yahya, the

---

[29] Al-Nuwayri, *BAS*, II, p. 154; At-Tijani, *BAS*, II, pp. 51–5; Ibn abi Dinar, *BAS*, II, pp. 289–90; Ibn al-Athir, *BAS*, I, pp. 454–5; *The Chronicle of Ibn al-Athir for the Crusading Period from al-Kamil fi'l-Ta'rikh. Part I: The Years 491–541/1097–1146: The Coming of the Franks and the Muslim Response*, trans. D. Richards (Aldershot, 2006), pp. 185–6; Ibn Khaldun, *BAS*, II, pp. 204–5; Ibn Hamdis, *BAS*, II, pp. 377–9.

[30] Al-Nuwayri, *BAS*, II, p. 154.

[31] At-Tijani, *BAS*, II, p. 52.

[32] Ibn al-Athir, *BAS*, I, p. 455; *Chronicle of Ibn al-Athir, Part I*, p. 186.

[33] Ibn al-Athir, *BAS*, I, p. 455; *Chronicle of Ibn al-Athir, Part I*, p. 186.

[34] *Chronica Monasterii Casinensis*, Bk IV, ch. 50, p. 516.

[35] Ibn Idari, *BAS*, II, p. 34; At-Tijani, *BAS*, II, p. 67.

[36] Al-Nuwayri, *BAS*, II, p. 156.

situation remained near the boiling point. The ill-feelings came to a head with the frightful plunder of Nicotera, Calabria in 1122. Ali's entreaties to the Almoravids had finally borne fruit. The depredation was committed by an Almoravid fleet led by Abu Abd Allah ibn Maymun, Ali ibn Yusuf's naval commander. Roger blamed the Zirids of Mahdiyah.[37] Accordingly, he decided to rid the realm of the vexation. In 1123, he ordered the preparation of a massive expedition to take Mahdiyah.

Roger amassed a huge armada. At-Tijani says it was composed of 300 ships carrying some 30,000 men and a thousand horses.[38] While these numbers seem clearly exaggerated, the force was probably quite formidable. Nonetheless, the endeavor would be a catastrophic failure, serving only to highlight the inexperience of Roger's regime in prosecuting naval warfare at the time. In short, the enterprise became an object lesson on how not to conduct a coordinated amphibious assault. Very little went right. While none of the Latin chroniclers makes note of the event, almost all the Muslim scholars of the era describe it in some detail. The fullest account is that of at-Tijani, who appears to have had access to the lost history of the Zirids of Mahdiyah by the early twelfth-century polymath Abu l-Salt Umayya.[39] To begin with, Roger evidently telegraphed the invasion by halting all traffic between Sicily and North Africa. The interruption of the hitherto steady flow of commerce between the two lands signaled the impending storm to al-Hasan. He began preparing for the inevitable by having the walls of Mahdiyah reinforced and by summoning the surrounding Arab tribes with a call to *jihad*. Roger then entrusted his armada to Christodoulos and George of Antioch, neither of whom seemed to have had much maritime experience at that point. After setting sail from Marsala, the two neophyte naval commanders allowed what both Ibn al-Athir and at-Tijani characterized as simply 'the wind' to scatter the fleet. The surviving vessels then managed to make the island of Pantelleria, which they seized amid much needless slaughter. On 21 July, the armada reached the environs of Mahdiyah, where the two Christian chiefs committed their most grievous blunder. They selected as their base camp the Jazirat al-Ahasi ('The Sisters'), a barren islet about ten miles to the north of Mahdiyah which at-Tijani says was 'all of burnt sand' and could easily be reached from the mainland by fording the shallow coastal waters.[40] Thus, not only was the site bereft of adequate water supplies, it was also quite exposed and vulnerable. Yet, neither commander apparently gave a thought to fortifying the camp or posting some sort of sentry system. As a consequence, when the two men set sail the next day to reconnoiter the defenses of Mahdiyah and its suburb of

---

[37] At-Tijani, *BAS*, II, p. 68; Ibn al-Athir, *BAS*, I, p. 456; *Chronicle of Ibn al-Athir, Part I*, p. 245; Ibn Idari, *BAS*, II, p. 34; Ibn Khaldun, *BAS*, II, p. 205.

[38] At-Tijani, *BAS*, II, p. 71.

[39] Johns, *Arabic Administration in Norman Sicily*, p. 85.

[40] Ibn al-Athir, *BAS*, I, pp. 456–7; *Chronicle of Ibn al-Athir, Part I*, p. 245; At-Tijani, *BAS*, II, pp. 71–2.

Zawilah, they returned to find the camp overrun, having suffered a loss of men and supplies they could ill afford.

There was a *ribat* (fortress) on the island called Qasr Ad-Dimas, which they managed to seize by suborning its Bedouin garrison, but when they posted their own troops inside, they failed to properly provision them before the next Arab assault. That attack came the following night and immediately prompted total panic among the Sicilians. They fled to their ships, leaving behind most of their horses and supplies. Clearly, they had been poorly trained and were ill-prepared for battle. The two commanders were clueless as to what to do next. They stood off in their ships for eight days, helpless to assist their comrades garrisoned in Ad-Dimas. Finally, low on water supplies, they returned home, abandoning the garrison. Despite the fact that the fortress was virtually impregnable, the defenders were annihilated only a few days later on 8 August 1123, because their paltry stocks of food and water had run out. Of the original 300-ship armada, barely a third reached the shores of Sicily.[41]

All in all, it was a miserable, bumbling performance. The scouting expedition alone revealed that the Sicilian admirals had very little notion of what they were up against. They had brought horses, for example, but had no idea what to do with them. Cavalry would have been of very little use besieging a city surrounded on three sides by water. The problem, of course, is that the two men were not military leaders. Rather they were essentially bureaucrats, making it up as they went along. The result was a fiasco of legendary proportions, which Muslim historians extolled for centuries. Al-Hasan had letters containing a blow-by-blow account of the victory, penned by the Zirid prince-historian Abd al-Aziz ibn Shaddad, dispatched to virtually every Muslim emir of North Africa.[42] Their Latin counterparts, on the other hand, studiously ignored it. Nevertheless, it was an opprobrium that the Normans and Roger, in particular, would never forget. Ibn Idari passes on this anecdote from Abu l-Salt's annals: 'Abd al-Rahman ibn Abd al-Aziz told me: "At the court of Roger in Sicily, I saw a man of the Franks with a long beard grasp the tip of his beard in his hand and swear that he would not cut one hair of it until he had taken vengeance upon the people of Mahdiyah. I asked what became of him, and I was told that, after the defeat, he tore at it until it bled."'[43] Neither Sicilian commander was overtly punished for the disaster, but Christodoulos would disappear from the scene by 1126.[44] As for George of Antioch, he managed to keep his sovereign's confidence and he would get better – much better.

---

[41] Ibn Idari, *BAS*, II, pp. 34–6; At-Tijani, *BAS*, II, pp. 68–74; Ibn abi Dinar, *BAS*, II, p. 290; Ibn al-Athir, *BAS*, I, pp. 455–8; *Chronicle of Ibn al-Athir, Part I*, pp. 245–6.

[42] At-Tijani, *BAS*, II, p. 70; Ibn al-Athir, *BAS*, I, p. 458; *Chronicle of Ibn al-Athir, Part I*, p. 246.

[43] Ibn Idari, *BAS*, II, p. 36. (English translation by Johns in *Arabic Administration in Norman Sicily*, p. 86.)

[44] Johns, *Arabic Administration in Norman Sicily*, pp. 70–1 and note 70.

At first, Roger persisted in pursuing his African designs. William of Tyre, who seems to be well-informed of events concerning Sicily, reports that Roger subsequently sent a 40-galley raiding expedition to the coast of Ifriqiyah, but the inhabitants, forewarned, met it with their own flotilla and chased the Norman ships back to Sicily.[45] The Muslim chroniclers attest that the Almoravids under Maymun then conducted a series of raids on Roger's realm, which culminated in the 1127 sacking of Syracuse, noted by William of Tyre as well.[46] Patti was also plundered, but Catania, having been alerted, was able to repulse the raiders.[47] These attacks became of such concern that Roger initiated negotiations with Count Raymond Berenguer III of Barcelona to join forces in a campaign against pirate bases in the Balearics. A treaty was even drawn up by which Roger was to provide Count Raymond with a fleet of 50 warships by the summer of 1129 while the Catalan prince would furnish the required open ports and logistical support.[48] The strategy made complete sense in light of Michele Amari's assertion that Abu Abd Allah ibn Maymun, who had twice now ravaged Roger's lands, was an Almoravid from Majorca.[49] The deal apparently fell through in January 1128 when Raymond inexplicably failed to ratify the treaty.[50] In any event, Roger acted himself in 1127 by taking Malta. Since its conquest in 1090–1 by his father, it had become a base for Muslim pirates, probably because Roger I had neglected to leave a garrison on the island.[51] Roger II's reconquest of Malta may have, in fact, been a preamble to a full-scale assault on the North African coast. His biographer, Alexander of Telese, records that Roger was intent on 'occupying other islands and lands' when his attention was diverted elsewhere.[52] William, duke of Apulia, had died in the summer of 1127 and Roger was determined to fight for what he believed was his rightful inheritance.[53] His African aspirations would have to wait.

---

[45] William of Tyre, *History of Deeds Done beyond the Sea*, II, Bk 13, ch. 22, p. 35; *Willelmi Tyrensis Chronicon*, Bk 13, ch. 22, p. 615.

[46] At-Tijani, *BAS*, II, pp. 74–5; Ibn Khaldun, *BAS*, II, p. 206; William of Tyre, *History of Deeds Done beyond the Sea*, II, Bk 13, ch. 22, p. 35; *Willelmi Tyrensis Chronicon*, Bk 13, ch. 22, p. 615.

[47] Amari, *Storia dei Musulmani di Sicilia*, III, p. 395.

[48] Amari, *Storia dei Musulmani di Sicilia*, III, pp. 395–8 (note 1 on p. 396 includes a transcription of the pact); *Rogerii II. Regis Diplomata Latina*, no. 9, pp. 22–4 (the preferred transcription).

[49] Amari, *Storia dei Musulmani di Sicilia*, III, pp. 384–5, note 5, anno 1127.

[50] Chalandon, *Histoire de la Domination Normande*, I, p. 378.

[51] Houben, *Roger II*, p, 41; Amari, *Storia dei Musulmani di Sicilia*, III, p. 395.

[52] Alexander of Telese, *Alexandri Telesini abbatis Ystoria Rogerii regis Sicilie, Calabria atque Apulie*, ed. L. De Nava (FSI, Rome, 1991), Bk I, ch. 4, p. 8. '... cumque ad alias iterum occupandas insulas terrasque attentius persisteret.'

[53] Alexander of Telese, *Ystoria Rogerii regis Sicilie*, Bk I, ch. 4, p. 8; *Annales Casinenses*, anno 1127, p. 309; *Annales Cavenses*, anno 1127, p. 191; *Chronica Ignoti Monachi Cisterciensis S. Mariae de Ferraria*, ed. A. Gaudenzi (Società Napolitana di Storia Patria, Monumenti Storici, ser.

Naval power in the establishment of Roger's *Regno*[54]

Absorbing the duchy of Apulia into his realm had long been part of Roger's plan. After all, whatever expansion plans he had for the south shore of the central Mediterranean were worthless without controlling the north shore. Accordingly, he had adopted his father's practice of extracting generous concessions from the duke of Apulia in return for his assistance. Falco of Benevento, the twelfth-century scribe and ardent Lombard patriot, reports that in 1122 Roger contributed 600 knights and 500 ounces of gold to Duke William's quarrel with Count Jordan of Ariano. In return, Falco contends, 'The Duke conceded to the Count his half of the city of Palermo, and Messina and the whole of Calabria, to secure his help in these affairs.'[55] Romuald, archbishop of Salerno and a fixture of the Norman royal court in the mid-twelfth century, testifies that the duke actually gave up much more to his young cousin:

> And because the foresaid duke was a liberal and generous man and since he had to be able to have the knights he was paying, he was first of all forced by necessity to place Calabria in pledge to the count for sixty thousand *bezants*.[56] Afterwards he sold to him [Roger] half of Palermo which belonged to him by hereditary right. Finally, when he was unable to have a son by his wife, he received a great deal of money from the count and at Messina instituted him as his heir to the duchy of Apulia and all his land.[57]

Alexander of Telese substantiates that William promised Roger that he would inherit the dukedom if William should die without an offspring.[58] This is why when Roger heard the news of William's demise in 1127, he immediately dropped everything and headed north to Salerno with a flotilla of seven

---

I: Cronache; Naples, 1888), anno 1127, p. 17; Romuald of Salerno, *Romualdi Salernitani Chronicon*, p. 214.

[54] The term '*Regno*' is commonly used to denote the *Regno di Sicilia* (Kingdom of Sicily).

[55] Falco of Benevento, *Chronicon Beneventanum*, ed. E. D'Angelo (Florence, 1998), p. 68. '*Medietatem suam Palormitanae civitatis, et Messanae et totius Calabriae dux ille eidem comiti concessit, ut ei super his omnibus auxilium largiretur; continuo sexcentos milites et quingentas uncias auri ei largitus est.*' (English translation by G. A. Loud at *Medieval History Texts in Translation*, University of Leeds, 2006, http://www.leeds.ac.uk/history/weblearning/MedievalHistoryTextCentre/medievalTexts/html.)

[56] The *bezant* was a Byzantine gold coin based on the Roman *solidus* of Constantine, weighing 4.5 grams. Grierson and Travaini, *Medieval European Coinage*, p. 3.

[57] Romuald of Salerno, *Romualdi Salernitani Chronicon*, p. 213. '*Et quia predictus dux homo erat liberalis et largus et quecumque habere poterat militibus erogabat, necessitate coactus primo Calabriam pro sexaginta milibus bisantiorum prephato comiti in pignore posuit. Postea mediam civitatem Panormi, que ei iure hereditario pertinebat, illi uendidit. Postremo cum de uxore sua filium habere non posset, recepta a prenominato comite multa pecunia, eum apud Messanam de ducatu Apulie et tota terra sua heredem instituit.*'

[58] Alexander of Telese, *Ystoria Rogerii regis Sicilie*, Bk I, ch. 4, p. 8.

vessels.[59] In doing so, he was practicing a medieval form of 'gunboat diplomacy'. The citizens of the former Norman capital balked at his claim of lordship at first, even assassinating one of his ambassadors, but Roger remained in the harbor for ten days on ships 'equipped with arms' and patiently cajoled them.[60] He finally got them to submit by agreeing to a number of concessions, which included allowing the upper citadel, the Torre Maggiore, to remain in the hands of the inhabitants. Before long, a legation from Benevento offered submission as well.[61] Amalfi saw the handwriting on the wall and followed suit.[62] Troia and Melfi were next, along with 'almost all of Apulia'.[63] Before the year was out, Romuald records that Roger was anointed prince of Salerno by Alfano, bishop of nearby Capaccio.[64] 'Soon pride turned his mind to the seizure of the ducal honor,' reports Falco, 'and he ordered all those dwelling in his lands to call him "Duke" Roger, which was done.'[65]

His moment of exultation, however, was short-lived. The claim on the dukedom was not well received by Pope Honorius II, who considered the investiture of the duke of Apulia a papal right based upon the precedent of Robert Guiscard's submission to the Holy See in 1059 and again in 1080. Alexander of Telese says Roger was still in Salerno when Honorius threatened him and his followers with excommunication, if he should persist in his claim. Roger attempted to change the pope's mind with bribes, but the pontiff remained adamant. He placed Roger under anathema.[66] The pope then cobbled together an alliance of mainland barons, which included, most notably, Count Rainulf of Caiazzo (called Rainulf of Alife in some documents) and Robert II of Capua. Others were Prince Grimoald of Bari, Count Godfrey of Andria, Tancred of Conversano and Count Roger of Ariano. Roger had no choice but to return to Sicily and gather his own forces.[67] The following spring the interpolator of Romuald of Salerno recounts that he crossed the strait with 2,000 knights, 3,000 infantrymen and 1,500 archers.[68] He swiftly moved through southern Apulia, seizing both Taranto and Otranto without a fight. Brindisi resisted,

[59] Alexander of Telese, *Ystoria Rogerii regis Sicilie*, Bk I, ch. 4–5, p. 8; *Chronica de Ferraria*, anno 1127, p. 17; Falco of Benevento, *Chronicon Beneventanum*, p. 86.

[60] Falco of Benevento, *Chronicon Beneventanum*, p. 86. '... *navigiis septem paratis in armis ...*'

[61] Falco of Benevento, *Chronicon Beneventanum*, pp. 86–8.

[62] Alexander of Telese, *Ystoria Rogerii regis Sicilie*, Bk I, ch. 7, p. 10; *Chronica de Ferraria*, anno 1127, p. 17; Falco of Benevento, *Chronicon Beneventanum*, p. 88.

[63] *Chronica de Ferraria*, anno 1127, p. 17. '... *maiorem partem Apulie ...*' Falco of Benevento, *Chronicon Beneventanum*, p. 88. '... *totius fere Apuliae partes ...*'

[64] Romuald of Salerno, *Romualdi Salernitani Chronicon*, p. 214.

[65] Falco of Benevento, *Chronicon Beneventanum*, p. 89. '*Continuo, consilio habito, ad ducatus arripiendum honorem animum impulit elatum, et precepit omnibus in terra sua manentibus, ut "ducem" Rogerium eum vocitarent; quod et factum est.*' (English version from an unpublished translation by G. A. Loud.)

[66] Alexander of Telese, *Ystoria Rogerii regis Sicilie*, Bk I, ch. 8–9, pp. 10–11.

[67] Alexander of Telese, *Ystoria Rogerii regis Sicilie*, Bk I, ch. 10–11, pp. 11–12.

[68] Romuald of Salerno, *Romualdi Salernitani Chronicon*, p. 216.

but he managed to reduce it after a prolonged siege.[69] Although not specifically mentioned by the sources, Roger must have had the support of his fleet in order to compel the submission of these well-fortified port cities. By then, the papal coalition had had time to react. Pope Honorius, with 200 knights, joined forces with Robert of Capua and Rainulf of Caiazzo, who had 5,000 troops, and marched southward.[70] Roger met them at the Brandano River in the Basilicata. He pitched camp on the opposite bank and waited.[71] As Houben points out, Roger's forces were paid professionals while many of those of the papal coalition were compelled only by feudal obligation and for a limited time, normally only 40 days.[72] Roger essentially waited the pope out. Inevitably, Honorius's allies melted away in the summer sun and the pope was forced to accept Roger's demands.[73] As a consequence, Roger received papal investiture as duke of Apulia, Calabria and Sicily on 22 August 1128 outside of Benevento.[74]

Thereafter, Duke Roger had only to consolidate his new status by reining in the Apulian towns and nobles still rebellious to his authority. Heavily fortified Troia frustrated him, but he was able to bring Melfi in line before returning to Sicily for the winter.[75] The next spring he was back with a still larger force: 3,000 knights and 6,000 infantrymen and archers, many of whom must have been Muslims.[76] Roger again rapidly moved eastward, terrorizing the countryside until he reached Brindisi, which Tancred of Conversano had recovered in the duke's absence. Thwarted, Roger took Taranto instead.[77] The key action, however, was prosecuted by his fleet, which, according to the interpolator of Romuald of Salerno, numbered 40 to 60 galleys. It succeeded in strangling into submission Bari, the traditional hotbed of Apulian resistance.[78] Afterwards, Roger accepted the surrender of most of the remainder of the rebellious barons on the condition that they help him reduce Troia. Thus, the latter city was finally

---

[69] Alexander of Telese, *Ystoria Rogerii regis Sicilie*, Bk I, ch. 12, pp. 12–13.

[70] *Chronica de Ferraria*, anno 1127, p. 17; Falco of Benevento, *Chronicon Beneventanum*, p. 100. Alexander of Telese, *Ystoria Rogerii regis Sicilie*, Bk I, ch. 13, p. 13, says the pope was accompanied by 300 knights.

[71] Alexander of Telese, *Ystoria Rogerii regis Sicilie*, Bk I, ch. 13–14, pp. 13–14.

[72] Houben, *Roger II*, p. 46.

[73] Alexander of Telese, *Ystoria Rogerii regis Sicilie*, Bk I, ch. 14, p. 14; Falco of Benevento, *Chronicon Beneventanum*, pp. 101–2.

[74] Alexander of Telese, *Ystoria Rogerii regis Sicilie*, Bk I, ch. 14, pp. 14–15; *Annales Casinenses*, anno 1128, p. 309; *Annales Cavenses*, anno 1128, p. 191; *Chronica de Ferraria*, anno 1127, p. 18; Falco of Benevento, *Chronicon Beneventanum*, p. 102; Romuald of Salerno, *Romualdi Salernitani Chronicon*, p. 217.

[75] Alexander of Telese, *Ystoria Rogerii regis Sicilie*, Bk I, ch. 15, p. 15.

[76] Romuald of Salerno, *Romualdi Salernitani Chronicon*, p. 218.

[77] Alexander of Telese, *Ystoria Rogerii regis Sicilie*, Bk I, ch. 16, p. 15; Romuald of Salerno, *Romualdi Salernitani Chronicon*, p. 218.

[78] Romuald of Salerno, *Romualdi Salernitani Chronicon*, p. 216.

induced to surrender after an arduous siege.[79] Subsequently in September, the duke declared a general peace at Melfi, returning in triumph to Sicily shortly afterwards.[80]

Roger capitalized on this success by taking advantage of a schism in the papacy following the demise of Honorius II in 1130. The College of Cardinals had split on a successor: one faction controlled by the Frangipane family elected Innocent II, while the other patronized by the Pierleoni family chose Anacletus II.[81] The latter purchased his popularity with the Roman masses through ostentatious acts of philanthropy,[82] so Innocent II traveled to France where he won the backing of Bernard, the charismatic abbot of the Cistercian abbey of Clairvaux who, in turn, eventually persuaded most of Europe's sovereigns to declare their support.[83] Meanwhile, Anacletus, in need of a powerful ally, turned to Roger. The two met at Avellino where Roger offered his allegiance in return for recognition as king of Sicily.[84] Anacletus had little choice but to accede. Accordingly, in 1130 the papal pretender signed a sweeping bull that gave Roger everything he could possibly have wanted. It not only 'conceded, granted and authorized the crown of the kingdom of Sicily, Calabria and Apulia' to Roger and his heirs, but it also conferred upon him 'the principality of Capua, as well as the lordship of Naples and entitlement to the support of the people of Benevento'.[85] It is particularly interesting to note that the document specifically 'establishes Sicily as the head of the kingdom', leaving little doubt as to the strategic significance Roger assigned to the island.[86] The Hauteville heir was subsequently crowned amid much fanfare in Palermo on Christmas day of 1130 (see Figure 3).[87] It was an event that was to have dire repercussions for both Anacletus and Roger, for it probably forced

---

[79] Alexander of Telese, *Ystoria Rogerii regis Sicilie*, Bk I, ch. 18–19, pp. 16–18; *Annales Casinenses*, anno 1129, p. 309.

[80] Alexander of Telese, *Ystoria Rogerii regis Sicilie*, Bk I, ch. 21, pp. 18–19.

[81] *Chronica de Ferraria*, anno 1130, p. 18; Falco of Benevento, *Chronicon Beneventanum*, p. 106.

[82] *Liber Pontificalis*, II, *Vita Innocentii II*, p. 380.

[83] Bernard of Clairvaux, *The Letters of St Bernard of Clairvaux*, trans. B. James (London, 1953), no. 127, pp. 188–9; *Sancti Bernardi Opera*, VII and VIII, EP, eds J. Leclercq and H. Rochais (Rome, 1974), VII, no. 124, pp. 305–7. See also I. Robinson, *The Papacy 1073–1198: Continuity and Innovation* (Cambridge, 1990), pp. 69–77.

[84] *Chronica de Ferraria*, anno 1130, p. 18; Falco of Benevento, *Chronicon Beneventanum*, p. 106.

[85] J. Deér, *Das Papsttum und die Süditalienischen Normannenstaaten, 1053–1212* (Göttingen, 1969), pp. 62–4; Caspar, *Roger II*, Reg. no. 65, pp. 506–7; *Regesta pontificum Romanorum*, no. 8411. '… concedit et donat et auctorizat coronam regni Siciliae et Calabriae et Apuliae … principatum Capuanum, honorem quoque Neapolis et auxilium hominum Beneventi.'

[86] Deér, *Das Papsttum*, p. 63; Caspar, *Roger II*, Reg. no. 65, pp. 506–7; *Regesta pontificum Romanorum*, no. 8411. 'Siciliam caput regni constituit.'

[87] Alexander of Telese, *Ystoria Rogerii regis Sicilie*, Bk II, ch. 3–6, pp. 25–6; *Annales Casinenses*, anno 1130, p. 309; *Annales Cavenses*, anno 1130, p. 191; *Chronica de Ferraria*, anno 1130, p. 18; Falco of Benevento, *Chronicon Beneventanum*, p. 108; Romuald of Salerno, *Romualdi Salernitani Chronicon*, p. 218.

Fig. 3. Roger II's Coronation. A Byzantine-style mosaic in the Santa Maria dell'Ammiraglio of Palermo (also called La Martorana) depicts the coronation of Roger II by the hand of Christ. (Credit: The Art Archive/Church of Martorana Palermo/Alfredo Dagli Orti)

Lothair III, the powerful German monarch, to formally join Innocent's camp at Liège on 21 March 1131 and become Roger's implacable adversary.[88]

The new king understood that his coronation was likely to foster discontent even in his own realm, especially among the cities of Campania. After all, they would chafe at their historic place of power in the *Mezzogiorno* being upstaged by distant Palermo. More vitally, Roger must have realized that the most potent opposition would come from the great port cities clustered around Naples Bay and the Sorrento Peninsula. Naples, Amalfi and Salerno were the only entities in the region that possessed the naval power to vie with his own. Salerno, he had humbled just prior to his coronation by blockading it until the citizens finally agreed to turn over to him custody of the upper citadel.[89] He later besieged Troia and Melfi until the inhabitants of those two towns consented to rebuild the ducal fortresses, which they had destroyed following William's death in 1127.[90] Now it was Amalfi's turn. Alexander of Telese testifies that the king demanded the Amalfitans turn over to him the city's fortifications.[91] They refused, so in the spring of 1131, in order to preempt all resistance, Roger ordered the *Amiratus* John to lay siege to Amalfi with land forces while George of Antioch, now '*Maximus Ammiratus*', blockaded the port with the fleet. George quickly occupied Capri, Trivento and Gallo Lungo. Roger himself came by sea to join in the reduction of Ravello. The eventual destruction of Ravello's fortifications intimidated Amalfi into submission.[92] Naples surely would have been next, had Sergius, the *magister militum* ('master of soldiers' or more accurately, 'military commander') of the city, not taken the hint and surrendered his allegiance without a fight.[93]

At this point, Roger may have felt relatively secure and free to enjoy a respite, but it was not to be. By giving his sister Matilda and her son refuge in his court, he had made an intractable enemy of Rainulf of Caiazzo, her husband.[94] Rainulf, in collaboration with Robert of Capua, would continue to be a vexation to Roger for the remainder of the decade. In 1132, the two fomented a renewed rebellion in Apulia. Sergius of Naples saw his chance and sided with the rebels.[95] Roger reacted once again by first seeking the submission of the port cities under rebel

---

[88] Robinson, *Papacy 1073–1198*, pp. 442–6.

[89] Alexander of Telese, *Ystoria Rogerii regis Sicilie*, Bk I, ch. 22, pp. 19–20; *Annales Cavenses*, anno 1130, p. 191; *Chronica de Ferraria*, anno 1130, p. 18.

[90] Alexander of Telese, *Ystoria Rogerii regis Sicilie*, Bk I, ch. 24, pp. 20–1; *Chronica de Ferraria*, anno 1131, p. 18.

[91] Alexander of Telese, *Ystoria Rogerii regis Sicilie*, Bk II, ch. 7, p. 26.

[92] Alexander of Telese, *Ystoria Rogerii regis Sicilie*, Bk II, ch. 8–11, pp. 27–8; *Annales Casinenses*, anno 1131, p. 309; *Annales Cavenses*, anno 1130, p. 191; *Chronica de Ferraria*, anno 1131, p. 18; Falco of Benevento, *Chronicon Beneventanum*, p. 108; Romuald of Salerno, *Romualdi Salernitani Chronicon*, pp. 218–19.

[93] Alexander of Telese, *Ystoria Rogerii regis Sicilie*, Bk II, ch. 12, pp. 28–9.

[94] Alexander of Telese, *Ystoria Rogerii regis Sicilie*, Bk II, ch. 12–17, pp. 29–31; Falco of Benevento, *Chronicon Beneventanum*, pp. 120–2.

[95] Falco of Benevento, *Chronicon Beneventanum*, p. 122.

control. He began by confiscating Taranto from Godfrey of Andria; then he blockaded Bari by land and sea, attaining the acquiescence of its inhabitants after only three weeks. The Bariots even handed over the rebellious Prince Grimoald, who was led off in chains to Sicily.[96] When Roger marched on Brindisi and besieged it as well, Tancred of Conversano knew his days were numbered, so he quickly agreed to turn the city over to the king in return for his life, albeit in exile to Jerusalem.[97] Both Rainulf of Caiazzo and Robert of Capua still refused to offer Roger fealty unless the king returned Rainulf's wife and son along with the towns of Avellino and Mercogliano, which the king had commandeered.[98] Instead of complying, Roger attacked Nocera, which belonged to Robert. There, Rainulf handed the king a terrible defeat. Nonetheless, Roger did what he would routinely do after suffering a setback: he simply retreated to safe ground, in this case, first to Salerno, but ultimately, as always, to Sicily.[99]

After gathering even greater forces, including some 60 ships, the twelfth-century *Chronica Ignoti Monachi Cisterciensis S. Mariae de Ferraria* says he returned to the mainland in the spring of 1133 more determined than ever.[100] The king gained the upper hand in due course and savagely subjugated most of Apulia. City after city fell to him: Acquabella, Corato, Barletta, Minervino, Grottole, Armento, Matera, Montepeloso, Acerenza, Bisceglie, Sant' Agata, Ascoli, Troia, Melfi and Bari.[101] Though hardly impartial, Falco of Benevento may not have been far from the mark when he characterized the cruelty of the king's campaign as follows: 'The aforementioned King Roger had depopulated the cities and towns of Apulia and savagely massacred their men and women …'[102] He goes on to describe a tragic incident, which he believes was brought on by Roger's brutality:

---

[96]   Alexander of Telese, *Ystoria Rogerii regis Sicilie*, Bk II, ch. 18–20, pp. 31–2; *Annales Casinenses*, anno 1132, p. 309; *Annales Cavenses*, anno 1132, p. 191; *Chronica de Ferraria*, anno 1131, p. 18; Falco of Benevento, *Chronicon Beneventanum*, p. 120. Falco says it only took 15 days to gain the surrender of Bari, as does the *Chronica de Ferraria*, which drew much from Falco's work.

[97]   Alexander of Telese, *Ystoria Rogerii regis Sicilie*, Bk II, ch. 21, p. 32; Falco of Benevento, *Chronicon Beneventanum*, p. 120.

[98]   Alexander of Telese, *Ystoria Rogerii regis Sicilie*, Bk II, ch. 22, pp. 32–3.

[99]   Alexander of Telese, *Ystoria Rogerii regis Sicilie*, Bk II, ch. 29–35, pp. 36–40; *Annales Casinenses*, anno 1132, p. 309; *Annales Cavenses*, anno 1132, p. 191; *Chronica de Ferraria*, anno 1132, p. 19; Falco of Benevento, *Chronicon Beneventanum*, pp. 134–42; Romuald of Salerno, *Romualdi Salernitani Chronicon*, p. 220.

[100]   *Chronica de Ferraria*, anno 1133, p. 19.

[101]   Alexander of Telese, *Ystoria Rogerii regis Sicilie*, Bk II, ch. 37–52, pp. 41–8; *Chronica de Ferraria*, anno 1133, pp. 19–20; Falco of Benevento, *Chronicon Beneventanum*, pp. 150–60; Romuald of Salerno, *Romualdi Salernitani Chronicon*, pp. 220–1.

[102]   Falco of Benevento, *Chronicon Beneventanum*, p. 158. 'Prefatus rex Rogerius civitates Apuliae et oppida, viros et mulieres eorum crudeli manu depopulatus est …' (English version from an unpublished translation by G. A. Loud.)

Furthermore we have heard that twenty-three ships, loaded with gold, silver and property which he [Roger] had looted from the cities of Apulia, sank to the bottom of the sea, and in these ships were many men, women and children from all the cities of Apulia, who were being taken captive into exile, never to see their homeland or relatives again.[103]

Only Benevento, Capua and Naples had escaped his wrath thus far. Robert of Capua fled north to seek the help of the Pisans.[104] Without sufficient naval assets, there was no way to combat Roger's advantage in sea power or prevent him from ferrying countless numbers of Muslim troops across the Strait of Messina. Over the course of several months, Robert pleaded with the Pisans for help. 'Jealous of the growing maritime power of Sicily,' observes William Heywood, an authority on medieval Tuscany, 'the Pisans lent a favorable ear to his petition.'[105] They promised 100 ships by March of the following year in return for 3,000 pounds of silver. But apparently King Roger offered them a better deal, because the promises of the Pisans proved empty. All that Pisa ever sent that year were two consuls and 100 troops. The ships never came.[106] A clue as to why can be found in an early 1134 letter of Bernard of Clairvaux to the Genoese in which he acerbically observes, 'We have heard you have received messengers from duke Roger...' He then admonishes them to 'not fight their neighbors and friends.'[107] Erich Caspar, Ferdinand Chalandon, William Heywood and Camillo Manfroni are unanimous in their interpretation: the clear implication is that the Genoese had been bribed by Roger to make trouble for the Pisans in the absence of their fleet.[108] Hence the Pisans prudently decided not to dispatch their ships.

Meanwhile, Rainulf of Caiazzo held out as long as he could, hoping that King Lothair, who was in Rome at the time, would come to their aid. But Lothair was not ready for a fight; he had only 2,000 troops with him and, most importantly, no naval forces to counteract those of Roger. He returned, instead, north of the Alps with what he had come for: the imperial crown, set upon his head by

---

[103] Falco of Benevento, *Chronicon Beneventanum*, pp. 158–60. *'Audivimus preterea viginti et tria navigia auro et argento onerata, et mobilium, quae de civitatibus Apuliae expoliaverat, in profundo maris submersisse; in quibus navigiis multi viri et mulieres ex omnibus civitatibus Apuliae, et infantes ligati exules ducebantur, patriam parentesque suos nunquam visuri.'* (English version from an unpublished translation by G. A. Loud.)

[104] Alexander of Telese, *Ystoria Rogerii regis Sicilie*, Bk II, ch. 37, p. 41.

[105] Heywood, *History of Pisa*, p. 83.

[106] Alexander of Telese, *Ystoria Rogerii regis Sicilie*, Bk II, ch. 37 and 56, pp. 41 and 50; *Chronica de Ferraria*, 1134, p. 20; Falco of Benevento, *Chronicon Beneventanum*, pp. 160 and 168.

[107] Bernard of Clairvaux, *Letters of St Bernard of Clairvaux*, no. 131, pp. 200–1; *Sancti Bernardi Opera*, VII, no. 129, pp. 322–4. *'Audivimus venisse ad vos nuntios ducis Rogerii ...'; '... non equidem id praesumendum adversus vicinos et amicos.'* (Note that Bernard pointedly refuses to acknowledge Roger's regal status by calling him 'duke'.)

[108] Caspar, *Roger II*, pp. 142–5; Chalandon, *Histoire de la Domination Normande*, II, pp. 34–5; Heywood, *History of Pisa*, p. 83; Manfroni, *Storia della Marina italiana*, I, p. 186.

Innocent II.[109] In the spring of 1134, Roger sailed into Salerno with nearly 60 galleys, which he immediately hurled against Naples. Although initially repulsed, the Sicilian fleet devastated the neighboring Neapolitan fortifications while the king ravaged the surrounding countryside with his land forces.[110] Resistance finally collapsed when the king took Nocera and the rebels realized that no help would be forthcoming from either the German emperor or Pisa. Both Rainulf of Caiazzo and Sergius of Naples were finally compelled to genuflect before the king and profess their loyalty once again.[111]

And once again Roger had little time to revel in his victory. He had scarcely returned to Sicily before he was afflicted with a serious illness. He recovered only to see his beloved wife, Queen Elvira, consumed by sickness, perhaps the same sickness that had nearly killed him. Alexander of Telese says he became so distraught that he shut himself up in chambers, giving birth to the rumor that he had perished.[112] His mainland enemies took the rumor for fact and attempted to seize the perceived opportunity. Robert of Capua returned from Pisa with a force of 20 ships and around 8,000 combatants to be welcomed at Naples by the *Magister Militum* Sergius. Rainulf of Caiazzo soon joined the conspiracy.[113] Stirred into action by his advisors, Roger hastily gathered his forces, which the *Annales Pisani* says included a fleet of 60 ships. Once more he rushed north, sailing into Salerno in mid-June.[114] After retaking Aversa and ravaging the region, the king sealed up the rebels inside Naples.[115]

Meanwhile, the Pisan fleet, freshly reinforced, decided to make a diversionary assault on Amalfi, mercilessly pillaging its old rival.[116] Both Alexander of Telese and Falco of Benevento testify that the original 20-ship flotilla was joined by 20

---

[109] Alexander of Telese, *Ystoria Rogerii regis Sicilie*, Bk II, ch. 36–7, pp. 40–1; *Annales Casinenses*, anno 1133, p. 309; *Annalista Saxo*, ed. K. Nass (MGH, SS, XXXVII, Hanover, 2006), p. 595; Falco of Benevento, *Chronicon Beneventanum*, p. 158.

[110] *Chronica de Ferraria*, anno 1134, p. 20; Falco of Benevento, *Chronicon Beneventanum*, p. 168.

[111] Alexander of Telese, *Ystoria Rogerii regis Sicilie*, Bk II, ch. 62–7, pp. 52–6; *Annales Casinenses*, anno 1134, p. 309; *Annales Cavenses*, anno 1134, p. 191; Falco of Benevento, *Chronicon Beneventanum*, pp. 170–2.

[112] Alexander of Telese, *Ystoria Rogerii regis Sicilie*, Bk III, ch. 1, p. 59.

[113] Alexander of Telese, *Ystoria Rogerii regis Sicilie*, Bk III, ch. 1–2, 7, pp. 59–60, 63; *Annales Casinenses*, anno 1134, p. 309; *Chronica de Ferraria*, anno 1135, p. 20; Falco of Benevento, *Chronicon Beneventanum*, p. 173.

[114] Alexander of Telese, *Ystoria Rogerii regis Sicilie*, Bk III, ch. 9, p. 64; Bernardo Maragone, *Annales Pisani*, p. 10.

[115] Alexander of Telese, *Ystoria Rogerii regis Sicilie*, Bk III, ch. 19, pp. 69–70; *Annales Casinenses*, anno 1135, p. 309; *Annales Cavenses*, anno 1135, p. 191; *Chronica de Ferraria*, anno 1135, p. 20; Falco of Benevento, *Chronicon Beneventanum*, pp. 172–4.

[116] Alexander of Telese, *Ystoria Rogerii regis Sicilie*, Bk III, ch. 24–5, pp. 72–3; *Annales Cavenses*, anno 1135, p. 191; *Chronica de Ferraria*, anno 1135, p. 20; Falco of Benevento, *Chronicon Beneventanum*, p. 174; Bernardo Maragone, *Annales Pisani,* pp. 9–10; Romuald of Salerno, *Romualdi Salernitani Chronicon*, p. 220.

more, but Bernardo Maragone's *Annales Pisani* claims that a total of 46 vessels were involved in the assault.[117] In any event, the attack was utterly devastating. Amalfi had been left virtually defenseless. Roger had directed four Amalfitan '*liburnae*' (probably a classicized reference to small, swift galleys) 'filled with men' ('*cum liburnis quattuor, armatorum refertis copia*') to harass Neapolitan shipping and had conscripted most of the rest of the able-bodied men into his own forces.[118] 'So when the Pisans arrived at dawn and stormed the city they found no resistance and cruelly sacked it,' recounts Alexander of Telese.[119] Maragone adds that they captured seven galleys and two larger ships, burning many others. The towns of Atrani, Maiori, Minori and Ravello followed suit.[120] 'And when the city had been completely ravaged and all the booty carried down to the fleet,' continues Alexander of Telese, 'they then seized the town of Scala and the other fortresses of Amalfi, and lastly launched an assault on the fortress called Fratta [near Ravello].'[121]

When Roger realized what was happening, he force-marched his army from recently subdued Aversa over the mountains of the Sorrento Peninsula to surprise the Pisans while they were attacking Fratta.[122] Maragone says Roger descended upon the Pisans with 7,000 soldiers. He also says the king had brought all 60 of his ships, *gatti* as well as galleys, but that they did not engage the Pisans.[123] Manfroni, however, is right to question why a battle-hardened fleet of 60 warships would decline to attack a fleet of only 46 vessels encumbered by booty.[124] In any event, Roger subjected the Pisans to a crippling defeat: over 1,500 men were killed or captured, including three consuls. The thrashing had so seriously compromised the Pisan fleet's combat effectiveness that it was soon compelled to withdraw its 43 remaining vessels.[125] Twenty-three days later, after

---

[117] Falco of Benevento, *Chronicon Beneventanum*, p. 174; Bernardo Maragone, *Annales Pisani*, pp. 9–10.
[118] Alexander of Telese, *Ystoria Rogerii regis Sicilie*, Bk III, ch. 25, p. 72.
[119] Alexander of Telese, *Ystoria Rogerii regis Sicilie*, Bk III, ch. 25, p. 72. '*Venientes itaque ipsi Pisani subito, inchoante aurore luce, invaserunt urbem, nulloque resistente eam funditus impieque depopulantur.*' (English translation by G. A. Loud at www.leeds.ac.uk/history/weblearning/MedievalHistoryTextCentre/medievalTexts/html.)
[120] Bernardo Maragone, *Annales Pisani*, p. 10.
[121] Alexander of Telese, *Ystoria Rogerii regis Sicilie*, Bk III, ch. 25, pp. 72–3. '*Cumque, urbe tota depopulata, universa ad classem spolia transportata fuissent, mox Scala oppido ceterisque Amalfie munitionibus invasis, novissime quoddam munimen, quod dicitur Fracta, oppugnare nituntur.*' (English translation by G. A. Loud at www.leeds.ac.uk/history/weblearning/MedievalHistoryTextCentre/medievalTexts/html.)
[122] Alexander of Telese, *Ystoria Rogerii regis Sicilie*, Bk III, ch. 26, p. 73; *Annales Cavenses*, anno 1135, p. 191; Bernardo Maragone, *Annales Pisani*, p. 10; Romuald of Salerno, *Romualdi Salernitani Chronicon*, p. 221.
[123] Bernardo Maragone, *Annales Pisani*, p. 10.
[124] Manfroni, *Storia della Marina italiana*, I, p. 188.
[125] Alexander of Telese, *Ystoria Rogerii regis Sicilie*, Bk III, ch. 26, p. 73.

plundering undefended Ischia out of spite, it returned to Pisa.[126] The rebels had lost their all-important naval support. The king once more had the advantage.

The siege of Naples, however, dragged on. Falco of Benevento reports that Roger made another maritime assault on the well-defended city immediately following the departure of the Pisans, but a storm broke up his fleet. Many of his ships had to seek shelter in the harbor of Pozzuoli and the king was compelled to send the remainder of his armada home for the winter. He, himself, returned to his island sanctuary to await further developments.[127] The situation changed dramatically in 1136. Innocent II, seeking to remove both Anacletus, his rival claimant to the papal throne, and Roger, the pretender's prime benefactor, finally convinced the German Emperor Lothair III to invade.[128] What is more, the Pisans, at last, committed to providing the 100 warships purchased years earlier with Campanian silver.[129] No specific reason is given for the change of heart, but it is not inconceivable that the pope had pressed for a renewal of the peace pact between the Pisans and the Genoese, which he had brokered at Grosseto in 1133.[130] Both he and his highly persuasive chief promoter, Bernard of Clairvaux, were present at the Council of Pisa in 1135.[131] In fact, the *Chronica de Ferraria* notes that the Genoese had also promised some support.[132] This would have allowed Pisan participation in the enterprise without fear of attack from Genoa. And, of course, the Pisans would have been anxious to avenge their disastrous defeat at the hands of the Normans at Fratta.

In 1137, after some delays consolidating his power in northern Italy, Lothair marched down the Adriatic coast toward Apulia, stopping long enough to subjugate Ancona with the help of the Venetians.[133] He was welcomed at Trani where the inhabitants handed over the royal garrison. Thirty-three Sicilian vessels attempted to contest the takeover, but eight were sunk and the fleet commander was killed.[134] Erich Caspar, author of a study still considered a standard work on Roger II, speculates that the Venetians were to blame,[135] but Willy Cohn, his German countryman and expert on Sicilian sea power, feels that it may have

---

[126] Bernardo Maragone, *Annales Pisani*, p. 10; Romuald of Salerno, *Romualdi Salernitani Chronicon*, p. 221.

[127] *Chronica de Ferraria*, anno 1135, p. 20; Falco of Benevento, *Chronicon Beneventanum*, p. 174.

[128] Falco of Benevento, *Chronicon Beneventanum*, pp. 174–6.

[129] Falco of Benevento, *Chronicon Beneventanum*, p. 186.

[130] Caffaro, *Annales Ianuenses* in *Annali genovesi di Caffaro e de'suoi continuatori dal MXCIX al MCCXCIII*, eds L. Belgrano and C. Imperiale di Sant'Angelo (5 vols, FSI, Genoa, 1890–1929), I, pp. 26–7.

[131] Bernardo Maragone, *Annales Pisani*, p. 9.

[132] *Chronica de Ferraria*, anno 1137, p. 21.

[133] *Annalista Saxo*, p. 605. See also Caspar, *Roger II*, p. 186.

[134] *Annalista Saxo*, pp. 606–7.

[135] Caspar, *Roger II*, p. 188.

been the citizens of Trani itself.[136] Manfroni seems to concur. He has concluded from charter evidence (discussed below) that the Venetians remained neutral in the war between Lothair and Roger, because the latter had bought them off.[137] Twenty-five more of Roger's ships were captured at Brindisi, which also willingly submitted to the emperor.[138] Many of the rebels, including Robert of Capua, joined the imperial army at Bari, which was reduced after a four-week siege.[139] After that, Falco of Benevento insists, 'The whole coastline right down to Taranto as well as Calabria decided to submit itself in fealty to the Emperor.'[140]

Lothair paused at Lagopesole in the highlands ten miles west of Acerenza to wait out the heat of summer before marching on to the last royal bastion remaining to Roger in Campania: Salerno.[141] In the meantime, the Pisan fleet of 100 ships arrived at Naples and again set about intimidating Amalfi and Atrani into submission. 'Then,' recounts Falco, 'the latter [the Pisans] marched against Ravello and Scala, entered them, plundered the inhabitants of all their goods and ravaged them with fire and sword.'[142] According to the *Annales Pisani*, in three days, starting from 3 July 1137, 'the whole of the duchy of the Amalfitani was placed under tribute.'[143] When Lothair reached Campania, he immediately laid siege to Salerno, with the help of the Pisans who joined in with 40 of their warships.[144] The *Annalista Saxo*, the mid-twelfth-century Saxon annals of the German kings, contends they were supported by 80 Genoese vessels, but this is unlikely since Caffaro, the chief Genoese annalist of the period, makes no mention of it.[145] The only other source to attest to the presence of the Genoese is the *Chronica de Ferraria*, and it gives no numbers of ships.[146] Furthermore, the *Annalista Saxo*'s suggestion that 300 Amalfitan vessels had entered the fray on the side of the imperial forces is preposterous, considering how Amalfi and its fleet were nearly expunged by the Pisans only two years earlier.[147]

All the while, Roger did the only sensible thing he could do. Having long since abandoned the siege of Naples, he had withdrawn to 'fortress Sicily', where

---

[136] Cohn, *Die Geschichte der normannisch-sicilischen Flotte*, pp. 32–3.

[137] Manfroni, *Storia della Marina italiana*, I, pp. 189–90.

[138] *Annalista Saxo*, p. 610.

[139] *Annalista Saxo*, p. 608; *Annales Casinenses*, anno 1137, p. 309; Falco of Benevento, *Chronicon Beneventanum*, p. 186.

[140] Falco of Benevento, *Chronicon Beneventanum*, p. 186. '*Inde maritima omnis usque ad Tarentum et Calabriam ad imperatoris fidelitatem alligari satagebat.*' (English version from an unpublished translation by G. A. Loud.)

[141] *Chronica de Ferraria*, anno 1137, p. 21; Falco of Benevento, *Chronicon Beneventanum*, p. 186.

[142] Falco of Benevento, *Chronicon Beneventanum*, p. 186. '*Inde super Rabellam et Scalam properantes eas invadunt, et universa eorum bona diripientes in ore ignis et gladii eas consumunt.*'

[143] Bernardo Maragone, *Annales Pisani*, p. 11. '*… totum ducatum Malfitanorum sub tributo posuerunt.*'

[144] Bernardo Maragone, *Annales Pisani*, p. 11.

[145] *Annalista Saxo*, p. 609.

[146] *Chronica de Ferraria*, anno 1137, p. 21.

[147] *Annalista Saxo*, p. 609.

he remained with the bulk of his naval and land forces, safe and unscathed.[148] He was badly overmatched, but he knew his enemies well. The odd alliance of imperial forces, papal troops, profit-motivated Pisans and Norman rebels could not last. He even gave orders to his chancellor and the commander of his 400-man garrison at Salerno, Robert of Selby, to retreat into the Torre Maggiore and relinquish the city to the imperial alliance without a fight, thereby sparing it a needless pillaging.[149] It was a stroke of genius. The negotiated settlement with Lothair on 8 August 1137 left his Pisan allies without the plunder upon which they had been counting. Their outrage propelled them into Roger's camp. They sent a galley to Sicily in search of a deal. They evidently found one to their liking, probably some form of cash compensation and/or trade concessions. The Pisans gathered their fleet and deserted the alliance.[150]

Without naval support, the invasion quickly foundered and fell apart in dissension. The pope and the German Emperor quarreled over who had the legitimate right to appoint Rainulf duke of Apulia. In the end, they compromised. Both performed the ceremony.[151] Their relationship, however, remained in tatters. Fifteen days later, Lothair departed for Germany only to die along the way, leaving Innocent II and the rebel leader Rainulf of Caiazzo to their own devices.[152] The Sicilian sovereign, once again, assembled his forces, returned to the mainland, and began swiftly reacquiring all that he had lost.[153] There were some reverses. In late October 1137, Rainulf managed to hand Roger a setback at Rignano on the western slopes of Monte Gargano.[154] A couple of months later, at the end of January 1138, Anacletus passed away.[155] The impact of these events was, nonetheless, minimal and only temporary. Rainulf, his arch-enemy, died

---

[148] Romuald of Salerno, *Romualdi Salernitani Chronicon*, p. 222.

[149] *Annales Casinenses*, anno 1137, p. 309; *Annales Cavenses*, anno 1137, p. 192; *Chronica de Ferraria*, anno 1137, pp. 21–2; Falco of Benevento, *Chronicon Beneventanum*, p. 188; Bernardo Maragone, *Annales Pisani*, p. 11; Romuald of Salerno, *Romualdi Salernitani Chronicon*, pp. 222–3.

[150] *Chronica de Ferraria*, anno 1137, pp. 21–2; Falco of Benevento, *Chronicon Beneventanum*, p. 188; Bernardo Maragone, *Annales Pisani*, p. 11; Romuald of Salerno, *Romualdi Salernitani Chronicon*, p. 223.

[151] *Annalista Saxo*, p. 610; *Chronica de Ferraria*, anno 1137, p. 22; Falco of Benevento, *Chronicon Beneventanum*, pp. 188–90; Romuald of Salerno, *Romualdi Salernitani Chronicon*, pp. 223–4.

[152] *Annales Casinenses*, anno 1137, p. 309; *Annales Cavenses*, anno 1137, p. 192; *Annalisto Saxo*, pp. 610–11; *Chronica de Ferraria*, anno 1137, p. 22; Falco of Benevento, *Chronicon Beneventanum*, pp. 194, 206; Romuald of Salerno, *Romualdi Salernitani Chronicon*, p. 224.

[153] *Chronica de Ferraria*, anno 1137, p. 22; Falco of Benevento, *Chronicon Beneventanum*, pp. 194–6; Romuald of Salerno, *Romualdi Salernitani Chronicon*, p. 224.

[154] *Annales Cavenses*, anno 1137, p. 192; Falco of Benevento, *Chronicon Beneventanum*, pp. 196–8; Romuald of Salerno, *Romualdi Salernitani Chronicon*, p. 225.

[155] *Annales Casinenses*, anno 1138, p. 309; *Chronica de Ferraria*, anno 1138, p. 24; Falco of Benevento, *Chronicon Beneventanum*, p. 206; Romuald of Salerno, *Romualdi Salernitani Chronicon*, p. 225.

suddenly in 1139.[156] In that same year, Pope Innocent II was cornered at Galluccio near San Germano and forced to confirm Roger as king of Sicily while investing his son, also named Roger, with the duchy of Apulia and another son, Alfonso, with the principality of Capua.[157] Soon afterwards, the king crowned his victory with the successful siege, by land and sea, of Bari in September 1139.[158] Roger had finally thwarted the designs of the papacy and the Western Empire, thereby securing his mainland domains. He would turn his eyes southward again, but there would be one more distraction before he could complete his long-postponed plans to claim the coast of North Africa.

Naval campaigns against Greece

The German Empire was not the only imperial challenge to Roger's rule. The Byzantine emperors still harbored great enmity toward the Normans for expropriating what they had historically deemed as theirs. Moreover, the attempts of Roger's uncle, Robert Guiscard, and his son, Bohemond, to conquer the Byzantine Empire in the waning years of the preceding century had not been forgotten. It was only a matter of time before the Sicilian monarch provoked the Eastern Empire into acting against him. That provocation came in 1135. Two events in that year were to cause the court of Constantinople grave concern. First of all, William of Tyre relates that when Bohemond II of Antioch passed away, Roger claimed 'Antioch with all its possessions as belonging to him by hereditary right'.[159] In fact, when the nobles of said city decided to invite Raymond, son of Count William of Poitou, to marry Bohemond's daughter and heir, Constance, Roger 'made arrangements in every coastal city of Apulia to waylay him'.[160] Raymond slipped through the net, but Roger later managed to have Ralph, the patriarch of Antioch, intercepted at Brindisi in hopes of pressuring the prelate into supporting his claim. Instead, Roger ended up befriending the cleric and even had him escorted home with a flotilla of his own ships after

---

[156] *Annales Casinenses*, anno 1139, p. 309; *Annales Cavenses*, anno 1138, p. 192; Falco of Benevento, *Chronicon Beneventanum*, p. 216; Romuald of Salerno, *Romualdi Salernitani Chronicon*, p. 226.

[157] *Annales Casinenses*, anno 1139, p. 309; *Annales Cavenses*, anno 1138, p. 192; *Chronica de Ferraria*, anno 1139, p. 25; Falco of Benevento, *Chronicon Beneventanum*, pp. 220–2; Romuald of Salerno, *Romualdi Salernitani Chronicon*, p. 225.

[158] *Annales Casinenses*, anno 1139, p. 309; *Annales Cavenses*, anno 1138, p. 192; Falco of Benevento, *Chronicon Beneventanum*, pp. 226–30; Romuald of Salerno, *Romualdi Salernitani Chronicon*, p. 226.

[159] William of Tyre, *History of Deeds Done beyond the Sea*, II, Bk 14, ch. 9, pp. 59–60; *Willelmi Tyrensis Chronicon*, Bk 14, ch. 9, p. 641. 'Nam Rogerus tunc Apulie dux, postmodum autem rex, Antiochiam cum omnibus pertinentiis suis, quasi iure sibi debitam hereditario ...'

[160] William of Tyre, *History of Deeds Done beyond the Sea*, II, Bk 14, ch. 20, pp. 77–8; *Willelmi Tyrensis Chronicon*, Bk 14, ch. 20, p. 657. '... unde in singulis Apulie urbibus maritimis pretenderat insidias ut eum comprehenderet ...'

Ralph had completed his business in Rome.[161] The whole effort was half-hearted and nothing ever came of it. Distracted by Lothair's invasion of his mainland domains, the king soon dropped the matter. Nonetheless, the incident could not have gone unnoticed by the Byzantine *basileus*, who had long been anxious to regain a principality he regarded, by right, as belonging to the Eastern Empire.

The second incident was, perhaps, even more troubling. Following the capitulation of Rainulf and the rebellious barons of Campania in 1135, Roger must have felt he had some breathing space from his struggles on the Italian mainland to continue his African aspirations. He sent George of Antioch to capture Jerba, an island off the coast of Tunisia in the Gulf Gabes. It was a notorious enclave of Muslim pirates, which, according to Ibn al-Athir, even the Zirids felt compelled to chastise on occasion.[162] A host of Muslim chroniclers recount how the Sicilian fleet surrounded the island, slaughtered many of the men and took the womenfolk captive.[163] Ibn Khaldun notes that when the survivors asked for *aman* (amnesty), 'the Franks left them on the island, but made them pay the *jizya* [tribute] and put them under their yoke.'[164] Since the primary occupation of the island's inhabitants was piracy, the only way they could pay said tribute was to continue their buccaneering ways at the behest of the king of Sicily. This is exactly what Hubert Houben, among others, has concluded.[165] And apparently, this seaborne brigandage remained as indiscriminate as before. The Venetians were so outraged at suffering some '4,000 *talents*' worth of damage to their merchants from piracy in the vicinity of Jerba that they went to the Emperor John II Komnenos in hopes of enlisting the Byzantines in an anti-Norman alliance.[166] They must have found a willing audience. Chalandon describes Constantinople's concerns: 'There was a real danger for Byzantine commerce of finding the Normans in Africa, in Antioch, and on the coasts of the Adriatic; and the attempts of the king of Sicily to command all the great maritime routes could not have been viewed with complacency in the court of Constantinople.'[167] Consequently, the Byzantines joined with the Venetians to propose an anti-Norman alliance to Lothair at the German imperial court at Merseburg in 1136.[168] Based

---

[161]   William of Tyre, *History of Deeds Done beyond the Sea*, II, Bk 15, ch. 12–13, pp. 113–15; *Willelmi Tyrensis Chronicon*, Bk 15, ch. 12–13, pp. 691–5.

[162]   Ibn al-Athir, *Chronicle of Ibn al-Athir, Part I*, p. 175.

[163]   Al-Nuwayri, *BAS*, II, pp. 156–7; At-Tijani, *BAS*, II, p. 55; Ibn abi Dinar, *BAS*, II, pp. 291–2; Ibn al-Athir, *BAS*, I, p. 461; *Chronicle of Ibn al-Athir, Part I*, pp. 321–2; Ibn Idari, *BAS*, II, p. 37; Ibn Khaldun, *BAS*, II, pp. 220–2.

[164]   Ibn Khaldun, *BAS*, II, p. 220.

[165]   Houben, *Roger II*, pp. 77–8.

[166]   *Annales Erphesfurtenses*, ed. G. Pertz (MGH, SS, VI, Hanover, 1844), anno 1135, p. 540. A *talent* was a classical unit of weight. In ancient Greece, a *talent* of silver was equivalent to around 25.8 kilos. Thus, '4,000 *talents*' could have referred to about 100 metric tons of silver. There is no way of knowing for sure.

[167]   Chalandon, *Histoire de la Domination Normande*, II, pp. 124–5.

[168]   *Annales Erphesfurtenses*, anno 1135, p. 540; *Annalista Saxo*, p. 610.

upon charter evidence (discussed in some detail further on), Manfroni believes that Roger found out about the putative pact and managed to detach the Venetians with trading privileges.[169] The Byzantines then ended up simply offering some limited financial support for Lothair's planned invasion of southern Italy. The Byzantine throne remained too preoccupied by its campaigns in Asia Minor to do more.[170]

The Emperor John II Komnenos did not desist, however. In 1140, he sent more emissaries to the court of King Conrad III of Germany, Lothair's successor, proposing a marriage alliance. Otto of Freising, Frederick Barbarossa's biographer, makes the purpose clear: 'They sought to renew the bond of union between the two empires, I mean the western and eastern, because of the insolence of Roger of Sicily.'[171] The enmity that both monarchs harbored for King Roger was, no doubt, stoked by bitter Norman exiles, such as Alexander of Conversano and Robert of Capua, known to have resided in each court.[172] Negotiations continued for some time with several exchanges of envoys.[173] Roger evidently got wind of these parleys, because he attempted to sabotage them by brokering a marriage alliance of his own with John II Komnenos in 1143. Nothing came of it because John died shortly afterwards.[174] So Roger made the same proposition to his son and successor, Manuel, and the latter reciprocated by sending his own ambassador. Discussions broke down, however, over Roger's claim to kingship of lands that the Byzantine *basileus* still considered as having been usurped from the Eastern Empire, namely the old *thema* of Longobardia (Apulia).[175] Shortly afterwards, Manuel dispatched the Patrikios Nikephoros to resume talks with the German court.[176] The alliance was subsequently brought to fruition by the marriage of Bertha of Sulzbach, Conrad's adopted daughter, to Manuel I

---

[169] Manfroni, *Storia della Marina italiana*, I, pp. 189–90.

[170] John Kinnamos, *Deeds of John and Manuel Comnenus*, trans. C. Brand (New York, 1976), Bk I, ch. 5–8, pp. 20–5.

[171] Otto of Freising, *The Deeds of Frederick Barbarossa*, trans. C. Mierow (New York, 1953), Bk I, ch. 24, p. 54; *Gesta Frederici: Ottonis et Rahewini Gesta Friderici I. Imperatoris*, ed. G. Waitz (MGH, SRG, Hanover–Leipzig, 1912), Bk I, ch. XXIV, p. 37. '... *tam confederationis, vinculum ob Rogerii Siculi insolentiam inter duo imperia, Hesperiae videlicet et Orientis, renovare cupientes* ...'

[172] John Kinnamos, *John and Manuel Comnenus*, Bk II, ch. 4, 12, pp. 37–8, 58; Otto of Freising, *Deeds of Frederick Barbarossa*, Bk I, ch. 25, p. 59; *Gesta Frederici*, Bk I, ch. XXV, pp. 42–3.

[173] Otto of Freising, *Deeds of Frederick Barbarossa*, Bk I, ch. 24–5, pp. 54–7; *Gesta Frederici*, Bk I, ch. XXIV–XXV, pp. 37–40.

[174] John Kinnamos, *John and Manuel Comnenus*, Bk III, ch. 2, p. 75.

[175] John Kinnamos, *John and Manuel Comnenus*, Bk III, ch. 2, pp. 75–6; Romuald of Salerno, *Romualdi Salernitani Chronicon*, p. 227.

[176] Otto of Freising, *Deeds of Frederick Barbarossa*, Bk I, ch. 24, pp. 57–9; *Gesta Frederici*, Bk I, ch. XXIV, pp. 40–3.

Komnenos in January 1146. This must have signaled to Roger that a combined assault on his kingdom by the two empires was imminent.[177]

Ironically, what spared the Sicilian *Regno* on this particular occasion was the Atabeg of Mosul, Imad al-Din Zanki ibn Aqsunqur. He conquered Edessa from the Franks in December 1144, raising grave concerns in the West over the fate of the Latin East.[178] This, in turn, set in motion a set of events that would divert the attention of the German and Byzantine courts. First of all, King Louis VII of France was prompted to announce on Christmas day of 1145 his intention to embark upon a crusade.[179] Pope Eugenius III subsequently tasked Bernard of Clairvaux with preaching the crusade, and the latter,[180] in turn, convinced a reluctant Conrad to join the Church-sanctioned expedition on Christmas of 1146.[181] Hence, an allied imperial invasion of Roger's realm was postponed.

The Sicilian monarch sought first to capitalize on the situation by making an ally of Louis in order to counterbalance the enmity of the Greek and German sovereigns. He sent envoys to the pre-crusade conference at Etampes, who offered, on his behalf, to provide ships and supplies, should the crusaders choose to journey through his kingdom. He even offered his personal participation or that of one of his sons.[182] The use of his fleet in such a manner would have displayed Norman naval power and served to intimidate both the Germans and the Greeks. But Louis declined, electing to take the overland route through Constantinople instead.[183] Thus rebuffed, Roger quickly abandoned any further thought of involvement. Besides, he saw another angle he could exploit. Since he knew the crusade would occupy Conrad, he had only to deal with Manuel. The latter provided just the opportunity Roger wanted. The Byzantine Emperor, rightfully fearing the hordes of crusaders descending upon his capital, sought to protect it as best he could.[184] This effort led him to make a costly miscalculation. 'The *basileus*,' observes Chalandon, 'had not foreseen that the king of Sicily would dare, at the risk of impeding the crusade, open hostilities, and he had committed the mistake of degarrisoning troops from the majority of the cities of the coast.'[185] Roger pounced.

---

[177] John Kinnamos, *John and Manuel Comnenus*, Bk II, ch. 4, pp. 36–7.

[178] Ibn al-Athir, *Chronicle of Ibn al-Athir, Part I*, pp. 372–3.

[179] Odo of Deuil, *De Profectione Ludovici VII in Orientem*, ed. and trans. V. Berry (New York, 1948), Bk I, pp. 6–7.

[180] Otto of Freising, *Deeds of Frederick Barbarossa*, Bk I, ch. 35, pp. 70–1; *Gesta Frederici*, Bk I, ch. XXXV, pp. 54–5.

[181] Otto of Freising, *Deeds of Frederick Barbarossa*, Bk I, ch. 40, pp. 74–5; *Gesta Frederici*, Bk I, ch. XL, p. 59.

[182] Odo of Deuil, *De Profectione*, Bk I, pp. 10–11.

[183] Odo of Deuil, *De Profectione*, Bk I, pp. 12–15.

[184] John Kinnamos, *John and Manuel Comnenus*, Bk II, ch. 12–13, pp. 58–61, Bk III, ch. 2, p. 76; Niketas Choniates, *O City of Byzantium! Annals of Niketas Choniates*, trans. H. Magoulias (Detroit, 1984), p. 36.

[185] Chalandon, *Histoire de la Domination Normande*, II, p. 135.

In April 1147, he launched a sizable armada against the Adriatic coast of main-land Greece.[186] No numbers are given, but Romuald of Salerno says the fleet was composed of 'very many galleys and transport ships'.[187] He also noted that it had been assembled at Otranto under the command of an *'ammiratus'* called Salernus.[188] (Most modern historians, however, believe the fleet commander was actually George of Antioch, though no source mentions him by name.[189]) Alternatively, Niketas Choniates, a twelfth-century Byzantine court official and historian, characterizes the vessels as 'swift-sailing ships' and indicates they were launched from Brindisi,[190] while Otto of Freising identifies the vessels as 'triremes and biremes which are now ordinarily called galleys or *sagitteae* [derived from the Latin word *sagitta*, meaning 'arrow', also implying speed]'.[191] Plainly, the force appears to have been assembled chiefly for raiding and not conquest. It struck strategically vital Corfu first.[192] The island commanded the Strait of Otranto between the heel of Apulia and the Balkan Peninsula, which, in turn, controlled access to the upper Adriatic. Yet its approaches were left totally unguarded.[193] This was not just because the Emperor Manuel had stripped the region of troops, but it was also because his predecessor, the Emperor John II Komnenos, had allowed the Byzantine navy to atrophy so completely that it virtually ceased to exist. Niketas Choniates gives a caustic description of the deleterious results produced by following the advice of John of Poutze, the 'grand commissioner and inspector of accounts':

> Thanks to this man's counsel, a measure for the common welfare and salutary for all the islands perpetuated by the former emperors was abolished by Emperor John with great harm. Whatever contributions were collected by ship-money levies and designated in the past for the fleet, he diverted into the treasury by the use of convincing arguments and very nearly scuttled the manned triremes

[186] *Chronica de Ferraria*, anno 1147, p. 28.

[187] Romuald of Salerno, *Romualdi Salernitani Chronicon*, p. 227. '... *galeas et naves plurimas* ...'

[188] Romuald of Salerno, *Romualdi Salernitani Chronicon*, p. 227. Andrea Dandolo, *Chronica Per Extensum Descripta*, p. 242, also says the fleet was gathered at Otranto.

[189] Caspar, *Roger II*, pp. 376–7; Cohn, *Die Geschichte der normannisch-sicilischen Flotte*, pp. 40–1; Chalandon, *Histoire de la Domination Normande*, II, p. 136, note 2; Manfroni, *Storia della Marina italiana*, I, p. 200.

[190] Niketas Choniates, *O City of Byzantium!*, p. 43.

[191] Otto of Freising, *Deeds of Frederick Barbarossa*, Bk I, ch. 34, p. 69; *Gesta Frederici*, Bk I, ch. XXXIV, p. 53. '... *triremibus et biremibus, quas modo galeas seu sagitteas* ...'

[192] *Annales Cavenses*, anno 1147, p. 192; Niketas Choniates, *O City of Byzantium!*, p. 43; Andrea Dandolo, *Chronica Per Extensum Descripta*, p. 242; *Historia ducum Veneticorum*, ed. H. Simonsfeld (MGH, SS, XIV, Hanover, 1883), p. 75; *Testi Storici Veneziani (XI–XIII secolo)*, ed. and trans. L. Berto (Padua, 1999), pp. 12–15; John Kinnamos, *John and Manuel Comnenus*, Bk III, ch. 2, p. 76; Otto of Freising, *Deeds of Frederick Barbarossa*, Bk I, ch. 34, p. 69; *Gesta Frederici*, Bk I, ch. XXXIV, p. 53; Romuald of Salerno, *Romualdi Salernitani Chronicon*, p. 227.

[193] Andrea Dandolo, *Chronica Per Extensum Descripta*, p. 242.

provided on demand by the islands. Arguing that the state and public did not always have need of the triremes and that the expenditures made on their behalf were a heavy annual burden, and that these funds, therefore, should be deposited in the treasury and that supplies and pay should be provided the navy by the imperial treasury only when needed, he appeared to be the best of men and an expert in the nature of public affairs – he who resorted to the pirate's plot of throwing his captive overboard. By proposing such measures, he diverted the emperor from excessive expenditures and, in turn, the chancellor was pleased by the moderation of expenses. Now, as a result of this ill-advised policy or penny pinching, pirates rule the seas, and the Roman maritime provinces are harassed by pirate ships, and the enemy gloats.[194]

Byzantine provincial misgovernment made the Norman armada's task all the easier. An odious tax collector had so incensed the local populace that the citizens of Kerkyra greeted the Sicilians with open arms, handing over the citadel without a fight.[195]

After leaving a garrison of 1,000 knights, the fleet continued southward on a protracted raid of Greek islands and coastal areas. The exact routing is difficult to follow, because each of the various Greek and Latin sources describes only a portion of it, providing a confused, incomplete picture. That being said, Niketas Choniates furnishes the most detailed account of the expedition by far, and it is possible, using his narrative as a template, to trace the path of the Sicilian fleet.[196] Basically, it circumnavigated the Peloponnesos counterclockwise from Corfu to the Isthmus of Corinth; then returned by the same route to enter the Gulf of Corinth from the west, raiding all the way to Corinth, itself, before proceeding back to Corfu (see Map 6). To recapitulate in greater detail, the fleet first ravaged Cephalonia, according to the *Annales Cavenses*.[197] The Sicilians then moved south to burn Methone on the southwest coast of the Peloponnesos.[198] They probably assaulted Neapolis at the northwestern base of the Malea Peninsula next.[199] At that point, they rounded Cape Malea (the very southern tip of the Peloponnesos) and attempted to take the citadel at Monemvasia on the east side of the peninsula, but failed. They subsequently tried to reverse course and head west again around Cape Malea, but Niketas Choniates testifies that storms, frequent to the area, blew them east and northward toward the eastern side of the Isthmus of Corinth.[200] It was likely at this juncture that they devastated Nauplion in the Gulf of Argolis.[201] Otto of Freising says even Athens was

---

[194] Niketas Choniates, *O City of Byzantium!*, pp. 32–3.

[195] Niketas Choniates, *O City of Byzantium!*, p. 43.

[196] Niketas Choniates, *O City of Byzantium!*, pp. 43–5.

[197] *Annales Cavenses*, anno 1147, p. 192.

[198] Otto of Freising, *Deeds of Frederick Barbarossa*, Bk I, ch. 34, p. 69; *Gesta Frederici*, Bk I, ch. XXXIV, p. 53.

[199] *Annales Cavenses*, anno 1146, p. 192.

[200] Niketas Choniates, *O City of Byzantium!*, p. 43.

[201] Houben, *Roger II*, p. 84.

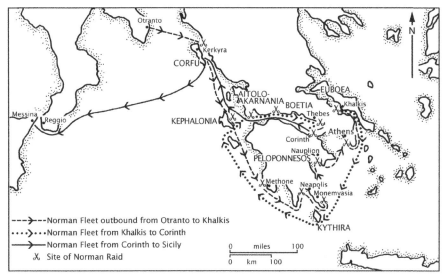

6. Norman raid on the Greek mainland in 1147. (Credit: C. Stanton with P. Judge)

struck, so it logically would have been at this time.[202] Next, the fleet must have sacked Negroponte, modern-day Khalkis, on the west side of the Aegean island of Euboea (Evvoia), if Andrea Dandolo can be believed.[203] From there, the fleet must have turned back and headed toward Cape Malea, where Chalandon says the Sicilians established fortified positions on the island of Kythira, ten miles to the south of the cape, and on the cape itself.[204] After this, they had to have ventured northward again to the western entrance of the Gulf of Corinth, where they would complete the final and most ruinous phase of their raiding expedition.

The Sicilians plundered the region just north of the Gulf of Patra, called Aitolo-Akarnania. They then penetrated into the Gulf of Corinth, anchoring at the port of Krissaios on the north shore at present-day Itea, where they disembarked and pillaged the *thema* of Boeotia. They eventually made their way to the great commercial city of Thebes, which they sacked unmercifully.[205] Choniates excoriates the commander's greed, 'A measure of his cupidity was his order that all or most of his ships should sink to the third stripe [wale –horizontal plank in the hull] from the weight of the monies.'[206] Not content with material wealth, Choniates insists that the captain also carried off those who 'had mastered the

[202] Otto of Freising, *Deeds of Frederick Barbarossa*, Bk I, ch. 34, p. 69; *Gesta Frederici*, Bk I, ch. XXXIV, p. 53.
[203] Andrea Dandolo, *Chronica Per Extensum Descripta*, p. 242.
[204] Chalandon, *Histoire de la Domination Normande*, II, p. 136.
[205] Niketas Choniates, *O City of Byzantium!*, pp. 43–4.
[206] Niketas Choniates, *O City of Byzantium!*, p. 44.

weaver's art'.[207] Romuald of Salerno concurs.[208] As economic historian Wilhelm Heyd points out, Thebes was an important center for the production of silk.[209] Otto of Freising, thus, not only seconds Choniates' assertion that the Sicilians kidnapped the silk weavers, but even goes on to allege that they used these captives to transplant the silk industry to Sicily: 'There they carried off a great amount of booty and, as an insult to the emperor and in compliment to their own prince, they led away captive even the workers who were accustomed to weave silken goods. Establishing them in Palermo, the metropolis of Sicily, Roger bade them teach his craftsmen the art of silk weaving'.[210] In point of fact, the art of silk weaving was already flourishing in Sicily, as is evinced by Roger's magnificent coronation mantle, bordered with Kufic script proudly proclaiming that it was produced for the king in the royal workshop in Palermo in 1133. It is still on display in the Kunsthistorisches Museum of Vienna.[211] Nonetheless, as scholar of the *Regno* Donald Matthew points out, the Normans were not above forcibly augmenting their stable of skilled silk artisans.[212]

The Normans reboarded their vessels and headed off for the richest prize of all: Corinth. Fortuitously situated on the Isthmus, the prosperous city possessed two harbors: one on the east for the Asian trade and one on the west to receive merchant vessels from Italy and beyond. It also had a heavily fortified mountain acropolis called Akrocorinth, but the city fell to the invaders as easily as the others. The reason was not because the inhabitants were taken by surprise, but precisely the opposite. Word of the Norman depredations in Boeotia had apparently preceded the raiders to Corinth. Many of those from the surrounding areas had thus sought refuge in the citadel, straining the limited provisions to the point where withstanding a long siege was impossible. More importantly, news of the marauders' truculence had served to intimidate the garrison's pusillanimous commander, a certain Nikephoros Chalouphes, who offered almost no resistance.[213] As a consequence, the Sicilians were able to loot Akrocorinth so thoroughly that Niketas Choniates offers the following hyperbole: 'One might have said, with good reason, that the Sicilian triremes were not pirate ships but merchantmen of large tonnage, so over-laden were they with fine merchandise

---

[207] Niketas Choniates, *O City of Byzantium!*, p. 44.

[208] Romuald of Salerno, *Romualdi Salernitani Chronicon*, p. 227.

[209] W. Heyd, *Histoire du commerce du Levant au moyan âge* (2 vols, Leipzig, 1885), I, p. 247.

[210] Otto of Freising, *Deeds of Frederick Barbarossa*, Bk I, ch. 34, pp. 69–70; *Gesta Frederici*, Bk I, ch. XXXIV, pp. 53–4. '... maxima ibidem preda direpta opifices etiam qui sericos pannos texere solent ob ignominiam imperatoris illius suique principis gloriam captivos deducunt. Quos Rogerius in Palermo Siciliae metropoli collocans artem illam texendi suos edocere precepit ...'

[211] A. Cilento and A. Vanoli, *Arabs and Normans in Sicily and the South of Italy* (New York, 2007); F. Gabrieli and U. Scerrato, *Gli Arabi in Italia* (Milan, 1979), pp. 138–9; Houben, *Roger II*, p. 125, fig. 7.

[212] D. Matthew, *The Norman Kingdom of Sicily* (Cambridge, 1992), pp. 127–8. See also Houben, *Roger II*, p. 163.

[213] Niketas Choniates, *O City of Byzantium!*, pp. 44–5.

that they were submerged very nearly to the level of the upper rower's bench.'[214] Afterwards, the Sicilians returned to Corfu and then presumably to Sicily.

Once news of the incursions arrived in Constantinople, the Emperor Manuel Komnenos reacted in predictable fashion. Since he had a moribund naval force, he immediately took steps to bolster it. John Kinnamos, the imperial secretary at the time, claims with evident exaggeration, 'He prepared a fleet of upwards of five hundred triremes, as well as an entire thousand horse-transports and supply ships ...'[215] Niketas Choniates is just as extravagant:

> The fleet was put in repair and new triremes were built and made ready to put out to sea. Fire-bearing ships were fitted out with liquid fire which had not hitherto been employed and projected. Fifty-oared ships rallied, and small pirate galleys mobilized. Cavalry transports were caulked, merchantmen were laden with provisions, and light pirate skiffs were outfitted. A fleet of nearly one thousand ships was collected and the infantry forces were mustered in the tens of thousands.[216]

More significantly, he enlisted the considerable naval support of the Venetians by granting them another *chrysobull* (imperial decree) extending generous commercial privileges.[217] The actual document is lost, but Manfroni speculates that it confirmed previous trading rights in the empire and included commercial concessions on the islands of Cyprus and Rhodes, excluded from the preceding treaties.[218] The Venetians probably would not have required much inducement in any case: Norman possession of both Otranto and Corfu could have conceivably confined them to the upper Adriatic. They simply could not have allowed it. The exact size of the Venetian contribution is elusive. Martino da Canale, a thirteenth-century Venetian chronicler thought to be a customs official, notes 29 ships, but this number is widely rejected as too low.[219] Nonetheless, the *Historia ducum Veneticorum* (also thirteenth-century) indicates it must have been substantial, because it included huge siege machines and '*gatti*' war vessels among its '*exercitus copiosus*' [ample force].[220]

The expedition to liberate the fortress of Kerkyra on Corfu from the Normans began in the early spring of 1148, but there were some unavoidable delays. The Venetian Doge Piero Polani passed away just as the fleet got under way and had to be replaced by his brother Giovanni and his son Raniero.[221] On the Greek side, the Emperor Manuel was already on the march with his

---

[214] Niketas Choniates, *O City of Byzantium!*, p. 45.
[215] John Kinnamos, *John and Manuel Comnenus*, Bk III, ch. 2, p. 76.
[216] Niketas Choniates, *O City of Byzantium!*, p. 45.
[217] Andrea Dandolo, *Chronica Per Extensum Descripta*, pp. 242–3; *Historia ducum Veneticorum*, p. 75; *Testi Storici Veneziani*, pp. 12–13.
[218] Manfroni, *Storia della Marina italiana*, I, p. 201.
[219] Martino Da Canale, *Les Estoires de Venise*, ed. A. Limentani (Firenze, 1972), Pt I, ch. XXIV, pp. 36–7.
[220] *Historia ducum Veneticorum*, p. 75; *Testi Storici Veneziani*, pp. 14–15.
[221] Andrea Dandolo, *Chronica Per Extensum Descripta*, p. 243.

army when he received word that the Cumans (Turkic nomads) had crossed the River Istros (the Danube) and were ravaging Byzantine lands. While he dealt with this incursion, he sent most of the ships ahead with his brother-in-law, the grand duke Kontostephanos (nicknamed 'Short Stephen' owing to his short stature, according to John Kinnamos), as commander of the fleet.[222] The *Megas Domestikos* (Grand Domestic), John Axouchos, was given charge of the infantry. Even when most of the allied forces were gathered at Kerkyra, they made little progress. The citadel was situated on a craggy precipice, overhanging the sea. Thus, despite the enormous size of the besieging force, it was impregnable.[223] At one point, Kontostephanos had a huge scaling ladder constructed of various ship components: 'Planks used in shipbuilding were fitted together, and masts from the large ships were joined with those which fell short of the necessary height that were braced by bands.'[224] The base of the ladder was anchored on the decks of a pair of large vessels while the top was propped against the walls of the fortress. Unfortunately, the weight of the ascending assailants who were being pelted by enormous projectiles caused the ladder to collapse. Some of the resulting debris struck 'Short Stephen' and killed him.

John Axouchos took over as overall commander, but further assaults remained fruitless.[225] Worse yet, the more protracted the siege became, the testier the besiegers got. Soon a bitter brawl broke out between the Venetians and Greeks, who had no great love for one another in the first place. Men were killed and wounded despite the initial attempts of the officers to quell the outbreak. The outnumbered Venetians were eventually driven back to their ships, which they sailed to the island of Asteris between Ithaca and Cephalonia. From there, they repeatedly ambushed Greek vessels. In the commission of such piracy, they managed to seize the imperial barge upon which they propped up a dark-skinned Ethiopian slave as a mock emperor in order to lampoon the swarthily complected Manuel. They then paraded the regally decked-out vessel before the Greek army at Kerkyra. The emperor apparently arrived at this juncture and, though deeply insulted, made peace with Venetians in order to resume the siege.[226] As Niketas Choniates points out, 'He should not maintain a thousand pirates on his own land, allowing Kerkyra to become a naval station and shipyard for the Sicilian triremes sailing against the Romans.'[227]

While all this was going on, George of Antioch was advancing King Roger's African aspirations with the conquest of Zirid possessions in Ifriqiyah and the

[222] John Kinnamos, *John and Manuel Comnenus*, Bk III, ch. 3–4, pp. 76–9.
[223] Niketas Choniates, *O City of Byzantium!*, p. 46.
[224] Niketas Choniates, *O City of Byzantium!*, p. 48.
[225] Niketas Choniates, *O City of Byzantium!*, pp. 46–50; John Kinnamos, *John and Manuel Comnenus*, Bk III, ch. 4, p. 79.
[226] Niketas Choniates, *O City of Byzantium!*, pp. 50–1; John Kinnamos, *John and Manuel Comnenus*, Bk III, ch. 5, p. 80.
[227] Niketas Choniates, *O City of Byzantium!*, p. 51.

Maghrib.[228] However, in the spring of 1149, Roger decided to dispatch his great admiral on a diversionary raid of Byzantine territories. Ostensibly the purpose was to draw pressure off his besieged garrison at Corfu,[229] but there may have been a more momentous motivation. John Kinnamos reports that in the winter of 1148–9 the Emperor Manuel, while still dealing with the Cumans, had met in Thessaloniki with King Conrad who was returning from the Second Crusade. There, Kinnamos contends, 'The emperor reminded him [Conrad] of what had been previously agreed; this was, that Italy [i.e., Apulia and Calabria] should be restored to the empress Irene [Bertha] for her marriage gift, as she was his [Conrad's] relative and he had betrothed her to the emperor.'[230] Chalandon surmises that the two sovereigns signed a pact at this meeting to jointly attack Roger the following spring; that they had, in fact, already divided up his kingdom.[231] The northern European sources seemed to confirm this.[232] If the continuator of the chronicle of Sigebert of Gembloux in present-day Belgium knew of this treaty, then Roger almost certainly did. Thus, George's mission of the subsequent spring appears to have been an effort to further distract the Byzantine Emperor so that he would be unable to follow through with the planned joint invasion of the Kingdom of Sicily.

Essentially, the diversion involved penetrating the Dardanelles and the Bosporus all the way to Constantinople with a fleet of 60 warships.[233] In the process three separate engagements with Byzantine naval forces occurred. Unfortunately, the exact sequence of events remains shrouded in confusion, because none of the various Latin and Greek narratives agree. The primary account is that of John Kinnamos, but his rendition defies logic. Kinnamos contends that the emperor, having learned that Roger had sent a fleet, divided his own fleet and dispatched a flotilla under the command of a certain Chouroup to intercept the Sicilian armada. The combined Greco-Venetian fleet did just that at Cape Malea and subjected the Sicilians to a resounding defeat, but Kinnamos says that 40 of their vessels escaped and continued on to Constantinople where they wreaked havoc on the Damalis district (modern Üsküdar). On its way back, according to Kinnamos, the Sicilian fleet encountered another Greek squadron bringing annual tax revenues from Crete. The Sicilians supposedly got the worst of it

---

[228] Abulfeda, *BAS*, II, pp. 101–2; Andrea Dandolo, *Chronica Per Extensum Descripta*, p. 243; At-Tijani, *BAS*, II, pp. 76–8; Ibn abi Dinar, *BAS*, II, pp. 294–6; Ibn al-Athir, *BAS*, I, pp. 469–75; *The Chronicle of Ibn al-Athir for the Crusading Period from al-Kamil fi'l-Ta'rikh. Part 2: The Years 541–589/1146–1193: The Age of Nur al-Din and Saladin*, trans. D. Richards (Aldershot, 2007), pp. 18–20.
[229] John Kinnamos, *John and Manuel Comnenus*, Bk III, ch. 5, p. 80.
[230] John Kinnamos, *John and Manuel Comnenus*, Bk II, ch. 19, p. 72.
[231] Chalandon, *Histoire de la Domination Normande*, II, pp. 141–2.
[232] Otto of Freising, *Deeds of Frederick Barbarossa*, Bk I, ch. 44, p. 103; *Gesta Frederici*, Bk I, ch. XLIV, p. 90; *Sigeberti Gemblacensis Chronica: Continuatio Praemonstratensis*, ed. D. Bethman (MGH, SS, VI, Hanover, 1844), anno 1149, p. 454.
[233] Andrea Dandolo, *Chronica Per Extensum Descripta*, p. 243.

again, the remnants limping back home.[234] All of this he describes in Chapter 5 of Book III, but in Chapter 19 of Book II, he notes in passing that a Sicilian fleet managed to rescue King Louis VII from the clutches of Chouroup, presumably at Cape Malea, by embarking the French sovereign on a Norman ship flying the colors of a Greek ally (probably Venice).[235]

None of this makes any sense. No naval commander in his right mind would continue some 500 miles from Cape Malea with the King of France in tow into hostile seas, through the confined waterways of the Dardanelles, the Sea of Marmara and the Bosporus to attack a heavily fortified imperial capital after losing a third or more of his fleet in a naval battle. In fact, the *Historia ducum Veneticorum* claims that a total of 40 Norman ships were sunk or captured at Cape Malea.[236] Clearly, Kinnamos was confused, yet Chalandon, of all scholars, seems to fundamentally accept this incongruous chronology.[237] Houben not only supports this view, but he even intimates that the battle at Cape Malea and the raid on Constantinople were a year apart.[238] And Cohn so misreads the text that he accuses Kinnamos of not noting the big battle with Chouroup's Greco-Venetian fleet at all,[239] even though the Byzantine historian pointedly describes it as follows: 'When the Sicilian fleet came to grips with Chouroup [commander of the combined Greco-Venetian armada], most of it was overcome, but forty of their ships avoided peril and reached Byzantion.'[240] Caspar's reading of the event is also flawed. His suggestion that the Normans chanced upon Chouroup's fleet and the Greek tax flotilla at the same place and at the same time is highly improbable.[241] Conversely, Manfroni's interpretation, based, in part, on Andrea Dandolo's account, is the most logical and, thus, the preferred version.[242] Andrea Dandolo reports that George's fleet of 60 warships avoided Chourop's flotilla but seized Louis from other Greek ships on the way to Constantinople, where the Normans burned the suburbs and fired flaming arrows at the imperial palace.[243] Interestingly, Dandolo's description of this incident is supported by the great Kurdish historian, Ibn al-Athir, who notes the Normans also 'captured several

---

234 John Kinnamos, *John and Manuel Comnenus*, Bk III, ch. 5, pp. 81–2.
235 John Kinnamos, *John and Manuel Comnenus*, Bk II, ch. 19, p. 72.
236 *Historia ducum Veneticorum*, p. 75; *Testi Storici Veneziani*, pp. 14–15.
237 Chalandon, *Histoire de la Domination Normande*, II, pp. 143–5.
238 Houben, *Roger II*, p. 85.
239 Cohn, *Die Geschichte der normannisch-sicilischen Flotte*, pp. 46–7. '*Dazu kommt aber ein schwerwiegender Grund, um den Bericht des Kinnamos als falsch zu bezeichnen. Er weiss nichts von der bald darauf stattfindenden grossen Seeschlacht zwischen Normannen und Greichen-Vene-tianern.*' ('In addition, there is a more serious reason for considering Kinnamos' report wrong. He knows nothing of the large naval battle between the Normans and the Greco-Venetians which took place soon thereafter.')
240 John Kinnamos, *John and Manuel Comnenus*, Bk III, ch. 5, pp. 81–2.
241 Caspar, *Roger II*, p. 394.
242 Manfroni, *Storia della Marina italiana*, I, pp. 203–5.
243 Andrea Dandolo, *Chronica Per Extensum Descripta*, p. 243.

Byzantine galleys and took a number of prisoners'.[244] Even the twelfth-century continuation of the *Sigeberti Gemblacensis Chronica* of the Abbey of Afflighem in modern-day Belgium confirms the basic outline of the entire Greek enterprise, including the episode at Constantinople.[245] Dandolo goes on to assert that it was on its return that the Sicilian fleet ran into the Greco-Venetian fleet and lost 19 ships in the subsequent battle.[246]

The actual sequence of events will, in all likelihood, never be known, but the most plausible scenario is as follows. George of Antioch's 60 ships probably made it unmolested all the way to the harbor of Constantinople, where they made nuisance attacks on the environs for several days. The Emperor Manuel probably learned of the raid from messengers who could have traveled along the old Roman road, Via Egnatia, to Durazzo, then by ship to Corfu.[247] It would have been at this time that he would have dispatched Chouroup with a portion of the Greco-Venetian fleet. Therefore, Chouroup would have been heading eastward around the Peloponnesos toward Constantinople while George would have been coming westward from the Byzantine capital, resulting in their chance meeting at Cape Malea. As for the encounter with the tax fleet, there would have been no reason for Greek ships en route from Crete to Constantinople to be as far west as Cape Malea. The Sicilian fleet most likely came upon the tax fleet from Crete while transiting along the eastern coast of the Peloponnesos. And contrary to the Kinnamos rendition, the Sicilian fleet would have easily overcome what was probably a smaller squadron of Greek vessels, some of which surely were not warships.

As for the incident involving King Louis VII, the French monarch and his queen (Eleanor of Aquitaine) may have actually been succored from the Greeks by a separate Sicilian squadron. A diploma of Roger II recognizes a certain George of Landolina as 'the commander of two royal triremes of the maritime fleet which, with divine help and the loyal courage and prudence of our knights and their commanders, expelled the ships and triremes of the Greek enemy, and at length released from captivity the most illustrious King Louis VII and his great men and magnates of Gaul'.[248] The document has been labeled an obvious forgery, in part because it is dated 22 January 1146 – three years before the actual event, but, like most forgeries, it is probably based upon a nucleus of truth. After

---

[244] Ibn al-Athir, *BAS*, I, p. 476; *Chronicle of Ibn al-Athir, Part 2*, p. 32.

[245] *Sigeberti Gemblacensis Chronica*, anno 1148–9, pp. 453–4.

[246] Andrea Dandolo, *Chronica Per Extensum Descripta*, p. 243. Romuald of Salerno, *Romualdi Salernitani Chronicon*, p. 227, called the battle a Norman victory, but he is alone in this assertion.

[247] Loud, *Age of Robert Guiscard*, pp. 85, 216.

[248] *Rogerii II. Regis Diplomata Latina*, Appendix I, no. VIII, pp. 253–4. '... *tamquam praefectus de duobus nostris regis triremibus nostris classae maritimae cum divino auxilio cooperante et nostrum militum eorumque praefectorum fortitudine fidelitate et prudentia non procul Graecorum hostium eorumque naves et triremes expulisti, et tandem à captivitate illustrissimum regem Lugdovicum VII. suosque proceres et Galliae magnates manu misisti.*'

all, why would ships bearing the king and queen of France returning from the Holy Land be passing storm-rich Cape Malea? According to John Pryor and *The Atlas of the Crusades* edited by Crusades scholar Jonathan Riley-Smith, the normal east–west trunk route from Palestine ran south of both Cyprus and Crete.[249]

In the end, the Norman castellan of Kerkyra, Theodore, sued for terms and the fortress fell into Byzantine hands.[250] Nonetheless, Roger had essentially accomplished his goal. He had distracted and delayed the Byzantines with the added benefit of seeing the already testy relationship with their maritime allies, the Venetians, poisoned still further. Be that as it may, Manuel would still attempt to mount an invasion of the Norman kingdom in the summer of 1149. He massed his troops and ships at Avlona with the intention of making the crossing to Sicily. Once again, however, fate intervened on behalf of Roger's *Regno*. A freak summer storm shredded the Greek armada.[251] As for the German threat, Chalandon thinks Roger successfully sidetracked Conrad by subsidizing the revolt of Welf VI of Bavaria against the Hohenstaufen crown in early 1150.[252] Conrad later succumbed to an unspecified illness at Bamberg in February 1152. Otto of Freising was inclined to attribute that unfortunate occurrence to Roger's chicanery as well.[253] Though unsubstantiated, the supposition probably would not have displeased the Sicilian sovereign in the least. Whatever the reasons, no joint Byzantine–German assault was ever carried out against the Kingdom of Sicily during Roger's reign.

The use of sea power in the subjugation of North Africa

At last secure in his own domain by the 1140s, Roger was able to direct his attention southward again and resume what he had postponed for so long. He was finally ready to wrest Ifriqiyah and the Maghrib coast from the Zirids. Ironically, the seeds for the conquest of the Muslims of North Africa had been sowed long ago by the Muslims themselves. About the middle of the eleventh century, al-Mu'izz ibn Badis, the Zirid emir of Qayrawan, shook off the yoke of his overlords, the Fatimid caliphs of Cairo, over differences in religious dogma. (The Fatimids were Shiite while the Zirids had become Sunni.) The Caliph al-Mustansir bi-Allah retaliated by 'granting' the Maghrib to the Banu Hilal and the Banu Sulaym, two warlike nomadic tribes from Upper Egypt. In 1051–2,

---

[249] Pryor, *Geography, Technology, and War*, p. 7; J. Riley-Smith, *The Atlas of the Crusades* (New York, 1991), pp. 50–1.
[250] Niketas Choniates, *O City of Byzantium!*, pp. 51–2.
[251] Niketas Choniates, *O City of Byzantium!*, p. 52; John Kinnamos, *John and Manuel Comnenus*, Bk III, ch. 6, pp. 82–3.
[252] Chalandon, *Histoire de la Domination Normande*, II, pp. 145–7.
[253] Otto of Freising, *Deeds of Frederick Barbarossa*, Bk I, ch. 70, pp. 110–11; *Gesta Frederici*, Bk I, ch. LXX, p. 98.

50,000 Bedouin warriors swept into the region, bringing utter devastation. They drove the Zirids out of Qayrawan and penned them up in Mahdiyah.[254] With Zirid power broken, dozens of petty emirs emerged, resulting in disunity and fragmentation. Amid the disorder, irrigation systems were left unattended and agricultural production collapsed. Thereafter, only famine ruled the region.[255] Writing in the mid-twelfth century, the Sicilian court geographer al-Idrisi describes Tripoli after the invasion:

> Before the current epoch, it [Tripoli] sheltered beautiful buildings on all sides and its environs were covered with olive trees, fig trees, date trees and all kinds of fruit trees. But various tribes attacked it, as well as its surrounding areas; in this way they made the population flee and emptied the countryside. They changed the general condition, destroyed the plantations and dried up the springs.[256]

As a consequence, the Muslims of North Africa became dependent on Sicilian grain. Roger used wheat like a weapon. He cultivated food dependency into political dependency until it reached the point that the Zirid emir of Mahdiyah, al-Hasan, was a virtual vassal in his own state.[257] By 1135, Roger was ready to exploit that unequal relationship.

Al-Hasan himself provided the invitation. In the summer of 1135, the emir of Bejaïa, Yahya ibn al-Aziz ibn Hammad, had sent a huge force under the command of Muttarif ibn Hamdun to besiege Mahdiyah, by land and sea. Ibn al-Athir contends that it arose from the favoritism al-Hasan had displayed toward a particular Arab tribal leader,[258] but Ibn abi Dinar, a seventeenth-century compiler of chronicles who wrote a history of Tunis, insists that it was because of his treaty with the Christian king of Sicily. Short on friends, al-Hasan had little recourse but to beseech the Sicilian monarch for help. Roger responded by directing George of Antioch to the rescue. Arriving swiftly with 20 warships, George not only broke the blockade, but threatened to destroy Muttarif's fleet.[259] The grateful al-Hasan, however, stopped him in order to spare Muslim lives and, according to Ibn abi Dinar, 'wrote to King Roger a letter, thanking him for the favor and saying to him that he would now obey his every command and prohibition.'[260] From that moment on, al-Hasan's tributary relationship to the Sicilian sovereign was explicit. Roger knew that his subsequent attack on Jerba in the Gulf of Gabes that same year would elicit no objection. Ostensibly, the reason was to clear the island of pirates that plagued the Sicilian Channel,

254 Abun-Nasr, *History of the Maghrib*, pp. 68–71.
255 Abulafia, 'Norman Kingdom of Africa', pp. 27–8.
256 Al-Idrisi, *La première géographie de l'Occident*, III, 2, p. 199.
257 Abulafia, 'Norman Kingdom of Africa', p. 33.
258 Ibn al-Athir, *BAS*, I, p. 459; *Chronicle of Ibn al-Athir, Part 1*, pp. 320–1.
259 Ibn abi Dinar, *BAS*, II, pp. 290–1; Ibn al-Athir, *BAS*, I, pp. 459–60; *Chronicle of Ibn al-Athir, Part I*, pp. 320–1; Ibn Khaldun, *BAS*, II, pp. 206–7; At-Tijani, *BAS*, II, p. 75.
260 Ibn abi Dinar, *BAS*, II, p. 291.

but in actuality it was a prelude to invasion.[261] After Jerba's subjugation, pirate activity continued under the auspices of the Norman king and may have actually increased. Not even al-Hasan was spared.[262]

In 1142, George of Antioch himself led 25 ships into the port of Mahdiyah where he seized several merchantmen, including a vessel loaded with gifts for al-Hafiz li-din Allah, the Caliph of Egypt.[263] According to Ibn abi Dinar, the raid was in punishment for al-Hasan's failure to pay for 'certain goods' (probably wheat), but any arrears in his grain payments to Roger were, in all likelihood, simply a pretext for intimidation.[264] It worked. Al-Hasan assumed a submissive posture. Instead of protesting the raid, Ibn al-Athir testifies that he 'renewed the truce for the sake of transporting grain from Sicily to Ifriqiyah because there was a serious famine there and high mortality.'[265] Ibn abi Dinar's language is blunter: 'He [al-Hasan] offered him obedience, so that he became as an ordinary *amil* [vassal] of Roger.'[266] It was only a matter of time before Roger removed him altogether.

In the meanwhile, the insatiable Sicilian sovereign used his position as protector of the Zirid emirate to make further inroads into North Africa. Tripoli traditionally fell within the al-Hasan's sphere of authority as ruler of Ifriqiyah, yet the inhabitants refused to submit to him. This conveniently provided Roger with the rationale to direct a fleet against the Barbary city in June 1143.[267] The exact size of the fleet is not specified, but it was apparently modest since it disembarked only 300 knights.[268] Moreover, George of Antioch is not mentioned as the fleet commander. As soon as the Sicilian-Normans had established a siege of the city, the surrounding Bedouin tribes attacked and the city's citizens sallied forth. The result was a Norman rout. The Sicilians fled to their ships, abandoning their weapons and animals. After returning to Sicily to re-equip, the fleet took out its frustrations on hapless little Djidjelli (Jijel), between Bejaïa and Bona (Annaba), that same year.[269] The following year (1144) the Sicilians conquered Bresk or Brashk, today the small port of Sidi Brahim on the western Maghrib

[261] Al-Nuwayri, *BAS*, II, pp. 156–7; At-Tijani, *BAS*, II, p. 55; Ibn abi Dinar, *BAS*, II, pp. 291–2; Ibn al-Athir, *BAS*, I, p. 461; *Chronicle of Ibn al-Athir, Part I*, pp. 321–2; Ibn Idari, *BAS*, II, p. 37; Ibn Khaldun, *BAS*, II, pp. 220–2.

[262] Chalandon, *Histoire de la Domination Normande*, II, p. 159.

[263] Ibn Idari, *BAS*, II, p. 37; At-Tijani, *BAS*, II, pp. 75–6; Ibn abi Dinar, *BAS*, II, pp. 292–3; Ibn al-Athir, *BAS*, I, pp. 461–2; *Chronicle of Ibn al-Athir, Part I*, p. 365.

[264] Ibn abi Dinar, *BAS*, II, p. 292.

[265] Ibn al-Athir, *BAS*, I, pp. 461–2; *Chronicle of Ibn al-Athir, Part I*, p. 365.

[266] Ibn abi Dinar, *BAS*, II, pp. 292–3.

[267] Ibn al-Athir, *BAS*, I, p. 463; *Chronicle of Ibn al-Athir, Part I*, p. 366.

[268] *Chronica de Ferraria*, anno 1143, p. 27.

[269] *Chronica de Ferraria*, anno 1143, p. 27; Al-Idrisi, *BAS*, I, p. 131; *La première géographie de l'Occident*, III, 1, p. 173; Ibn abi Dinar, *BAS*, II, p. 293; Ibn al-Athir, *BAS*, I, pp. 462–3; *Chronicle of Ibn al-Athir, Part I*, pp. 366–7; Ibn Khaldun, *BAS*, II, pp. 222–3.

coast.[270] In 1145 they pillaged and occupied the island of Kerkenna, just opposite Sfax on the Tunisian coast.[271] By this time, al-Hasan must have known what was coming. Kerkenna fell within Mahdiyah's purview. He weakly raised an objection on the grounds that Roger was violating the treaties between them, but the Norman king brushed it aside, saying the island's inhabitants were not al-Hasan's subjects.[272] Maritime supremacy in the Sicilian Channel now belonged to the Normans. The end of Zirid rule in Ifriqiyah was both inevitable and imminent, but first there was the unfinished business in the Tripolitania.

Roger was so determined to conquer Tripoli that he signed a seven-year truce in late 1144 with Pope Lucius II, suspending a contentious struggle over Capua, Benevento and the papal lands bordering the kingdom.[273] His priorities were plainly on the central Mediterranean. On 15 June 1146, the Sicilians once again appeared before the walls of Tripoli – this time with a resolve not to be deterred. Ibn abi Dinar specifies that there were 200 ships in the armada,[274] while at-Tijani identifies George of Antioch as its admiral.[275] The *Chronica de Ferraria* mentions 20,000 fighters on 100 ships as being involved in the expedition.[276] Regardless of exact numbers, it was a substantial, well-led force. Furthermore, the timing turned out to be fortuitous. Factional strife had broken out in the city only a few days previously. One group of the inhabitants had driven out the Banu Matruh (Arab) leadership and installed one of the 'Veiled Ones' (Almoravids – Berbers) as sheik. On the third day after George had established the land–sea siege of the city, fighting broke out within the walls. The Arab party had attempted to restore the Banu Matruh by force and the Berber faction resisted. George seized the opportunity. He had his men swiftly scale the walls using ladders. The Sicilians then subjected both sides to the sword and quickly quelled all opposition. George soon announced an *aman* (amnesty), inviting all those who had fled to return to the city. Judging from the near unanimous assessment of the Muslim chroniclers, the Norman admiral showed admirable restraint by medieval standards. Clearly his intention was to establish normalcy as rapidly as possible. He stayed for six months, repairing the city's fortifications and installing loyal leadership. After careful consideration of both factions, probably to determine which would be the more acceptable to the citizenry and faithful to the crown, he left one of

---

[270] Al-Idrisi, *BAS*, I, p. 130–1; *La première géographie de l'Occident*, III, 1, p. 163; Ibn al-Athir, *BAS*, I, p. 463; *Chronicle of Ibn al-Athir, Part I*, p. 375.

[271] Ibn abi Dinar, *BAS*, II, p. 293; Ibn al-Athir, *BAS*, I, pp. 464–5; *Chronicle of Ibn al-Athir, Part I*, p. 378.

[272] Ibn al-Athir, *BAS*, I, p. 465; *Chronicle of Ibn al-Athir, Part I*, p. 378.

[273] *Chronica de Ferraria*, anno 1145, p. 28. 'Volens interim rex acquirere africanum regnum et Tripolim de Barbaria treuguam, quam contradixerat fieri filiis suis adhuc viventibus inter ipsos et eundem papam Lucium, quatenus per septennium quiescerent infestare Beneventanos et Romanorum fines, ipsam treguam concessit et confirmavit.'

[274] Ibn abi Dinar, *BAS*, II, p. 293.

[275] At-Tijani, *BAS*, II, p. 60.

[276] *Chronica de Ferraria*, anno 1146, p. 28.

the Banu Matruh in charge, taking with him several hostages.[277] Subsequently, Roger issued a proclamation by which Ibn al-Athir claims, 'The people of Sicily and the Byzantines were obliged to travel there and it quickly flourished and its affairs prospered.'[278] Thus, Roger turned Tripoli into a trading entrepôt for the benefit of his realm.[279] In so doing, the Norman king signaled his intentions for the entirety of Ifriqiyah and the Maghrib. He was not merely bent on conquest for conquest's sake, but wanted to harness the commercial capability of the coast.

There are indications that the Norman triumph at Tripoli may have triggered a domino effect, which very rapidly gave Roger the rest of the Maghrib coast between Tripoli and Cape Bon. The next link in the chain reaction was Gabes. Ibn abi Dinar explains: 'At the news of Tripoli, the terror grew so much more throughout Ifriqiyah that the prince of Gabes wrote to Roger most humbly and servilely, delivering to him the country which he held and being satisfied to become an *amil* [vassal-governor] of the king.'[280] Ibn al-Athir and Ibn Khaldun paint Yusuf, the lord of Gabes, as a scurrilous freedman who had usurped power upon the death of his master, the Emir Rushayd ibn Kamil ibn Jamil; then abused his position by molesting his former master's women. When complaints reached al-Hasan, nominally still lord of Ifriqiyah, the emir of Mahdiyah demanded that the former desist. Yusuf refused. Al-Hasan mobilized his military. This, in turn, prompted Yusuf to go to Roger. Even so, both Arab historians connect Yusuf's defection to the fall of Tripoli.[281] Ibn al-Athir quotes Yusuf as saying to Roger, 'I want you to give me a robe of honor and appoint me governor of Gabes to be your deputy, just as you did with the Banu Matruh in Tripoli.'[282] Subsequently in early 1148, al-Hasan had Gabes besieged, prompting the citizenry to revolt. Yusuf was seized and tortured to death in a horrendously humiliating fashion, involving the rearrangement of his genitals.[283] Roger must have been secretly overjoyed, because the murder of his *amil* gave him the pretext he wanted to crown his African strategy.

The opportunity had such urgency for Roger that he elected to proceed even though his garrison at Corfu was under siege by the Byzantines and Venetians at the time. There could hardly have been a more propitious moment to do so. Ibn al-Athir speaks of the privation that then plagued North Africa:

---

[277] Abulfeda, *BAS*, II, p. 100; Al-Nuwayri, *BAS*, II, pp. 157–8; At-Tijani, *BAS*, II, p. 60; *Chronica de Ferraria*, anno 1147, p. 28; Ibn abi Dinar, *BAS*, II, p. 293; Ibn al-Athir, *BAS*, I, pp. 465–6; *Chronicle of Ibn al-Athir, Part I*, p. 380.

[278] Ibn al-Athir, *BAS*, I, p. 466; *Chronicle of Ibn al-Athir, Part I*, p. 380.

[279] D. Abulafia, 'L'Attività commerciale genovese nell'Africa normanna: la città di Tripoli', in *Atti del Congresso Internazionale di Studi sulla Sicilia Normanna (395–402)* (1973), pp. 1–8, especially 3.

[280] Ibn abi Dinar, *BAS*, II, p. 293.

[281] Ibn al-Athir, *BAS*, I, pp. 466–8; *Chronicle of Ibn al-Athir, Part 2*, pp. 13–14; Ibn Khaldun, *BAS*, II, pp. 226–8.

[282] Ibn al-Athir, *BAS*, I, p. 467; *Chronicle of Ibn al-Athir, Part 2*, p. 14.

[283] Ibn al-Athir, *BAS*, I, pp. 467–8; *Chronicle of Ibn al-Athir, Part 2*, p. 14.

This year [1147–8] there was a famine in Ifriqiyah, which lasted a long time. It had begun in the year 537 [1142–3]. It had a terrible effect on the population, who even resorted to cannibalism. Because of starvation the nomads sought out the towns and the townspeople closed the gates against them. Plague and great mortality followed. The country was emptied and from whole families not a single person survived. Many people traveled to Sicily in search of food and met with great hardship.[284]

He goes on to unequivocally state that Roger took advantage of this situation by amassing an immense fleet of war. He and several other Muslim scholars put the number of ships at 250 while at-Tijani asserts there were 300.[285] Al-Maqrizi, writing in the fifteenth century, says there were even more and denotes some of the ship types: '... the *shawani-hi* [warships] amounted to two hundred *shini* [galleys] and one hundred *taride* [oared horse carriers], not counting the *al-hammala* [transports]'.[286] In June 1148, this great armada sailed from Sicily under the command of none other than George of Antioch. The objective was Mahdiyah itself.[287]

The fleet put into Pantelleria first, doubtless to replenish food and water supplies. There they encountered a merchantman from Mahdiyah. Fearing it would alert the Zirid capital of the impending assault, George had the ship seized. He then took the precaution of having one of the vessel's crew send a message back to Mahdiyah by carrier pigeon, saying the Norman fleet was bound for Constantinople, a credible ruse considering Roger was engaged in an ongoing conflict with the Byzantine emperor at the time. It might have actually worked had not nature interceded on behalf of al-Hasan. George's intention was to surprise the city at dawn, but just as the armada came within sight, a fierce offshore wind held it out to sea. It could barely make way, even under oars. George attempted to dissemble with a message saying their real goal was Gabes, but al-Hasan knew his nominal rule of Mahdiyah was at an end.[288] 'I fear that he will disembark and beleaguer us by land and by sea and cut us off from our supplies,' he reportedly told his advisors. 'We do not have enough to feed us for a month.'[289] So he gathered his family and followers along with what valuables they could carry and vacated the city. Many of the inhabitants followed suit before the wind finally abated, allowing the Sicilian fleet to enter the port late in the afternoon. The Normans seized the city unopposed.[290]

Once again, George demonstrated remarkable restraint in victory. He permitted the city to be plundered for only two hours (probably just enough to

[284] Ibn al-Athir, *BAS*, I, p. 469; *Chronicle of Ibn al-Athir, Part 2*, pp. 16–17.

[285] Abulfeda, *BAS*, II, p. 101; Ibn al-Athir, *BAS*, I, p. 470; *Chronicle of Ibn al-Athir, Part 2*, p. 18; Ibn Khaldun, *BAS*, II, p. 226; At-Tijani, *BAS*, II, p. 76.

[286] Al-Maqrizi, translated by Johns in *Arabic Administration in Norman Sicily*, p. 82.

[287] Ibn al-Athir, *BAS*, I, p. 470; *Chronicle of Ibn al-Athir, Part 2*, p. 18.

[288] Ibn al-Athir, *BAS*, I, pp. 470–2; *Chronicle of Ibn al-Athir, Part 2*, pp. 18–19.

[289] Ibn al-Athir, *BAS*, I, p. 471; *Chronicle of Ibn al-Athir, Part 2*, p. 19.

[290] Ibn al-Athir, *BAS*, I, p. 472; *Chronicle of Ibn al-Athir, Part 2*, p. 19.

compensate his combatants) before declaring a general amnesty. He even sent out messengers to inform those who had fled that it would be safe to return. Within a week most had accepted the offer of safe-conduct and were rewarded with provisions and even monetary loans.[291] George's generosity was probably without precedent in the region. Clearly, his intention was to win hearts and minds, not just masonry. This was no mere raid. As was the case with Tripoli, the Normans had come to stay. They quickly strove to capitalize on their conquest by moving up the remainder of the coast of Ifriqiyah. George dispatched squadrons to nearby Susa and Sfax. Susa gave in without a fight. The governor was al-Hasan's son, Ali, and he joined his father on the run. Sfax attempted to put up some resistance, but the Sicilian attackers, using a feigned flight maneuver, inveigled the defenders into making an ill-advised sally. The Normans quickly surrounded and slaughtered them.[292] After the fall of Sfax, Ibn abi Dinar says even the caravan leaders came to offer their allegiance.[293] George's forces attempted to take the fortress of Kelibia (modern Iqlibiya) on the eastern side of Cape Bon Peninsula, but the Muslim sources insist the castle proved too obdurate.[294] Both Andrea Dandolo and the continuator of Sigebert of Gembloux indicate that the fortress fell to the Sicilians, but their contention is suspect since neither source provides any details.[295] It is more likely that George decided that the citadel was not worth more Sicilian blood. After all, it had no port and no commercial value. Nor did it threaten their previous gains.

At-Tijani provides an indication of how completely the Normans now controlled the Sicilian Channel. Al-Hasan had fled to his ally Muhriz ibn Ziyad at Mu'allaqa, the site of ancient Carthage not far from Tunis. After a few months, he purchased a ship for a planned journey to the court of the Caliph al-Hafiz in Egypt, but George of Antioch, who apparently had already established a network of spies, learned of his intentions and sent 20 warships to intercept him. Al-Hasan then judged that the likelihood of capture was such that he was better advised seeking refuge instead with the emir of the Almohads, Abd al-Mu'min, in Marrakech.[296] Ibn al-Athir confirms the basic facts of the episode.[297] Such command of the sea passage between the eastern and western Mediterranean had a profound and immediate impact on commerce. Already the Sicilian fisc

---

[291] Ibn abi Dinar, *BAS*, II, p. 295; Ibn Khaldun, *BAS*, II, p. 226; Ibn al-Athir, *BAS*, I, p. 473; *Chronicle of Ibn al-Athir, Part 2*, p. 19; At-Tijani, *BAS*, II, p. 78.

[292] Ibn abi Dinar, *BAS*, II, p. 295; Ibn al-Athir, *BAS*, I, p. 475; *Chronicle of Ibn al-Athir, Part 2*, p. 20; Ibn Khaldun, *BAS*, II, pp. 227–8.

[293] Ibn abi Dinar, *BAS*, II, pp. 295–6.

[294] Ibn abi Dinar, *BAS*, II, p. 296; Ibn al-Athir, *BAS*, I, p. 475; *Chronicle of Ibn al-Athir, Part 2*, p. 20; Ibn Khaldun, *BAS*, II, p. 228.

[295] Andrea Dandolo, *Chronica Per Extensum Descripta*, p. 243; *Sigeberti Gemblacensis Chronica*, anno 1148, p. 454.

[296] At-Tijani, *BAS*, II, p. 78.

[297] Ibn al-Athir, *BAS*, I, p. 475; *Chronicle of Ibn al-Athir, Part 2*, p. 20; At-Tijani, *BAS*, II, p. 78.

was benefiting substantially from regular visits by Christian and Muslim shipping bound through Palermo and Messina for Syria, Egypt, Spain, northern Italy and most other corners of the Mediterranean,' observes David Abulafia. 'Roger's conquests in north Africa effectively cut off the alternative, non-Sicilian route for traffic from east to west – Tunis being the only stopping-point not under direct Norman dominion.'[298] In fact, if Andrea Dandolo is to be believed, even Tunis became a tributary of the Norman court of Palermo.[299]

It should be noted at this juncture that Roger coveted only those coastal areas just south of the Sicilian Channel. His African ambitions extended no further eastward than Tripoli. In point of fact, Romuald of Salerno records that Roger made peace with the 'rege Babylonie' ('the king of Babylon', i.e., the caliph of Cairo) at about the same time Tripoli was taken.[300] This was, in all probability, a renewal of an existing treaty with the Fatimid Caliph al-Hafiz. A royal diploma of 1137 to the city of Salerno, which included trading privileges in Alexandria, indicates that some sort of pact with the caliphate was already in place.[301] This may have, in actuality, been the accord which George of Antioch himself originally negotiated with the court of Cairo when he first entered Roger's service more than a quarter of a century before.[302] Perhaps the most compelling evidence of ongoing amicable relations between the two rulers is a remarkable letter from al-Hafiz to Roger dated to the same timeframe as the Salerno privilege mentioned above. Preserved by Ahmad Abd Allah al-Qalqashandi, a fourteenth-century Mameluk compiler of chancery manuals, the letter has been partially translated by Marius Canard, a French Orientalist, and paraphrased in some detail by Jeremy Johns.[303] In it, al-Hafiz seems not only to condone Roger's recent (1135) conquest of Jerba, an infamous pirates' nest, but he also expresses gratitude for the protection provided one of the caliph's merchantmen called 'the Bride' and, in return, 'ordered his admiral to afford the same protection to Roger's ships.'[304] Moreover, the body of the letter reveals that it was but one in a continuing exchange of cordial correspondence.[305]

The king of Sicily would consolidate his African gains over the next few years by continuing the compassionate policies initially implemented by his brilliant first minister. Ibn abi Dinar says of him, 'Roger strengthened his dominion in

---

[298] Abulafia, 'Norman Kingdom of Africa', pp. 35–6.

[299] Andrea Dandolo, *Chronica Per Extensum Descripta*, p. 243.

[300] Romuald of Salerno, *Romualdi Salernitani Chronicon*, p. 227.

[301] *Rogerii II. Regis Diplomata Latina*, no. 46, pp. 129–31.

[302] At-Tijani, *BAS*, II, p. 66.

[303] M. Canard, 'Une lettre du calife Fātimite al-Hafiz (524–544/1130–1149) à Roger II', in *Studi Ruggeriani, VIII Centenario della morte di Ruggero II, Atti del Convegno internazionale di studi ruggeriani (Palermo, 21–25 aprile 1954)* (2 vols, Palermo, 1955), I, pp. 125–46 (reprinted in Canard, *Miscellanea Orientalia*, London, 1973); Johns, *Arabic Administration in Norman Sicily*, pp. 259–65.

[304] Johns, *Arabic Administration in Norman Sicily*, p. 260.

[305] Johns, *Arabic Administration in Norman Sicily*, p. 264.

most of that region; he collected the *kharaj* [harvest tax] from his subjects with kindness and temperance; he became reconciled with the disposition of the people and governed with humanity and justice.'[306] While garrisons were left in the major cities, a high level of autonomy was permitted. Interference in local religious and civil affairs was assiduously avoided. Accordingly, most Muslim scholars concede that life on the coast of Ifriqiyah under the Normans was more prosperous than it had been under the Zirid princes. Grain imports from Sicily came in an uninterrupted flow while gold caravans streamed in from across the Sahara. Traders from all Christendom began to frequent the region's ports.[307]

While the Muslim chroniclers provide most of the details of the Norman conquest of North Africa, the event was not unknown in the Latin West. The *Chronica de Ferraria*, which offers more specifics than many of the others, declares that 'the kingdom [of Sicily] held Africa, Tripoli and Apulia.'[308] Romuald of Salerno echoes the sentiment: 'He [Roger] conquered Susa, Bona, Gabes, Sfax and Tripoli and rendered them tributaries to himself.'[309] The so-called 'Hugo Falcandus', a Sicilian court observer who mostly covered the reign of Roger's son William, is more effusive still: 'For he [Roger] subjugated Tripoli in Barbary, Africa, Sfax, Gabes and numerous other barbarian cities through many personal efforts and dangers.'[310] The *Annales Casinenses* starkly states, 'King Roger seized Africa.'[311] The conquest was even known in northern Europe. The continuator of the chronicler Sigebert of Gembloux goes so far as to record that Roger seated an 'archbishop of Africa' ('*archiepiscopum Affricae*').[312] The conquest is also noted by several English authors, the most prominent of whom was Gervase of Tilbury who proclaims in the twelfth-century *Otia Imperialia* that Roger had a sword engraved with the inscription: 'Apulian and Calabrian, Sicilian and African alike serve me.'[313] Andrea Dandolo of Venice repeated the story in the fourteenth century almost verbatim.[314] Clearly, the Norman kingdom of Sicily under Roger II and his gifted admiral, George of Antioch, had achieved its apogee.

[306] Ibn abi Dinar, *BAS*, II, p. 296.

[307] Abulafia, 'Norman Kingdom of Africa', p. 36.

[308] *Chronica de Ferraria*, anno 1154, p. 29. '… *haberet regnum Africe, Tripolis et Apulie.*'

[309] Romuald of Salerno, *Romualdi Salernitani Chronicon*, p. 227. '*Susas Bonam Capsim Sfaxim et Tripolim expugnavit et sibi tributarias reddidit.*'

[310] 'Hugo Falcandus', *The History of the Tyrants of Sicily, 1154–1169*, ed. and trans. G. A. Loud and T. Wiedemann (Manchester, 1998), p. 57; 'Ugo Falcando', *La historia o liber de regno Sicilie e la epistola ad Petrum Panormitane urbis thesaurarium di Ugo Falcando*, ed. G. Siragusa (FSI, XXII, Rome, 1904), pp. 5–6. '*Tripolim namque Barbarie, Affricam, Faxum, Capsiam aliasque plurimas barbarorum civitates multis sibi laboribus ac periculis subiugavit.*'

[311] *Annales Casinenses*, anno 1147, p. 310. '*Rex Roggerius cepit Africam.*'

[312] *Sigeberti Gemblacensis Chronica*, anno 1148, p. 454.

[313] Gervase of Tilbury, *Otia Imperialia* (*Recreation for an Emperor*), ed. and trans. S. Banks and J. Binns (OMT, Oxford, 2002), pp. 464–5. '*Appulus et Calaber, Siculus mihi seruit et Afer.*' (Ralph de Diceto and Ralph Niger also note the epigram.)

[314] Andrea Dandolo, *Chronica Per Extensum Descripta*, p. 243.

Fig. 4. George of Antioch. A Byzantine-style mosaic in the Santa Maria dell'Ammiraglio of Palermo (La Martorana) portrays the church's benefactor, George of Antioch, bearing the white mane of old age.
(Credit: The Art Archive/Church of Martorana Palermo/Alfredo Dagli Orti)

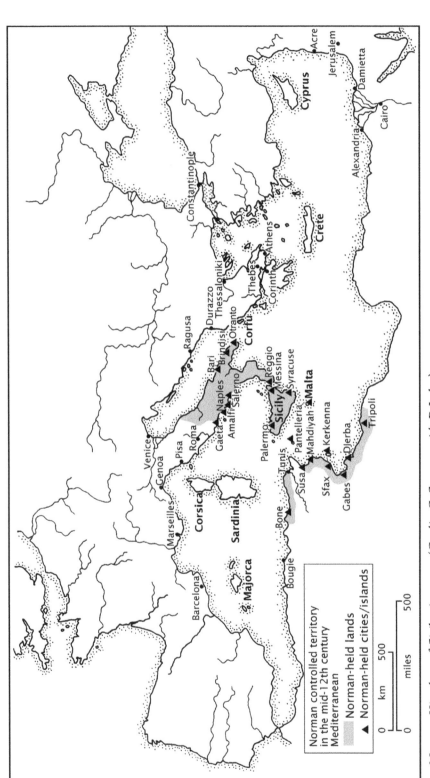

7. Norman Kingdom of Sicily circa 1154. (Credit: C. Stanton with P. Judge)

Meanwhile the encroaching power of the Almohads under Abd al-Mu'min became a growing concern. Their conquest of the Hammadids of Bejaïa in 1152–3 made it clear that they were a problem Roger could not ignore.[315] He even went so far as to offer the emirs of the other Arab tribes of the Maghrib the aid of 5,000 Norman knights to stave off the relentless Almohad advance. They politely declined, saying (according to Ibn al-Athir), 'We do not need your help.'[316] They were demonstrably wrong. Abd al-Mu'min subsequently ambushed them in the mountains near Setif, Algeria, handing them a crushing defeat.[317] There was little to stop him at that point. Unfortunately, Roger had to deal with this challenge deprived of the sagacious counsel and acknowledged competence of his 'Maximus Ammiratus'. According to Ibn al-Athir, George of Antioch, Roger's 'emir of emirs' for most of his reign, succumbed to hemorrhoids and gallstones in the year 546 (1151–2) of the Hegira (see Figure 4).[318]

Roger apparently attempted to replace the irreplaceable with a Muslim eunuch converted to Christianity by the name of Philip of Mahdiyah. 'Having found him [Philip] faithful in deed and reliable in carrying out his business,' reports the interpolator of Romuald of Salerno, 'he [Roger] gave him precedence over everybody in his palace and appointed him as master of his household.'[319] In late 1153, he sent Philip at the head of a fleet to capture Bona or Bône (ancient Hippo and now modern Annaba) on the Maghrib coast, possibly hoping to establish it as a western bulwark against Almohad incursions.[320] The new admiral of the fleet not only succeeded, but also reasserted Norman authority over the rebellious islands of Jerba and Kerkenna at the same time.[321] Nonetheless, Philip apparently did not enjoy the same bond of trust his predecessor had shared with the Sicilian sovereign. He was accused of being a Christian in name only because he allegedly showed excessive leniency toward his former coreligionists at Bona. He had allowed most of the wealthier Muslims to escape with their belongings and was relatively mild toward the remaining inhabitants of the city where he lingered for only ten days.[322] According to the interpolator of Romuald of Salerno, Roger found the charges credible, despite the fact that Philip seemed to be simply following in the forbearing footsteps of his predecessor. The king allowed his *amiratus* to be judged, found guilty and burned at

---

[315] Ibn al-Athir, BAS, I, pp. 477–8; Chronicle of Ibn al-Athir, Part 2, pp. 42–3.

[316] Ibn al-Athir, BAS, I, pp. 478–9; Chronicle of Ibn al-Athir, Part 2, pp. 62–3.

[317] Ibn al-Athir, BAS, I, p. 479; Chronicle of Ibn al-Athir, Part 2, p. 63.

[318] Ibn al-Athir, BAS, I, p. 476; Chronicle of Ibn al-Athir, Part 2, p. 32.

[319] Romuald of Salerno, Romualdi Salernitani Chronicon, p. 234. 'Et quia ipsum in agendis suis fidelem et negotiorum suorum idoneum exsecutorum inuenerat, uniuerso hunc prefecit palatio, et totius domus sue statuit esse magistrum.' (English translation provided by G. A. Loud in Houben, Roger II, p. 110.)

[320] Ibn al-Athir, BAS, I, p. 479; Chronicle of Ibn al-Athir, Part 2, p. 63; Ibn Khaldun, BAS, II, p. 229.

[321] Al-Idrisi, BAS, I, pp. 132–3; La première géographie de l'Occident, III, 2, pp. 204–6.

[322] Ibn al-Athir, BAS, I, p. 479; Chronicle of Ibn al-Athir, Part 2, pp. 63–4.

the stake as an apostate.[323] The testimony of Ibn al-Athir supports this.[324] It was a tragic ending to an enlightened reign, marked by pragmatism and tolerance. Old and tired, bereft of the sagacious counsel of his great admiral, King Roger himself expired the next year.[325] He had, however, bequeathed to his son William a virtual maritime empire with a stranglehold on the central Mediterranean (see Map 7). The great Muslim historian Ibn al-Athir would later admiringly write: 'Having organized a large fleet, he made himself lord of the islands which lie between Mahdiyah and Sicily, such as Malta, Pantelleria, Jerba and Kerkenna. And he extended his dominion to the coast of Africa, [where] … he did so much pleasing to God.'[326]

King Roger's naval strategy

In the final analysis, the greatest bequest of Roger II to his successors, however, was not a strong and wealthy kingdom. It was the naval strategy by which that kingdom had been established and maintained. At its core this strategy was based upon simple geography. At the heart of the realm was Sicily, and Sicily was at the heart of the Mediterranean, astride the east–west shipping channels. The maritime technology of the era meant that a ship could pass by the island undetected only with great difficulty. This was essentially because the vessels of the era were dependent upon adjacent shores for navigation, food, shelter and, most vitally, water. Roger understood this and sought to magnify its effect by incorporating both the north and south shores of the central Mediterranean into his kingdom, along with all the major islands in-between. Once this was accomplished, he possessed near total control of both the Strait of Messina (3 miles wide) and the Sicilian Channel (100 miles wide). Hardly a vessel could transit from Western Europe or the Maghrib to the East and vice versa without permission from the king of Sicily. Roger, guided by the financial acumen of his shrewd first minister, George of Antioch, knew to convert this singular advantage into extraordinary wealth.

The strategic significance of Sicily's geography could not have been lost upon Roger II. After all, it was he who had commissioned Abu Abdallah Muhammad ibn Muhammad ibn Idris al-Ali bi-amr Allah al-Idrisi, one of the greatest geographers of the Middle Ages. At Roger's behest, al-Idrisi produced the *Kitab Nuzhat al-mushtaq fi-khtiraq al-afaq* ('The Pleasure Excursion of One Who Is Eager to Traverse the Regions of the World'), which he later named simply

---

[323] Romuald of Salerno, *Romualdi Salernitani Chronicon*, pp. 234–6.
[324] Ibn al-Athir, *BAS*, I, pp. 479–80; *Chronicle of Ibn al-Athir, Part 2*, pp. 63–4.
[325] Ibn al-Athir, *BAS*, I, p. 480; *Chronicle of Ibn al-Athir, Part 2*, p. 64; Romuald of Salerno, *Romualdi Salernitani Chronicon*, p. 236.
[326] Ibn al-Athir, *BAS*, I, p. 450.

the *Kitab Rujar* ('Book of Roger') in honor of his benefactor.[327] It was a highly detailed textual description of the world as inspired by the work of Hellenized Egyptian geographer, Claudius Ptolemy (died circa 170), but based largely on the eyewitness reports of observers dispatched from Sicily. The work provided exact distances and traveling times by ship between the various inhabited islands and between major ports. It described harbor facilities, often including notations about the availability of food and water. Observations on crop and livestock production were also almost always included.[328] Accompanying the geographical treatise was a map of the world, which came to be known in Latin as the *Tabula Rugeriana* ('Map of Roger'). It showed the 'known world' divided into Ptolemy's seven climatic zones, depicting Eurasia and North Africa with the Mediterranean featured prominently in-between.[329] Furthermore, Roger ordered al-Idrisi to construct an 'enormous and immense' planisphere of pure silver, which was to be engraved with 'countries and districts, coasts and lands, gulfs and seas, watercourses and river mouths ...'[330] The planisphere is lost but the *Tabula Rugeriana* and the *Kitab Rujar* survive in several copies. A 1553 reproduction of the book preserved at the Bodleian Library of Oxford (Ms Pococke 375) contains dozens of brightly colored maps (see Map 8). Of special interest is the chart of the western Mediterranean spread across folios 187v–188r, which clearly shows the close proximity of Sicily to Calabria and Cape Bon as well as to such surrounding islands as the Aeolians, Malta and Pantelleria (see Map 9). Al-Idrisi may have intended the work as an altruistic addition to man's knowledge of the world, but, in fact, to the pragmatic mind of the Norman king, it must have represented a treasure trove of useful intelligence. The description of the island of Lampedusa, halfway between Malta and Mahdiyah, is a case in point:

> As for the island of Lampedusa, the distance which separates it from the nearest point in Africa, that is to say from Qabudiah [a peninsula near Mahdiyah], is two days' navigation. Lampedusa is endowed with a port sheltered from all winds, which can hold many ships of war and is situated on the southwest of the island. One finds neither fruits nor animals there.[331]

Al-Idrisi managed to complete his prodigious task only a few weeks before Roger's death, but the Arab geographer contends that the king was involved in the project's research for the entire fifteen years it took to compile the information. In the prologue to the *Kitab Rujar*, al-Idrisi insists the monarch was motivated by the desire 'to know his lands sufficiently and exactly, while being based on unquestionable and proven knowledge.'[332] And al-Idrisi emphasized

327 Ibn Khaldun, *BAS*, II, p. 203. See also Houben, *Roger II*, pp. 102–4.
328 Al-Idrisi, *BAS*, I, pp. 31–131; *La première géographie de l'Occident*.
329 H. Bresc and A. Nef, 'Note sur la présente édition', *La première géographie de l'Occident*, pp. 19–22.
330 Al-Idrisi, *BAS*, I, pp. 40–1; *La première géographie de l'Occident*, 'Prologue', p. 61.
331 Al-Idrisi, *BAS*, I, p. 54; *La première géographie de l'Occident*, IV, 2, p. 305.
332 Al-Idrisi, *BAS*, I, p. 36; *La première géographie de l'Occident*, 'Prologue', p. 60.

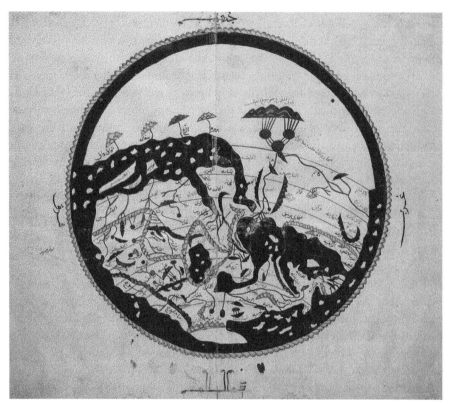

8. Circular world map of al-Idrisi. This circular world map from a sixteenth-century copy of al-Idrisi's *Kitab Rujar* ('Book of Roger') is centered on the Mediterranean with North Africa at the top of the image and the whole of Eurasia at the bottom. (Credit: Ms Pococke 375, fols 3v and 4r of the sixteenth century, reproduced here by permission of the Bodleian Libraries, University of Oxford ©, with all rights reserved)

that Roger was interested in specifics: 'He wanted to know the borders of these territories, their routes by land and by sea, the climate in which they were situated, the seas and gulfs which were found there.'[333] Roger seemed to nurture a particular interest in key waterways and obstacles to navigation. For example, Gervase of Tilbury, an English writer who briefly served in the court of King William II, relates a fanciful but revealing anecdote in which Roger hires a famous diver, Nicholas Pipe, to investigate why the Strait of Messina was so treacherous to shipping.[334] Some of the details of the tale are obviously imagined, but the character Nicholas Pipe seems to have actually existed. Walter Map, another twelfth-century writer from the British Isles, even speaks of him in

---

[333] Al-Idrisi, *BAS*, I, p. 36; *La première géographie de l'Occident*, 'Prologue', p. 60.
[334] Gervase of Tilbury, *Otia Imperialia*, pp. 332–5.

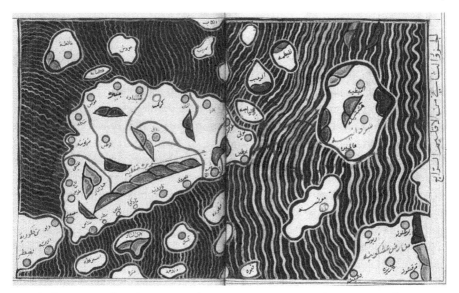

9. Al-Idrisi map of Sicily. Among the many maps contained in a sixteenth-century copy of the *Kitab Rujar* from Cairo was al-Idrisi's depiction of the central Mediterranean, showing Sicily's close proximity to the Tunisia (top) and the Italian mainland (bottom) as well as the surrounding islands. (Credit: Ms Pococke 375, fols 187v and 188r of the sixteenth century, reproduced here by permission of the Bodleian Libraries, University of Oxford ©, with all rights reserved)

De Nugis Curialium ('Courtiers' Trifles').[335] And Roger's apparent curiosity about the currents that run through the strait seems perfectly logical. John Pryor notes that local pilots were often needed to navigate this difficult passage between Calabria and Sicily.[336] Such pilots were undoubtedly provided for a fee, a portion of which surely found its way into the royal treasury. The point is that Roger assuredly was aware that he owned the principal chokepoint of the Mediterranean and he most likely knew to profit from that happy circumstance.

Moreover, Roger essentially owned the island that stood in the center of that chokepoint. Excluding property apportioned to a handful of *familiares* (members of the inner circle) and a few dozen ecclesiastical institutions under royal patronage, Sicily was the demesne of the Hauteville family. This meant that, with scant exception, Roger controlled every pasture, forest, town and strip of coastline on the island along with the adjacent waters.[337] The royal registers edited by CarlRichard Brühl, Erich Caspar and Karl Kehr are rife with diplomas showing that the king maintained a monopoly on virtually every-

---

[335] Walter Map, *De Nugis Curialium*, ed. and trans. M. James (OMT, Oxford, 1983, reprinted 2002), pp. 368–71.
[336] Pryor, *Geography, Technology, and War*, p. 92.
[337] Abulafia, 'Crown and the Economy under Roger II and his Successors', *Dumbarton Oaks Papers*, XXXVII (Washington, DC, 1983), pp. 1–14, especially 2–3.

thing associated with this royal demesne, from pitch and lumber production to fishing and salt procurement.[338] It is clear from charter evidence that, unless specifically exempted, anyone using royal property for nearly anything had to pay a tax. Consequently, any merchant vessel that pulled into a Sicilian port had to pay an *anchoraticum* (anchorage fee) and a *commercium* or *plateaticum* (ten percent levy on all merchandise).[339] A June 1104 privilege to the monastery of San Pancrazio near Taormina lists the *falangaticum* (coastal dues), the *decima* (a tariff of a tenth on all merchandise) and the *ius portus* (port taxes) collected by the *custodes maris* (coast guard), *portulani* (harbor masters) and *officiales littorales* (beach officials).[340] All exports and imports were strictly monitored and taxed. A January 1134 privilege in favor of Lipari–Patti prohibits the monastery from importing foreign cereals for commercial purposes,[341] while another privilege of the same year permits the monastery of Santissimo Salvatore of Messina to export a small amount (200 *salme*)[342] of grain to Africa in exchange for necessities only.[343] Tight regulation of grain exports is quite understandable when one considers that wheat subsidies were a primary tool for controlling the crown's African holdings. There was even a duty on all trade goods transported on royal roads.[344] Ibn Jubayr relates in the late twelfth century how he and his companions were challenged by a customs official upon leaving Termini on the road to Palermo.[345]

Furthermore, the crown maintained tight control on the materials needed for ship maintenance and revictualing. Pitch for rendering a vessel watertight, for instance, was a monopoly of the king. In 1124, Roger granted to Bishop Angerius of Catania a furnace for cooking pitch, a function that the diploma indicated was normally reserved for the crown.[346] Nor could one harvest lumber from the realm's forests without the king's permission. In 1132, Roger gave leave to the citizens of Cefalu to utilize wood, but only for the construction of houses.[347] Even fish, especially tuna, and the salt needed to preserve it were regulated by the royal fisc. For example, in May 1134 the king conferred upon the archimandrite[348] of Santissimo Salvatore of Messina the right to 'fifty *barrilia* [barrels] of tuna from

---

[338] Brühl, *Rogerii II. Regis Diplomata Latina*; Caspar, *Roger II*, Regesten, pp. 473–580; K. Kehr, *Die Urkunden der Normannisch-Sicilischen Könige* (Innsbruck, 1902), Urkunden, pp. 405–502.

[339] Abulafia, 'Crown and the Economy under Roger II', pp. 8–9.

[340] C. Minieri Riccio, *Saggio di Codice Diplomatico, formato sulle antiche scritture dell'Archivio di Stato di Napoli* (2 vols, Napoli, 1878), I, no. 6, pp. 6–9.

[341] Caspar, *Roger II*, Reg. no. 93, p. 521.

[342] A *salma* was a medieval Sicilian measure of dry volume equivalent to about eight bushels.

[343] Caspar, *Roger II*, Reg. no. 95, pp. 522–3.

[344] Abulafia, 'Crown and the Economy under Roger II', p. 9.

[345] Ibn Jubayr, *Travels of Ibn Jubayr*, p. 347; BAS, I, pp. 158–9.

[346] Caspar, *Roger II*, Reg. no. 44, pp. 494–5.

[347] *Rogerii II. Regis Diplomata Latina*, no. 19, pp. 52–3.

[348] The abbot of a Basilian (Greek Orthodox) monastery.

the tuna fishing at Milazzo per year and one hundred *salme* of salt from the salt works at Faro', implying that all others either had no such privilege or were required to pay for it.[349] Thus, after Roger had consolidated his power on the Italian mainland and conquered the adjacent coastlines of North Africa, ships passing through the central Mediterranean had no easy access to markets, food, water supplies, shelter and repair materials without contributing to the royal fisc of the king of Sicily. And George of Antioch, his astute and ever-reliable first minister who had initially gained notoriety as an efficient collector of taxes for the Zirid princes, doubtless used the formidable Sicilian fleet to ensure that few vessels escaped payment. Moreover, Roger's control of the North African coast assured him a portion of the profits from the caravan trade, particularly in gold from sub-Saharan Africa.[350] The Sicilian *tarì* (a quarter *dinar* gold coin about a gram in weight) was almost the only gold coinage produced in Western Europe in the twelfth century.[351] In other words, Roger II and George of Antioch most likely turned the island of Sicily into a massive tollgate. No wonder the realm was legendary for its opulence. And, of course, that opulence was skillfully translated into power, both diplomatic and military.

Sicily was not only Roger's principal source of wealth, but it was also his sanctuary from all the enemies of his rule. And he was not above using his wealth to keep it as such. He knew that no adversary, no matter how strong militarily, could unseat him from his throne unless it possessed some sort of sea power. Since the two empires that coveted his kingdom, German and Byzantine, both lacked sufficient maritime resources at the time, this meant they needed to effect some sort of alliance with one or more of the Italian maritime powers of the age, that is, Genoa, Pisa or Venice. Consequently, Roger's diplomacy consisted largely of detaching one or the other of these seafaring city-states from any imperially inspired anti-Norman league.

A prime example is revealed in the events of 1134. Robert of Capua, one of the leaders of the baronial revolt against King Roger, attempted to purchase the aid of Pisa with 3,000 pounds of silver, ultimately winning the promise of 100 vessels. Genoa supposedly also committed support, and Falco of Benevento notes that the doge of Venice may have pledged assistance as well. But nothing happened. No fleet was sent that year from any of the maritime republics.[352] As was discussed earlier, two outraged letters from Bernard of Clairvaux, one to the citizens of Pisa and the other to those of Genoa, explain why. In these

---

[349] Pirro, *Sicilia sacra*, II, pp. 976–7. '... *de tonnara Milatii quolibet anno tunnina barrilia quinquaginta, et de salina Phari salmas salis centum.*'

[350] Abulafia, 'Norman Kingdom of Africa', pp. 27–8.

[351] Grierson and Travaini, *Medieval European Coinage*, pp. 2–4; G. A. Loud, 'Norman Sicily in the twelfth century', *New Cambridge Medieval History, Volume IV, c.1024–c.1198, Part II*, ed. D. Luscombe and J. Riley-Smith (Cambridge, 2004), p. 468.

[352] Falco of Benevento, *Chronicon Beneventanum*, pp. 162–70. See also Heywood, *History of Pisa*, pp. 83–4.

missives, the anti-Norman cleric beseeches the Genoese and the Pisans not to be corrupted by Roger's enticements.[353] Clearly, the king of Sicily had suborned the profit-minded merchants of the two mercantile city-states with promises of largesse and commercial concessions. This should hardly have been surprising, at least in the case of Genoa. It had enjoyed a small colony on Sicily since 1116, when Roger granted the Genoese consul Ogerius Capra a plot of land near Messina.[354] Moreover, pacts of mutual maritime cooperation concluded in 1127–8 between the city of Savona, a Genoese protectorate, and the court of Palermo demonstrate ongoing amicable relations with the mariners of Liguria.[355]

As for the seamen of Tuscany, Roger had success enticing them away from his enemies as well. The best example occurred when the imperial–papal coalition led by Lothair III of Germany swept through Apulia and Campania in 1137. After the capitulation of Salerno, it must have seemed all but inevitable that Calabria would soon fall as well, possibly leading to an assault on Sicily itself. Yet on the brink of total victory, the coalition collapsed. The Pisans' own Bernardo Maragone leaves little doubt as to what happened:

> Strongly besieged for fifteen days, with mangonels and siege castles and *gatti* [battering rams], it [Salerno] finally surrendered itself to the Emperor Lothair and the Pisans. Afterwards the king [Lothair] entered into conflict with the Pisans; who sent a galley with wise men and these men conferred with the wise men of the king of Sicily whose men were in the Torre Maggiore [of Salerno], and thus they made peace with him, and afterwards the Pisans returned home on 13 October. [356]

The Pisans apparently felt that the negotiated surrender of Salerno had cheated them out of their spoils. Alternatively, Romuald of Salerno says the breakdown arose from Lothair's failure to help prevent the burning of a costly Pisan siege engine, but he confirms the fundamental result: 'Whence the Pisans, moved to anger by the emperor, who had not offered them aid in this matter, withdrew and afterwards were in agreement with King Roger.'[357] Whatever the reason for the falling out, it can easily be surmised from the foregoing that Roger had adeptly capitalized on the Pisans' dissatisfaction to lure them away with silver or commercial privileges. As a consequence, the Pisans immediately abandoned the imperial–papal coalition. Stripped of sea power to combat the potent Norman

---

353   Bernard of Clairvaux, *Letters of St Bernard of Clairvaux*, nos 131 and 132, pp. 200–2; *Sancti Bernardi Opera*, VII, nos 129 and 130, pp. 322–6.

354   S. Cusa, ed., *I diplomi greci et arabi di Sicilia* (2 vols, Palermo, 1868–81), I, pp. 359–60.

355   Abulafia, *Two Italies*, pp. 65–8.

356   Bernardo Maragone, *Annales Pisani*, p. 11. '*Que per quindecim dies fortiter obsessa, cum manganis et castellis et gattis, tandem reddidit se imperatori Lotario et Pisani. Postea idem rex contristas est cum Pisanis; qui Pisani miserunt unam galeam com sapientibus et hoc fecerunt cum consilio sapientum regis Sicilie qui erant in Turri Maiore, et sic fecerunt pacem cum eo, postea Pisas reversi sunt XIII kal. octubris.*'

357   Romuald of Salerno, *Romualdi Salernitani Chronicon*, p. 223. '*Unde Pisani in iram commoti ab imperatore, qui eis super hoc auxilium non prestiterat, recesserunt et postmodum sunt cum rege Roggerio concordati.*'

fleet, the league was doomed. Lothair himself headed home only two weeks later, leaving Pope Innocent II and his Apulian allies to fend for themselves.[358] Roger was, therefore, able to reverse all of their gains in short order.

Roger also proved that greed was a more powerful motivator than enmity with respect to the Venetians. As noted earlier, Venice, enraged over Sicilian pirate activity in the vicinity of Jerba, formed an anti-Norman alliance with Constantinople and sent envoys to enlist Lothair at the German imperial court at Merseburg in 1136.[359] Roger, however, had been informed of the negotiations and evidently managed to detach the Venetians from the proposed anti-Norman league by offering a trade deal that the merchants of La Serenissima could not refuse. Traces of the concession are found in a pair of September 1175 diplomas issued concurrently in Palermo by King William II in favor of the Venetians. The first assures that 'the Venetians shall be safe and secure on land and sea in their persons and their money from our men, our fleet and galleys, with the exception of corsairs and those who act against our kingdom, and with the exception of those who are in the service of the Emperor of Constantinople...'[360] The second concedes that 'the Venetians coming to our kingdom will henceforth give only half of what is customary to give from their ships and merchandise brought to or taken away from our kingdom according to privileges in the time of the most glorious lord King Roger, our grandfather, and the most magnificent master King William, our father of blessed memory'.[361] Camillo Manfroni has concluded that the concession represented by these two charters is a confirmation of an earlier charter, now lost, which Roger bestowed on the Venetians around the year 1136.[362] Abulafia seems to concur: 'Roger had already, it seems, granted Venice commercial rights as long ago as the 1130s or early 1140s...'[363] And, most significantly, Manfroni is convinced that the concession was in 'compensation for the neutrality of the Venetians'.[364]

Moreover, Abulafia contends that the Normans probably intimidated the Venetians into maintaining an amicable relationship.[365] The Historia ducum

---

[358] Heywood, History of Pisa, p. 88.

[359] Annales Erphesfurtenses, p. 42; Annalista Saxo, pp. 601–2.

[360] G. Tafel and G. Thomas, Urkunden zur älteren Handels-und Staatsgeschichte der Republik Venedig (2 vols, Fontes Rerum Austriacum, XII, Vienna, 1856), I, no. LXV, pp. 172–4. 'Venetici salvi et securi erunt per terram et mare in personis suis et eorum pecuniis de hominibus nostris et stolio nostro et galeis nostris, exceptis cursalibus et illis, qui contra regnum nostram egerint, et exceptis illis, qui fuerint in auxilio Imperatoris Constantinopolitani...'

[361] Tafel and Thomas, Urkunden der Republik Venedig, I, no. LXVI, pp. 174–5. 'Venetici venientes in regnum nostrum, de navibus et mercibus eorum, quas in regnum attulerint, vel a regno reportaverint, de justiis, quas temporibus domini gloriosissimi regis Rogerii, avi nostri, et domini magnificentissimi, regis Willelmi, patris nostri beate memorie, dare soliti sint, amodo nonnisi medietatem tandem dent de hoc, quod hactenus dare soliti sunt.'

[362] Manfroni, Storia della Marina italiana, I, p. 189.

[363] Abulafia, Two Italies, pp. 88–9, 142–3.

[364] Manfroni, Storia della Marina italiana, I, pp. 189–90.

[365] Abulafia, Two Italies, pp. 80–3.

Fig. 5. Saracen watch tower. The tenth-century Torre Saracena at Piràino on the northeast coast of Sicily has an unimpeded view of the Aeolian Islands and is typical of the fortifications the Normans took over to form their coastal watch system. (Credit: C. Stanton)

Veneticorum plainly implies that Roger exerted unremitting pressure on the Venetians by confiscating their merchandise and subjecting them to state-sponsored piracy, whenever he felt the need.[366] Accordingly, Abulafia later points out, 'In the 1150s, while Roger was still alive, the Venetians agreed to make peace with the King of Sicily, and recovered in consequence their trading rights, probably in the form granted to them ten or twenty years before.'[367] In any event, there is no evidence that Venice ever participated in Lothair's invasion of the *Regno*. In fact, in a February 1144 privilege, Roger granted permission to some Venetian citizens to rebuild a church dedicated to Saint Mark in the Seralkadi quarter of Palermo, indicating there was probably some sort of Venetian enclave in the royal capital contemporaneous with the events in question.[368] Nor did the Venetians join the Byzantine emperor in his planned attack on Apulia in 1149. A Greek presence on both sides of the Strait of Otranto was no more attractive a proposition to the Venetians than Norman dominance of this lone exit from the Adriatic. As it happens, none of the Italian maritime powers was ever involved in an assault on Sicily during Roger's reign.

Roger II used military means to achieve his goals only when he felt there was no practical alternative. Even then, he made the island of Sicily the flagship of his strategy. The *Chronica de Ferraria* attests that he safeguarded his domains with a well-developed coastal watch system complete with towers:

> The king so fortified the points of entry to his kingdom that it was scarcely possible for anyone to enter it against his will. For the frontiers of this kingdom were barred either by rivers, which could only be crossed by bridges, or by mountains – the valleys through which were defended by walls. The other sides were surrounded by the sea, the coasts of which were furnished with towers and guards, so that if an [enemy] fleet should approach by sea, he would immediately be informed of its size and whereabouts by signals displayed along the coasts.[369]

The *Catalogus Baronum*, an inventory of military obligations for Apulia and Capua commissioned by Roger, provides some evidence that these towers were manned through feudal obligation.[370] Moreover, the system of watch towers seems to have been particularly prominent along the shores of the extreme toe of Calabria and the northeastern corner of Sicily. Ruins of such towers or fortresses (some Byzantine or 'Saracen') on high points spaced roughly every three miles

366 *Historia ducum Veneticorum*, p. 75; *Testi Storici Veneziani*, pp. 16–17.
367 Abulafia, *Two Italies*, p. 89.
368 Caspar, *Roger II*, Reg. no. 163, p. 552.
369 *Chronica de Ferraria*, anno 1151, pp. 26–7. 'Cuius regni ingressus idem rex sic munivit, quod vix posset aliquis illic ingredi contra eius libitum. Nam clausum est idem regnum aut fluminibus, que nisi per pontes transiri non possunt, aut montibus, quorum valles clausit muris. Per ceteras vero partes habet maria, quorum horas munivit turribus aut custodibus, ut si superveniret super maria navalis exercitus, per fanones apparentes in oris maninis quot et ubi essent cito percipi posset.' (English translation by G. A. Loud in Houben, *Roger II*, p. 156.)
370 *Catalogus Baronum*, ed. E. Jamison (FSI, Rome, 1972), pp. 33–4, 36–8.

Fig. 6. Aci Castello. Constructed of black lava stone from Mount Etna, this Norman fortress guards the approach to Catania and is part of a chain of fortifications that girds the northeastern littoral of Sicily. (Credit: C. Stanton)

still guard the eastern and western approaches to the Strait of Messina (see Figures 5 and 6). Additionally, Roger ultimately made certain that he retained control of the primary fortifications of each great port city. A case in point was Amalfi. Alexander of Telese describes Roger's motivation for attacking the city in 1131:

> The king began to consider carefully the problem of how he might strengthen his kingdom in that perpetual peace which he greatly desired, and how to prevent anybody having the opportunity to resist him. Thus he began to demand urgently and peremptorily from the Amalfitans that they hand over to him all those fortifications which had been left in their hands to guard, for he would in no way consent to nor allow any further agreement by which they might hold these while serving him.[371]

---

[371]   Alexander of Telese, *Ystoria Rogerii regis Sicilie*, Bk II, ch. 7, p. 26. '*Cepit Rex sollicitus intra mentis sue volvere archanum, qualiter deinde regnum suum, quod multum desiderabat, perpetua solidaretur pace nullusque adversum se resistendi facultatem posset habere. Unde ab amalfitanis vehementius instanterque cepit exhigere quatinus cunctas suas dimittentes munitiones, sibi eas custodiendas traderent; alioquin nullo modo nulloque pacto ulterius pateretur, ut ipsi eas sibi servandas tenerent.*' (English translation by G. A. Loud at www.leeds.ac.uk/history/weblearning/MedievalHistoryTextCentre/medievalTexts/html.)

In keeping with this policy, Roger similarly took over the fortifications of Salerno and Bari despite earlier agreements with the citizenry of those cities that he would not.[372] Moreover, he often garrisoned them with his loyal 'Saracen' troops.[373]

Perhaps more significantly, Roger made certain that command of his formidable fleet, based in Palermo and Messina, remained a primary duty of his first minister,[374] his *amiratus amiratorum*[375] or *maximus ammiratus*,[376] who for most of his reign was George of Antioch.[377] Defended by his well-led armada, Roger was virtually unassailable by either imperial forces or papal minions while he remained on Sicily. Thus, his basic tactic whenever threatened militarily or recovering from a battlefield setback on the mainland was to withdraw onto his nearly impregnable island, the flagship of his fleet, and wait until inevitable dissension within the ranks of his enemies caused the collapse of their coalition. This was precisely how he dealt with the invasion of Emperor Lothair III in 1137.[378] He well understood the expeditionary nature of imperial incursions into southern Italy. Since the days of Charlemagne, no emperor had ever ventured into southern Italy and stayed. Roger knew that, sooner or later, imperial armies would always return north, leaving his papal enemies and rebellious nobles to deal with him alone. He also knew that any accommodation between his fractious nobles and the pope would also eventually break down as it did under Pope Honorius II at Benevento in 1128.[379] All he had to do was wait.

Offensively, Roger used his redoubtable armada chiefly to strengthen his hold on the central Mediterranean. These aggressive efforts were mostly directed at North Africa. Almost from the inception of his majority until his death, he sought by a persistent campaign of conquest to secure the southern shore of the Sicilian Channel. Once he had done so, predominately through the victories of his adept admiral, he was able to take a sizable share of east–west commerce, while profiting from a hugely lucrative trade in Sicilian grain for sub-Saharan gold.[380]

---

[372] Alexander of Telese, *Ystoria Rogerii regis Sicilie*, Bk I, ch. 22, pp. 19–20; Bk II, ch. 34, p. 39; Falco of Benevento, *Chronicon Beneventanum*, p. 186.
[373] *Annalisto Saxo*, p. 608; Falco of Benevento, *Chronicon Beneventanum*, p. 186. See also Chalandon, *Histoire de la Domination Normande*, II, p. 67.
[374] L. Mott, *Sea Power in the Medieval Mediterranean: The Catalan–Aragonese Fleet in the War of the Sicilian Vespers* (Gainesville, 2003), p. 54.
[375] *Rogerii II. Regis Diplomata Latina*, no. 24, pp. 66–8.
[376] Alexander of Telese, *Ystoria Rogerii regis Sicilie*, Bk II, ch. 8, p. 27.
[377] Ménager, *Amiratus*, pp. 44–54.
[378] Romuald of Salerno, *Romualdi Salernitani Chronicon*, pp. 222–3.
[379] Alexander of Telese, *Ystoria Rogerii regis Sicilie*, Bk I, ch. 14–15, pp. 14–15; Falco of Benevento, *Chronicon Beneventanum*, pp. 100–2; Romuald of Salerno, *Romualdi Salernitani Chronicon*, pp. 216–17.
[380] Abulafia, 'Norman Kingdom of Africa', pp. 35–6.

The fleet of war itself was no small part of Roger's success.[381] Many of the ships were, doubtless, procured through feudal obligation from the subject port cities (described in Appendix A),[382] but a goodly number must also have come from the established royal arsenals in Palermo and Messina.[383] The ships were crewed primarily through the *datium marinariorum* ('mariners' duty'), which required lordships, abbeys and townships to supply a specified number of mariners for the fleet.[384] According to the recent analysis of John Pryor, the primary warship of his fleet was a distinctly Italian version of the *galea*, a descendant of the *dromōn*. Instead of two or more levels of rowers, one above the other, stroking from a sitting position, Pryor believes that Sicilian galleys employed the relatively efficient *alla sensile* oarage system in which the rowers sat two per bench at deck level, each manipulating his own oar in a stand-and-sit stroke fashion. This enabled greater power, possibly resulting in greater speed while allowing for greater load-carrying capacity below deck.[385] In other words, Roger's galleys may have been faster with greater range than those of their adversaries – ideal for raiding and interdiction at sea. (A fuller description of the *galea* is provided in Appendix A.) Complaints of harassment by Norman warships contained in various Latin, Greek and Arab annals seem to substantiate this.[386] In point of fact, while a certain amount of state-sponsored piracy probably occurred, Roger's fleets almost certainly fostered commercial activity through the central Mediterranean by quelling Muslim marauding. It was in his best interest to do so.

Roger also used his fleets in an aggressive manner to project his power and to keep his enemies at bay. Examples of this tactic were the raids against Greece conducted by George of Antioch in 1147 and 1149. Again, the fast *galea*, with improved endurance, was exemplary for such forays. It enabled George to strike wherever he wished and depart again before his adversaries could act. This was particularly true in 1149 during his audacious harassment of Constantinople and its environs.[387] In truth, Roger's fleets did not always prevail in engagements with enemy fleets, particularly those of Pisa and Venice, but their performance

[381] Manfroni, *Storia della Marina italiana*, I, p. 182.

[382] *Tancredi et Willelmi III Regum Diplomata*, ed. H. Zielinski (CDRS, Ser. I, V, Cologne, 1982), no. 18, pp. 42–6. See also Mott, *Sea Power in the Medieval Mediterranean*, pp. 56–7.

[383] Al-Idrisi, *BAS*, I, pp. 60, 68; *La première géographie de l'Occident*, IV, 2, pp. 308, 312.

[384] Caspar, *Roger II*, Reg. no. 69, p. 472; Pirro, *Sicilia sacra*, II, p. 999. See also R. Gregorio, *Considerazioni sopra la Storia di Sicilia* (6 vols, Palermo, 1805–16), II, pp. 81–3.

[385] Peter of Eboli, *Liber ad honorem Augusti sive de rebus Siculis, Codex 120 II der Burgerbibliothek Bern*, eds T. Kolser and M. Stahli, trans. G. Becht-Jordens (Sigmaringen, 1994), p. 131, fol. 119r. See also Pryor and Jeffreys, *Dromōn*, pp. 423–44.

[386] *Annales Erphesfurtenses*, p. 540; Ibn al-Athir, *BAS*, I, pp. 461–2; *Chronicle of Ibn al-Athir, Part I*, p. 365; Niketas Choniates, *O City of Byzantium!*, p. 45.

[387] Andrea Dandolo, *Chronica Per Extensum Descripta*, pp. 242–4; Niketas Choniates, *O City of Byzantium!*, pp. 45–53; Ibn al-Athir, *BAS*, I, p. 476; *Chronicle of Ibn al-Athir, Part 2*, p. 32; John Kinnamos, *John and Manuel Comnenus*, Bk III, ch. 4–5, pp. 78–82; Romuald of Salerno, *Romualdi Salernitani Chronicon*, p. 227.

was sufficient to discourage a full-scale assault on Sicily – that is, at least while Roger sat on the throne.

In summary, controlling the central Mediterranean was the essence of Roger's naval strategy, and Sicily, with its strategic setting, was his primary means for doing that. Accordingly, he sought to bolster this advantage by strengthening his grip on the lands to the north and the south of the island and by developing a strong, swift fleet to protect it and deter unsanctioned shipping through the adjacent straits. This enabled him to monitor both military and commercial ships sailing through the central Mediterranean, a development which, according to the letters of Jewish traders contained in the Cairo Geniza (the storeroom of the Ben Ezra synagogue of Fustat), produced lasting changes in trading patterns on the 'middle sea', particularly with respect to Muslim commerce.[388] In other words, the Geniza documents provide evidence that Roger's establishment of maritime supremacy in the central Mediterranean facilitated the expansion of West Italian sea power eastward and permitted him to assume control of trade emanating from Muslim North Africa. This does not imply that Roger attempted to restrict the flow of commercial traffic in any way; it merely means that he did his best to route that traffic through Palermo and Messina so that he could exact a portion of the profits.[389] In fact, Hubert Houben makes the argument that Roger's conquest of the Maghrib coast including the islands of Jerba and Kerkenna promoted trade by stemming Muslim piracy in the Sicilian Channel.[390] Thus, Roger became the envy of his world by parlaying Sicily's strategic advantage into enormous wealth and power. It was also the key to the kingdom's survival against a host of adversaries until very nearly the end of the century. As long as his successors adhered to the principle of dominating the central Mediterranean while keeping their enemies off-balance and divided, the Norman Kingdom flourished. Once they strayed from that fundamental blueprint, they and the maritime empire that Roger had founded were doomed.

---

[388] Goitein, *A Mediterranean Society*, I, pp. 32, 39–40.
[389] Specific examples from the Geniza documents are provided in Chapter 4 below, 'The Impact'.
[390] Houben, *Roger II*, p. 83.

3

The Eclipse (1154 to 1194)

It had taken the Hautevilles nearly a century to establish the maritime empire that Roger II bequeathed to his successors. It took those successors only a few decades to fritter it away. By 1194, the Hauteville dynasty was at an end, replaced by the German House of Hohenstaufen. There are, of course, myriad reasons why this occurred, but the most salient single answer is: Roger's heirs deviated from the core naval strategy that he had so painstakingly developed, a strategy that focused on dominance of the central Mediterranean. Gradually, the last Hautevilles lost their grip on the north and south shores of the 'middle sea'; they allowed their adversaries to ally with the great Italian sea powers of the age; and, worst of all, they exhausted their naval power on ill-advised adventurism in distant lands, eventually allowing the once-daunting Sicilian fleet to fall into desuetude. Each succeeding sovereign contributed his own peculiar set of blunders to the tragic decline.

Naval operations of William I

Prior to his demise, Roger II did everything he could to prepare William, his only surviving son, for what he knew would be a difficult reign. He even gave him a head start on his regal duties by having him crowned co-sovereign on Easter Sunday 1151.[1] But he could not give him the one advantage that he himself had enjoyed for most of his rule and what his son needed most: an advisor of the caliber of George of Antioch. George, of course, passed away the very year Roger invited William to share the throne. George's successor, Philip of Mahdiyah, was executed for treason against God a short time later in 1153 and Roger himself succumbed the year after. According to the court observer, the so-called 'Hugo Falcandus', William further complicated the transition himself by imprisoning or exiling the remaining coterie of his father's advisors. He then selected as his 'admiral of admirals' a vice chancellor and former notary by the name of Maio

---

[1] *Annales Casinenses*, anno 1151, p. 310; 'Hugo Falcandus', *History of the Tyrants of Sicily*, p. 59; *Liber de Regno Sicilie*, p. 7; Romuald of Salerno, *Romualdi Salernitani Chronicon*, p. 231.

of Bari.[2] While Maio was probably nowhere near as odious and incompetent as the highly biased 'Falcandus' makes him out to be, the new first minister had no apparent military or foreign policy experience. As a consequence, it is highly doubtful that he had a grasp of the naval strategy upon which the Kingdom of Sicily's survival was based. Thus, king and counselor were decidedly unprepared for what was to come.

The two men gave evidence of this by immediately diverging from the policy blueprint carefully laid out by those who had preceded them. Both Greek and Arabic sources note that they ordered an ill-advised raid on the caliphate of Cairo in 1154, thereby abrogating the long-lasting pact of friendship between the two courts. The Sicilian armada apparently ravaged the Nile delta region and sacked Tinnis (southwest of Port Said).[3] An entry in the *Al-Mawa iz wa-l-i tibar bi-dhikr al-khitat wa-l-athar* ('Topographical and Historical Description of Egypt') by al-Maqrizi indicates the size and scope of the Sicilian expedition was significant. This same source says that the Sicilians had around 60 ships and that they raided Rosetta (modern Rashid), Damietta and Alexandria as well. Al-Maqrizi dated the action to late 1145, but he was writing in the fifteenth century and may well have confused the chronology.[4] In any event, such distant adventurism cost King William and his 'emir of emirs' a friend they could ill afford to lose and drained away precious naval assets that they would need to deal with imminent threats. Both Michele Amari and Camillo Manfroni speculate that the Pisans, who had concluded a trade treaty with the caliphate of Egypt in 1154, had poisoned Egyptian relations with the Sicilians, but neither scholar offers any real proof of this.[5] The bottom line is that the raid was a precedent-setting departure from past policies, which signaled the eventual demise of the dynasty.

All the forces that had acted upon the *Regno* during Roger's reign were still there after his death and descended upon his heir nearly all at once. The most immediate and pressing challenge to William's rule would come from the throne of Byzantium. In fact, Constantinople's hostile intentions were portended by a Greek attack on the Sicilian fleet mentioned above as it returned from Egypt. The primary account of this clash is that of John Kinnamos, who says that it was preceded by a peace proposal from William. The king sent envoys to the Emperor Manuel Komnenos offering to return 'all the persons and property' appropriated by George of Antioch during the 1147 assault on Thebes and Corinth, but the Byzantine *basileus* rejected the olive branch and instead ordered

2   *Guillelmi I. Regis Diplomata*, ed. H. Enzensberger (CDRS, Ser. I, III, Cologne, 1996), no. 2, pp. 7–8; 'Hugo Falcandus', *History of the Tyrants of Sicily*, p. 60; *Liber de Regno Sicilie*, pp. 7–8; Romuald of Salerno, *Romualdi Salernitani Chronicon*, pp. 234–7.
3   Ibn al-Athir, *BAS*, I, p. 480; *Chronicle of Ibn al-Athir, Part 2*, p. 65; John Kinnamos, *John and Manuel Comnenus*, Bk III, ch. 13, pp. 95–6.
4   Al-Maqrizi, *BAS*, II, pp. 591–2.
5   Amari, *Storia dei Musulmani di Sicilia*, III, pp. 475–6; Manfroni, *Storia della Marina italiana*, I, p. 218.

an invasion fleet assembled under the command of his uncle, Constantine Angelus.[6] He had instructed Angelus to wait at Monemvasia on the southern tip of the Peloponnesos for further fleet reinforcements, but the latter, having learned of the Sicilian fleet's return from the Nile Delta, moved to intercept it with what vessels he had. Kinnamos does not give a specific number for the Byzantine flotilla but describes the Greek fleet as being inferior to that of the Sicilians. The continuator of the *Sigeberti Gemblacensis Chronica*, on the other hand, says 140 Greek ships faced a much smaller number of Sicilian vessels, but this seems to be a wild, uncorroborated estimate.[7] Kinnamos was in a better position to know and, given the outcome of the encounter, his account seems more credible. If, indeed, the Greeks were outnumbered, Angelus may have logically assumed that the enemy ships would be rendered ponderous by a surfeit of booty. He evidently was wrong. Upon the approach of the Greek squadron, the Sicilians began to withdraw in good order until they realized that they were dealing with an inferior force. They then adroitly outmaneuvered their disorderly opponents and took the wind advantage. The result was a rout in which Constantine Angelus was captured.[8] Although the encounter was a Norman victory, William should have been forewarned: Manuel was determined to attack him.

The Byzantine *basileus* first attempted to revive the anti-Norman alliance with the German throne. He had been in on-again, off-again negotiations with Conrad's successor, Frederick I Barbarossa, over a marriage alliance since September 1153.[9] Now, in the summer of 1155, Manuel dispatched a pair of *sebastoi* ('August Ones' – members of the imperial family), Michael Palaiologos and John Doukas, along with the exiled Norman noble, Alexander of Conversano, to parley with the German sovereign near Ancona, Italy.[10] Frederick, however, remained unwilling to commit, probably because he was hesitant to allow the Greeks another foothold on the Italian peninsula. There was little he could do at the moment in any case. He had just been crowned Holy Roman Emperor in Rome by Pope Hadrian IV, but a bloody battle with the citizenry combined with disease brought on by the heat of August made his nobles recalcitrant. They compelled him to retreat north of the Alps.[11]

[6] John Kinnamos, *John and Manuel Comnenus*, Bk III, ch. 12, pp. 94–5.

[7] *Sigeberti Gemblacensis Chronica*, anno 1154, p. 456.

[8] John Kinnamos, *John and Manuel Comnenus*, Bk III, ch. 13, pp. 95–6; Niketas Choniates, *O City of Byzantium!*, pp. 55–6.

[9] John Kinnamos, *John and Manuel Comnenus*, Bk IV, ch. 1, p. 106; Otto of Freising, *Deeds of Frederick Barbarossa*, Bk II, ch. 11, pp. 123–4; *Gesta Frederici*, Bk II, ch. XI, pp. 111–12.

[10] John Kinnamos, *John and Manuel Comnenus*, Bk IV, ch. 1, pp. 106–7; Otto of Freising, *Gesta Frederici*, Bk II, ch. XXXVI, pp. 144–5; *Deeds of Frederick Barbarossa*, Bk II, ch. 36, p. 154.

[11] *Annales Casinenses*, anno 1155, p. 311; *Annales Cavenses*, anno 1156, p. 192; Otto of Freising, *Deeds of Frederick Barbarossa*, Bk II, ch. 32–7, pp. 150–5; *Gesta Frederici*, Bk II, ch. XXXII–XXXVII, pp. 140–5; Romuald of Salerno, *Romualdi Salernitani Chronicon*, pp. 238–9;

Undeterred, the three Byzantine envoys entered into discussions with Robert II of Bassonville, the disaffected Norman count of Loritello, who himself had been unsuccessful in convincing Frederick to form a coalition against the Sicilian sovereign. The two parties soon agreed to join forces in an assault on Apulia.[12] Their timing was fortuitous. William had taken deathly ill in the month of September and was even rumored to have perished.[13] Worse still, a revolt led by a certain Bartholomew of Garsiliato erupted at Butera on Sicily.[14] And, as if that were not enough, Robert of Sorrento, erstwhile Prince of Capua, took advantage of the opportunity to reclaim his old Campanian domains.[15] The *Annales Casinenses* reports, 'Robert of Sorrento seized the whole of the principality of Capua all the way up to Naples and Salerno.'[16] William was even in a state of virtual war with Pope Hadrian IV, who had refused to recognize him as king and had excommunicated him.[17]

The circumstances could hardly have been better for the odd alliance of Greek troops and Norman rebels. Well-financed with Byzantine gold and supported by 10 warships, Palaiologos and his coalition soon bought the submission of the port cities of Vieste, Bari and Trani.[18] Andria also sued for peace when Richard, its lord, was killed in battle. Mottola was easily overcome. Montepeloso and Gravina rapidly followed, along with 'many other towns and fortresses.'[19] William

William of Tyre, *History of Deeds Done beyond the Sea*, II, Bk 18, ch. 2, 7, pp. 237, 247–8; *Willelmi Tyrensis Chronicon*, Bk 18, ch. 2, 7, pp. 811, 819.

[12] 'Hugo Falcandus', *History of the Tyrants of Sicily*, p. 66; *Liber de Regno Sicilie*, p. 14; John Kinnamos, *John and Manuel Comnenus*, Bk IV, ch. 2, pp. 107–8; Romuald of Salerno, *Romualdi Salernitani Chronicon*, p. 239; William of Tyre, *History of Deeds Done beyond the Sea*, II, Bk 18, ch. 2, p. 238; *Willelmi Tyrensis Chronicon*, Bk 18, ch. 2, p. 811.

[13] 'Hugo Falcandus', *History of the Tyrants of Sicily*, p. 65; *Liber de Regno Sicilie*, p. 13; *Annales Casinenses*, anno 1155, p. 311; Bernardo Maragone, *Annales Pisani*, p. 15; Otto of Freising, *Deeds of Frederick Barbarossa*, Bk II, ch. 49, p. 166; *Gesta Frederici*, Bk II, ch. XLIX, p. 157.

[14] 'Hugo Falcandus', *History of the Tyrants of Sicily*, pp. 71–2; *Liber de Regno Sicilie*, pp. 18–20; Romuald of Salerno, *Romualdi Salernitani Chronicon*, p. 238.

[15] *Annales Casinenses*, anno 1155, p. 311; Bernardo Maragone, *Annales Pisani*, p. 15; *Chronica de Ferraria*, anno 1154, p. 29; 'Hugo Falcandus', *History of the Tyrants of Sicily*, p. 66; *Liber de Regno Sicilie*, p. 14; Otto of Freising, *Deeds of Frederick Barbarossa*, Bk II, ch. 37, pp. 154–5; *Gesta Frederici*, Bk II, ch. XXXVII, p. 145; Romuald of Salerno, *Romualdi Salernitani Chronicon*, p. 239; William of Tyre, *History of Deeds Done beyond the Sea*, II, Bk 18, ch. 7, p. 247; *Willelmi Tyrensis Chronicon*, Bk 18, ch. 7, p. 819.

[16] *Annales Casinenses*, anno 1155, p. 311. 'Robert de Sorrento cepit omnem principatum Capuae usque Neapolim et Salernum.'

[17] William of Tyre, *History of Deeds Done beyond the Sea*, II, Bk 18, ch. 2, p. 237; *Willelmi Tyrensis Chronicon*, Bk 18, ch. 2, pp. 810–11.

[18] Niketas Choniates, *O City of Byzantium!*, p. 53; John Kinnamos, *John and Manuel Comnenus*, Bk IV, ch. 2–4, pp. 107–10; Otto of Freising, *Deeds of Frederick Barbarossa*, Bk II, ch. 49, pp. 165–6; *Gesta Frederici*, Bk II, ch. XLIX, pp. 156–7; Romuald of Salerno, *Romualdi Salernitani Chronicon*, p. 239.

[19] John Kinnamos, *John and Manuel Comnenus*, Bk IV, ch. 4–7, pp. 113–18.

of Tyre attests that Taranto was also captured at this time.[20] Monopoli resisted vigorously, but, with the help of the Greek fleet, it too was compelled to surrender.[21] In the meantime, however, Palaiologos passed away of fever in Bari, leaving John Doukas in command of the Greek forces.[22] Nonetheless, by 14 April 1156 Doukas was able to stand before the walls of Brindisi and write to the emperor that, thus far, the expedition had been successful. John Kinnamos ascribes the following words to him: 'Know that until this day everything has proceeded according to our intent, as we have overcome almost all the cities which exist in Italy [Apulia] and on the Ionian Gulf [Adriatic Sea], and have been victorious in great battles in a fashion worthy of your empire and of the Romans' race.'[23] Only Brindisi remained unconquered on the Adriatic coast. Unfortunately, the effort to take it would be their undoing.

John Doukas knew what was coming even as he wrote his victory missive to the emperor, for, in that same message, he pleaded for reinforcements. The King of Sicily was on his way.[24] Like his father, some twenty years prior, William had recovered from his life-threatening malady. He immediately laid siege to Butera, eventually gaining the submission of the rebels through negotiation.[25] He then quickly assembled a large force from 'all parts of Sicily and Calabria' and marched directly for Brindisi.[26] John Kinnamos attests that he also launched 'a fleet of numerous ships'.[27] Doukas, fearing he would be caught between the hammer that was William and the walls of Brindisi, made a frantic effort to seize the city. A frightened citizenry opened the gates to the coalition forces, but the Norman garrison still held the citadel and remained firm. William's fleet arrived ahead of his land forces and immediately pressed the attack. This was ill-advised. The physical layout of the port of Brindisi is in the shape of an inverted 'Y' with a constricted entranceway (about 100 meters wide) at the base of the stem. Thus, the Sicilian ships were forced to assemble in groups of ten and navigate through the narrow opening in single file. This enabled Doukas to place his soldiers and projectile-launching machines along the shoreline of the harbor while his 14 ships contested each Sicilian vessel as it entered the inner harbor. As a result, the Sicilians took a beating, losing four of their ships and over 2,000 fighters.[28] It was only a brief respite, however, and Doukas knew it. His situation was

[20] William of Tyre, *History of Deeds Done beyond the Sea*, II, Bk 18, ch. 7, p. 247; *Willelmi Tyrensis Chronicon*, Bk 18, ch. 7, p. 819.
[21] John Kinnamos, *John and Manuel Comnenus*, Bk IV, ch. 9, p. 119.
[22] John Kinnamos, *John and Manuel Comnenus*, Bk IV, ch. 7, p. 117; Otto of Freising, *Deeds of Frederick Barbarossa*, Bk II, ch. 49, p. 165; *Gesta Frederici*, Bk II, ch. XLIX, p. 157.
[23] John Kinnamos, *John and Manuel Comnenus*, Bk IV, ch. 10, pp. 122–3.
[24] John Kinnamos, *John and Manuel Comnenus*, Bk IV, ch. 10, p. 122.
[25] 'Hugo Falcandus', *History of the Tyrants of Sicily*, pp. 71–2; *Liber de Regno Sicilie*, pp. 14–20.
[26] William of Tyre, *History of Deeds Done beyond the Sea*, II, Bk 18, ch. 8, p. 250; *Willelmi Tyrensis Chronicon*, Bk 18, ch. 8, p. 821. '… ex universa Sicilia et Calabria…'
[27] John Kinnamos, *John and Manuel Comnenus*, Bk IV, ch. 10, p. 122.
[28] John Kinnamos, *John and Manuel Comnenus*, Bk IV, ch. 10–11, pp. 123–5.

desperate. The Greeks and the Norman rebels allied with them had to breach the fortifications of the citadel before William arrived with his army.

They constructed a 'tortoise', probably of wood and hides, and maneuvered it against the outer curtain wall of the fortress. Using it to shield themselves from projectiles launched from the battlements above, they burrowed beneath the base of the wall until they had created a hollow, which they filled with timbers. These they set on fire, eventually weakening the masonry to the point of collapse. The defenders, however, simply retreated to the inner bastion and the siege went on. Robert of Bassonville was one of the first to recognize how dire the situation had become and unilaterally abandoned the effort. He fled north to the Abruzzi (the region north of Apulia and east of Rome). A group of mercenaries from the march of Ancona then demanded double pay. They departed the moment they were refused.[29] Not long afterwards, a cadre of rebel Norman knights defected to William's side.[30] John Doukas's only hope was that help from the emperor would reach Brindisi before the bulk of the Norman army.

Manuel had, in fact, heeded the call. He had appointed Alexios Bryennios, son of Anna Comnena and Nikephoros Bryennios, as *megas doux* ('grand duke' or 'high admiral') of a Byzantine relief fleet.[31] Unfortunately, the rash young noble departed for Apulia without having recruited sufficient forces to counter those of the approaching Norman army. Once he had arrived at Brindisi, Doukas realized that the Greeks and their allies remained hopelessly outnumbered. Retreating to Bari, a much more defensible position, was discussed and rejected in favor of one more last-ditch assault on the citadel. This one, however, was no more successful than the others. The Greeks apparently attempted to use the outer fortifications to launch the attack, but these had been so heavily damaged by sapping and constant bombardment that they collapsed, killing many of the attackers.[32] By the time this last ill-fated effort had played itself out, William was upon them. On 28 May 1156, William's army enveloped the Greek land contingent arrayed around the harbor while the Sicilian fleet, which had been anchored at the Pedagne Islets barely a mile and half from the entrance, moved to block the escape of the Byzantine fleet. William's forces crushed the remnants of the coalition like a closing fist (see Map 10). Both Byzantine commanders were captured along with all of the Greek vessels, which the *Annales Pisani* says numbered about 30 ships.[33]

[29] John Kinnamos, *John and Manuel Comnenus*, Bk IV, ch. 11–12, pp. 126–7.

[30] John Kinnamos, *John and Manuel Comnenus*, Bk IV, ch. 13, p. 128.

[31] Niketas Choniates, *O City of Byzantium!*, p. 55; John Kinnamos, *John and Manuel Comnenus*, Bk IV, ch. 12, p. 126.

[32] John Kinnamos, *John and Manuel Comnenus*, Bk IV, ch. 12, pp. 126–7.

[33] *Annales Casinenses*, anno 1156, p. 311; *Annales Ceccanenses*, anno 1156, p. 284; *Chronica de Ferraria*, anno 1156, p. 29; 'Hugo Falcandus', *History of the Tyrants of Sicily*, p. 73; *Liber de Regno Sicilie*, pp. 20–1; John Kinnamos, *John and Manuel Comnenus*, Bk IV, ch. 13, pp. 128–9; Bernardo Maragone, *Annales Pisani*, p. 15; Otto of Freising, *Deeds of Frederick Barbarossa*, Bk II, ch. 49, p. 166; *Gesta Frederici*, Bk II, ch. XLIX, p. 157; Romuald of Salerno, *Romualdi*

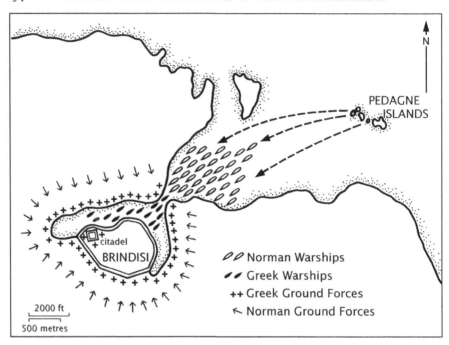

10. Battle of Brindisi in 1156. (Credit: C. Stanton with P. Judge)

William's victory was total. He had his prisoners 'bound together in fetters and irons like hens' and packed off to Sicily,[34] while he took his vengeance out on Bari.[35] The inhabitants had demolished the royal citadel, hence William, whom later writers would call 'the Bad', so thoroughly obliterated the city that four years afterwards Jewish traveler Benjamin of Tudela would write, 'Neither Jews nor Gentiles live there at the present day in consequence of its destruction.'[36] Robert of Capua was betrayed by one of his own vassals while attempting to cross the River Garigliano into the Abruzzi, then was turned over to William who had him blinded and imprisoned in Sicily.[37] As for Pope Hadrian IV, boxed into a

Salernitani Chronicon, pp. 239–40; William of Tyre, History of Deeds Done beyond the Sea, II, Bk 18, ch. 8, p. 250; Willelmi Tyrensis Chronicon, Bk 18, ch. 8, p. 821.

[34] Guillelmi I. Regis Diplomata, no. 13, pp. 36–7. '... quas gallinas compendibus et ferreis nessibus ...'

[35] Annales Casinenses, anno 1156, p. 311; Annales Ceccanenses, anno 1156, p. 284; Chronica de Ferraria, anno 1156, p. 29; 'Hugo Falcandus', History of the Tyrants of Sicily, pp. 73–4; Liber de Regno Sicilie, pp. 21–2; Romuald of Salerno, Romualdi Salernitani Chronicon, p. 240.

[36] Benjamin of Tudela, The Itinerary of Bejamin of Tudela, trans. M. Adler (London, 1907), p. 9.

[37] Annales Casinenses, anno 1156, p. 311; Annales Ceccanenses, anno 1156, p. 284; Chronica de Ferraria, anno 1156, p. 29; 'Hugo Falcandus', History of the Tyrants of Sicily, pp. 74–5; Liber de Regno Sicilie, p. 22; Romuald of Salerno, Romualdi Salernitani Chronicon, p. 240; William of Tyre, History of Deeds Done beyond the Sea, II, Bk 18, ch. 8, pp. 250–1; Willelmi Tyrensis Chronicon, Bk 18, ch. 8, pp. 821–2.

corner at Benevento and bereft of his erstwhile allies, he was compelled, like his predecessors, to invest another Hauteville 'with the kingdom of Sicily with one banner, with the duchy of Apulia with another and with the principality of Capua with a third'.[38] These events all served to elevate William's standing in the region, a fact recognized by Genoa, which dispatched Ansaldo Auria and Guglielmo Vento in November 1156 to negotiate a new treaty with the court of Palermo, which David Abulafia says recognized 'King William's authority in the *Regno* in exchange for commercial rights'.[39]

But William's thirst for revenge was yet to be sated. In 1157 he dispatched a large fleet under Stephen, brother of Maio of Bari, to inflict his wrath upon Byzantium itself.[40] According to Maragone, there were 140 *galeae* along with 24 transport *dromōns*, carrying 400 knights. By chance, Stephen encountered 'a very great fleet of the Emperor Manuel' ('*maximum stolium Emmanuelis imperatoris*') in the narrow Euripos Strait between Boeotia and the island of Euboea, and engaged it on land and sea. He defeated it, capturing many Greeks and burning their ships. Afterwards, the Sicilian fleet sacked Negroponte (modern Khalkis). It then proceeded north to the Gulf of Pagasitikos and attacked a Pisan colony at Almira (near present-day Volos, Thessaly), burning a tower there.[41] Niketas Choniates narrates that the Sicilian armada pressed on to penetrate the Helles-pont (Dardanelles) all the way to Constantinople, where it paraded before the walls to proclaim William 'lord and emperor of Sicily, Apulia, Capua, and Calabria, and all the provinces and islands between them'. For good measure, the Sicilian admiral was then said to have had his crews fire silver-shafted arrows at the Blachernai Palace before departing.[42]

Chalandon wonders if Choniates might have actually been referring to the 1149 raid of the Byzantine capital directed by Roger II,[43] but this bit of bravado seems in character for the unimaginative William who may well have simply copied his father's example. Besides, Choniates specifically names Maio as commander of the Sicilian fleet, probably mistaking Stephen for his brother.[44] If he had been referring to the 1149 episode, he would likely have identified George of Antioch as the fleet's admiral or no one at all. Moreover, the plunder of Almira, just north of the Euripos Strait, indicates that Constantinople was

---

[38] *Annales Casinenses*, anno 1156, p. 311; Deér, *Das Papsttum*, pp. 92–3; Romuald of Salerno, *Romualdi Salernitani Chronicon*, pp. 240–1. '… *papa ipsum per unum uexillum de regno Sicilie, per aliud de ducatu Apulie, per tercium de principatu Capue inuestiuit*.'
[39] *Codice Diplomatico della Repubblica di Genova*, ed. C. Imperiale di Sant'Angelo (FSI, 3 vols, Rome, 1936), I, no. 280, pp. 341–2. See also Abulafia, *Two Italies*, pp. 90–1.
[40] Romuald of Salerno, *Romualdi Salernitani Chronicon*, p. 241.
[41] Bernardo Maragone, *Annales Pisani*, p. 17.
[42] Niketas Choniates, *O City of Byzantium!*, p. 57. The Blachernai Palace was the preferred residence of the Komnenian emperors and was located in a quarter by the same name in the northwest of the city.
[43] Chalandon, *Histoire de la Domination Normande*, II, p. 248.
[44] Niketas Choniates, *O City of Byzantium!*, p. 57.

logically the fleet's ultimate destination. No matter, the foray apparently had its desired effect. Manuel agreed to a thirty-year peace pact with his reviled Sicilian rival the very next year.[45] Not surprisingly, the Greek chroniclers contend that it was the Sicilians who had initiated the negotiations. Both Kinnamos and Choniates purport that William's envoys petitioned for peace by promising to return all the booty garnered during the 1147 raid in the Gulf of Corinth as well as the Greek commanders captured at Brindisi in 1156.[46] The primary Latin source, Romuald of Salerno, of course, tells a different story: 'Learning that many of his men had been captured by the King of Sicily and that he could not fight them on equal terms, the emperor sent a series of envoys and came to an agreement with the king, and so a treaty of peace was sworn between them.'[47] In this case, Romuald's report appears to be more accurate. Ferdinand Chalandon explains why: 'It is, moreover, probable that the successive failures, of which we have spoken, had considerably diminished the Byzantine fleet, which had lost a great number of ships.'[48] Simply said, the Byzantines no longer possessed the naval power necessary to challenge the Norman fleet.

It was a success William would not be able to savor long. Even as he was dealing with the Byzantine threat, he was already in the process of losing his royal holdings in North Africa. A revolt of his Muslim subjects was kindled in Sfax where, as it turns out, William's father had unwittingly provided the spark almost a decade before. In the aftermath of the city's conquest in 1148, Roger had taken the sheik Abu l-Hasan al-Furrayani as a hostage to guarantee the loyal rule of his son, Umar ibn Abi l-Hasan al-Furrayani, who served as Roger's *amil*. When Abu'l-Hasan observed the dissension of the nobles on Sicily and the distraction caused by the Greeks and rebels in Apulia at the beginning of William's reign, he wrote to his son from Palermo advising him that the time was ripe for a revolt, regardless of the fact it would mean his own death. On 25 February 1156, Umar acted upon his father's advice. That night, at a prearranged hour, the citizens revolted and slaughtered the Christians living there. William's knee-jerk response was to execute Abu l-Hasan. It only exacerbated matters. The old sheik was considered a martyr.[49] Norman control of North Africa came crashing down.

Ibn al-Athir records that the islands of Jerba and Kerkenna soon shrugged off the Sicilian yoke as well.[50] In Tripoli, at-Tijani says William's royal representa-

[45] *Annales Casinenses*, anno 1158, p. 311.

[46] Niketas Choniates, *O City of Byzantium!*, pp. 56–7; John Kinnamos, *John and Manuel Comnenus*, Bk IV, ch. 15, p. 134.

[47] Romuald of Salerno, *Romualdi Salernitani Chronicon*, p. 241. '*Imperator autem cognoscens multos de suis a rege Sicilie captos, nec posse cum eo de pari contendere, missis frequentibus nuntiis, cum rege concordatus est, et pacis federa sunt hinc inde iurata.*' [English translation in *History of the Tyrants of Sicily*, Loud and Weidemann.]

[48] Chalandon, *Histoire de la Domination Normande*, II, p. 248.

[49] Ibn al-Athir, *BAS*, I, pp. 480–1; *Chronicle of Ibn al-Athir*, *Part 2*, pp. 76–7; Ibn Khaldun, *BAS*, II, pp. 229–30; At-Tijani, *BAS*, II, pp. 50–1.

[50] Ibn al-Athir, *BAS*, I, p. 481; *Chronicle of Ibn al-Athir*, *Part 2*, p. 76.

tives hastened their own downfall by insisting that the Banu Matruh speak ill of the encroaching Almohads from the pulpit. This was enough to prompt the Arab *amil*, Abu Muhammad ibn Matruh, to follow Umar's lead and foment an uprising in his own city. He encouraged his people to erect barricades in the streets overnight so that when the alarmed Norman cavalry burst forth from their fortifications in the morning, they were quickly halted and overwhelmed.[51] Muhammad ibn Rushayd ibn Kamil similarly roused the citizenry of Gabes.[52] And, at the same time, the Almohads under Abd al-Mu'min took Bona.[53]

Soon, only Susa, Mahdiyah and the adjacent town of Zawilah remained to the Normans. Elated by what he had started, Umar encouraged the inhabitants of Zawilah to follow Sfax's lead. They did so, with the help of the neighboring Arab tribes and the men of Sfax. After assuming control of the town, they joined forces to put Mahdiyah itself under siege. On this occasion, however, William swiftly responded with a relief flotilla of 20 ships. Reinforced with additional men and supplies, the Norman garrison bribed the Bedouin tribesmen among the besiegers to abandon the siege. When they complied, the Normans knights immediately capitalized. They sortied out of Mahdiyah and caught the rebels by surprise on the exposed isthmus between the two towns. Many of the men of Sfax fled by ship while most of those of Zawilah were slain. Zawilah was subsequently retaken.[54] William had purchased himself a short reprieve.

That reprieve was brought to a brutal end in 1159 by Abd al-Mu'min, the Almohad lord of the western Maghrib. Ibn Khaldun relates how the survivors of the slaughter at Zawilah in 1157 made their way to the Almohad caliph's court in Marrakech to bemoan the savagery that they had suffered at the hands of the 'Frank' and 'to implore his help'.[55] They found a receptive audience. Ibn al-Athir tells of the prodigious preparations undertaken by Abd al-Mu'min: 'He wrote to all his lieutenants in the West – and he ruled nearly up to Tunis – ordering them to keep all the grain that was harvested, to leave it in the ear and store it in special places, and also to dig wells along the route.' His governors responded by gathering three years' worth of harvests. 'They transferred it to depots, which they sealed with clay and which became like hills.'[56] The gargantuan effort was necessary. In early spring of 1159, Ibn al-Athir insists Abd al-Mu'min marched out of Marrakech at the head of an army of 100,000, not including the various sorts of camp-followers. Although this is clearly an exaggeration, the number was

[51] At-Tijani, *BAS*, II, p. 61.
[52] Ibn al-Athir, *BAS*, I, p. 482; *Chronicle of Ibn al-Athir, Part 2*, pp. 76–7; Ibn Khaldun, *BAS*, II, p. 230.
[53] Ibn al-Athir, *BAS*, I, p. 481; *Chronicle of Ibn al-Athir, Part 2*, p. 76; Ibn Khaldun, *BAS*, II, p. 230.
[54] Ibn al-Athir, *BAS*, I, p. 482; *Chronicle of Ibn al-Athir, Part 2*, pp. 76–7; Ibn Khaldun, *BAS*, II, pp. 230–1.
[55] Ibn Khaldun, *BAS*, II, p. 231.
[56] Ibn al-Athir, *BAS*, I, p. 485; *Chronicle of Ibn al-Athir, Part 2*, p. 103.

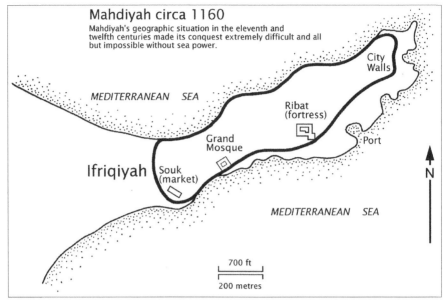

11. Mahdiyah circa 1160. (Credit: C. Stanton with P. Judge)

certainly substantial.[57] He reached the city of Tunis on 13 July and laid siege to it with the help of a fleet of 70 ships, which included galleys, *taride* and *shalandi*. The city quickly capitulated. Shadowed by his fleet, Abd al-Mu'min then moved on to his ultimate objective: Mahdiyah. He arrived on 5 August. The Almohad forces found Zawilah evacuated, so they immediately made it their headquarters, completely repopulating the town in a day.[58]

The Norman garrison at Mahdiyah was reported to have numbered 3,000 knights (probably an inflated figure at that), but a quick boat tour of the sea wall by the Almohad leader convinced him that it might as well have been ten times that number.[59] The city was surrounded on three sides by water and attached to the mainland by an isthmus, not 300 meters wide. 'It was like a hand in the sea with its wrist connected to the mainland,' describes Ibn al-Athir (see Map 11).[60] Abd al-Mu'min knew that his only recourse was to starve them out. As a consequence, morale among the defenders was high at first. They subjected the besiegers to frequent sorties, wreaking havoc upon them. Ibn al-Athir says the outskirts of Zawilah were a mere 'bow shot distant' from the west gate of Mahdiyah, so it would have been relatively easy to surprise the unwary. Abd al-Mu'min finally had to compel his men to build a protective revetment on the

57 Ibn al-Athir, *BAS*, I, p. 485; *Chronicle of Ibn al-Athir, Part 2*, p. 103.
58 Ibn al-Athir, *BAS*, I, pp. 485–7; *Chronicle of Ibn al-Athir, Part 2*, pp. 103–4; Ibn Khaldun, *BAS*, II, pp. 231–2.
59 Chalandon, *Histoire de la Domination Normande*, II, p. 239.
60 Ibn al-Athir, *BAS*, I, p. 487; *Chronicle of Ibn al-Athir, Part 2*, p. 104.

isthmus in order to prevent the attacks.[61] Relieved with sufficient provisions, the Normans could have held out indefinitely.

That relief appeared on the horizon on 8 September in the form of a fleet of 150 galleys, according to the Muslim chroniclers.[62] 'Hugo Falcandus' gives the figure 160.[63] In any case, the Almohad armada, on the surface, appeared to be no match for it. The Sicilian fleet, however, had just been recalled from a raiding expedition in the Balearic Islands, probably burdened with plunder and prisoners from Ibiza.[64] In addition to lumbering low in the water, the ships may have been short on water supplies, the crews fatigued. Whatever the cause, the Norman fleet was defeated. 'Hugo Falcandus' would have us believe that its admiral, Peter the Caid, turned stern and fled as a part of some conspiracy cooked up by Maio of Bari to embarrass the king,[65] but the Muslim chroniclers tell a far different tale. At-Tijani speaks of a sudden storm that scattered the Sicilian ships just as they were lowering their sails to enter the harbor. The Almohad admiral, the renowned Abu Abd Allah ibn Maymun, saw his opportunity and seized it. He launched his fleet into their midst and managed to cull out those Sicilian ships separated from the main body of the Norman armada.[66] As a result, he was able to capture seven or eight of their galleys.[67] This seems quite plausible when one considers that the southern Mediterranean is prone to strong southeasterly sirocco winds in the spring and summer. If this was the case, the wind was probably blowing onto the bows of the Sicilian vessels, holding them offshore, while the Muslim ships had the same wind at their sterns, that is, they had the wind advantage. In any event, Peter the Caid, given the circumstances, probably had little choice but to return home.

The discouraged garrison held out for an additional four months hoping for another relief fleet, during which Abd al-Mu'min added Sfax, Gabes and Tripoli to his dominion.[68] Meanwhile, the court of Palermo had decided to abandon Mahdiyah. Both 'Hugo Falcandus' and the Chronica de Ferraria indicate that Maio of Bari deliberately deceived William on how dire the situation had become in the belief that holding the city was not worth additional relief

[61] Ibn al-Athir, BAS, I, pp. 487–8; Chronicle of Ibn al-Athir, Part 2, p. 104; At-Tijani, BAS, II, p. 79.

[62] Ibn al-Athir, BAS, I, p. 489; Chronicle of Ibn al-Athir, Part 2, p. 105; Ibn Khaldun, BAS, II, p. 233; At-Tijani, BAS, II, p. 80.

[63] 'Hugo Falcandus', History of the Tyrants of Sicily, p. 78; Liber de Regno Sicilie, p. 25.

[64] Ibn al-Athir, BAS, I, p. 489; Chronicle of Ibn al-Athir, Part 2, p. 105; 'Hugo Falcandus', History of the Tyrants of Sicily, p. 78; Liber de Regno Sicilie, p. 25; Ibn Khaldun, BAS, II, p. 233; Romuald of Salerno, Romualdi Salernitani Chronicon, p. 242.

[65] 'Hugo Falcandus', History of the Tyrants of Sicily, pp. 79–80; Liber de Regno Sicilie, pp. 26–7.

[66] At-Tijani, BAS, II, p. 80.

[67] Ibn al-Athir, BAS, I, p. 489; Chronicle of Ibn al-Athir, Part 2, p. 105; 'Hugo Falcandus', History of the Tyrants of Sicily, p. 79; Liber de Regno Sicilie, p. 26; At-Tijani, BAS, II, p. 80.

[68] Ibn al-Athir, BAS, I, p. 488; Chronicle of Ibn al-Athir, Part 2, p. 105; Ibn Khaldun, BAS, II, p. 233.

efforts.[69] Finally, it became apparent to the defenders that no help from Palermo would be forthcoming.[70] Ibn al-Athir reports, 'Their provisions were exhausted so that they had eaten their horses.'[71] The garrison yielded in return for their lives and passage back to Sicily.[72] Abd al-Mu'min entered Mahdiyah on the morning of 21 January 1160. He installed one of his own tribesmen in the city as *amil*, but he also left there none other than al-Hasan ibn Ali ibn Yahya, whom George of Antioch had forced out twelve years previously.[73] Now al-Hasan was back to witness the ouster of the Normans from North Africa. The Kingdom of Sicily had lost control of the south shore of the central Mediterranean only a dozen years after seizing it. Norman dominance of the Sicilian Channel was over. The decline had begun.

Even if William did not realize it, the loss of the African possessions was a devastating blow, economically and militarily, to the maritime empire that his father had built. Nevertheless, he can be forgiven to a certain extent. There were mitigating circumstances. William was dealing with numerous and varied distractions at the time. His low-born first minister was wildly unpopular among his still restive Norman nobility.[74] His court seethed with intrigues. A faction led by Matthew Bonnellus, the lord of Caccamo and Prizzi, ultimately engineered Maio's assassination in November 1160 and, later, even had the king imprisoned in his own palace.[75] William was freed by a popular uprising and Matthew Bonnellus was eventually arrested, but revolts later flared on both Sicily and the mainland.[76] Roger Sclavus, the illegitimate son of Count Simon of Policastro, and one of Matthew Bonnellus's former associates, incited some North Italians (probably followers of the Aleramici family of Liguria) to occupy Butera and Piazza Armerina, while in February 1161 Robert of Loritello was once again stirring up trouble in Apulia. William reacted swiftly, demolishing Piazza Armerina and besieging Butera. After gaining Butera's capitulation, he flattened it as well and forced Roger Sclavus into exile. Once Sicily was pacified, William transited the strait with a large army and marched on Taverna, causing it to suffer the

---

[69] *Chronica de Ferraria*, anno 1158–9, p. 29; 'Hugo Falcandus', *History of the Tyrants of Sicily*, p. 80; *Liber de Regno Sicilie*, p. 27.

[70] 'Hugo Falcandus', *History of the Tyrants of Sicily*, p. 80; *Liber de Regno Sicilie*, pp. 27–8; Romuald of Salerno, *Romualdi Salernitani Chronicon*, p. 242.

[71] Ibn al-Athir, *BAS*, I, p. 490; *Chronicle of Ibn al-Athir, Part 2*, p. 106.

[72] Ibn al-Athir, *BAS*, I, p. 490; *Chronicle of Ibn al-Athir, Part 2*, p. 106; 'Hugo Falcandus', *History of the Tyrants of Sicily*, pp. 80–1; *Liber de Regno Sicilie*, pp. 27–8; Ibn Khaldun, *BAS*, II, p. 233; Romuald of Salerno, *Romualdi Salernitani Chronicon*, p. 242; At-Tijani, *BAS*, II, p. 81.

[73] *Annales Casinenses*, anno 1160, p. 311; Ibn al-Athir, *BAS*, I, pp. 490–1; *Chronicle of Ibn al-Athir, Part 2*, p. 106; Ibn Khaldun, *BAS*, II, pp. 233–4.

[74] Romuald of Salerno, *Romualdi Salernitani Chronicon*, p. 245.

[75] *Chronica de Ferraria*, anno 1158–9, p. 29; 'Hugo Falcandus', *History of the Tyrants of Sicily*, pp. 95–110; *Liber de Regno Sicilie*, pp. 41–57; Romuald of Salerno, *Romualdi Salernitani Chronicon*, pp. 245–6.

[76] 'Hugo Falcandus', *History of the Tyrants of Sicily*, pp. 122–3; *Liber de Regno Sicilie*, pp. 71–2; Romuald of Salerno, *Romualdi Salernitani Chronicon*, p. 248.

same fate as Butera. As he approached Taranto, Robert of Loritello again chose discretion over valor and retreated to the Abruzzi.[77] Romuald of Salerno reports that the king completed his campaign by expelling Count Richard of Aquila and having his fortress on Monte Arcano (believed to have been on the coast of the Principality of Capua) seized by his 'galliots' (light galleys).[78] The *Annales Ceccanenses* places these events in March 1162.[79]

No sooner had the king suppressed this latest insurrection than ominous clouds began to appear on the northern horizon. From the beginning, Frederick Barbarossa had harbored the same imperial designs on the Hauteville domains as his predecessors, and William had done little to assuage that animus. In 1159, following the death of Pope Hadrian IV, William had been one of the first monarchs of Europe to recognize Alexander III as the true pope in opposition to Victor IV, who was championed by the German imperial court.[80] The Sicilian king had subsequently campaigned for Frederick's ensuing excommunication in 1160.[81] Then, as if to salt the wound, William had sent four of his ships to help Pope Alexander evade the clutches of the imperial party by escorting him from Terracina in January 1162 to Genoa from where he eventually reached the safety of Provence.[82] The only thing which had prevented Barbarossa from acting sooner against Sicily was his long war with Milan. So, when the recalcitrant Lombard commune finally fell in March 1162, Frederick was ready to redirect his attentions further south.[83] At the very moment William was subduing rebels in Apulia and Campania, the German emperor was brokering a treaty with Pisa, offering huge pieces of the Kingdom of Sicily in return for the sea power needed to conquer it. The resulting 6 April 1162 privilege from Frederick promised the Tuscan city-state the right to conduct commerce in Sicily, Apulia, Calabria and in the Principality of Capua exempt from all duties while granting them, in fief, half of Palermo, Messina, Salerno and Naples; all of Gaeta, Mazara and Trapani along with a street in every other city of the *Regno*, plus one-third of William's treasury. Moreover, he granted the Pisans the entire Tyrrhenian littoral from Portovenere to Civitavecchia with the right to exclude rival merchants of their

---

[77] *Annales Casinenses*, anno 1160–2, p. 311; *Annales Ceccanenses*, anno 1161–2, p. 285; 'Hugo Falcandus', *History of the Tyrants of Sicily*, pp. 121–8; *Liber de Regno Sicilie*, pp. 70–7; Romuald of Salerno, *Romualdi Salernitani Chronicon*, pp. 248–51.

[78] Romuald of Salerno, *Romualdi Salernitani Chronicon*, p. 251.

[79] *Annales Ceccanenses*, anno 1162, p. 285.

[80] Romuald of Salerno, *Romualdi Salernitani Chronicon*, pp. 243–4.

[81] Otto of Freising, *Deeds of Frederick Barbarossa*, Bk IV, ch. 62, pp. 294–5; *Gesta Frederici*, Bk IV, ch. LXII, p. 304.

[82] *Liber Pontificalis*, II, *Vita Alexandri III*, p. 404; Romuald of Salerno, *Romualdi Salernitani Chronicon*, p. 249.

[83] *Annales Casinenses*, anno 1162, p. 312; *Annales Cavenses*, anno 1163, p. 192; *Annales Ceccanenses*, anno 1162, p. 285; Otto of Freising, *Deeds of Frederick Barbarossa*, Appendix, p. 335; *Gesta Frederici*, Appendix, p. 347.

choosing.[84] It was a sweeping concession, conceived to ensure their enthusiastic involvement in the invasion of William's realm.

A clause that obligated the emperor to lend support to Pisa in the case of hostilities with Genoa may well have spurred Pisa's Ligurian competitors to seek a similar deal with Frederick out of self-defense. Not long afterwards, Genoese ambassadors entered into a dialogue with the German court at Pavia. They came away with a generous privilege of their own, although not as lucrative as the one granted to Pisa. Frederick guaranteed the Genoese all of Syracuse, in fief, along with 250 'knights' fees' of land ('*ducentas quinquaginta caballarias*') in the Val de Noto as well as a *fondaco* (warehouse/market quarter) in each of the *Regno*'s maritime cities and a quarter of William's treasury. In addition, they were allowed a street with a church and a bakery in each port city. Like the Pisans, they were also to be exempt from imposts everywhere in the kingdom. As for the Tyrrhenian coast, it was to be theirs from Portovenere to Monaco and they could exclude whomever they wanted, including their Provençal rivals.[85] While it was far less than that promised to the Pisans, it was a dramatic improvement over the treaty secured from William in 1156, which was basically a non-aggression pact embellished with tax exemptions and trading concessions in the major ports of Sicily as well as the right to ban the merchants of Provence.[86] William had essentially been outbid for his own kingdom. David Abulafia feels, however, that Genoa may have been attempting 'to show William of Sicily that it did not aim at the conquest of his kingdom so much as at the security from conquest of Liguria; in other words, that the oath to Frederick I was lip-service'.[87] There are subtle signs that this was true. The *Annales Pisani* records the seizure in October 1162 of all Pisans found in William's domains along with their property and ships in retribution for the agreement with the German emperor.[88] No such reprisals were meted out to the Genoese.[89]

Nonetheless, William was in a perilous position. Barbarossa had intended to begin the campaign that summer and he clearly had the dedicated naval support he required for the invasion of Sicily. But an unforeseen event would postpone it indefinitely. A few days after the treaty of Pavia was signed on 9 June 1162, an altercation broke out between Genoese and Pisan merchants in Constantinople. The Pisans attacked the Genoese *fondaco* in force: blood was shed and property

---

[84] *Constitutiones et Acta Publica Imperatorem*, no. 205, pp. 282–7; *Friderici I. Diplomata* (1158–1167), ed. H. Appelt (MGH, DRIG, X, II, Hanover, 1979), no. 356, pp. 198–203. See also Abulafia, *Two Italies*, pp. 124–5.

[85] Caffaro, *Annales Ianuenses*, I, pp. 65–6; CDG, I, no. 308, pp. 395–404; *Constitutiones et Acta Publica Imperatorem*, no. 211, pp. 292–7; *Friderici I. Diplomata*, no. 367, pp. 220–5. See also Abulafia, *Two Italies*, pp. 127–9.

[86] Caffaro, *Annales Ianuenses*, I, pp. 46–7; CDG, I, no. 280, pp. 341–2. See also Abulafia, *Two Italies*, pp. 90–6.

[87] Abulafia, *Two Italies*, p. 131.

[88] Bernardo Maragone, *Annales Pisani*, p. 28.

[89] Manfroni, *Storia della Marina italiana*, I, p. 230.

destroyed. The Genoese were forced to flee for their lives. The resultant ill-will between the two West Italian maritime powers quickly escalated into a full-scale war.[90] The Norman Kingdom of Sicily had once again been granted a stay of execution, but the means of its destruction had been formulated. It was only a matter of time.

In summary, William had done a mediocre job of preserving Hauteville suzerainty over southern Italy and the central Mediterranean. He had quelled the various insurrections and kept the Byzantines at bay, but he had lost North Africa and had been unable to prevent the German emperor from recruiting two of the most powerful maritime republics of the era into an anti-Norman alliance. At its most fundamental level, he had abandoned his father's naval strategy for ensuring the strength and security of the Sicilian *Regno*, yet had adopted none of his own. As a result he lurched from crisis to crisis, reacting to events as they occurred. Furthermore, he lacked his father's foresight and shrewdness. He was, instead, a blunt instrument, imposing punishment without considering the damage done to his own designs. The total devastation of Bari over the ruin of the royal citadel by its citizens was a case in point. It was nothing more than a self-defeating temper tantrum that did not serve the crown. The elimination of Bari removed from the realm a major port city on the Adriatic along with all of its revenues for the royal fisc, not to mention its contribution in sailors and ships to the king's fleet. His father would probably have, instead, punished the leaders and compelled the townspeople to rebuild the citadel, just as he had done at Troia and at Melfi in 1130.[91] Worse yet, William had lost the focus on the central Mediterranean that had served his father and his father's father so well. He had begun to use the fleet for far-flung adventurism such as the 1154 attack on Egypt and, especially, the 1159 plunder of the Balearics at a time when the Almohads were marching upon Mahdiyah. He would have been far better off using his fleet to protect his North African assets. As it was, William was responsible for the loss of Norman naval supremacy in the central Mediterranean.[92]

Naval campaigns of William II

When William I died of dysentery and tertian fever in May 1166,[93] he bequeathed to his heir a monarchy weaker and poorer than the one he had inherited.

---

[90] Caffaro, *Annales Ianuenses*, I, pp. 67–71.

[91] Alexander of Telese, *Ystoria Rogerii regis Sicilie*, Bk I, ch. 24, p. 20.

[92] G. A. Loud, 'William the Bad or William the Unlucky? Kingship in Sicily 1154–1166', *Haskins Society Journal*, VIII (1996), pp. 99–113, provides an alternative view on William's performance.

[93] *Annales Casinenses*, anno 1166, p. 312; *Annales Cavenses*, anno 1165, p. 192; *Annales Ceccanenses*, anno 1166, p. 285; *Chronica de Ferraria*, anno 1166, p. 30; 'Hugo Falcandus', *History of the Tyrants of Sicily*, p. 137; *Liber de Regno Sicilie*, pp. 87–8; Romuald of Salerno, *Romualdi Salernitani Chronicon*, p. 253.

However, if 'William the Bad' was an appropriate sobriquet for the second sovereign of the Kingdom of Sicily, in terms of preserving its autonomy, then 'William the Worse' would have been suitable for his son. While William I had made the realm vulnerable to ruin, William II virtually assured it. As it was, he was known as 'William the Good', perhaps because later chroniclers, remembering the chaos that prevailed after his death, tended to look back upon his reign with nostalgia. The author of the *Chronica de Ferraria*, for instance, eulogized him in this manner: 'He was pious, just, peaceful, illustrious and kind; he held the kingdom of Sicily, Apulia and the Terra di Lavoro in peace.'[94] Nonetheless, his policies spelled the end of Hauteville rule.

Little actual harm was done initially. William II was only about thirteen when his father passed away, so rule of the realm fell to his mother, Queen Margaret, who acted as regent.[95] Margaret's concerns were those of survival for the young king. 'Hugo Falcandus' praises her for acting quickly to forestall any internal attempts to seize the throne: 'So the queen, in order to make both the people and the nobles grateful towards her and her son, decided to win their support by countless good deeds, and to extract their loyalty, if possible, by granting them enormous favors.'[96] She then attempted to centralize administrative power under a master chamberlain and a handful of *familiares regis*. She honored her husband's deathbed wish and invested Peter the Caid with overall administrative authority,[97] but when palace intrigues forced the latter into exile, she appointed a relative, Stephen of Perche, as chancellor.[98] He, too, fell victim to court conspiracy and was eventually ousted when one of his advisors, a certain Odo Quarrel, was suspected of siphoning off port fees from ships transiting through Messina.[99] As for external threats, Frederick Barbarossa took the opportunity presented by William I's death to invade Italy anew with the intention of absorbing the Kingdom of Sicily into his empire.[100] His allies, the Pisans, had even prepared for the purpose 'a great fleet of fifty galleys and thirty-five *sagittae*

---

94   *Chronica de Ferraria*, anno 1189, p. 31. '*Hic fuit pius, iustus, pacificus, pulcer et benignus; pacifice regnum Sicilie, Apulie et Terre Laboris tenuit.*' (The Terra di Lavoro means 'Land of Work' and refers to the royal province, which roughly corresponds to modern Lazio and northern Campania.)

95   'Hugo Falcandus', *History of the Tyrants of Sicily*, pp. 137–8; *Liber de Regno Sicilie*, pp. 88–9; Romuald of Salerno, *Romualdi Salernitani Chronicon*, pp. 253–4. ('Hugo Falcandus' says William II was fourteen at the time, while Romuald attests that he was twelve.)

96   'Hugo Falcandus', *History of the Tyrants of Sicily*, p. 139; *Liber de Regno Sicilie*, p. 90. '*Itaque regina, ut plebem ac proceres sibi filioque gratos efficeret, statuit eorum gratiam copia meritorum elicere, et fidem, si fieri posset, immensis saltem benificiis extorquere.*'

97   'Hugo Falcandus', *History of the Tyrants of Sicily*, pp. 137–9; *Liber de Regno Sicilie*, pp. 88–90.

98   'Hugo Falcandus', *History of the Tyrants of Sicily*, pp. 147, 161; *Liber de Regno Sicilie*, pp. 98–9, 110–11; Romuald of Salerno, *Romualdi Salernitani Chronicon*, pp. 254–5.

99   'Hugo Falcandus', *History of the Tyrants of Sicily*, pp. 200, 213–14; *Liber de Regno Sicilie*, pp. 147, 160–1; Romuald of Salerno, *Romualdi Salernitani Chronicon*, p. 257.

100   Romuald of Salerno, *Romualdi Salernitani Chronicon*, p. 255.

and many other ships and an ample multitude of men, arms and victuals'.[101] But luck remained with the Hautevilles. He reached as far as Rome before dysentery reduced his army and forced his retreat.[102] In the aftermath, the regency was even adept enough to enter into a beneficial pact with the Pisans. The consul Bulgarino Anfosso led a delegation to Sicily to negotiate a peace in November 1167, but went away empty-handed.[103] The Normans probably were not willing to concede much at that point, because they knew no imperial attack was imminent. They were more responsive two years later, however, when the consul Gerardo Cortovecchia led another embassy to Palermo and 'the King of Sicily received them with great honor and honorably established perpetual peace with them'.[104]

One of the most striking aspects of the regency was the lack of foreign adventures. The only one alleged to have occurred was Sicilian participation in the failed Christian siege of Damietta in 1169. Michele Amari cites as proof of Norman involvement a passage of Ibn al-Athir in which the Arab scholar tells how the Franks of Syria dispatched messengers 'to the Franks who were in Sicily, Andalusia and elsewhere, appealing for aid' in an assault on Damietta.[105] Ibn al-Athir does not actually indicate whether the Sicilians responded positively or not. For evidence of that, Amari points to this passage of the Egyptian historian al-Maqrizi: 'And they [the Franks of Syria] asked for the help of their brothers in Sicily; who aided them with money and arms, and sent a great number of their men equipped with *gatti* [leather canopy-covered battering rams, in this case] and mangonels'.[106] But al-Maqrizi was writing in the fifteenth century and may simply have assumed that Sicilian support had been forthcoming. Besides, he says nothing of any Sicilian ships. Chalandon counters the argument by referring to Abu Samah al-Muqaddasi, a thirteenth-century anthologist, who quotes a letter from Saladin to the caliph of Baghdad making it clear that the only Christian forces at Damietta in 1169 were those of Constantinople and the Latin Kingdom of Jerusalem.[107] The letter reveals that the king of Sicily only learned of the Christian campaign after the fact. Indeed, Saladin's letter contends that it was the desire to avenge the debacle at Damietta suffered by his eastern coreligionists that inspired William to assemble the massive naval force which he launched upon Alexandria in 1174.[108] Moreover, William of Tyre confirms that

[101] Bernardo Maragone, *Annales Pisani*, p. 43. '... *magnum stolum L galearum et XXXV sagittarium atque aliarum multarum navium, ac copiosam multitudinem virorum, armorum et victualium...*'
[102] Romuald of Salerno, *Romualdi Salernitani Chronicon*, pp. 255–6.
[103] Bernardo Maragone, *Annales Pisani*, p. 44.
[104] Bernardo Maragone, *Annales Pisani*, p. 49. '... *Rex Sicilie cum honore magno recepit, et pacem honorifice cum eis perpetuo firmavit.*'
[105] Amari, *Storia dei Musulmani di Sicilia*, III, p. 515; Ibn al-Athir, *BAS*, I, pp. 491–3; *Chronicle of Ibn al-Athir*, Part 2, p. 183.
[106] Al-Maqrizi, *BAS*, II, p. 593.
[107] Chalandon, *Histoire de la Domination Normande*, II, pp. 394–5.
[108] Abu Samah, *BAS*, I, p. 540.

envoys were, indeed, dispatched from the Holy Land to seek assistance from the Christian monarchs of the West, including William of Sicily, but he says, 'They accomplished little, however, in the matter which had been entrusted to them.'[109] Nor does William of Tyre mention a Sicilian presence in his lengthy account of the failed 50-day siege of Damietta.[110] The evidence appears unequivocal: it was only after William II reached his majority in 1171 that the Kingdom of Sicily began to embark upon the grand naval expeditions to the East that would eventually sap the strength of its sea power.

The last known royal document bearing the name of Queen Margaret as regent ('cum domina Margarita gloriosa regina matre sua' – 'with the glorious mistress Margaret our queen mother') is a diploma in favor of the church of Girgenti, dated March 1171.[111] All succeeding documents bear only William's name, styled 'rex Sicilie ducatus Apulie et principatus Capue' ('king of Sicily, duke of Apulia and prince of Capua').[112] Once William II ruled alone, the external policies of the Regno took a decided turn from defensive to offensive. It was not long before the young king began to project the realm's naval power eastward. His first major foreign policy decision was to dispatch against Egypt a maritime force so gargantuan that, if Abu Samah is credible, it took the Sicilian sovereign five years to amass it.[113] Ibn al-Athir describes it in some detail: 'The ruler of Sicily equipped a large fleet, numbering two hundred galleys carrying men, thirty-six transports carrying horses, six large ships carrying war materials and forty vessels with provisions. In the fleet were 50,000 infantry, 1,500 knights and 500 turcopoles.'[114] (What the Syrian scholar saw as 'turcopoles' were probably some of William's vaunted 'Saracen' archers.) Ibn al-Athir's estimate is roughly in line with the Latin sources. William of Tyre confirms 200 Sicilian ships,[115] while the Annales Pisani notes 150 galleys and 50 transport dromōns.[116] The objective was Alexandria. According to the Arab sources, disaffected Fatimid officials in Cairo, indignant over the elimination of the Fatimid caliphate by Saladin, conjured up a conspiracy against him. They invited King Amalric of Jerusalem and King William of Sicily to invade Egypt in order to draw Saladin

[109]   William of Tyre, History of Deeds Done beyond the Sea, II, Bk 20, ch. 12, pp. 360–1; Willelmi Tyrensis Chronicon, Bk 20, ch. 12, p. 926. '… parum tamen in negocio quod eis iniunctum fuerat proficientes.'
[110]   William of Tyre, History of Deeds Done beyond the Sea, II, Bk 20, ch. 15–16, pp. 363–8; Willelmi Tyrensis Chronicon, Bk 20, ch. 15–16, pp. 929–33.
[111]   P. Collura, ed., Le più antiche carte dell'archivio capitolare di Agrigento (1092–1282) (DSS, Ser. I. XXV, Palermo, 1960), no. 22, pp. 54–6; Kehr, Urkunden, no. 21, pp. 439–40.
[112]   Kehr, Urkunden, no. 22, p. 441. See also Chalandon, Histoire de la Domination Normande, II, p. 351.
[113]   Abu Samah, BAS, I, p. 540.
[114]   Ibn al-Athir, BAS, I, p. 496; Chronicle of Ibn al-Athir, Part 2, p. 229.
[115]   William of Tyre, History of Deeds Done beyond the Sea, II, Bk 21, ch. 3, p. 399; Willelmi Tyrensis Chronicon, Bk 21, ch. 3, p. 963.
[116]   Bernardo Maragone, Annales Pisani, p. 61.

out of Cairo so that they could foment a popular uprising that would sweep the Ayyubids (Saladin's Kurdish dynasty) from power.[117] Hence, the two Christians kings had apparently decided upon a coordinated assault on Alexandria. Two unforeseen events conspired against them to doom the enterprise. First, Saladin learned of the plot and had all the conspirators executed.[118] Second, Amalric succumbed to dysentery not three weeks before the arrival of the Sicilian armada at Alexandria.[119] Thus, when the Sicilians came ashore on 28 July 1174, they had neither the element of surprise nor the supporting ground forces from the Latin Kingdom that they were expecting.

A predictable fiasco ensued. The inhabitants of Alexandria, knowing that they simply needed to stall the Sicilians long enough for Saladin to arrive, blocked the port by scuttling a few vessels at the entrance.[120] They then let the invaders disembark and begin the siege of the city. The defenders were even confident enough to execute a daring sortie on the third night of the siege, slaughtering many of the attackers and burning most of their siege machines.[121] The successful sally also served to underline the poor quality of Sicilian leadership, which was caught by surprise even though the armed sally was a common siege-breaking technique routinely used everywhere at the time. Chalandon concludes that the overall commander was Tancred of Lecce,[122] based upon Ibn al-Athir's characterization of him as 'the cousin of the ruler of Sicily'.[123] Even when it was learned that Saladin's army was approaching by forced march, Tancred failed to take proper precautions or even fortify the camp.

Saladin's soldiers overran the Sicilians in their tents at night and literally drove them into the sea. Some survived by boarding their vessels; others drowned. A small group of 300 knights managed to hold out on a hilltop until daybreak, at which time they were finally overcome.[124] William of Tyre sums up the resulting shambles as follows: 'During the stay of five or six days made before the city, through the lack of caution displayed by the governors and leaders, both the infantry and cavalry forces sustained great losses by death and capture and were

---

[117] Ibn al-Athir, *BAS*, I, pp. 493–4; *Chronicle of Ibn al-Athir, Part 2*, pp. 218–19; Ibn Khaldun, *BAS*, II, pp. 234–5.

[118] Ibn al-Athir, *BAS*, I, p. 495; *Chronicle of Ibn al-Athir, Part 2*, pp. 219–20; Ibn Khaldun, *BAS*, II, p. 235.

[119] William of Tyre, *History of Deeds Done beyond the Sea*, II, Bk 20, ch. 31, p. 395; *Willelmi Tyrensis Chronicon*, Bk 20, ch. 31, pp. 956–7.

[120] Abu Samah, *BAS*, I, p. 538.

[121] Abu Samah, *BAS*, I, p. 538; Ibn al-Athir, *BAS*, I, p. 497; *Chronicle of Ibn al-Athir, Part 2*, p. 229; Ibn Khaldun, *BAS*, II, p. 236.

[122] Chalandon, *Histoire de la Domination Normande*, II, p. 496.

[123] Ibn al-Athir, *BAS*, I, p. 496; *Chronicle of Ibn al-Athir, Part 2*, p. 229.

[124] Abu Samah, *BAS*, I, pp. 538–9; Ibn al-Athir, *BAS*, I, p. 498; *Chronicle of Ibn al-Athir, Part 2*, p. 230; Ibn Khaldun, *BAS*, II, p. 236.

finally obliged to retire in confusion.'[125] Not surprisingly, Romuald of Salerno, a member of William's court, makes no mention of the disaster, and few of the south Italian chronicles note the episode at all. The *Annales Casinenses* says simply, 'The royal fleet went to Alexandria in the month of August [1174].'[126] The *Chronica de Ferraria* adds little, but, at least, alludes to the defeat: 'King William II sends his fleet to Alexandria, where many are retained by the Saracens.'[127]

Unchastened, William sent his fleet back the very next year. This time the target was Tinnis. Al-Maqrizi cryptically documents the arrival in 1175 of 40 Sicilian ships, which besieged the port for only two days before weighing anchor. He is more descriptive of a raid that occurred a couple of years later in 1177. On this occasion a Sicilian flotilla of 40 ships actually captured the city and, after a short but intense spate of fighting, prevented its rescue by the sailors of an Egyptian squadron evidently from Damietta. The Sicilians then made a brief raid on Alexandria, returning with 'a great abundance of plunder and prisoners.'[128] After remaining for only four days, they inexplicably departed.

Admittedly, William's naval policy did not entirely consist of offensive operations. There was some positive diplomatic activity, occasionally involving commerce. In September 1175, William issued the two privileges in favor of Venice mentioned above. They represented a treaty of alliance between the *Regno* and *La Serenissima* for a period of at least twenty years. It was essentially an anti-Byzantine pact that included trade concessions.[129] As previously described, the first document promised protection for Venetian vessels throughout the Kingdom of Sicily except those involved in piracy or in the service of the Byzantine Empire and guaranteed the territories of the Republic freedom from attack by Sicilian ships.[130] The second document confirmed to Venice trading privileges granted by the previous Norman kings and halved the fees due the crown in Messina, Palermo and the other ports of Sicily.[131] The accord quite effectively shielded the Kingdom of Sicily from Byzantine attack. Constantinople's debilitated fleet could not possibly have contended with the joint maritime forces of Venice and Sicily.

Five years later, William concluded a highly beneficial trade pact with the Almohad emir of Tunis. In 1180, Sicilian warships supposedly seized an Almohad ship carrying the sultan's daughter. William returned her to her father unharmed.

[125] William of Tyre, *History of Deeds Done beyond the Sea*, II, Bk 21, ch. 3, pp. 399–400; *Willelmi Tyrensis Chronicon*, Bk 21, ch. 3, p. 963. 'Ubi dum eius procuratores et primicerii incautius se habent, amissis ex utroque ordine quampluribus tam captivatis quam peremptis gladio, post moram quinque aut sex dierum, quam circa urbem fecerant, confusi recesserunt.'

[126] *Annales Casinenses*, anno 1174, p. 312. 'Mense Augusti stolium regis ivit Alexandriam.'

[127] *Chronica de Ferraria*, anno 1174, p. 31. 'Rex Gullielmus ij mictit storium suum in Alexandriam, ubi plures retinentur a Sarracenis.'

[128] Al-Maqrizi, *BAS*, II, p. 591.

[129] Abulafia, *Two Italies*, pp. 142–3.

[130] Tafel and Thomas, *Urkunden der Republik Venedig*, I, no. LXV, pp. 172–4.

[131] Tafel and Thomas, *Urkunden der Republik Venedig*, I, no. LXVI, pp. 174–5.

In gratitude, the emir granted the Kingdom of Sicily a ten-year truce, which included commercial concessions similar to those that had existed in Roger II's day along with a *fondaco* in both Mahdiyah and Zawilah.[132] But what is striking about these agreements is that William apparently initiated neither of them. In both cases, ambassadors were sent to William. Andrea Dandolo notes that it was Venice that had instigated negotiations by dispatching Aureo Mastropetro and Aureo Dauro to Palermo.[133] As for the pact with the Almohads of North Africa, the *Annales Casinenses* specifically states: 'Our lord king made a truce at Palermo ['*apud Panormum*'] with the king of the Almohads for ten years in the month of August.'[134] In other words, William did not send envoys: they came to him. Therefore, one must assume that he did not actively pursue diplomacy as an integral part of any conscious maritime strategy to further Norman interests in the Mediterranean. His diplomatic role was largely passive. He remained primarily married to large-scale, risky offensives against distant adversaries.

In the summer of 1181, William sent out another grand expedition, this time to the Balearics, ostensibly to suppress Almoravid pirates operating from those islands. Once again the south Italian chronicles hardly speak of it, but the annals of Genoa and Pisa note it prominently. Bernardo Maragone's son, Salem, writes in the *Annales Pisani* that the force was composed of 184 galleys, 45 horse transports and 40 supply ships, carrying victuals, a host of archers and siege machines.[135] Ottobono Scriba, a continuator of the *Annales Ianuenses* (*Annali Genovesi*), describes it as 'a great fleet of galleys and very many *uscerii* [horse transports]' under the command of Walter of Moac, William's '*Regni fortunati stoli amiratus*' ('Admiral of the Blessed Royal Fleet').[136] It was so substantial that when Saladin learned of its preparations, he feared it was bound for Egypt.[137] Salem recounts that the armada anchored first at San Pietro Island off the southwest coast of Sardinia before continuing on.[138] At some point, according to Ottobono Scriba, it pulled into Genoa, perhaps to persuade the Genoese to join the expedition.[139] But the commune must have demurred, because, instead, Genoa renewed its truce with the Sultan of Majorca.[140] A raging pestilence in

---

[132] L. de Mas Latrie, *Traités de paix et de commerce et documents divers concernant les relations des Chrétiens avec les Arabes de l'Afrique septentrionale au Moyen Age* (2 vols, Paris, 1866), I, pp. 51–2.

[133] Andrea Dandolo, *Chronica Per Extensum Descripta*, p. 262.

[134] *Annales Casinenses*, anno 1181, p. 312. '*Dominus noster rex fecit treuguam apud Panormus cum rege Maxamutorum usque ad decem annos mense Augusto.*'

[135] Salem Maragone, *Annales Pisani*, p. 72.

[136] Ottobono Scriba, *Annales Ianuenses*, *Annali genovesi di Caffaro e de'suoi continuatori*, II, pp. 15–16. '… *maximo stolo de galeis et plurimis uxeriis…*'

[137] William of Tyre, *History of Deeds Done beyond the Sea*, II, Bk 22, ch. 8, p. 458; *Willelmi Tyrensis Chronicon*, Bk 22, ch. 8, p. 985.

[138] Salem Maragone, *Annales Pisani*, p. 72.

[139] Ottobono Scriba, *Annales Ianuenses*, II, p. 16.

[140] Abulafia, *Two Italies*, p. 157.

Genoa soon obliged Walter of Moac to move the fleet to nearby Vado Liguria for the winter.[141] He apparently attempted to attack Majorca on his own the next spring, but Salem says that 'the angry sea and adverse winds' forced the fleet to turn away before reaching its objective.[142] William of Tyre paints a picture direr still: 'Driven by unfavorable winds, practically the entire fleet was wrecked in the vicinity of the coastal cities of Savona, Albenga and Ventimiglia, where the tumultuous waves dashed the ships upon the shore.'[143] An anonymous Sicilian chronicle of the thirteenth century contained in the massive *Historia Diplomatica Friderici Secundi* of Jean Louis Alphonse Huillard-Bréholles reports that around 40 vessels were lost.[144] Yet again, another of William's ambitious undertakings had ended in disaster.

Perhaps because William personally led not a single expedition on land or sea, catastrophic failure never seemed to dull his taste for the far-reaching enterprise. In 1185 he would mount one so massive that its collapse would signal the eclipse of Norman sea power in the Mediterranean altogether. His goal was nothing less than the conquest of the Eastern Empire. The genesis of this audacious ambition was manifold. First of all, it was born of a family predilection. The Hautevilles had nurtured an enmity for the Byzantine Empire ever since Tancred's sons had first set foot in southern Italy. The dream of finishing what Robert Guiscard had begun over a century prior must have been very tantalizing. Secondly, William undoubtedly harbored a grudge against the throne of Constantinople. After some considerable negotiation, he had been betrothed to the Emperor Manuel's daughter, Maria, but when it had come time to meet his new bride in Taranto in 1172, he had been humiliatingly stood up.[145] Thirdly, the time was ripe. The court of Constantinople was in even greater upheaval than usual. Manuel had passed away in 1180, leaving as his successor his young son, Alexios II, under the regency of his mother, Mary of Antioch.[146] The unpopularity of her regency prompted Andronikos Komnenos, the emperor's first cousin, to usurp the crown in 1182,

[141] Ottobono Scriba, *Annales Ianuenses*, II, pp. 15–16.

[142] Salem Maragone, *Annales Pisani*, p. 72. '… il mare adirato et li venti contrari …' (Salem Maragone's portion of the *Annales Pisani* survives only in an abridged seventeenth-century Italian translation.)

[143] William of Tyre, *History of Deeds Done beyond the Sea*, II, Bk 22, ch. 8, p. 458; *Willelmi Tyrensis Chronicon*, Bk 22, ch. 8, pp. 1017–18. '… ubi infausta navigatione et sinistris acta flatibus tota pene deperiit, circa Saonam, Albenguenam et Vigintimiliam urbes maritimas freto intumes-cente littoribus allisa.'

[144] J. Huillard-Bréholles, ed., *Historia Diplomatica Friderici Secundi* (6 vols in 12 parts, Paris, 1852–61), I, Pt 2, p. 890. See also Amari, *Storia dei Musulmani di Sicilia*, III, p. 529.

[145] Romuald of Salerno, *Romualdi Salernitani Chronicon*, p. 261.

[146] Eustathios of Thessaloniki, *The Capture of Thessaloniki*, trans. J. Melville Jones (Canberra, 1988), ch. 14, pp. 20–1; Ibn Jubayr, *BAS*, I, pp. 168–9; *Travels of Ibn Jubayr*, p. 354; Niketas Choniates, *O City of Byzantium!*, pp. 124–8.

which, in turn, led to further discontent.[147] When a pretender to the throne claiming to be Alexios II appeared on Sicily, William, much like Robert Guiscard before him, saw an opportunity. According to Archbishop Eustathios of Thessaloniki, who is the primary source for this event, a certain monk by the name of Sikountenos Philadelphenos of 'Bagentia' (probably *Vagenetia*, the coastal region of Epirus opposite Corfu) arrived in Sicily with a young lad rumored to be Alexios, Manuel's son and heir.[148] In point of fact, Eustathios confirms that Andronikos had ordered both Alexios II and his mother strangled and thrown into the sea.[149] Nonetheless, Ibn Jubayr says some Genoese merchants passing through Palermo confirmed the lad's identity to William as the genuine heir to the throne of Byzantium. It is not known whether William really believed it or not, but he treated the boy as such anyway in order to provide an additional pretext for war.[150]

So intent was he on hurling the full military might of the realm at Constantinople that in October 1184 William made a commitment that would ultimately bring a halt to Hauteville rule. In order to preclude any possibility of German pressure during the campaign, he consented to the marriage of his aunt Constance, the posthumous daughter of Roger II, to Henry VI, the heir to the Hohenstaufen crown – knowing full well that if he died without an heir, the Kingdom of Sicily would be absorbed by the German Empire.[151] The *Annales Casinenses* purports that the king even had the realm's nobility, including his cousin Tancred of Lecce, swear fealty to Constance as his legal heir at Troia in 1185.[152] In other words, William wagered his kingdom on the virility of his loins. It was a bad bet.

Preparations for the expedition must have been on a staggering scale. Eustathios speaks of 'more than two hundred ships of various kinds, including cavalry transports'.[153] Ibn Jubayr, who was traveling through Sicily as the fleet was being equipped, reports, 'As to numbers, some say there are three hundred sail, between galleys and dromonds, while others say there are more, and that a hundred ships carrying victuals are to accompany it.'[154] Given that Eustathios estimates the land forces at 80,000 plus 5,000 knights, 400 or more vessels does not seem too outlandish an approximation.[155] Indeed, the old French continua-

---

[147] *Chronica de Ferraria*, anno 1183, p. 31; Eustathios of Thessaloniki, *Capture of Thessaloniki*, ch. 21–48, pp. 27–59; Ibn Jubayr, *BAS*, I, pp. 169–70; *Travels of Ibn Jubayr*, p. 354; Niketas Choniates, *O City of Byzantium!*, pp. 129–52.
[148] Eustathios of Thessaloniki, *Capture of Thessaloniki*, ch. 51, pp. 60–1.
[149] Eustathios of Thessaloniki, *Capture of Thessaloniki*, ch. 35, 42–3, pp. 40–1, 52–3.
[150] Ibn Jubayr, *BAS*, I, pp. 169–74; *Travels of Ibn Jubayr*, pp. 354–6.
[151] *Annales Casinenses*, anno 1185, p. 312; Chalandon, *Histoire de la Domination Normande*, II, pp. 386–7.
[152] *Annales Casinenses*, anno 1190, p. 314. See also Houben, *Roger II*, p. 172.
[153] Eustathios of Thessaloniki, *Capture of Thessaloniki*, ch. 51, pp. 62–3.
[154] Ibn Jubayr, *BAS*, I, p. 169; *Travels of Ibn Jubayr*, p. 354.
[155] Eustathios of Thessaloniki, *Capture of Thessaloniki*, ch. 138, p. 151.

tion of William of Tyre provides an indication that William recruited from far and wide at great expense:

> He [William] sent to the land of Outremer and all the lands nearby and recruited knights and sergeants and gave them pay in accordance with each man's status. He also retained the pilgrims from other lands who were passing through his kingdom. So for two years he held up the passage so that no one could cross to the land of Outremer.[156]

Indeed, the chronicle goes so far as to blame this extraordinary recruitment effort for having divested the Latin Kingdom of Jerusalem of able-bodied men, thus making it vulnerable to eventual conquest by Saladin.[157] William was so obsessed with the project that Ibn Jubayr reports that he came to Messina to personally oversee the outfitting of the fleet.[158] Wars in any era are prohibitively expensive. This one may have, in fact, irreparably weakened the financial solvency of the Kingdom of Sicily. Eustathios, for one, categorically states with evident credibility, 'His [William's] treasury was emptied and left bare.'[159]

William presaged the start of the campaign in January 1185 by imposing an embargo on all ships departing from Sicily.[160] The vast armada finally set sail in June under the command of Tancred of Lecce. The land forces were led by Richard of Acerra and a certain Baldwin.[161] They reached Durazzo on 24 June and apparently intimidated the city into an immediate surrender.[162] After leaving a garrison, the army proceeded to Thessaloniki, presumably by way of the Via Egnatia through Edessa, arriving at the walls of the Macedonian capital on 6 August. The fleet appeared in the harbor nine days later after rounding the Peloponnesos. With the arrival of their ships, the Sicilians were able to gird the entire city.[163] The west side, on which stood the harbor and Golden Gate

---

[156] 'The old French Continuation of William of Tyre, 1184–1197', *The Conquest of Jerusalem and the Third Crusade*, trans. P. Edbury (Aldershot, 1996), ch. 72, pp. 73–4; *La continuation de Guillaume de Tyr (1184–1197)*, ed. M. Morgan (Paris, 1982), ch. 72, p. 82. 'Il … manda en la terre d'outremer et en toutes les terres qui pres estoient chevaliers et serjanz, et lor doneit soz selonc ce que chascun esteit, et si retint les pelerins qui d'autres terres aloient par sa terre por passer. Et tint ensii II ans le passage, que de gens qui ne vindrent d'outremer.'

[157] 'The old French Continuation of William of Tyre, 1184–1197', ch. 72, p. 74; *La continuation de Guillaume de Tyr (1184–1197)*, ch. 72, p. 82.

[158] Ibn Jubayr, *BAS*, I, pp. 142–3; *Travels of Ibn Jubayr*, pp. 337–8.

[159] Eustathios of Thessaloniki, *Capture of Thessaloniki*, ch. 51, pp. 62–3.

[160] Ibn Jubayr, *BAS*, I, p. 168; *Travels of Ibn Jubayr*, p. 353.

[161] *Annales Ceccanenses*, anno 1185, p. 287.

[162] *Annales Casinenses*, anno 1185, p. 313; *Annales Ceccanenses*, anno 1185, p. 287; *Annales Cavenses*, anno 1185, p. 193; Eustathios of Thessaloniki, *Capture of Thessaloniki*, ch. 53, pp. 64–5; Niketas Choniates, *O City of Byzantium!*, p. 164; 'The old French Continuation of William of Tyre, 1184–1197', ch. 73, p. 74; *La continuation de Guillaume de Tyr (1184–1197)*, ch. 73, pp. 82–3.

[163] Eustathios of Thessaloniki, *Capture of Thessaloniki*, ch. 54–6, pp. 66–9; Niketas Choniates, *O City of Byzantium!*, p. 164.

(the main entrance to the city through which ran the Via Egnatia), presented something of a problem, because the water depth remained so shallow in the summer months that the Sicilians could not bring their ships close enough to the walls to effectively engage the defenders with projectiles.[164] In fact, the defenders were able to back the besiegers off with their own missile barrages.[165] So, the Sicilians beached their ships and attempted to simply maintain the integrity of the blockade on the west side while they concentrated their efforts on the east side where stood the Asomatoi Gate. The circumvallation here was in a state of disrepair and weaker. The Sicilians, thus, set their sappers to work under the cover of missile fusillades directed from the masts of ships and two large deck-mounted catapults.[166]

The siege lasted only nine days after the arrival of the fleet, largely because of the incompetence of the city's *strategos*, a certain David Komnenos. He was apparently a pusillanimous palace appointee who possessed no military experience and poor leadership skills.[167] Not only had he failed to shore up the east wall, but he had botched a hasty repair of the acropolis's cistern by filling it before the lining had properly set. As a result, it would hold no water.[168] Therefore, there was virtually no chance that the city could have endured a prolonged siege. As it was, the sappers managed to complete their work on the east wall by 24 August. Once a hollow had been excavated out of the base of the circumvallation, they filled it with timbers and torched the lot. The wall soon crumbled and admitted the Sicilians, mostly sailors at first.[169] At approximately the same time, other invaders penetrated the west wall, presumably through the Golden Gate. They had apparently suborned a German contingent tasked with guarding that gate.[170] The Norman forces flooded into the city from both sides. And, despite the best efforts of their commanders, the invaders subjected the inhabitants to the usual unspeakable atrocities for which medieval armies teeming with mercenaries were predisposed. Over 7,000 of the city's citizens were slaughtered, according to Eustathios. The archbishop also claims that over 3,000 invaders perished of their own excesses. Pestilence spawned by rotting corpses strewn

---

[164] Eustathios of Thessaloniki, *Capture of Thessaloniki*, ch. 59, pp. 74–5.
[165] Eustathios of Thessaloniki, *Capture of Thessaloniki*, ch. 75, pp. 94–5.
[166] Eustathios of Thessaloniki, *Capture of Thessaloniki*, ch. 59, 81, pp. 74–5, 98–9.
[167] Eustathios of Thessaloniki, *Capture of Thessaloniki*, ch. 6–12, pp. 8–19; Niketas Choniates, *O City of Byzantium!*, pp. 164–5.
[168] Eustathios of Thessaloniki, *Capture of Thessaloniki*, ch. 62, pp. 76–9.
[169] *Annales Casinenses*, anno 1185, p. 313; *Annales Ceccanenses*, anno 1185, p. 287; *Annales Cavenses*, anno 1185, p. 193; *Chronica de Ferraria*, anno 1184, p. 31; Eustathios of Thessaloniki, *Capture of Thessaloniki*, ch. 82–6, pp. 100–5; Niketas Choniates, *O City of Byzantium!*, p. 165; 'The old French Continuation of William of Tyre, 1184–1197', ch. 73, p. 74; *La continuation de Guillaume de Tyr (1184–1197)*, ch. 73, pp. 82–3.
[170] Eustathios of Thessaloniki, *Capture of Thessaloniki*, ch. 73–4, pp. 92–3.

through the streets must have heightened the horror and added to the death toll of victors and vanquished alike.[171]

Although the rule of Andronikos had devolved into megalomania, he was, at least, cognizant of the Latin incursion. He took steps to counter it and protect the capital. When he first heard of the Sicilian armada's approach, he dispatched a certain John Branas to lead the defense of Durazzo. Branas arrived only a few days before the Normans, however – just in time to capitulate and be taken captive back to Sicily. In the meantime, the emperor had also directed Greek land forces toward Thessaloniki. He, however, made the cardinal tactical error of dividing those forces into five parts. One division he assigned to his incompetent son John, another to the *chartoularios* ('keeper of records') Theodore Choumnos, another to Andronikos Palaiologos, yet another to the eunuch and *parakoimomenos* ('High Chamberlain') Nikephoros and the last to Alexios Branas.[172] Having received erroneous messages from the *strategos* David Komnenos that Thessaloniki was prepared to withstand a long siege, Andronikos gave orders to his military commanders to merely harass the besieging forces.[173] Of the five commanders, only Choumnos actually attacked the Normans.[174] By itself, his unit was too small to do any real damage, but Eustathios reveals that if the governor of the city had chosen to make a sally at that time, the Byzantines might have temporarily, at least, broken the siege: 'We learned from the reports of the Latins themselves that if, at that moment when Choumnos attacked them, the defenders of the city had made a sortie by the harbor, they would have captured their opponents' siege equipment and driven their army back, and would have been able to burn every single ship which they had.'[175] Without such support, Choumnos was forced to retreat into the nearby mountains, where, like his comrades, he watched from a safe distance.[176]

Once Thessaloniki was pacified, Baldwin and Richard of Acerra marched the Sicilian army towards Constantinople in two corps. The main body proceeded directly for the capital while the other ravaged the region of Serrai (modern Serres) in Macedonia. The fleet remained intact, at first, to defend Thessaloniki from assault by Byzantine forces, which were known to be nearby. As the army progressed towards its objective, Tancred of Lecce eventually took the warships and headed for the Bosporus, leaving behind the transport vessels.[177] Meanwhile, Andronikos oversaw the repair of Constantinople's walls and ordered a flotilla of 100 vessels outfitted for the defense of the city. Nonetheless, the outlook was bleak. Word arrived that the Sicilians had captured Amphipolis (in central

[171]   Eustathios of Thessaloniki, *Capture of Thessaloniki*, ch. 98–106, pp. 112–21.

[172]   Niketas Choniates, *O City of Byzantium!*, p. 175.

[173]   Eustathios of Thessaloniki, *Capture of Thessaloniki*, ch. 57, pp. 70–1.

[174]   Niketas Choniates, *O City of Byzantium!*, p. 175.

[175]   Eustathios of Thessaloniki, *Capture of Thessaloniki*, ch. 67, pp. 86–7.

[176]   Niketas Choniates, *O City of Byzantium!*, p. 176.

[177]   Niketas Choniates, *O City of Byzantium!*, pp. 198–201.

Macedonia) and an advanced guard now neared Mosynopolis (near modern Komotini in Thrace), less than 200 miles from the capital.[178] An event then transpired that dramatically altered the situation: Andronikos was overthrown by a popular revolt in September and Isaakios Angelos was placed on the throne in his stead. The latter immediately dispatched another army with Alexios Branas, a *protosebastos* and thus an exalted member of the imperial family, at its head.[179]

At first, Branas simply shadowed the Sicilian force near Mosynopolis, awaiting his opportunity. Arrogance and a breakdown of discipline among the invaders provided that opportunity. 'They separated according to companies,' writes Niketas Choniates, 'each going its separate way, and scattered in the hope of despoiling anyone coming out of or carrying provisions into Mosynopolis.'[180] Branas' troops began to attack these small groups of pillagers and harry the rear ranks of the advance guard. Finally, in early November, the Byzantines engaged the enemy vanguard in a pitched battle and drove it back on to the main body of the Sicilian army camped on the banks of the Strymon near Amphipolis. Choniates says Baldwin attempted 'to sue for peace', but the Greeks sensed total victory was at hand and attacked.[181] The Sicilians tried to weather the onslaught but eventually wavered and broke. Most were either killed or captured, including the two Norman commanders. The survivors along with those Sicilian soldiers who had been plundering the Serrai made their way back to Thessaloniki as best they could. Thessaloniki was evacuated in haste, the remnants of the Sicilian army boarding the supply ships still in the harbor.[182] Those who could find no room on the ships had to make the overland trek to Durazzo, still in Sicilian hands. Eventually, even Durazzo was abandoned.[183]

Meanwhile, Tancred of Lecce arrived in the Sea of Marmara with his 200 galleys, expecting to join the land forces in a siege of Constantinople. Instead, he found the entrance to the Bosporus blocked by a Byzantine fleet of 100 galleys. Furthermore, Greek troops with bows and various projectile-launching devices held the shore on either side of the strait and prevented the Sicilians from disembarking. Unaware of the debacle at Amphipolis, Tancred waited in vain for 17 days among the islands of Marmara for the arrival of the Sicilian army. Finally, after ravaging the island of Imrali Adasi and the banks of the Dardanelles, the Sicilian fleet set sail for home.[184] According to Niketas Choniates, few ships arrived: 'It is said that many ships, men and all, sank in the deep when

[178] Niketas Choniates, *O City of Byzantium!*, p. 176.
[179] *Annales Casinenses*, anno 1185, p, 313; Niketas Choniates, *O City of Byzantium!*, pp. 188–94, 198.
[180] Niketas Choniates, *O City of Byzantium!*, p. 198.
[181] Niketas Choniates, *O City of Byzantium!*, p. 199.
[182] *Annales Ceccanenses*, anno 1185, p. 287; Niketas Choniates, *O City of Byzantium!*, p. 199; 'The old French Continuation of William of Tyre, 1184–1197', ch. 73, p. 74; *La continuation de Guillaume de Tyr (1184–1197)*, ch. 73, p. 83.
[183] Niketas Choniates, *O City of Byzantium!*, p. 200.
[184] *Annales Casinenses*, anno 1185, p, 313; Niketas Choniates, *O City of Byzantium!*, pp. 200–1.

they encountered tempestuous winds, while famine and disease emptied out others.'[185] Recounting the demise of retreating enemy fleets from storms seems to be *de rigueur* for medieval chroniclers of all ethnic origins, but the time of year (late November) and the circumstances of the Sicilian withdrawal argue more strongly for the veracity of this particular account. 'Thus, no less than ten thousand fighting men were lost in these campaigns,' notes Choniates who adds, 'The captives taken in both battles, numbering more than four thousand, were incarcerated in public houses.'[186]

An army annihilated and an armada decimated, yet William remained unrepentant and thirsting for revenge. The very next year he sent a new admiral, Margaritus of Brindisi, with another fleet to aid Isaakios Komnenos, the self-styled emperor of Cyprus. The Byzantine Emperor Isaakios Angelos had deemed the adventurer from Isauria (an old Roman region of south-central Anatolia) a tyrant and a potential threat to the throne, so he had sent an armada of 70 'long ships' under the command of John Kontostephanos and Alexios Komnenos, both of royal blood, to oust him. Isaakios Komnenos, however, was waiting for them. As soon as the Byzantine forces disembarked amid a storm, the Cypriot ruler attacked and quickly defeated them. At the same time, Margaritus surprised the Byzantine fleet, easily seizing its ships, probably because they were bereft of fighting men. As a reward, Isaakios Komnenos allowed Margaritus to take the Greek captains back with him as prisoners.[187]

The incident, for which Niketas Choniates is the sole source, introduces a personality who would figure prominently for the remainder of Hauteville rule in Sicily. Margaritus would be the fleet admiral for the Norman kingdom until the end. A diploma of July 1192 in favor of San Nicola de Peratico exalts him as '*Margaritus de Brundusio Dei et regia gratia comes Malte et victoriosus Regij stolij amiratus*' ('Margaritus of Brindisi, by grace of God and king, count of Malta and victorious admiral of the Royal fleet').[188] Yet, his origins remain a mystery. Nothing is known of his career up to this point, except that, ironically, he was apparently quite famous at the time. The twelfth-century English chronicler Roger of Howden mentioned him in both his *Chronica* and the *Gesta Regis Henrici Secundi*.[189] Léon-Robert Ménager lists more than a dozen other northern European chronicles containing references to Margaritus, several of which iden-

185 Niketas Choniates, *O City of Byzantium!*, p. 201.
186 Niketas Choniates, *O City of Byzantium!*, p. 201.
187 Niketas Choniates, *O City of Byzantium!*, p. 204.
188 C. Garufi, 'Margarito di Brindisi Conte di Malta e Ammiraglio del Re di Sicilia', in *Miscellanea di Archeologia, Storia e Filologia dedicata al Prof. Antonino Salinas* (Palermo, 1907), pp. 273–82.
189 Roger of Howden, *The Annals of Roger de Hoveden*, trans. H. Riley (2 vols, London, 1853), II, p. 156; *Chronica Magistri Rogeri de Houedene*, ed. W. Stubbs (4 vols, RS 51, London, 1868–71, reprint 1964), III, p. 66; *Gesta Regis Henrici Secundi Benedicti Abbatis*, ed. W. Stubbs (2 vols, RS 49, London, 1867, reprint 1965), II, p. 128.

tify him as a pirate.[190] Indeed, Niketas Choniates himself calls Margaritus 'the most formidable pirate on the high seas at that time.'[191] Michele Amari even speculates that Margaritus was actually the pirate leader called 'Siphantos,'[192] whom Eustathios credits as having spared him during the sacking of the Thessaloniki.[193] He presents no evidence, however, and the half-hearted argument forwarded by Ménager in support of the theory is labored and inconclusive.[194] Nonetheless, it appears evident that Margaritus was some sort of buccaneer chief, which begs the question: Were the ships he commanded his or William's? Niketas says only that 'he [Margaritus] recognized the tyrant of the island [Sicily] as his lord.'[195] Not only may Margaritus have had a flotilla of his own, some scholars hold that he had a vested interest in assisting Isaakios Komnenos because he was the latter's brother-in-law.[196] Moreover, it only seems logical that William would have had some difficulty equipping a new fleet of his own so soon after having suffered such a devastating loss during the campaign against Constantinople.

That being said, Margaritus was back in the eastern Mediterranean at William's behest in 1188. The reason was the total defeat of the Latin Kingdom's forces by Saladin at the Horns of Hattin in July of the year before.[197] What remained of the Latin East in Syria and Palestine had been rendered defenseless in the face of Saladin's onslaught. William was the first monarch of the Christian West to receive the urgent entreaties for help brought that same summer by Joscius, the Archbishop of Tyre at the time.[198] He responded by sending Margaritus in command of a sizable armada the following summer. The various versions of the 'Old French Continuation of William of Tyre' put the number of vessels

---

[190] Ménager, *Amiratus*, pp. 96–9.

[191] Niketas Choniates, *O City of Byzantium!*, p. 204.

[192] Amari, *Storia dei Musulmani di Sicilia*, III, pp. 535–6.

[193] Eustathios of Thessaloniki, *Capture of Thessaloniki*, ch. 83, pp. 100–1.

[194] Ménager, *Amiratus*, pp. 97–8.

[195] Niketas Choniates, *O City of Byzantium!*, p. 204.

[196] R. Rudt de Collenberg, 'L'empereur Isaac de Chypre et sa fille (1155–1207)', *Byzantion*, XXXVIII (1968), pp. 123–53, especially 145–6.

[197] Ambroise, *The History of the Holy War: Ambroise's Estoire de la Guerre Sainte*, trans. M. Ailes (2 vols, Woodbridge, 2003), I, lines 2526–73, p. 41; II, pp. 68–9; Baha' al-Din ibn Shaddad, *The Rare and Excellent History of Saladin*, trans. D. Richards (Aldershot, 2002), pp. 72–5; *Das Itinerarium Peregrinorum*, ed. H. Mayer (Stuttgart, 1962), ch. 5, pp. 257–9; *The Chronicle of the Third Crusade: The Itinerarium Peregrinorum et Gesta Regis Ricardi*, trans. H. Nicholson (Aldershot, 1997), Bk 1, ch. 5, pp. 32–3; *Itinerarium Peregrinorum et Gesta Regis Ricardi*, *Chronicles and Memorials of the Reign of Richard I*, ed. W. Stubbs (2 vols, RS 38, London, 1864, reprint 1964), I, Bk I, ch. V, pp. 14–16; Ibn al-Athir, *Chronicle of Ibn al-Athir, Part 2*, pp. 322–4; 'The old French Continuation of William of Tyre, 1184–1197', ch. 40–2, pp. 45–7; *La continuation de Guillaume de Tyr (1184–1197)*, ch. 40–2, pp. 52–4; Roger of Howden, *Annals of Roger de Hoveden*, II, pp. 64–5; *Chronica Magistri Rogeri de Houedene*, II, pp. 319–20; *Gesta Regis Henrici Secundi*, II, pp. 10–14.

[198] 'The old French Continuation of William of Tyre, 1184–1197', ch. 74, p. 75; *La continuation de Guillaume de Tyr (1184–1197)*, ch. 74, p. 83. See also Riley-Smith, *The Crusades, A Short History* (London, 1987), p. 110.

somewhere between 400 and 200.[199] The *Itinerarium Peregrinorum's* estimate of 50 ships,[200] however, is more in line with contemporary Arab observers, Ibn al-Athir and Imad ad-Din al-Isfahani, who both attest to 60 galleys.[201] Whatever the exact size of the fleet, it appears it was effective in buying some time for what was left of the Latin Kingdom. 'Who can doubt that it was a miracle that, with the help of the king's [William's] forces, Antioch was held, Tripoli defended, Tyre saved and the inhabitants of these cities kept secure from famine and the sword?' muses the *Itinerarium Peregrinorum*, adding, 'Margarit was in command of the royal fleet, a great man of action.'[202] Imad ad-Din obliquely lends credence to that claim by calling Margaritus 'the worst of the foulest of tyrants and the most dreadful of demons.'[203] Since the latter was secretary to Saladin, he was probably an eyewitness to the events at hand. The demonstrably biased scholar-rhetorician attempts to dissemble by characterizing Margaritus as indecisive and ineffectual, but then goes on to describe how the Sicilian admiral succeeded in impeding Saladin's march up the Syrian coast.[204]

The truth is that Margaritus's arrival in July 1188 probably deterred Saladin from attacking Tripoli. The Sicilian admiral then hounded the sultan as he progressed northward.[205] When Saladin was passing Maraclea, Margaritus anchored his ships in a line just off the beach below the Margat, the glowering Hospitaller fortress perched on a precipice above the shore. Armed with *ballistae*, arbalests and hosts of archers, the galleys rendered the narrow passageway between the shoreline and the Margat impassable. Saladin finally had to have mantles and palisades constructed and arranged along the pathway facing seaward in

---

[199] 'The old French Continuation of William of Tyre, 1184–1197', ch. 73, p.74; *La continuation de Guillaume de Tyr (1184–1197)*, ch. 73, p. 83.

[200] *Das Itinerarium Peregrinorum*, ch. 14, p. 271; *Chronicle of the Third Crusade: The Itinerarium Peregrinorum*, Bk I, ch. 14, p. 43; *Itinerarium Peregrinorum et Gesta Regis Ricardi, Chronicles and Memorials of the Reign of Richard I*, I, Bk I, ch. XIV, p. 27. (The *Itinerarium Peregrinorum*, as published by William Stubbs, is a Latin prose narrative of the Third Crusade probably compiled in the early thirteenth century from first-hand accounts by Richard de Templo, the prior of Holy Trinity priory in London.)

[201] Ibn al-Athir, *BAS*, I, pp. 499–500; *Chronicle of Ibn al-Athir, Part 2*, p. 345; Imad ad-Din, *BAS*, I, p. 340.

[202] *Das Itinerarium Peregrinorum*, ch. 14, p. 271; *Chronicle of the Third Crusade: The Itinerarium Peregrinorum*, ch. 14, p. 43; *Itinerarium Peregrinorum et Gesta Regis Ricardi, Chronicles and Memorials of the Reign of Richard I*, I, Bk I, ch. XIV, pp. 27–8. 'Ejus ergo beneficium esse quis dubitat, quod Antiocha retenta, quod Tripolis defensa, quod Tyrus servata, qui harum urbium incolas a fame et gladio viribus suis securos conservat? Margaritus classi regiae regendae praeerat, vir admodum strenuus.'

[203] Imad ad-Din, *BAS*, I, p. 341.

[204] Imad ad-Din, *BAS*, I, pp. 339–42.

[205] *Das Itinerarium Peregrinorum*, ch. 14, p. 271; *Itinerarium Peregrinorum et Gesta Regis Ricardi, Chronicles and Memorials of the Reign of Richard I*, I, Bk I, ch. XIV, pp. 27–8; *Chronicle of the Third Crusade: The Itinerarium Peregrinorum*, ch. 14, p. 43. See also Riley-Smith, *Atlas of the Crusades*, pp. 60–1; *Crusades*, p. 110.

order to reach Jabala.[206] The episode seems to reflect an early and highly efficacious employment of ship-to-shore battery tactics. Margaritus was obviously a
skilled naval commander. He shadowed Saladin all the way up to Latakia and,
although he could not prevent the latter city's capture, he was, according to both
Ibn al-Athir and Imad ad-Din, able to confer with the great Kurdish general
himself, in hopes of dissuading him from his path of conquest.[207] Needless to
say, he failed, but the tale of the attempt reveals the measure of respect he had
earned from the Muslim opposition.

The 'Old French Continuation of William of Tyre' indicates that William II,
deeply moved by the plight of the Christians in Palestine, was preparing an even
larger relief expedition to the Latin East and that he had even made definite
plans to go himself: 'Then he had a large fleet of ships and galleys made ready on
which he intended coming with the king of England, the brother of his wife.'[208]
If so, this would have fitted into an identifiable pattern with respect to naval
policy. Roughly every five or six years throughout his reign, William had organized a massive naval expedition comprising 200 or more ships. The first was the
assault on Alexandria in 1174; the second was the raid on the Balearics in 1181;
and the most colossal undertaking of them all was the invasion of Byzantium
in 1185 (see Map 12). While the exact cost of these extravagant enterprises is
impossible to gauge, there can be no argument that they all took months to
mount and must have drained huge sums from the royal coffers. They, therefore,
served only to debilitate the kingdom, especially since all of them were spec-
tacular failures accompanied by epic losses of manpower and equipment. Even
if they had succeeded, none of these enterprises, except possibly the conquest of
Constantinople, would have realistically resulted in territorial gains or additional
revenue for the realm. Yet, had not fate truncated his plans, William would have,
as early as 1190, embarked on still another great adventure that promised little
or no profit to the realm. His death on 18 November 1189, however, doomed his
designs.[209] It also condemned his kingdom, for he died without a direct heir.

[206] Ibn al-Athir, BAS, I, pp. 499–500; Chronicle of Ibn al-Athir, Part 2, p. 345; Imad ad-Din,
BAS, I, pp. 341–2. See also Riley-Smith, Atlas of the Crusades, pp. 60–1.
[207] Ibn al-Athir, BAS, I, pp. 500–1; Chronicle of Ibn al-Athir, Part 2, pp. 346–7; Imad ad-Din,
BAS, I, pp. 342–4.
[208] 'The old French Continuation of William of Tyre, 1184–1197', ch. 73, p. 74; La continuation
de Guillaume de Tyr (1184–1197), ch. 73, p. 83. 'Apres fist faire grant estoire de nes et de galies par
quei il venist avec le rei d'Engleterre cui seror il aveit a feme'
[209] Annales Casinenses, anno 1189, p. 314; Annales Cavenses, anno 1189, p. 193; Annales Ceccanenses, anno 1189, p. 288; Chronica de Ferraria, anno 1189, p. 31; Richard of San Germano,
Ryccardi de Sancto Germano Notarii Chronica, ed. C. Garufi (RIS, 2nd edn, VIIb, Bologna,
1938), Explicit Prologus, pp. 4–6.

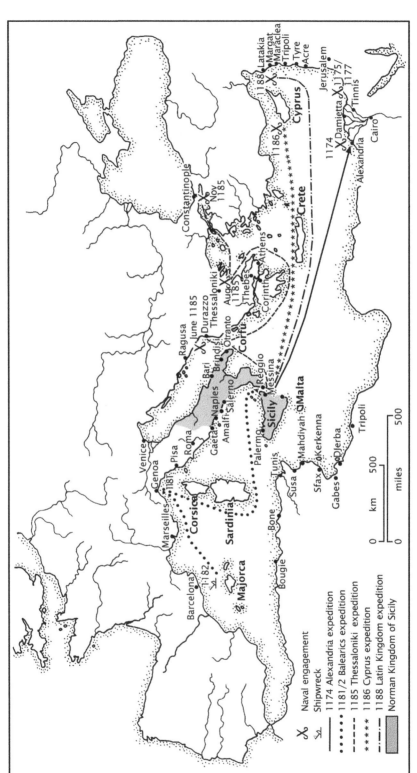

12. Norman naval expeditions under William II. (Credit: C. Stanton with P. Judge)

Dissolution of Norman sea power under Tancred

When William II died, Tancred of Lecce, his cousin, claimed the crown of Sicily. The problem was that William had designated as his successor Constance, his aunt and the last daughter to Roger II, now the wife of Henry of Hohenstaufen.[210] Along with the *Annales Casinenses*, Richard of San Germano (a notary at Montecassino at the time) leaves little doubt of this, attesting 'that all the counts of the kingdom took an oath on the king's orders that if this same king [William II] should happen to die without children, then they would become the subjects of this same aunt [Constance] and her husband the said King of Germany [Henry]'.[211] Yet, in January 1190, the *Annales Ceccanenses* declares, 'And therefore all the archbishops, bishops, abbots and the counts of the court of Sicily mutually coming together, elected Count Tancred, and honorably crowned him king'.[212] According to the *Annales Casinenses*, the election even earned the consent of Pope Clement III, who had no desire to see the Holy See surrounded by the German Empire: 'Count Tancred of Lecce ... was called to Palermo by the magnates of the court and, with the assent and favour of the Roman Curia, was crowned as king in the month of January'.[213]

Nonetheless, while Tancred had the support of most of the nobility and the tacit backing of the papacy, William's previous public designation of Constance as his rightful heir called into question Tancred's legitimacy. And legitimacy counted for something among the Normans. This was why Robert Guiscard had sought investiture as Duke of Apulia, Calabria and Sicily from Pope Nicholas II at Melfi in 1059 and why his brother, Roger, had so carefully guarded his status as Robert's vassal. Tancred's disputed legitimacy meant that members of the Norman nobility had some legal cover or, at least justifiable rationale, for choosing between him and Constance's husband, Henry of Hohenstaufen, as it advantaged them. Count Richard of Acerra, for instance, sided with Tancred because he was the latter's brother-in-law,[214] but Count Roger of Andria, who

[210] Roger of Howden, *Gesta Regis Henrici Secundi*, II, pp. 101–2.
[211] Richard of San Germano, *Ryccardi de Sancto Germano Notarii Chronica, Explicit Prologus*, p. 6. '... ut ad regis ipsius mandatum omnes regni comites sacramentum prestiterint, quod si regem ipsum absque liberis mori contingeret, ammodo de facto regni tamquam fideles ipsi sue amite tenerentur et dicto regi Alamannie viro eius.' (English translation by G. A. Loud at www.leeds.ac.uk/history/weblearning/ MedievalHistoryTextCentre/medievalTexts/html.)
[212] *Annales Ceccanenses*, anno 1189, p. 288. 'Et sic omnes archiepiscopi episcopi abbates et universi aulici comites Siciliae invicem convenientes, elegerunt comitem Tancredum, et honorifice in regem coronaverunt.'
[213] *Annales Casinenses*, anno 1190, p. 314. 'Tancredus comes Licii ... Panormum vocatus a magnatibus curiae, de assensu et favore curiae Romanae coronatur in regem mense Ianuarii.' (English translation by G. A. Loud at www.leeds.ac.uk/history/weblearning/MedievalHistoryTextCentre/medievalTexts/html.)
[214] *Annales Casinenses*, anno 1190, p. 314; Richard of San Germano, *Ryccardi de Sancto Germano Notarii Chronica*, anno 1190, p. 9.

'had been Master Justiciar of the whole realm in the time of the aforesaid King William and who had then exercised full authority in Apulia', could not condescend to be subordinate to Tancred, so he chose Henry as his liege lord.[215] Therefore, Tancred had to buy the loyalty of the nobility. Richard of San Germano explains: 'Then he [Tancred] used the royal wealth and for a long time did not hesitate to break open the public treasury, so that he might convert the other counts and barons of the kingdom to fealty and obedience to him.'[216]

The point of all this is that Tancred could not depend on traditional feudal obligation to provide him with the military manpower and equipment he would need to stay in power. It had to be purchased at a very high price, a fact that had perilous implications for Norman naval power going forward. Tancred was compelled to dip deeply into a royal treasury that must have been much diminished. Not only had William financed one extravagant enterprise after another, but he had subsidized the construction of the magnificent Cathedral of Monreale, to this day one of the most opulent ecclesiastical edifices in Christendom.[217] Worse yet, the flow of funds into the royal fisc was nothing like what it had been during the reign of Roger II, when revenues poured in from the kingdom's African territories. Tancred himself reduced revenue still more through concessions to the ports of the kingdom in order secure their fidelity. A June 1190 privilege to Naples is a case in point.[218] 'Naples was exempted from feudal service in the royal fleet and its citizens were to be free from the payment of commercial dues throughout the kingdom,' summarizes Abulafia in *Two Italies*.[219] At the same time, Tancred needed funds to suppress the inevitable insurrections. The south Italian chronicles are rife with reports of rebellion, often fomented and aided by the German throne. He even had to quell a Muslim uprising in Palermo instigated by local Christians barely days after his coronation.[220] And it was doubtful his martial prowess could make up for what he lacked in financial wherewithal, given the fact that he had presided over the collapse of the Alexandria campaign of 1174 and the botched Byzantine invasion of 1185, two of the worst military reverses in the history of the realm. In other words, Tancred was a weak monarch, destined to get weaker.

He would not even have a chance to put his house in order before some

---

[215]   Richard of San Germano, *Ryccardi de Sancto Germano Notarii Chronica*, anno 1190, p. 9. '… *cum tempore memorati regis Guillelmi totius regni magister Iustitiarius fuerit, et in Apulia plenum tunc dominium exerceret.*'
[216]   Richard of San Germano, *Ryccardi de Sancto Germano Notarii Chronica*, anno 1190, p. 9. '… *atque ut ceteros regni comites et barones ad suam fidelitatem converteret et mandatum, regales effudit opes, et diu servatas est ausus frangere gazas.*' (English translation by G. A. Loud at www. leeds.ac.uk/history/weblearning/ MedievalHistoryTextCentre/medievalTexts/html.)
[217]   Richard of San Germano, *Ryccardi de Sancto Germano Notarii Chronica*, Explicit Prologus, pp. 4–5.
[218]   *Tancredi et Willelmi III Regum Diplomata*, no. 6, pp. 15–19.
[219]   Abulafia, *Two Italies*, p. 173.
[220]   Richard of San Germano, *Ryccardi de Sancto Germano Notarii Chronica*, anno 1190, p. 9.

very powerful and demanding guests showed up on his shores: the kings of England and France. The promises of his predecessor forced Tancred to host an unruly army of crusaders on Sicilian soil. It was something the first ruler of the realm, Roger I, had refused to do. Tancred was to learn why, and the lesson would be a costly one. Philip II Augustus of France and Richard I Lion-heart of England had agreed to meet at Messina in the summer of 1190.[221] Philip, who had joined his fleet at Genoa, arrived first in a single ship with little pomp on 16 September.[222] The Lion-heart, on the other hand, had intended to intercept his fleet at Marseilles, but when it failed to arrive as expected, Roger of Howden says 'he hired ten large busses [transport ships] and twenty well-armed galleys' and proceeded on his own.[223] He pulled into Messina amid much fanfare on 23 September.[224] The *Itinerarium Peregrinorum* describes the event in great glittering detail:

> Then, when rumours spread that the noble-minded king of England was approaching, the people rushed out in crowds, wanting to see him. Pouring on to shore they struggled to stand where they could see him coming in. Look! Far away they saw the sea covered with innumerable galleys, and from afar the sound of war-trumpets echoed in their ears, the clarions resounding clear and shrill. As the fleet came nearer, they saw galleys rowing in good order, adorned and laden throughout with various sorts of weapons, with countless standards and pennants on the tips of spear shafts fluttering in the air in beautiful array. The prows of the galleys were each painted differently, with shields glittering in the sun on each bow. You would have seen the sea boil as the great number of rowing oars approached. The ears of the onlookers rang with the thundering of war-trumpets – known as *trompes* – and they were thrilled with delight at the approach of this diverse uproar.[225]

---

[221] *Itinerarium Peregrinorum et Gesta Regis Ricardi, Chronicles and Memorials of the Reign of Richard I*, I, Bk II, ch. IX, p. 150; *Chronicle of the Third Crusade: Itinerarium Peregrinorum*, Bk 2, ch. 9, p. 151.

[222] *Itinerarium Peregrinorum et Gesta Regis Ricardi, Chronicles and Memorials of the Reign of Richard I*, I, Bk II, ch. XIII, p. 156; *Chronicle of the Third Crusade: Itinerarium Peregrinorum*, Bk 2, ch. 13, pp. 156–7.

[223] Roger of Howden, *Annals of Roger de Hoveden*, II, p. 143; *Chronica Magistri Rogeri de Houedene*, III, p. 39; *Gesta Regis Henrici Secundi*, II, p. 112. '... conduxit decem bucias magnas, et viginti galeas bene armatas...'

[224] Roger of Howden, *Annals of Roger de Hoveden*, II, pp. 157–8; *Chronica Magistri Rogeri de Houedene*, III, p. 54; *Gesta Regis Henrici Secundi*, II, pp. 125–6.

[225] *Chronicle of the Third Crusade: Itinerarium Peregrinorum*, Bk 2, ch. 13, p. 157; *Itinerarium Peregrinorum et Gesta Regis Ricardi, Chronicles and Memorials of the Reign of Richard I*, I, Bk II, ch. XIII, pp. 156–7. 'Porro rex Angliae ille magnanimus, ex quo fama praedicante divulgabatur adventare, catervatim ruunt populi, illum cernare cupientes, et in littus se ingerentes certatem occupant sedes illum ascendentem visuri. Et ecce! eminus prospiciunt mare galeis opertum innumeris, et vox a longe intonabat in aures eorum tubarum reboantium, et lituorum clarius et acutius resonantium. Interea propius accedentibus fuit videre galeas seriatim remigantes, variis undique ornatas et refertas armaturis, ventilantibus ad auram innumeris ordine decoro signis et penuncellis, in hastilium summitatibus, rostris galearum varietatibus picturarum distinctis, appensorum in singulis proris scintillantibus radiis scutorum. Videres ex multitudine adventantium remigantium

To be precise, this passage only portrays the arrival of the 30 Provençal vessels that Richard had hired in Marseilles. According to the *Itinerarium Peregrinorum*, his main fleet, consisting of 108 galleys and an undisclosed quantity of transport vessels, had reached Sicily ahead of him.[226]

It was a sizable force, which must have included a goodly number of ruffians to roil the sensibilities of the Sicilians. That and Richard's well-documented high-handedness (he had apparently commandeered a Basilian monastery upon arrival) made some sort of eruption inevitable.[227] Both Ambroise and the *Itinerarium Peregrinorum* allege that an altercation over a loaf of bread mushroomed into a full-blown battle at the very moment that Richard and Philip were conferring with Jordan del Pin, the city's governor, and Margaritus, admiral of the fleet, on ways to keep the peace. Richard, never one to restrain himself, joined the fray and led his troops in a full-scale assault on the city.[228] Curiously, Margaritus did nothing, leaving the defense of the harbor to Philip, who was able to fend off an assault by Richard's galleys.[229] The Sicilian admiral later fled the city with Jordan del Pin.[230] In any event, the English were not to be deterred. 'They took Messina in less time than it takes a priest to say Matins,' boasts Ambroise, a Norman poet in Richard's entourage.[231] There was, of course, an excess of looting, but the worst damage to the realm may have occurred in the harbor. 'What is more, their galleys were set on fire and burned to ashes,' reports the *Itinerarium Peregrinorum*.[232] Ambroise echoes the statement, using different words: '... and the galleys, which were neither poor nor mean, were burned.'[233] Messina was the primary arsenal and the homeport of the Sicilian fleet. That

---

mare fervescere, tubarum intonationibus, quas trumpas vulgo dicunt, audientium aures tinnire, et ex vario tumultuantium accessu delectationem excitari.'

[226] *Chronicle of the Third Crusade: Itinerarium Peregrinorum*, Bk 2, ch. 7, p. 149; *Itinerarium Peregrinorum et Gesta Regis Ricardi, Chronicles and Memorials of the Reign of Richard I*, I, Bk II, ch. VII, p. 148.

[227] Roger of Howden, *Annals of Roger de Hoveden*, II, p. 158; *Chronica Magistri Rogeri de Houedene*, III, p. 56; *Gesta Regis Henrici Secundi*, II, p. 127.

[228] Ambroise, *Estoire de la Guerre Sainte*, I, lines 714–36, p. 12; II, p. 41; *Itinerarium Peregrinorum et Gesta Regis Ricardi, Chronicles and Memorials of the Reign of Richard I*, I, Bk II, ch. XV–XVI, pp. 158–64; *Chronicle of the Third Crusade: Itinerarium Peregrinorum*, Bk 2, ch. 15–16, pp. 159–63.

[229] *Itinerarium Peregrinorum et Gesta Regis Ricardi, Chronicles and Memorials of the Reign of Richard I*, I, Bk II, ch. XVI, pp. 159; *Chronicle of the Third Crusade: Itinerarium Peregrinorum*, Bk 2, ch. 16, p. 160.

[230] Roger of Howden, *Annals of Roger de Hoveden*, II, p. 169; *Chronica Magistri Rogeri de Houedene*, III, p. 64; *Gesta Regis Henrici Secundi*, II, p. 138.

[231] Ambroise, *Estoire de la Guerre Sainte*, I, lines 808–9, p. 13; II, p. 42. 'Plus tost eürent pris Meschines c'uns prestres n'ad dit ses matines.'

[232] *Chronicle of the Third Crusade: Itinerarium Peregrinorum*, Bk 2, ch. 16, p. 163; *Itinerarium Peregrinorum et Gesta Regis Ricardi, Chronicles and Memorials of the Reign of Richard I*, I, Bk II, ch. XVI, p. 164. 'Praeterea galea ipsorum igne supposito succensae sunt in pulverem.'

[233] Ambroise, *Estoire de la Guerre Sainte*, I, lines 816–17, p. 14; II, p. 42. 'Si furent lor galees arses, qui n'ierent povres n[ë] escharses.'

was undoubtedly why Margaritus was there. The inescapable conclusion is that on that awful day, 3 October 1190, Richard's crusaders may have destroyed the royal fleet and, perhaps, even the arsenal for rebuilding it.

Aggravating the injury, Richard extorted a huge sum from Tancred, which caused him to deplete the royal fisc still further, thereby severely hampering his efforts to replace what he had lost at Messina. After making peace with each other, both Richard and Philip dispatched messengers to Tancred, demanding reparations for all the alleged injustices perpetrated on their people by the citizens of Messina. In addition, Richard's representatives insisted on full compensation for the dower of his sister, Joanna, who was William's widow, along with her rightful claim to a share of the royal treasury.[234] Roger of Howden gives a full accounting:

> For he had demanded of king Tancred Mount Saint Angelo [on the Gargano promontory in Apulia], with the whole earldom and its other appurtenances, on behalf of his sister Joanna, which William, the former king of Sicily, her husband, had assigned her for her dower, as also a gilded chair for the said Joanna, according to the custom of the queens of that kingdom; and for his own use a gilded table twelve feet in length, and a foot and half in breadth; also, a large tent of silk, of such size that two hundred knights might sit at table beneath it, and two gilded trestles to support the said gilded table, besides the four and twenty cups, and as many dishes, of silver, and sixty thousand measures of corn, as many of barley, and as many of wine, and a hundred armed galleys, with all their equipments, and victuals for the galley-men for two years.[235]

Tancred, without a fleet and short on friends in the face of a strong German claim to his throne, had no choice but to accede to the exactions as best he could. Of all the demands, the 'one hundred armed galleys' was probably the most difficult to satisfy. Ultimately, he bought Richard off, mostly with hard currency. In November, he paid the king of England 20,000 ounces of gold for Joanna's dower and another 20,000 ounces of gold, part in compensation for all the other demands and part as dowry for his daughter, promised to Arthur of Brittany,

---

234 Ambroise, *Estoire de la Guerre Sainte*, I, lines 866–73, p. 14; II, p. 43; *Itinerarium Peregrinorum et Gesta Regis Ricardi, Chronicles and Memorials of the Reign of Richard I*, I, Bk II, ch. XVIII, pp. 165–6; *Chronicle of the Third Crusade: Itinerarium Peregrinorum*, Bk 2, ch. 18, pp. 164–5.

235 Roger of Howden, *Annals of Roger de Hoveden*, II, p. 163; *Chronica Magistri Rogeri de Houedene*, III, p. 61. 'Ipse enim a rege Tancredo exigebat Montem Sancti Angeli, cum toto comitatu et aliis pertinentiis suis, ad opus Johannae sororis suae, quem Willelmus quandam rex Siciliae, maritus ejus, dedit ei in dodarium; et cathedram auream ad opus ejusdem Johannae de consuetudine reginarum illius regni; et ad opus sui ipsius mensam auream de longitudine duodecim pedum, et de latitudine unius pedis et semis; et quoddam tentorium de serico magnum adeo quod ducenti milites in eo possint simul manducare: et duo tripodes aureos ad praedictam mensam auream sustinendam, et viginti quator cuppas argenteas, et totidem discos argenteos, et sexaginta millia salmes de frumento, et totidem de hordeo, et totidem de vino, et centum galeas armatas cum toto apparatu, et cum victu galiotarum ad duos annos.'

Richard's nephew. Richard split the largesse with Philip.[236] Even so, Tancred had to endure his unwelcome guests for another six months, not seeing the sterns of their ships until around Easter of the following year. In yet another sign that Norman sea power was a mere shadow of its former self, the *Itinerarium Peregrinorum* said this about the departure of the English fleet: 'The city of Messina may justly and uniquely boast that never in times past had such a great fleet left its shores, and neither perhaps would its like ever be seen again.'[237] Given that Messina was the primary arsenal of the kingdom and that it had launched an armada of some 400 vessels five years previously, that is a remarkable statement. The *Gesta Regis Henrici Secundi* records that Richard sailed out on 10 April 'with one hundred fifty large ships and with fifty-three galleys',[238] a significant ship complement, to be sure, but it should not have been able to awe the Sicilians.

By then, the threat from the German throne had come to a head. Frederick Barbarossa, having taken the overland route to the Holy Land, had drowned in June 1190 while crossing the River Seleph (Goksu) in Anatolia.[239] This had served to elevate his son Henry to the German throne and embolden him to make good on what he believed was rightfully his as Constance's husband: the crown of the Kingdom of Sicily. In February 1191, he was in Pisa negotiating the renewal of the anti-Norman pact that his father had formed with the Tuscan mariners in 1162. The resulting privilege of 1 March mirrored what Barbarossa had issued nearly thirty years before: the Pisans were promised half of Palermo, Messina, Salerno and Naples while being granted all of Gaeta, Mazara and Trapani. Most all of the other tenets remained the same as the previous pact.[240] In April, about the same time as Tancred was finally bidding farewell to the kings of England and France, the king of Germany was being crowned in St Peter's by Pope Clement

---

[236] Ambroise, *Estoire de la Guerre Sainte*, I, lines 981–1049, pp. 16–17; II, pp. 45–6; *Itinerarium Peregrinorum et Gesta Regis Ricardi, Chronicles and Memorials of the Reign of Richard I*, I, Bk II, ch. XXI, pp. 169–70; *Chronicle of the Third Crusade: Itinerarium Peregrinorum*, Bk 2, ch. 21, p. 168; Roger of Howden, *Annals of Roger de Hoveden*, II, pp. 166–7; *Chronica Magistri Rogeri de Houedene*, III, pp. 65–6; *Gesta Regis Henrici Secundi*, II, pp. 133–5.

[237] *Chronicle of the Third Crusade: Itinerarium Peregrinorum*, Bk 2, ch. 26, p. 174; *Itinerarium Peregrinorum et Gesta Regis Ricardi, Chronicles and Memorials of the Reign of Richard I*, I, Bk II, ch. XXVI, pp. 176–7. '*Civitas quidem Messana non immerito poterit singulari gloriari jactantia, nunquam a retroactis temporibus, classem talem et tamtam a finibus illis egressam, nec forte ullo tempore ibidem ulterius videndam consimilem.*'

[238] Roger of Howden, *Gesta Regis Henrici Secundi*, II, p. 162. '*... cum centum quinquaginta magnis navibus, et cum quinquaginta tribus galeis.*'

[239] *Annales Casinenses*, anno 1190, p. 314; *Das Itinerarium Peregrinorum*, ch. 24, pp. 300–1; *Itinerarium Peregrinorum et Gesta Regis Ricardi, Chronicles and Memorials of the Reign of Richard I*, I, Bk I, ch. XXIV, pp. 54–5; *Chronicle of the Third Crusade: Itinerarium Peregrinorum*, I, ch. 24, pp. 64–5; 'The old French Continuation of William of Tyre, 1184–1197', ch. 94, pp. 87–8; *La continuation de Guillaume de Tyr (1184–1197)*, ch. 94, pp. 96–7; Richard of San Germano, *Ryccardi de Sancto Germano Notarii Chronica*, anno 1190, p. 10.

[240] *Constitutiones et Acta Publica Imperatorem*, no. 333, pp. 472–7. See also Abulafia, *Two Italies*, p. 180.

III as the Emperor Henry VI. By the end of the month the newly minted 'Prince of the Romans' (*'principem Romanorum'*) had crossed the northern frontier of the *Regno* and had laid siege to Naples.[241] The effort, however, did not go as well as planned. It seems his Pisan allies were unable to complete the blockade of the port. Henry sent for reinforcements. Meeting in May with the Genoese emissaries, Ugolino Mallonus and Ido Picio, he essentially reinstated his father's 1162 concession to the Ligurian maritime power with a few minor embellishments.[242] Ottobono Scriba encapsulates: 'For he confirmed the old customs and privileges, and the march and county [of Genoa?], the mountain of Monaco, the *castrum* of Gavi [a fortress town 20 miles north of Genoa], the city of Syracuse with everything belonging to it, and 250 knights' fees [*caballarii*] of land in the Val di Noto, as well as many other things which are contained in the privilege.'[243]

Tancred responded in the only manner he could. In July, he granted a sweeping concession to Gaeta in return for its 'fervor of faithfulness' (*'fervor fidelitatis'*). The privilege basically conferred upon the citizens of Gaeta civil and judicial autonomy in their city and in the surrounding territories while exempting or reducing such royal taxes on commerce as the *falangagium* and the *catenacii*. Perhaps most tellingly, it decreased their obligation to provide armed galleys to the royal fleet from two to one.[244] There could only be one reason why Tancred would have elected to grant such a dispensation precisely at the time the kingdom was being invaded by enemy naval forces. Like Naples, he expected Gaeta to use its naval assets to defend itself.[245] After all, the port would have needed little additional incentive. Its citizens surely must have known that the German Emperor had pledged their city to the Pisans at this point, just as those of Naples must have been aware that half of their city had been sold to Pisa in payment for its sea power.

In the meantime, the Genoese made good on their vow to join the imperial coalition's attack on Campania. A force of 33 galleys under the consuls Bellobruno and Rolando di Carmadino sailed south in August. By the time they reached '*Castelli de mare*' (Castel Vulturno, on the Vulturno River six miles south of Mondragone), it was apparent that they were too late. Ottobono Scriba reports that a fleet headed by the famous Admiral Margaritus had blockaded the Pisan

---

[241] *Annales Casinenses*, anno 1191, p. 314; *Annales Cavenses*, anno 1190, p. 193; *Annales Ceccanenses*, anno 1191, p. 288; Otto of St Blasien, *Ottonis de Sancto Blasio Chronica*, ed. A. Hofmeister (MGH, SRG, Hanover, 1912), p. 55; Richard of San Germano, *Ryccardi de Sancto Germano Notarii Chronica*, anno 1191, pp. 11–12.

[242] CDG, III, no. 2, pp. 4–12; *Constitutiones et Acta Publica Imperatorem*, no. 337, pp. 479–83.

[243] Ottobono Scriba, *Annales Ianuenses*, II, pp. 38–9. '*Confirmauit enim ueteres consuetudines et priuilegia, et marchiam et comitatum, podium Monachi, castrum Gaui, Syracusanam civitatem cum omnibus suis pertinentiis, et CCL caballariis terrae in ualle Noth, et alia plurima quae in eodem priuilegio continentur.*' (English translation by G. A. Loud at www.leeds.ac.uk/history/weblearning/MedievalHistoryTextCentre/medievalTexts/html.)

[244] *Tancredi et Willelmi III Regum Diplomata*, no. 18, pp. 42–6.

[245] Abulafia, *Two Italies*, p. 173.

fleet at the mouth of the Vulturno. It turns out that the siege of Naples had been lifted owing to disease within the imperial army, disease that had laid low even the emperor himself. At a loss, the Genoese proceeded to Ischia, according to Ottobono. From there, the two consuls inexplicably elected to head in the dark of night to the Ponziane Islands, 53 miles to the west. Somehow during the night the two became separated. Bellobruno found himself the next morning with 23 vessels and Rolando di Carmadino nowhere in sight with the rest of the ships. For reasons again unexplained, the consul then chose to head due north. When the small flotilla came abeam Capo Circeo, a headland 25 miles west of Gaeta, it caught sight of another fleet.[246] Ottobono Scriba describes the encounter:

> Behold Margaritus appeared with King Tancred's fleet, comprising 72 galleys, two *sagittei* and two *scurzati* [?], and challenged the aforesaid 22 [23] galleys. Seeing this, our galleys raised their sails and took up arms, wishing to attack King Tancred's fleet. Finally it happened that Margaritus and the royal fleet turned tail and steered towards the island of Ischia, and the Genoese fleet steered towards Rome.[247]

Ottobono Scriba is the only source for this episode, and his account is not credible. The details simply do not add up. First of all, he claims that the Pisan fleet escaped a Sicilian blockade at night. This hardly seems possible. Castel Vulturno is on the south bank of the river a few hundred meters inland from the mouth and the mouth is barely one hundred meters wide. The Pisan ships would have to have been nearly invisible to slip out unchallenged. In any event, the *Annales Pisani* makes no mention of the incident. More to the point, why would the Genoese consuls choose to continue south from Castel Vulturno once they had learned the siege of Naples had been lifted? And, why did they decide upon Ischia as a destination? Most curiously, why would supposedly seasoned mariners opt to sail west from Ischia to Ponza at night? That is a journey of 53 miles out into the open sea in darkness, probably into the prevailing winds. At a sprightly average speed of seven knots, it would have taken over seven and a half hours to complete. And the tale of the chance encounter the next day at Capo Circeo seems altogether suspect. If the mandate of the Sicilian fleet was to break the siege of Naples, what was it doing 76 miles to the north with Henry's imperial army still in the area (at Capua)? And more glaringly, why would the vaunted Margaritus, known in multiple sources as either 'king of the sea' or 'Neptune',[248]

---

[246] Ottobono Scriba, *Annales Ianuenses*, II, pp. 38–9.

[247] Ottobono Scriba, *Annales Ianuenses*, II, p. 39. '*Ecce Margaritus cum stolio regis Tanclerii, uidelicet cum galeis LXXII et duabus sagitteis et duabus scurzatis, apparuit, et predictus XXII [XXIII] galeis dedit insultum. Quibus uisis, galeae nostrae erexerunt uexilla, et ceperunt arma, uolentes aggredi exercitum regis Tanclerii. Tandem contigit quod Margaritus cum stolio regis dedit terga, et tenuerunt uersus insulam Yscle; et exercitus Ianuae tenuit uersus Romam.*' (English translation by G. A. Loud at www.leeds.ac.uk/history/weblearning/MedievalHistoryText-Centre/medievalTexts/html.)

[248] Garufi, 'Margarito di Brindisi Conte di Malta e Ammiraglio del Re di Sicilia', p. 273.

at the head of 76 ships turn tail and run at the sight of a flotilla numbering a mere 23? If he did not intend to engage, what was he doing so far north? These unanswered questions engender a deep incredulity. As if that were not enough, Ottobono's description of the action is unrealistic. He says, '... our galleys raised their sails and took up arms, wishing to attack king Tancred's fleet',[249] yet galley fleets usually lowered their sails prior to engagement.[250] John Pryor explains why: 'Masts were normally lowered before going into battle if at all possible in order to prevent their smashing the hulls and causing loss of life if they came crashing down.'[251] Ottobono's account of an encounter with the Sicilian fleet is, thus, most probably a concoction.

Theodore Toeche, author of *Kaiser Heinrich VI*, for one, was convinced that the incident was a fiction fabricated by Ottobono to exalt the exploits of his countrymen.[252] On the other hand, Dione Clementi, in her 1954 paper entitled 'Some Unnoticed Aspects of the Emperor Henry VI's Conquest of the Norman Kingdom of Sicily', used what she euphemistically termed 'a spirited translation of the passage' to come up with the rather bizarre interpretation that the Genoese had pressed on to Ischia then Ponza in search of the Pisan fleet in order to confer with them on the next course of action.[253] A more appropriate description of her translation would be 'imaginative', for it is difficult to envision Genoese mariners seeking out their Pisan counterparts for any purpose other than battle. Graham Loud offers a more straightforward translation, which includes no speculation about a Genoese attempt to rendezvous with the Pisans and it is to be preferred.[254] And her explanation that the Sicilian fleet might have balked at an engagement with an inferior force at Capo Circeo because 'the other enemy fleet might be harrying the coasts of the kingdom' is strained and tenuous.[255]

A much more plausible explanation is that the fleet that Bellobruno saw at Capo Circeo, if he saw one at all, was not the Sicilian royal fleet under Margaritus's command. Ottobono may have only conjured up the name of the famous admiral to cast his compatriots in a more heroic light. The fact is that the Sicilian royal fleet may have ceased to exist at this juncture. It is most probable that

---

[249] Ottobono Scriba, *Annales Ianuenses*, II, p. 39. '... *galeae nostrae erexerunt uexilla, et ceperunt arma, uolentes aggredi exercitum regis Tanclerii*.' (English translation by G. A. Loud at www.leeds.ac.uk/history/weblearning/MedievalHistoryTextCentre/medievalTexts/html.)

[250] Coates, Morrison, Rankov, *Athenian Trireme*, p. 43.

[251] Pryor and Jeffreys, *Dromōn*, p. 231.

[252] T. Toeche-Mittler, *Kaiser Heinrich VI* (Leipzig, 1867), p. 202, note 2.

[253] D. Clementi, 'Some Unnoticed Aspects of the Emperor Henry VI's Conquest of the Norman Kingdom of Sicily', *Bulletin of the John Rylands Library*, XXXVI (Manchester, 1954), pp. 328–59, especially 341–2.

[254] G.A. Loud, 'The Genoese Annals of Ottobuono Scriba', *Medieval History Texts in Translation* (University of Leeds, 2006), http://www.leeds.ac.uk/history/weblearning/MedievalHistoryTextCentre/medievalTexts/html.

[255] Clementi, 'Emperor Henry VI's Conquest of the Norman Kingdom of Sicily', p. 343.

Richard Coeur de Lion had burned it to the waterline at the port of Messina the year before.[256] This would explain why there is no other reliable account in any chronicle or annals of any ethnic origin describing a single naval action of the Sicilian royal fleet led by Margaritus or any other Norman commander after Richard's sack of Messina in the fall of 1190. Peter of Eboli's manuscript contains an illustration of a single ship 'of Tancred' ('*Tancredini*') fancifully warding off an imperial cavalry charge at the siege of Naples, but the vessel could just as well have belonged to one of Tancred's subject cities, like Naples itself.[257] Besides, the text of Peter's poem makes no mention of Sicilian ships at the siege of Naples.[258] Such a dearth of information on Sicilian sea power in the final years of the Norman Kingdom prompted William Heywood to muse in dismay, 'Margaritus and the Norman navies have disappeared from the scene as if by magic.'[259]

The ships that the Genoese flotilla encountered in August 1191 may have, in fact, belonged to Gaeta, Naples or both. After all, those two Campanian cities would have had a vested interest in defending themselves from imperial conquest. Both cities must certainly have known that it had been imperial policy since 1162 to carve up the *Regno* and dole out the various parts to the emperor's allies in the aftermath of the conquest. These two ports could not have been ignorant of the fact that they had been promised to their Ligurian and Tuscan competitors as prizes of war. They would have needed little further inducement to put up a vigorous defense. All Tancred had to do was to convince them that life would be much better under him than the imperialist party, especially the hated Pisans who had repeatedly assaulted Campanian ports throughout the twelfth century as the seaborne henchmen of the German emperor. Accordingly, Abulafia theorizes that Tancred offered generous concessions to Naples and Gaeta in 1190 and 1191 respectively to encourage them to resist the emperor of their own volition.[260] If he is right, and all evidence indicates that he is, this is precisely what they did. Gaeta, in particular, would have been motivated to contest the presence of the Pisans at Castel Vulturno. The July 1191 royal concession to Gaeta granted it suzerainty over a number of fortlets and small ports from Marina Lago di Patria, 10 miles south of the Vulturno, to Lido di Fondi, 13 miles northwest of Gaeta and only 14 miles east of Capo Circeo.[261] Indeed, the diversion of the Genoese fleet by way of Ponza can be explained by the desire to avoid a belligerent and aroused Gaeta on the journey homeward.

---

[256] Ambroise, *Estoire de la Guerre Sainte*, I, lines 816–17, p. 14; II, p. 42; *Itinerarium Peregrinorum et Gesta Regis Ricardi* in *Chronicles and Memorials of the Reign of Richard I*, II, Bk II, ch. XVI, p. 164; *Chronicle of the Third Crusade: Itinerarium Peregrinorum*, Bk 2, ch. 16, p. 163.

[257] Peter of Eboli, *Liber ad honorem Augusti sive de rebus Siculis*, fol. 110r, p. 95.

[258] Peter of Eboli, *Liber ad honorem Augusti sive de rebus Siculis*, fol. 108v, p. 89.

[259] Heywood, *History of Pisa*, p. 224.

[260] Abulafia, *Two Italies*, p. 173.

[261] *Tancredi et Willelmi III Regum Diplomata*, no. 18, p. 44.

Further evidence that the Norman royal navy had ceased to exist as an effective fighting force is provided by two of the most reliable accounts of the Tancred era, the *Annales Casinenses* and the chronicle of Richard of San Germano. Neither mentions the use of a Sicilian sea power in the struggle to stave off conquest by Henry VI. As a matter of fact, the only other source to indicate that the kingdom still possessed any warships at all is Peter of Eboli's manuscript. It displays three illustrations depicting such vessels, two of which show the same ship – the one that transported Constance from Salerno to Messina in 1191.[262] The contemporary narratives describe in detail the various land confrontations between Tancred's allies and the assorted proxies of Henry VI, but no naval engagements are noted. The efforts of Tancred himself to retain control of Apulia, Calabria and the Terra di Lavoro are also chronicled without allusion to any naval assistance. Nor are any naval exploits of Margaritus mentioned in the waning years of the Hauteville era.

Even so, Tancred did the best that he could with what he had. Henry's long absence from Italy had allowed this last Hauteville claimant to the crown of Sicily to mark some successes. On the battlefield, Tancred managed to outlast Henry's man, Count Berthold of Königsberg, and drive imperial opposition to the frontiers of Apulia and the Terra di Lavoro.[263] Thanks to the duplicity of the citizens of Salerno, Tancred even had the Empress Constance in his grasp for a time, although he ended up sending her back to Henry as a goodwill gesture at the pope's urging.[264] His most promising accomplishment was the conclusion of a marriage pact with the Byzantine Emperor, Isaakios Angelos, whereby the latter's daughter, Irene, exchanged nuptials with Tancred's son and designated successor, Roger, at Brindisi in the spring of 1193.[265] It all fell apart, however, shortly afterwards. In December of that same year, Roger fell gravely ill and died on Christmas Eve. Tancred followed him to the crypt on 20 February of the following year, leaving his young son William III as his successor under the regency of Queen Sibylla.[266] At that point, the demise of the Norman Kingdom of Sicily was a foregone conclusion.

Henry, in the meantime, had consolidated his position inside Germany and had gained an unexpected windfall. One of his vassals, Duke Leopold V of Austria, had captured King Richard on his return from the Third Crusade. The German Emperor made the English monarch pay a steep price for his free-

---

[262] Peter of Eboli, *Liber ad honorem Augusti sive de rebus Siculis*, fols 110r on p. 95, 119r on p. 131 and 120r on p. 135.

[263] *Annales Casinenses*, anno 1193, pp. 316–17; Richard of San Germano, *Ryccardi de Sancto Germano Notarii Chronica*, anno 1193, pp. 15–16.

[264] *Annales Casinenses*, anni 1191–2, pp. 315–16; *Annales Ceccanenses*, anno 1193, p. 292; Otto of St Blasien, pp. 55–7; Richard of San Germano, *Ryccardi de Sancto Germano Notarii Chronica*, anno 1191, p. 13.

[265] *Annales Casinenses*, anno 1193, p. 317; *Chronica de Ferraria*, anno 1193, p. 32.

[266] *Annales Casinenses*, anno 1194, p. 317; *Chronica de Ferraria*, anno 1193, p. 32; Richard of San Germano, *Ryccardi de Sancto Germano Notarii Chronica*, anno 1193, p. 16.

dom.[267] Roger of Howden lists the terms of his release: 'The king of England shall give to the emperor of the Romans one hundred thousand silver marks as his ransom, and shall find fifty galleys, with all their equipments, and two hundred knights for his service for one year.'[268] Those 50 fully armed galleys doubtless complemented the fleets of both Genoa and Pisa, as Henry headed south with his armies in the spring of 1194 to finally complete the conquest of the Norman Kingdom of Sicily. Nowhere did he encounter any substantial resistance. Naples capitulated to the Pisans, while Henry took Salerno by storm and subjected it to a terrible sacking in vengeance for having held his queen hostage for a time.[269] The *Annales Casinenses* says, 'Then he marched into Apulia, and meeting no resistance came through Calabria to Messina.'[270] The only naval battle of the whole campaign was between the Genoese and the Pisans, squabbling over spoils at Messina.[271] The Norman navy was nowhere to be seen. In the end, the great admiral Margaritus was reduced to making a last stand, not on the deck of a ship of war, but at Queen Sibylla's side in the Castellammare of Palermo – that is, until his own garrison surrendered to the enemy. Henry marched triumphant into the capital and was crowned king in the cathedral on Christmas day.[272] The Norman Kingdom of Sicily was dead, due in no small part to the fact that its naval power had predeceased it.

The sources are silent on the fate of the royal fleet. No explanation is offered anywhere as to why there was no navy to contest the final Hohenstaufen conquest of the island. The dismaying disappearance of the Norman fleet piqued even the consternation of Camillo Manfroni who laments:

---

[267] *Annales Casinenses*, anno 1192, p. 316; *Itinerarium Peregrinorum et Gesta Regis Ricardi* in *Chronicles and Memorials of the Reign of Richard I*, I, Bk VI, ch. XXXVII, pp. 442–3; *Chronicle of the Third Crusade: Itinerarium Peregrinorum*, Bk 6, ch. 37, p. 383; 'The old French Continuation of William of Tyre, 1184–1197', ch. 144–6, pp. 122–3; *La continuation de Guillaume de Tyr (1184–1197)*, ch. 144–6, pp. 155–7; *Otto of St Blasien*, pp. 57–8; Richard of San Germano, *Ryccardi de Sancto Germano Notarii Chronica*, anno 1193, p. 15; Roger of Howden, *Annals of Roger de Hoveden*, II, p. 270; *Chronica Magistri Rogeri de Houedene*, III, p. 186.

[268] Roger of Howden, *Annals of Roger de Hoveden*, II, p. 288; *Chronica Magistri Rogeri de Houedene*, III, p. 205. 'Quod rex Angliae dabit imperatori Romanorum centum millia marcarum argenti de redemptione, et inveniet ei quinquaginta galeas cum omni apparatu per unum annum in servitio suo, et cc milites per unum annum in servitio suo.'

[269] *Annales Casinenses*, anno 1194, p. 317; *Annales Cavenses*, anno 1194, p. 193; *Annales Ceccanenses*, anno 1194, p. 292; *Chronica de Ferraria*, anno 1194, p. 32; *Otto of St Blasien*, pp. 59–60; Richard of San Germano, *Ryccardi de Sancto Germano Notarii Chronica*, anno 1194, p. 16.

[270] *Annales Casinenses*, anno 1194, p. 317. 'Deinde transit in Apuliam, et nullo resistente per Calabriam venit Messanam.'

[271] Ottobono Scriba, *Annales Ianuenses*, II, pp. 48–9.

[272] *Annales Casinenses*, anno 1194, p. 317; *Annales Cavenses*, anno 1194, p. 193; *Annales Ceccanenses*, anno 1194, p. 292; Richard of San Germano, *Ryccardi de Sancto Germano Notarii Chronica*, anno 1194, p. 17. See also Chalandon, *Histoire de la Domination Normande*, II, pp. 485–7.

Sicily, which, from the Norman conquest up to then, had always been able to glory in the possession of a flourishing armada, fell into the power of Swabia, without a single ship to dispute the crossing of the strait by the invaders, without a feat of arms of any kind to cancel the shame of its fall, to testify to the existence of that navy, which one day had made the Greek empire tremble.[273]

Tancred, in truth, was responsible for neither the ruin of the royal fleet nor the collapse of the kingdom. He was merely present at the last gasp. The series of concessions he issued to many of the maritime cities of the realm served to illuminate the lack of legitimacy bequeathed to him by William, which forced the king to give away the merchandise in order to keep the store. Inevitably, he ran out of merchandise and the store was forfeit. The July 1191 privilege to Gaeta in which Tancred reduced the ship quota due the royal fleet from two to one is particularly endemic of a pattern that undermined the king's ability to sustain the fleet. The very concessions that he made in an effort to purchase the loyalty he needed, prevented him from building up or even maintaining the naval power upon which the kingdom depended.

---

[273] Manfroni, *Storia della Marina italiana*, I, p. 294.

4

The Impact

The establishment of Norman naval supremacy in the central Mediterranean during the twelfth century was far-reaching and momentous. The impact went well beyond the Normans in particular and southern Italy in general. It was at the very nexus of change on the 'middle sea', a change that would affect the course of events not only in Europe, but also in the Middle East and North Africa for generations. It would not be an overstatement to characterize it as a multifaceted, pivot point in history with wide-ranging military, political and economic effects on a large number of peoples in vastly varied regions. That being said, the impact can best be broken down into four major and immediate consequences: firstly, the Norman conquest of the central Mediterranean facilitated the eastward expansion of West Italian sea power, namely that of Genoa and Pisa, in conjunction with the Crusading movement; secondly, it engendered Western commercial growth both north-to-south and east-to-west; thirdly, it altered forever Muslim trading patterns across the Mediterranean; and finally, it laid the groundwork for the resurgence of Sicilian sea power under Frederick II.

Eastward expansion of West Italian sea power

Prior to the eleventh century, Muslim domination of the central Mediterranean acted as a brake on Western commercial expansion. Muslim control of Sicily and the lands immediately to the north and south meant that West Italian maritime commerce was largely restricted to the Tyrrhenian basin. Genoa and Pisa were effectively barred from partaking in the lucrative trade with Byzantium, the Levant and Egypt. Only such long-time Muslim trading partners as the merchants of Amalfi were allowed to transit freely to the East. Muslim piracy, in particular, plagued the efforts of Genoa and Pisa to extend their trade routes eastward. Norman advances in southern Italy and Sicily, beginning in the second half of the eleventh century, provided the long-awaited opportunity to break the 'Saracen' stranglehold. For once, Christian ground forces in the form of Norman knights were making sustainable gains on the land masses constricting the Mediterranean at its middle.

The Pisans, especially, were aching to join the fray. Barely two years after the Hauteville brothers seized the Strait of Messina (1061), the men of Tuscany set their sights on Palermo, doubtless a hotbed of Aghlabid pirates in years past. Amatus even implies that they did so at the behest of Robert Guiscard. The Norman chronicler writes, 'While the duke was striving to take Bari, he requested and sought the aid of the Pisans so that the Saracens might not be allowed a long respite to bring supplies into the land and that he might not delay too long in destroying them.'[1] Although the reference is to Bari, it is clear from Amatus' chapter summary that the target of the attack was Palermo ('Chapter 28: How the Pisans came to the aid of the duke and besieged Palermo and fought against the Saracens on land and on sea').[2] Amatus' subsequent description of that attack is borne out by other sources, but he got the chronology wrong: the Pisan raid on Palermo took place in 1063,[3] whereas Robert's siege of Bari did not begin until 1068.[4] Furthermore, it is doubtful that the Pisans made their foray at Guiscard's urging. Geoffrey Malaterra insists instead that they did so at their own instigation, motivated by profit and vengeance for the ill-treatment of their traders: 'The merchants of Pisa, who frequently visited Palermo to profit from maritime commerce, sought to avenge certain injuries that they had suffered at the hands of the people of Palermo.'[5]

Malaterra goes on to infer that the Pisans were taking advantage of Norman successes on Sicily to advance their own military and commercial interests. He records that it was actually the Pisans who first approached the Normans. In early September 1063, they attempted to inveigle Robert's younger brother Roger into supporting the proposed assault on Palermo with his cavalry. But Roger demurred.[6] William Heywood (*History of Pisa*) surmises that he did so because he had no intention of sharing the prize with the pecuniarily minded Pisans.[7] While there was probably some truth to this, the more likely explanation is that Roger simply did not have the manpower to oblige. It would not be until 1064 that he would attempt to take Palermo himself and, even then, it was only because his older brother and liege lord, Robert, came to the island with an

---

[1] Amatus, *History of the Normans*, Bk V, ch. 28, p. 146; *Storia de' Normanni*, Bk V, ch. XXVIII, pp. 255–6. 'En cellui temps, quant lo Duc se combatoit pour prendre la cité de Bar, demanda et requist l'ajutoire de cil de Pise, à ce qui li Sarrazin non soient leissiez o lonc repos et non fornissent la terre par lonc temps; et que lo Duc non demorast trop pour les destruire.'

[2] Amatus, *History of the Normans*, Bk V, ch. summary, p. 132; *Storia de' Normanni*, Bk V, p. 222. 'Capitula XXVIII. Coment li Pisen vindrent en aide à lo Duc et mistrent siege entor Palerme, et combatirent contre li Sarrazin par mer et par terre.'

[3] Bernardo Maragone, *Annales Pisani*, p. 5.

[4] Malaterra, *Deeds of Count Roger*, Bk 2, ch. 40, p. 117; *De rebus gestis Rogerii*, Bk II, ch. XL, p. 48.

[5] Malaterra, *Deeds of Count Roger*, Bk 2, ch. 34, p. 111; *De rebus gestis Rogerii*, Bk II, ch. XXXIV, p. 45. 'Pisani ergo mercatores, qui saepius navali commercio Panormum lucratum venire soliti erant, quasdam injurias ab ipsis Panormitanis passi vindicari cupientes.'

[6] Malaterra, *Deeds of Count Roger*, Bk 2, ch. 34, pp. 111–12; *De rebus gestis Rogerii*, Bk II, ch. XXXIV, p. 45.

[7] Heywood, *History of Pisa*, pp. 27–8.

army of some 500 additional knights.[8] This effort, ironically, failed because it lacked naval support, but the point remains that Roger just was not ready a year earlier. Besides, he was too busy consolidating his hold on the Val Demone. The fact that the Pisans had sent emissaries to Troina to beseech the aid of Roger's ground forces is, however, quite telling about their purposes. It is apparent that the Pisans were intent upon far more than simply a looting expedition. It appears probable that they wanted Palermo to be taken and held in order to make the western approach to the Strait of Messina safer and more passable. Such an objective is also implied by the huge scale of the enterprise. There is an inscription commemorating the event just to the left of the main door of the eleventh-century cathedral of Pisa, which purports that 'all the old, middle-aged and also the young' of the city participated in the undertaking.[9] The force was of such size that it was able to penetrate the port and seize six large merchantmen, with the 'Saracen' citizenry apparently helpless to prevent it. The Pisan armada even disembarked a substantial body of infantry near the mouth of the River Oreto, which then ravaged the outskirts of the city with impunity for several days despite an armed sortie by the inhabitants. The plunder acquired from the enterprise was evidently enough to finance the construction of the magnificent Romanesque Duomo of Pisa.[10]

Continued Norman successes on Sicily emboldened an even grander assault on the Muslims of the central Mediterranean by the mariners of Pisa in 1087. This time the objective was Mahdiyah. Its Zirid emir, Tamim, had apparently converted his capital into a bastion of Muslim piracy that plagued 'the middle sea' far and wide. Such is attested by the anonymous *Carmen in victoriam Pisanorum*: 'There is no place in all the world nor the islands of the sea that Temin would not throw into disorder with his horrible perfidy; Rhodes, Cyprus as well as Crete and Sardinia are violently harassed together with the noble men of Sicily.'[11] Hyperbole notwithstanding, even Muslim authors agree that Tamim had engendered the enmity of the coastal communities of the Christian West. Ibn al-Athir writes, 'The cause was that the Emir Tamim 'ibn 'al Mu'izz 'ibn Badis, prince of the country, was making frequent maritime raids against the Rum, laying waste to the towns and upsetting their populations.'[12] In any case, there can be little doubt that the activities of the Zirid fleet probably curtailed trade traffic through the Sicilian Channel, and served as one last obstruction to the eastward expansion of Christian commerce. It was a circumstance that Pisa

---

[8]   Malaterra, *Deeds of Count Roger*, Bk 2, ch. 36, p. 114; *De rebus gestis Rogerii*, Bk II, ch. XXXVI, pp. 46–7.

[9]   Bernardo Maragone, *Annales Pisani*, p. 5. '*Omnes maiores, medii, pariterque minores …*' (Maragone preserved the inscription in its entirety in the *Annales Pisani*.)

[10] Bernardo Maragone, *Annales Pisani*, pp. 5–6.

[11] *Carmen in victoriam Pisanorum*, p. 24, par. 8: '*Non est locus toto mundo neque maris insula, quam Timini non turbaret orrenda perfidia; Rodus Ciprus Creta simul et Sardinia, vexabatur et cum illis nobilis Sicilia.*'

[12] Ibn al-Athir, *BAS*, I, p. 440.

could no longer abide. As William Heywood so aptly observed, 'So long as Sicily remained in Mussulman hands, voyages to the Levant were probably rare and isolated; but the Norman conquests opened the Straits of Messina to Christian merchantmen, and the day had now arrived when a great pirate sea-port of the north coast of Africa could no longer be tolerated.'[13] So determined were the Pisans to remove this hindrance that they joined forces with their reviled Ligurian competitors, the Genoese. The Amalfitans, heretofore inveterate allies of the Muslims, must also have grown tired of the harassment, for they too offered their support.[14] Roger was summoned to join the cause as well, but, as was noted earlier, the 'Great Count' had evidently contracted a non-aggression pact with Tamim and, accordingly, declined.[15]

Under the aegis of Pope Victor III (formerly Desiderius, the pro-Norman abbot of Montecassino), the maritime powers of western Italy assembled an enormous fleet for the undertaking.[16] The *Carmen in victoriam Pisanorum* purports that they 'collected a thousand ships in only three months'.[17] The Muslim sources estimate the number was a more modest but still substantial 300 to 400 vessels, which Ibn al-Athir contends took the Genoese and Pisans four years to accumulate.[18] Furthermore, at-Tijani and Ibn abi Dinar insist the armada carried some 30,000 fighters.[19] Whatever the actual size of the force, the consensus is that it descended first upon the island of Pantelleria, which it easily occupied.[20] When the armada landed at Zawilah, Mahdiayah's suburb, on Saint Sixtus Day (6 August) the timing could not have been more opportune.[21] Tamim was away with the core of his army, apparently contending with the marauding Bedouins who had tormented the Maghrib at the behest of the Fatimid caliphs of Cairo since the middle of the century.[22] Ironically, it was probably the Arab warriors of the Banu Hilal and the Banu Sulaym who had prompted Tamim to resort to piracy in the first place. They had so devastated the agriculture and commerce of North Africa that the Zirids had little choice but to seek revenue from alternative sources. They would now, indirectly, cost the Zirids even more, for the West Italians stormed ashore virtually unopposed. According to the *Carmen in victo-*

[13] Heywood, *History of Pisa*, p. 34.

[14] *Carmen in victoriam Pisanorum*, p. 25, par. 11–13.

[15] Ibn al-Athir, *BAS*, I, p. 451; Malaterra, *Deeds of Count Roger*, Bk 4, ch. 3, pp. 193–4; *De rebus gestis Rogerii*, Bk IV, ch. III, p. 179.

[16] *Chronica Monasterii Casinensis*, Bk III, ch. 71, p. 453.

[17] *Carmen in victoriam Pisanorum*, p. 24, par. 10. '... component mille naves solis tribus mensibus.'

[18] Ibn al-Athir, *BAS*, I, p. 441.

[19] Ibn abi Dinar, *BAS*, II, p. 283; At-Tijani, *BAS*, II, p. 62.

[20] *Carmen in victoriam Pisanorum*, p. 25, par. 15; Ibn al-Athir, *BAS*, I, p. 441; Al-Nuwayri, *BAS*, II, p. 153.

[21] Bernardo Maragone, *Annales Pisani*, p. 6.

[22] At-Tijani, *BAS*, II, p. 63; Ibn abi Dinar, *BAS*, II, p. 283; Ibn al-Athir, *BAS*, I, p. 441; Al-Nuwayri, *BAS*, II, p. 153.

riam Pisanorum, the result was a bloodbath of epic proportions.[23] 'The enemy assaulted our country in such numbers, that they seemed like clouds of locusts or swarms of vermin,' reads a *qasidah* (poem) relayed by at-Tijani describing the event.[24] By the time Tamim returned, he could do nothing but seek refuge in the royal citadel and watch helplessly while the Christian raiders completed a horrific sacking of both Zawilah and Mahdiyah.

In the end, he was able to buy them off at considerable expense. Ibn al-Athir says Tamim was compelled to release all his Christian prisoners and pay a tribute of 30,000 gold *dinars*.[25] Al-Nuwayri puts the ransom figure at 80,000.[26] But the concession that probably meant the most to the merchants of Genoa and Pisa was the clause contained in the *Carmen in victoriam Pisanorum* whereby the Zirid ruler 'swore by God in heaven according to his own written word to henceforth not impose treacherous attacks on Christians and not to levy duties' on their shipping.[27] The door to the East had been flung wide open. Only the Normans, who held Sicily and the Strait of Messina, could stand in the way and it was not in their best interest to do so. Taxing east–west trade promised to be a lucrative enterprise for the House of Hauteville. All that was needed was a catalyst to stimulate the spread of West Italian sea power eastward. That spark was provided by the Crusades.

Pope Urban II's call to take up the cross reached Genoa and Pisa at perhaps the most propitious juncture in their development. The inclination toward independent republican governments that began in the early eleventh century had achieved realization. During the last quarter of the century the two cities had succeeded in establishing domestic peace and achieving some measure of autonomy from imperial control. In Genoa, feuding between liberal bourgeois elements and the old aristocratic families who were descended from the viscounts had withered away to be replaced by the *compagna*, the beginnings of a commune style of government.[28] The arbitration of Archbishop Daimbert had effected a similar development in Pisa. Years of internecine conflict between the margraves[29] of Tuscany and the urban nobility of Pisa had effectively been brought to a conclusion by the 1094 *Concordia*, a document that recognized the authority of the communal assembly. By the end of the century both cities were electing consuls.[30] At the same time, the two burgeoning mercantile powers had won preeminence over the northern Tyrrhenian. By 1050 the two had ousted

[23] *Carmen in victoriam Pisanorum*, p. 26, par. 37–9.
[24] At-Tijani, *BAS*, II, p. 64.
[25] Ibn al-Athir, *BAS*, I, p. 441.
[26] Al-Nuwayri, *BAS*, II, p. 153.
[27] *Carmen in victoriam Pisanorum*, p. 28, par. 58. 'Iuravit per Deum celi suas legens litteras, iam ammodo Christianis non ponet insidias, et non tollet tulineum…'
[28] S. Epstein, *Genoa and the Genoese, 958–1528* (Chapel Hill, 1996), p. 33.
[29] Margraves were descended from the German *Markgrafen* ('march counts') who had responsibility for protecting royal or imperial borderlands.
[30] Heywood, *History of Pisa*, pp. 9–10.

Muslim pirates from Sardinia, and in 1077 Pisa held sway over Corsica as well. The mariners of Genoa and Pisa had become so bold that in the last decades of the eleventh century they were raiding the coasts of Muslim Spain (Al-Andalus) and the Balearics.[31] At peace internally and secure in the western Mediterranean, the opportunity to send their warships east with the crusading movement must have been irresistible. It would be under the banner of the faithful that West Italian sea power would sally forth to firmly ensconce itself in the eastern Mediterranean.

While Norman naval power did not participate directly in the First Crusade, it most certainly facilitated the participation of the West Italian fleets. Given the exigency imposed by geography, Norman domination of the central Mediterranean meant that neither the Genoese nor the Pisans could freely transit to the East without at least the tacit approval of the House of Hauteville. In point of fact, there were only two choices for entering the Ionian Sea from the west: the Sicilian Channel or the Strait of Messina. John Pryor observes, 'From the Sicilian Channel or the Straits of Messina, ships could either cross the Ionian Sea directly to Modon or Crete or alternatively follow the coasts of Sicily, Calabria, Apulia, and the Balkans.'[32] Between the two routes, the coastal one through the strait was overwhelmingly preferred. Pryor notes, for example, that 'Genoese galleys bound for the Levant or Romania and entering from the Straits of Messina almost always took the coastal route'. He goes on to state, 'In fact galleys of all persuasions would normally have taken the coastal route, because even in summer the weather in the Ionian is unpredictable.'[33] Indeed, William Heywood speculates that the Pisan expedition of 1099 commanded by Archbishop Daimbert 'seems to have sailed round the heel of Italy to Apulia, and thence after crossing the Strait of Otranto, along the Greek coast to Cape Matapan [at the end of the Mani Peninsula of Laconia, Greece], never venturing out of sight of land'.[34] This is based on Bernardo Maragone's testimony that the Pisan fleet paused to plunder the islands of Leucadia and Cephalonia along the way.[35]

Since the more convenient access to this coastal route would have been the Strait of Messina, it stands to reason that most western fleets traversing the central Mediterranean in the crusading period would have done so through the Strait of Messina. Ruth Gertwagen, an expert in medieval Mediterranean port facilities, cites al-Idrisi to reinforce that supposition from a logistical standpoint: 'Galley fleets that did not provision in Sicily would have to have put into Reggio, where there was abundant water, attested to by the existence of bathhouses, and

---

[31] Lewis, *Naval Power and Trade*, pp. 232–4.

[32] Pryor, *Geography, Technology, and War*, pp. 92–3.

[33] Pryor, *Geography, Technology, and War*, p. 93.

[34] Heywood, *History of Pisa*, p. 93.

[35] Bernardo Maragone, *Annales Pisani*, p. 7. 'Profiscendo vero Lu'catam et Cefaloniam, urbes fortissimas, expugnantes expoliaverunt, quoniam Ierosolimitanum iter impedire consueverunt.'

whose markets provided fruits and vegetables.'[36] It bears repeating that the Strait of Messina, less than three miles wide, was tightly controlled on both shores by the Normans. They even held sway over the Lipari Islands, monitoring the western approach. It is, thus, inconceivable that any sizable armed force could have passed through that very narrow corridor without the knowledge and consent of the Hautevilles. Yet there is no record of them hindering, much less preventing, any armada from proceeding East under the auspices of the cross.

In truth, the Strait of Messina probably became a virtual turnstile for Western sea power during the Crusades, especially West Italian sea power. The Genoese appear to have been the first of the maritime cities to join the fray. In early 1097, Pope Urban II dispatched Bishops Hugh Chateauneuf d'Isère of Grenoble and William I of Orange to preach the crusade in the church of San Siro in Genoa. In July a flotilla of 12 galleys and a supply ship (sandanum) set sail for the Holy Land.[37] It is hardly surprising that it apparently had no difficulty passing through the strait, given that Roger de Hauteville's wife at the time was Adelaide del Vasto of Liguria. And fittingly, as fortune would have it, the first contingent of crusaders that the Genoese would aid was led by a Hauteville, Bohemond of Taranto, son of Robert Guiscard. By November, the small squadron had made its way to the Port of Saint Symeon at the mouth of the River Orontes, about ten miles from Antioch.[38] Its timing could not have been better. The crusaders besieging the city under Bohemond and Raymond of Toulouse (St Gilles) were growing short of supplies. 'The siege had already lasted five months,' reports William of Tyre, 'when some ships of Genoa, carrying pilgrims and provisions, sailed into the mouth of the river from the sea.'[39] So keen on acquiring the support of the Genoese was Bohemond that he himself led a force of 100 men to escort a party of them back to Antioch. The Genoese dispatched some 600 men with him, including, interestingly enough, 25 mounted combatants, implying the small flotilla had brought horses with them.[40]

Following the eventual capture of Antioch, Bohemond rewarded his Genoese allies for their part in the siege by granting them the first of their many concessions in the Levant. On 14 July 1098, they received from the Norman lord a

[36] Al-Idrisi, *La première géographie de l'Occident*, p. 341. See also R. Gertwagen, 'Harbours and facilities along the eastern Mediterranean sea lanes to Outremer', in *Logistics of Warfare in the Age of the Crusades*, ed. J. Pryor (Aldershot, 2006), pp. 95–118, especially 104.

[37] Caffaro, *Liberatio Orientis* in *Annali genovesi*, I, pp. 101–2.

[38] Raymond of Aguilers, *Historia Francorum qui ceperunt Iherusalem*, trans. John and Laurita Hill (Philadelphia, 1968), ch. IV, p. 32; *Raimundi de Aguilers canonici Podiensis historia Francorum qui ceperunt Iherusalem*, *Recueil des historiens des croisades*, *Historiens occidentaux*, ed. Académie des Inscriptions et Belles Lettres (5 vols, Paris, 1844–95), III, ch. V, p. 242.

[39] William of Tyre, *History of Deeds Done beyond the Sea*, I, Bk 5, ch. 4, p. 229; *Willelmi Tyrensis Chronicon*, Bk 5, ch. 4, p. 274. 'Cumque iam in mensem quintum se protraxisset obsidio, naves quedam Ianuensium, peregrinos et victualia deferentes, infra fauces fluminis egresse a pelago se contulerant ...'

[40] Caffaro, *Liberatio Orientis*, pp. 102–3.

charter allotting them a quarter that included 30 houses, a fountain and a market arrayed around the church of Saint John. The charter also guaranteed trade in Antioch free from all duties for Genoese merchants. In return, the Genoese agreed to help maintain Bohemond's communications with Norman Italy.[41] It was a pattern that would repeat itself for both Genoa and Pisa throughout the crusading movement of the twelfth century.

The vessels of the first Genoese expedition apparently remained in the area for some time afterwards because the crusaders continued to depend on them for supplies. In fact, the leaders of the Frankish army deemed it prudent to proceed from Antioch to Jerusalem by way of the coast instead of the Damascus route, because these ships along with some English vessels could provision them with victuals from Cyprus, Byzantium and other Christian-controlled lands.[42] The decision proved wise, because these vessels were able to sustain the crusaders with grain, wine, barley and pork during the ill-fated first siege of Acre.[43] The vital importance of seaborne replenishment to the success of the crusades had been firmly established.

A second, even smaller Genoese expedition arrived at the port of Jaffa on 17 June 1099. There were only two vessels, but they carried two brothers whose descendants would eventually control nearly all the Genoese possessions in Palestine: Guglielmo and Primo Embriaco.[44] Once again the arrival of the Ligurian ships along with four English vessels was most timely for the crusaders, for the siege of Jerusalem was going poorly. As was the case before the walls of Antioch, thirst and famine were their most formidable adversaries.[45] Moreover, several attempts to breach the walls had failed, because the Franks possessed few ladders and no siege towers.[46] The Genoese would provide the remedy for both shortfalls. The mariners were well-stocked, judging from the reception of bread, wine and fish they provided the party of Frankish knights that had come to seek their aid.[47] Caffaro reports that they then disassembled their vessels and carried the wood back to Jerusalem in order to construct siege machinery, devices used in the ultimate reduction of the city.[48]

[41] CDG, I, no. 7, pp. 11–12; Regesta regni Hierosolymitani 1097–1291, ed. R. Rohricht (Innsbruck, 1893), no. 12, p. 2.

[42] Raymond of Aguilers, Historia Francorum, Hill, ch. XI, p. 85; RHC, Occ, III, ch. XIV, p. 274.

[43] Raymond of Aguilers, Historia Francorum, Hill, ch. XI, p. 88; RHC, Occ, III, ch. XV, p. 276.

[44] Caffaro, Liberatio Orientis, p. 110.

[45] Peter Tudebode, Historia de Hierosolymitano Itinere, trans. John and Laurita Hill (Philadelphia, 1974), ch. XI, p. 113; RHC, OCC, III, ch. XIV, p. 103.

[46] Raymond of Aguilers, Historia Francorum, Hill, ch. XIV, p. 117; RHC, Occ, III, ch. XX, p. 293.

[47] Raymond of Aguilers, Historia Francorum, Hill, ch. XIV, p. 120; RHC, Occ, III, ch. XX, p. 295.

[48] Caffaro, Liberatio Orientis, pp. 110–11.

The Pisans made their initial appearance in the East somewhat belatedly, arriving only after the capture of Jerusalem. Unlike their Ligurian competitors, however, it was on a much larger scale and bore the backing of the entire commune. Moreover, the city's most prominent citizen, Archbishop Daimbert himself, assumed the role of standard-bearer for the undertaking. The mariners, soldiers, carpenters and merchants who filled its ships must have nearly emptied the Tuscan city-state. According to Bernardo Maragone, the fleet was comprised of 120 vessels.[49] Anna Comnena's penchant for exaggeration drove her to claim, 'He [Daimbert] equipped triremes, dromons and other fast vessels to the number of 900, and so left for Syria.'[50] Regardless of the exact number, it bears emphasizing that a fleet of such size could hardly have passed through the Strait of Messina on its way to the Holy Land, unnoticed by the Normans. It is certain that its appearance in the eastern Mediterranean caused quite a stir. The sack of the Greek islands of Leucadia and Cephalonia prompted the Emperor Alexios to send a fleet of his own against the Pisans. Daimbert's armada managed to elude the Byzantines, but a second expedition from Pisa that same year numbering about 50 ships was waylaid off Rhodes by the fleet of Alexios' main maritime ally, Venice.[51] It is instructive that the movement of West Italian sea power in force through the central Mediterranean toward the Orient triggered great alarm among the Christian powers of the East, but not the Normans of southern Italy. It is also noteworthy that the first crusader leader to take advantage of this newly available sea power was, appropriately, an opportunistic Hauteville. Bohemond of Taranto immediately sought to enlist the Pisan fleet in his siege of Latakia, a Greek seaport at the time.[52]

The investment of Latakia was soon abandoned for a host of reasons, not the least of which was the shame of warring on a Christian city. Nonetheless, the alliance between Daimbert and Bohemond persisted.[53] The two later joined forces with Raymond of Toulouse for an inconclusive attack on Jabala, after which they marched together to Jerusalem, with the Pisan fleet protecting their seaward flank.[54] Upon their arrival, just before Christmas of 1099, Daimbert immediately demanded the patriarchate of Jerusalem. Godfrey de Bouillon, who was 'Defender of the Holy Sepulcher', had little choice but to accede to the Pisan archbishop's demands. Bohemond had brought superior forces with him, and Godfrey needed the help of the Pisan fleet to secure the coastal cities for his nascent Latin Kingdom. As a consequence, Daimbert was elected Patriarch of

[49] Bernardo Maragone, *Annales Pisani*, p. 7.

[50] Anna Comnena, *Alexiad*, p. 360; *Alexiade*, III, Bk XI, ch. X, pp. 41–2.

[51] Anna Comnena, *Alexiad*, pp. 360–3; *Alexiade*, III, Bk XI, ch. X, pp. 42–5. See also Manfroni, *Storia della Marina italiana*, I, pp. 141–2.

[52] Albert of Aachen, *Historia Ierosolimitana*, Bk VI, ch. 55, pp. 476–7; Bernardo Maragone, *Annales Pisani*, p. 7.

[53] Albert of Aachen, *Historia Ierosolimitana*, Bk VI, ch. 59, pp. 482–3.

[54] R. Yewdale, *Bohemond I, Prince of Antioch* (Princeton, 1924), p. 89.

Jerusalem, replacing Arnulf of Chocques. At the same ceremony, Bohemond was recognized as lord of Antioch.[55] It is, perhaps, by no accident that the most prominent Norman-Italian lord of the crusading movement managed to ally himself to both great West Italian maritime powers.

While there is scant testimony as to what the Pisan fleet contributed to the Latin Kingdom thereafter, it stands to reason that Godfrey would not have hesitated to use this valuable military resource. After all, he had paid a very dear price for the services of Daimbert's armada. Not only had he acquiesced in the archbishop's election as patriarch, the duke had also, by Easter 1100, acceded to the prelate's demand that he be given a fourth part of the port of Jaffa and all of the Holy City, including the tower of David.[56] To begin with, Godfrey probably employed the expertise of the Pisan sailors to refurbish and fortify the ancient port of Jaffa so that it might serve as a naval base for reducing the other coastal cities of Palestine.[57] Indeed, it appears that the Pisans assisted in the sieges of several of these ports.

Even if the bulk of Daimbert's fleet returned to Pisa later in 1100 as Camillo Manfroni suggests,[58] many of its mariners must have remained behind. Albert of Aachen testifies that Pisans were present in many of the subsequent coastal actions undertaken by the crusaders. He reports that they were among those who took Arsuf in the spring of 1101 as well as Caesarea in June of that same year.[59] And he notes that Pisan ships had joined those of the Genoese in helping Baldwin blockade Jubayl and Acre, gaining the submission of both in the spring of 1104.[60] They apparently were also at the siege of Sidon in August 1107.[61] Albert even mentions them as being among those who occupied Tripoli in the summer of 1109, and he says that it was on Pisan ships that Bertrand, son of Count Raymond, sailed from Tripoli to begin the blockade of Beirut in December of that same year.[62] While Albert's testimony can be called into question since he himself never set foot in the 'Holy Land',[63] active Pisan participation in the crusades can be corroborated by the commercial concessions conceded to them in

---

[55] Albert of Aachen, *Historia Ierosolimitana*, Bk VII, ch. 7, pp. 496–7; Fulcher of Chartres, *A History of the Expedition to Jerusalem, 1095–1127*, trans. F. Ryan and ed. H. Fink (Knoxville, 1969), Bk I, ch. XXXIII, par. 20 and note 11, p. 132; *Fulcheri Carnotensis Historia Hierosolymitana*, ed. H. Hagenmeyer (Heidelberg, 1913), Bk I, ch. XXXIII, par. 20, pp. 333–4; William of Tyre, *History of Deeds Done beyond the Sea*, I, Bk 9, ch. 15, pp. 402–3; *Willelmi Tyrensis Chronicon*, Bk 9, ch. 15, p. 440.

[56] William of Tyre, *History of Deeds Done beyond the Sea*, I, Bk 9, ch. 16, pp. 403–4; *Willelmi Tyrensis Chronicon*, Bk 9, ch. 16, pp. 441–2.

[57] Albert of Aachen, *Historia Ierosolimitana*, Bk VII, ch. 12, pp. 502–3. See also S. Runciman, *A History of the Crusades* (3 vols, Cambridge, 1951), I, p. 308.

[58] Manfroni, *Storia della Marina italiana*, I, p. 144.

[59] Albert of Aachen, *Historia Ierosolimitana*, Bk VII, ch. 54–5, pp. 562–5.

[60] Albert of Aachen, *Historia Ierosolimitana*, Bk IX, ch. 26–8, pp. 670–5.

[61] Albert of Aachen, *Historia Ierosolimitana*, Bk X, ch. 46, pp. 760–1.

[62] Albert of Aachen, *Historia Ierosolimitana*, Bk XI, ch. 13–15, pp. 782–7.

[63] S. Edgington, 'Introduction', *Historia Ierosolimitana*, pp. xxiii–xxiv.

the Latin East during the twelfth century.[64] For instance, Tancred, Bohemond's nephew and eventual heir as prince of Antioch, granted the Pisans a quarter not only in Antioch, but also in Latakia, suggesting the Pisans may have had a hand in Tancred's reduction of that city in 1108.[65] 'Thus, in less than a century from the expedition under Daimbert,' concludes Heywood, 'they [the Pisans] had colonies in Laodicea [Latakia], Antioch, Tripoli, Tyre, Acre, Jaffa, and probably also in Jerusalem and Caesarea.'[66]

The Genoese contribution to the establishment of the Latin Kingdom of Jerusalem is far less obscure thanks to the involvement of the primary Genoese chronicler of the period, Caffaro di Caschifellone. He sailed with the first substantial fleet to leave Genoa after the capture of Jerusalem by the crusaders. Consisting of 26 galleys and six supply ships ('*XXVI galeas et naves VI*'), it arrived in the East in the autumn of 1100 under the leadership of Guglielmo Embriaco.[67] Caffaro was an eyewitness to many of the succeeding events and wrote, in addition to the *Annales Ianuenses*, the *Liber de liberatione civitatum orientis* ('The Book of the liberation of the cities of the East') recounting the Genoese contribution to the First Crusade.[68] It is quite revealing that the first order of business for the leaders of Caffaro's expedition when it pulled into Latakia was to request confirmation of Bohemond's earlier concessions in Antioch. The mission was obviously motivated by more than mere matters of faith. More importantly, the Genoese seemed quite keen on maintaining the bond with their Norman allies. Bohemond had been captured by Kumushtakin ibn Danishmend, the Turkish emir of Sivas, late that summer,[69] so it was his regent, Tancred, with whom the Genoese dealt.[70] Wishing to retain the Genoese in his own campaign of conquest, the Norman lord acceded to their wishes and added several more grants of his own. He promised them a third of the port revenues of Saint Symeon, half the revenues of Latakia along with a quarter in that city, a quarter in Jubayl and a quarter in any other city taken with Genoese assistance.[71]

After wintering in Latakia, the same fleet headed south to Jaffa, where it was met by Baldwin of Boulogne in April 1101. The latter had assumed rule of Jerusalem upon the death of his brother Godfrey the summer before and now

---

[64] Manfroni, *Storia della Marina italiana*, I, pp. 505–11.

[65] G. Müller, *Documenti sulle relazioni delle Città Toscane coll'Oriente Cristiano e coi Turchi fino all'anno MDXXXI* (Florence, 1879), doc. I, p. 3.

[66] Heywood, *History of Pisa*, p. 115.

[67] Caffaro, *Annales Ianuenses*, I, p. 5; *Liberatio Orientis*, p. 112. (The *Liberatio Orientis* specifies four *naves* vice six.)

[68] Epstein, *Genoa and the Genoese*, p. 28.

[69] Fulcher of Chartres, *Expedition to Jerusalem*, Bk I, ch. XXXV, par. 2–3, p. 135; *Historia Hierosolymitana*, Bk I, ch. XXXV, par. 2–3, pp. 344–7; Ibn al-Athir, *Chronicle of Ibn al-Athir*, Part I, p. 32. See also Yewdale, *Bohemond I*, pp. 92–3.

[70] Fulcher of Chartres, *Expedition to Jerusalem*, Bk II, ch. VII, par. 1, pp. 150–1; *Historia Hierosolymitana*, Bk II, ch. VII, par. 1, pp. 390–3.

[71] CDG, I, no. 12, pp. 16–18; RRH, no. 35, p. 5.

needed sea support to win the coast for the kingdom. Accordingly, he offered the Genoese generous terms: a third of the booty and slaves of any city captured with their aid as well as a street in each conquered city to be held as a hereditary possession complete with extraterritoriality. Baldwin lost little time capitalizing on this treaty. He immediately laid siege to Arsuf, a town that his brother had been unable to reduce for want of sea power. The city capitulated in less than a month. The very next month the coalition encircled Caesarea, capturing it in a little over two weeks.[72] During the blockade, the Genoese manifested their resourcefulness by constructing a wooden siege tower from the masts and oars of several of their ships.[73] As agreed, the Ligurian mariners received their quarter within the walls and a third part of the booty. Caffaro describes the distribution of the spoils as follows:

> First, they set aside from the money in the encampment one tenth and one fifth to the galleys [ship-owners]. But all the remaining money they divided among the eight thousand men. And they gave 48 solidi Poitevin and two pounds of pepper to each as his share, apart from the honorarium of the consuls, the ship-masters, and the better men, which was a great sum.[74]

It is worth noting that the Genoese seemed to feel safest making such an apportionment in Norman territory. Caffaro testifies, 'The Genoese with their galleys and the entire expeditionary force went to the beach of San Parlerio near Solino and encamped there.'[75] Both Luigi Belgrano (editor of the *Annali genovesi*) and Robert S. Lopez (a medieval economic historian) have identified the locality as Saint Symeon, the ancient port of Antioch.[76]

Caffaro records that the Genoese fleet returned home in the fall of 1101, but another flotilla must have made its way out to the Levant shortly thereafter.

---

[72] Albert of Aachen, *Historia Ierosolimitana*, Bk VII, ch. 54–5, pp. 562–5; Caffaro, *Annales Ianuenses*, I, pp. 9–12; Fulcher of Chartres, *Expedition to Jerusalem*, Bk II, ch. VIII, par. 1–3, pp. 151–2; *Historia Hierosolymitana*, Bk II, ch. VIII, par. 1–3, pp. 393–8; Ibn al-Qalanisi, *The Damascus Chronicle of the Crusades*, ed. and trans. H. A. R. Gibb (London, 1932), p. 51; William of Tyre, *History of Deeds Done beyond the Sea*, I, Bk 10, ch. 14, pp. 433–5; *Willelmi Tyrensis Chronicon*, Bk 10, ch. 14, pp. 469–71.

[73] Fulcher of Chartres, *Expedition to Jerusalem*, Bk II, ch. IX, par. 1–5, pp. 153–4; *Historia Hierosolymitana*, Bk II, ch. IX, par. 1–5, pp. 400–3; William of Tyre, *History of Deeds Done beyond the Sea*, I, Bk 10, ch. 15, pp. 435–7; *Willelmi Tyrensis Chronicon*, Bk 10, ch. 15, pp 471–2.

[74] Caffaro, *Annales Ianuenses*, I, p. 13; R. Lopez and I. Raymond, trans., *Medieval Trade in the Mediterranean World, Illustrative Documents* (New York, 1955), doc. 31, pp. 88–9. '... et de peccunia campi decimam et quintum galearum primum extraxerunt. Aliud vero, quod remansit, inter uiros octo milia diuiserunt, et unicuique per partem solidos XLVIII de pictauinis et libras II piperis dederunt, preter honorem consulum et naucleriorum et meliorum uirorum, quod magnum fuit.'

[75] Caffaro, *Annales Ianuenses*, I, p. 13; *Medieval Trade in the Mediterranean World*, doc. 31, p. 89. 'Postea uero Ianuenses cum galeis et toto exercitu iuxta Sulinum in plagia sancti Parlerii uenerunt, et campum fecerunt...'

[76] Belgrano, *Annali genovesi*, I, p. 13, note 2; Lopez, *Medieval Trade in the Mediterranean*, p. 89, note 5.

This is because he also notes that 'eight galleys and other oared warships and supply ships' ('*VIII galeis et goribis et navi*') commanded by a certain Mauro de Platea Longa and Paganus de Volta with 'many other noble men' ('*cum multis aliis nobilibus uiris*') helped take Tortosa in April 1102.[77] In the spring of 1104, perhaps as many as 40 Genoese vessels joined Raymond of Toulouse in an assault on Tripoli. When that foundered, the combined force easily took Jubayl, winning for the Genoese a third of that town's territory.[78] In May of that same year, William of Tyre writes that Baldwin contracted a fleet of 70 Genoese galleys to help him bring Acre to heel.[79] The *Damascus Chronicle* of Ibn al-Qalanisi claims there were 'over ninety vessels in all',[80] but Fulcher of Chartres, Baldwin's chaplain and an eyewitness, supports William's account, attesting 'the Genoese came with a fleet of seventy beaked ships'.[81] William also reliably reports that their assistance did not come cheap. He says the Geneose finally agreed to participate in the siege according the following terms: 'On condition that they [the Genoese] should be given in perpetuity a third part of the returns and revenues collected at the port of Acre from sea-borne import and in addition be granted a church in the city and full jurisdiction over one street, the Genoese consented to lend loyal aid in taking the aforesaid city.'[82] Baldwin had failed to take the town the spring before, but, thanks to the Genoese blockade, succeeded on this attempt.[83]

To ensure continued Genoese collaboration, Baldwin effected a sweeping treaty that went well beyond the terms previously agreed upon. It not only confirmed the concessions in Arsuf, Caesarea and Acre, but it also pledged an annual subsidy of 300 bezants, streets in Jerusalem and Jaffa, and a third of any city the Genoese should help capture in the future. Furthermore, the security of their persons and property throughout the realm was assured while the king abjured his rights to the property of any Genoese man who should die intestate

---

[77] Caffaro, *Liberatio Orientis*, pp. 118–19; Fulcher of Chartres, *Expedition to Jerusalem*, Bk II, ch. XVII, par. 1, p. 166; *Historia Hierosolymitana*, Bk II, ch. XVII, par. 1, pp. 433–4.

[78] Albert of Aachen, *Historia Ierosolimitana*, Bk IX, ch. 26, pp. 670–1; Caffaro, *Annales Ianuenses*, I, pp. 13–14; *Liberatio Orientis*, pp. 120–1.

[79] William of Tyre, *History of Deeds Done beyond the Sea*, I, Bk 10, ch. 28, p. 454; *Willelmi Tyrensis Chronicon*, Bk 10, ch. 27, p. 486.

[80] Ibn al-Qalanisi, *Damascus Chronicle*, p. 61.

[81] Fulcher of Chartres, *Expedition to Jerusalem*, Bk II, ch. XXV, par. 1, p. 176; *Historia Hierosolymitana*, Bk II, ch. XXV, par. 1, p. 462. '… venerunt Ianuenses cum classe LXX navium rostratarum.'

[82] William of Tyre, *History of Deeds Done beyond the Sea*, I, Bk 10, ch. 28, pp. 455–6; *Willelmi Tyrensis Chronicon*, Bk 10, ch. 27, pp. 486–7. '… responsum dederunt quod si redditum et obventionum, que ex marino accessu in portu colligerentur, tercia pars illis in perpetuum concederetur et in civitate ecclesia et in vico iurisdicto plena daretur, ad capiendam predictam urbem fideliter elaborarent.'

[83] Albert of Aachen, *Historia Ierosolimitana*, Bk IX, ch. 27–8, pp. 670–5; Caffaro, *Annales Ianuenses*, I, p. 14; *Liberatio Orientis*, p. 121; Fulcher of Chartres, *Expedition to Jerusalem*, Bk II, ch. XXV, par. 3–4, p. 176; *Historia Hierosolymitana*, Bk II, ch. XXV, par. 3–4, p. 464.

within the kingdom.[84] Baldwin confirmed these grants in May 1105 along with all other Genoese possessions and privileges throughout the Latin Kingdom in return for fealty.[85] And, according to Albert of Aachen, Genoese mariners apparently proved their loyalty by participating in the lengthy siege of Sidon, begun in the autumn of 1107.[86]

Bertrand of Toulouse, Raymond's son, provided the Genoese with yet another opportunity to aggrandize property in the Levant. He engaged 70 galleys in the early spring of 1109 to invest Tripoli for the second time by promising the Genoese a third of the city, plus all of Jubayl. Once again the effort stalled before the walls, but Baldwin soon joined the fray, tipping the balance of the battle in favor of the crusaders. The citizens finally surrendered. Bertrand reneged on his pledge to the Genoese, who reacted by occupying all of Jubayl anyway.[87] The Ligurian mariners completed their contribution to the First Latin Kingdom of Jerusalem by helping Baldwin besiege Beirut in the spring of 1110 with around 40 ships. It fell the following year.[88] When it was all said and done, the Genoese had helped the crusaders capture nearly every coastal city of the Levant with the exception of Tyre, which was seized in 1124, chiefly with the aid of the Venetians.

The tale of precisely how it was all done remains a bit muddled, partly owing to the fact that Caffaro penned the *Liberatio Orientis* from memory about half a century after the events in question, but it is plain that the Genoese contribution was an ongoing one involving considerable maritime assets. Steven Epstein makes the following astute observation in *Genoa and the Genoese*: 'The most plausible explanation for the tangled story of what the Genoese accomplished in the east in this decade is that every year some Genoese fought in the Latin states and that the chronicles noted only major fleets and their deeds.'[89] This was most likely also true of the Pisans. And they were not the only ones.

Raymond of Aguilers, who traveled with Raymond of Toulouse, speaks of a flotilla of 30 English ships early on in the campaign:

---

[84] *CDG*, I, no. 15, p. 20; *RRH*, no. 43, p. 8.

[85] *CDG*, I, no. 16, pp. 21–2; *RRH*, no. 45–6, pp. 8–9.

[86] Albert of Aachen, *Historia Ierosolimitana*, Bk X, ch. 46, pp. 760–1; Ibn al-Qalanisi, *Damascus Chronicle*, p. 87.

[87] Albert of Aachen, *Historia Ierosolimitana*, Bk XI, ch. 13–15, pp. 782–7; Caffaro, *Annales Ianuenses*, I, p. 14; *Liberatio Orientis*, pp. 123–4; Fulcher of Chartres, *Expedition to Jerusalem*, Bk II, ch. XLI, par. 1–3, p. 195; *Historia Hierosolymitana*, Bk II, ch. XLI, par. 1–3, pp. 531–3; Ibn al-Qalanisi, *Damascus Chronicle*, pp. 88–90; William of Tyre, *History of Deeds Done beyond the Sea*, I, Bk 11, ch. 9–10, pp. 475–8; *Willelmi Tyrensis Chronicon*, Bk 11, ch. 9–10, pp. 507–10.

[88] Caffaro, *Annales Ianuenses*, I, p. 15; Fulcher of Chartres, *Expedition to Jerusalem*, Bk II, ch. XLII, par. 1–3, pp. 196–7; *Historia Hierosolymitana*, Bk II, ch. XLII, par. 1–3, pp. 534–6; Ibn al-Qalanisi, *Damascus Chronicle*, pp. 99–100; William of Tyre, *History of Deeds Done beyond the Sea*, I, Bk 11, ch. 13, pp. 484–6; *Willelmi Tyrensis Chronicon*, Bk 11, ch. 13, pp. 515–16.

[89] Epstein, *Genoa and the Genoese*, p. 31.

These English, upon receipt of news of the crusades launched in the name of God's vengeance against those who desecrated the land of Christ's nativity and His apostles, set sail on the Anglican sea, and thus rounding the coast of Spain, bearing across the Ocean and ploughing through the waves of the Mediterranean, after great trials arrived at Antioch and Latakia in advance of our army. The English as well as the Genoese assured us commerce from Cyprus and other islands and so proved helpful. Daily these ships sailed to and fro over the sea thereby frightening the Saracens and thus making Greek shipping safe.[90]

There was even a Scandinavian expedition under Sigurd, King of Norway.[91] In fact, Sigurd stopped on his way to the Holy Land at the Norman court in Palermo in 1109, prompting the following entry in the early thirteenth-century *Heimskringla* ('Circle of the World' – a saga of the old Norse kings by the Icelandic poet and politician Snorre Sturlason):

In the spring King Sigurd came to Sicily, where he stayed for a long time. Rothgeir [Roger] was duke then there, and he greeted the king well and bade him come to a banquet. King Sigurd went and many men were with him. It was a noble welcome, and each day of the feast Duke Rothgeir stood and did service at King Sigurd's table. On the seventh day of the feast, when the men had taken their baths, King Sigurd took the duke by the hand, led him up to the high-seat, and gave him the name of king and the right of being king over the realm of Sicily; before that time there had been jarls [earls] over the realm.[92]

During the long siege of Antioch (October 1097–June 1098), Albert of Aachen tells of a 'Winemer of Boulogne, master of pirates, and certain Christians' who led a significant force of ships manned by men of the Lowlands who joined forces with those of Provence to besiege Latakia:

These people assembled ships drawn from different kingdoms and lands, namely from Antwerp, Tiel, Frisia [coastal area of the North Sea from the Netherlands to Denmark], and Flanders, and joined by sea the Provençals in the land of Saint-Gilles who were subject to Count Raymond and sailed around the world to that same city of Latakia. They took possession of it and conquered it ...[93]

---

[90] Raymond of Aguilers, *Historia Francorum*, ch. XIII, p. 113; *Le 'Liber' de Raymond D'Aguilers*, ed. J. and L. Hill, trans. P. Wolff (Paris, 1969), ch. XIII, p. 135; *RHC, Occ*, III, ch. XVIII, p. 290. '*Etenim Angli audito nomine ulcionis Domini in eos qui terram nativitatis Ihesu Christi et apostolorum eius indigne occupaverant, ingressi mare anglicum, et circinata Ispania tranfretantes per mare oceanum, atque civitatem Laodicie, antequam exercitus noster per terram illuc veniret laboriose obtinuerunt. Profuerunt nobus eo tempore tam istorum naves quam et Genuensium. Habebemus enim ad obsidionem per istas naves et per securitatem eorum commercia a Cypro insula et a reliquis insulis. Quippe hee naves cotidie discurrebant per mare, et ob ea Grecorum naves secure erant, quia Sarraceni eis incurrere formidabant.*'

[91] William of Tyre, *History of Deeds Done beyond the Sea*, I, Bk II, ch. 14, pp. 486–8; *Willelmi Tyrensis Chronicon*, Bk II, ch. 14, pp. 517–19.

[92] Snorre Sturlason, *Heimskringla or The Lives of the Norse Kings*, ed. and trans. E. Monsen and A. H. Smith (Cambridge, 1932), p. 610.

[93] Albert of Aachen, *Historia Ierosolimitana*, Bk III, ch. 59, pp. 230–1; Bk VI, ch. 55, pp. 476–9. '*Hii collectione nauium a diuersis regnis et terris contracta, uidelicet ab Antwerpia, Tila,*

The town was subsequently lost.

The bottom line is that the First Crusade provoked a prodigious jump in traffic through the central Mediterranean, in general, and the Strait of Messina, in particular. In this regard, the Normans of Italy had to have been complicit. John Pryor, who has determined that the Sicilian Channel and the Strait of Messina formed a major trunk route in the medieval Mediterranean, concluded, 'Had mastery of the trunk routes for Christendom not been secured in the tenth and eleventh centuries, the Crusader states in Palestine and Syria could not have survived in the twelfth, even if the overland First Crusade had succeeded in establishing them.'[94] In other words, the Latin Kingdom of Jerusalem probably would never have been founded and certainly not sustained, if the Normans under the Hauteville banner had not secured the central Mediterranean and facilitated the flow of Western shipping to the East, particularly that of Genoa and Pisa.

Revitalization of Western commerce in the Mediterranean

Though momentous, the contribution of Norman naval supremacy in the central Mediterranean to Western military expansion paled in comparison to its impact upon the growth of Western commerce. The ultimate benefit of Norman dominance of the Sicilian Channel and the Strait of Messina was not that it enabled West Italian sea power to support the establishment of the Latin Kingdom of Jerusalem. Rather it was that it fostered the founding of a West Italian commercial empire in the East. As a result of their participation in the Crusades, Genoa and Pisa were able to set up merchant outposts, *fondaci*, in the Levant that negated their geographic disadvantage and opened the golden spigot that was trade with the Orient. Consequently, merchandise flowed more freely east-to-west, and Western Europe was the primary beneficiary.

In *Naval Power and Trade in the Mediterranean*, A. R. Lewis made this stark observation about the economic environment of the Tyrrhenian Sea in the ninth century: 'In startling contrast to the humming cities and busy trade of Moslem Spain and North Africa the Christian coastline from Barcelona to the Tiber was dead and all but deserted.'[95] An overstatement? Perhaps, but few could argue that the commercial activity of such north Tyrrhenian port cities as Genoa and Pisa offered even a hint of what it would become. Christian shipping was almost certainly depressed compared to Muslim maritime commerce of the era. This dismal state of affairs persisted through the tenth century and

---

Frisia, Flandria, per mare Prouincialibus in terra sancti Egidii de potestate comitis Reimundi associati, nauigio in circuitu orbis terre usque ad ipsam urbem Laodicie appulsi sunt. Quam occupantes et expugnantes …'
[94] Pryor, *Geography, Technology, and War*, pp. 7, 111.
[95] Lewis, *Naval Power and Trade*, p. 177.

into the eleventh – as long as the Muslims held the central Mediterranean. Once the House of Hauteville seized it for the West, Genoa and Pisa were able to send their merchantmen East relatively unhindered. They did so in the wake of the Crusading movement in great numbers. Christian commerce on the 'middle sea' surged and Western Europe flourished. And, correspondingly, so did the Norman Kingdom of Sicily.

What was begun with the First Crusade grew exponentially thereafter in large measure because of the continued forbearance of the Norman lords of Sicily and southern Italy. The Genoese and the Pisans strove to increase their respective holdings in the Levant throughout the First Latin Kingdom. Whenever the opportunity presented itself, they proffered the support of their sea power to the Latin principalities in return for more concessions. Insecure and still quite vulnerable, the rulers of the new Christian realm continued to grant the West Italians the concessions that they sought.

Since Genoa had already been ceded a considerable dominion during the First Crusade, it was Pisa that benefited more from these later grants. Even though it was primarily the Venetian fleet of the Doge Domenico Michieli that supported the successful siege of Tyre in 1124,[96] Baldwin II awarded the Pisans five houses around the harbor in that city along with exemption from export/import fees.[97] In 1156 Baldwin III confirmed his father's grants and enlarged them. He not only gave the Pisans more land in Tyre, but he also conferred upon them the *vicecomitatus*, which allowed the Pisans to live in the city under the protection of their own laws.[98] Such grants of extraterritoriality were extremely important because they enabled the Italian maritime states to establish their possessions in Syria as autonomous, commercial enclaves, free from royal interference.

The Pisans derived even greater benefits from their involvement with King Amalric. The latter subscribed to the notion that the best way to ensure the long-term security of the Latin Kingdom was to subdue Egypt. To that end he sought to enlist the Italian maritime powers, especially the Pisans, in a campaign of conquest. While Amalric was still count of Ascalon and Jaffa (1157), he bestowed upon his Tuscan allies half of all the port revenues of Jaffa, exemption from taxes on their merchandise and an area for construction of a market and adjacent houses.[99] As king of Jerusalem in 1165, Amalric sought to retain the favor of the Pisans for an expedition against Alexandria by granting them still more land in Tyre 'between the buildings of the city and the waters of the port'.[100] In recip-

---

[96]   Fulcher of Chartres, *Expedition to Jerusalem*, Bk III, ch. XXVIII, pp. 255–6; *Historia Hierosolymitana*, Bk III, ch. XXVIII, pp. 695–6; William of Tyre, *History of Deeds Done beyond the Sea*, I, Bk 12, ch. 25, pp. 552–6; *Willelmi Tyrensis Chronicon*, Bk 12, ch. 25, pp. 577–81.

[97]   Heyd, *Histoire du commerce*, I, p. 150; Heywood, *History of Pisa*, p. 108.

[98]   *RRH*, no. 322, pp. 82–3.

[99]   *RRH*, no. 324, p. 83.

[100] *RRH*, no. 412, p. 107. '... *inter civitatis domos et aquam portus.*'

rocation, Bernardo Maragone records that in 1167, 'The Pisans courageously in aid to the aforesaid king sent the Consul Burgense with ten galleys.'[101] In recompense 'for the good service which they showed to him in the siege of Alexandria,' Amalric assigned his Tuscan allies a merchant quarter in Acre together with the coveted *vicecomitatus*.[102] These concessions in Acre were confirmed in 1182 by Amalric's successor, Baldwin IV, who added the grant of a street leading down to the harbor.[103] Amalric beseeched the Pisans to continue their participation in the Egyptian campaigns, but they initially balked, probably for fear of rupturing the remunerative Egyptian trade relations that they had enjoyed since 1153 when they were given *fondaci* in both Alexandria and Cairo.[104] In September 1169, however, the sovereign tendered them an enticement that they simply could not reject:

> Freedom of all commerce throughout the entire land which he might occupy in Egypt; an assembly house in the city of Fustat; a church, house, bakery, mill and a bath adjacent to a merchant quarter in each of Cairo, Fustat and Rosetta; and henceforth one thousand bezants of the royal revenues in either Cairo or Fustat each year without service; and every sort of commerce in Alexandria, Damietta and Tinnis as he might acquire them.[105]

The Pisans did, in fact, contribute a contingent to the subsequent campaign, but the effort all came do naught when Amalric's ambitions for Egypt fell apart.[106]

Other Latin lords of the Levant also catered to the Pisans. In 1154 Rainald and Constance of Antioch ceded them lands in Latakia as well as Antioch. The Pisans were also permitted the right to adjudicate legal altercations among themselves in both cities.[107] Raymond of Tripoli followed suit in 1179 with the grant of a house in his city.[108] Three years later they were given the opportunity to purchase yet another edifice in Tripoli.[109] By the end of the First Latin Kingdom of Jerusalem, Pisan merchants had property and privileges in nearly every major port of the Levant.[110]

The Genoese had already earned concessions in many of these cities during

---

[101] Bernardo Maragone, *Annales Pisani*, p. 45. '*Pisani viriliter in auxilium iamdicti regis miserunt Burgensem Consulem cum X galeis.*'

[102] *RRH*, no. 449, p. 117. '...*vpro bono servitio quod in obsidione Alexandrie Pisani sibi exhibuerunt* ...'

[103] *RRH*, no. 617, p. 163.

[104] Manfroni, *Storia della Marina Italiana*, I, p. 508.

[105] *RRH*, no. 467, pp. 122–3. '... *libertatem de omni jure negotiationis per totam terram, quam occupaverit in Aegypto, et curiam in urbe Babylonis, ecclesiam, domum, furnum, molendinum et balnea juxta fundam mercatorum, eadem apud Cahiram in platea Belbecanti et apud Rassit, deinde M bisantios in funda regali sive Babylone sive Cahirae singulis annis sine servitio, quosque de omnimodo jure negotiationis ipsum commune acquietaverit Alexandriae, Damiatae et Tani.*'

[106] Bernardo Maragone, *Annales Pisani*, p. 47.

[107] *RRH*, no. 292, p. 74.

[108] *RRH*, no. 585, pp. 155–6.

[109] *RRH*, no. 621, pp. 164–5.

[110] Heywood, *History of Pisa*, p. 115.

the early consolidation of the kingdom. Such grants were merely confirmed in the years following. As was previously noted, Baldwin I renewed all royal privileges to the Genoese in Jerusalem, Antioch, Acre, Latakia, Tortosa, Jubayl, Caesarea, Arsuf and Saint Symeon in 1105.[111] The princes of Antioch also remained quite generous to the Genoese. Their possessions in that north Syrian city were confirmed several times, beginning in 1127 when Bohemond II upheld the grants of his predecessor, Bohemond I.[112] The gifts of both Bohemonds were renewed in 1144 by Rainald and Constance.[113] Finally, in 1169 Bohemond III reaffirmed all existing privileges, possessions and exemptions while promising the redress of any Genoese grievance in the royal court 40 days after the complaint.[114]

The importance of these concessions to the growth of Western commerce in the Mediterranean cannot be overemphasized. The quarters granted to the mariners of Genoa and Pisa by the Latin conquerors of Syria were in no way colonies. Rather they were merchant enclaves bestowed not on the West Italian city-states themselves but on the merchants of those maritime republics. Nor were they normally ceded to named individuals. With a few exceptions such as the concessions made to the Embriaco brothers in Jubayl, these grants were hereditary endowments made to the collective citizenry of the city of origin and their descendants.[115] This is precisely why the charters often did not specify a particular person or persons as recipients. The diplomas, instead, usually designated as beneficiary an institution that represented the city as a whole, like the cathedral. For example, King Baldwin's charter of 1104, which confirmed Genoese possessions in Acre, Arsuf, Caesarea, Jaffa and Jerusalem, was actually conferred upon the city's cathedral church of San Lorenzo.[116] In fact, even merchants of other Ligurian towns were able to benefit from Genoese privileges in the East by claiming Genoese citizenship. The same was true of other Tuscans who crowded under the Pisan banner. This practice was permitted as long as these other West Italian merchants recognized the jurisdiction of the appropriate Genoese or Pisan magistrate while in Syria.[117]

Moreover, these enclaves in the Latin Kingdom could not be considered colonies in the strictest sense of the word because they were never inhabited by a permanent group of settlers. Rather, such mercantile quarters were, for the most part, used only seasonally by a steady of flow of merchants, most of whom resided in the mother city. The unambiguous explanation for this state of affairs is that these possessions were acquired not as aggrandized territory for exploi-

---

[111] *RRH*, no. 45–6, pp. 8–9.
[112] *RRH*, no. 119, pp. 29–30.
[113] *RRH*, no. 228, p. 57.
[114] *RRH*, no. 471, p. 124.
[115] J. Prawer, *The Crusaders' Kingdom: European Colonialism in the Middle Ages* (New York, 1972), pp. 489–90.
[116] *RRH*, no. 43, p. 8.
[117] Prawer, *Crusaders' Kingdom*, pp. 90–2.

tation, but as economic bases for the facilitation of Eastern trade. Genoa and Pisa had contributed to the conquest of Palestine expressly for the purpose of obtaining such trading posts in a congenial economic environment. The Israeli historian Joshua Prawer adroitly encapsulates the phenomenon: 'The Italians used the kingdom [Latin Kingdom] as a base of operations, a market, for their merchandise and a market of primary and finished products to be exported elsewhere, wherever good roads, friendly winds and demand–supply relations promised profits.'[118] After all, the merchant quarter was frequently called a *fondaco*, which literally meant 'warehouse'. Such a 'warehouse' quarter formed the core of a self-sufficient community distinct from the crusader city in which it existed. Each *fondaco* had its own church, market, bath, mill, oven and houses for rent to transient merchants. The members of the *fondaco* lived apart from the local inhabitants of the city and enjoyed a special status. They were not subjects of the Latin Kingdom, but retained the citizenship of the mother city. They remained Genoese and Pisan businessmen organized into an autonomous political and social entity for the sole purpose of pursuing commercial aims.[119]

The existence of these *fondaci* in Latin Syria meant that the risks to the merchants of Genoa and Pisa brought about by the distance of their mother cities from the Levant were drastically reduced. Eastern traders, Muslim and otherwise, passed through the gates of the host port cities of the Latin Kingdom on the landward side and sold to the West Italian merchants in their *fondaci* the commodities so highly prized in the West (such as pepper, cassia, nutmeg, dye pigments and precious stones) in exchange for gold and silver.[120] On the seaward side, Genoese and Pisan ships loaded the goods into their holds and carried them back to their mother cities from where the commodities were distributed to destinations throughout the western Mediterranean. A large quantity of this merchandise was sold to Western Muslims who had developed an appetite for the goods of the Levant. Genoa, in particular, became a commercial intermediary between the Muslims of the East and those of the West.[121] Significant amounts of dye pigments, pearls and spices found their way to Tunis, Bejaïa and Ceuta on Genoese ships. The West Italians also supplied the Muslim coasts of the southern Mediterranean with linens, cotton cloths and fine silks, all of European manufacture. They even furnished the 'infidels' with such maritime matériel as wood, iron and pitch.[122]

---

[118] Prawer, *Crusaders' Kingdom*, p. 483.
[119] Heyd, *Histoire du commerce du Levant*, pp. 153–4.
[120] H. Krueger, 'The Wares of Exchange in the Genoese–African Traffic of the Twelfth Century', *Speculum*, XII (1937), pp. 57–71, especially 65 and 71; R. Lopez, 'Market Expansion: The Case of Genoa', *Journal of Economic History*, XXIV (1964), pp. 445–64, especially 450; Prawer, *Crusaders' Kingdom*, pp. 496–7; J. Riley-Smith, 'Government in Latin Syria and the commercial privileges of foreign merchants', in *Relations between East and West in the Middle Ages*, ed. D. Baker (Edinburgh, 1973), pp. 109–32, especially 115–22.
[121] Prawer, *Crusaders' Kingdom*, p. 496.
[122] Krueger, 'Wares of Exchange in the Genoese–African Traffic', pp. 59–61, 70–1.

Thus, trade relations, which had begun so tentatively in the late eleventh century between the West Italians and their North African adversaries, blossomed into a considerable commercial traffic. It was enabled in no small measure by the Norman Kingdom of Sicily. David Abulafia, who illuminates the close commercial connection between the Normans of southern Italy and the northern communes in *Two Italies*, points out that 'the Normans encouraged Italian merchants to travel to their African possessions and to help build up commercial life after years of devastation and famine'.[123] The Genoese and Pisans sold finished textiles in the Maghrib in exchange for sub-Saharan gold, for instance – the same gold used to purchase Oriental commodities in the Levant. Such a thriving trade was formalized in many cases by treaties.[124] Several examples from the Cairo Geniza prove that Pisa as well as Genoa shared in the trade with the Muslim Maghrib. As a case in point, there was mention of a Pisan concordat in 1133 with the Sultan Yahya Ibn Aziz of Bejaïa, which pledged mutual friendship.[125] There is also evidence of an 1157 pact with the sheik of Tunis whereby the latter promised the Pisans that he would not trade in Pisan slaves, and that he would renounce customs duties on unsold Pisan merchandise taken back by sea.[126]

More important than this flourishing commerce with Western Islam, however, was the transmittal of Eastern trade to Western Europe. Genoa and Pisa almost certainly played a prominent role in revitalizing the economic activity of the north; and the conduit through which they provided such an infusion of commerce was probably Provence. David Abulafia found evidence in the notarial registers of Genoa that the Ligurian commune was handling Toulouse's trade with Sicily and the East. He also notes that in the twelfth century the Pisans carried a considerable amount of Marseilles' commerce with the Latin Levant.[127] Indeed, Benjamin of Tudela confirms that both Genoa and Pisa served as intermediaries for the eastern commerce of Provence. Speaking of the city of Montpellier, he observes: 'People of all nations are found there doing business through the medium of the Genoese and Pisans.'[128] Using Provence as a conduit, the West Italians serviced the great emporia of Western Europe, the trade fairs, with the luxury items of the East. The rich feudal nobility paid exorbitant prices for the spices, rugs, pearls and perfumes brought mostly by sea on the decks of Ligurian and Tuscan round ships.[129] The Genoese and Pisans became so successful as suppliers of these goods that they were compelled to seek out more Western markets in Spain and southern France. To that end, the Genoese, for example, established

---

[123] Abulafia, *Two Italies*, p. 86.
[124] Abulafia, *Two Italies*, pp. 48, 86.
[125] Goitein, *A Mediterranean Society*, I, p. 310.
[126] Mas Latrie, *Traités de paix et de commerce*, I, pp. 37–9.
[127] Abulafia, *Two Italies*, pp. 95–6.
[128] Benjamin of Tudela, *Itinerary*, p. 2.
[129] A. Atiya, *Crusade, Commerce and Culture* (New York, 1962), pp. 172, 177–8, 184–5.

fondaci in Toulouse, Montpellier, Narbonne, Almeria and Tortosa.[130] Trade in
Europe had never fully ceased, but in the twelfth century it surged ahead with
renewed vigor. It bears stressing once again that none of this would have been
possible had not the Normans seized naval supremacy from the Muslims in the
central Mediterranean.

As a result, investment in Eastern trade increased steadily throughout the
twelfth century. Before the First Crusade, such commerce had been negligible,
but by the end of the First Latin Kingdom of Jerusalem in 1187, over a third of
all Genoese mercantile traffic, for instance, was with the Orient.[131] In addition to
cargo, the ships of the West began transporting huge numbers of pilgrims. Based
on eye-witness reports, John Pryor speculates, 'Hundreds of ships carrying tens
of thousands of pilgrims must have made the voyage from the West to the Holy
Land every year.'[132] Nautical technology improved as the demand for capacity
increased. Cargo vessels rapidly evolved from small coastal ships on the order of
the single-masted, open-hulled Serçe Limani ship of the early eleventh century
to the two-masted, multi-decked sailing ships of the mid-twelfth century, which
often sported both sterncastles and forecastles.[133] And, blessed with the security
of their newly acquired commercial empires in the East, the West Italian maritime powers led the way. In short, the merchant enclaves of Genoa and Pisa in
the Latin Levant were, in the aggregate, an enormous engine that powered an
economic explosion in Western Europe. Hence, David Abulafia was prompted
to assert, 'These bases were taps at the end of a long Middle Eastern pipeline
bringing spices and drugs and dyes and fabrics from Mesopotamia and beyond
to the Frankish settlements, and thence via Messina or Palermo to continental
Europe.'[134]

Accordingly, unless the West Italians somehow absurdly elected to portage
their vessels over the Apennines, the entirety of this dramatically enlarged volume
of traffic had to transit either the Strait of Messina or the Sicilian Channel. The
island of Sicily under Norman suzerainty controlled both. While it was a fairly
simple matter to regulate traffic through the narrow strait, the 100-mile-wide
channel appears, on the surface, to have been more problematic. It actually was
not. John Pryor provides clues as to why:

> The Sicilian Channel between Sicily and Tunisia could be dangerous because of
> Sherki bank about 50 miles north of Cape Bon, which has Keith reef on it with

[130] E. Byrne, 'Genoese Colonies in Syria', in *The Crusades and other Historical Essays presented
to Dana C. Munro by his former students*, ed. L. Paetow (New York, 1928), pp. 139–82, especially 143.

[131] Prawer, *Crusaders' Kingdom*, p. 399.

[132] J. Pryor, 'Mediterranean Round Ship', in *Cogs, Caravels and Galleons: The Sailing Ship,
1000–1650*, ed. R. Gardiner (London, 1994), p. 70.

[133] Byrne, *Genoese Shipping in the Twelfth and Thirteenth Centuries* (Cambridge, MA, 1930),
pp. 3, 5–8; Pryor, 'Mediterranean Round Ship', pp. 69–70.

[134] Abulafia, *Two Italies*, p. 53.

only about 1.8m of water over the reef and strong currents and heavy seas around it. But galleys would keep close in to the Sicilian coast, staying well clear of such dangers. By doing so, they would also avoid the danger of being pushed south into the Gulf of Gabes with its dangerous sandbanks by the prevailing northerly winds in the channel.[135]

The Strait of Messina was, therefore, the funnel through which flowed the vast majority of east–west mercantile traffic on the Mediterranean. This meant that Messina, the home port of the royal fleet of the Norman Kingdom of Sicily, became the primary transshipment point for the Levant trade. Such was again confirmed by Benjamin of Tudela who notes, 'Here [Messina] most of the pilgrims assemble to cross over to Jerusalem, as this is the best crossing.'[136] This latter fact led Abulafia to flatly state, 'Messina was a Norman phenomenon and a phenomenon of the Crusades.'[137]

Messina offered other vital advantages. 'The peacefulness and productivity of Sicily and southern Italy encouraged the north Italians to make Messina and Palermo their bases from which to trade with north African, Spanish and, above all, eastern ports,' points out Abulafia, who also notes that 'the Sicilian Navy was sufficiently strong to make a reality of royal promises to protect alien merchants.'[138] The port city's unrivalled attributes were lost on neither Genoa nor Pisa. Both sought to establish some sort of settlement there.[139] The Genoese were the first to take root. As was previously noted, in September 1116 Roger II granted to the Genoese consul, Ogerius Capra, and his brother Amicus a tract of land adjacent to the comital castle at Messina. While the grant seems to have been a personal one bestowed upon the consul's family by the young count 'in recognition for their loyalty to him',[140] it was clearly intended for commercial usage. The plot was very small, only 10 cubits wide (about 15 feet), but it had access to the sea and was specifically allotted for the construction of a lodging, presumably for mariners. Moreover, the concession exempted the Capra brothers from taxes on the importation and exportation of merchandise from Sicily up to a value of sixty *tarì*.[141] It was not a grand concession, but it was the germinating seed for a commercial quarter that would grow along with Genoa's Levant trade. Further evidence of a long-standing Genoese base in Messina is found

[135] Pryor, 'Geographical Conditions of Galley Navigation in the Mediterranean', in *Age of the Galley*, pp. 206–216, especially 215–16.
[136] Benjamin of Tudela, *Itinerary*, p. 76.
[137] Abulafia, *Two Italies*, p. 42.
[138] D. Abulafia, 'Pisan commercial colonies and consulates in twelfth-century Sicily', *English Historical Review*, IXIII (1978), pp. 68–81, especially 69–70.
[139] D. Abulafia, 'The merchants of Messina: Levant trade and domestic economy', *Papers of the British School at Rome*, LIV (1986), pp. 196–212, especially 197–9.
[140] Caspar, *Roger II*, Reg. no. 82, p. 490.
[141] Caspar, *Roger II*, Reg. no. 82, pp. 490–1; Cusa, ed., *Diplomi greci et arabi di Sicilia*, I, pp. 359–60.

in the privilege granted to them by King William I in 1156.[142] It omitted the usual provision for a quarter in the port, which was common for such commercial charters of the era, implying one already existed.[143] After all, the Hauteville family had nurtured an affinity for the Ligurians ever since the marriage of Adelaide del Vasto of the powerful Aleramici margraves of Savona to Roger's father, the 'Great Count'. Two of Adelaide's sisters were betrothed to Roger I's sons and her uncle Henry married one of the count's daughters.[144] It is believed that many of the Aleramici family came with Adelaide and eventually settled in Sicily.[145] It is, then, no surprise that by 1194 the Genoese establishment in Messina would grow to include a *fondaco* named after Saint John and a palace given to them by Margaritus of Brindisi.[146]

The Pisans were allied with the imperial party for much of the Hauteville era, but even they were able to establish an enclave in Messina. Although it is not known precisely when, it is possible it may have been as early as Roger II's reign. After all, Roger seems to have offered both Genoa and Pisa concessions in order to detach them from the anti-Norman league led by Lothair. Bernard of Clairvaux's letters to both communes in 1134, beseeching them not to be tempted by the Norman lord's overtures, are exhibits 'A' and 'B'.[147] And it seems likely that Roger offered the Tuscan mariners some compelling concessions in 1137 in order to get them to quit Lothair's coalition after the fall of Salerno.[148] Indeed, it would appear that the Pisans may even have been present in Messina previous to these episodes. Caffaro speaks of an incident in 1129 in which a small Pisan flotilla harried by a Genoese fleet of 16 ships sought refuge in Messina. There, they apparently found the support of some of their compatriots already in port, perhaps as part of some permanent presence. King Roger was forced to mediate.[149] More definitively, a September 1189 document (erroneously dated 9 October 1190) discovered in the archives of the Certosa di Calci ('Charterhouse of Calci' – a former Carthusian monastery near Pisa) refers to a 'hospice of the consul of the Pisans of Messina'.[150] Abulafia, who has preserved the contents of the diploma in his 1978 paper entitled 'Pisan commercial colonies and consulates in twelfth-century Sicily', believes it 'provides further evidence that Messina had become the focus of Pisan trade in the Mediterranean, a base from which the

---

[142] CDG, I, no. 279 and 280, pp. 338–42.

[143] Abulafia, *Two Italies*, pp. 92–3.

[144] Houben, *Roger II*, p. 24; Malaterra, *Deeds of Count Roger*, Bk 4, ch. 14, pp. 189–90; *De rebus gestis Rogerii*, Bk IV, ch. XIV, p. 93.

[145] Abulafia, *Two Italies*, pp. 64–5; Amari, *Storia dei Musulmani di Sicilia*, III, pp. 235–7.

[146] Ottobono Scriba, *Annales Ianuenses*, II, p. 48.

[147] Bernard of Clairvaux, no. 131 and 132, pp. 200–2; *Sancti Bernardi Opera*, no. 129 and 130, pp. 322–6.

[148] Bernardo Maragone, *Annales Pisani*, p. 11.

[149] Caffaro, *Annales Ianuenses*, I, p. 24.

[150] Abulafia, 'Pisan commercial colonies and consulates in twelfth-century Sicily', *Appendix*, doc. II, pp. 79–80. '... *hospitio consulum pisanorum Messane*.'

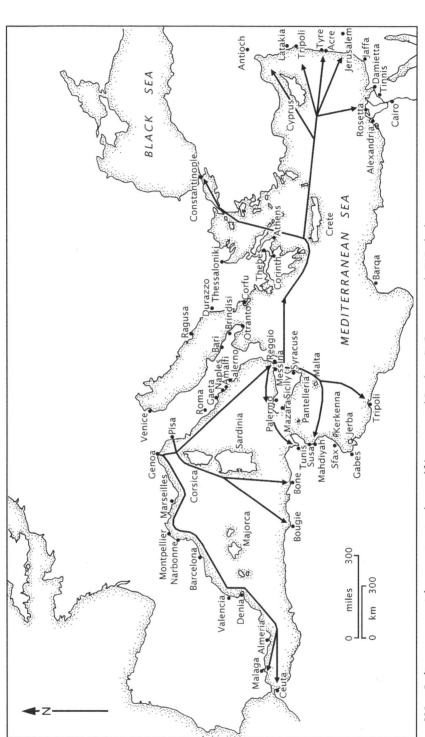

13. West Italian commercial expansion in the twelfth century. (Credit: C. Stanton with P. Judge)

Pisans radiated to other foreign ports'.[151] The same could doubtless be said of the Genoese. There can be no denying that Messina's fortuitous geography with respect to east–west Mediterranean trade made it a highly desirable stopover point for both West Italian maritime powers. This is precisely why Genoa and Pisa agreed to assist the German Emperor Henry VI in his invasion of Sicily in 1194. And it was no accident that the fleets of these two cities, though ostensibly allies at the time, engaged in a full-scale naval battle over control of Messina.[152]

Despite occasionally squabbling over the spoils, the Genoese and Pisans accrued enormous advantages from Norman Sicily. Not only did the Norman conquest of the island open the doorway to the exotic riches of the East, it provided the conduit for a decidedly lucrative north–south commerce. With his ground-breaking *Two Italies*, David Abulafia eloquently established that the two northern communes benefited from an extremely profitable trade in finished textiles and silver for Sicilian wheat and cotton.[153] With the overt encouragement of the Norman kings, the two West Italian republics also used Sicily as a convenient stepping stone to engage in trade with North Africa, an enterprise that allowed them to tap into the sub-Saharan caravan traffic in gold bullion.[154] As a result, peaceful commerce with the Muslims became a familiar scene in the West as well as the East. Within a relatively short period of time – hardly more than a century – Genoese and Pisan merchants could be found in every major port of the Mediterranean, Christian and Muslim alike (see Map 13). Not only had they helped make large-scale east–west trade possible once more, but they became the major carriers of it. Thanks to the Norman subjugation of southern Italy, Sicily and, for a time, the Maghrib coast, the Genoese and Pisans began to ply the waters of the Mediterranean so freely that their merchant fleets became the principal medium of transportation and communication from one end of the sea to the other. According to the papers of the Cairo Geniza, whenever Muslim or Jewish traders traveled or corresponded in the twelfth century, they usually did so on the vessels of the West Italians.[155]

In a perverse way, even the most ardent competitors of the West Italians, the Venetians, profited from emergent Norman naval power. The threat from Robert Guiscard's fleet in 1081 provoked the Eastern Emperor Alexios I into offering Venice a sweeping set of concessions in return for naval support. They included an annual donation of 20 pounds of gold to St Mark's basilica, the Byzantine title of *protosebastos* ('first venerable one') in perpetuity for the doge with an attendant stipend, a similar honorific and salary for the Venetian patriarch and a *fondaco* in Constantinople that included lodging, four docking slips in the harbor and a bakery. Alexios even granted an annuity to the Venetian church of St Andrew in

---

[151] Abulafia, 'Pisan commercial colonies and consulates in twelfth-century Sicily', p. 72.
[152] Ottobono Scriba, *Annales Ianuenses*, II, pp. 48–9.
[153] Abulafia, *Two Italies*, pp. 283–4.
[154] Abulafia, *Two Italies*, pp. 98–9.
[155] Goitein, *Mediterranean Society*, I, pp. 40, 59 and 211.

Durazzo and obligated the Amalfitans to pay a tax to St Mark's in order to retain their quarter in the capital. But, most significantly, he authorized the Venetians to trade in very nearly every major port in the Greek Empire with the exception of those on Cyprus and Rhodes free from taxes.[156] Alexios essentially handed *La Serenissima* an insurmountable competitive edge in the maritime commerce of the empire that would assure its dominance in the eastern Mediterranean basin for centuries. As Camillo Manfroni put it in somewhat melodramatic fashion, 'From this moment the lion of Saint Mark spreads its great wings toward the Orient and makes its roars heard.'[157] Norman naval assaults on Corfu and the Greek mainland under George of Antioch in 1147 goaded the Emperor Manuel into not only confirming the above-described trading privileges, but even extending them to encompass Cyprus and Rhodes as well. At the same time, the Venetian enclave in Constantinople was enlarged at the expense of the Amalfitan quarter, which, for a time, was abolished altogether.[158]

From the foregoing, it is apparent that there was one Italian mercantile power that did not fare nearly as well: Amalfi. Prior to the Norman conquest of southern Italy and Sicily, Amalfi was what Armand O. Citarella of St Michael's College called 'the seat of a commercial center, without doubt, the most important in the Western Mediterranean.'[159] What is now hardly more than a fishing village with a tiny harbor nestled on the south side of the Sorrento Peninsula between the much larger maritime cities of Naples and Salerno was, in the ninth and tenth centuries, a prosperous mercantile power with a network of trade routes that the extended the breadth of the Mediterranean.[160] Admittedly, little hard evidence of its past seafaring glory remains. There are no compendious notarial cartularies of the sort found in the Archivio di Stato of Genoa.[161] Indeed, few Amalfitan commercial contracts from the era survive.[162] Nonetheless, the anecdotal and testimonial substantiation is overwhelming. In the tenth-century *Kitab Surat al-Ard* ('Configuration of the Earth', also known as the 'Book of the Routes and the Kingdom'), Ibn Hawqal writes of Amalfi, 'This latter city is, in Lombardy, one of the most productive, most beautiful, which enjoys some of the best conditions and is distinguished by its wealth and opulence.'[163] In the eleventh century, William of Apulia says of the Campanian port, 'None is

---

[156]   Anna Comnena, *Alexiad*, p. 191; *Alexiade*, II, Bk VI, ch. V, pp. 54–5; Tafel and Thomas, *Urkunden der Republik Venedig*, I, pp. 51–4.

[157]   Manfroni, *Storia della Marina italiana*, I, pp. 124–5.

[158]   Tafel and Thomas, *Urkunden der Republik Venedig*, I, pp. 109–13.

[159]   Citarella, 'Relations of Amalfi with the Arab World before the Crusades', p. 299.

[160]   Heyd, *Histoire du commerce du Levant*, pp. 98–108.

[161]   Abulafia, *Two Italies*, pp. 11–19.

[162]   Kreutz, *Before the Normans*, pp. 92–3.

[163]   Ibn Hawqal, *La Configuration de la Terre*, ed. and trans. J. Kramers and G. Wiet (2 vols, Paris, 1964), I, p. 197.

richer in silver, gold and textiles from all sorts of different places.'[164] He goes on to name Antioch and Alexandria as examples of its far-flung foreign markets.[165] Moreover, contemporary historians testify that the Amalfitans enjoyed a special status throughout the eastern Mediterranean basin in both Byzantine and Arab lands. Bishop Liudprand of Cremona, the Lombard chancellor to Berengar II of Italy, claims that 'Venetian and Amalfitan merchants' ('*Veneticis et Amelfitanis institoribus*') were so active in Constantinople at the time of his second embassy to the imperial court in the mid-tenth century that 'street walkers and conjurors' ('*obolariae mulieres et mandrogerontes*') in Italy wore the purple cloth of Byzantine nobility.[166] And William of Tyre describes how the privileged standing which the Amalfitans enjoyed with the caliph of Cairo enabled them to establish hospices in the coastal cities of the Levant from Alexandria to Latakia and even in Jerusalem.[167]

Amalfi's singular success had to have arisen from some special circumstance that gave them a unique advantage no other Tyrrhenian-based port city enjoyed at that time. Matteo Camera, the city's favorite son and author of a magisterial two-volume history of the duchy, would have us believe that Amalfi's merchants flourished in the Orient principally because the court of Constantinople considered Amalfi a dependency of the Eastern Empire.[168] This has some merit. After all, the tenth-century *De Administrando Imperio* of Constantine Porphyrogenitus unequivocally declares, 'Naples and Amalfi and Sorrento have always been subject to the Emperor of the Romans.'[169] And by 922, Amalfi's rulers proudly bore such Byzantine titles as *imperialis patricius* ('imperial patrician') and *protospatarius* ('first sword bearer').[170] The Amalfitans, thus, almost certainly took full advantage of their perceived status to trade freely in the Empire. This would, however, have done them little good, had not been able to sail safely to the Orient through the central Mediterranean, which, by the end of the ninth century, was held by the Muslims of North Africa and Sicily.

Accordingly, the special circumstance exclusive to the Amalfitans that enabled them to establish a mercantile empire in the East must have been amicable relations with the Muslims, particularly those of North Africa. Indeed, this is the

---

[164] William of Apulia, *La Geste de Robert Guiscard*, Bk III, lines 478–9, pp. 190–1. '*Nulla magis locuples argento, vestibus, auro, partibus innumeris.*' (Translation by G. A. Loud at www.leeds.ac.uk/history/ weblearning/MedievalHistoryTextCentre/medievalTexts/html.)

[165] William of Apulia, *La Geste de Robert Guiscard*, Bk III, lines 481–2, pp. 190–1.

[166] Liudprand of Cremona, *De Legatione Constantinopolitana, Works of Liudprand of Cremona*, ch. LIV–LV, pp. 267–8; *Die Werke Liudprands von Cremona*, ch. LIV–LV, pp. 204–5.

[167] William of Tyre, *History of Deeds Done beyond the Sea*, II, Bk 18, ch. 4–5, pp. 241–5; *Willelmi Tyrensis Chronicon*, Bk 18, ch. 4–5, pp. 814–17.

[168] M. Camera, *Memorie storico-diplomatiche dell'antica città e ducato di Amalfi* (2 vols, Salerno, 1881), I, pp. 88–9.

[169] Constantine VII Porphyrogenitus, *De Administrando Imperio*, ch. 27, pp. 116–17.

[170] *Codice diplomatico amalfitano*, ed. R. Filangieri di Candida (2 vols, Naples, 1917), I, doc. 2, p. 3.

thesis of Armand Citarella's watershed 1967 article, 'The Relations of Amalfi with the Arab World Before the Crusades'.[171] There are tantalizing clues that the Amalfitans did, in fact, cultivate the Muslims of North Africa as trading partners. First of all, two Amalfitan commercial contracts from the early tenth century contain prices in *tarì*, the gold for which could only have come from North Africa.[172] There were no known sources for the metal in medieval Europe. Modern historians commonly acknowledge that Amalfi was minting its own gold *tarì* coins by the middle of the tenth century, indicating ongoing trade with the Muslims of North Africa.[173] Then there is the testimony of William of Apulia, who pointedly notes that the Amalfitans 'know the Arabs, the Libyans, the Sicilians and Africans'.[174] There are many other signs but the most compelling indication is the obvious fact that the Amalfitans were able to transit with impunity the Muslim-dominated central Mediterranean en route to the commercially promising East. Letters of Jewish traders from the Cairo Geniza reveal that in the early eleventh century travel between Amalfi and such Muslim destinations as Alexandria in Egypt and Mahdiyah in the Maghrib via Sicily was commonplace.[175] This gave the Amalfitans a clear competitive edge over their West Italian rivals as well as those from Provence and Catalonia. Citarella contends that the resultant 'freedom of trade in the great emporium on the Bosphorus [Constantinople] and especially the ports of North Africa gave the Amalphitans a monopoly shared only with Venice, in the sale of ceremonial clothes, spices, and other oriental products in Italy'. When what Citarella calls 'the catastrophe of the Norman conquest' occurred under the auspices of the unremitting Hautevilles in the late eleventh century, the Amalfitans lost their special circumstance.[176] The seizure of the central Mediterranean from the Muslims leveled the playing field and released the expansive energies of Genoa and Pisa eastward.

And the Hautevilles as overlords did not help matters much. In fact, falling under the power of the Normans aggravated the situation for the Amalfitans and hastened their decline. When the harassment of Guaimar IV, prince of Salerno, compelled the Amalfitans in 1073 to seek the protection of the latter's brother-in-law, Robert Guiscard, their fortunes took a precipitous tumble.[177] Their new suzerain's designs on the Eastern Empire in the early 1080s prompted a Byzantine

[171] Citarella, 'Relations of Amalfi with the Arab World', p. 300.

[172] *Codice diplomatico amalfitano*, I, doc. 2 and 3, pp. 3–5.

[173] Grierson and Travaini, *Medieval European Coinage*, p. 3; Kreutz, *Before the Normans*, p. 82; Loud, *Age of Robert Guiscard*, pp. 50–1.

[174] William of Apulia, *La Geste de Robert Guiscard*, Bk III, line 483, pp. 190–1. 'His Arabes, Libi, Siculi noscuntur et Afri.'

[175] S. Goitein, *Letters of Medieval Jewish Traders* (Princeton, 1973), no. 3 and 4, pp. 39–45; TSC-ULC, doc. 144, 12" glasses, fragment 1.10 *et seq.*; TSC-ULC, 8" vols, Arabic J series, vol. 1, fol. 5.

[176] Citarella, 'Relations of Amalfi with the Arab World', pp. 301, 312.

[177] Amatus, *History of the Normans*, Bk VIII, ch. 7–8, p. 191; *Storia de' Normanni*, Bk VIII, ch. VII–VIII, pp. 348–9; Malaterra, *Deeds of Count Roger*, Bk 3, ch. 3, p. 135; *De rebus gestis*

backlash against Amalfi. Amalfitan commercial interests in Constantinople were downgraded in favor of their arch-competitors, the Venetians. As was discussed above, the expansion of Venetian privileges in Constantinople and throughout the empire eventually displaced those of Amalfi.[178] The Normans did little to compensate their new subjects for the loss. Instead, they regularly drained off Amalfitan maritime assets for their own enterprises. Soon after accepting sovereignty over the city, Guiscard conscripted Amalfitan ships for his investment of Salerno.[179] Following Salerno's eventual capitulation, he then sent Amalfitan men and ships to assist his newfound ally, Richard of Capua, in the abortive siege of Naples.[180] And there can be little doubt that Amalfitan sailors and ships were included in the fleets that Robert hurled against the Greek mainland in 1081 and 1084.[181]

By 1096 it must have become evident to the Amalfitans that subservience to the Hautevilles was not in their best interest. They revolted. The Normans led by Roger, the 'Great Count', and Roger Borsa, Duke of Apulia, immediately laid siege to the city. Only the advent of the First Crusade and Bohemond's defection to take up the cross spared Amalfi.[182] It was purely a provisional postponement, however. The 'Great Count's' son, Roger II, would employ his formidable fleet commanded by George of Antioch to bring the city to heel in early 1131, shortly after his coronation.[183] It would be the first of several humiliating and crippling violations of its sovereignty that the city would suffer. The Pisans, as the maritime henchmen of the German Emperor Lothair III, would sack Amalfi in 1135 so savagely that it would never recover its past seafaring glory. The city had been unable to put up even a ghost of a resistance because Roger had siphoned off what few martial means remained to it for the long siege of Naples.[184] The

Rogerii, Bk III, ch. III, p. 58; William of Apulia, La Geste de Robert Guiscard, Bk III, lines 412–20, pp. 186–7.

[178] Anna Comnena, Alexiad, p. 191; Alexiade, II, Bk VI, ch. V, pp. 54–5; Tafel and Thomas, Urkunden der Republik Venedig, I, pp. 51–4, 109–13.

[179] Malaterra, Deeds of Count Roger, Bk 3, ch. 3, p. 135; De rebus gestis Rogerii, Bk III, ch. III, p. 58.

[180] Amatus, History of the Normans, Bk VIII, ch. 25, p. 200; Storia de' Normanni, Bk VIII, ch. XXV, p. 366.

[181] Anna Comnena, Alexiad, p. 188; Alexiade, II, Bk VI, ch. IV, pp. 50–1; William of Apulia, La Geste de Robert Guiscard, Bk IV, lines 122–33, pp. 210–11.

[182] Malaterra, Deeds of Count Roger, Bk 4, ch. 24, pp. 204–5; De rebus gestis Rogerii, Bk IV, ch. XXIV, p. 102.

[183] Alexander of Telese, Bk II, ch. 8–11, pp. 27–8; Annales Casinenses, anno 1131, p. 309; Annales Cavenses, anno 1130, pp. 185–97, especially 191; Chronica de Ferraria, anno 1131, p. 18; Falco of Benevento, Chronicon Beneventanum, p. 108; Romuald of Salerno, Romualdi Salernitani Chronicon, pp. 218–19.

[184] Alexander of Telese, Bk III, ch. 24–5, pp. 72–3; Annales Cavenses, anno 1135, p. 191; Chronica de Ferraria, anno 1135, p. 20; Falco of Benevento, Chronicon Beneventanum, p. 174; Bernardo Maragone, Annales Pisani, pp. 9–10; Romuald of Salerno, Romualdi Salernitani Chronicon, p. 220.

Pisans would repeat the depredation two years later, again as a member of an anti-Norman imperial alliance.[185]

By the end of the Norman Kingdom, Amalfi was a mere shadow of its former self. It had long since lost its standing in the Byzantine Empire and the First Crusade, of course, caused it to lose virtually all of its holdings in the Holy Land. Amalfi's properties in Palestine were conceded by the Fatimid Caliph of Cairo whose forces had been evicted by the crusaders.[186] Taking the place of the Amalfitans in the Latin Kingdom of Jerusalem were their West Italian competitors, Genoa and Pisa, the very sea powers whose eastward expansion in support of the Crusades the Norman conquest had facilitated.

Indeed, the Normans appear to have made little effort to intercede on behalf of their Amalfitan subjects in their own commercial dealings with the East. King Roger, for example, ensured that a mid-1130s treaty with the Caliph of Cairo contained preferential trading rights in Alexandria for his mainland capital, Salerno, but apparently made no such provision for Amalfi.[187] In truth, the Normans had little incentive to support Amalfitan commercial endeavors, because the kingdom derived most of its maritime revenues not from its own mercantile shipping, but from the duties it charged other merchant fleets to transit the central Mediterranean. Indeed, the only Amalfitan legacy that seems to have survived the Norman era was a set of maritime laws reflected in the famed *Tabula de Amalpha*.[188]

Nevertheless, the fact remains that emergent West Italian sea power as represented chiefly by Genoa and Pisa benefited immensely from Norman dominance in the central Mediterranean. The displacement of an inimical Muslim hegemony in the region by a Christian naval power meant that, for the first time in centuries, Christian merchants from Western Europe could easily traverse the Sicilian Channel or the Strait of Messina to the East. This allowed Genoa and Pisa to profitably participate in the crusades without having to fight their way past Sicily and the Maghrib coast. Indeed, the Crusading movement itself was dependent, at least initially, on the support of West Italian sea power. As a result, Genoa and Pisa were able to establish highly lucrative merchant enclaves in the Latin Kingdom. This, of course, increased the volume of trade through the central Mediterranean – trade that the Norman Kingdom happily taxed for the benefit of its burgeoning treasury. The Normans thus profited as much as the West Italian mercantile republics with only a fraction of the risk. It was a successful business model and it financed their dominion in the region to the end of the era. But the biggest beneficiary was probably Western Europe, as

[185] Bernardo Maragone, *Annales Pisani*, p. 11; Falco of Benevento, *Chronicon Beneventanum*, p. 186.

[186] William of Tyre, *History of Deeds Done beyond the Sea*, II, Bk 18, ch. 4–5, pp. 241–5; *Willelmi Tyrensis Chronicon*, Bk 18, ch. 4–5, pp. 814–17.

[187] *Rogerii II. Regis Diplomata Latina*, no. 46, pp. 129–31.

[188] *Tabula de Amalpha*, ed. V. Giuffre (Cava dei Tirreni, 1965).

a whole, because the resultant ease of travel to the East for its merchants and merchandise energized its economic ascendancy.

Altered trading patterns of Muslim commerce

If the impact of the Norman conquest of the central Mediterranean on the West Italian city-states and consequently Europe was profoundly positive, it was utterly stultifying on Muslim North Africa. Muslim commerce from Morocco to Egypt was irreparably altered by the Norman seizure of Sicily. In fact, in his monumental study of the Cairo Geniza documents, *A Mediterranean Society*, Shelomo Goitein forthrightly states, 'The eleventh century ... witnessed a complete translocation of the Mediterranean trade routes.'[189] His research pinpointed a clear cause: 'In the West, the dominating feature was the rise of the Italian maritime cities on one hand, and the foundation and development of the Norman kingdom of the "two Sicilies" [Sicily and southern Italy] on the other.'[190]

The evidence provided by the Cairo Geniza is compelling. Though it stems from a single source – the *geniza* (storeroom) of the Ben Ezra synagogue of Fustat (Old Cairo), it is highly reliable. First of all, the cache of documents is voluminous. It is comprised of nearly 250,000 literary leaves, at least 10,000 of which are document-length, spread out over a score of modern collections, the largest of which is the Taylor-Schechter Collection of the University Library of Cambridge.[191] What makes the source almost unimpeachable, however, is the nature of the documents. The vast majority are letters from Jewish merchants to family, friends and colleagues. They were deposited in the *geniza* because it was believed that any document that contained the name of 'God' should be preserved.[192] This implies that they were, in fact, testimonials to God and, as such, would not contain intentional falsehoods. In other words, the authors of these letters believed that what they had written was true. These are letters to loved ones and friends; therefore, from the heart. Their contents would not normally have been filtered through the lens of ethnocentricity or subject to religious and political bombast, that is, they are as close to an objective portrayal of existing circumstances as the modern medieval scholar is likely to acquire.

Moreover, the Geniza records are uniquely suited to support the study at hand. The documents encompass almost exactly the timeframe of Mediterranean history in question. Goitein, who considered the classical period of the Cairo Geniza to be from the Fatimid conquest of Egypt in 969 to the fall of the Ayyubids in 1250, writes this of the era:

---

[189] Goitein, *Mediterranean Society*, I, p. 32.
[190] Goitein, *Mediterranean Society*, I, pp. 39–40.
[191] Goitein, *Mediterranean Society*, I, pp. 4–5, 13.
[192] Goitein, *Mediterranean Society*, I, p. 1.

It was a time of profound and lasting changes on the Mediterranean scene. Naval superiority shifted from the Muslim south to the Christian north. On the African coast, the center of gravity moved from Tunisia, which had been the nucleus of Fatimid power during the tenth century, eastward toward Egypt. Along the north shore the trend was westward: Byzantium, in its role as the protagonist of Christendom, was replaced by the Italian republics, the Normans, and later on, by the kingdoms of France and Spain.[193]

The Cairo Geniza, thus, essentially contains an objective account from an independent source of the rise of Norman sea power and its impact on the region. On top of that, the source is centered on the central Mediterranean, precisely the area affected by the Norman conquest. 'The most surprising feature in the contents of the Geniza,' observes Goitein, 'as far as its geographical distribution is concerned is the overwhelming preponderance in it of people from Tunisia and Sicily, especially from the time of its inception around 1000 down to the last quarter of the eleventh century.' He estimates that at least eighty percent of all business correspondence in the period originates from the Jewish merchants of the Maghrib, because the Palestinian–Rabbanite leaders of the Ben Ezra synagogue actively recruited the relatively wealthy merchants of the Maghrib in the aftermath of the synagogue's destruction by the Fatimid caliph al-Hakim in 1012 in order to finance its rebuilding.[194] Finally, the one aspect of daily life that the Geniza documents illuminate well is travel and seafaring.[195] Therefore, the Cairo Geniza supplies invaluable, unbiased corroboration for Latin, Greek and Arabic accounts of this pivotal point in Mediterranean history. Goitein himself confirms this: 'The struggle for Sicily and southern Italy, in which Byzantines, Muslims, local Italians, and Normans took part, as well as the successful attacks of the two latter on various points of the North African coast, is copiously reflected in the Geniza.'[196]

The Cairo Geniza provides a dramatic before-and-after portrait of conditions in the central Mediterranean. Prior to the appearance of the Normans, the letters of the Jewish merchants describe a thriving Muslim trade structure that stretched the breadth of Mediterranean from Fatimid Egypt to Ummayyad Spain. The Zirid Maghrib and Sicily stood at its heart, and the Muslim vessels that sailed the sea almost unmolested frequently stopped at both. 'During the tenth and earlier parts of the eleventh centuries,' says Goitein, 'Tunisia and Sicily formed the hub of the Mediterranean selling the goods of the East to the West and vice versa.'[197] Indeed, Sicily and the Zirid Maghrib seemed to have been considered a single economic unit and the preferred destination for merchantmen originating from ports in Egypt until the middle of the eleventh century. Travel

---

[193] Goitein, *Mediterranean Society*, I, p. 29.
[194] Goitein, *Mediterranean Society*, I, pp. 20–1.
[195] Goitein, *Mediterranean Society*, I, p. 27.
[196] Goitein, *Mediterranean Society*, I, p. 40.
[197] Goitein, *Mediterranean Society*, I, p. 212.

between Tunisia and Sicily was constant, making Palermo and Mazara the most important ports on the island.[198] Based on his Geniza research, Goitein finds that Mazara on the southwestern tip of Sicily nearest the Maghrib was 'a major distribution center of the Mediterranean trade during the eleventh century'.[199] Messina on the northeastern tip, on the other hand, is hardly mentioned in the Geniza documents. Therefore, most east–west shipping seems to have passed through the Sicilian Channel rather than the Strait of Messina. Accordingly, vessels originating in Egypt, mostly from Alexandria and Damietta, navigated along the southern shores of the Mediterranean by way of Tripoli, Mahdiyah, Tunis and Mazara to Bona, Bejaïa and Ceuta in the western Maghrib and from there to ports of call in the Al-Andalus of Spain like Malaga, Almeria and Denia (see Map 14). Only such Christian trading partners as Amalfi and Gaeta would have found it convenient to use the Strait of Messina for their eastern trade.

Until the latter half of the eleventh century, the Cairo Geniza shows that east–west commerce on the Mediterranean was almost exclusively carried by Muslim vessels or Christian collaborators like Amalfi and Venice. 'All seafaring was done on ships whose proprietors, whether Muslims, Christians, or Jews, bear Arabic or Arabicized names,' discovered Goitein.[200] The Pisans and Genoese, for instance, are not mentioned until the twelfth century.[201] Those few Christian merchantmen who dared to sail the central Mediterranean had to contend with a plague of piracy – piracy that sought to prey especially on the ships of the 'infidels'. 'Piracy was part and parcel of the Holy War against Christendom,' explains Goitein.[202] But, of course, with the relative dearth of Christian vessels to victimize, the marauders also became a problem for Muslim merchantmen. The pirate enclave of Jerba, the small island opposite Gabes on the Maghrib coast, proved particularly vexing. Ibn al-Athir records that the Zirid emir, Ali ibn Yahya ibn Tamim, was forced to dispatch a fleet to the island in 1115–16 because 'the inhabitants had been interrupting commerce and seizing merchants'.[203]

Moreover, Islamic leaders were not opposed to using such buccaneers against their coreligionists for political purposes. Goitein notes that Jabbara, the emir of Barqa on the Libyan coast, and his father Muktar appear often in the Geniza documents of the early eleventh century, victimizing not just Byzantine shipping but also that of Tunisia. 'It seems that the Fatimid rulers of Egypt used the pirates of Barqa for chastising the Sunnite West in the same way in which they employed the Bedouin hordes of the Hilal and Sulaym, namely to destroy a

---

[198] Goitein, *Mediterranean Society*, I, p. 215.
[199] Goitein, *Mediterranean Society*, I, p. 302.
[200] Goitein, *Mediterranean Society*, I, p. 40.
[201] A. Citarella, 'A Puzzling Question concerning the Relations between the Jewish Communities of Christian Europe and Those Represented in the Geniza Documents', *Journal of the American Oriental Society*, XCI (1971), pp. 390–7, especially 397.
[202] Goitein, *Mediterranean Society*, I, p. 327.
[203] Ibn al-Athir, *Chronicle of Ibn al-Athir*, I, p. 175.

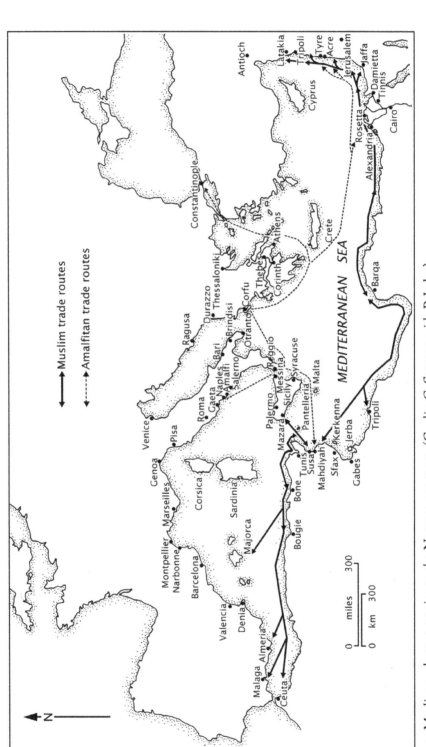

14. Muslim trade routes prior to the Norman conquest. (Credit: C. Stanton with P. Judge)

country whose prosperity was a thorn in their sides,' concludes Goitein.[204] As a result, ships sailing between Egypt and Tunisia regularly went in convoy with a man-of-war to protect them. There are many examples in the Geniza. 'The ships are ready to set sail,' explains a letter from Alexandria written around 1023. 'They wait only until the *ustūl* [heavy warship] will be repaired.'[205] It suffices to say that the central Mediterranean was a very dangerous place for all concerned in the years before Norman naval supremacy had been established. It was a particularly inimical environment for Christian shipping.

Auguries of change began to appear toward the middle of the eleventh century. First, there was the Byzantine invasion of Sicily in 1038 under Giorgios Maniakes. It was a massive undertaking, lasting nearly four years. It included a contingent of Normans led by the first of the Hauteville brothers, and was supported by a sizeable Byzantine fleet, commanded by a relative of the *basileus*. Goitein noted serious signs of disruption in the Geniza's correspondence during that four-year period. The presence of the Byzantine fleet off Sicily meant traders not only avoided the island, but the Zirid Maghrib as well. The direct route between Egypt and Tunisia by sea was out of the question. The author of a letter written circa 1040 from Mahdiyah laments: 'I hope, however, that there will be traffic on the Barqa route. Therefore, repack the bales into camel-loads – half their original size – and send them via Barqa. Perhaps I shall get a good price for them and acquire antimony with it this winter. For dear brother, if the merchandise remains in Alexandria year after year, we shall make no profit.' Later he tellingly adds, 'During the whole of last summer I was in Qayrawan to arrange for the dispatch of consignments belonging to M. Abu l-Faraj [Ibn 'Allah] and found no one wanted to undertake an overseas journey this year.'[206]

Next, about 1051, came the onslaught of the Banu Hilal and the Banu Sulaym, flung like the proverbial plague of locusts upon the Zirid Maghrib by the Fatimid caliphate of Cairo. The upheaval and dislocation this event caused drastically impacted commerce in the region. Traders were trapped in their cities, unable to move freely about the countryside for fear of being slaughtered by marauding bands of Bedouins. Around 1055 a learned Jewish merchant from Fustat, named Nahray, relates how his brother had been unable to leave the city of Qayrawan for eight months. 'Finally, a group of Muslims and among them some [Jews?] left the city,' he writes, 'but the Arabs [meaning: the Bedouins] killed them, cutting their stomachs open and saying: "You have swallowed dinars".'[207] Aside

[204] Goitein, *Mediterranean Society*, I, p. 327.
[205] Goitein, *Letters of Medieval Jewish Traders*, no. 69–70, pp. 306–15, especially 310; Bodleian Library, Oxford, Hebrew Mss d 66, no. 2878, *Catalogue of the Hebrew Manuscripts of the Bodleian Library*, fol. 15; TSC-ULC, 13" vols, J series, vol. 17, fol. 3.
[206] Goitein, *Letters of Medieval Jewish Traders*, no. 18, pp. 101–7; Bodleian Library, Oxford, Hebrew Mss a 2, no. 2805, CHMBL, fol. 17.
[207] Goitein, *Letters of Medieval Jewish Traders*, no. 31, pp. 153–8, especially 155; British Museum, catalogue no. Or. 4452, fol. 9, letter to merchant-banker and scholar Nahray b. Nassim.

from such lurid tales of depredation, the ultimate upshot of the Hilali invasions was that they weakened the Zirid dynasty at a time when the Normans were amassing power in the area and beginning to threaten Sicily. The ravages of the Bedouin raiders in the hinterlands had to have seriously hampered the ability of the Zirids to maintain a credible naval force, for instance.

The Zirids were, thus, in no position to prevent the next calamity from occurring: the Norman invasion of Sicily. The beginning of the island's conquest by the Hautevilles is described in mournful detail by the Jewish chief judge of Mahdiyah around 1061: 'The situation deteriorates constantly, and everyone is terribly disturbed about the progress of the enemy [the Normans] who has already conquered most of the island.' The judge goes on to explain why this is such a great tragedy: 'The prices here [Mahdiyah] go up, for this place must rely for its supply of grain entirely on Sicily.' This last is an obvious reference to the devastation to agriculture wrought by the Arab Bedouins in the hinterland of the Maghrib. He finishes by relating some of the human toll brought about by the Norman incursion: 'Twelve families of our coreligionists have been taken captive, and countless numbers of Muslims. May God protect all those of Israel who have remained there. [Messina (?) was conquered] by the sword and a number of Jews died there.'[208]

The letters of the Geniza reveal that it was not long before the Norman offensive on Sicily began to adversely affect maritime commerce. One written about 1062 recounts how a force led by Ibn al-Thumnah, the erstwhile emir of Syracuse and Catania who had allied himself with Roger de Hauteville, had intercepted a merchantman from the Maghrib near Girgenti and purloined its load of textiles.[209] Another letter dated in August of the same year offers some hope of respite. Some Spanish coreligionists traveling on a ship from Mazara 'reported good and reassuring news, namely that Ibn al-Thumna had been killed and that the situation [on the island] had become settled.'[210] The hope, of course, proved false. The Norman offensive only took a pause. A missive composed around 1063/4 tells of a boat on its way from Mazara to the Maghrib that was forced to evade 'the enemy' by fleeing to the nearby port of Sciacca. The same letter refers to a widespread 'burning of the ships' at the time.[211] This would, of course, conform to a Norman strategy of disrupting trade while preventing Sicily's Muslim defenders from being resupplied. And, as Goitein points out, 'No

---

[208] Goitein, *Letters of Medieval Jewish Traders*, no. 33, pp. 163–8, especially 167; Institute Narodov Azii, St Petersburg, D-55, doc. no. 13.
[209] Goitein, *Mediterranean Society*, I, p. 330; TSC-ULC, doc. no. 372, 12" glasses, fragment 1.10.
[210] Goitein, *Letters of Medieval Jewish Traders*, no. 34, pp. 168–73, especially 169; TSC-ULC, 13" vols, J series, vol. 19, fol. 20.
[211] Goitein, *Mediterranean Society*, I, p. 330; Dropsie College, Philadelphia, doc. no. 389, fragment 1.32.

clear-cut distinction between piracy and war can be made in the period under discussion.'[212]

As the Norman conquest progressed, fewer letters from the region made their way into the *geniza* of the Ben Ezra synagogue of Fustat. The turmoil to travel and trade caused by the Normans on Sicily and the despoliation of the Maghrib countryside perpetrated by the Bedouin tribes not only dampened commerce but also precipitated a general diaspora. This is reflected in a drastic falloff in letters from the Jewish traders of the Maghrib at the time. Goitein points out, 'There are not many of them during the first half of the twelfth century and even fewer from its second half.'[213] Two of those dwindling dispatches from the beginning of the twelfth century illustrate just how far Zirid fortunes had fallen. The first, written around 1100, describes a blockade of the port of Mahdiyah by attackers whom Goitein surmises were the Normans:

> What I have to tell you about the news of war is that an Andalusian ship set sail from al-Mahdiyya, the enemy fought it, but the night separated them and it returned safely to Sfax. Then, when a second ship set sail, the enemy rammed it and took everything which was in it, merchandise and people, and left the ship turned upside down.[214]

A second letter written at about the same time by a merchant from Alexandria complained of rampant piracy between Mahdiyah and Sicily. Goitein deduced from the foregoing 'that the rulers of Tunisia had entirely lost their former maritime supremacy.'[215]

As Zirid naval power atrophied, that of the Normans reached its zenith under Roger II. Norman fleets raided the coasts of Ifriqiyah and the Maghrib throughout the latter's reign. These attacks took an ominous turn from simple plundering to outright conquest and occupation in the 1130s. A certain Abu Sa'id, while traveling on a Christian ship from Egypt around 1135, writes of encountering a Norman fleet that had just seized the island of Jerba.[216] There are several other letters that echo the event. One composed in Egypt on 14 October 1136 reports, 'Today there arrived the prisoners from Jerba [apparently to be ransomed].'[217] The same Abu Sa'id dispatched another letter circa 1140 from Palermo to Fustat, which infers that the Norman navy had effectively severed

---

[212] Goitein, *A Mediterranean Society*, I, p. 330.

[213] Goitein, *Letters of Medieval Jewish Traders*, p. 231.

[214] S. Goitein, 'Glimpses from the Cairo Geniza on naval warfare in the Mediterranean and on the Mongol invasion', *Studi Orientalistici in onore di Giorgio Levi della Vita* (Rome, 1956), pp. 393–408, especially 402; University Library of Cambridge, Or 1081, J series, vol. 27.

[215] Goitein, 'Glimpses from the Cairo Geniza on naval warfare', p. 395; Bodleian Library, Oxford, Hebrew Mss b11, fols 5 and 11.

[216] Goitein, *Letters of Medieval Jewish Traders*, p. 324; TSC-ULC, 8" vols, series J, vol. 23, fol. 13.

[217] Goitein, *Letters of Medieval Jewish Traders*, p. 324, note 1; TSC-ULC, K series, box 6, fol. 47.

Ifriqiyah's sea link with the East. He writes, 'I entered Sicily with my family coming from Tunis because of the privations suffered there ...' He adds tellingly, 'I intended to travel to Egypt via Sicily, for it is no longer possible to travel to Egypt directly from Ifriqiyah.'[218] Abu Sa'id was a spice merchant; thus, Goitein believes that growing Norman naval supremacy in the Sicilian Channel caused his business to shrivel and die. The end was near.

It came in 1148 with the Norman capture of Mahdiyah and the adjacent cities on the Maghrib coast. A letter dated 11 September 1149 from a Jewish India trader named Abraham Yiju in Aden to his family in Mahdiyah poignantly reflects the aftermath: 'I heard what happened to the coastline of Ifriqiya, Tripoli, Jerba, Qarqanna [Kerkenna], Sfax, al-Mahdiya, and Susa. No letter, however, from which I could learn who died and who remained alive, has arrived.' Yiju's letter finally reached his family not in Mahdiyah, but in Sicily where they had been 'reduced to a single loaf of bread'. He invites them to join him in Aden, Fustat or Alexandria, fearing 'it will not be possible ... to go to al-Mahdiya or to Ifriqiya, namely, to Tunis or Qayrawan.'[219] The clear implication is that commerce had been so disrupted by the actions of the Norman navy and the subsequent conquest of North Africa that many of the merchants of the Maghrib had been forced to migrate elsewhere.

The impact on travel and trade was pronounced. Muslims from the Maghrib could no longer routinely journey on Muslim ships along the southern shore of the Mediterranean. Travel was now aboard Christian ships, which almost invariably proceeded by way of Sicily, specifically Palermo and Messina. This is illustrated by the itinerary adopted in 1153 by Perahya ibn Joseph, the nephew of Abraham Yiju mentioned above, in response to Yiju's invitation.[220] Goitein explains:

> Perahya's family had left Tunisia, probably in 1148, when it was partly occupied by the Normans, and settled in Mazara, a port on the southwestern coast of Sicily. During the eleventh century, Mazara was a lively trading entrepôt, serving as a bridgehead to Tunisia and a terminal for ships going to the Levant. After the Norman conquest of Sicily, however, and the subsequent severing of close relations between Tunisia and the island, Mazara lost its importance as a seaport. Perahya had to look for another way to get to Egypt. He turned first north overland to Palermo and from there went by boat to Messina on the east coast of Sicily.[221]

The Norman occupation of the Maghrib coast lasted only a dozen years. A letter written in the autumn of 1156 was a harbinger of its fall. It told of an

---

[218] Goitein, *Letters of Medieval Jewish Traders*, no. 74, pp. 323–7, especially 325; TSC-ULC, 13" vols, series J, vol. 26, fol. 10.

[219] Goitein, *Letters of Medieval Jewish Traders*, no. 41, pp. 201–6, especially 203–4; TSC-ULC, 10" vols, J series, vol. 10, fol. 15.

[220] Goitein, *Letters of Medieval Jewish Traders*, no. 75, pp. 327–30; Elkan N. Adler Collection, Jewish Theological Seminary of America, New York, no. 151, catalogue no. 2557.

[221] Goitein, *Letters of Medieval Jewish Traders*, p. 325.

Almohad fleet of 40 vessels assembled at Bejaïa.[222] The Almohads would take Mahdiyah and the other Norman-held ports of North Africa by early 1160. Nonetheless, the change wrought by the establishment of Norman naval dominance in the central Mediterranean was permanent. Christian maritime might now held sway from one end of the sea to the other. Venice remained a great maritime presence in the eastern Mediterranean, but, beginning in the early twelfth century, the Cairo Geniza shows Genoa and Pisa emerging as major sea powers in both the East and the West. By this time most merchants from Muslim lands rode on the ships of the two West Italian republics.[223] Between 1183 and 1185 Ibn Jubayr, for instance, traveled on Genoese ships from Ceuta to Alexandria, from Acre to Sicily and, finally, from Sicily to Andalusia.[224] And, of course, the West Italians became dominant players in commerce everywhere. A letter from Fustat to Aden circa 1103 intimates that the imprisonment of Genoese merchants in Fustat by the Fatimid vizier al-Afdal ibn Badr, for all intents and purposes, temporarily shut down the markets of Egypt.[225] About thirty years later, a 9 January 1133 dispatch from Fustat reinforces the impression: 'This year business is at a standstill, for no one had come from the West [Muslim Andalusia and the Maghrib] …'[226] Muslim hegemony on the Mediterranean was long a memory, never to return. The Norman conquest had opened the floodgate that was the central Mediterranean and released a torrent of Western maritime ascendancy that could not and would not be reversed.

The resurgence of Sicilian sea power under Frederick II

The Hohenstaufen seizure of Sicily did not spell the end of Sicilian sea power. It would enjoy a great renaissance in the years that followed. But it would not be Henry VI Hohenstaufen who would effect that renaissance. Henry was crowned King of Sicily on Christmas Day 1194, yet he remained in Palermo only until April 1195 when events in Germany forced his return. He was not able to come back to the kingdom until November 1196 and he only set foot on Sicily again in March 1197. By the end of September 1197, he was dead of a sudden illness, having spent barely thirteen months on the island.[227] There simply was not enough time and opportunity for him to imprint any sort of Hohenstaufen stamp on the

---

[222] Goitein, *Mediterranean Society*, I, p. 308; Bodleian Library, Oxford, Hebrew Mss bII, no. 2874, *CHMBL*, fol. 15, fragment 1.28.

[223] Goitein, *Mediterranean Society*, I, pp. 40, 59; 'Glimpses from the Cairo Geniza on naval warfare', p. 397.

[224] Ibn Jubayr, *Travels of Ibn Jubayr*, pp. 26–9, 327–37, 357–65.

[225] Goitein, *Mediterranean Society*, I, p. 45; Bodleian Library, Oxford, Hebrew Mss b 3, no. 2806, *CHMBL*, fol. 26.

[226] Goitein, *Mediterranean Society*, I, p. 45; TSC-ULC, 13" vols, series J, vol. 33, fol. 1.

[227] Richard of San Germano, *Ryccardi de Sancto Germano Notarii Chronica*, anni 1196–7, pp. 17–18.

administration of the kingdom, much less institute a reorganization of the fleet. There was no Hohenstaufen naval tradition to speak of, anyway. He and his father, Frederick I Barbarossa, had purchased their naval power from the great maritime republics of Genoa and Pisa. Any naval expertise he may have acquired as a result of the conquest, he squandered by having the last Norman admiral, Margaritus of Brindisi, blinded and packed off to his castle at Trifels where the former 'king of the sea' reportedly perished.[228] Moreover, the collapse of central authority in Sicily following Henry's death sabotaged any basis for building a new Sicilian fleet. During the subsequent regency, Queen Constance, in order to curry favor with the kingdom's clergy, repeatedly granted exemptions to the royal levies upon which fleet funding depended.[229] The man who would ultimately resurrect Sicilian sea power would be Henry's son and successor, Frederick II, and it would not be Hohenstaufen methods of rule that Frederick would utilize; it would be those of the Hautevilles.

Frederick II may have been officially designated as heir to the Hohenstaufen dynasty, but he had Hauteville blood coursing through his veins, pumped by a thoroughly Norman heart. His mother, Constance, was the last daughter of Roger II, the greatest of the Norman kings, and her actions during her brief regency suggest that she wanted Frederick to follow in her father's footsteps. 'Her aim was to restore the Norman monarchy,' states Abulafia unambiguously.[230] Indeed, when the young prince was born the day after Henry's coronation, the *Annales Casinenses* notes that he was called 'Frederick Roger or Roger Frederick' after his two famous grandfathers.[231] Following Henry's death, the queen surrounded her son with local advisors and even attempted to banish the self-proclaimed *imperii senescalcum* (imperial seneschal), Markward von Anweiler, from the kingdom. Unfortunately, her untimely demise in November 1198 prevented her from doing more. In her will, however, she managed to shield her son somewhat from the designs of the German princes by having Pope Innocent III appointed as his guardian.[232]

Nonetheless, his minority was a difficult and chaotic one in which Markward von Anweiler and his German henchmen, notably Count Diepold of Acerra, conspired to take control of the kingdom, even making the young king captive at one point. The threat only ended with Markward's death from dysentery in 1202.[233] Meanwhile, the Genoese and Pisans competed incessantly for control

---

228   E. Jamison, *Admiral Eugenius of Sicily, his life and work* (London, 1975), Appendix II, no. 23, pp. 347–8; Ménager, *Amiratus*, p. 102.
229   Mott, *Sea Power in the Medieval Mediterranean*, pp. 61–2.
230   Abulafia, *Frederick II*, p. 93.
231   *Annales Casinenses*, anno 1194–5, pp. 317–18. '... *Fredericum Roggerium seu Roggerium Fredericum* ...'
232   Richard of San Germano, *Ryccardi de Sancto Germano Notarii Chronica*, anno 1198, p. 19.
233   Richard of San Germano, *Ryccardi de Sancto Germano Notarii Chronica*, anni 1199–1202, pp. 19–23. See also Abulafia, *Frederick II*, pp. 94–102; Matthew, *Norman Kingdom of Sicily*, pp. 300–2.

of Sicily's great trading ports, particularly Syracuse, which saw major engagements between the two in 1204 and 1205.[234] It was a minor miracle that Frederick survived to reach his majority in December 1208 at the callow age of fourteen.[235] Barely four years later he was compelled to travel north to claim his German imperial inheritance.[236] It was not until 1220 that he was able to come south again to tend to his Sicilian kingdom. Now a tested monarch of twenty-six, he wasted little time. Within a matter of days after his imperial coronation in Rome on 22 November,[237] he was in Capua issuing the first of several landmark bodies of law, the so-called Assizes of Capua, which harkened back to the old Norman legal structure and system of government. The 'assizes' were actually a series of decrees by which, contends Abulafia, 'Frederick sought to reestablish the Sicilian monarchy in the spirit that it had been exercised by Roger II and William II.'[238] Specifically, they invoked *de resignandis privilegiis*, which essentially abrogated all the royal privileges that had issued since the death of William II in 1189 and required them to be reconfirmed. This enabled Frederick to reverse the ruinous exemptions from feudal service granted by his father and to restore many of the royal prerogatives usurped by the baronage in his minority.[239] More pertinently, it allowed the crown to regain control over the old Norman system of tithes and taxes on communities so crucial for funding any sort of military capability, like a fleet.

This consolidation of royal authority and the resultant revitalization of royal revenues evidently began to pay dividends quite quickly. By April 1221, Frederick was able to appoint Henry of Malta, a known Genoese pirate and highly regarded naval commander, as *marini stolii ammiratum* ('admiral of the fleet') and dispatch him with 40 galleys to aid the armies of the Fifth Crusade at Damietta.[240] This was to be in partial fulfillment of the crusading vows the emperor had made to Honorius III at his imperial investiture, but, unfortunately, the crusaders capitulated before Henry's flotilla could even see action. Frustrated by the failure, Frederick imprisoned his new admiral and had him stripped of

[234] Ogerio Pane, *Annales Ianuenses*, II, pp. 96–8.
[235] Richard of San Germano, *Ryccardi de Sancto Germano Notarii Chronica*, anno 1208, p. 26.
[236] Richard of San Germano, *Ryccardi de Sancto Germano Notarii Chronica*, anno 1212, p. 46.
[237] Richard of San Germano, *Ryccardi de Sancto Germano Notarii Chronica*, anno 1220, pp. 82–3.
[238] Abulafia, *Frederick II*, p. 140.
[239] J. Powell, *The Liber Augustalis or Constitutions of Melfi Promulgated by the Emperor Frederick II for the Kingdom of Sicily in 1231* (Syracuse, 1971), Introduction, p. XXX.
[240] Marchiso Scriba, *Annales Ianuenses*, II, p. 178; Richard of San Germano, *Ryccardi de Sancto Germano Notarii Chronica*, anno 1221, p. 95. See also D. Abulafia, 'Henry Count of Malta and his Mediterranean Activities, 1203–1230', in *Medieval Malta: Studies on Malta before the Knights*, ed. A. T. Luttrell (Supplementary Monograph of the British School at Rome) (1975), pp. 104–25, especially 119–22.

Malta.[241] Notwithstanding, the episode served notice that the Kingdom of Sicily was once again a naval power and that more was to come.

Frederick began planning for a new crusade, the Sixth, the very next year. By March 1224, he reported to Honorius III that he was amassing a fleet of *centum galeas* ('one hundred galleys') and *quinquaginta vero usseria* ('fifty usceriis [also called uxeriis]' –oared cavalry transports with stern-mounted disembarkation ramps).[242] In July 1225 at San Germano, he promised Honorius' successor, Pope Gregory IX, to embark upon the crusade within two years with *quinquaginta galeas* ('fifty galleys') and *centum calandras* ('one hundred *chelandia*' – oared transports).[243] There were many delays, the last one of which was in the summer of 1227 when illness forced Frederick to return to port shortly after setting sail. This prompted Gregory IX to excommunicate him in October, but, undeterred, the emperor ultimately departed from Brindisi in June 1228.[244] By the time he reached Limassol, Cyprus on 21 July, Philip of Novara, a lawyer in the service of the Ibelin family, testified that he had a fleet of 70 ships that included 'galleys, *taride* and other *naves*'.[245] The galleys were undoubtedly warships while the *taride* were oared horse transports and the *naves* were probably other transports for carrying troops, provisions and equipment – indicating a multifaceted fleet of a relatively sophisticated naval force. Moreover, Frederick had dispatched in advance an unspecified number of ships under Riccardo Filangieri, the imperial marshal, and Herman von Salza, the master of the Teutonic knights.[246] Since almost all of these ships were most likely oared vessels of one kind or another, crewed by 100 to 150 men per ship who doubled as combatants, they represented a substantial infantry component. As a consequence, John Pryor convincingly argues that Fredrick's naval force was formidable enough for him to bargain from a position of strength with Sultan al-Kamil of Egypt, who held Palestine.[247] This, combined with the fact that al-Kamil was locked in a dire dynastic struggle for control of the region, enabled Frederick to induce the sultan to cede Jerusalem (save Temple Mount) along with Bethlehem and Nazareth in a negotiated

---

[241] Richard of San Germano, *Ryccardi de Sancto Germano Notarii Chronica*, anno 1221, p. 100.

[242] Huillard-Bréholles, *Historia Diplomatica Friderici Secundi*, II, Pt I, p. 410.

[243] Huillard-Bréholles, *Historia Diplomatica Friderici Secundi*, II, Pt I, pp. 501–3.

[244] Richard of San Germano, *Ryccardi de Sancto Germano Notarii Chronica*, anno 1228, p. 151.

[245] Philip of Novara, *The Wars of Frederick II against the Ibelins in Syria and Cyprus*, trans. J. LaMonte with M. Hubert (New York, 1936), Bk II, ch. XVIII, p. 73; *Mémoires (1218–1243)*, ed. Charles Kohler (Paris, 1913), Bk II, ch. XVIII, p. 12. '... et mena o luy setante entre gualees et tarydes et autre navie.' (The translation is my own, because LaMonte and Hubert did not interpret the ship types precisely.)

[246] Huillard-Bréholles, *Historia Diplomatica Friderici Secundi*, III, p. 44; Richard of San Germano, *Ryccardi de Sancto Germano Notarii Chronica*, anno 1228, p. 150.

[247] J. Pryor, 'The Crusade of Emperor Frederick II, 1220–29: The Implications of the Maritime Evidence', *American Neptune*, 52 (1992), pp. 113–32, especially 131–2.

settlement.[248] Frederick declared victory and crowned himself King of Jerusalem in the Church of the Holy Sepulcher on 18 March 1229.[249]

The negotiated success of the Sixth Crusade did not, however, heal the rupture between Frederick and the papacy. While Frederick was still in Palestine, Gregory IX sponsored an invasion of his kingdom, beginning in January 1229.[250] The emperor returned to Brindisi in June on a flotilla commanded by his reinstated admiral, Henry of Malta, and immediately embarked upon a campaign to regain lost lands.[251] Frederick soon obtained the upper hand militarily, compelling the pontiff to reluctantly come to the negotiating table at San Germano. Richard of San Germano, the leading source on the Hohenstaufen era and an official in Frederick's court through much of the 1230s, describes an arduous arbitration process in which prominent German princes and members of the church hierarchy interceded with the pope on Frederick's behalf before the talks finally culminated in the Treaty of San Germano on 20 July 1230. Even then, there were further discussions at Ceprano, and the pope did not personally absolve Frederick from anathema until 1 September at Anagni.[252] Frederick must have harbored no illusions that his absolution meant a permanent mending of relations with the Holy See. Pope Gregory was implacably opposed to imperial designs in Italy.

Frederick had already tasked his jurists as early as July of that year to begin working on a comprehensive legal code for the kingdom that would further shore up his power and enable the machinery of his government to function effectively even in his absence.[253] The result was the *Liber Augustalis*, otherwise known as the *Constitutions of Melfi*, promulgated on 1 September 1231.[254] The extent to which this set of laws is based upon Norman precedent is truly remarkable. According to medieval legal historian Kenneth Pennington, Frederick's *Constitutions* included 39 of the 69 statues that composed the so-called Assizes of Ariano issued by his grandfather, Roger II, nearly a century before. An additional 27 *Constitutions* were derived directly from laws instituted by kings William I and II.[255] While none of the *Constitutions* dealt directly with the fleet or the admi-

[248] Huillard-Bréholles, *Historia Diplomatica Friderici Secundi*, III, pp. 93–9, especially 97.
[249] *L'estoire de Eracles empereur et la conqueste de la terre d'Outremer, RHC, Occ*, ed. AIBL (5 vols, Paris, 1844–95), II, p. 375.
[250] Abulafia, *Frederick II*, pp. 197–8; Matthew, *Norman Kingdom of Sicily*, p. 334.
[251] Huillard-Bréholles, *Historia Diplomatica Friderici Secundi*, I, Pt 2, p. 902. See also Abulafia, 'Henry Count of Malta', p. 123.
[252] Richard of San Germano, *Ryccardi de Sancto Germano Notarii Chronica*, anno 1230, pp. 166–72. See also Abulafia, *Frederick II*, pp. 200–1; Matthew, *Norman Kingdom of Sicily*, p. 335.
[253] Abulafia, *Frederick II*, pp. 202–26; Matthew, *Norman Kingdom of Sicily*, p. 342.
[254] Huillard-Bréholles, *Historia Diplomatica Friderici Secundi*, IV, Pt 1, pp. 1–178; W. Stürner, ed., *Die Konstitutionen Friedrichs II für das Königreich Sizilien* (CAPIR, II, Supplementum, Hanover, 1996); Powell, trans., *Constitutions of Melfi*.
[255] K. Pennington, 'The Normans in Palermo: King Roger II's Legislation', *Haskins Society Journal*, XVIII (2006), pp. 140–67, especially 162.

ralty, this body of law was so sweeping that it touched upon nearly every aspect of rule within the realm and centralized royal authority to a degree not seen since the halcyon days of the Norman kingdom. 'Many of the laws concern the rights and obligations of the feudal barons in southern Italy, and the confirmation of the controls claimed over them by Roger II,' observes Abulafia, who later adds that Frederick also attempted to provide for 'a "loyal" economy subservient to his needs and adaptable to the demands of foreign wars'.[256]

Given that the period immediately following Frederick's temporary rapprochement with the papacy was relatively placid, he may not have felt the need to address regulations concerning the admiralty. After all, when Henry of Malta passed away in 1232, he apparently saw no immediate need to replace him.[257] That all changed dramatically on Palm Sunday (20 March) 1239, when Pope Gregory IX excommunicated the emperor for a second time. From prior experience Frederick must have known what was coming next; thus, it is extremely doubtful that he was unaware that, by September, the pope had enlisted two of the greatest naval powers of the era, Genoa and Venice, to collaborate against him.[258] In December 1239, Frederick not only designated a new *regni nostri Sicilie ammiratus* ('admiral of our kingdom of Sicily'), Nicola Spinola, but, in the same document, he also decreed the *Capitula pertinentia ad Officium Ammiratae* ('Capitularies pertaining to the Office of Admiral'), the first set of medieval regulations governing a royal admiralty.[259]

Since Frederick's previous proclamations were all based on Norman practices, it would be imprudent to assume that the *Capitula Ammiratae* edict was not. Thus, for the subject matter at hand, some further analysis of the document is warranted. On its most basic level, the *Capitula* simply sought to describe the rights and responsibilities of the realm's admiral of the fleet. But the document's overarching goal was to concentrate control over the kingdom's maritime matters, particularly with respect to organizing and maintaining a strong naval capability, in a single office. Written as a solitary, unbroken block of prose, the *Capitula* are perhaps best examined according to four broad categories:

> **Equipping and manning the fleet.** First and foremost, the admiral was responsible for the construction and repair of the fleet's ships. This, of course, meant that he had oversight of the royal arsenals and, thus, the authorization to appoint one or two magistrates ('*probos et legales viros*' – 'honest and proper men') in each shipyard to administer it and keep track of its accounts.[260] He also had the right to assign or dismiss galley commanders called *comiti* (two

[256] Abulafia, *Frederick II*, pp. 213, 225.
[257] Abulafia, 'Henry Count of Malta', p. 124.
[258] Abulafia, *Frederick II*, pp. 315–16.
[259] Huillard-Bréholles, *Historia Diplomatica Friderici Secundi*, V, Pt I, pp. 577–83.
[260] Huillard-Bréholles, *Historia Diplomatica Friderici Secundi*, V, Pt I, p. 578.

per vessel), except where hereditary feudal entitlement prevented it.[261] In order
to fund the maintenance of the fleet, the admiral had but to present receipts
to the royal curia, which was then obligated to supply the required capital
without further query.[262] The admiral was free to augment these resources
with whatever spare equipment could be found in and around the arsenals as
well as from captured enemy vessels.[263]

Policing the sea. This duty was largely concerned with the management
of piracy: either its promotion or prevention. Piracy was an acknowledged
component of medieval commerce in the Mediterranean. Frederick enter-
tained no notions of wanting to eradicate it. He simply wished his admiral
to influence it in his favor. First of all, the admiral himself was expected to
engage in it. Prizes garnered from piracy were considered a legitimate source
of revenue for the royal fisc as well as a sanctioned means for ship commanders
and crews to supplement their compensation. More importantly, the *Capitula*
obliged the admiral to regulate maritime raiding by restricting it to those
whom he furnished licenses. In order to obtain such a license, a privateer had
to provide a deposit to insure that neither the realm's shipping nor that of its
allies would be attacked. The ordinance prescribed ample financial incentives
to encourage aggressive enforcement. The admiral was empowered to collect
from violators total restitution for any transgressions over and above what
fines he may charge. If the culprit could not be made to pay, then appropriate reparations would be gleaned from the offender's community or compatriots. Furthermore, to preclude any possibility of collusion on the part of the
admiral, the latter was liable for any shortfalls in the perpetrator's deposit.[264]

Maritime adjudication. The admiral was accountable for keeping the peace
within the fleet both at sea and in port. He and his deputies were required to
be fully cognizant of all aspects of maritime justice, both criminal and civil,
and be prepared to mete it out in an expeditious manner 'in accordance with
the law and custom of the fleet' from 15 days before the arming of the ships
until 15 days after their deactivation. This jurisdiction was extended to include
the admiral's direct subordinates and those employed in the royal arsenals.[265]

Compensation. Nicola Spinola, the man whom the emperor appointed as
admiral of his fleet in the same instrument that he issued the *Capitula*, was
Genoese, but it is highly doubtful that Frederick fretted over his loyalty. The
Capitula contained an extremely generous compensation package, virtually
guaranteeing the admiral's fidelity. The ordinance mandated a base annual

[261] Huillard-Bréholles, *Historia Diplomatica Friderici Secundi*, V, Pt I, p. 580.
[262] Huillard-Bréholles, *Historia Diplomatica Friderici Secundi*, V, Pt I, p. 583.
[263] Huillard-Bréholles, *Historia Diplomatica Friderici Secundi*, V, Pt I, pp. 581–2.
[264] Huillard-Bréholles, *Historia Diplomatica Friderici Secundi*, V, Pt I, pp. 578–9.
[265] Huillard-Bréholles, *Historia Diplomatica Friderici Secundi*, V, Pt I, pp. 579–80. '…
secundum statum et consuetudinem armate…'

salary of 100 *salme* of wheat and 100 *salme* of wine from royal lands, plus one ounce of gold per day from the crown curia to cover expenses. The admiral was also authorized to equip four galleys at his discretion in the service of the king or any 'other required business', and he was permitted to move merchandise through the ports of the kingdom exempt from all royal duties. And that was just a start. The real reward was in prizes. Frederick clearly wanted to supply sufficient incentive for aggressive action on the part of his admiral. To begin with, the latter was given rights to the person and property of any captured commander. He was entitled to one *palma* of the cargo of any captured grain vessel.[266] He was also due one-twentieth of the spoils from seized 'Saracen' ships and, if he or his subordinates should manage to collect tribute from liable communities of the Barbary coast, he was owed one-tenth. The *Capitula* even granted him the right to salvage ships wrecked on the shores of the kingdom. Finally, the emperor conceded to the admiral 'all rights [probably some sort of levy] which his predecessors had customarily received, by virtue of their office, from mariners of the court and others sailing on the sea'.[267]

David Abulafia regards the latter phraseology as an indication that 'the *Capitula* themselves probably crystallized rather than created many of the Admiral's duties', implying that they were based upon a prior naval tradition.[268] Léon-Robert Ménager, being of a similar mind, cites the same passage and also refers to an earlier one that mentions the concept of the 'hereditary *comiti* from the time of the Norman kings'. 'One thing is certain,' he concludes, 'it is that these regulations represent in no way an original and spontaneous creation, but rather a kind of codification of what can be considered long-established customs'.[269] Medieval nautical historian Lawrence Mott feels that these passages were taken out of context, but he concurs that the *Capitula* 'crystallized' some past practices.[270] Indeed, the evidence is far from definitive, even circumstantial, but it all points in one direction: that the *Capitula* were substantially based on practices that had to have originally been put in place by the Normans.

The supervision of the Sicilian fleet in accordance with the dictates of the *Capitula* proved efficacious before long. As it turns out, Nicola Spinola died in early 1241, hardly more than a year after the new regulations were instituted. Frederick replaced him in March with yet another Genoese mariner, Ansaldo

---

[266] A *palma* was actually a measure of length (about 3 inches), so the presumption is that it referred to that depth of whatever grain was contained in the cargo hold of the captured ship.
[267] Huillard-Bréholles, *Historia Diplomatica Friderici Secundi*, V, Pt I, pp. 580–2. '*Predicto enim ammirato concedimus quod habeat et habere debeat omnia jura que ammirati alii predecessores sui ratione ammiratie officii habuerunt tam a curia inferendis quam a marinariis et aliis per mare navigantibus consueverant recipere et habere.*'
[268] Abulafia, 'Henry Count of Malta', p. 121.
[269] Ménager, *Amiratus*, pp. 118–19.
[270] Mott, *Sea Power in the Medieval Mediterranean*, pp. 65 and 279, note 67.

de Mari. Less than two months later, the latter led a combined Sicilian–Pisan fleet in excess of 60 galleys against around 30 Genoese vessels, carrying Guelph prelates summoned from northern Europe by Pope Gregory IX. The two fleets engaged near Giglio Island off the coast of Tuscany on 3 May. The imperial armada won an overwhelming victory, sinking three of the Genoese galleys and capturing 22 along with over 100 of the inimical clergy. It was the worst defeat Genoa had ever suffered up to that point.[271]

Between that battle and Frederick's death on 13 December 1250, the Sicilian royal fleet and its Ghibelline allies, principally the Pisans, were embroiled in almost constant conflict with Guelph naval forces, notably the Genoese. The Genoese had thrown their lot in with the renewed Lombard League led by Milan to oppose Ghibelline goals in northern Italy. Thus, the Genoese became the papacy's main maritime ally and Frederick's primary opposition at sea. The death of Gregory IX served only to aggravate the enmity between the Ligurian republic and the imperial throne, because Sinibaldo Fieschi of Genoa was elected in his place in June 1243. As Innocent IV, this first Genoese pope had Frederick formally deposed at the Council of Lyon in July 1245.[272] Accordingly, the Sicilian fleet spent much of its time attacking Genoa and harassing its interests on Corsica and the Riviera. Either under the command of Ansaldo de Mari or his son, Andreoulus, Sicilian squadrons, numbering anywhere from 10 ships to 60 and often basing out of Savona, ranged from the coast of western Provence all the way to North Africa. Sicilian naval forces established such a presence in the north Tyrrhenian by the end of Frederick's reign that Willy Cohn was inspired to somewhat exuberantly proclaim that the Sicilian fleet had achieved naval supremacy in the region.[273]

The impact of Frederick's *Capitula*, however, went well beyond his reign. As the first document to ordain the rights and responsibilities of an admiralty in the medieval Mediterranean, it served as a template for future such ordinances. The *Capitula officii ammiratiae* ('Capitularies of the office of the Admiral') that Charles I of Anjou enacted in March 1269 is similar in form and function.[274] And Mott has called the instructions issued to the Aragonese admiral, Roger of Lauria, several years later 'a virtual restatement of the *Capitula* of Frederick II in format and text, with only a few important changes'.[275] Ménager insists that 'it purely and simply restored the *Capitula Friderici II*'.[276] While Mott has

[271] W. Cohn, *Die Geschichte der sizilischen Flotte unter der Regierung Freidrichs II.* (1197–1250) (Breslau, 1926), pp. 47–53.
[272] Abulafia, *Frederick II*, pp. 348–54.
[273] Cohn, *Flotte unter der Regierung Freidrichs II*, pp. 62–82; Epstein, *Genoa and the Genoese*, pp. 124–7.
[274] Ménager, *Amiratus*, pp. 115–16.
[275] Mott, *Sea Power in the Medieval Mediterranean*, pp. 94–5.
[276] Ménager, *Amiratus*, p. 116.

persuasively argued that these documents diverge decisively from the *Capitula pertinentia ad Officium Ammiratae* in practical application, the influence of Frederick's ground-breaking proclamation is undeniable.[277] Therefore, the impact of the Norman precedent upon which it is based must also be incontrovertible.

---

[277] Mott, *Sea Power in the Medieval Mediterranean*, pp. 78 and 95.

Conclusion

On the eve of the Norman conquest of southern Italy and Sicily, the central Mediterranean resided in the sphere of Islam. Aggressive elements of its faithful dominated the north and south shores and the islands in-between at the very middle of the sea. Muslim pirates plagued both the Strait of Messina and the Sicilian Channel. Constantinople, remnant of the Eastern Roman Empire, fought fitfully to hold on to what little it still possessed on the lower Italian Peninsula. Meanwhile, the papacy was powerless to assert itself over the region, and the so-called Holy Roman Empire under the German kings only sporadically intervened in the chaotic affairs that prevailed south of Rome. The 'middle sea' was effectively divided in half, and east–west commerce was limited to Muslim and Jewish merchants along with a handful of their Western trading partners such as the Amalfitans. All dynamism on the sea seemed to emanate from the East. The rise of Norman sea power in the central Mediterranean under the inexorable Hautevilles irrevocably transformed the geopolitical and economic impetus on the sea and gave it a decided tilt to the West. The Mediterranean world would never be the same again. It was, quite literally, a sea change.

At the height of the Kingdom of Sicily under Roger II, the Normans held sway over both the north and south littorals of the central Mediterranean and the intervening islands. They had supplanted the 'Saracens' and swept their pirates from the sea, replacing them with Sicilian ships under the command of a gifted *amiratus*, George of Antioch. As a result, the 'middle sea' was opened to Christian as well as Muslim commerce – for a price. Traffic between western Islam (southern Spain and the Maghrib) and the Arab dynasties of the East in Egypt and Syria continued, but Catalan, Genoese, Pisan and Provençal merchants began to enjoy the fruits of eastern trade with ever greater frequency. And, of course, the Normans grew wealthy and powerful by taxing that trade. Perhaps more significantly, Christian control of southern Italy and Sicily rendered the region a springboard for, arguably, the most aggressive movement in the history of the medieval Mediterranean: the Crusades. It is no accident that they began just after the conquest was completed and continued for hundreds of years afterward. Many of these expeditions, enthusiastically assisted by the West Italian maritime republics, transited either the Kingdom of Sicily or the seaways it controlled.[1] Norman naval power participated only peripherally in this phenomenon, but its hold on the central Mediterranean served as a catalyst for the eventual eclipse of eastern sea power. Indeed, the first three Crusades put Arab fleets on the defen-

---

[1] Riley-Smith, *Atlas of the Crusades*, pp. 30–1, 34, 49, 62–3, 94–7.

sive, while the Fourth Crusade ended in the capture of the Constantinople not a decade after the last Hauteville was forced from power in Palermo.

Moreover, the impact of the Norman accomplishment did not end with the coronation of Henry VI Hohenstaufen as King of Sicily on Christmas Day in 1194. The very next day his son and successor was born to the Empress Constance, Roger II's last daughter. Frederick II would not only bring Hauteville blood back to the throne of Sicily, but he would also restore Norman administrative practices.[2] One of his proclamations, the *Capitula pertinentia ad Officium Ammiratae*, probably codified many of the principles by which the fleet had been governed under the Norman kings.[3] While Norman methods of rule eventually waned, Sicily and southern Italy became more deeply ensconced in the Western world. A succession of German, French and Spanish rulers followed the Normans, but the central Mediterranean would never again drift into the orbit of the East. On the obverse, eastern sea power was driven into a state of atrophy. The Byzantine navy never regained its former glory and the Muslim fleets of the East did not venture into the western Mediterranean in any consequential numbers until the Ottoman forays of the late fifteenth century.[4] Even then, it is instructive to note that the resurgence of Muslim sea power at the instigation of the Ottomans was blunted in 1571 at Lepanto by a host of West European naval powers that had, prior to the battle, mustered at Messina.[5] Due in great measure to the maritime legacy left by the Normans, Sicily's strategic significance to the West would endure into the modern era.

[2]   Abulafia, *Frederick II*, pp. 140–2, 202–26.
[3]   Huillard-Bréholles, *Historia Diplomatica Friderici Secundi*, V, Pt I, pp. 577–83. See also Mott, *Sea Power in the Medieval Mediterranean*, pp. 61–77.
[4]   A. Lewis and T. Runyan, *European Naval and Maritime History, 300–1500* (Bloomington, 1985), pp. 82–5.
[5]   Rodgers, *Naval Warfare under Oars*, pp. 167–79.

Appendix A

The Fleet (ships, sailors, shipyards, and strategies)

If recounting the events of Norman naval history is challenging owing to the lack of maritime expertise among the relevant chroniclers, then describing the naval infrastructure, that is, the fleet itself, is problematic in the extreme. First of all, there is very little documentation on the matter specific to the Normans. There are no medieval equivalents to the Royal Navy's *Admiralty Manual of Seamanship* or Jane's *Fighting Ships*.[1] There is no extant handbook of naval organization from the period and, pending further analysis of the Yenikapi galleys,[2] no warship of the eleventh or twelfth century has ever been discovered. The few pictorial representations of medieval ships that exist are simplified, primitive and not to scale. Verbal descriptions are equally scarce and uniformly inadequate, because contemporary authors almost invariably lacked a knowledge of things nautical and had a penchant for using anachronistic and inaccurate terminology. In other words, we have no precise picture of what Norman vessels of war were like or how they were crewed and commanded. The answers, then, must lie within the Norman *modus operandi*. These clever, resourceful adventurers were not innovators; they rarely developed techniques and tactics on their own. They were, instead, masters of accommodation and adaptation. They took whatever was available, borrowing or commandeering it from others to make it their own. Accordingly, any understanding of the Norman fleets of the Hauteville era must be inferred from clues gleaned from a number of indirect sources such as Byzantine and Muslim naval practices, medieval maritime archaeology and contemporary documentation on Norman naval campaigns in the Mediterranean. This appendix will attempt to do exactly that in order to portray, in turn, the ships, shipyards, sailors and strategies of the Norman fleets.

Ships: types and procurement

In the beginning, there was no particular ship type readily identifiable as peculiarly Norman. The Normans had long since forgotten the seafaring ways of their

---

[1] Admiralty of Great Britain, *Manual of Seamanship* (London, 1894); F. Jane, ed., *All the World's Fighting Ships* (London, 1898–1904).
[2] U. Kocabaş, ed., *The 'Old Ships' of the 'New Gate', Yenikapi Shipwrecks, Vol. I* (Istanbul, 2008), pp. 176–83.

Viking forebears. Thus, they would have availed themselves of whatever maritime technology was prevalent in the Mediterranean at the time of their arrival, adapting it to their needs as the circumstances dictated. This means that the type of ships that they initially employed were, in all probability, of Byzantine design. The Byzantines had bequeathed their maritime tradition to the mariners of Italy and Sicily through centuries of rule prior to the Norman conquest. The Emperor Constans II established a strong Byzantine naval presence in Sicily in 662 when he moved his court to Syracuse.[3] The island became a base for the Byzantine provincial fleet as early as 717 when the Emperor Leo III 'the Isaurian' came to power and began reorganizing the imperial navy into naval *themata* and provincial fleets.[4] In fact, it was the provincial fleet commander, the *tourmarches* Euphemios, who abetted the Muslim conquest of the island in 827 by offering the Aghlabids his support in return for the governorship.[5] Even after the Muslim invasion had begun, a Byzantine provincial fleet persisted in the northeast portion of the island and in Calabria (considered a part of the *thema* of Sicily) as well as Apulia (the *thema* of Longobardia). Ibn al-Athir reports a raid by 'ten *chelandia* of the Rum' on Mondello near Muslim Palermo in 848.[6] These *chelandia* were probably from a Byzantine flotilla based in southern Italy that was tasked with guarding the coasts and participating in campaigns against the 'Saracens' of Sicily. In 877 and again in 879, Pope John VIII, seeking to curtail Muslim pirates operating along the Tyrrhenian coast, wrote to the Emperor Basil I to beseech the aid of ten *chelandia* controlled by 'Gregory', the imperial governor of Longobardia.[7] An episode from the *Vita S. Nili Abbatis* ('Life of the Abbot St Nilus'), which took place around 965, reveals that a squadron continued to exist in southern Italy well after the Byzantines were expelled from Sicily following the Aghlabid capture of Taormina in 902. It seems that the abbot had to intervene with the *doux* (provincial governor) Nikephoros Magistros on behalf of the inhabitants of Rossano. The latter, outraged over an order to outfit additional *chelandia* for the defense of the *thema*, had burnt the existing ships and massa-

---

3   Theophanes, *annus mundi* 6153, p. 487. See also J. Bury, 'Naval Policy of the Roman Empire in Relation to the Western Provinces, from the seventh to the ninth century', *Centenario della Nascita de Michele Amari* (Palermo, 1910), pp. 21–34, especially 24; Pryor and Jeffreys, *Dromōn*, p. 25.
4   Theophanes, *annus mundi* 6210, pp. 549–50. See also H. Ahrweiler, *Byzance et la la mer: la marine de guerre, la politique et les institutions maritimes de Byzance au VII–XV siècles* (Paris, 1966), pp. 31–4, 90; E. Eickhoff, *Seekrieg und Seepolitik zwischen Islam und Abendland: das Mittelmeer unter Byzantinischer und Arabischer Hegemonie, 650–1040* (Berlin, 1966), pp. 84–5, 96–9.
5   Ibn al-Athir, *BAS*, I, pp. 364–5; John Skylitzes, *Synopsis historiōn*, pp. 44–5. See also A. Toynbee, *Constantine Porphyrogenitus and his world* (London, 1973), pp. 325–6.
6   Ibn al-Athir, *BAS*, I, p. 376.
7   Pope John VIII, *Papae Registrum*, no. 47, p. 45 and no. 245, p. 214.

cred the ships' masters.[8] Thietmar of Merseburg noted that the Emperor Nike-phoros II Phocas (963–969) expected a quota of two *chelandia* per year from Calabria filled with tribute.[9] The *themata* of Calabria and Longobardia (Apulia) continued to provide vessels for imperial naval expeditions in the region well into the eleventh century.[10] As late as 1038, Malaterra indicates that the Byzantine general Giorgios Maniakes gathered ships from imperial possessions in Calabria and Apulia for his invasion of Sicily, an expedition that included a Norman contingent led by William de Hauteville.[11] Thus, a Byzantine maritime tradition must surely have continued to exist in southern Italy long after the arrival of the Normans, leading Ekkehard Eickhoff, the German maritime medievalist, to categorically assert: 'It is no coincidence that, along with Amalfi, Calabria constituted contingents of the first Norman fleet against Bari, thus providing the germinating seed for the foundation of the magnificent Norman sea power of the next century.'[12]

Identifying the specific types of ships the Normans may have used from contemporary textual materials has been a maddeningly perplexing and frustrating process. This is because medieval chroniclers employed a bewildering array of appellations for contemporary vessels, which varied according to the era and ethnic origin of the author. The term *chelandion* may have had a much different meaning to a tenth-century Greek writer than to an eleventh-century Latin annalist. 'As a result,' explains John Pryor in *The Age of the ΔPOMΩN*, his landmark treatise on the Byzantine navy, 'large sections of this study have evolved into an etymological and philological hunt for linguistic chimerae.'[13] The academic aristocracy of Byzantine maritime historians like Pryor, Eickhoff and Hélène Ahrweiler has devoted hundreds of pages in the quest to elucidate meaning from the maze of nautical terminology proffered by medieval authors with only modest success. It would be fruitless to attempt to replicate their noble efforts here. Instead, the focus will be on a handful of basic ship types commonly found in those annals and chronicles describing the naval exploits of the Normans in the Mediterranean: the *dromōn*, its variant the *chelandion*, the *galea*, the *cattus/gattus*, the *navis* (supply ship), the *sagitta*, and the horse transport.

[8] *Vita S. Nili Abbatis*, *Acta Sanctorum*, ed. Societé des Bollandistes (68 vols, Antwerp and Brussels, 1643–1940), *Septembris* VII, ch. IX, sect. 60–2, pp. 318–20.

[9] Thietmar of Merseburg, *Ottonian Germany*, Bk III, ch. 23, pp. 145–6; *Die Chronik*, Bk III, ch. 23, pp. 126–9.

[10] Gay, *Italie méridionale et l'empire byzantine*, pp. 343–9.

[11] Malaterra, *Deeds of Count Roger*, Bk I, ch. 7, pp. 55–6; *De rebus gestis Rogerii*, Bk I, ch. VII, p. 20.

[12] E. Eickhoff, 'Byzantinische Wachtflotillen in Unteritalien im 10 Jahrhundert', *Byzantinische Zeitschrift*, XLV (1952), pp. 340–4.

[13] Pryor and Jeffreys, *Dromōn*, p. 5.

Dromōn

The principal war galley of the medieval Mediterranean from the late fifth century to the early twelfth century was the Byzantine *dromōn*. Therefore, it stands to reason that the Normans employed them during the era of conquest. In fact, Malaterra confirms *dromōns* were present during the initial Norman invasion of Sicily;[14] and Anna Comnena says 'horses and armed knights were embarked on *dromōns*' in Robert Guiscard's first assault on Byzantium.[15] The *dromōn* is believed to have evolved from the *liburnae*, light warships of the late Roman period patterned after the pirate vessels of the Liburni people of Illyria.[16] The first known depiction is folio 77r of the late fifth-century *Roman Vergil* (Ms Vat. Lat. 3867) in the Biblioteca Apostolica Vaticana.[17] It shows two galleys, each with a single level of oar ports, twin steering oars, a single lateen sail and a chain-supported 'spur' instead of an *embolos* or waterline ram. The replacement of shell-first ship construction with frame-first techniques rendered the waterline ram ineffective, so the 'spur' was apparently used to smash the oars of an enemy vessel and, perhaps, to hold the vessel fast for boarding.[18]

The first verbal description of *dromōns* was provided by Procopius of Caesarea in his sixth-century *History of the Wars*: 'They were single banked ships covered by decks, in order that the men rowing them might, if possible, not be exposed to the bolts of the enemy. Such boats are called "dromones" ["runners"] by those of the present time; for they are able to obtain a great speed.'[19] Pryor's research suggests that they were originally fully decked, monoreme galleys (one bank of rowers per side) with about 50 rowers each. By the tenth century they had developed into bireme galleys (two banks of rowers per side) with 100 or more oarsmen.[20] The *Naumachika* ('Concerning naval warfare' – circa 905) of the Emperor Leo VI prescribes:

> Each of the dromons should be long and [well] proportioned with two *elasiai* [oar-banks], one below and one above. Each [oar-bank] should have a minimum of twenty-five *zygoi* [thwarts], on which the oarsmen will be seated, so that in all there are twenty-five thwarts below and similarly twenty-five above, making a total of fifty. Two oarsmen should sit on each of these [thwarts], one on the right

---

[14] Malaterra, *Deeds of Count Roger*, Bk 2, ch. 8, p. 90; *De rebus gestis Rogerii*, Bk II, ch. VIII, p. 31.

[15] Anna Comnena, *Alexiad*, p. 131; *Alexiade*, I, Bk III, ch. XII, p. 139.

[16] Hocker, 'Late Roman, Byzantine, and Islamic Galleys and Fleets', pp. 86–100, especially 88 and 94.

[17] D. Wright, *The Roman Vergil and the Origins of Medieval Book Design* (London, 2001), p. 25.

[18] Pryor and Jeffreys, *Dromōn*, pp. 143–4.

[19] Procopius, *History of the Wars*, trans. H. Dewing (8 bks, London, 1916), Bk III, ch. XI, pp. 104–5.

[20] For a painstakingly detailed rendering of a tenth-century Byzantine *dromōn*, see John Pryor's drawing on the frontispiece of *Dromōn*.

and the other on the left, so that all the oarsmen together themselves [are] also soldiers, both those above and those below, [total] one hundred men.[21]

The *dromōn* also occasionally depended upon sails for propulsion. The length of the vessel makes it evident that there were at least two masts: a foremast and a main mast.[22] By closely examining the description of a ship-mounted siege tower in John Kaminiates' account of the capture of Thessaloniki by Leo of Tripoli in 904, the maritime historian R. H. Dolley was able to determine that the ships of the day were undoubtedly rigged with lateen sails.[23] Even so, an extensive table of reported voyages of ancient and medieval galleys compiled by Pryor reveals that galley fleets rarely averaged more than six knots for short voyages (under a day) and usually cruised at less than four knots over the course of longer voyages.[24]

The *dromōn*'s primary armament was the siphon for discharging 'Greek fire' at opposing vessels. One was usually mounted on the prow beneath a reinforced platform, a sort of forecastle upon which stood projectile-launching marines. There were also castles amidships on either side of the main mast as well as a sterncastle called a *krabatos* where the *kentarchos* or ship's commander was stationed.[25] Liudprand of Cremona makes it clear that these other castles, too, could have housed siphons. He quotes the Emperor Romanos I Lekapenos (920–944), who instructed his shipwrights to 'put the fire-throwers not only at the bows but at the stern and both sides as well'.[26] But 'Greek fire' was no longer the decisive weapon it had been when it was first contrived in the seventh century by the Syrian inventor Kallinikos.[27] By the eleventh century, others were said to have possessed its secret. Malaterra even describes how the Venetians employed it against the Normans at Durazzo.[28] The weapon had a limited range and could only be used under certain narrow conditions, such as calm or following winds.[29] Liudprand of Cremona describes how God answered

[21] Leo VI, *The naval warfare of the Emperor Leo* (*Taktika*, Constitution XIX), *Dromōn*, Appendix Two, par. 7–8, pp. 486–7; Nikephoros Ouranos, *On fighting at sea*, *Dromōn*, Appendix Five, par. 6–7, pp. 574–5.

[22] R. Dolley, 'The Warships of the later Roman Empire', *Journal of Roman Studies*, XXXVIII (1948), pp. 47–53, especially 51–2; Pryor and Jeffreys, *Dromōn*, p. 238.

[23] John Kaminiates, *The Capture of Thessaloniki*, trans. D. Frendo and A. Fotiou (Perth, 2000), ch. 32, pp. 55–6. See also R. Dolley, 'The rig of early medieval warships', *The Mariner's Mirror*, XXXV (1949), pp. 51–5, especially 52–3.

[24] Pryor and Jeffreys, *Dromōn*, pp. 343–51.

[25] Leo VI, *The naval warfare of the Emperor Leo* (*Taktika*, Constitution XIX), *Dromōn*, Appendix Two, par. 8, pp. 486–9; Nikephoros Ouranos, *On fighting at sea*, *Dromōn*, Appendix Five, par. 7, pp. 574–7.

[26] Liudprand of Cremona, *Antapodosis*, *Works of Liudprand of Cremona*, Bk V, ch. XV, p. 186; *Die Werke Liudprands von Cremona*, Bk V, ch. XV. p. 138. '... quo ignis proicitur, non in prora solum, verum etiam in puppi, insuper in utrisque lateribus ponite.'

[27] Pryor, *Dromōn*, Appendix Six, pp. 607–13, 621.

[28] Malaterra, *Deeds of Count Roger*, Bk 3, ch. 26, p. 156; *De rebus gestis Rogerii*, Bk III, ch. XXVI, p. 73.

[29] Pryor and Jeffreys, *Dromōn*, pp. 383–5.

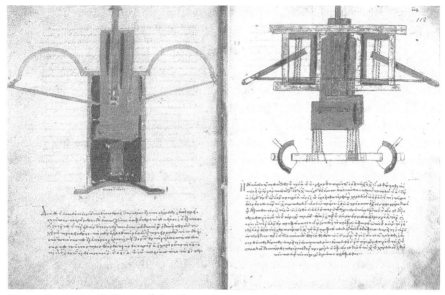

Fig. 7. Byzantine *ballistae* of the eleventh century. The Byzantine bow-*ballistae* pictured in an eleventh-century manuscript of the *Poliorketika* of Philon of Byzantium are examples of the type that may have been mounted on Norman war galleys of the eleventh century. (Credit: Ms Vat. Gr. 1164, fols 110v and 112r of the eleventh century, reproduced here by permission of the Biblioteca Apostolica Vaticana ©, with all rights reserved)

the prayers of the Byzantines in their use of 'Greek fire' against an attacking Rus fleet in 941: 'Therefore He lulled the winds and calmed the waves; for otherwise the Greeks would have had difficulty in hurling their fire.'[30]

A more practical weapon was the bow-*ballista*, a large crossbow-type device powered by a torsion mechanism (usually of twisted cord) (see Figure 7). As early as the sixth century, the Byzantine Emperor Maurice promulgated, 'On the prows of all, or at least most, of the fighting ships, mount small *ballistae*, covered with heavy cloth, so their fire may repel any attacks by the enemy while they are still a good distance away.'[31] The Emperor Constantine VII Porphyrogenitus compounded that requirement substantially in *De Cerimoniis Aulae Byzantinae* by specifying that each *dromōn* be outfitted with 'twenty platforms with hand-spanned bow-*ballistae* with silken strings.'[32] It is therefore probable that Norman warships of the eleventh century employed such *ballistae* vice siphons

[30] Liudprand of Cremona, *Antapodosis, Works of Liudprand of Cremona*, Bk V, ch. XV, p. 186; *Die Werke Liudprands von Cremona*, Bk V, ch. XV. p. 138. '... *ventis tunc placidum reddidit mare; secus enim ob ignis emissionem Grecis esset incommodum.*'

[31] Maurice, *Strategikon*, trans. G. Dennis (Philadelphia, 1984), Bk XII, ch. 21, p. 157.

[32] Constantine VII Porphyrogenitus, *De Cerimoniis Aulae Byzantinae*, Chapters II, 44 and 45 of Book II, trans. J. Haldon in 'Theory and Practice in Tenth-Century Military Adminis-

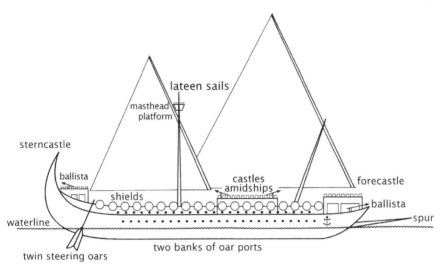

Fig. 8. Norman-Italian war galley of the eleventh century. This drawing illustrates the author's concept of an eleventh-century Norman-Italian war galley highlighting the major features, particularly the deployment of ballistae. (Credit: C. Stanton with P. Judge)

(see Figure 8). Both Dolley and Pryor contend that these mechanically operated *ballistae* launched iron quarrels, dubbed *mues* ('mice') or *muiai* ('flies').[33] Added to these were a host of horrific projectiles from conventional arrows and javelins to jars filled with *naphtha* (a petroleum-based incendiary, probably 'Greek fire'), unslaked lime or even various venomous creatures such as snakes and scorpions.[34] Thus, sea battles were often reduced to missile exchanges, which eventually led to grappling and hand-to-hand combat on the decks of engaged ships,[35] a development that may well have favored the battle-hardened Normans.

A variant of the *dromōn* that appears often in medieval texts is the *chelandion*. The name likely stemmed from the classical Greek *kelēs*, meaning 'courser', referring to a fast-sailing monoreme merchant galley or a riding horse. Pryor believes that '*chelandion* almost certainly originated as a term for horse transports'.[36] It eventually became applied to warships. Ibn al-Athir claims a Byzantine armada of 300 *chelandia* was defeated by the Aghlabids off Messina in 859.[37] In the

tration: Chapters II, 44 and 45 of the *Book of Ceremonies*', *Travaux et Memoires*, XIII (2000), pp. 201–352, especially 224–5.

[33] Dolley, 'Warships of the later Roman Empire', p. 352; Pryor and Jeffreys, *Dromōn*, p. 379.

[34] Leo VI, *The naval warfare of the Emperor Leo* (*Taktika*, Constitution XIX), *Dromōn*, Appendix Two, par. 60, pp. 508–9; Nikephoros Ouranos, *On fighting at sea*, *Dromōn*, Appendix Five, par. 57, pp. 596–7.

[35] Pryor and Jeffreys, *Dromōn*, pp. 402–4.

[36] Pryor and Jeffreys, *Dromōn*, p. 167.

[37] Ibn al-Athir, *BAS*, I, pp. 380–1.

late tenth century Thietmar of Merseburg described the *chelandion* as 'a ship of marvelous length and speed, having two banks of oars on each side with space for one hundred and fifty sailors'. He added that these galleys were outfitted with 'fire which was only extinguishable with vinegar'.[38] The maritime historian Frederick Hocker contends that they became synonymous with large *dromōns*, capable of accommodating 200 oarsmen each.[39] Indeed, Constantine VII Porphyrogenitus seems to use the terms interchangeably in his inventory for the 949 expedition to Crete.[40] William of Apulia identifies the Greek vessels that Robert Guiscard defeated at Corfu in 1084 as 'chelindros' (*chelandia*).[41] The Arabic name for the vessel was *shalandī*, apparently derived from the Greek name, and the Muslims may have employed them well into the twelfth century.[42] Ibn al-Athir describes them as being among the seventy ships which Abd al-Mu'min used to blockade the Normans at Mahdiyah in 1159–60.[43]

Galea

Beginning sometime in the late eleventh century, the *dromōn* underwent a subtle transformation from warship to transport vessel. By the early twelfth century it had given way altogether to a product of Western maritime technology: the *galea*. Both Camillo Manfroni and Willy Cohn hail the development,[44] but it is John Pryor who pinpoints the wellspring of the innovation and why it occurred. Pryor convincingly argues that the transition began in Norman Italy, because the term *galea* first appears in late eleventh-century Italo-Norman chronicles, referring to some sort of small, fast galley.[45] William of Apulia records that, following Guiscard's death, his wife 'embarked on the *galeram* which she knew to be very fast'.[46] Geoffrey Malaterra describes an episode in which the bishop of Nicastro's vessel was attacked 'by two pirate ships, which were called *galeas*'.[47] And Amatus

---

[38] Thietmar of Merseburg, *Ottonian Germany*, Bk 3, ch. 23, pp. 145–6; *Die Chronik*, Bk III, ch. 23, pp. 126–9. 'Hec [salandria] est, ut prefatus sum, navis mire longitudinis et alacritatis, et utroque latere duos habet ordines remorum et centum quinquaginta nautas.'; '... inextinguibilemque ab omni re preter acetum ferentes ignem ...'

[39] Hocker, 'Late Roman, Byzantine, and Islamic Galleys and Fleets', pp. 94–5.

[40] Constantine VII Porphyrogenitus, *De Cerimoniis*, II, Chapter 45, trans. Haldon in 'Theory and Practice in Tenth-Century Military Administration', pp. 218–19.

[41] William of Apulia, *La Geste de Robert Guiscard*, Bk V, lines 155–78, pp. 244–7.

[42] A. Fahmy, *Muslim Sea Power in the Eastern Mediterranean from the Seventh to the Tenth Century* (London, 1950), pp. 129–31.

[43] Ibn al-Athir, *BAS*, I, p. 486; *Chronicle of Ibn al-Athir*, Part 2, pp. 103–4.

[44] Cohn, *Die Geschichte der normannisch-sicilischen Flotte*, p. 92; Manfroni, *Storia della Marina italiana*, I, Appendix I, pp. 452–3.

[45] Pryor and Jeffreys, *Dromōn*, pp. 423–4.

[46] William of Apulia, *La Geste de Robert Guiscard*, Bk V, lines 339–40, p. 254. 'Quamque magis celerem cognoverat esse galeram scandit ...'

[47] Malaterra, *Deeds of Count Roger*, Bk 4, ch. 25, p. 206; *De rebus gestis Rogerii*, Bk IV, ch. XXV, p. 103. '... a duabus piratarum navibus, quas galeas appellant ...'

of Montecassino relates how Guiscard and his brother Roger boarded 'two very fast and maneuverable *galéez*' to reconnoiter the port of Messina.[48]

All of this is perfectly logical when one considers the long exposure of southern Italy to Byzantine maritime models, including small scouting ships called *galeai* in imperial military treatises.[49] In fact, Pryor goes on to definitively state, 'It is also clear that these early Western *galeae* were emulated from Byzantine *galeai*, most probably from those encountered by the Normans and others in South Italy.'[50] Further substantiation of this may ultimately be provided by the Yenikapi Shipwrecks Project of Istanbul University. Examination has been initiated on only one of the four galleys discovered in the Theodosian Harbor of old Constantinople, but preliminary observations indicate that this vessel, designated YK-16, was probably one of these *galeai*, the Byzantine precursors of the *galeae*. Its length (22.5 meters or 73.8 feet), width (2.4 meters or 7.8 feet) along with the remnants of oarsmen's thwarts signify that it was a light monoreme galley propelled by 25 oars per side, 50 in all.[51] It was found at approximately the same sediment level in the harbor as the cargo vessel YK-12, which is dated to the ninth and tenth centuries.[52] There is much yet to be determined, but it seems very likely that this vessel is one of the '*galeai* or *monēreis*, speedy and light', described in Constitution XIX of Leo VI's *Taktika*, written in the early tenth century.[53]

Pryor points to the miniatures of three manuscripts, all tied to Italy and dated from the middle of the twelfth century to the first years of the thirteenth century, to conclude that the West, and particularly Italy, had developed a galley based upon a new and more efficient oarage system called *alla sensile*.[54] It is a configuration in which the oarsmen are all on one level, sitting two or more per bench on each side of the ship with each man manipulating his own oar.[55] Pryor first draws attention to a set of seven ship images in the Paris manuscript of the *Annales Ianuenses* (Ms Suppl. Lat. 773 of the Bibliothèque Nationale). The first three, which accompany entries for the years 1125, 1136 and 1165, indicate two superimposed banks of oars while each of the last four miniatures for twelfth century shows a single row of oar ports, inferring that the oarsmen were all

---

48 Amatus, *History of the Normans*, Bk V, ch. 14, p. 138; *Storia de' Normanni*, Bk V, ch. XIV, p. 235. '… II galéez subtilissime et molt velocissime.'
49 Leo VI, *The naval warfare of the Emperor Leo* (*Taktika*, Constitution XIX), *Dromōn*, Appendix Two, par. 10, pp. 488–9; Nikephoros Ouranos, *On fighting at sea*, *Dromōn*, Appendix Five, par. 9, pp. 576–7.
50 Pryor and Jeffreys, *Dromōn*, p. 284.
51 Kocabaş, *Yenikapi Shipwrecks*, pp. 176, 182.
52 Kocabaş, *Yenikapi Shipwrecks*, pp. 114, 214.
53 Leo VI, *The naval warfare of the Emperor Leo* (*Taktika*, Constitution XIX), *Dromōn*, Appendix Two, par. 10, pp. 488–9.
54 Pryor and Jeffreys, *Dromōn*, pp. 424–31.
55 M. Bandioli, R. Burler and A. Zysberg, 'Oar Mechanics and Oar Power in Medieval and Later Galleys', in *Age of the Galley*, pp. 172–205, especially 172–5.

Fig. 9. Sicilian *galea* of the twelfth century. This illustration from the Bern manuscript of Peter of Eboli's *Liber ad honorem Augusti sive de rebus Siculis* seems to show a twelfth-century Sicilian bireme *galea*, employing the *alla sensile* oarage system. (Credit: Codex 120 II, fol. 119r of the twelfth century, reproduced here by permission of the Burgerbibliothek Bern ©, with all rights reserved)

seated on one level: the deck.[56] Thus, the transition to a new oarage system may have taken place. Pryor subsequently references the illustration on folio 146v of the Codex Vitr. 26–2 manuscript of John Skylitzes' *Synopsis historiōn* in the Biblioteca Nacional of Madrid which shows oarsmen on one level working two files of oars: one through oar ports in the hull, the other with oars above the gunnel.[57] Finally, he points to folio 119r of the Bern manuscript of Peter of Eboli's *De rebus Siculis carmen* (Codex 120 II) in the Burgerbibliothek as clear evidence that the *alla sensile* oarage system had been adopted (see Figure 9). The illustration contains an elaborate image of what Pryor believes to be a *galea* in which two files of rowers are depicted at deck level. One set of oars is worked through oar ports in a wale (horizontal plank in the hull) above the level of the spur while another set is manipulated through what appears to be a rudimentary outrigger, which would have increased stroking power by providing extra lever-

---

[56] Pryor and Jeffreys, *Dromōn*, pp. 424–6.
[57] Tsamakda, *Chronicle of Ioannes Skylitzes*, fig. 363, fol. 146r. See also Pryor and Jeffreys, *Dromōn*, pp. 426–9.

Fig. 10. Sculpture of oarsmen from the twelfth century. Entitled 'rameurs dans un bateau', this sculpture on a capital from the twelfth-century Romanesque priory of Notre Dame de la Daurade of Toulouse (Musée des Augustins) seems to show oarsmen on the deck of a ship executing the stand-and-sit-stroke rowing technique. (Credit: C. Stanton)

age.[58] Both files of rowers on this bireme galley sat side-by-side, two men per thwart (bench), each working his own oar – the outboard oarsman through the outrigger and the inboard rower through an oar port in the hull. This seating arrangement is what permitted all of the rowers to work in synchronization at deck level. Further substantiation that this transition had occurred seems to be provided by a Romanesque capital from the twelfth-century priory of Notre Dame de la Daurade of Toulouse in which all the 'rameurs' ('rowers') are clearly depicted on deck (see Figure 10).[59]

The fact that all oarsmen were at deck level offered enormous advantages. Because none of the men were cramped by a low overhead, as would be the case with rowers below deck, each man could rise during the stroke motion and, thus, execute the more powerful stand-and-sit stroke technique.[60] The air would

[58] Peter of Eboli, *Liber ad honorem Augusti sive de rebus Siculis*, fol. 119r, p. 131. See also Pryor and Jeffreys, *Dromōn*, pp. 429–31.
[59] *Rameurs dans un bateau* in the Musée des Augustins of Toulouse, France.
[60] Pryor and Jeffreys, *Dromōn*, pp. 433–4.

have been fresh instead of fetid, allowing for greater endurance. And, perhaps, most important of all, having all the rowers above deck would have created extra cargo space below deck for provisions, particularly water – the fuel on which all galleys operated. Moreover, the removal of the need for a second deck would have theoretically allowed shipwrights to construct sleeker hulls, offering less water resistance.[61] In other words, these vessels may well have been faster with far greater range. In fact, John Pryor observes from the Italo-Norman sources that 'they were known to have had fine lines and to have been very fast'.[62] Just as advantageous was the size of the vessels. Pryor points out that the stand-and-sit stroke of the *alla sensile* oarage system necessitated an increased *inter-scalmium* (the distance between tholepins upon which the oars pivoted, that is, the length of an oarsman's stroke). It must have been around 1.2 meters for the *galea* as opposed to the standard *dromōn*, which had an *interscalmium* of less than a meter. This meant that the *galea* probably had the same length as an Angevin galley of the late thirteenth century, 39.5 meters – a good deal larger than the standard *dromōn*, which was only around 31.5 meters long.[63] And in medieval maritime warfare size mattered. No wonder the bireme *galea* made the bireme *dromōn* obsolete.

If Pryor is correct in his hypothesis that the innovation had its origins in southern Italy, this would have given the Kingdom of Sicily a distinct technological edge over its Muslim and Byzantine adversaries. All indications are that this was exactly the case. It appears that the *galea* was the mainstay of Roger II's fleet even before his 1130 coronation. In 1128, he agreed to send Count Raymond of Barcelona 'galeas quinquaginta' ('50 galeae') to deal with Almoravid pirates in the Tyrrhenian.[64] According to the interpolator of Romuald of Salerno, that same year he dispatched 60 'ueloces galee' ('fast galeae') to blockade recalcitrant Bari.[65] In 1134 Falco of Benevento says he attacked rebellious Naples with another 60 'galeas'.[66] In the 1140s Roger used them extensively to project his power against Byzantium. Romuald of Salerno says that the fleet that George of Antioch commanded in his 1147 raid of the Peloponnesos and the Gulf of Corinth was composed of 'galeas et naves plurimas' ('very many galeae and supply ships').[67] And Andrea Dandolo asserts that the famed admiral led an armada of 60 'galearum' on yet another assault on Greece in 1149, the one in which he penetrated the Dardanelles to shower the Blachernai palace with arrows.[68]

[61] Pryor and Jeffreys, *Dromōn*, p. 443.
[62] Pryor, 'A view from a masthead', p. 130.
[63] Pryor and Jeffreys, *Dromōn*, pp. 434–4; Pryor, 'A view from a masthead', pp. 129–30.
[64] *Rogerii II. Regis Diplomata Latina*, no. 9, pp. 22–4. See also Amari, *Storia dei Musulmani di Sicilia*, III, pp. 396–7, note 1.
[65] Romuald of Salerno, *Romualdi Salernitani Chronicon*, p. 216.
[66] Falco of Benevento, *Chronicon Beneventanum*, p. 168.
[67] Romuald of Salerno, *Romualdi Salernitani Chronicon*, p. 227.
[68] Andrea Dandolo, *Chronica Per Extensum Descripta*, p. 243.

While the term *galea* could have simply been a generic reference to any sort of oared vessel, one would expect that Romuald of Salerno and Andrea Dandolo, both citizens of seafaring cities, would have been more precise, especially since both identify other types of ships in their writings. The same is true of Bernardo Maragone of Pisa who testifies that Roger's son William I sent '*CXL galearum et XXIIII dermonum*' ('140 *galeae* and 24 *dromōns*') on a raid of Constantinople in 1157, similar to the one in 1149.[69] Accordingly, Maragone's son Salem must also have been referring to specific ships types when he described the composition of William II's ill-fated expedition to the Balearics in 1181/2: '*galee 184 sechi 45 per portare mille cavalieri, nave and altri legni 40 con molta vettovaglia*' ('184 *galeae*, 45 transports for carrying a thousand horses and 40 other ships with victuals').[70] Ottobono Scriba of Genoa called the same armada '*maximo stolo de galeis et plurimis uxerii*' ('a great fleet of very many *galeae* and *uscerii* [horse transports]').[71] Perhaps, the most compelling argument is the *galea*'s presumed performance capability. Its speed and endurance would seem to have made it ideal for such long-range raiding expeditions, and its extra cargo capacity would have offered the bonus of being able to bring back more booty.

Cattus/Gattus

A ship type often mentioned in the chronicles, but thinly described and never pictured, is the *cattus* or *gattus*. It was apparently a large, oared fighting ship that evoked considerable respect. As was previously noted in Chapter 1, Geoffrey Malaterra emphasized the disadvantage the Hautevilles faced in their initial invasion of Sicily by pointing out that the opposing Muslim fleet possessed *catti*.[72] Amatus of Montecassino substantiated that *catti* were present at the time and also offered cause for concern.[73] Indeed, Amatus later conveys the confidence of the Normans on the eve of the 1071 siege of Palermo when he states that Guiscard's galley 'was accompanied by ten *catti* and forty other ships'.[74] These vessels were also apparently in Robert's fleet at the siege of Durazzo in 1081. It was a '*cattus*' that Malaterra famously described as having been burned by 'Greek fire'

---

[69] Bernardo Maragone, *Annales Pisani*, p. 17.

[70] Salem Maragone, *Annales Pisani*, p. 72. (Salem's section survives only as a seventeenth-century Italian translation.)

[71] Ottobono Scriba, *Annales Ianuenses*, II, p. 16.

[72] Malaterra, *Deeds of Count Roger*, Bk 2, ch. 8, p. 90; *De rebus gestis Rogerii*, Bk II, ch. VIII, p. 32. '*Nam, quamvis noster navalis exercitus plurimus esset, eorum tamen amplior et fortioribus navibus abundantior erat. Nostri denique tantummodo germundos et galeas, Sicilienses vero cattos et golafros, sed et dromundos et diversae fabricae naves habebunt.*'

[73] Amatus of Montecassino, *History of the Normans*, Bk V, ch. 13, p. 138; *Storia de' Normanni*, Bk V, ch. XIII, pp. 234–5.

[74] Amatus, *History of the Normans*, Bk VI, ch. 14, p. 156; *Storia de' Normanni*, Bk VI, ch. XIV, pp. 276–7. '*... estoit acompaingnié X gat et XL autres nez.*'

in the initial encounter with the Venetians.[75] The Normans continued to employ the vessels well into the twelfth century. Bernardo Maragone bears witness that King Roger's fleet at the siege of Naples in 1134 consisted of 'sixty *galeae* and *gatti* and *naves* with a multitude of infantry'.[76] The most definitive description of these vessels comes from a pair of chroniclers of the Crusades. Albert of Aachen tells of an Egyptian fleet in the summer of 1110: 'Then, after some days, a matchless navy sailed out from the realm of Egypt, comprising galleys, biremes, and triremes, commonly called *catti*, turreted and equipped for war ...'[77] Similarly, William of Tyre makes special note of them in his description of the armada of the Venetian Doge Domenico Michieli: 'There were in this fleet certain beaked vessels larger than galleys which were called *gatti*. Each ship was equipped with a hundred oars, for each of which two oarsmen were required.'[78] Oarage systems with two or more men manipulating the same oar had not yet been adopted in the West, so William may simply have erred in an effort to create the impression of size. *Catti/gatti* were apparently significantly larger than other galleys, since William later observes that the *gatti* 'were placed in front so that if the enemy happened to catch sight of them from a distance, he might take them for merchant ships rather than an enemy's fleet'.[79] Pryor believes the name was probably drawn from the Arab word *qit'a*, defined simply as a twelfth-century Muslim warship.[80] Therefore, from the foregoing it could be deduced that the *cattus/gattus* was a large, high-profile war galley of Muslim derivation, possibly a trireme (meaning three files of oars per side) topped with castles.

Navis

Literally, the word *navis* merely means 'ship' in Latin, but contemporary historians routinely used it to designate 'transport vessels'. For example, William of Apulia, in recounting Robert Guiscard's 1084 expedition to the Balkans, says that in addition to 120 warships, 'The duke also brought *naves oneraria* [cargo

---

[75] Malaterra, *Deeds of Count Roger*, Bk 3, ch. 26, p. 156; *De rebus gestis Rogerii*, Bk III, ch. XXVI, p. 73. '... quandam navem de nostris, quam cattum nominant, dolose inter ipsas liquidi aequoris undas comburunt.'

[76] Bernardo Maragone, *Annales Pisani*, p. 10. '... sexaginta galeis et gattis et navibus cum multitudine peditum ...'

[77] Albert of Aachen, *Historia Ierosolimitana*, Bk XI, ch. 27, pp. 800–1. 'Dehinc, post dies aliquot, incomparabilis naualis exercitus a regno Babylonie in galidis, in biremibus et triremibus, dictis vulgariter cattis, turritis et bello compositis ...'

[78] William of Tyre, *History of Deeds Done beyond the Sea*, I, Bk 12, ch. 22, p. 548; *Willelmi Tyrensis Chronicon*, Bk 12, ch. 22, p. 574. 'Erant sane in eadem classe quedam naves rostrate, quas gatos vocant, galeis maiores, habentes singule remos centenos, quibus singulis duo erant remiges necessarii.'

[79] William of Tyre, *History of Deeds Done beyond the Sea*, I, Bk 12, ch. 22, p. 548; *Willelmi Tyrensis Chronicon*, Bk 12, ch. 22, p. 574. 'Has cum gatis priore ordinant, ea intentione, ut si ab hostibus forte de remoto conspicerentur, non putaretur hostium exercitus sed mercatorum naves; galee vero subsequebantur.'

[80] Pryor, 'From Dromōn to Galea', p. 108. (Definition on p. 250 of *Age of the Galley*.)

ships] filled with horses, supplies and arms, and various things for use on the sea.'[81] The reference to *naves* was normally generic and did not denote a specific ship type. A *navis* could be any kind of vessel other than a war galley used to carry supplies. In fact, if chroniclers mention transport ships at all, they often designate them simply as 'other ships'. For instance, Bernardo Maragone describes the Pisan fleet that was to accompany Frederick Barbarossa on his intended invasion of the *Regno* in 1167 as '50 *galearum* and 35 *sagittae* and *aliarum multarum navium* [many other ships] and an ample multitude of men, arms and victuals'.[82] Frequently, supply ships are omitted altogether from descriptions of fleet inventories in much the same way as foot soldiers and support personnel are excluded from accounts of land armies. Only warships are mentioned in the former, while just the number of knights is given in the latter. Nonetheless, these supply vessels had to have been of critical importance, for they carried the extra water and provisions required for large-scale, long-range expeditions. In the beginning, the supply ships that the Normans used were merchant vessels, because this was the type of ship they normally found in the harbors of port cities brought under their control. In fact, these merchant vessels probably formed the bulk of Norman flotillas in the first years of the conquest. Only later did the Normans have transport vessels specially constructed to carry large numbers of infantry, cavalry and siege machines.

Fortunately, modern maritime archaeology offers some clues as to the general nature of these vessels – something, ironically, that it could not do for warships. Almost all that is known about Mediterranean transport vessels in the Norman period comes from the discoveries of four shipwrecks: the seventh-century Yassi Ada wreck, the ninth-century cargo vessel at Bozburun, the eleventh-century Serçe Limani find and the early thirteenth-century Contarini hull. Basically all of these vessels were what are called 'round ships', owing to their lower length-to-width ratio and the rounded appearance of the hull. All were lateen rigged sailing ships with directional control provided by twin steering oars.[83] The oldest, the Yassi Ada, discovered off an islet of the same name near Bodrum in southwestern Turkey, is 20.52 meters (67.3 feet) long with 5.22 meters (17.1 feet) of beam, giving it a length-to-beam ratio of 4:1. It is estimated to have had a displacement of 72.86 metric tons and is presumed to have had only one mast. Its significance lies in the fact that it seems to show the transition in hull construction from the shell technique to the stronger skeleton style.[84] The Serçe Limani,

[81] William of Apulia, *La Geste de Robert Guiscard*, Bk V, lines 147–9, pp. 244–5. 'Duxit praeterea naves oneraria quarum lex erat, has et equis sumtuque replevit et armis et variis rebus, quas aequoris exigit usus.'
[82] Bernardo Maragone, *Annales Pisani*, p. 43. '... L galearum et XXXV sagittariarum atque aliarum multarum navium, ac copiosam multitudinem virorum, armorum et victualium ...'
[83] Pryor, 'Mediterranean Round Ship', pp. 59–76, especially 59–60.
[84] G. Bass and F. Van Doorninck, *Yassi Ada: A Seventh-Century Byzantine Shipwreck* (College Station, 1982), pp. 69, 84–6.

also found off southwestern Turkey (opposite Rhodes), is nearly four hundred years younger, but is much smaller: 15.66 meters (54.4 feet) long and 5.12 meters in beam (16 feet), with a length-to-beam ratio of 3:1 and only 35 metric tons of displacement. It probably, however, had two masts, a foremast and mainmast.[85] The Contarini vessel from the Po Delta, though similar in size to the Yassi Ada, at 20.98 meters (68.8 feet) in length and 5.2 meters (17 feet) in beam for a ratio of 4:1, also possessed two masts. Both the Serçe Limani and the Contarini ships were built entirely frame first.[86] The smallest is the Byzantine boat found full of wine amphorae near the Bozburun Peninsula of southern Turkey: 15 meters (49 feet) by 5 meters (16 feet).[87] The ongoing examination of the nine 'trade ships' excavated at Yenikapi, thus far, will doubtless yield more information, but all of these vessels are even smaller than those discussed above. The longest (YK-15) extends only 11.45 meters (37.6 feet) and the widest (YK-18) has a beam of only 3.2 meters (10.5 feet).[88] And that is the trouble. None of these single-decked ships seems to answer to the adjective 'large', often used to describe *naves* by contemporary chroniclers of the Norman era.

Amatus recounts that Robert Guiscard, in order to move the main body of his army across the Strait of Messina in 1061, requisitioned from Reggio all sorts of vessels 'especially the [big] ships'.[89] Roger of Howden describes the fleet of Richard Coeur de Lion that departed from Sicily in the spring of 1191 as being composed of 'one hundred fifty *magnis navibus* [large ships] and with fifty-three galleys'.[90] Given that *naves* are often mentioned in association with galleys, one would expect them to be at least as large as *dromōns* and *galeae*, estimated at around 31–39 meters long.[91] Pryor has managed to fill in some of the information gap and provide a more complete picture with his painstaking examination of the contracts of King Louis IX of France with Genoa, Marseilles and Venice, stipulating the ships to be built for his two mid-thirteenth-century Crusades (1248 and 1270). All of St Louis's transport ships were two-masted with either two or three decks, varying in length from 28.9 meters (94 feet) to 35.2 meters (115.5 feet) and in width from 7.75 meters (25.4 feet) to 9.5 meters (31.1 feet), yielding

---

[85] G. Bass, S. Matthews, J. Steffy and F. Van Doorninck, *Serçe Limani: An Eleventh-Century Byzantine Shipwreck* (College Station, 2004), pp. 153–87.

[86] Pryor, 'Mediterranean Round Ship', pp. 62–4.

[87] F. Hocker, 'Sampling a Byzantine Vintage: Bozburun, Turkey', in *Beneath the Seven Seas*, ed. G. Bass (New York, 2005), pp. 100–5.

[88] Kocabaş, *Yenikapi Shipwrecks*, pp. 103–75, 214.

[89] Amatus, *History of the Normans*, Bk V, ch. 19, pp.139–40; *Storia de' Normanni*, Bk V, ch. XIX, pp. 237–8. 'Adont comanda que diverse maniere de navie et de mariniers venissent devant la soë presence, et particulerement devissent aler les nez.' (Prescott Dunbar rightly translates the word 'nez' in the context of the subject passage as meaning 'big ships.')

[90] *Gesta Regis Henrici Secundi*, II, p. p. 162. '... centum quinquaginta magnis navibus, et cum quinquaginta tribus galeis.'

[91] Pryor and Jeffreys, *Dromōn*, p. 205, Fig. 20.

a displacement tonnage of between 323 and 806 metric tons.[92] In simple terms, the specifications of St Louis's ships reveal a huge size disparity with the medieval shipwrecks discovered by nautical archaeologists. Here is the difference: the wrecks discussed above were all short-range, medium-capacity merchant vessels, while St Louis's ships were all military-style transports, purpose-built to carry large numbers of men, horses and provisions. Thus, even though the construction features of Norman *naves* must have been similar to the Serçe Limani and the Contarini wrecks, their size, at least in the twelfth century, must have been more like St Louis's vessels.

Sagitta

Its very name seems to signify what kind of vessel it was. *Sagitta* is Latin for 'arrow', implying a swift ship. Often employed for raiding, it appears to have been a small galley used predominantly in the West from the eleventh through the thirteenth century.[93] A forerunner may have been the *sagena*, a vessel of Balkan Slavic origin often mentioned as a pirate vessel in the ninth and tenth centuries.[94] The *De Administrando Imperio* of Constantine Porphyrogenitus describes the *sagena* as a galley of the Croatian navy, crewed by 40 men.[95] Its speed and versatility must have been appealing, because its use was apparently widely adopted. In his 1970 article 'Sagena piscatoris', Kennerly Woody identifies the *sagena* as 'a small, fast ship used by Saracen pirates, by residents of the maritime cities of Italy, and by the inhabitants of the Dalmatian coast'.[96] When Pope John VIII wrote to the Byzantine Emperor Basil I in 877 beseeching naval assistance, it was to combat raiding by 'the *sagene* of the Agarenes [Sicilian Arabs]'.[97] Barbara Kreutz believes that the Amalfitans originally adopted this type of vessel from the Muslims, their frequent trading partners, and then transmitted the technology to the rest of southern Italy.[98]

As Woody observes, however, almost all mention of the *sagena* disappears from the sources by the middle of the tenth century.[99] Taking its place in the eleventh century, particularly with the mariners of Italy, seems to have been the *sagitta*. Otto of Freising records that *sagittae* figured prominently in the Sicilian

[92] J. Pryor, 'The Naval Architecture of Crusader Transport Ships: A Reconstruction of some Archetypes for Round-hulled Sailing Ships', *The Mariners Mirror*, LXX (1984), pp. 171–219, 275–92, 363–6, especially 202–13; Pryor, 'Mediterranean Round Ship', p. 64.

[93] Pryor, 'From Dromōn to Galea', p. 108.

[94] Gardiner, *Age of the Galley*, p. 250.

[95] Constantine VII Porphyrogenitus, *De Administrando Imperio*, pp. 150–1.

[96] K. Woody, 'Sagena piscatoris: Peter Damiani and the papal election decree of 1059', *Viator*, VII, (1970), pp. 33–54, especially 40.

[97] Pope John VIII, *Papae Registrum*, no. 47, p. 45. '... Agarenorum sagene ...'

[98] B. Kreutz, 'Ships, Shipping, and the Implications of Change in the Early Medieval Mediterranean', *Viator*, VII (1976), pp. 79–109, especially 101–3.

[99] Woody, 'Sagena piscatoris', p. 44.

fleet that raided the Peloponnesos in 1147.[100] Cohn, Manfroni and Pryor concur that it was an oared galley, smaller than the Byzantine *galeai*, but they are not sure how small since the number of oars it employed seems to vary widely according to the source and the time period.[101] Lawrence Mott contends that the version of the *sagitta* employed by the Normans was, in fact, quite small, with no more than 16 oars.[102] Supporting that notion, the medieval arsenal of Amalfi displays a replica of a *sagitta* that is about 40 feet long by four feet wide with eight thwarts, suggesting 16 oarsmen. In addition to raiding, the vessel was used for dispatching messages and scouting. Geoffrey Malaterra testifies that on the eve of his 1084 attack on Syracuse, Roger dispatched a certain 'Philip, son of the patrician Gregory, with a very fast *sagacia* [probably a *sagitta*] toward Syracuse to reconnoiter the whole area.'[103] The *sagittae* were apparently used in significant numbers throughout the Norman period. Reference to the vessel is found with increasing frequency in Italian sources in the latter half of the twelfth century. Both the *Annales Ianuenses* of Caffaro and the *Annales Pisani* of Bernardo Maragone, for instance, contain several references to '*multas sagitteas*' during the Genoese–Pisan conflict of 1162.[104] The Normans continued to employ them until late in the Hauteville dynasty. In October 1182, William II renewed a privilege of August 1176 that granted the monastery of Santa Maria Nuova di Monreale five *sagittae*. This type of vessel was not normally used for fishing and hauling foodstuffs. This and the fact that the concession specified that these ships were to be kept in the port of Palermo implies that they were liable to be conscripted by the crown in time of need.[105]

Horse transports

The Normans, at least in the beginning, would have placed a heavy tactical emphasis on these vessels. After all, their whole strategy was about getting battle-winning cavalry to the point of attack. There was no specific ship type associated with carrying horses initially, because the Normans would have 'made do' with whatever vessels they could find in the ports under their control at the time. Indeed, the Emperor Leo VI noted the need for horse transports in his

---

[100] Otto of Freising, *Deeds of Frederick Barbarossa*, Bk I, ch. 34, p. 69; *Gesta Friderici*, Bk I, ch. XXXIV, p. 53.

[101] Cohn, *Die Geschichte der normannisch-sicilischen Flotte*, pp. 95–6; Manfroni, *Storia della Marina italiana*, I, p. 457; Pryor, 'From Dromōn to Galea', p. 108.

[102] Mott, *Sea Power in the Medieval Mediterranean*, p. 57.

[103] Malaterra, *Deeds of Count Roger*, Bk 4, ch. 2, p. 178; *De rebus gestis Rogerii*, Bk IV, ch. II, p. 86. '*Philippum, filium Gregorii patricii, cum velocissima sagacia versus Syracusam, omnem terram exploratum, mandant.*'

[104] Caffaro, *Annales Ianuenses*, I, pp. 69–71; Bernardo Maragone, *Annales Pisani*, p. 27.

[105] C. A. Garufi, *I Documenti inediti dell'epoca Normanna in Sicilia* (DSS, ser. 1, 18, Palermo, 1899), doc. 73, pp. 175–83.

early tenth-century *Taktika*, but declined to describe a definite ship type.[106] This is probably because a variety of vessels was used. As early as 762, Theophanes the Confessor reported that the Emperor Constantine V used *chelandia* to transport horses in his wars against the Bulgars.[107] A miniature at the top of folio 31v of the Madrid manuscript of John Skylitzes' *Synopsis historion* shows what appears to be a generic galley transporting horses in Thomas the Slav's fleet as it moved on Abydos in 821.[108] In *De Cerimoniis*, the Emperor Constantine VII Porphyrogenitus reports that in 935 the Emperor Romanos Lekapenos dispatched to Longobardia under the *Patrikios* Kosmas an expedition of 11 *chelandia* that included 1,453 cavalry.[109] While it would have been impossible for these few *chelandia* to carry an equivalent number of steeds, they may have transported a small contingent of mounts. In recounting the invasion of Crete in 960, Leo the Deacon designates the horse carriers simply as 'transport ships', saying Nikephoros Phocas 'had brought ramps with him on the transport ships, which he set up on the beach, and thus transferred the army, fully armed and mounted, from sea onto dry land'.[110] No horse transports are mentioned among Giorgios Maniakes' fleet when he assaulted Sicily in 1038, but clearly horses must have been employed because the army that he had ferried across the strait included a contingent of at least 300 Norman knights who almost certainly were mounted. Moreover, the Madrid manuscript of Skylitzes' *Synopsis historion* illustrates a Byzantine cavalry charge executed against Islamic adversaries during the campaign.[111]

Again, when the Hautevilles commenced their conquest of Sicily in 1061, they dispatched a preliminary force of knights (presumably mounted) across the Strait of Messina under the cover of darkness, yet no precise vessel type was identified. Amatus says Roger transferred his mounted contingent across the strait on '*nefs*', old French for 'ships',[112] while Malaterra notes that Roger used *naves*, also meaning 'ships' in the same general sense.[113] The Hauteville brothers probably just utilized whatever merchant ships were in the harbor of Reggio at the time.[114] They continued to use existing cargo ships to accommodate their

---

[106] Leo VI, *The naval warfare of the Emperor Leo* (*Taktika*, Constitution XIX), *Dromon*, Appendix Two, par. 11, pp. 488–9; Nikephoros Ouranos, *On fighting at sea*, *Dromon*, Appendix Five, par. 10, pp. 576–7.

[107] Theophanes the Confessor, *annus mundi* 6254, p. 599.

[108] Tsamakda, *Chronicle of Ioannes Skylitzes*, fig. 61, fol. 31v.

[109] Constantine VII Porphyrogenitus, *De Cerimoniis Aulae Byzantinae*, Chapters II, 44 and 45, trans. Haldon in 'Theory and Practice in Tenth-Century Military Administration', pp. 212–15.

[110] Leo the Deacon, *History of Leo the Deacon*, Bk I, ch. 3, pp. 60–1.

[111] Tsamakda, *Chronicle of Ioannes Skylitzes*, fig. 504, fol. 213r.

[112] Amatus, *History of the Normans*, Bk V, ch. 15, p. 138; *Storia de' Normanni*, Bk V, ch. XV, pp. 235–6.

[113] Malaterra, *Deeds of Count Roger*, Bk 2, ch. 10, pp. 90–1; *De rebus gestis Rogerii*, Bk II, ch. X, p. 33.

[114] D. Waley, '"Combined Operations" in Sicily, A.D. 1060–1078', *Papers of the British School at Rome*, XXII (1954), pp. 118–25, especially 120.

Fig. 11. Mosaic of horse embarkation from the fourth century. The remnants of a fourth-century Roman mosaic at the Villa Imperiale del Casale of Piazza Armerina displays the embarkation of horses onto a ship by way of a gangplank, similar to how the Normans may have accomplished the task. (Credit: C. Stanton)

horse transportation needs at least through the summer of 1071 when, prior to the siege of Palermo, Guiscard had a hill at Otranto leveled in order to make the embarkation of horses easier.[115] For short, over-water operations such as crossing the Strait of Messina, the Norman penchant for pragmatic adaptation would have served them well.[116] They probably handled the evolution very much as it had been done for centuries. There are several images, for example, among the fourth-century Roman mosaics of the Villa Imperiale del Casale at Piazza Armerina in Sicily, which depict horses and other animals being embarked on open vessels by way of a gangplank (see Figure 11).[117] The Bayeux Tapestry shows horses being offloaded directly over the gunnel.[118] Transporting horses by sea over short distances apparently posed no insurmountable challenge. The

[115] Malaterra, *Deeds of Count Roger*, Bk 2, ch. 43, p. 122; *De rebus gestis Rogerii*, Bk II, ch. XLIII, p. 51.

[116] J. Pryor, 'Transportation of horses by sea during the era of the Crusades: eighth century to 1285 A.D., *The Mariner's Mirror*, LXVIII (1982), pp. 9–27, 103–25, especially 12–13.

[117] L. Casson, *Ships and Seamanship in the Ancient World* (Princeton, 1971), fig. 141; B. Pace, *I mosaici di Piazza Armerina* (Rome, 1955), fig. 25.

[118] L. Musset, *La Tapisserie de Bayeux* (Paris, 2002), scene 39, pp. 202–3.

animals could have been stabilized for short crossings by a combination of slings and ropes.[119] Longer voyages would have required more sophisticated methods, including some modifications incorporated into the design of the ships. Essentially the horses needed more space to accommodate their physiological needs. They required enormous amounts of breathable air, sustenance and water, all of which was converted into waste, which had to be evacuated in an efficient manner.[120]

It was apparently not until the invasion of the Balkans in 1081 that Robert Guiscard began using vessels built for the purpose. Anna Comnena relates that 'horses and armed knights embarked on *dromōns*'.[121] Pryor's studies indicate that an appropriately modified *dromōn* or *chelandion* could have accommodated a dozen or so steeds along the keel.[122] In the twelfth century, the Normans almost certainly employed vessels designed for the purpose. The first Norman expedition against Mahdiyah in 1123 was said to have included around a thousand horses.[123] Transporting mounts in that number would surely have required specially crafted vessels. By the time King Roger ordered the second assault on Mahdiyah in 1148, purpose-built horse transports were definitely in use. Al-Maqrizi tallied 100 *taride* (oared horse transports) in George of Antioch's armada.[124] Indeed, a wreck of what appears to be a twelfth-century horse transport was discovered in 1989 off the south coast of Sicily at Camarina.[125] Ibn al-Athir counted 36 *taride* in William II's invasion fleet at Alexandria in 1174,[126] while the *Annales Pisani* claims there were, instead, '50 *dromōns* for carrying horses'.[127] And Ottobono Scriba records that the Sicilian admiral Walter of Moac had with him 'very many horse transports' ('*plurimis uxeriis*') on his ill-fated raiding expedition to the Balearics in 1181.[128] Since '*uxeriis*' or '*usceriis*' (as it occasionally appears) logically comes from the medieval Latin word '*uscerium*', which means 'door', such vessels may have had stern hull ports for disembarking the horses.[129] These sorts of ships could be backed onto a beach, enabling fully mounted knights to emerge ready for battle under the protection of sterncastles manned by archers.[130] On

[119] Pryor and Jeffreys, *Dromōn*, pp. 318–19.

[120] Pryor and Jeffreys, *Dromōn*, pp. 326–33.

[121] Anna Comnena, *Alexiad*, p. 131; *Alexiade*, I, Bk III, ch. XII, p. 139.

[122] Pryor and Jeffreys, *Dromōn*, pp. 322–5.

[123] At-Tijani, *BAS*, II, p. 71; Ibn al-Athir, *BAS*, I, p. 456; *Chronicle of Ibn al-Athir, Part I*, p. 245; Ibn Khaldun, *BAS*, II, p. 206.

[124] Al-Maqrizi, translated by Johns in *Arabic Administration in Norman Sicily*, p. 82.

[125] G. di Stefano, 'Antichi relitti nella baia di Camarina', in *Atti, IV rassegna di archeologia subacquea*, ed. P. Gianfrotta (Messina, 1991), pp. 127–34. (Note: Camarina is near Capo Scalambri from where Roger I launched his 1091 invasion of Malta.)

[126] Ibn al-Athir, *BAS*, I, p. 496; *Chronicle of Ibn al-Athir, Part 2*, p. 229.

[127] Bernardo Maragone, *Annales Pisani*, p. 61. '... L dermonum pro equis portandis ...'

[128] Ottobono Scriba, *Annales Ianuenses*, II, pp. 5–16.

[129] W. Rodgers, *Naval Warfare under Oars, 4th to 16th Centuries: A Study of Strategy, Tactics and Ship Design* (Annapolis, 1940), p. 113.

[130] Pryor, 'Transportation of horses by sea during the era of the Crusades', p. 19.

the other hand, the term 'usceriis' may simply be derived from 'ushari', the Arab word for transport galley.[131] In any case, it is highly improbable that the Normans ever employed anything like the mammoth, multi-decked sailing *taride*, commissioned by St Louis for the Sixth and Seventh Crusades. The lack of established port facilities in the medieval Mediterranean would have ensured that oared horse transports would have been preferred well into the thirteenth century because they could be beached for offloading, whereas sailing ships could not.[132] The Normans would have placed a high premium on coming ashore battle-ready.

Procurement

The Normans, mounted knights with little or no exposure to the ways of the sea, initially acquired the vessels they needed the time-honored Norman way: they simply appropriated them from the port cities they conquered. Amatus relates that the Hautevilles commandeered ships from Reggio to begin the conquest of Sicily in 1061.[133] Later, in order to complete the blockade of Bari in 1068, William of Apulia explains, 'The duke [Robert Guiscard] fortified his camp with knights and filled the sea with the ships of the Calabrians.'[134] Once Bari was reduced in 1071, Lupus Protospatarius records that Robert then departed from Bari with 58 ships to accomplish the siege of Palermo.[135] In the early stages of the conquest, the Normans most likely took whatever vessels were available and most of these probably were not warships. There must have been few such vessels in the ports of Calabria and Apulia at the time. The Byzantine navy was in atrophy and war galleys were of no commercial use, since they possessed scant room for excess cargo. Moreover, the maritime communities of southern Italy would have had little incentive to build and maintain warships apart from providing protection from piracy for their own commercial fleets. Thus, the Normans would have had to settle mostly for merchant vessels, hastily outfitted for war. This would explain their initial hesitancy to engage Muslim fleets of war, as was the case in 1061 when they avoided contact with the Muslim fleet sent from Palermo to block their intended assault on Messina.[136] It was not until the first expedition against Byzantium in 1081 that Guiscard employed vessels built for the task, and even then, William of Apulia says the duke had to rent some specialized transports from Dalmatia to carry supplies, arms and combatants.[137] Accord-

---

[131]   Fahmy, *Muslim Sea-Power*, pp. 150–1; Pryor and Jeffreys, *Dromōn*, pp. 258–9, note 319.

[132]   Pryor, 'Transportation of horses by sea during the era of the Crusades', pp. 103–4.

[133]   Amatus, *History of the Normans*, Bk V, ch. 8–11, pp. 136–7; *Storia de' Normanni*, Bk V, ch. VIII–XI, pp. 230–4.

[134]   William of Apulia, *La Geste de Robert Guiscard*, Bk II, lines 485–6, pp 158–9. '*Dux munit milite castra, atque replet Calabris advectis navibus aequor.*'

[135]   Lupus Protospatarius, *Annales*, anno 1071, p. 60.

[136]   Malaterra, *Deeds of Count Roger*, Bk 2, ch. 8–9, pp. 89–90; *De rebus gestis Rogerii*, Bk II, ch. VIII–X, p. 32.

[137]   William of Apulia, *La Geste de Robert Guiscard*, Bk IV, lines 134–7, pp. 210–11.

ingly, for most of the era of conquest, the Norman fleets were composed largely of commandeered vessels.

These confiscations from conquered port cities were doubtless *ad hoc* arrangements imposed at sword point as the need arose. A system of expected contributions may have gradually evolved from these precedents in a manner similar to the one described by Norman specialist Elizabeth van Houts in 'The Ship List of William the Conqueror'.[138] According to the *Brevis Relatio*, William 'ordered that, as quickly as possible, each magnate of Normandy, according to his own means, should prepare ships, by which he and his whole army which he would bring with him could be transported to England'.[139] Van Houts believes that these *ad hoc* arrangements between lord and vassal resulted in the 'Ship List', which formed the basis of a 'quota system in use in later times'.[140] A similar quota system probably emerged in Norman Italy when the Hautevilles imposed repeated demands on the maritime cities of Apulia, Calabria and Campania to support their ongoing campaigns. In so doing, they may have been able to build upon an existing Byzantine quota system to which Thietmar of Merseburg alluded when he noted in the tenth century that two *chelandia* were required from the *thema* of Calabria each year.[141]

The resulting obligations were subsequently codified in ducal and royal charters. The diploma issued by King Tancred to the city of Gaeta in July 1191, which reduced the required contribution to the royal fleet from two galleys to one, proves that such a quota system existed.[142] Further evidence is offered by an exchange of letters between the Emperor Frederick II and his admiral, Henry of Malta. In response to Frederick's urgent call for 40 galleys to assist in the siege of Gaeta in 1230, Henry blames the difficulty in complying on the fact that 'all of coastal Apulia, Sicily and Calabria had failed to fulfill its obligation of service'. He goes on to explain, 'Territory, for instance, that in the time of King William [II] customarily provided three galleys, could scarcely be depended upon for two and that which was accustomed to arming two, guaranteed only one'.[143] Documents such as these led Lawrence Mott, author of *Sea Power in the Medieval Mediterranean*, to unequivocally conclude: 'Besides men and money,

[138]   E. van Houts, 'The Ship List of William the Conqueror', *Anglo-Norman Studies*, X (1988), pp. 159–83.

[139]   Van Houts, trans., 'The *Brevis Relatio de Guillelmo nobilissimo comite Normannorum* written by a Monk of Battle Abbey', *Camden Miscellany*, 5th series, X (1997), pp. 1–48, especially 29. '... *precepit ut quamcicius possent omnes barones Normannie unusquisque secundum suam possibilitatem naues prepararent quibus ipse et omnis militia quam secum ducturus esset in Angliam transuehi posset.*'

[140]   Van Houts, 'Ship List of William the Conqueror', p. 172.

[141]   Thietmar of Merseburg, *Ottonian Germany*, Bk 3, ch. 23, pp. 145–6; *Die Chronik*, Bk III, ch. 23, pp. 126–9.

[142]   *Tancredi et Willelmi III Regum Diplomata*, no. 18, pp. 42–6.

[143]   K. Hampe, ed., *Die Aktenstücke zum Frieden von San Germano, 1230* (MGH, EP Selectae, IV, Berlin, 1926), no. 8–9, pp. 107–9. '... *tota maritima Apulie, Scicilie et Calabrie deficiat servi-*

the Normans required that cities and regions provide galleys for the fleet on a regular basis. These obligations are inferred from Hohenstaufen documents in which the government based its claims on feudal rights established under the Normans.'[144] Moreover, Mott theorizes that the Sicilian court may have even expected ecclesiastical institutions under royal patrimony to maintain some vessels for use in the royal fleet in time of need.[145] As an example, he points to the five *sagittae* William II entrusted to Santa Maria Nuova di Monreale.[146] The granting of five such galleys to a monastery was highly unusual. The inference is that these vessels were intended for a military application.

And, of course, during the *Regno*, the Normans produced and maintained their own fleet of warships. In 1177, Romuald of Salerno, as an emissary of William II, boasted to the Emperor Frederick Barbarossa that the king 'prepared his biremes each year'.[147] To do so, the Norman kingdom funded and operated royal arsenals.

Shipyards: location and operation

In the *Kitab Rujar* ('Book of Roger'), al-Idrisi, the court geographer of Roger II, describes the ports of the kingdom in some detail. He even mentions several places where ships were built, like Gaeta, Sorrento and Bari, but he identifies only two arsenals: Palermo and Messina.[148] These two ports almost certainly contained the royal shipyards that outfitted the ships of the Norman navy.

The Normans inherited the arsenal of Palermo from their predecessors, the Muslims. Indeed, the very name 'arsenal' is derived from the Arabic term *dar as-sina'ah*, meaning simply 'house of manufacture'.[149] The tenth-century Arab geographers, Muhammad ibn Ahmad al-Muqaddasi and Abu al-Qasim Muhammad Ibn Hawqal, place the arsenal in the Al Halisah quarter in the southern portion of the city, abutting the Gulf of Palermo (see Map 3). It was the same district that included the emir's palace, the *diwan* (administrative offices) and the Great Mosque.[150] Ibn abi Dinar, writing in the seventeenth century, also notes the existence of an 'arsenal for the construction of ships' in the Al Halisah

---

ciis adimplendis. Terra enim, que a tempore regis Guillelmi in tribus galeis solita est servire, vix nititur in duabus, et unam vix repromittit, que duas consuevit armare.'
[144] Mott, *Sea Power in the Medieval Mediterranean*, p. 56.
[145] Mott, *Sea Power in the Medieval Mediterranean*, p. 57.
[146] Garufi, *I Documenti inediti dell'epoca Normanna in Sicilia*, doc. 73, pp. 175–83.
[147] Romuald of Salerno, *Romualdi Salernitani Chronicon*, p. 290. '... singulis annis biremes suas preparat.'
[148] Al-Idrisi, *BAS*, I, pp. 60–8; *La première géographie de l'Occident*, IV, 2, pp. 301–12; V, 2, pp. 377–83.
[149] Manfroni, *Storia della Marina italiana*, I, p. 472.
[150] Ibn Hawqal, *BAS*, I, pp. 11–12; Al-Muqaddasi, *BAS*, II, pp. 670–1.

at the time.[151] The Spanish Muslim pilgrim Ibn Jubayr confirms that it was still there late in the twelfth century.[152] In the nineteenth century, Michele Amari narrowed the location down to the general area of the Piazza Marina on the southeastern side of La Cala, the old harbor. While little remained, Amari, with the help of a civil engineer friend, was able to discern the general outline of the arsenal. He estimated it to have covered an area of nearly 52,000 square meters, a considerable expanse.[153]

The Muslim sources also indicate that the environs of Palermo offered the arsenal all the raw materials necessary to support the fleet. In describing the north coast of the island, al-Idrisi observes, 'With the wood found in the surrounding mountains, they construct vessels.'[154] Both he and Ibn Hawqal speak of abundant springs flowing through the city and the River Oreto, which runs along the southern boundary, suggesting that the fleet would have had access to ample water supplies.[155] Ibn Hawqal also noted that adjacent to the river were extensive marshes covered with reeds, 'the majority of which is twisted into cord for the rigging of ships'. And on the west side, the geographer tells of the *Ayn al-hadid* ('Iron Spring') where 'there is actually a mine of this metal, possessed today by the Sultan, from which iron [ore] is extracted for use in the fleet.'[156] Nor would the revictualing of the fleet with foodstuffs have presented a problem. The city lies on the edge of a fertile plain known as the Conca d'Oro ('bowl of gold', as in the sense of a 'horn of plenty').

It is difficult to believe that the Hautevilles would not have availed themselves of this facility. Camillo Manfroni, for one, has no doubt of it: 'Certainly Roger, having remained to complete the conquest and govern the island, would have taken possession of the Arab arsenal and ships.'[157] This would have, in turn, infused the nascent Norman naval force with a strong Arab influence. Manfroni supports this deduction by adding, 'Thus, any new ship constructions would have replicated Arab type warships, celebrated for their lightness and great solidity.'[158]

While Roger may have been happy to assume control of the arsenal of Palermo, he soon made Messina the primary shipyard of his demesne. Geoffrey Malaterra relates how, in 1081, the count 'brought in skilled masons from all around and began to lay the foundations for a fortress and tower in Messina'.[159]

---

[151]   Ibn abi Dinar, *BAS*, II, p. 288.
[152]   Ibn Jubayr, *Travels of Ibn Jubayr*, p. 343; *BAS*, I, p. 150.
[153]   Amari, *BAS*, I, pp. 12–13, note 3.
[154]   Al-Idrisi, *BAS*, I, p. 66; *La première géographie de l'Occident*, IV, 2, p. 311.
[155]   Al-Idrisi, *BAS*, I, pp. 60–2; *La première géographie de l'Occident*, IV, 2, pp. 308–9; Ibn Hawqal, *BAS*, I, pp. 13–14.
[156]   Ibn Hawqal, *BAS*, I, p. 22.
[157]   Manfroni, *Storia della Marina italiana*, I, p. 118.
[158]   Manfroni, *Storia della Marina italiana*, I, p. 118.
[159]   Malaterra, *Deeds of Count Roger*, Bk 3, ch. 32, pp. 162–3; *De rebus gestis Rogerii*, Bk III, ch. XXXII, p. 77. '… *undecumque terrarum artificiosis caementariis conductis, fundamenta castelli, turresque apud Messanam jacens, aedificare coepit.*'

It stands to reason that he would have refurbished the arsenal there at the same time. One quite probably remained from when the island was a Byzantine *thema*. After all, the very northeastern corner persisted as part of the Byzantine Empire until the summer of 902, when the Lord High Admiral Eustathios Argyros was finally forced to quit Taormina by the armies of Ibrahim II ibn Ahmad.[160] Even after the Muslim conquest, the people of the Val Demone region remained overwhelmingly Greek in ethnicity. They would have had every incentive to maintain something of what the Byzantines had built there in Messina. Roger surely would have taken over such a facility just as he had the arsenal of Palermo. Messina's easy access to Norman domains in Calabria and Apulia along with its strategic position commanding the strait would have made such action imperative.

Evidence that he did so comes only a few years later. In response to the depredations of Ibn el-Werd, the emir of Syracuse, Malaterra reports that Count Roger ordered a fleet to be outfitted on 1 October 1084. It was ready on 20 May 1085, and while the chronicler does not say precisely where the armada was prepared, it is clear from his description of its route to Syracuse that it was done in Messina. On the first night, Roger's fleet stopped at Taormina, about 28 miles or four hours' journey to the south. The next night, it pulled into Lognina (probably Ognina, just north of Catania), 25 miles further south, and on the third, it rendezvoused with the land forces at a place called Rasesalix, which Ferdinand Chalandon deduced was Capo Santa Croce near present-day Augusta, another 20 miles south.[161] Moreover, establishing a shipyard at Messina, with its Greek population, would have given Roger access to Byzantine shipbuilding techniques. Thus, he would have had the advantages of both Byzantine and Muslim maritime traditions in his quest to turn Norman Sicily into a sea power.

If a Norman arsenal at Messina was a definite possibility under Roger I in the eleventh century, it was a veritable certainty in the twelfth century under his son, Roger II. Al-Idrisi, the latter's court geographer, bears witness: 'Here is an arsenal; here vessels are constructed, here is a continuous docking and anchoring, offloading and loading of vessels, originating from all the maritime lands of the Rum; here gather the great ships: the travelers and the merchants, either from the land of the Rum or from the Muslims, are drawn here from every group.'[162] As he did with Palermo, al-Idrisi itemizes the city's natural advantages. He notes that it is surrounded by mountains to the west bearing ample quantities of iron, not to mention wood. He describes the courses of 'excellent water' that wash through it. He especially extols the excellence of its deep-water harbor facility:

---

[160]　Ibn al-Athir, *BAS*, I, pp. 393–4; Al-Nuwayri, *BAS*, II, pp. 151–2; John Skylitzes, *Synopsis historiōn*, p. 152. See also R. Dolley, 'The Lord High Admiral Eustathios Argyros and the Betrayal of Taormina to the African Arabs in 902', *Atti dello VIII congresso internazionale di studi byzantini* (Rome, 1953), I, pp. 340–53.

[161]　Malaterra, *Deeds of Count Roger*, Bk 4, ch. 2, pp. 177–8; *De rebus gestis Rogerii*, Bk IV, ch. II, pp. 85–6. See also Chalandon, *Histoire de la Domination Normande*, I, pp. 338–9.

[162]　Al-Idrisi, *BAS*, I, p. 68; *La première géographie de l'Occident*, IV, 2, p. 312.

'The port is a great marvel, renowned in all the world, because the largest ships can anchor so near the shore that from dry land one can take by hand what is found aboard the vessels.'[163] Thirty years later, in 1184, during the reign of William II, the Almohad traveler Ibn Jubayr echoed al-Idrisi's observations: 'In Messina, the King has a shipyard containing fleets of uncountable numbers of ships.'[164] He, too, greatly admired the natural setting of the port:

> Messina leans against the mountains, the lower slopes of which adjoin the entrenchments of the town. To its south is the sea, and its harbor is the most remarkable of maritime ports, since large ships can come into it from the seas until they almost touch it. Between them and the shore is thrown a plank over which men come and go and porters take up the baggage; thus no boats are needed for loading and unloading save for ships anchored far out. You will observe ships ranged along the quay like horses lined at their pickets or in their stables. This is all because of the great depth here of the sea which forms the strait, some three miles wide, that separates the island from the continent.[165]

Ibn Jubayr gives compelling testimony that Messina had, in fact, become the primary arsenal of the Norman Kingdom of Sicily by the late twelfth century. He personally witnessed King William II overseeing the preparation at Messina of the massive Norman armada that invaded Byzantium in 1185.[166] Further proof is provided by a privilege of Roger II in favor of Messina dated 15 May 1129. It essentially recognizes Messina's special status and grants sweeping exemptions and prerogatives to its citizens, but it also contains a curious clause that seems to establish the city as the base for the royal galley: 'Whenever the army or fleet of this city is being prepared, a galley is to be outfitted in which the royal person will pass over the sea; and which galley, with the royal insignia and that of city, will be honored and placed before all others.'[167] Unfortunately, the royal charter itself is widely regarded as a self-serving, fifteenth-century forgery.[168] Another charter of 20 August 1160, supposedly signed by William I, confirms Roger's concessions, but it also has been dubbed false by a host of historians.[169] There is, however, a reference in the *Liber de Regno Sicilie* of 'Hugo Falcandus' that lends credence to the forged privilege's basic content, though it does not specifically mention ships. 'Falcandus' contends that the leading citizens of the city petitioned Stephen of Perche, the chancellor during William II's minority,

---

[163] Al-Idrisi, *BAS*, I, p. 68; *La première géographie de l'Occident*, IV, 2, p. 312.

[164] Ibn Jubayr, *Travels of Ibn Jubayr*, p. 343; *BAS*, I, p. 150.

[165] Ibn Jubayr, *Travels of Ibn Jubayr*, p. 339; *BAS*, I, pp. 144–5.

[166] Ibn Jubayr, *Travels of Ibn Jubayr*, p. 338; *BAS*, I, p. 144.

[167] *Capitoli e Privilegi di Messina*, ed. C. Giardina (Palermo, 1937), doc. IV, pp. 6–14; *Rogerii II. Regis Diplomata Latina*, no. 11, pp. 29–35. 'Et quoties statuetur exercitus aut stolus in eadem civitate et ex eisdem civibus armaretur galea, eum qua regia persona transfretabit, que galea cum signis regiis et civitatis ab omnibus aliis honorabitur et preponetur.'

[168] *Capitoli e Privilegi di Messina*, pp. XXX–XXXV.

[169] *Capitoli e Privilegi di Messina*, pp. XXXV, 17–19; *Guillelmi I. Regis Diplomata*, no. 20, p. 111.

Fig. 12. Arsenale della Repubblica di Amalfi. Pictured above is the remainder of
one of two long bays of the Arsenale della Repubblica di Amalfi. It dates from
the eleventh century and is the only medieval arsenal in Italy still extant from the
Norman era. (Credit: C. Stanton)

'and emphatically urged him to have the privilege restored to them which King Roger had granted'.[170] The chancellor apparently acceded to their wishes. 'Hugo Falcandus' later supplies some additional circumstantial evidence. When the people of Messina rose up against Stephen the next year, he says they bragged that they could raise 60 armed galleys in a day – a boast only a city that was home base for the royal fleet could have made.[171]

Lastly, a royal magistracy that was critical to the maintenance and administration of the fleet resided in Messina. It was the *Comitum Galeae Messanae* and it consisted of a 'count of the galleys' and a five-member commission. Among its responsibilities was the collection of the *statutum navale tributum*, a sort of land tax assessed for the funding of the fleet. A charter of 1176 from the archives of the monastery of Santa Maria Vallis Giosafat in Messina gives an insight as to the agency's function. A man named Basil sought permission from the magistrate, a certain Bartholomaeus, to sell a vineyard in order to obtain relief from the three *tarì* impost, but the 'count of the galleys' and his board authorized the sale only if Basil used the proceeds to purchase another property bearing the same tax obligation.[172] Although no other documentary evidence remains, it is assumed that the *Comitum Galeae Messanae* exacted other goods and services as well. A 1209 diploma of Frederick II confirms a concession of land made by William II to Nicosia, Sicily in return for 296 sailors and an annual contribution of wood made to the arsenal.[173] It seems logical that the *Comitum Galeae Messanae* or an entity like it would be charged with the collection of such levies of manpower and matériel. Exemptions granted to certain select ecclesiastical institutions make it clear that the crown tightly controlled such key shipbuilding materials as pitch and lumber. For instance, Roger II's authorization for the bishopric of Catania to operate a furnace for the preparation of pitch in 1124 was unique.[174] Furthermore, the right to harvest lumber from the forests of the island was granted only to a favored few, like the citizens of Cefalu, the monks of Sant'Angelo di Brolo and the clerics of San Giovanni degli Eremiti in Palermo. Even then, it was allowed only to the extent needed to provide for the maintenance of those communities.[175] A bureau along the lines of the *Comitum Galeae Messanae* would have

---

[170] 'Hugo Falcandus', *History of the Tyrants of Sicily*, p. 183; *Liber de Regno Sicilie*, p. 131. '... rogabant eum instantissime ut privilegium eis reddi faceret quod olim Rogerius rex supra quibusdam ... factum ...'

[171] 'Hugo Falcandus', *History of the Tyrants of Sicily*, p. 204; *Liber de Regno Sicilie*, p. 151.

[172] Cusa, *Diplomi greci et arabi di Sicilia*, I, pp. 368–71; Gregorio, *Considerazioni supra la storia di Sicilia*, II, p. 83, note 19 [contains a Latin version of the original Greek text of the diploma].

[173] W. Koch, *Die Urkunden Friedrichs II. 1198–1212* (MGH, DRIG, XIV, Hanover, 2002), no. 93, pp. 181–3.

[174] Caspar, *Roger II*, Reg. no. 44 and 48, pp. 494–6.

[175] Caspar, *Roger II*, Reg. no. 73, p. 513; *Rogerii II. Regis Diplomata Latina*, no. 19 and 76, pp. 52–3, 217–23; Pirro, *Sicilia sacra*, II, p. 1021.

been the most likely means of enforcing such strictures. It may even have had oversight of the maintenance and operation of the arsenal itself. Nothing remains of the arsenals at Palermo and Messina. As a matter of fact, there is only one medieval arsenal still left from the Norman era in all of southern Italy: the Arsenale della Repubblica di Amalfi (see Figure 12). It, however, gives an excellent insight as to how the arsenals of the *Regno* may have been structured and operated. The arsenal of Amalfi originally consisted of two long tufa stone bays divided by 22 pilasters. It dates from the eleventh century, although the ogival arches and Gothic rib vaulting suggest it was built much later.[176] This is most likely because Frederick II ordered it restored in 1240 along with several other shipyards in the kingdom.[177] The footprint of the facility, however, apparently remained the same. Each bay reportedly could accommodate two galleys, meaning the arsenal could have sustained the outfitting of four galleys at once. Unfortunately, only half of each bay separated by 10 pilasters survives. A devastating storm and resulting landslide claimed the rest on 25 November 1343.[178] Nonetheless, much information can be gleaned from what remains. Careful measurement of the interior floor space of the arsenal confirms earlier estimates of its capacity. The remainder of each bay is 140 feet long, 21 feet wide and 35 feet high: more than enough space to accommodate a standard-size *dromōn*, *chelandion* or *galea* of approximately 110–120 feet in length by 14–16 feet of maximum beam. Adjacent to the arsenal were a number of warehouses containing tools and materials for the construction and repair of the vessels.[179] Some were said to have contained furnaces for the production of pitch.

Not all of the work was performed within the arsenal's vaulted bays. For one thing, there was a satellite shipyard at nearby Atrani.[180] Furthermore, hull construction was also performed in slipways built into a portion of Amalfi's east beach, called the *scarium*. Medieval docks and slipways found beneath the waters of the marina provide proof of this. The road that runs along the shoreline of this city still bears the name 'Lo Scario'.[181] While the vaulted arsenal of Amalfi provides some visual cues as to what the arsenals of Messina and Palermo may have been like, the *scarium* of Amalfi provides proof that similar open dockyards must have existed in other ports of the Norman domain. There may well have been an open dockyard at Otranto, for instance. Robert Guiscard gathered his naval assets at this Apulian port for his assault on Palermo in 1071.[182] He did so

---

[176] M. Camera, *Memorie Storico-Diplomatiche dell'Antica Città e Ducato di Amalfi* (2 vols, Salerno, 1881), I, p. 32.

[177] A. D'Antuono, *Amalfi, L'Antica Repubblica Marinara* (Salerno, 2000), p. 55.

[178] Camera, *Memorie Storico-Diplomatiche*, I, pp. 32–4; M. Del Treppo and A. Leone, *Amalfi Medioevale* (Naples, 1977), p. 64.

[179] D'Antuono, *Amalfi, L'Antica Repubblica Marinara*, p. 55.

[180] Del Treppo and Leone, *Amalfi Medioevale*, p. 64.

[181] D'Antuono, *Amalfi, L'Antica Repubblica Marinara*, p. 58.

[182] Malaterra, *Deeds of Count Roger*, Bk 2, ch. 43, p. 122; *De rebus gestis Rogerii*, Bk II, ch. XLIII, p. 51.

again for his first Byzantine expedition in 1081,[183] as well as his last in 1084.[184] In the twelfth century, Romuald of Salerno records that Roger II launched his 1147 raid of the Peloponnesos from Otranto.[185] No arsenal has been noted there in the sources, but surely there must have been some facility for repairing and outfitting the Norman fleet. Indeed, there probably was some sort of shipyard in all the major ports of the *Regno*. Al-Idrisi specifically notes a shipyard at Bari, for instance, and says of Gaeta, 'They construct large and small ships there.'[186]

Sailors: recruitment and organization

The war galley was the most labor-intensive military machine of the Middle Ages. Although it had two lateen sails, its primary means of propulsion was provided by multiple files of oarsmen. A light bireme galley, whether it be a *dromōn* of the eleventh century or a *galea* of the twelfth century, required a crew of 144 to 154 trained, able-bodied men including at least two *comiti* (masters), four *nauclerii* (helmsmen), 34 to 40 *supersalienti* (marines) and 104 to 108 *marinarii* (oarsmen).[187] That means that a fleet of 100 galleys required around 15,000 men just to man the ships – a sizable recruiting challenge.

Recruitment
The Normans initially satisfied their need for mariners the same way they acquired their ships: they conscripted them. The Hautevilles drafted sailors together with their ships from conquered ports at sword point, if need be. For example, when Robert Guiscard needed to have his army ferried across the Strait of Messina from Reggio in 1061, Amatus says the duke 'ordered that various kinds of ships and mariners be brought before him'.[188] After taking Bari in 1071, Robert commandeered its citizens and directed them to prepare the necessary maritime muscle to blockade Palermo. And William of Apulia reports, 'The citizens of Bari executed his orders.'[189] At first, the Hautevilles enlisted the bodies they needed to fill their ships from wherever they could obtain them, and they

[183] Malaterra, *Deeds of Count Roger*, Bk 3, ch. 14, pp. 145–6; *De rebus gestis Rogerii*, Bk III, ch. XIV, pp. 65–6.

[184] Malaterra, *Deeds of Count Roger*, Bk 3, ch. 40, pp. 170–1; *De rebus gestis Rogerii*, Bk III, ch. XL, pp. 81–2.

[185] Romuald of Salerno, *Romualdi Salernitani Chronicon*, p. 227.

[186] Al-Idrisi, *La première géographie de l'Occident*, V, 2, pp. 377, 382–3.

[187] Pryor and Jeffreys, *Dromōn*, pp. 254–61; J. Pryor, 'The galleys of Charles I of Anjou, King of Sicily: ca. 1269–84', *Studies in Medieval and Renaissance History*, XIV (1993), pp. 33–103, especially 81–9.

[188] Amatus, *History of the Normans*, Bk V, ch. 19, pp. 139–40; *Storia de' Normanni*, Bk V, ch. XIX, pp. 237–8. 'Adont comanda que diverse maniere de navie et de mariniers venissent devant la soë presence.'

[189] William of Apulia, *La Geste de Robert Guiscard*, Bk III, line 187, pp. 174–5. 'Actu Barenses huius praecepta secuti.'

probably were neither very discriminating nor very temperate in their demands. When Robert was trying to encourage recalcitrant recruits to join him on the 1084 expedition to the Balkans, William of Apulia relates that 'the duke reinforced his gentle persuasions with threats, and forced many to go'.[190] Anna Comnena is less tactful: 'From all quarters of Lombardy and Apulia he gathered them, over age and under age, pitiable objects who had never seen armor even in their dreams.'[191] While the crews of the first Norman fleets were not slaves, they probably were not enthusiastic participants either.

These incidents of *ad hoc* extortions of manpower from coastal communities to support Norman naval enterprises during the era of conquest eventually became regularized into a quota system much like that for ships described earlier. Repeated demands for mariners to meet the exigencies of the conquest created precedents, which ultimately became codified after Norman suzerainty became established. The quota for sailors began to appear in ducal or royal diplomas as the *datium marinariorum*. A May 1131 charter of Roger II in favor of San Salvatore of Messina is a case in point. It exempted 40 of the monastery's sailors from the *datium marinariorum*.[192] The port cities of the *Regno* probably bore the brunt of the burden, but this exaction was also assessed on certain grants of land. Frederick II's diploma of May 1209 on behalf of Nicosia (mentioned earlier) reveals that the grant of Migeti to the city by William II entailed an obligation to provide 'three hundred sailors minus four' to the royal fleet.[193] Similarly, a charter of William I, dated May 1160, assessed a contribution of 250 mariners to the fleet annually from the citizens of Caltagirone for the concessions of Judica and Fatanaxim granted by his father, Roger II.[194] Unless otherwise exempted, even ecclesiastical institutions were expected to supply sailors. Until spared by William II's privilege of November 1177, the bishop of Lipari and Patti had to provide 20 mariners annually, for instance.[195] In fact, Graham Loud has determined that 'such concessions should be seen as decidedly unusual'.[196]

Finally, individual Norman barons were also held responsible under feudal obligation to provide manpower for the fleet. The *quaternus magne expeditionis*, now known as the *Catalogus Baronum*, contains several references to a *custodia*

---

[190] William of Apulia, *La Geste de Robert Guiscard*, Bk IV, lines 131–3, p. 210. '… *sed verba minantia blandis dux addens precibus, multos properare coegit.*' (English translation by G. A. Loud at www.leeds.ac.uk/history/weblearning/MedievalHistoryTextCentre/medievalTexts/html.)

[191] Anna Comnena, *Alexiad*, p. 65; *Alexiade*, I, Bk I, ch. XIV, p. 52.

[192] Caspar, *Roger II*, Reg. no. 69, p. 511; R. Starraba, *I Diplomi della Cattedrale di Messina* (Palermo, 1888), Pt II, no. II, pp. 342–7. (Starraba dates the diploma to May 1130, but Caspar correctly places it in 1131, after Roger's coronation, since it is obviously a royal charter.)

[193] Koch, *Die Urkunden Friedrichs II*, no. 93, pp. 181–3. '… *tricentos marinarios minus quator* …'

[194] *Guillelmi I. Regis Diplomata*, no. 29, pp. 78–9; Kehr, *Urkunden*, no. 16, pp. 434–6.

[195] Kehr, *Urkunden*, no. 24, pp. 444–5.

[196] G. A. Loud, *The Latin Church in Norman Italy* (Cambridge, 2007), pp. 359–60.

maritima (coastal watch).[197] Designated fief-holders were required to supply personnel to man watch towers along the southern littoral of Italy. There is even an entry requiring a noble of Policastro near Salerno to fulfill his feudal obligation by serving on a galley: 'Jordan, as it is said, holds seven villeins and performs his duty on a galley.'[198] The fact that there are few other such notations in the *Catalogus Baronum* can be explained by the nature of the document. Begun under Roger II, it was an inventory of military obligations owed to the crown in the duchy of Apulia and the principality of Capua only.[199] During the *Regno*, the royal fleet was based almost exclusively out of Sicily. Therefore, as a matter of practical necessity, most of the manpower would have had to come from the island. Moreover, medieval rulers had no modern concept of an 'army' and a 'navy'. In other words, they did not view naval service as a separate branch of the armed forces like modern sovereigns do. Rather, the fleet was regarded simply as a component of the realm's overall military capability. Thus, some of the entries listed in the *Catalogus Baronum* could well have been intended to support naval requirements. There is no way of knowing.

While it is assumed that the *datium marinariorum* fell most heavily upon the port cities of the Norman kingdom, the dearth of documentary evidence attesting to that presumption is dismaying. The charters detailing Caltagirone's assessment may offer some clues as to why. The original charter concerning Caltagirone, now lost, was not an assessment for the royal fleet at all. It was a privilege from Roger II, dated 1 September 1143, which conceded to the citizens of Caltagirone the nearby territory of Judica,[200] conquered by the 'Great Count' in 1076.[201] As far as it is known, there was no other *quid pro quo* than the 40,000 *tarì* price cited. It was not until William I's charter of May 1160 that the price for Judica, plus an additional property called Fatanaxim, was adjusted to 5,000 *tarì* annually and the required service of 250 sailors per year was added.[202] William II confirmed the concession in August 1182.[203] Frederick II confirmed it again in February 1202 and reduced the annual requirement of mariners from 250 to 150.[204] In the late eighteenth century, the Sicilian historian Rosario Gregorio found still another confirmation of the privilege in the archives of Caltagirone, this one from Conrad IV in 1254.[205] The point here is that the citizens of Caltagirone were motivated to preserve the privilege, even going to the extent of petitioning

---

[197] *Catalogus Baronum*, pp. 33–8.
[198] *Catalogus Baronum*, p. 106. 'Jordanus sicut dixit tenet villanos septem et serviet de officio suo in galeis.'
[199] *Catalogus Baronum*, p. XV.
[200] Kehr, *Urkunden*, no. 9, pp. 423–4.
[201] Malaterra, *Deeds of Count Roger*, Bk 3, ch. 10, p. 140; *De rebus gestis Rogerii*, Bk III, ch. X, p. 62.
[202] *Guillelmi I. Regis Diplomata*, no. 29, pp. 78–9; Kehr, *Urkunden*, no. 16, pp. 434–6.
[203] Kehr, *Urkunden*, no. 27, pp. 452–3.
[204] Koch, *Die Urkunden Friedrichs II*, no. 40, pp. 81–3.
[205] Gregorio, *Considerazioni supra la storia di Sicilia*, II, p. 384.

several confirmations. They wanted to conserve their claim to the conceded land. Port cities such as Catania, Syracuse, Mazara, Trapani, etc., would have had no such inclination, because, in all probability, they would have been expected to contribute maritime manpower as a duty incumbent upon a maritime city of the realm. So if the royal chancery had lost documents detailing these obligations, such as might have occurred during the pillaging of the palace in 1161,[206] the seafaring cities would not have been eager to hold on to their copies.

Moreover, there is ample evidence that once the conquest of Sicily was well under way Roger I relied heavily on the conquered Muslim enclaves of the island to fill the ranks of both his land and naval forces. Initially, these cadres of Muslim men were probably raised as part of an annual tribute demanded of the conquered communities of the island. The Latin chroniclers provide plentiful testimony that 'Saracens' formed the nucleus of Roger's military. Malaterra reported that 'many thousands of Saracens' were among Roger's forces at the siege of Cosenza in 1091.[207] He made virtually the same observation for the investment of Castrovillari in 1094.[208] And, at the siege of Capua in 1098, the chronicler claimed that the 'Saracens constituted the largest part of his army'.[209] Eadmer of Canterbury, St Anselm's biographer, who was in the archbishop's entourage at the siege of Capua, provided this eyewitness account: 'There were indeed some pagans [Saracens], for the count of Sicily, a vassal of duke Roger, had brought many thousands of them with him on the expedition.'[210] Roger, thus, almost certainly incorporated large numbers of Muslims from the conquered territories of Sicily into his naval forces. His son, Roger II, continued the practice, though it is likely he paid for their services. Ibn abi Dinar writes, 'The armadas of this king [Roger II] were full of Muslims and of Franks: with which he took many Muslim lands.'[211] Later, he confirms Muslims were present in the Sicilian armada that conquered Jerba in 1135.[212] Muslim archers must have been a particularly prized element on the decks of Roger's ships. Albert of Aachen provides an indication of their crucial role in his description of the fleet that transported Roger's mother, Adelaide, to her nuptials in the Latin Kingdom in 1113: 'In one of the seven ships Saracen men, who were very strong archers and glittered with the brilliance of their precious garments, were brought as a gift for the king, and

---

[206] 'Hugo Falcandus', *History of the Tyrants of Sicily*, p. 109; *Liber de Regno Sicilie*, p. 56.

[207] Malaterra, *Deeds of Count Roger*, Bk 4, ch. 17, p. 194; *De rebus gestis Rogerii*, Bk IV, ch. XVII, p. 96. '... *multa Saracenorum millia...*'

[208] Malaterra, *Deeds of Count Roger*, Bk 4, ch. 22, p. 200; *De rebus gestis Rogerii*, Bk IV, ch. XXII, p. 100. '... *multa millia Saracenorum...*'

[209] Malaterra, *Deeds of Count Roger*, Bk 4, ch. 26, p. 208; *De rebus gestis Rogerii*, Bk IV, ch. XXVI, p. 104. '... *Saracenorum, quorum maxima pars exercitui intererat.*'

[210] Eadmer, *Life of St Anselm*, trans. R. Southern (London, 1962), pp. 111–12. '*Siquidem nonnulli talium [Paganorum]; nam eorum multa milia in ipsam expeditionem secum adduxerat homo ducis Rogerius comes de Sicilia.*'

[211] Ibn abi Dinar, *BAS*, II, p. 288.

[212] Ibn abi Dinar, *BAS*, II, pp. 291–2.

their skill at archery was considered inferior to none in the region of Jerusalem.'[213] In fact, flotillas from Sicily were undoubtedly crewed mostly with 'Saracens'.

Feudal obligation and outright conscription were not the only means by which the Normans recruited crew complements for their ships. The lure of largesse from the royal fisc attracted many to the king's galleys, particularly in the latter half of the twelfth century. Indeed, it seems most mariners, whether bound by feudal service or volunteers, were recompensed by the crown. King Tancred's 1191 concession to Gaeta pledged that its sailors serving in the royal fleet would 'receive the same [pay] as the mariners of galleys armed in the principality of Salerno'.[214] Furthermore, the Normans were not above renting the manpower they needed. Even in the era of conquest, the Hautevilles hired mercenaries. William of Apulia recounts how Ragusan archers prevented a Norman rout at the hands of the Venetians before the walls of Durazzo in 1081: 'The men from Ragusa and Dalmatia who accompanied the duke covered the sea with flights of arrows, but did not dare to take their ships very far from the harbour.'[215] Additional anecdotal evidence suggests that a large component of mercenary mariners also served the Kingdom of Sicily. William II, in particular, tapped the reservoirs of the royal treasury to the limit to man the ambitious undertakings of his reign. Niketas Choniates describes William's recruitment effort for the expedition against the Byzantine Empire in 1185: 'Marshaling his military forces in full array, he selected a large number of mercenaries whom he enthused with large stipends and swollen promises and thus enrolled thousands of knights.'[216] Eustathios of Thessaloniki seconds the sentiment: '... there was a movement of forces mustered by the Sicilian and enrolling themselves under his leadership.'[217]

For some, the mere promise of plunder was sufficient to enlist their participation in the crown's expeditions. Indeed, booty was a major form of compensation throughout the era everywhere. Even when the city of Mahdiyah capitulated unconditionally to George of Antioch in 1148, he was compelled to allow the members of his expedition, presumably including ships' crews, at least two hours of looting before declaring *aman*.[218] It was expected. Every enterprise must have attracted significant numbers of freebooters whose only enticement was a share of the spoils. Eustathios of Thessaloniki insists that the pirate Siphantos and

---

[213] Albert of Aachen, *Historia Ierosolimitana*, Bk XII, ch. 13, pp. 842–5. '*In una de septem nauibus uiri Sarraceni et sagittarii fortissimi, claritate preciosarum uestium fulgentes, inerant, dono regi adducti, et qui nullis in regione Ierusalem sagittandi arte inferiores haberentur.*'

[214] *Tancredi et Willelmi III Regum Diplomata*, no. 18, p. 45. '*... sicut recipiunt eas alii marinarii galearum, que armabuntur in principatu Salerni.*'

[215] William of Apulia, *La Geste de Robert Guiscard*, Bk IV, lines 302–4, p. 220. '*Gens comitata ducem cum Dalmaticis Ragusea telorum crebis consternit iactibus aequor; non tamen a portu procul audent ducere naves.*' (English translation by G. A. Loud at www.leeds.ac.uk/history/weblearning/MedievalHistoryTextCentre/medievalTexts/html.)

[216] Niketas Choniates, *O City of Byzantium!*, p. 164.

[217] Eustathios of Thessaloniki, *Capture of Thessaloniki*, ch. 52, p. 63.

[218] Ibn al-Athir, *BAS*, I, p. 473; *Chronicle of Ibn al-Athir, Part 2*, p. 19.

the crews of his ships who joined the Sicilian assault on Thessaloniki in 1185 'were not receiving anything from the king, but put their trust in the gifts of fortune'.[219] Indeed, piracy, state-sponsored or otherwise, was a burgeoning business of the period eagerly pursued by the inhabitants of all seafaring cities, those of the *Regno* included. Donald Matthew's assessment of the prevailing ethos seems particularly apropos:

> Royal expeditions against the Greeks or Muslims were only conceivable because the sailors of the kingdom were already engaged in enterprises of their own requiring skill, audacity and an eye to the main chance. To this extent, the king's most important and elaborate military adventures did not have so much to be paid in full by taxation, as launched with public enthusiasm in the expectation of considerable profit. Royal summons to battle under William II may therefore have been greeted enthusiastically by his subjects, not resisted as unwelcome duty.[220]

Organization

A clear picture of the fleet's command structure is also elusive. There is no extant organizational chart for the Norman navy. Modern historians have been left to puzzle out paltry pieces of information from obscure titles styled on royal diplomas in order to divine the duties of court dignitaries associated with the fleet. This has led to the sort of speculation adopted by Evelyn Jamison, the doyenne of Italo-Norman history, which assumes that the designation *amiratus* implies overall command of the fleet.[221] Léon-Robert Ménager counters that notion by correctly pointing out that no document exists that expressly delineates command of the fleet as a primary duty of the *amiratus*.[222] Instead, Ménager's rather pedantic study of Norman court titles has led him to conclude that the dignity *amiratus* was merely a Latinization of the Arabic word *amīr* for 'emir' ('commander') and that the official who bore the title, at least under King Roger, was the equivalent of a 'first minister'.[223] Indeed, medieval Muslim scholars such as al-Maqrizi most often refer to such an official as a 'vizier',[224] defined by Arabist D. S. Richards as 'first minister of the civilian bureaucracy'.[225] Accordingly, Ménager assumes that the *amiratus* had no official connection to the fleet: 'We need first of all to clearly settle a point: the *amirati* are not admirals. Nothing in the exercise of their responsibility, nothing in the past and in the semantic context of the term justifies such a translation.'[226] Unfortunately, the French academic's treatise on the subject amounts to little more than a myopic exercise

[219] Eustathios of Thessaloniki, *Capture of Thessaloniki*, ch. 138, p. 151.

[220] Matthew, *Norman Kingdom of Sicily*, p. 262.

[221] E. Jamison, *Admiral Eugenius of Sicily, his life and work* (London, 1975), p. 33.

[222] Ménager, *Amiratus*, pp. 79–80.

[223] Ménager, *Amiratus*, pp. 51–2.

[224] Al-Maqrizi, translated by Johns in *Arabic Administration in Norman Sicily*, pp. 80–2.

[225] Richards, *Chronicle of Ibn al-Athir, Part I*, p. 8.

[226] Ménager, *Amiratus*, p. 80.

in philology, which overlooks the duties actually performed by those holding the title. The principal, overriding responsibility of the first minister was to ensure the survival of the kingdom against its many persistent enemies and, since it was essentially an island kingdom, his main tool for accomplishing that task was the fleet. That is why nearly every first minister who bore some form of the title *amiratus*, from Christodoulos to Margaritus, had at some point commanded at least one major naval expedition. Hence, the title eventually became associated with command of the fleet. This was made readily apparent when William II bestowed the dignity *regii fortunati stolii amiratus* ('Admiral of the Blessed Royal Fleet') on Walter of Moac in 1177.[227]

In the beginning, it is true that the position had little to do with the fleet. The first *amiratus* was a Norman knight named Robert whom Guiscard installed in Palermo as a military governor following the city's capitulation in 1072. The duke dubbed the official 'amiratus', meaning 'emir', in deference to his new subjects.[228] A successor named Peter Bido, probably appointed by Roger, appears on two 1086 diplomas with the title *armerati Palermi*.[229] Hiroshi Takayama, an expert on the *Regno's* governmental practices, surmises that he was only a local official responsible for the administration of Palermo and its immediate environs.[230] By the time Christodoulos appeared with the title in 1107,[231] the duties of the position had expanded to include the administration of all Sicily and Calabria.[232] That being said, he seems to have been nothing more than a high-level bureaucrat, having little or no involvement with the fleet. It is only after George of Antioch defected to the Sicilian court from the Zirid emirate centered at Mahdiyah in 1108/9 that the office began to take on a naval aspect.[233] George became Christodoulos' right-hand man on the eve of Norman naval expansion in the central Mediterranean. The disastrous 1123 attempt on Mahdiyah was the first known naval experience for either man. It was also the last for Christodoulos, probably because, as the overall commander of the expedition, he bore the brunt of the blame for its failure.[234] George, on the other hand, saw his career soar along with the interventionist naval strategy of his sovereign. Indeed, Roger II's drive to seize the coast of Ifriqiyah and the eastern Maghrib was, no doubt, inspired by the man who would eventually become his 'maximus ammiratus' ('supreme admiral').[235] George's many exploits at the head of victorious Norman fleets did much to give the title *amiratus* the connotation of 'naval commander'.

---

227 Ménager, *Amiratus*, p. 94, note 4.
228 William of Apulia, *La Geste de Robert Guiscard*, Bk III, lines 340–3, pp. 182–3.
229 L.-R. Ménager, *Recueil des Actes des Ducs Normands d'Italie (1046–1127), I: Les Premiers Ducs (1046–1087)* (Bari, 1980), no. 52–3, pp. 181–4.
230 Takayama, *Administration of the Norman Kingdom of Sicily*, p. 36.
231 *Rogerii II. Regis Diplomata Latina*, no. 1, pp. 3–4.
232 Jamison, *Admiral Eugenius*, p. 33.
233 Al-Maqrizi, translated by Johns in *Arabic Administration in Norman Sicily*, p. 81.
234 Johns, *Arabic Administration in Norman Sicily*, p. 74.
235 Alexander of Telese, *Ystoria Rogerii regis Sicilie*, Bk II, ch. 8, p. 27.

His successor as fleet commander, Philip of Mahdiyah, was a converted Muslim who extended the concept of a key minister with ties to Muslim North Africa capable of leading naval enterprises. He orchestrated the successful capture of Bona in 1153 and, even though his career ended in flames on suspicion of being an apostate,[236] the Sicilian crown's predilection for naval commanders of Muslim extraction did not end there. When Mahdiyah was besieged by the Almohads in 1159, William I dispatched Peter the Caid, a Muslim by birth, to the rescue at the head of the Sicilian fleet.[237] Despite the failure of the effort, William soon promoted Peter to master chamberlain and, on his death bed, elevated the eunuch to first among *familiares Regis* – in effect, prime minister.[238] Following William's demise, palace intrigue forced Peter to flee. 'Hugo Falcandus' concurs with Romuald of Salerno, who contends that he defected 'to the king of the Almohads.'[239] The Latin sources say no more of him, but Muslim chroniclers pick up the thread of his story and go on to portray a brilliant career as the naval commander for Abu Yusuf Ya'qub ibn Abd al-Mum'in, the Almohad caliph of Morocco. Ibn Khaldun tells the tale of Ahmad as-Siqilli ('Ahmad the Sicilian') who, having been taken prisoner as a youth during the Norman capture of Jerba in 1135, subsequently served in the court of the Christian ruler of Sicily. The Arab scholar tells how Ahmad later fled Sicily out of fear for his life following the sovereign's death and eventually found employment with Yusuf. 'He [the caliph] entrusted him with the command of his fleets,' recounts Ibn Khaldun, 'and thus he [Ahmad] distinguished himself in the *jihad* against the nations of Christendom.'[240] Michele Amari has convincingly identified Ahmad as-Siqilli as none other than Peter the Caid.[241] The point here is that Peter the Caid was an accomplished naval commander who seamlessly transitioned from a Sicilian naval system to an Almohad one. Moreover, he apparently did so with great success. Ibn Khaldun makes the grandiose statement: 'In his [Ahmad's] time, the fleets of the Muslims reached a size and fame which they attained neither before nor since.'[242] All of this begs the question: Was the Sicilian fleet, at least in the early stages of the *Regno*, organized in a manner similar to the Muslim fleets of the Western Mediterranean? Given the heavy Muslim influence on the Norman court through the reigns of the first two kings of Sicily, it certainly seems so.

---

[236] Ibn al-Athir, *BAS*, I, p. 479; *Chronicle of Ibn al-Athir, Part 2*, pp. 63–4; Ibn Khaldun, *BAS*, II, p. 229; Romuald of Salerno, *Romualdi Salernitani Chronicon*, pp. 234–6.

[237] 'Hugo Falcandus', *History of the Tyrants of Sicily*, p. 78; *Liber de Regno Sicilie*, p. 25; Romuald of Salerno, *Romualdi Salernitani Chronicon*, p. 242.

[238] 'Hugo Falcandus', *History of the Tyrants of Sicily*, pp. 133, 137–9; *Liber de Regno Sicilie*, pp. 83, 88–90.

[239] 'Hugo Falcandus', *History of the Tyrants of Sicily*, pp. 146–7; *Liber de Regno Sicilie*, pp. 97–9; Romuald of Salerno, *Romualdi Salernitani Chronicon*, p. 254. '... ad Masmordorum regem.'

[240] Ibn Khaldun, translated by Johns in *Arabic Administration in Norman Sicily*, p. 227.

[241] Amari, *Storia dei Musulmani di Sicilia*, III, pp. 505–506.

[242] Ibn Khaldun, translated by Johns in *Arabic Administration in Norman Sicily*, p. 227.

Therefore, Ibn Khaldun's thumbnail description of the Muslim admiralty of the Maghrib at the time is most germane to the discussion of the Sicilian fleet's command structure:

> The fleet was assembled from all provinces. Each region where ships were used contributed one unit under the supervision of a commander in charge of everything connected with fighting, weapons and combatants alike. There was also a captain who directed the movement of the fleet, using either the wind or oars. He also directed its anchoring in port. When the whole fleet was assembled for a large-scale raid or for important government business, it was manned in its home port. The ruler loaded it with men from his best troops and clients, and placed them under the supervision of one commander, who belonged to the highest class of the people of this realm and to whom all were responsible. He then sent them off, and awaited their victorious return with booty.[243]

It was not until William II's majority and the return to the expansionist policies of Roger II that the notion of an *amiratus*/fleet commander once again came to the fore. It did so in a very overt manner with the elevation of Walter of Moac. Not only was he designated as *regii fortunati stolii amiratus* in 1177, but his title was expanded in 1178 to *regii fortunati stolii ammiratus et magister regie duane baronum et de secretis* ('Admiral of the Blessed Royal Fleet and Master of the Royal Office of Barons and the Office of Private Matters').[244] Takayama defines the *duana de secretis* essentially as the royal office of land management for Sicily and Calabria, and the *duana baronum* as the office that performs the same function for the royal demesne in southern Italy, save Calabria. In other words, by the reign of William 'the Good', the minister who commanded the fleet may also have controlled many of the purse strings by which the fleet was funded. Moreover, the *amiratus* may now, at the pleasure of the king, have had oversight not only of royal revenues but also the ship and personnel quotas used to arm the armadas of the realm. The commander of the fleet, thus, continued to be a key officer in the royal administration, but the title of *amiratus* had most definitely become associated with command of the fleet in the later days of the Norman regime in Sicily.[245] Margaritus of Brindisi evidently inherited at least the mantle of fleet commander and held it until the end of the Hauteville dynasty. He bore the title *Dei et regia gratia comes Malte et victoriosus regii stolii amiratus* ('By grace of God and King, Count of Malta and Admiral of the Victorious Royal Fleet').[246]

There is no document from the Norman era that delineates the actual duties of the *amiratus*; however, the decrees of Frederick II may provide some clues, since it has already been well-established that the emperor reinvigor-

[243] Ibn Khaldun, *Muqaddimah*, pp. 209–10.
[244] Jamison, *Admiral Eugenius*, Appendix II, no. 7, p. 336.
[245] Takayama, *Administration of the Norman Kingdom of Sicily*, pp. 131–5, 152–5.
[246] Garufi, 'Margarito di Brindisi Conte di Malta e Ammiraglio del Re di Sicilia', doc. no. I, p. 280.

ated Norman administrative practices (see the section entitled 'The resurgence of Sicilian sea power under Frederick II' in Chapter 5). So, from the evidence of the *Capitula pertinentia ad Officium Ammiratae*, it is reasonable to assume that the Norman *amiratus* was probably authorized to oversee the operation of the realm's arsenals, to administer crown-sponsored piracy by issuing letters of marque, to ensure the fleet was properly manned, to assign galley commanders, to dispense justice within the naval forces and to request appropriate funding for fleet expenditures including pay and provisions.[247] In addition, an 8 April 1240 directive from Frederick shows that the admiral was also responsible for provisioning both the fleet and the arsenals with all the necessary matériel and equipment.[248] Another imperial document, dated 16 December 1239, furnishes some indication as to how the admiral was expected to acquire fleet funding. It mentions an 'assisam galee' ('galley tax'), an 'assise lignaminum' ('wood tax') and the 'marinaria' collected by 'doanam nostram' ('our *duana* – apparently referring to the *duana de secretis* and the *duana baronum* established during the Norman era).[249] Under Frederick, the admiral then obtained fleet funding from these two offices through the royal curia. In Norman times, the admiral may even have controlled these offices directly.[250]

Little is known of the naval chain of command between the *amiratus* and the ordinary galley oarsman. This is probably because, judging from Ibn Khaldun's description of contemporary Muslim naval command structure, it was rather simplified. The concept of a large military bureaucracy is an invention of more modern times. The *amiratus* doubtless depended on small magistracies like the *Comitum Galeae Messanae* to administer the *datium marinariorum* for collecting the levies in money, men and materials needed to equip the fleet.[251] Beneath them were the *portulani* responsible for the management of the realm's harbors and the security of the coasts.[252] There may even have been administrators of naval districts who supervised shipyards and arsenals like the *prothontini* of the Hohenstaufen and Aragonese periods. Matteo Camera noted that such officers existed in Amalfi, for instance.[253]

Operationally, a squadron commander may have served beneath the *amiratus* under the nom de guerre *comes galearum* (count of galleys). The position could

247 Huillard-Bréholles, *Historia Diplomatica Friderici Secundi*, V, Pt 1, pp. 577–83.
248 Huillard-Bréholles, *Historia Diplomatica Friderici Secundi*, V, Pt 2, p. 885.
249 Huillard-Bréholles, *Historia Diplomatica Friderici Secundi*, V, Pt 1, pp. 588–92, especially 590–1.
250 Mott, *Sea Power in the Medieval Mediterranean*, p. 69; Takayama, *Administration of the Norman Kingdom of Sicily*, p. 131.
251 Cusa, *Diplomi greci et arabi di Sicilia*, no. II, pp. 368–71. See also Gregorio, *Considerazioni supra la storia di Sicilia*, II, p. 83, note 19.
252 Minieri Riccio, *Saggio di Codice Diplomatico*, I, no. 6, pp. 6–9. See also Mott, *Sea Power in the Medieval Mediterranean*, p. 75.
253 Camera, *Memorie Storico-Diplomatiche*, I, pp. 526–8.

have evolved from the Byzantine *komēs*, delineated by the Emperor Leo VI in the *Naumachika* as an officer in charge of three to five galleys.[254] For instance, when Robert Guiscard assigned five galleys to each of his sons prior to the Battle of Corfu in 1084, he was using each of them as a sort of *comes galearum*.[255] Then, of course, there were the two *comiti* (ship's masters) for each galley. Under these were the *nauclerii* (helmsmen), *protelati* (stroke oarsmen), *prodei* (prow hands), *palamarii* (mooring hands), *supersalienti* (marines) and, finally, the *marinarii* (oarsmen). Sailors on transport sailing vessels were most often called *nautae*.[256]

Strategy and tactics

John Pryor has written the perfect preamble to any discussion on medieval naval strategy and tactics: 'Appreciation of the fact that all medieval naval warfare was essentially coastal and amphibious warfare is important since many of the recommended strategies and tactics were devised in that context.'[257] Much of the success enjoyed by the Normans in the Mediterranean in the eleventh and twelfth centuries stems from the fact that they understood and embraced this basic concept. Their heritage as a people proficient in land warfare gave them an intuitive grasp of the critical importance of seizing and maintaining control of the land adjacent to seas, because as Pryor has previously pointed out, 'Control of the land meant control of the sea.'[258] From the very beginning, their whole strategy for conquering the central Mediterranean was founded upon that fundamental principle. The Normans quickly learned that in order to subjugate southern Italy and Sicily, they would have to subdue the coastal cities. And, in order to do that they would need to acquire and employ ships.

Strategy

The Norman strategy of using their fleets to capture and control the coastal areas of the central Mediterranean depended on their execution of four fundamental naval operations: the amphibious assault, the blockade, the coastal watch and the engagement at sea.

The challenge of conquering the island of Sicily convinced the Normans that they would have to master the art of the amphibious assault. Their previous experience was almost exclusively with land warfare where they could use their

---

[254] Leo VI, *The naval warfare of the Emperor Leo* (*Taktika*, Constitution XIX), *Dromōn*, Appendix Two, par. 25, pp. 494–5; Nikephoros Ouranos, *On fighting at sea*, *Dromōn*, Appendix Five, par. 23, pp. 582–3.

[255] William of Apulia, *La Geste de Robert Guiscard*, Bk V, lines 157–60, pp. 244–5.

[256] Pryor, 'Galleys of Charles I of Anjou, King of Sicily', pp. 81–3.

[257] Pryor and Jeffreys, *Dromōn*, p. 391.

[258] Pryor and Jeffreys, *Dromōn*, p. 390.

vaunted heavy cavalry tactics. So, initially, they viewed ships merely as a means of transporting their knights along with horses and infantry to whatever military objective they had chosen. This was initially how they employed Reggio's ships in 1061: to transport their army across the Strait of Messina so that they could besiege the city of the same name. A Muslim fleet from Palermo employing more specialized warships nearly prevented the Hautevilles from making the crossing, however.[259] They managed do so only by subterfuge, using the cover of darkness. Robert put the lessons of the Sicily campaign to use on a massive scale for his Balkan expeditions in 1081[260] and 1084.[261] He had dozens of vessels specially built and equipped for the purpose.[262] He even contracted with the Dalmatians to provide large transports, crewed by experienced mariners.[263] Concurrently, his younger brother, Roger, had fleets of his own equipped for specific missions, such as the siege of Trapani in 1077,[264] followed by the assault on Syracuse in 1085.[265] And finally, there was the invasion of the Muslim maritime enclave of Malta in 1091.[266]

The fleets of Roger II, guided by George of Antioch, perfected the amphibious assault on the shores of Ifriqiyah and the eastern Maghrib in the first half of the twelfth century while William II made such large-scale naval evolutions emblematic of his reign in its second half. Moreover, all the Hauteville sovereigns engaged in a particularly virulent form of amphibious warfare in order to extend their power and intimidate potential enemies: coastal raiding. Roger II was particularly adept at employing this strategy. Arab writers indicate that Roger's fleets routinely raided the smaller ports of North Africa like Jijel in 1143[267] and Brashk in 1144.[268] And, George of Antioch plagued Greek territories

[259] Amatus, *History of the Normans*, Bk V, ch. 13–16, pp. 138–9; *Storia de' Normanni*, Bk V, ch. XIII–XVI, pp. 234–6; Malaterra, *Deeds of Count Roger*, Bk 2, ch. 8–10, pp. 9–1; *De rebus gestis Rogerii*, Bk II, ch. VIII–X, pp. 31–2.

[260] Anna Comnena, *Alexiad*, p. 69; *Alexiade*, I, Bk I, ch. XVI, p. 56.

[261] Anna Comnena, *Alexiad*, pp. 188–9; *Alexiade*, II, Bk VI, ch. V, pp. 50–1.

[262] Malaterra, *Deeds of Count Roger*, Bk 3, ch. 14, p. 145; *De rebus gestis Rogerii*, Bk III, ch. XIV, pp. 65–6.

[263] William of Apulia, *La Geste de Robert Guiscard*, Bk IV, lines 123–36, pp. 210–11.

[264] Malaterra, *Deeds of Count Roger*, Bk 3, ch. 11, pp. 140–2; *De rebus gestis Rogerii*, Bk III, ch. XI, pp. 62–4.

[265] Malaterra, *Deeds of Count Roger*, Bk 4, ch. 2, pp. 177–9; *De rebus gestis Rogerii*, Bk IV, ch. II, pp. 85–6.

[266] Malaterra, *Deeds of Count Roger*, Bk 4, ch. 16, pp. 192–4; *De rebus gestis Rogerii*, Bk IV, ch. XVI, pp. 94–5.

[267] Al-Idrisi, *BAS*, I, p. 131; *La première géographie de l'Occident*, III, 1, p. 173; Ibn abi Dinar, *BAS*, II, p. 293; Ibn al-Athir, *BAS*, I, pp. 462–3; *Chronicle of Ibn al-Athir, Part I*, pp. 366–7; Ibn Khaldun, *BAS*, II, pp. 222–3.

[268] Al-Idrisi, *BAS*, I, pp. 130–1; *La première géographie de l'Occident*, III, 1, p. 163; Ibn al-Athir, *BAS*, I, p. 463; *Chronicle of Ibn al-Athir, Part I*, p. 375.

so successfully in 1147[269] and 1149[270] that the Emperor Manuel was never able to mount his intended invasion of the *Regno*. William I repeated the stratagem in 1157 by raiding the environs of Constantinople itself, thereby bullying the *basileus* into a peace treaty.[271]

In 1064 the Hautevilles endured an epiphanic experience that impressed upon them the vital importance of the maritime blockade. They failed miserably in their first attempt to reduce Palermo, because there was nothing to prevent the Palermitans from receiving ample revictualing from their coreligionists in North Africa by way of the open harbor. Robert and Roger understood at that point that unless they learned to close off the seaward approaches, sieges of port cities would be ineffective and they would be unable to complete the conquest.[272] The two brothers made no further attempts on Palermo until they had gathered sufficient naval forces to establish a tight blockade of the port. Accordingly, they used Calabrian ships to strangle Bari into submission in 1071 by establishing a seemingly impenetrable cordon of chained ships around the port, cutting off its sea link with Byzantium.[273] Once they gained control of Bari's maritime assets, the Hautevilles then employed them to completely encircle the port of Palermo that same year.[274] Investment by sea was a major tool of Roger II in his effort to subdue rebellious Apulian and Campanian ports like Bari,[275] Amalfi[276] and Naples.[277] And, as shown earlier, William II's fleet orchestrated a spectacularly

---

[269] *Annales Cavenses*, anno 1147, p. 192; Niketas Choniates, *O City of Byzantium!*, p. 43; Andrea Dandolo, *Chronica Per Extensum Descripta*, p. 242; *Historia ducum Veneticorum*, p. 75; *Testi Storici Veneziani*. pp. 12–17; John Kinnamos, *John and Manuel Comnenus*, Bk III, ch. 2, p. 76; Otto of Freising, *Deeds of Frederick Barbarossa*, Bk I, ch. 34, p. 69; *Gesta Frederici*, Bk I, ch. XXXIV, p. 53; Romuald of Salerno, *Romualdi Salernitani Chronicon*, p. 227.

[270] Andrea Dandolo, *Chronica Per Extensum Descripta*, p. 243; Ibn al-Athir, *BAS*, I, p. 476; *Chronicle of Ibn al-Athir*, Part 2, p. 32; *Sigeberti Gemblacensis Chronica*, anno 1148--9, pp. 453–4.

[271] Niketas Choniates, *O City of Byzantium!*, p. 57; Bernardo Maragone, *Annales Pisani*, p. 17; Romuald of Salerno, *Romualdi Salernitani Chronicon*, p. 241.

[272] Amatus, *History of the Normans*, Bk V, ch. 26, p. 143; *Storia de' Normanni*, Bk V, ch. XXVI, pp. 246–8.

[273] Amatus, *History of the Normans*, Bk V, ch. 27, p. 143; *Storia de' Normanni*, Bk V, ch. XXVII, pp. 248–55; Lupus Protospatarius, *Annales*, anno 1071, p. 60; William of Apulia, *La Geste de Robert Guiscard*, Bk II, lines 479–528, pp 158–61.

[274] Amatus, *History of the Normans*, Bk VI, ch. 13, pp. 155–6; *Storia de' Normanni*, Bk VI, ch. XIII, pp. 275–6; Malaterra, *Deeds of Count Roger*, Bk 2, ch. 43, p.122; *De rebus gestis Rogerii*, Bk II, ch. XLIII, p. 51.

[275] Romuald of Salerno, *Romualdi Salernitani Chronicon*, p. 216.

[276] Alexander of Telese, *Ystoria Rogerii regis Sicilie*, Bk II, ch. 8–11, pp. 27–8; *Annales Casinenses*, anno 1131, p. 309; *Annales Cavenses*, anno 1130, p. 191; *Chronica de Ferraria*, anno 1131, p. 18; Falco of Benevento, *Chronicon Beneventanum*, p. 108; Romuald of Salerno, *Romualdi Salernitani Chronicon*, pp. 218–19.

[277] Alexander of Telese, *Ystoria Rogerii regis Sicilie*, Bk II, ch. 62–7, pp. 52–6; *Annales Casinenses*, anno 1134, p. 309; *Annales Cavenses*, anno 1134, p. 191; *Chronica de Ferraria*, anno 1134, p. 20; Falco of Benevento, *Chronicon Beneventanum*, pp. 168–72.

successful siege in 1185 at Thessaloniki by positioning its vessels close enough to the walls for ship-mounted catapults and *ballistae* to pummel the defenders.[278]

Once the coastlines were conquered, the core of Norman naval strategy was to deny those coastal areas to all others unless they paid for the privilege. In doing so, they were able to effectively and profitably dominate the central Mediterranean. The state of nautical technology at the time meant that to deny access to land was to deny foreign flotillas the lifeblood of any medieval galley fleet: fresh water, provisions and shelter from the vagaries of weather. The Normans accomplished this not with ships, because patrolling the sea lanes was simply not a realistic option at the time. The vulnerability of galleys to high winds (velocities in excess of 4–5 on the Beaufort scale: 16–17 knots),[279] slow closing speeds (less than 10 knots)[280] and poor line of sight capability (6 to 10 miles),[281] even from mastheads, made interdiction at sea impracticable. Accordingly, the Normans set up a highly efficient coastal watch system. Roger I probably began it by taking over Byzantine and Saracen watch towers and fortlets along the northeastern corner of Sicily, each no more than two or three miles from the next (see Figures 5 and 6). The *Chronica de Ferraria* bears witness that Roger II expanded it by decreeing that a similar system be maintained through feudal obligation on the southern shores of the Italian Peninsula.[282] The *custodia maritima* (coastal watch) was eventually incorporated into the *Catalogus Baronum*, which was revised in 1168, ensuring that the system endured until late in the Hauteville era.[283]

As far as engagements at sea were concerned, the Normans sensibly sought to avoid them. In the beginning, their relative inexperience at sea naturally prompted them to steer clear of hostile confrontations with enemy fleets. This proved to be a sound strategy because seaborne battles were rarely decisive and often subject to vagaries of weather and chance. After all, as Pryor succinctly puts it, 'The first priority of a *strategos* [commander] was to preserve his own forces intact and then to search for any opportunity or strategy that would enable him to attack the enemy with the least risk to his own forces.'[284] To dare an engagement, even

---

[278] *Annales Casinenses*, anno 1185, p. 313; *Annales Ceccanenses*, anno 1185, p. 287; *Annales Cavenses*, anno 1185, p. 193; Eustathios of Thessaloniki, *Capture of Thessaloniki*, ch. 53, 59, 81, pp. 64–5, 74–5, 98–9; Niketas Choniates, *O City of Byzantium!*, pp. 164–5; 'The old French Continuation of William of Tyre, 1184–1197', ch. 73, p. 74; *La continuation de Guillaume de Tyr (1184–1197)*, ch. 73, pp. 82–3.

[279] J. Pryor, 'Types of ships and their performance capabilities', in *Travels in the Byzantine World: Papers from the Thirty-fourth Spring Symposium of Byzantine Studies*, ed. R. Macrides (Aldershot, 2002), pp. 33–58, especially 47.

[280] Coates, Morrison, Rankov, *Athenian Trireme*, pp. 102, 239–40.

[281] Pryor and Jeffreys, *Dromōn*, pp. 388–9.

[282] *Chronica de Ferraria*, anno 1151, pp. 26–7.

[283] *Catalogus Baronum*, pp. XVII, 33–8.

[284] J. Pryor, 'Byzantium and the Sea: Byzantine Fleets and the History of the Empire in the Age of the Macedonian Emperors, C. 900–1025 CE', in *War at Sea in the Middle Ages and the Renaissance*, eds J. Hattendorf and R. Unger (Woodbridge, 2003), p. 99.

when numerically superior, was to risk a resounding defeat. Pryor was speaking specifically of the Byzantines, but the strategy seemed to have applied to the Normans as well. Their first pitched sea battle against the Venetians during the siege of Durazzo ended in near disaster when Robert's son, Bohemond, recklessly charged the 'sea harbor' that the Venetians had formed by chaining their larger ships together. The much smaller Norman ships, probably *dromōns* or *galeae*, were holed and sunk by heavy projectiles thrown from platforms constructed in the masts of the much taller Venetian vessels.[285] The Normans shunned all contact with the Venetian fleet for the rest of that campaign. In later years, they tended to engage in pitched naval battles only when offered no alternative. In fact, throughout the remainder of their naval operations they mostly adopted the advice espoused by the Emperor Leo VI in Constitution XIX of the *Taktika*:

> You must indeed deal with the enemy through attacks and other practices and stratagems, either with the whole of the naval fleet under you or with part of it. However, without some urgent compelling reason for this, you should not rush into a general engagement. For there are many obstacles [in the workings] of so-called Tyche [Fate] and events in war [are] contrary to expectation.[286]

Tactics

When unavoidably forced into a battle at sea, the Normans waged it much the same as any protagonist of the era. Tactics had changed little since the late Roman period, largely because naval military technology had changed little. There was no ship-killing weapon like a waterline ram or *rostrum*, because the frame-first hull architecture adopted well before the eleventh century obviated the ram's effectiveness.[287] 'Greek fire', useful to the Byzantines in the seventh and eighth centuries, was difficult to acquire and dangerous to deploy.[288] Besides, there is no proof that the Normans ever possessed or used it. Thus, all adversaries were confined to the same basic principles of engagement enunciated by the Emperor Leo VI and various other Byzantine naval tacticians of the ninth and tenth centuries. To begin with, an encounter with an opposing force had to be anticipated in order to seize the initiative, and the best way of doing this was to deploy scouts. Accordingly, the ninth-century treatise on naval warfare composed by Syrianos Magistros prescribed the use of scout ships: 'There should be four of these, two keeping about six miles ahead of the main fleet and the other two in between so that the second group are informed of the disposition of

---

[285] Anna Comnena, *Alexiad*, pp. 137–9; *Alexiade*, I, Bk IV, ch. II, pp. 147–8; Malaterra, *Deeds of Count Roger*, Bk 3, ch. 26, p. 156; *De rebus gestis Rogerii*, Bk III, ch. XXVI, p. 70. See also Manfroni, *Storia della Marina italiana*, I, pp. 126–7.

[286] Leo VI, *The naval warfare of the Emperor Leo* (*Taktika*, Constitution XIX), *Dromōn*, Appendix Two, par. 36, pp. 498–9; Nikephoros Ouranos, *On fighting at sea*, *Dromōn*, Appendix Five, par. 34, pp. 586–7.

[287] Pryor and Jeffreys, *Dromōn*, pp. 134–52.

[288] Pryor, *Dromōn*, Appendix Six, pp. 607–21.

Fig. 13. Battle between two *dromōns* of the eleventh century. This illustration from the eleventh-century *Kynegetika* manuscript of Pseudo-Oppian depicts two *dromōns* embroiled in the kind of close combat typical of medieval sea engagements. (Credit: Ms Gr. 479, fol. 23r from the Biblioteca Nazionale Marciana di Venezia, with the permission of the Art Archive/Gianni Dagli Orti)

the enemy by the former through certain signals which they will have arranged with each other, and should have done the same with the fleet.'[289]

Being thus forewarned of an encounter, the commander could prepare his fleet for battle. This meant drawing up into battle formation. The favored formation was the classic crescent-shaped line abreast, with the flagship in the middle and the larger, more formidable ships at the tips of the horns. From the concave center of the crescent, the commander would theoretically be in a perfect position to watch the battle unfold and signal the horns to envelope the enemy flotilla at the appropriate point.[290] Eventually, all encounters devolved into engagements of individual ships. Folio 23r of the eleventh-century *Kynegetika* manuscript of Pseudo-Oppian (Ms Gr. 479, Biblioteca Marciana of Venice) illustrates two *dromōns* embroiled in this sort of close combat at sea (see Figure 13). The first phase of such engagements was the heavy exchange of missiles, which normally meant arrows or small iron rods (*mues* or *muiai*). These missiles were often

---

[289] Syrianos Magistros, *Naval Battles of Syrianos Magistros*, trans. Jeffreys, *Dromōn*, Appendix One, par. 3, pp. 460–1.
[290] Leo VI, *The naval warfare of the Emperor Leo* (*Taktika*, Constitution XIX), *Dromōn*, Appendix Two, par. 50, pp. 504–5; Nikephoros Ouranos, *On fighting at sea*, *Dromōn*, Appendix Five, par. 48, pp. 592–3.

Fig. 14. Sea combat from the thirteenth century. This miniature from a thirteenth-century manuscript of Vegetius' *De Re Militari* portrays a classic sea engagement between two opposing vessels with crossbows, pikes, grapnels and stone projectiles clearly visible. (Credit: Ms Marlay Add. 1, fol. 86r of the thirteenth century, reproduced here by permission of the Fitzwilliam Museum of Cambridge ©, with all rights reserved)

fired from hand-held crossbows as well as bow-*ballistae* mounted on castles at the prow, stern and either side of the main mast.[291] Once galleys closed on one another, the objective was to immobilize the enemy ship by riding up over the oars with the spur or possibly capsizing the vessel.[292] Additionally, iron caltrops (spiked projectiles) and large stones were frequently dropped from the masts in the hope of holing the hull of the enemy ship.[293] The crews would then seek to couple with the opposing vessel using grappling hooks and pikes. Folio 86r

[291] Leo VI, *The naval warfare of the Emperor Leo* (*Taktika*, Constitution XIX), *Dromōn*, Appendix Two, par. 60, pp. 508–9; Nikephoros Ouranos, *On fighting at sea*, *Dromōn*, Appendix Five, par. 57, pp. 596–7.
[292] Pryor and Jeffreys, *Dromōn*, pp. 143–4.
[293] Leo VI, *The naval warfare of the Emperor Leo* (*Taktika*, Constitution XIX), *Dromōn*, Appendix Two, par. 62, 65, pp. 508–9; Nikephoros Ouranos, *On fighting at sea*, *Dromōn*, Appendix Five, par. 59–60, pp. 596–7.

of Ms Marlay Add. 1, a thirteenth-century Vegetius manuscript in the Fitz-william Museum of Cambridge, clearly depicts such pikes and hooks as well as stones being hurled from masts (see Figure 14). The final phase of the battle was boarding with the resultant hand-to-hand combat invariably determining the outcome of the encounter.[294]

Given the inherent unpredictability of such clashes, the Normans strove, as much as possible, to replicate land-based battle conditions where their fighting skills gave them an edge. The previously described cordon of ships and land bridges that Robert established around the port of Bari in 1068 is a case in point. It was specifically conceived in such a manner so that he could direct his infantry out onto the vessels to augment the crews in case of attack from either the city or the sea (see Map 2).[295] The Normans seemed to instinctively understand that galley warfare was fundamentally coastal in nature. Most of their confrontations with enemy fleets occurred near shores where they enjoyed the presence of their own land forces, such as at Bari in 1071, when Roger I's flotilla attacked and defeated the Byzantine relief fleet under Jocelyn of Molfetta with Guiscard's besieging army looking on,[296] and at Brindisi in 1156, when William I's ships bottled up the Greek fleet in the city's harbor surrounded by the king's ground forces (see Map 9).[297] Roger II, in particular, seemed to grasp that his control of Sicily made his fleet almost invincible when operating in the central Mediter-ranean. After all, the island provided it with an unending supply of water, food and reinforcements, not to mention a coastline of countless safe havens. Sicily was the unsinkable flagship of his fleet. That is why, with few exceptions, like the two raids on the Greek mainland in the 1140s, he limited the activities of his navy to the central Mediterranean.

---

[294] Leo VI, *The naval warfare of the Emperor Leo* (*Taktika*, Constitution XIX), *Dromōn*, Appendix Two, par. 68, pp. 508–11; Nikephoros Ouranos, *On fighting at sea*, *Dromōn*, Appendix Five, par. 62, pp. 596–9; Pryor and Jeffreys, *Dromōn*, pp. 403–4.

[295] Amatus, *History of the Normans*, Bk V, ch. 27, p. 143; *Storia de' Normanni*, Bk V, ch. XXVII, pp. 248–9; Malaterra, *Deeds of Count Roger*, Bk 2, ch. 40, pp. 117–18; *De rebus gestis Rogerii*, Bk II, ch. XL, pp. 48–9; William of Apulia, *La Geste de Robert Guiscard*, Bk II, lines 479–528, pp 158–61.

[296] Amatus, *History of the Normans*, Bk V, ch. 27, p. 145; *Storia de' Normanni*, Bk V, ch. XXVII, pp. 253–4; Malaterra, *Deeds of Count Roger*, Bk 2, ch. 43, pp. 120–2; *De rebus gestis Rogerii*, Bk II, ch. XLIII, pp. 50–1; William of Apulia, *La Geste de Robert Guiscard*, Bk III, lines 112–38, pp 170–3.

[297] *Annales Casinenses*, anno 1156, p. 311; *Annales Ceccanenses*, anno 1156, p. 284; *Chronica de Ferraria*, anno 1156, p. 29; 'Hugo Falcandus', *History of the Tyrants of Sicily*, p. 73; *Liber de Regno Sicilie*, pp. 20–1; John Kinnamos, *John and Manuel Comnenus*, Bk IV, ch. 13, pp. 128–9; Bernardo Maragone, *Annales Pisani*, p. 15; Otto of Freising, *Deeds of Frederick Barbarossa*, Bk II, ch. 49, p. 166; *Gesta Frederici*, Bk II, ch. XLIX, p. 157; Romuald of Salerno, *Romualdi Salernitani Chronicon*, pp. 239–40; William of Tyre, *History of Deeds Done beyond the Sea*, II, Bk 18, ch. 8, p. 250; *Willelmi Tyrensis Chronicon*, Bk 18, ch. 8, p. 821.

Appendix B

The Sources

Curiously, modern historians have largely overlooked this critical aspect of Mediterranean history. There are no major works whatsoever on Norman sea power. The only extant study devoted to the subject is a 104-page booklet produced in German by Willy Cohn a century ago.[1] While Cohn deserves credit for recognizing the significance of the study and identifying valuable sources, his work unfortunately is flawed by almost all accounts. It is basically an amalgamation of narratives on Norman naval engagements excerpted from the Norman chronicles and accompanied by superficial analysis. He devotes little attention to ship types, crew composition, recruitment, naval organization or tactics; and there is almost no mention at all of the impact on the medieval Mediterranean.

Aside from these glaring deficiencies, Cohn's approach was tainted by a number of misconceptions. For instance, he makes the unwarranted assumption that the early Norman conquerors, specifically Robert and Roger de Hauteville, designed and built their own vessels from the very beginning. There is no evidence of this.[2] In fact, the Norman chronicler William of Apulia was probably quite right when he asserted, 'The Norman race had up to this point known nothing of naval warfare.'[3] Cohn also made the peculiar decision to concentrate only on the Sicilian fleets of Roger I and Roger II, based upon the unsubstantiated notion that the fleets of Robert Guiscard and Roger were entirely separate. The premise of separate fleets was invalid. Roger was Robert's vassal. This meant that Roger undoubtedly supplied Robert with ships when called upon. Roger's chronicler, Geoffrey Malaterra, testifies that this was exactly what occurred when Robert mounted his massive expeditions against the Greek empire in the

Note: For the sake of convenience, full initial citations are repeated for all of the sources discussed in this appendix.

[1]   W. Cohn, *Die Geschichte der normannisch-sicilischen Flotte unter der Regierung Rogers I. und Rogers II. (1060–1154)* (Breslau, 1910).
[2]   D. Waley, '"Combined Operations" in Sicily, A.D. 1060–1078', *Papers of the British School at Rome*, XXII (1954), pp. 118–25, especially 119–20.
[3]   William of Apulia, *La Geste de Robert Guiscard*, trans. M. Mathieu (Palermo, 1961), Bk III, lines 132–3, pp. 170–1. '*Gens Normannorum navalis nescia belli hactenus …*' (Translation by G. A. Loud at www.leeds.ac.uk/history/weblearning/MedievalHistoryTextCentre/medievalTexts/html.)

1080s.[4] Moreover, the notion of separate fleets implies the existence of standing navies, something that the Hautevilles were simply not in a position to maintain. Instead, flotillas were gathered for specific undertakings for limited periods of time. Cohn's coverage of Norman naval power during the *Regno* (the Norman Kingdom of Sicily) is stronger, perhaps because he was able to rely on the relatively sound scholarship of Erich Caspar,[5] but, even then, he only dealt with the reign of Roger II, thus leaving out the critical final episode in Norman naval history: the naval exploits of William I and William II and the ultimate collapse of Norman sea power under Tancred of Lecce. Only by studying this final phase may a full understanding be gained of the strategy by which Roger II hoisted Sicilian sea power to its apex and preserved his realm against all comers. It was only when his successors deviated from that strategy that the Hauteville dynasty began its descent to demise.

Ironically, a more comprehensive treatment is provided by the Italian maritime scholar, Camillo Manfroni, who addressed the topic in his monumental *Storia della Marina Italiana* over a decade before Willy Cohn's work.[6] He wove the story of the Normans into a colossal narrative of all the Italian maritime powers of the age, but for those willing to sift it out, his history of Norman sea power is enhanced by the careful analysis of a historian knowledgeable in nautical matters. The result is a more complete picture. In addition to detailed accounts of all known Norman naval engagements, he includes useful appendices on possible ship types, recruitment, fleet organization and strategy. His basic conclusion was that the Normans had simply appropriated the ships and crews they needed for their expeditions from the port cities that they conquered in Byzantine Calabria and Apulia. The work's primary detractions are that his secondary sources are unavoidably antiquated and that the narrative on Norman sea power seems discursive because the passages concerning it are distributed throughout the larger narrative embracing all the great Italian maritime powers.

Even those who have written extensively on the Normans in the south, such as Ferdinand Chalandon and John Julius Norwich, have only touched upon the Normans' use of ships in the course of their historical narratives while providing little accompanying analysis. They have addressed naval power only in passing, simply assuming that it must have been formidable in order to create such a strong island kingdom. In the *Normans in the South*, for instance, Norwich indicates Norman sea power was substantial, but provides no substantiation. He

---

[4]   Geoffrey Malaterra, *The Deeds of Count Roger of Calabria and Sicily and of his brother Duke Robert Guiscard*, trans. K. Wolf (Ann Arbor, 2005), Bk 3, ch. 40, p. 170; *De rebus gestis Rogerii Calabriae et Siciliae comitis et Roberti Guiscardi ducis fratris eius*, ed. E. Pontieri (RIS, 2nd edn, Bologna, 1927--8), Bk III, ch. XL, p. 81.

[5]   E. Caspar, *Roger II. (1101–1154) und die Gründung der Normannisch-sicilischen Monarchie* (Innsbruck, 1904).

[6]   C. Manfroni, *Storia della Marina italiana dalle invasioni barbariche al trattato di Ninfeo, anni di C. 400–1261*, I (3 vols, Livorno, 1899).

simply says, 'Nation and navy were one and inseparable; it is hardly possible to conceive of one without the other.'[7] Moreover, Norwich's capacious two-volume account, *The Normans in the South 1016–1130* and *The Kingdom in the Sun 1130–1194*, is so vivid that it blurs the line between vigorous historical narrative and imaginative storytelling.[8] His effort is, therefore, not totally reliable.

On the other hand, Ferdinand Chalandon's two-volume treatise *Histoire de la Domination Normande en Italie et en Sicile* is more prosaic but extremely well-researched and painstakingly documented.[9] It, thus, furnishes a solid foundation for more targeted research. His use of primary sources is, by far and away, the most wide-ranging and thorough. In fact, his discussion of the contemporary chroniclers is still the most comprehensive of any single study. He provides nearly all the relevant references needed to research the topic along with several very useful appendices on Norman administration and military organization. Furthermore, his objectivity and clear chronological narrative offer the best available background on the Norman experience in the central Mediterranean. His study remains fundamental. Nevertheless, he rarely dwells on maritime matters and often gives short shrift to sea engagements.

Those few scholars who have chosen to tackle the maritime exploits of the Normans in the Mediterranean have long decried the dearth of documentary evidence on the subject. Matthew Bennett, who wrote an article entitled 'Norman Naval Activity in the Mediterranean c. 1060–c. 1108', quips: '[Willy] Cohn's thin hull should have warned me, perhaps.'[10] The reason, of course, is that there are no surviving organizational manuals or maritime decrees from the period setting out how the Norman fleets were to be composed, manned and operated. There is no Norman equivalent to the *Naumachika* ('Concerning naval warfare')[11] of the Byzantine Emperor Leo VI or the *Epitoma Rei Militaris* ('Epitome of Military Science')[12] by Vegetius.

Accordingly, historians have been forced to rely primarily on the narratives of the Norman chroniclers, most of whom were clerics ignorant of things nautical and heavily biased. The lack of impartiality is certainly true of those chroniclers covering the era of conquest. Amatus, a Cassinese monk from Salerno, wrote his *Historia Normannorum* at the behest of Abbot Desiderius to commemorate the achievements of the abbey's two main benefactors at the time: Richard of

---

[7]   J. Norwich, *The Normans in the South, 1016–1130* (London, 1967), p. 291.

[8]   J. Norwich, *The Normans in the South* (London, 1967); *The Kingdom in the Sun, 1130–1194* (London, 1970).

[9]   F. Chalandon, *Histoire de la Domination Normande en Italie et en Sicile* (2 vols, Paris, 1907).

[10]   M. Bennett, 'Norman Naval Activity in the Mediterranean c.1060–c.1108', *Anglo-Norman Studies*, XV (1993), pp. 41–58, especially 43.

[11]   A. Dain, ed., *Naumachica partim Adhuc Inedita in unum nunc primum congessit et indice auxit Alphonsus Dain* (Paris, 1943).

[12]   Vegetius, *Epitome of Military Science*, trans. N. P. Milner (Liverpool, 1993).

Capua and Robert Guiscard.[13] William of Apulia, probably a Lombard in the court of Roger Borsa, was commissioned by the latter to compose the *Gesta Roberti Wiscardi*, extolling the exploits of his father.[14] And Geoffrey Malaterra was a Norman monk at the monastery of St Agata in Catania when his bishop, a certain Angerius appointed by Count Roger, sponsored him to write *De rebus gestis Rogerii Calabriae et Siciliae comitis et Roberti Guiscardi ducis fratris eius*.[15]

The raconteurs of King Roger's reign are hardly more reliable. First of all, none of them focused on the use of sea power. Falco of Benevento, Alexander of Telese and Romuald of Salerno all concentrated almost exclusively on the king's struggles with Norman rebels often allied with the pope and his ongoing efforts to defend his kingdom against the intrusions of the German emperor. They paid little attention to the realm's maritime clashes with the Byzantine Empire and almost none at all to Roger's bid to control the Maghrib coast of North Africa. Moreover, like their predecessors, the objectivity of the later Norman chroniclers must be called into question. Alexander of Telese, the abbot of San Salvatore of Telese, was commissioned to compose the *Ystoria Rogerii regis Sicilie Calabrie atque Apulie* by the Countess Matilda, the king's sister.[16] The *Chronicon Beneventanum*,[17] which also detailed Roger's elevation to sovereign of all southern Italy as well as Sicily, was written by Falco of Benevento, a Lombard partisan who was vociferously anti-Norman.[18] Romuald, archbishop of Salerno, was a member of the royal court from 1161 to 1181 and played an active role in its intrigues.[19] His *Chronicon*, therefore, often seems contrived to commend his own contributions to the kingdom rather than maintain some semblance of detachment.[20]

For the final chapter of the Hauteville dynasty, there are, in addition to Romuald of Salerno, the so-called 'Hugo Falcandus' and Peter of Eboli. The anonymous author of the *Liber de Regno Sicilie*, named 'Hugo Falcandus' by historians, was obviously a witness to the inner workings of the court of William I and the early years of William II, but his palpable loathing of nearly everyone

[13] Amatus of Montecassino, *The History of the Normans*, trans. P. Dunbar (Woodbridge, 2004); *Storia de' Normanni*, ed. V. de Bartholomaeis (FSI, Rome, 1935). See also K. Wolf, *Making History: The Normans and Their Historians in Eleventh-Century Italy* (Philadelphia, 1995), p. 88.

[14] William of Apulia, *La Geste de Robert Guiscard*. See also Wolf, *Making History*, pp. 123–4.

[15] Malaterra, *Deeds of Count Roger*, p. 41; *De rebus gestis Rogerii Calabriae*, p. 3. See also E. Albu, *The Normans in their Histories* (Woodbridge, 2001), p. 111.

[16] Alexander of Telese, *Alexandri Telesini abbatis Ystoria Rogerii regis Sicilie, Calabria atque Apulie*, ed. L. De Nava (FSI, Rome, 1991).

[17] Falco of Benevento, *Chronicon Beneventanum*, ed. E. D'Angelo (Florence, 1998).

[18] Chalandon, *Histoire de la Domination Normande*, I, pp. XLI–XLIII.

[19] H. Houben, *Roger II of Sicily, A Ruler between East and West*, trans. G. A. Loud and D. Milburn (Cambridge, 1992), p. 183.

[20] Romuald of Salerno, *Romualdi Salernitani Chronicon*, ed. C. Garufi (RIS, 2nd edn, vol. VII, Citta di Castello, 1935).

involved, especially Maio of Bari, the first minister of William I, tainted much of what he wrote.[21] Similarly, Peter of Eboli's account of the last days of Norman rule, the *Carmen de Rebus Siculis*, was colored by his self-confessed antipathy toward Tancred of Lecce, the final Hauteville claimant to the monarchy.[22]

Bearing these detractions in mind, all of the above chroniclers were in a position to be well informed of the events about which they wrote and, therefore, serve as useful contemporary sources. They all describe Norman naval activity in varying detail. Amatus of Montecassino,[23] Geoffrey Malaterra[24] and William of Apulia,[25] for instance, all noted the use of ships in the sieges of Bari and Palermo during the era of conquest. Correspondingly, Romuald of Salerno,[26] Falco of Benevento[27] and Alexander of Telese[28] all give compelling accounts of King Roger's efforts to impose his authority over the maritime cities of Amalfi, Gaeta and Naples in the aftermath of his accession. Each chronicler had a tendency to color his narrative of the naval engagements either for or against the Normans, depending upon his perspective.

Nonetheless, modern scholars have a number of options for verifying the events in question. First of all, they can compare the various accounts, all written independently of one another, in an attempt to reconcile the discrepancies. Secondly, there are a number of abbatial annals like the *Annales Barenses*,[29] the *Annales Cavenses*,[30] the *Chronica ignoti monachi S. Mariae de Ferraria*[31] and the *Chronica Monasterii Casinensis*[32] that can also provide corroboration. Of course, this category of sources also has its problems with respect to reliability. The *Chronica Monasterii Casinensis*, for example, was begun by the relatively unprejudiced Leo Marsicanus (later archbishop of Ostia) in the late eleventh century, but was, unfortunately, continued into the mid-twelfth century by the notorious Peter the

---

[21] 'Hugo Falcandus', *The History of the Tyrants of Sicily, 1154–1169*, ed. and trans. G. A. Loud and T. Wiedemann (Manchester, 1998); *La historia o liber de regno Sicilie e la epistola ad Petrum Panormitane urbis thesaurarium di Ugo Falcando*, ed. G. Siragusa (FSI, XXII, Rome, 1904).
[22] Peter of Eboli, *Liber ad honorem Augusti sive de rebus Siculis, Codex 120 II der Burgerbibliothek Bern*, eds T. Kolser and M. Stahli, trans. G. Becht-Jordens (Sigmaringen, 1994).
[23] Amatus, *History of the Normans*, Bk V, ch. 27, pp. 143–6; Bk VI, ch. 14–16, p. 156; *Storia de' Normanni*, Bk V, ch. XXVII, pp. 248–54; Bk VI, ch. XIV–XVI, pp. 276–8.
[24] Malaterra, *Deeds of Count Roger*, Bk 2, ch. 40, p. 117; Bk 2, ch. 43, pp. 120–3; Bk 2, ch. 45, p. 124; *De rebus gestis Rogerii*, Bk II, ch. XL, p. 48; Bk II, ch. XLIII, pp. 30–1; Bk II, ch. XLV, pp. 52–3.
[25] William of Apulia, Bk III, lines 112–43, pp. 170–1; Bk III, lines 225–54, pp. 176–9.
[26] Romuald of Salerno, *Romualdi Salernitani Chronicon*, pp. 218–21.
[27] Falco of Benevento, *Chronicon Beneventanum*, pp. 108–70.
[28] Alexander of Telese, *Ystoria Rogerii regis Sicilie*, Bk II, ch. 9–11, pp. 27–8.
[29] *Annales Barenses*, ed. G. Pertz (MGH, SS, V, Hanover, 1844), pp. 51–6.
[30] *Annales Cavenses*, ed. G. Pertz (MGH, SS, III, Hanover, 1839), pp. 185–97.
[31] *Chronica Ignoti Monachi Cisterciensis S. Mariae de Ferraria*, ed. A. Gaudenzi (Società Napolitana di Storia Patria, Monumenti Storici, ser. I: Cronache; Naples, 1888).
[32] *Chronica Monasterii Casinensis*, ed. H. Hoffmann (MGH, SS, XXXIV, Hanover, 1980).

Deacon, whose unscrupulous attitude toward forgery made him and everything he touched suspect.[33] Naturally, these ecclesiastical chronicles were also written from the perspective of the institutions to which the authors belonged.

Moreover, the acquisitive nature of the Normans earned them the scrutiny of their competitors and enemies as well. The chroniclers of the Italian maritime powers such as Caffaro di Caschifellone of Genoa, Bernardo Maragone of Pisa and the Venetian doge, Andrea Dandolo, furnish yet another valuable, if slanted, layer of information on Norman maritime activities of the era. The naval encounters of each of these city-states with the Normans, peaceful or otherwise, are all documented in the *Annali genovesi*,[34] *Gli Annales Pisani*[35] and the *Chronica per Extensum Descripta* of Venice.[36] Also among the non-Norman, Latin observers are a handful of historians like William of Tyre,[37] Odo of Deuil[38] and the author of the *Itinerarium Peregrinorum*,[39] who recorded the later Sicilian *Regno*'s sporadic involvement in the Crusading movement.

The Greek observers are also very useful for providing the other side of various engagements with the Normans. Anna Comnena's description of the naval battles that occurred during Robert Guiscard's two Byzantine adventures is a case in point.[40] As the daughter of the Emperor Alexios I Komnenos and the wife of the Byzantine historian Nikephorus Bryennios, she provides the most detailed reports of both the siege of Durazzo in 1081 and the disastrous defeat of the Greco-Venetian fleet at Corfu in 1084, for example. Byzantine historians Niketas Choniates[41] and John Kinnamos[42] are almost alone in portraying George of Antioch's raids on Greek territories under Roger II in the 1140s. And the single most informative account of the ill-fated attempt to conquer Byzan-

---

33 Wolf, *Making History*, p. 89.
34 Caffaro, *Annales Ianuenses, Annali genovesi di Caffaro e de' suoi continuatori dal MXCIX al MCCXCIII*, eds L. Belgrano and C. Imperiale di Sant'Angelo (5 vols, FSI, Genoa, 1890–1929), I, pp. 5–75.
35 Bernardo Maragone, *Gli annales Pisani di Bernardo Maragone*, ed. M. Gentile (RIS, vol. VI, part II, Bologna, 1936).
36 Andrea Dandolo, *Chronica Per Extensum Descripta*, ed. E. Pastorello (RIS, vol. XII, Bologna, 1938–42).
37 William of Tyre, *A History of Deeds Done beyond the Sea*, trans. E. Babcock and A. Krey (2 vols, New York, 1943); *Willelmi Tyrensis Archiepiscopi chronicon*, ed. R. Huygens, H. Mayer and R. Gerhard (2 vols, CCCM, nos 63–63A, Turnholt, 1986).
38 Odo of Deuil, *De Profectione Ludovici VII in Orientem*, ed. and trans. V. Berry (New York, 1948).
39 *Itinerarium Peregrinorum et Gesta Regis Ricardi, Chronicles and Memorials of the Reign of Richard I*, ed. W. Stubbs (2 vols, RS 38, London, 1864, reprint 1964); *The Chronicle of the Third Crusade: The Itinerarium Peregrinorum et Gesta Regis Ricardi*, trans. H. Nicholson (Aldershot, 1997); *Das Itinerarium Peregrinorum*, ed. H. Mayer (Stuttgart, 1962).
40 Anna Comnena, *The Alexiad of Anna Comnena*, trans. E. Sewter (London, 1969); *Alexiade (Règne de l'Empereur Alexis I Comnène 1081–1118)*, ed. and trans. B. Leib (3 vols, Paris, 1937).
41 Niketas Choniates, *O City of Byzantium! Annals of Niketas Choniates*, trans. H. Magoulias (Detroit, 1984).
42 John Kinnamos, *Deeds of John and Manuel Comnenus*, trans. C. Brand (New York, 1976).

tium by William II ('the Good') is undoubtedly *The Capture of Thessaloniki* by Archbishop Eustathios of that same city.[43]

Additionally, were it not for the annals of the Islamic historians, faithfully preserved in Michele Amari's *Biblioteca Arabo-Sicula*, we would certainly have an incomplete view of Norman naval operations with respect to the conquest of Sicily under Roger I and the subjugation of North Africa under his son, Roger II. The observations of the Islamic historian Ibn al-Athir, the scholarly pilgrim Ibn Jubayr, the Sicilian court geographer al-Idrisi and many others are all represented in Amari's diligent two-tome Italian translation,[44] as well as in a number of more recent translations. The works of many of these contemporary Muslim historians have often been overlooked by Western scholars. Al-Idrisi's *Kitab Rujar* ('Book of Roger'),[45] for instance, contains a goldmine of information on the maritime infrastructure of the Mediterranean at the time, yet neither Willy Cohn nor Camillo Manfroni makes any reference to him at all. Together with their Christian counterparts, the Islamic historians provide a much more balanced view of Norman maritime policies in the Mediterranean.

It is an invaluable set of Byzantine sources, however, that furnishes specifics on how the Norman fleets may have been organized and operated. Over a century ago, the French scholar Jules Gay established that most of southern Italy at the time of the Normans' arrival was a Byzantine *catepanate* (governorship) composed of the *themata* (administrative units) of Calabria and Longobardia.[46] It was ruled in the name of the *basileus* (sovereign) by no less than an imperial *magistros* (master of offices). Therefore, Byzantine maritime methods must have predominated in the region. The Byzantine sources delineating these practices are in the form of military discourses generated by the imperial court of Constantinople in the tenth century. Contained within them are a series of treatises on naval warfare, which John Pryor affirms 'provide the most detailed information about ships and naval warfare to survive from anywhere in the Mediterranean world between antiquity and the thirteenth century'.[47]

Foremost among these is Constitution XIX of Emperor Leo VI's *Taktika*, otherwise known as *Naumachika Leontos Basileos* or 'Concerning the naval warfare of the Emperor Leo'.[48] Written at the beginning of the tenth century, it contains highly detailed prescriptions on how the various imperial vessels were to be constructed, manned and deployed. In 960, the *Patrikios* and *Parakoimōmenos*

---

43 Eustathios of Thessaloniki, *The Capture of Thessaloniki*, trans. J. Melville Jones (Canberra, 1988).

44 M. Amari, ed., *Biblioteca Arabo-Sicula* (2 vols, Turin, 1880–1).

45 Al-Idrisi, *BAS*, I, pp. 31–133; *La première géographie de l'Occident*, trans. P. Jaubert, eds H. Bresc and A. Nef (Paris, 1999).

46 J. Gay, *L'Italie méridionale et l'empire byzantine depuis l'avènement de Basile I jusqu'à la prise de Bari par les Normands (867–1071)* (Paris, 1904), pp. 343–9.

47 J. Pryor and E. Jeffreys, *The Age of ΔΡΟΜΩΝ (Dromōn), The Byzantine Navy ca 500–1204* (Leiden, 2006), p. 176.

48 Pryor and Jeffreys, *Dromōn*, p. 175.

(Grand Chamberlain) Basil, an illegitimate son of Emperor Romanos Lekapenos, commissioned a naval guide that describes not only the ships of the Byzantine fleets but also the various components of these ships and their uses. Later, the *strategos* Nikephoros Ouranos built upon the work of Leo VI with his own tome on naval tactics, describing the various formations and stratagems to be used in battle. Bundled together with these treatises in Alphonse Dain's *Naumachica partim Adhuc Inedita* was the truncated work of an official entitled 'Syrianos Magistros', which addresses, among other matters, the duties of the naval *strategos* (military commander).[49] Finally, the works of Constantine VII Porphyrogenitus add still more detail to the picture of naval operations at the time. Chapters 44 and 45 of Book II of *De Cerimoniis Aulae Byzantinae* ('Book of Ceremonies') specify the numbers of ships, men, horses and armaments involved in the expeditions to Crete in 911 and 949 as well as an expedition to Longobardia (Apulia) in 935,[50] while chapter 51 of *De Administrando Imperio* delineates the outfitting of the imperial galley.[51]

Latecomers to the Mediterranean, the Arabs initially learned their nautical skills from the Byzantines. An Arabic translation of Leo VI's *Naumachika* was found inserted in the *Al-Ahkam fi Fan al-Qital fi'l Bahr al Mulukiyah wa'l Dawabit al-Namusiyah* ('Royal rules and customary regulations for the art of naval warfare') of Ibn al-Manqali, a thirteenth-century official in the Mameluk sultanate of Egypt. This prompted Greek maritime historian Vassilios Christides to assert, 'The Arabs definitely made use of Byzantine military manuals.'[52] To these guides the Arabs contributed their own. In addition to Ibn al-Manqali's *Al-Ahkam*, cited above, a tenth-century customs official in Baghdad named Qudama Ibn Ja'far included in the *Kitab al-Kharaj* ('Book of Revenues') a chapter called the 'Form of instructions to the Commander of the Maritime Frontier'.[53] Muslim mariners, thus, must have added their own unique touches to ship design and strategy. It is inconceivable that the Normans would not have tapped into this reservoir of maritime knowledge as well. After all, they stood at the nexus of the two Mediterranean cultures. The Normans were likely exposed to the tenets of these naval manuals through their conquests of Byzantine southern Italy and 'Saracen' Sicily. Therefore, by studying these Byzantine and Arab naval

---

[49] Dain, *Naumachica*, pp. 43–55.
[50] Constantine VII Porphyrogenitus, *De Cerimoniis Aulae Byzantinae*, Chapters 44 and 45 of Book II, trans. J. Haldon in 'Theory and Practice in Tenth-Century Military Administration: Chapters II, 44 and 45 of the *Book of Ceremonies*', *Travaux et Memoires*, XIII (2000), pp. 201–352.
[51] Constantine VII Porphyrogenitus, *De Administrando Imperio*, ed. G. Moravcsik, trans. R. Jenkins (Budapest, 1949; 2nd edn, Washington, DC, 1967).
[52] V. Christides, 'Naval warfare in the Eastern Mediterranean (6th–14th centuries): an Arabic translation of Leo VI's Naumachica', *Graeco-Arabica*, III (1984), pp. 137–48.
[53] V. Christides, 'Two parallel naval guides of the tenth century; Qudama's document and Leo VI's Naumachica: a study on Byzantine and Moslem naval preparedness', *Graeco-Arabica*, I (1982), pp. 51–103.

treatises scholars may learn much about Norman naval practices. Fortunately, for those linguistically challenged scholars who have not as yet conquered Greek or Arabic, Elizabeth Jeffreys provides careful English translations for all of the above-cited Greek works in the Appendices of *The Age of ΔΡΟΜΩΝ (Dromōn), The Byzantine Navy ca 500–1204*,[54] as does Ahmad Shboul for Ibn al-Manqali's *Al-Ahkam*.[55]

At the turn of the twelfth century, numerous charters and privileges, such as those contained in the royal registers of CarlRichard Brühl,[56] Erich Caspar,[57] Horst Enzensberger,[58] Karl Kehr[59] and Herbert Zielinski[60] began to appear. Many of them offer still more clues as to how ships were procured and mariners recruited. By examining the maritime-related exemptions granted by some of these royal privileges one can obtain a sense of what was required of the various vassals, ecclesiastical institutions, ports and townships of the realm. One of the few administrative documents still extant from the Norman court is the *Catalogus Baronum*,[61] a register of military service owed by the fiefs of Apulia and Capua probably compiled at the behest of Roger II in the middle of the twelfth century and updated under his grandson, William II, in 1168. Among its many entries are a few additional shreds of information as to how the Norman kings may have raised manpower for their fleets and coastal watches.

There are very few existing depictions of medieval vessels that enable us to visualize what Norman warships may have looked like. One of the most tantalizing sources has been the illustrations of a handful of medieval manuscripts. The late fifth-century *Roman Vergil* (Biblioteca Apostolica Vaticana, Ms Vat. Lat. 3867, fol. 77r)[62] and the early sixth-century *Ilias Ambrosiana* (Biblioteca Ambrosiana di Milano, Cod. Ambros. F. 205) both appear to depict early versions of the *dromōn*.[63] The ninth-century *Sacra Parallela* manuscript of St John of Damascus (Paris Bibliothèque Nationale, Ms Gr. 923, fol. 207r) shows a pair of two-masted, lateen-rigged vessels with oarports, which may also be *dromōns*.[64] The Madrid manuscript of the *Synopsis historiōn* of John Skylitzes

---

[54] E. Jeffreys, *Dromōn*, Appendices 1–5, pp. 455–605.

[55] A. Shboul, *Dromōn*, Appendix 8, pp. 645–66.

[56] *Rogerii II. Regis Diplomata Latina*, ed. C. Brühl (CDRS, Ser. I, II, 1, Cologne 1987).

[57] Caspar, *Roger II*, Regesten, pp. 443–541.

[58] *Guillelmi I. Regis Diplomata*, ed. H. Enzensberger (CDRS, Ser. I, III, Cologne, 1996).

[59] K. Kehr, *Die Urkunden der Normannisch-Sicilischen Könige* (Innsbruck, 1902), Urkunden, pp. 405–502.

[60] *Tancredi et Willelmi III Regum Diplomata*, ed. H. Zielinski (CDRS, Ser. I, V, Cologne, 1982).

[61] *Catalogus Baronum*, ed. E. Jamison (FSI, Rome, 1972).

[62] D. Wright, *The Roman Vergil and the Origins of Medieval Book Design* (London, 2001), p. 25; Pryor and Jeffreys, *Dromōn*, pp. 138–9.

[63] Pryor and Jeffreys, *Dromōn*, pp. 139–42.

[64] Pryor and Jeffreys, *Dromōn*, p. 142, fig. 8; K. Weitzmann, *The miniatures of the Sacra parallela, Parisinus Graecus 923* (Princeton, 1979), pl. LIII, fig. 203.

(Biblioteca Nacional, Codex Vitr. 26–2) has numerous miniatures containing representations of mid-twelfth-century bireme galleys.[65] The first illustrations of the Italian *galea* appear as marginal miniatures in the twelfth-century Paris manuscript of Genoa's *Annales Ianuenses* (Bibliothèque Nationale, Ms Suppl. Lat. 773).[66] Finally, from the early thirteenth century, John Pryor has identified several illustrations of the Bern manuscript of Peter of Eboli's *Liber ad honorem Augusti sive rebus Siculis* (Bern Burgerbibliothek, Codex 120 II) as depictions of the Sicilian *galea*.[67]

The most exciting new revelations, however, are not coming from traditional documentary research. The fields of marine archaeology and medieval naval architecture have unearthed promising new paths of research in regard to sea power in the age of oared vessels. Many of the findings have the potential of answering long-held questions, particularly applicable to Norman naval power in the eleventh and twelfth centuries. Marine researchers from the Nautical Archaeology Program of Texas A&M University have lately made several crucial discoveries that shed new light on medieval ship technology and operating procedures. George Bass and Frederick van Doorninck have produced extensive findings from a seventh-century Byzantine shipwreck excavated at Yassi Ada[68] near Bodrum, Turkey and an eleventh-century Byzantine shipwreck found at Serçe Limani,[69] also on the southwest Turkish coast. And nearby, on the Bozburun Peninsula, Frederick Hocker began excavations in 1995 on the wreck of another Byzantine merchant vessel, this one from the ninth century.[70] In addition, remnants of medieval vessels have been found in Sicilian waters: a Greek boat at Pantano Longarini in 1965,[71] an Arab vessel near Marsala in 1985[72] and the hull of a horse transport at Camarino in 1989.[73] Most recently and perhaps most promising are the Yenikapi shipwrecks of Istanbul. In 2004 the construction of a

---

[65] V. Tsamakda, *The Illustrated Chronicle of Ioannes Skylitzes in Madrid* (Leiden, 2002); Pryor and Jeffreys, *Dromōn*, Appendix 7, pp. 633–44.

[66] Pryor and Jeffreys, *Dromōn*, pp. 424–6.

[67] Peter of Eboli, *Liber ad honorem Augusti sive de rebus Siculis*, pp. 95, 135, 179 and particularly 131. See also Pryor and Jeffreys, *Dromōn*, pp. 429–30.

[68] G. Bass and F. van Doorninck, *Yassi Ada: A Seventh-Century Byzantine Shipwreck* (College Station, 1982).

[69] G. Bass, S. Matthews, J. Steffy and F. Van Doorninck, *Serçe Limani: An Eleventh-Century Byzantine Shipwreck* (College Station, 2004).

[70] F. Hocker, 'A Ninth-century Shipwreck near Bozburun, Turkey', *Institute of Nautical Archeaology Quarterly*, 22.1 (1995), pp. 12–14; F. Hocker, 'Sampling a Byzantine Vintage: Bozburun, Turkey', in *Beneath the Seven Seas*, ed. G. Bass (New York, 2005), pp. 100–5.

[71] G. Bass, *A History of Seafaring based on Underwater Archaeology* (London, 1974), pp. 144–6.

[72] G. Purpura, 'Un relitto de eta normanna a Marsala', *Bolletino d'arte*, ser. VI, XXIX (1985), pp. 129–36.

[73] G. di Stefano, 'Antichi relitti nella baia di Camarina', in *Atti, IV rassegna di archeologia subacquea*, ed. P. Gianfrotta (Messina, 1991), pp. 127–34.

new subway system for the city revealed the fourth-century Theodosian Harbor of Constantinople at what will eventually be the Yenikapi metro stop on the Sea of Marmara. To date (May 2008), researchers of Istanbul University's Department of Conservation and Restoration under Prof. Sait Başaran have uncovered 31 Byzantine-era shipwrecks, four of which appear to be galleys.[74] Analysis and documentation of these wrecks have only begun, but the potential is enormous.

Perhaps even more auspicious is the work of a new crop of historians who analyze the actual operating conditions endured by mariners of the medieval Mediterranean. John Francis Guilmartin was one of the first to challenge conventional theories on medieval galley warfare in the Mediterranean. His ground-breaking work, *Gunpowder & Galleys, Changing Technology & Mediterranean Warfare at Sea in the 16th century*, established that Alfred Thayer Mahan's notion of maintaining naval superiority through control of the sea lanes as a 'fallacy' in the era of oared vessels.[75] 'Whether or not we consider control of the sea a militarily valid concept,' writes Guilmartin, 'we must accept the fact that sixteenth century naval warfare in the Mediterranean revolved around fleets of galleys, fleets which by their very nature could not "control the sea".'[76]

John Pryor followed this breakthrough in thinking with his landmark treatise, *Geography, Technology, and War: Studies in the maritime history of the Mediterranean, 649–1571*,[77] in which he used physical factors to evaluate the documentary evidence with a mind to forming a more accurate picture of commercial and military maritime operations in the Mediterranean during the Middle Ages. Pryor's examination of the effects of weather patterns, sea currents and coastal topography on the nautical technology of the era has rigorously tested the veracity of contemporary accounts, dispelling several long-standing misconceptions. Consequently, he has pushed Henri Pirenne's theories on the shift of economic centers in the Mediterranean world deeper into desuetude and dismissed entirely the applicability of Mahan's concept of sea power. Pryor did so by outlining the severe limitations imposed on galley operations throughout the Middle Ages. For example, he highlighted the vulnerability of galleys to the whims of adverse weather conditions and the requirement for enormous amounts of fresh water for their crews. Such real-world observations have forced medievalists to reevaluate their convictions on contemporary diplomacy, military strategy and trading patterns in the Mediterranean in light of the fact that control of the sea was

---

[74] U. Kocabaş, ed., *The 'Old Ships' of the 'New Gate', Yenikapi Shipwrecks, Vol. I* (Istanbul, 2008).

[75] J. Guilmartin, *Gunpowder & Galleys: Changing Technology & Mediterranean Warfare at Sea in the 16th Century* (Cambridge, 1974, revised 2003); A. Mahan, *The Influence of Sea Power upon History, 1660–1783* (London, 1890), p. 219.

[76] Guilmartin, *Gunpowder & Galleys*, pp. 32–3.

[77] J. Pryor, *Geography, Technology, and War: Studies in the maritime history of the Mediterranean, 649–1571* (Cambridge, 1988).

largely dependent upon control of its shores, because control of the shores meant control of the water sources and safe havens from inclement weather upon which galleys relied. This is why possession of certain islands, such as Sicily, Majorca and Crete was strategically crucial to the powers of the era.

Pryor's book, *The Age of ΔΡΟΜΩΝ (Dromōn), The Byzantine Navy ca 500–1204,*[78] may well prove seminal to the subject of medieval maritime power in the Mediterranean. This comprehensive collaboration with Elizabeth Jeffreys augments the venerable contributions of Hélène Ahrweiler[79] and Ekkhard Eickhoff[80] on Byzantine naval power and caps nearly a quarter of a century of work that has radically altered the perspective of maritime historians on the medieval Mediterranean. The tome tracks the development of the *dromōn*, the basic Byzantine warship, through the early Middle Ages. This type of warship proliferated throughout the Mediterranean world and was doubtless the first one encountered by the Normans who ventured into southern Italy. The work goes on to describe the transition to the Italian *galea* and the concomitant rise of the Latin West, at the center of which stood the Kingdom of Sicily.

Lastly, Pryor's theories concerning the performance and operating characteristics of oared vessels have found empirical endorsement in the findings of J. S. Morrison, J. F. Coates and N. B. Rankov. In the mid-1980s, Morrison, a maritime historian who has written numerous pieces on the warships of antiquity, collaborated with Coates, the former Chief Naval Architect and Deputy Director of Ship Design in the British Ministry of Defence, to bring about the building of an authentic Greek *triērēs* (trireme). The two men eventually managed to convince the Hellenic Navy to commission the construction of the *Olympias*, an Athenian trireme, which was ultimately launched in June 1987. Boris Rankov, of the University of London, then joined the team as rowing master for five seasons of sea trials between 1987 and 1994. These trials yielded a treasure trove of empirical data on the operation of oared vessels, applicable not only to antiquity but also to the medieval era.[81] The three scholars subsequently published those findings in minute detail and with ample illustration in the second edition of *The Athenian Trireme: The History and Reconstruction of an Ancient Greek Warship.*[82] The preliminary verdict of all these efforts thus far is that the galley fleets of the Middle Ages, merchant and military, faced severe limitations on their operations from fundamental technological constraints. Thus, those who

[78] Pryor and Jeffreys, *Dromōn.*
[79] H. Ahrweiler, *Byzance et la la mer: la marine de guerre, la politique et les institutions maritimes de Byzance au VII–XV siècles* (Paris, 1966).
[80] E. Eickhoff, *Seekrieg und Seepolitik zwischen Islam und Abendland: das Mittelmeer unter Byzantinischer und Arabischer Hegemonie, 650–1040* (Berlin, 1966).
[81] J. Coates and J. Morrison, 'The Sea Trials of the Reconstructed Athenian Trireme Olympias', *The Mariner's Mirror*, LXXIX (1993), pp. 131–41.
[82] J. Coates, J. Morrison and N. Rankov, *The Athenian Trireme, The History and Reconstruction of an Ancient Greek Warship* (2nd edn, Cambridge, 2000).

controlled extensive shorelines and islands with water sources in the Mediterranean possessed enormous control over maritime traffic. Accordingly, Norman dominance of the central Mediterranean was of such critical importance that it virtually guaranteed Western maritime ascendancy for centuries to come.

Bibliography

Manuscripts

Bern, Burgerbibliothek, Codex 120 II
Cambridge, Fitzwilliam Museum, Ms Marlay Add. I
Madrid, Biblioteca Nacional de España, Codex Vitr. 26–2
Oxford, Bodleian Library, Ms Pococke 375
Rome, Biblioteca Apostolica Vaticana, Ms Vat. Lat. 3225
Rome, Biblioteca Apostolica Vaticana, Ms Vat. Lat. 3867
Rome, Biblioteca Apostolica Vaticana, Ms Vat. Lat. 4936
Rome, Biblioteca Apostolica Vaticana, Ms Vat. Lat. 6202
Rome, Biblioteca Apostolica Vaticana, Ms Vat. Lat. 8782
Rome, Biblioteca Apostolica Vaticana, Ms Vat. Gr. 1605
Rome, Biblioteca Apostolica Vaticana, Ms Vat. Gr. 1164
Venice, Biblioteca Marciana, Ms Gr. 479

Printed Primary Sources

Abulfeda, *Biblioteca Arabo-Sicula*, ed. M. Amari (2 vols, Turin, 1880–1), II, 85–109.

Abu Samah, *Biblioteca Arabo-Sicula*, ed. M. Amari (2 vols, Turin, 1880–1), I, 544.

Albert of Aachen, *Historia Ierosolimitana, History of the Journey to Jerusalem*, ed. and trans. S. Edgington (Oxford Medieval Texts, Oxford, 2007).

Alexander of Telese, *Alexandri Telesini abbatis Ystoria Rogerii regis Sicilie, Calabrie atque Apulie*, ed. L. De Nava (Fonti per la storia d'Italia, Rome, 1991). English translation by G. A. Loud at *Medieval History Texts in Translation* (University of Leeds, 2006), http://www.leeds.ac.uk/history/weblearning/MedievalHistoryTextCentre/medievalTexts/html.

Al-Idrisi, *Biblioteca Arabo-Sicula*, ed. M. Amari (2 vols, Turin, 1880–1), I, 30–133.

Al-Idrisi, *La première geographie de l'Occident*, trans. P. Jaubert, eds H. Bresc and Annliese Nef (Paris, 1999).

Al-Maqrizi, *Biblioteca Arabo-Sicula*, ed. M. Amari (2 vols, Turin, 1880–1), II, 259–266.

Al-Nuwayri, *Biblioteca Arabo-Sicula*, ed. M. Amari (2 vols, Turin, 1880–1), II, 110–160.

Amari, M., ed., *Biblioteca Arabo-Sicula* (2 vols, Turin, 1880–1).

Amari, M., ed., *I diplomi arabi del Archivio fiorentino* (Florence, 1863–7).

Amato di Montecassino, *Storia De' Normanni*, ed. V. Bartholomaeis (Fonti per la storia D'Italia, Rome, 1935).

Amatus of Montecassino, *The History of the Normans*, trans. P. Dunbar, revised G. Loud (Woodbridge, 2004).

Ambroise, *The History of the Holy War: Ambroise's Estoire de la Guerre Saint*, ed. and trans. M. Ailes and M. Barber (2 vols, Woodbridge, 2003).

Andrea Dandolo, *Chronica Per Extensum Descripta*, ed. E. Pastorello (Rerum Italicarum Scriptores, vol. XII, Bologna, 1938–42).

Anna Comnena, *The Alexiad of Anna Comnena*, trans. E. Sewter (London, 1969).

Anne Comnena, *Alexiade (Règne de l'Empereur Alexis I Comnène 1081–1118)*, ed. and trans. B. Leib (3 vols, Paris, 1937).

Annales Barenses, ed. G. Pertz (Monumenta Germaniae Historica, Scriptores, V, Hanover, 1844), 51–56.

Annales Beneventani, ed. G. Pertz (Monumenta Germaniae Historica, Scriptores, III, Hanover, 1839), 173–185.

Annales Casinenses, a. 1000–1212, ed. G. Pertz, (Monumenta Germaniae Historica, Scriptores, XIX, Hanover, 1866), 303–320.

Annales Cavenses, ed. G. Pertz (Monumenta Germaniae Historica, Scriptores, III, Hanover, 1839), 185–197.

Annales Ceccanenses, ed. G. Pertz (Monumenta Germaniae Historica, Scriptores, XIX, Hanover, 1866), 275–302.

Annales Erphesfurtenses, ed. G. Pertz (Monumenta Germaniae Historica, Scriptores, VI, Hanover, 1844), 536–541.

Annalista Saxo, ed. K. Nass (Monumenta Germaniae Historica, Scriptores, XXXVII, Hanover, 2006).

Anonymi Barensis Chronicon, ed. L. Muratori (Rerum Italicarum Scriptores, V, Milan, 1726), 145–156.

Anonymi Vaticani Historia Sicula, ed. L. Muratori (Rerum Italicarum Scriptores, VIII, Milan, 1726), 745–780.

At-Tijani, *Biblioteca Arabo-Sicula*, ed. M. Amari (2 vols, Turin, 1880–1), II, 41–81.

Baha' al-Din Ibn Shaddad, *The Rare and Excellent History of Saladin*, trans. D. Richards (Aldershot, 2002).

Benjamin of Tudela, *The Itinerary of Benjamin of Tudela*, ed. M. Adler (London, 1907).

Bernard of Clairvaux, *The Letters of St Bernard of Clairvaux*, trans. B. James (London, 1953).

Bernard of Clairvaux, *Sancti Bernardi Opera*, VII–VIII, *Epistolae*, eds J. Leclercq and H. Rochais (Rome, 1974).

Bernardo Maragone, *Gli annales Pisani di Bernardo Maragone*, ed. L. Gentile (Rerum Italicarum Scriptores, 2nd edn, Bologna, 1936).

Brevis Relatio de Guillelmo nobilissimo comite Normannorum, ed. and trans. E. van Houts, *Camden Miscellany*, 5th series, vol. 10 (Cambridge, 1997), 1–48.

Caffaro, *Annales Ianuenses, Annali genovesi di Caffaro e de' suoi continuatori dal MXCIX al MCCXCIII*, eds L. Belgrano and C. Imperiale di Sant'Angelo (5 vols, Fonti per la storia d'Italia, Genoa, 1890–1929), I, 5–75.

Cambridge Chronicle, Biblioteca Arabo-Sicula, ed. M. Amari (2 vols, Turin, 1880–1), I, 277–292.

Carmen in victoriam Pisanorum, ed. H. E. J. Cowdrey, 'The Mahdia Campaign of 1087', *The English Historical Review*, CCCLXII (1977), 1–29, especially 24–29.

Catalogus Baronum, ed. E. Jamison (Fonti per la storia d'Italia, Rome, 1972).

Chronica Ignoti Monachi Cisterciensis S. Mariae de Ferraria, ed. A. Gaudenzi (Società Napoletana di Storia Patria, Monumenti Storici, ser. I, Napoli, 1888).

Chronica Monasterii Casinensis, ed. H. Hoffmann (Monumenta Germaniae Historica Scriptores, XXXIV, Hanover, 1980).

Chronicon Breve Nortmannicum, ed. L. Muratori (Rerum Italicarum Scriptores, V, Milan, 1726), 278 (I–VI).

Chronicon Casauriense auctore Johanne Berardi, ed. L. Muratori (Rerum Italicarum Scriptores, II 2, Milan, 1726), 775–1018.

Chronicon Salernitanum, ed. U. Westerbergh (Stockholm, 1956).

Chronicon di Sancti Bartolomeo di Carpineto, ed. E. Fuselli (L'Aquila, 1996).

Chronicon Vulturnense, ed. V. Federici (3 vols, Istituto Storico Italiano, Rome, 1925).

Codice Diplomatico Amalfitano, ed. R. Filangieri (Naples, 1917).

Codice Diplomatico della Repubblica di Genova, ed. C. Imperiale di Sant'Angelo (3 vols, Fonti per la storia d'Italia, Rome, 1936–42).

Collura, P., ed., *Le piu antiche carte dell'archivio capitolare di Agrigento (1092–1282)* (Documenti per servire alla storia di Sicilia, Ser. I. xxv, Palermo, 1960).

Constantine VII Porphyrogenitus, *De Administrando Imperio*, ed. G. Moravcsik and trans. R. Jenkins (Washington, DC, 1967).

Constantine VII Porphyrogenitus, *De Cerimoniis aulae byzantinae*, Bk II, Ch. 44 and 45, ed. and trans. J. Haldon, 'Theory and practice in tenth-century military administration: Chapters II, 44 and 45 of the *Book of Ceremonies*', *Travaux et Memoires*, 13 (2000), 201–352.

Constantine VII Porphyrogenitus, *De Cerimoniis aulae byzantinae*, Bk II, Ch. 44 and 45, ed. and trans. E. Jeffreys, *The Age of ΔΡΟΜΩΝ (Dromōn), The Byzantine Navy ca 500–1204* (Leiden, 2006), Appendix IV, 547–570.

Constitutiones et Acta Publica Imperatorem et Regum, ed. L. Weiland (Monumenta Germaniae Historica, Legum Sectio IV, Vol. I, Hanover, 1893).

Cronache veneziane antichissime, Vol. I, ed. G. Monticolo (Fonti per la storia d'Italia, XIX, Rome, 1890).

Cusa, S., ed., *I diplomi greci ed arabi di Sicilia* (Palermo, 1868–81).

Dain, A., ed., *Naumachica partim Adhuc Inedita in unum nunc primum congessit et indice auxit Alphonsus Dain* (Paris, 1943). Unpublished translation of the Greek to English by Professor Emeritus F. van Doorninck of Texas A&M University.

Deér, J., ed., *Das Papsttum und die süditalienischen Normannenstaaten 1053–1212* (Göttingen, 1969).

Del Re, G., ed., *Cronisti e Scrittori Sincroni della Dominazione normanna nel regno di Puglia e Sicilia* (2 vols, Naples, 1845–68).

Dennis, G., ed., *Three Byzantine Military Treatises* (Washington, D.C, 1985).

Dudo of St Quentin, *History of the Normans*, trans. E. Christiansen (Woodbridge, 1998).

Eadmer, *The Life of Saint Anselm, Archbishop of Canterbury*, trans. R. Southern (London, 1962).

Erchempert, *Historia Langobardorum Beneventanorum*, ed. G. Waitz (Monumenta Germaniae Historica, Scriptores rerum Langobardicarum et Italicarum, Hanover, 1878), 231–264.

L'estoire de Eracles empereur et la conqueste de la terre d'Outremer, Recueil des historiens des croisades, Historiens occidentaux, ed. Académie des Inscriptions et Belles Lettres (5 vols, Paris, 1844–95), I–II.

Eustathios of Thessaloniki, *The Capture of Thessaloniki*, trans. J. Melville Jones (Canberra, 1988).

Falco of Benevento, *Chronicon Beneventanum*, ed. E. D'Angelo (Florence, 1998). Unpublished English translation by G. A. Loud, University of Leeds.

Filangieri, R., ed., *I registri della cancellaria angioina* (33 vols, Naples, 1950–1).

Freshfield, E., trans., *A manual of later Roman law: the Ecloga ad Procheiron mutata ... including the Rhodian maritime law* (Cambridge, 1927).

Friderici I. Diplomata (1158–1167), ed. H. Appelt (Monumenta Germaniae Historica, Diplomata Regum et Imperatorum Germaniae, Vol. X, Pt II, Hanover, 1979).

Fulcher of Chartres, *A History of the Expedition to Jerusalem, 1095–1127*, trans. F. Ryan and ed. H. Fink (Knoxville, 1969).

Fulcher of Chartres, *Fulcheri Carnotensis, Historia Hierosolymitana (1095–1127)*, ed. H. Hagenmeyer (Heidelberg, 1913).

Garufi, C. A., ed., *I documenti inediti dell'epoca normanna in Sicilia* (Documenti per servire alla storia di Sicilia, ser. 1, 18, Palermo, 1899).

Geoffrey Malaterra, *De rebus gestis Rogerii Calabriae et Siciliae comitis et Roberti Guiscardi ducis fratris eius*, ed. E. Pontieri (Rerum Italicarum Scriptores, 2nd edn, vol. 5, Bologna, 1927–8). English translation by G. A. Loud at *Medieval History Texts in Translation* (University of Leeds, 2006), http://www.leeds.ac.uk/history/weblearning/MedievalHistoryTextCentre/medievalTexts/html.

Geoffrey Malaterra, *The Deeds of Count Roger of Calabria and Sicily and of His Brother Duke Robert Guiscard*, trans. K. Wolf (Ann Arbor, 2005).

Gervase of Tilbury, *Otia Imperialia: Recreation for an Emperor*, ed. and trans. S. Banks and J. Binns (Oxford Medieval Texts, Oxford, 2002).

Gesta Francorum. The Deeds of the Franks and the other Pilgrims to Jerusalem, ed. and trans. R. Hill (Oxford Medieval Texts, Oxford, 1962).

Giardina, C., ed., *Capitoli e Privilegi di Messina* (Palermo, 1937).

Goitein, S., ed. and trans., *Letters of Medieval Jewish Traders* (Princeton, 1973).

Guillelmi I. Regis Diplomata, ed. H. Enzensberger (Codex Diplomaticus Regni Siciliae, Ser. I, III, Cologne, 1996).

Hampe, K., ed., *Die Akenstücke zum Frieden von San Germano: 1230* (Monumenta Germaniae Historica, Epistolae Selectae, IV, Berlin, 1926).

Historia ducum Veneticorum, ed. E. Simonsfeld (Monumenta Germaniae Historica, Scriptores, XIV, Hanover, 1883), 72–97.

'Hugo Falcandus', *La historia o liber de regno Sicilie e la epistola ad Petrum Panormitane urbis thesaurarium di Ugo Falcando*, ed. G. Siragusa (Fonti per la storia d'Italia, XXII, Rome, 1904).

'Hugo Falcandus', *The History of the Tyrants of Sicily, 1154–69*, trans. and annotated by G. A. Loud and T. Wiedemann (Manchester, 1998).

Huillard-Bréholles, J., ed., *Historia Diplomatica Friderici Secundi* (6 vols in 12 parts, Paris, 1852–61).

Ibn abi Dinar, *Biblioteca Arabo-Sicula*, ed. M. Amari (2 vols, Turin, 1880–1), II, 273–297.

Ibn al-Athir, *Biblioteca Arabo-Sicula*, ed. M. Amari (2 vols, Turin, 1880–1), I, 353–507.

Ibn al-Athir, *The Chronicle of Ibn al-Athir for the Crusading Period from al-Kamil fi'l-Ta'rikh, Part I, The Years 491–541/1097–1146: The Coming of the Franks and the Muslim Response*, ed. and trans. D. Richards (Aldershot, 2006).

Ibn al-Athir, *The Chronicle of Ibn al-Athir for the Crusading Period from al-Kamil fi'l-Ta'rikh, Part II, The Years 541–589/1146–1193: the Age of Nur al-Din and Saladin*, ed. and trans. D. Richards (Aldershot, 2007).

Ibn-al-Qalanisi, *The Damascus Chronicle of the Crusades*, trans. H. Gibb (London, 1967).

Ibn Hawqal, *Biblioteca Arabo-Sicula*, ed. M. Amari (2 vols, Turin, 1880–1), I, 10–27.

Ibn Hawqal, *La Configuration de la Terre*, trans. J. Kramers and G. Wiet (2 vols, Paris, 2001).

Ibn Idari (Al-Bayan), *Biblioteca Arabo-Sicula*, ed. M. Amari (2 vols, Turin, 1880–1), II, 1–40.

Ibn Jubayr, *Biblioteca Arabo-Sicula*, ed. M. Amari (2 vols, Turin, 1880–1), I, 137–180.

Ibn Jubayr, *The Travels of Ibn Jubayr*, trans. R. Broadhurst (London, 1952).

Ibn Khaldun, *Biblioteca Arabo-Sicula*, ed. M. Amari (2 vols, Turin, 1880–1), II, 163–243.

Ibn Khaldun, *The Muqaddimah*, trans. F. Rosenthal (Princeton, 1967).

Imad ad-Din al-Isfahani, *Biblioteca Arabo-Sicula*, ed. M. Amari (2 vols, Turin, 1880–1), II, 429–490.

Imad ad-Din al-Isfahani, *Conquête de la Syrie et de la Palestine*, trans. H. Massé (Paris, 1972).

Italia Pontificia, ed. P. Kehr (10 vols, Berlin, 1905–74).

Itinerarium Peregrinorum et Gesta Regis Ricardi, Chronicles and Memorials of the Reign of Richard I, vol. I, ed. W. Stubbs (Rolls Series, Rerum Britannicarum Medii Aevi Scriptores, 38, London, 1864).

Itinerarium Peregrinorum et Gesta Regis Ricardi, The Chronicle of the Third Crusade, trans. H. Nicholson (Aldershot, 1997).

John VIII (Pope), *Papae Registrum*, ed. E. Caspar (Monumenta Germaniae Historica, Epistolae, VII, Berlin, 1928).

John the Deacon, *Chronicon Venetum, Cronache Veneziane Antichissime*, ed. G. Monticolo (Fonti per la storia d'Italia, IX, Rome, 1890), 55–171.

John the Deacon, *Gesta Episcoporum Neapolitanorum* (Monumenta Germaniae Historica, Scriptores rerum Langobardicarum et Italicarum, Hanover, 1878), 424–436.

John Kaminiates, *The Capture of Thessaloniki*, trans. D. Frendo and A. Fotiou (Perth, 2000).

John Kinnamos, *Deeds of John and Manuel Comnenus*, trans. C. Brand (New York, 1976).

John Skylitzes, *Empereurs de Constantinople (Synopsis historiōn)*, trans. B. Flusin (Paris, 2003).

John Skylitzes, *A Synopsis of Byzantine History 811–1057*, trans. J. Wortley (Cambridge, 2010).

Koch, W., ed., *Die Urkunden Friedrichs II. 1198–1212* (Monumenta Germaniae Historica, Diplomata Regum et Imperatorum Germaniae, XIV, Hanover, 2002).

The Liber Augustalis or Constitutions of Melfi Promulgated by the Emperor Frederick II for the Kingdom of Sicily in 1231, trans. J. Powell (Syracuse, 1971).

Le Liber censuum de l'eglise romaine, eds L. Duchesne and P. Fabre (3 vols, Bibliothèque des Écoles Françaises d'Athènes et de Rome 2, série 6, Paris, 1889–1952).

Le Liber Pontificalis, eds L. Duchesne and C. Vogel (3 vols, Bibliothèque des Écoles Françaises d'Athènes et de Rome 2, série 3, Paris, 1886–1957).

Leo the Deacon, *The History of Leo the Deacon (Byzantine Military Expansion in the Tenth Century)*, trans. A. Talbot and D. Sullivan (Washington, DC, 2005).

Leo VI, *L''Extrait Tactique' tiré de Léon VI le Sage*, French trans. A. Dain (Bibliotheque de l'École des Hautes Etudes, CCLXXXI, Paris, 1942).

Leo VI, 'La Naumachie de l'Empereur Byzantin Léon VI', French trans. J. Sottas, *Academie de Marine*, XIV (Paris, 1935), 17–31.

Leo VI, *The Naval Warfare of the Emperor Leo*, ed. and trans. E. Jeffreys, *The Age of ΔΡΟΜΩΝ (Dromōn), The Byzantine Navy ca 500–1204* (Leiden, 2006), Appendix II, 483–519.

Leo VI, *The Taktika of Leo VI*, trans. G. Dennis (Washington, DC, 2010).

Liudprand of Cremona, *Die Werke Liudprands von Cremona*, ed. J. Becker (Monumenta Germaniae Historica, 3rd edn, Scriptores rerum Germanicarum, XLI, Hanover, 1915).

Liudprand of Cremona, *The Works of Liudprand of Cremona*, trans. F. Wright (London, 1930).

Loud, G. A., ed., 'A Calendar of the Diplomas of the Norman Princes of Capua', *Papers of the British School of Rome*, XLIX (1981), 99–143.

Loud, G. A., ed. and trans., 'The Extant Charters of William II of Sicily (1166–89): A Calendar' (unpublished manuscript, University of Leeds, 2008).

Lupus Protospatarius, 'The Annales Barenses and the Annales Lupi Protospatharii: Critical Edition and Commentary', ed. and trans. W. Churchill (doctoral dissertation, University of Toronto, 1979).

Lupus Protospatarius, *Annales*, ed. G. Pertz (Monumenta Germaniae Historica, Scriptores, V, Hanover, 1844), 51–63.

Marchiso Scriba, *Annales Ianuenses*, *Annali genovesi di Caffaro e de' suoi continuatori dal MXCIX al MCCXCIII*, eds L. Belgrano and C. Imperiale di Sant'Angelo (5 vols, Fonti per la storia d'Italia, Genoa, 1890–1929), II, 156–202.

Marino Sanuto Torsello, *Liber secretorum fidelium crucis super Terrae Sanctae recuperatione et conservatione...*, ed. J. Bongars (1611, reprinted Jerusalem, 1972).

Martino Da Canale, *Les Estoires de Venise: Cronaca veneziana in linqua francese dalle origini al 1275*, ed. L. Olschki (Civiltà veneziana. Fonti e testi, 12, ser. III, Florence, 1972).

Mas Latrie, L. de, *Traités de paix et de commerce et documents divers concernant les relations des Chrétiens avec les Arabes de l'Afrique septentrionale au Moyen Age* (2 vols, Paris, 1866).

Maurice, *Strategikon*, trans. G. Dennis (Philadelphia, 1984).

Ménager, L., ed., *Recueil des actes des ducs normands d'Italie (1046–1127), I. Les premiers ducs (1046–1087)* (Società di storia patria per la Puglia, documenti e monografie, 45, Bari, 1981).

Michael Psellus, *Fourteen Byzantine Rulers*, trans. E. Sewter (London, 1953).

Minieri Riccio, C., *Saggio di Codice diplomatico, formato sulle antiche scritture dell'Archivio di Stato di Napoli* (Naples, 1878–83).

Muhammad ibn Mankali, *Al-adilla al-rasmiyya fi 'l-ta'abi al-harbiyya* and *Al-ahkam al-mulukiyya wa 'l-dawabit al-namusiyya*, trans. A. Shboul, *The Age of ΔΡΟΜΩΝ*

(*Dromōn*), *The Byzantine Navy ca 500–1204* (Leiden, 2006), Appendix VIII, 645–666.

Müller, G., *Documenti sulle relazioni delle Città Toscane coll'Oriente Cristiano e coi Turchi fino all'anno MDXXXI* (Florence, 1879).

Naval warfare commissioned by Basil, the patrikios and parakoimōmenos, ed. and trans. E. Jeffreys, *The Age of ΔΡΟΜΩΝ* (*Dromōn*), *The Byzantine Navy ca 500–1204* (Leiden, 2006), Appendix III, 521–545.

Nikephoros Ouranos, *On fighting at sea*, ed. and trans. E. Jeffreys, *The Age of ΔΡΟΜΩΝ* (*Dromōn*), *The Byzantine Navy ca 500–1204* (Leiden, 2006), Appendix V, 571–605.

Nikephoros, Patriarch of Constantinople, *Short History*, ed. and trans. C. Mango (Washington, DC, 1990).

Niketas Choniates, *O City of Byzantium!, Annals of Niketas Choniates*, trans. H. Magoulias (Detroit, 1984).

Odo of Deuil, *De Profectione Ludovici VII in Orientem*, ed. and trans. V. Berry (New York, 1948).

Ogerio Pane, *Annales Ianuenses, Annali genovesi di Caffaro e de' suoi continuatori dal MXCIX al MCCXCIII*, eds L. Belgrano and C. Imperiale di Sant'Angelo (5 vols, Fonti per la storia d'Italia, Genoa, 1890–1929), II, 67–154.

Orderic Vitalis, *Ecclesiastical History*, ed. and trans. M. Chibnall (6 vols, Oxford Medieval Texts, Oxford, 1969–80).

Otto of Freising, *Gesta Friderici: Ottonis et Rahewini Gesta Friderici I. Imperatoris*, ed. G. Waitz (Monumenta Germaniae Historica, Scriptores rerum Germanicarum, Hanover–Leipzig, 1912).

Otto of Freising, *The Deeds of Frederick Barbarossa*, trans. C. Mierow (New York, 1953).

Ottobono Scriba, *Annales Ianuenses, Annali genovesi di Caffaro e de' suoi continuatori dal MXCIX al MCCXCIII*, eds L. Belgrano and C. Imperiale di Sant'Angelo (5 vols, Fonti per la storia d'Italia, Genoa, 1890–1929), II, 3–66.

Peter of Eboli, *De rebus Siculis carmen*, ed. E. Rota (Rerum Italicarum Scriptores, ser. 2, vol. XXXI, part I, Città di Castello, 1904).

Peter of Eboli, *Liber ad honorem Augusti sive de rebus Siculis, Codex 120 II der Burgerbibliothek Bern*, eds T. Kolser and M. Stahli, trans. G. Becht-Jordens (Sigmaringen, 1994).

Peter Tudebode, *Historia de Hierosolymitano Itinere*, trans. J. and L. Hill (Philadelphia, 1974).

Peter Tudebode, *Petri Tudebodi seu Todebovis sacerdotis Sivracensis historia de Hierosolymitano itinere, Recueil des historiens des croisades, Historiens occidentaux*, ed. Académie des Inscriptions et Belles Lettres (5 vols, Paris, 1844–95), III, 1–117.

Philip of Novara, *Mémoires (1218–1243)*, ed. Charles Kohler (Paris, 1913).

Philip of Novara, *The Wars of Frederick II against the Ibelins in Syria and Cyprus*, trans. J. LaMonte with M. Hubert (New York, 1936).

Pirro, Roccho, *Sicilia sacra*, ed. A. Mongitore (2 vols, 3rd edn, Palermo, 1733).

Ralph of Caen, *The Gesta Tancredi of Ralph of Caen, A History of the Normans on the First Crusade*, trans. B. Bachrach and D. Bachrach (Aldershot, 2005).

Raymond of Aguilers, *Historia Francorum Qui Ceperunt Iherusalem*, trans. J. and L. Hill (Philadelphia, 1968).

Raymond of Aguilers, Le 'Liber' de Raymond D'Aguilers, ed. J. and L. Hill, trans. P. Wolff (Paris, 1969).

Raymond of Aguilers, Raimundi de Aguilers canonici Podiensis historia Francorum qui ceperunt Iherusalem, Recueil des historiens des croisades, Historiens occidentaux, ed. Académie des Inscriptions et Belles Lettres (5 vols, Paris, 1844–95), III, 235–309.

Regesta pontificum Romanorum ab condita ecclesia ad annum post Christum natum MCXCVIII, eds P. Jaffé, S. Loewenfeld, F. Kaltenbrunner and P. Ewald (2 vols, 2nd edn, Leipzig, 1885–8).

Regesta regni Hierosolymitani 1097–1291, ed. R. Rohricht (Innsbruck, 1893); Additamentum (Innsbruck, 1904).

Richard of San Germano, Ryccardi de Sancto Germano Notarii Chronica, ed. C. Garufi (Rerum Italicarum Scriptores, 2nd edn, Bologna, 1938), 3–25. Partial English translation by G. A. Loud at Medieval History Texts in Translation (University of Leeds, 2006), http://www.leeds.ac.uk/history/weblearning/MedievalHistory TextCentre/medievalTexts/html.

Robert of Clari, The Conquest of Constantinople, trans. E. McNeal (New York, 1936).

Rodulfus Glaber, Opera: The Five Books of the Histories, ed. and trans. J. France (Oxford Medieval Texts, Oxford, 1989).

Roger of Howden, The Annals of Roger de Hoveden, trans. H. Riley (2 vols, London, 1853).

Roger of Howden, Chronica, ed. W. Stubbs (4 vols, Rolls Series, Rerum Britannicarum Medii Aevi Scriptores, 51, London, 1868–71).

Roger of Howden, Gesta Regis Henrici Secundi, ed. W. Stubbs (2 vols, Rolls Series, Rerum Britannicarum Medii Aevi Scriptores, 49, London, 1867).

Rogerii II. Regis Diplomata Latina, ed. C. Brühl (Codex diplomaticus regni Siciliae, Ser. I. ii, 1, Cologne–Vienna, 1987).

Romuald of Salerno, Romualdi Salernitani Chronicon, ed. C. Garufi (Rerum Italicarum Scriptores, 2nd edn, vol. VII, Città di Castello, 1935).

Salem Maragone, Gli annales Pisani di Bernardo Maragone, ed. L. Gentile (Rerum Italicarum Scriptores, 2nd edn, Bologna, 1936), anni 1182–1192, 72–74.

Sigeberti Gemblacensis Chronica: Continuatio Praemonstratensis, a. 1113–1155, ed. D. Bethman (Monumenta Germaniae Historica, Scriptores, VI, Hanover, 1844), 447–456.

Snorre Sturluson, Heimskringla or The Lives of the Norse Kings, ed. and trans. E. Monsen and A. H. Smith (Cambridge, 1932).

Starrabba, R., ed., I Diplomi della cattedrale di Messina (Documenti per servire alla storia di Sicilia, Ser. I. I, Palermo, 1876–90).

Stürner, W., ed., Die Konstitutionen Friedrichs II für das Königreich Sizilien (CAPIR, II, Supplementum, Hanover, 1996).

Sullivan, D., ed. and trans., Siegecraft: Two Tenth-Century Instruction Manuals by 'Heron of Byzantium' (Washington, DC, 2000).

Syianos Magistros, Naval Battles of Syrianos Magistros, ed. and trans. E. Jeffreys, The Age of ΔΡΟΜΩΝ (Dromōn), The Byzantine Navy ca 500–1204 (Leiden, 2006), Appendix I, 455–481.

Tabula de Amalpha, ed. V. Giuffre (Cava dei Tirreni, 1965).

Tafel, G. and G. Thomas, eds, Urkunden zur älteren Handels- und Staatsgeschichte *der Republik Venedig* (2 vols, Fontes Rerum Austriacarum, section II, vol. XII, Vienna, 1856).

Tancredi et Willelmi III Regum Diplomata, ed. H. Zielinsky (Codex diplomaticus regni Siciliae, Ser. I. v., Cologne–Vienna, 1982).

Testi Storici Veneziani (XI–XIII secolo), ed. and trans. L. Berto (Padova, 1999).

Theophanes, *The Chronicle of Theophanes Confessor: Byzantine and Near Eastern History, AD 284–813*, ed. and trans. C. Mango and R. Scott (Oxford, 1997).

Thietmar of Merseburg, *Die Chronik von Bischofs Thietmar von Merseburg*, ed. R. Holtzman (Monumenta Germaniae Historica, Scriptores Rerum Germanicarum, Berlin, 1935).

Thietmar of Merseburg, *Ottonian Germany: The Chronicon of Thietmar of Merseburg*, trans. D. Warner (Manchester, 2001).

Vegetius, *Epitome of Military Science*, trans. N. Milner (Liverpool, 1993).

Vita S. Nili Abbatis, Acta Sanctorum, ed. Societé des Bollandistes (68 vols, Antwerp and Brussels, 1643–1940), *Septembris* VII, 279–343.

Wace, *The History of the Norman People (Roman de Rou)*, trans. G. Burgess, notes by G. Burgess and E. van Houts (Woodbridge, 2004).

Walter Map, *De Nugis Curialium (Courtiers' Trifles)*, ed. and trans. M. James (Oxford Medieval Texts, Oxford, 1983).

William of Apulia, *La Geste de Robert Guiscard*, ed. M. Mathieu (Istituto siciliano di studi bizantini e neoellenici, 4, Palermo, 1961). English translation by G. A. Loud at *Medieval History Texts in Translation* (Leeds, 2006), http://www.leeds.ac.uk/history/weblearning/MedievalHistoryTextCentre/medievalTexts/html.

William of Jumièges, Orderic Vitalis, and Robert of Torigini, *The Gesta Normannorum Ducum*, ed. and trans. E. van Houts (2 vols, Oxford Medieval Texts, Oxford, 1995).

William of Tyre, *A History of Deeds Done beyond the Sea*, trans. E. Babcock and A. Krey (2 vols, New York, 1943).

William of Tyre, *Historia rerum in partibus transmarinis gestarum*, ed. R. Huygens (Corpus Christianorum, Continuatio mediaevalis, 2 vols, Turnhout, 1986).

William of Tyre, *The Old French Continuation of William of Tyre 1184–1197, The Conquest of Jerusalem and the Third Crusade*, trans. P. Edbury (Aldershot, 1998).

Zecchino, O., *Le Assise di Ariano: Testo critico, traduzione e note* (Cava dei Tirreni, 1984).

Secondary Sources

Abulafia, D., 'Ancona, Byzantium and the Adriatic, 1155–1173', *Papers of the British School at Rome*, LII (1984), 195–216. Reprinted in D. Abulafia, *Italy, Sicily and the Mediterranean, 1100–1400* (London, 1987), essay no. IX.

Abulafia, D., 'L'Attività commerciale genovese nell'Africa normanna: la città di Tripoli', *Atti del Congresso Internazionale di Studi sulla Sicilia Normanna*, (395–402) (1973), 1–8. Reprinted in D. Abulafia, *Commerce and Conquest in the Mediterranean, 1100–1500* (Aldershot, 1993), essay no. IV.

Abulafia, D., *Commerce and Conquest in the Mediterranean, 1100–1500* (Aldershot, 1993).

Abulafia, D., 'The Crown and the Economy under Roger II and his Successors', *Dumbarton Oaks Papers*, XXXVII (1983), 1–14. Reprinted in D. Abulafia, *Italy, Sicily and the Mediterranean, 1100–1400* (London, 1987), essay no. I.

Abulafia, D., 'Dalmation Ragusa and the Norman Kingdom of Sicily', *The Slavonic and East European Review*, LIV (1976), 412–428. Reprinted in D. Abulafia, *Italy, Sicily and the Mediterranean, 1100–1400* (London, 1987), essay no. X.

Abulafia, D., *Frederick II, A Medieval Emperor* (London, 1988).

Abulafia, D., 'Henry Count of Malta and his Mediterranean Activities, 1203–1230', in *Medieval Malta: Studies on Malta before the Knights*, ed. A. T. Lutrell (Supplementary Monograph of the British School at Rome) (1975), 104–125. Reprinted in D. Abulafia, *Italy, Sicily and the Mediterranean, 1100–1400* (London, 1987), essay no. III.

Abulafia, D., ed., *Italy in the Central Middle Ages* (Oxford, 2004).

Abulafia, D., *Italy, Sicily and the Mediterranean, 1100–1400* (London, 1987).

Abulafia, D., ed., *The Mediterranean in History* (London, 2003).

Abulafia, D., 'The merchants of Messina: Levant trade and domestic economy', *Papers of the British School at Rome*, LIV (1986), 196–212. Reprinted in D. Abulafia, *Commerce and Conquest in the Mediterranean, 1100–1500* (Aldershot, 1993), essay no. XII.

Abulafia, D., 'The Norman Kingdom of Africa and the Norman Expeditions to Majorca and the Muslim Mediterranean', *Anglo-Norman Studies*, VII (1985), 26–49. Reprinted in D. Abulafia, *Italy, Sicily and the Mediterranean, 1100–1400* (London, 1987), essay no. XII.

Abulafia, D., 'Pisan commercial colonies and consulates in twelfth-century Sicily', *English Historical Review*, 93 (1978), 68–81. Reprinted in D. Abulafia, *Commerce and Conquest in the Mediterranean, 1100–1500* (Aldershot, 1993), essay no. VI.

Abulafia, D., *The Two Italies: Economic Relations between the Norman Kingdom of Sicily and the Northern Communes* (Cambridge, 1977).

Abulafia, D., *The Western Mediterranean Kingdoms 1200–1500: The Struggle for Dominion* (London, 1997).

Abun-Nasr, J., *A History of the Maghrib in the Islamic Period* (Cambridge, 1987).

Ahmad, A., *A History of Islamic Sicily* (Edinburgh, 1975).

Ahrweiler, H., *Byzance et la mer: la marine de guerre, la politique et les institutions maritimes de Byzance au VII–XV siècles* (Paris, 1966).

Albu, E., *The Normans in their Histories* (Woodbridge, 2001).

Alertz, U., 'The Naval Architecture and Oar Systems of Medieval and Later Galleys', in *The Age of the Galley, Mediterranean Oared Vessels since Pre-Classical Times*, eds R. Gardiner and J. Morrison (London, 1995), 142–162.

Amari, M., *Storia dei Musulmani di Sicilia*, ed. C. Nallino (3 vols, 2nd edn, Catania, 1935–9).

Anderson, R., *Oared Fighting Ships* (London, 1962).

Antoniadis-Bibicou, H., *Études d'histoire maritime de Byzance: à propos du 'Thème des Caravisiens'* (Paris, 1966).

Atiya, A., *Crusade, Commerce and Culture* (New York, 1962).

Bachrach, B., 'On the Origins of William the Conqueror's Horse Transports', *Technology and Culture*, XXVI (1985), 505–531.

Bachrach, B., 'Some Observations on the Military Administration of the Norman Conquest', *Anglo-Norman Studies*, VIII (1985), 1–25.

Basch, L., 'Ancient wrecks and the archaeology of ships', *The International Journal of Nautical Archaeology and Underwater Exploration*, I (1972), 1–58.

Bass, G., *History of seafaring based on underwater archaeology* (London, 1972).

Bass, G. and F. van Doorninck, 'An 11th century shipwreck at Serçe Liman, Turkey', *American Institute of Nautical Archaeology*, 7.2 (1978), 119–132.

Bass, G. and F. van Doorninck, *Yassi Ada: A Seventh-Century Byzantine Shipwreck* (College Station, 1982).

Bass, G., S. Matthews, J. R. Steffy and F. van Doorninck, *Serçe Limani: An Eleventh-Century Shipwreck* (College Station, 2004).

Beech, G., 'A Norman-Italian Adventurer in the East: Richard of Salerno 1097–1112', *Anglo-Norman Studies*, XV (1993), 25–40.

Bennett, M., 'Norman Naval Activity in the Mediterranean c.1060–c. 1108', *Anglo-Norman Studies*, XV (1993), 41–58.

Bennett, M., 'The Normans in the Mediterranean', in *A Companion to the Anglo-Norman World*, eds C. Harper-Bill and E. van Houts (Woodbridge, 2003), 87–102.

Bibicou, H., 'Une page d'histoire diplomatique de Byzance au XIe siècle: Michel VII Doukas, Robert Guiscard et la pension de dignitaires', *Byzantion*, XXIX–XXX (1959–60), 43–75.

Bonino, M., 'Lateen-rigged medieval ships. New evidence from wrecks in the Po Delta (Italy) and notes on pictorial and other documents', *The International Journal of Nautical Archaeology and Underwater Exploration*, 7.1 (1978), 9–28.

Bradbury, J., *The Medieval Siege* (Woodbridge, 1992).

Bragadin, M., *Histoire des republiques maritimes italiennes: Venise – Amalfi – Pise – Gênes* (Paris, 1955).

Bréhier, L., 'La Marine de Byzance du VIII au XI siècle', *Byzantion*, XIX (1949), 1–16.

Brown, R., *The Normans* (Woodbridge, 1984).

Bünemann, R., *Robert Guiskard 1015–1085. Eine Normanner erobert Süditalien* (Cologne, 1997).

Bury, J., 'The Naval Policy of the Roman Empire in Relation to the Western Provinces, from the 7th to the 9th century', *Scritti per Il Centenario della Nascita di Michele Amari*, II (Palemo, 1910, reprinted 1990), 1–14.

Busch, S., *Medieval Mediterranean Ports: The Catalan and Tuscan Coasts, 1100 to 1235* (Leiden, 2001).

Byrne, E., 'Genoese Colonies in Syria', in *The Crusades and other Historical Essays presented to Dana C. Munro by his former students*, ed. L. Paetow (New York, 1928), 139–182.

Byrne, E., *Genoese Shipping in the Twelfth and Thirteenth Centuries* (Cambridge, 1930).

Camera, M., *Istoria della Città e Costiera di Amalfi* (Napoli, 1836).

Camera, M., *Memorie storico-diplomatiche dell'antica città e ducato di Amalfi* (2 vols, Salerno, 1876–81).

Canard, M., 'Une lettre du calife Fātimite al-Hafiz (524–544/1130–1149) à Roger II', *Studi Ruggeriani, VIII Centenario della morte di Ruggero II, Atti del Convegno internazionale di studi ruggeriani (Palermo, 21–25 aprile 1954)* (2 vols, Palermo, 1955), I, 125–146. Reprinted in M. Canard, *Miscellanea Orientalia* (London, 1973).

Capitani, O., 'Specific Motivations and Continuing Themes in the Norman Chronicles of Southern Italy in the Eleventh and Twelfth Centuries', *The Normans in
Sicily and Southern Italy, The Lincei Lectures* (Oxford, 1977), 1–46.

Carile, A. and S. Cosentino, *Storia della Marineria Bizantina* (Bologna, 2004).

Caspar, E., *Roger II und die Gründung der Normannisch-sicilischen Monarchie* (Innsbruck, 1904).

Casson, L., 'Merchant Galleys', in *The Age of the Galley, Mediterranean Oared Vessels
since Pre-Classical Times*, eds R. Gardiner and J. Morrison (London, 1995), 117–126.

Casson, L., *Ships and Seamanship in the Ancient World* (Princeton, 1971).

Casson, L. and J. R. Steffy, eds, *The Athlit Ram* (College Station, 1991).

Chalandon, F., *Histoire de la Domination Normande en Italie et en Sicile* (2 vols, Paris,
1907).

Chibnall, M., *The Normans* (Oxford, 2000).

Christides, V., 'Arab–Byzantine Struggle in the Sea: Naval Tactics (7th–11th C.
A.D.): Theory and Practice', in *Aspects of Arab Seafaring: An Attempt to Fill in
the Gaps of Maritime History*, eds Y. Yousef Al-Hijji, V. Christides, P. Moschona
and C. Makrypoulias (Athens, 2002), 87–103.

Christides, V., *The Conquest of Crete by the Arabs (ca. 824): a turning point in the
struggle between Byzantium and Islam* (Athens, 1984).

Christides, V., 'Ibn al-Manqalī (Manglī) and Leo VI: new evidence on Arabo-Byzan-
tine ship construction and naval warfare', *Byzantinoslavica*, 56 (1995), 83–96.

Christides, V., 'Naval warfare in the Eastern Mediterranean (6th–14th centuries): an
Arabic translation of Leo VI's Naumachica', *Graeco-Arabica*, III (1984), 137–148.

Christides, V., 'Two parallel naval guides of the tenth century: Qudāma's document
and Leo VI's Naumachica: a study on Byzantine and Moslem naval preparedness',
Graeco-Arabica, I (1982), 51–103.

Cilento, A., and A. Vanoli, *Arabs and Normans in Sicily and the South of Italy* (New
York, 2007).

Citarella, A., 'A Puzzling Question concerning the Relations between the Jewish
Communities of Christian Europe and Those Represented in the Geniza Documents', *Journal of the American Oriental Society*, XCI (1971), 390–397.

Citarella, A., 'The Relations of Amalfi with the Arab World Before the Crusades',
Speculum, XLII (1967), 299–313.

Clementi, D., 'Some Unnoticed Aspects of the Emperor Henry's Conquest of the
Norman Kingdom of Sicily', *Bulletin of the John Rylands Library of the University
of Manchester*, XXXVI (1954), 328–359.

Cohn, W., *Die Geschichte der normannisch-sicilischen Flotte unter der Regierung Rogers
I. und Rogers II. (1060–1154)* (Breslau, 1910).

Cohn, W., *Die Geschichte der sizilischen Flotte unter der Regierung Frederichs II. (1197–
1250)* (Breslau, 1926).

Contamine, P., *La Guerre au moyen âge* (Paris, 1980).

Cowdrey, H., *Age of Abbot Desiderius: Montecassino, the Papacy, and the Normans in
the Eleventh and Early Twelfth Centuries* (Oxford, 1983).

Cowdrey, H., 'The Mahdia campaign of 1087', *The English Historical Review*,
CCCLXII (1977), 1–29.

Crawford, F., *The Rulers of the South* (2 vols, New York, 1900).

Cuozzo, E. and J. Martin, eds, *Cavalieri alla conquista del Sud* (Bari, 1998).

Curtis, E., *Roger of Sicily and the Normans in Lower Italy 1016–1154* (New York, 1912).

Dalli, C., *The Medieval Millennium* (Malta, 2006).

D'Antuono, A., *Amalfi, L'Antica Repubblica Marinara* (Salerno, 2000).

Davis, R., *The Medieval Warhorse* (London, 1989).

Davis, R., *The Normans and their Myth* (London, 1976).

Delarc, O., *Les Normands en Italie, depuis les premières invasions jusqu'à l'avénement de S. Grégoire VII (859–862, 1016–1073)* (Paris, 1883).

Del Treppo, M. and A. Leone, *Amalfi Medioevale* (Napoli, 1977).

Deuve, J., *Les Opérations Navales Normandes au Moyen Âge (900–1200)* (Condé-sur-Noireau, 2000).

Dimmock, L., 'The lateen rig', *The Mariner's Mirror*, XXXII, (1946), 35–41.

Di Stefano, G., 'Antichi relitti nella baia di Camarina', in *Atti, IV rassegna di archeologia subacquea*, ed. P. Gianfrotta (Messina, 1991), 127–134.

Di Stefano, G., *Monumenti della Sicilia Normanna* (Palermo, 1955).

Dolley, R., 'The Lord High Admiral Eustathios Argyros and the Betrayal of Taormina to the African Arabs in 902', *Atti dello VIII congresso di studi bizantini*, I (Rome, 1953), 340–353.

Dolley, R., 'Naval Tactics in the heyday of the Byzantine thalassocraty', *Atti dello VIII congresso di studi bizantini*, I (Rome, 1953), 324–339.

Dolley, R., 'The rig of early medieval warships', *The Mariner's Mirror*, XXXV (1949), 51–55.

Dolley, R., 'The warships of the later Roman empire', *Journal of Roman Studies*, XXXVIII (1948), 47–53.

Dotson, J., 'Economics and Logistics of Galley Warfare', in *The Age of the Galley, Mediterranean Oared Vessels since Pre-Classical Times*, eds R. Gardiner and J. Morrison (London, 1995), 217–223.

Dotson, J., 'Ships types and fleet composition at Genoa and Venice in the early thirteenth century', in *Logistics of Warfare in the Age of the Crusades*, ed. J. Pryor (Aldershot, 2006), 63–93.

Douglas, D., *The Norman Achievement 1050–1100* (London, 1969).

Drell, J., *Kinship and Conquest: Family Strategies in the Principality of Salerno during the Norman Period, 1077–1194* (Ithaca, 2002).

Ducellier, A., *La façade maritime de l'Albanie au Moyen Âge: Durazzo et Valona du Xle au Xve siècle* (Thessaloniki, 1981).

Ehrenkruetz, A., 'The place of Saladin in the naval history of the Mediterranean Sea in the Middle Ages', *Journal of the American Oriental Society*, LXXV (1955), 100–116.

Eickhoff, E., 'Byzantinische Wachtflottillen in Unteritalien im 10 Jahrundert', *Byzantinische Zeitschrift*, XLV (1952), 340–344.

Eickhoff, E., *Seekrieg und Seepolitik zwischen Islam und Abendland: das Mittelmeer unter byzantinischer und arabischer Hegemonie, 650–1040* (Berlin, 1966).

Epstein, S., *Genoa and the Genoese, 958–1528* (Chapel Hill, 1996).

Fahmy, A., *Muslim Sea Power in the Eastern Mediterranean from the Seventh to the Tenth Centuries* (London, 1950).

Fernández-Armesto, F., 'Naval Warfare after the Viking Age, c. 1100–1500', in *Medieval Warfare*, ed. M. Keen (Oxford, 1999), 230–252.

Fossier, R., ed., *The Cambridge Illustrated History of the Middle Ages, 950–1250*, II (Cambridge, 1997).

France, J., 'The occasion of the coming of the Normans to southern Italy', *Journal of Medieval History*, XVII (1991), 185–205.

France, J., *Victory in the East, A Military History of the First Crusade* (Cambridge, 1994).

France, J., *Western Warfare in the Age of the Crusades, 1000–1300* (Ithaca, 1999).

Gabrieli, F., trans. and ed., *Arab Historians of the Crusades*, trans. from Italian by E. J. Costello (Turin, 1957).

Gabrieli, F. and U. Scerrato, *Gli Arabi in Italia* (Milan, 1979).

Gardiner, R. and J. Morrison, eds, *The Age of the Galley, Mediterranean Oared Vessels since Pre-Classical Times* (London, 1995).

Gardner, R. and R. Unger, eds, *Cogs, Caravels and Galleons: The Sailing Ship 1000–1650* (London, 1994).

Garufi, C., 'Margarito di Brindisi Conte di Malta e Ammiraglio del Re di Sicilia', *Miscellanea di Archeologia, Storia e Filologia dedicata al Prof. Antonino Salinas* (Palermo, 1907), 273–282.

Gay, J., *L'Italie méridionale et l'empire byzantine depuis l'avènement de Basile I jusqu'à la prise de Bari par les Normands (867–1071)* (Paris, 1904).

Gertwagen, R., 'Harbours and facilities along the eastern Mediterranean sea lanes to Outremer', in *Logistics of Warfare in the Age of the Crusades*, ed. J. Pryor (Aldershot, 2006), 95–118.

Gillingham, J., 'An Age of Expansion, c. 1020–1204', in *Medieval Warfare*, ed. M. Keen (Oxford, 1999), 59–88.

Gillmor, C., 'Naval logistics of the cross-Channel operation, 1066', *Anglo-Norman Studies*, VII (1984).

Giovanni, V., *La topografia antica di Palermo dal secolo X al XV* (Palermo, 1890).

Goitein, S., 'Glimpses from the Cairo Geniza on naval warfare in the Mediterranean and on the Mongol invasion', *Studi Orientalistici in onore di Giorgio Levi della Vida*, I (Roma, 1956), 393–408.

Goitein, S., *A Mediterranean Society*, I, *Economic Foundations* (Berkeley and Los Angeles, 1967).

Gregorio, R., *Considerazioni supra la storia di Sicilia dai tempi dei Normanni sino ai presenti* (6 vols, Palermo, 1805–16).

Grierson, P. and L. Travaini, *Medieval European Coinage*, 14, *Italy (III) (South Italy, Sicily, Sardinia)* (Cambridge, 1998).

Guilmartin, J., *Gunpowder and Galleys: Changing Technology and Mediterranean Warfare at Sea in the 16th Century* (Cambridge, 1974, revised 2003).

Halphen, L., 'La conquête de la Méditerranée par les Européens au XI et au XII siècles', *Mélanges d'histoire offerts à Henri Pirenne*, I (1926), 175–180.

Harper-Bill, C. and E. van Houts, eds, *A Companion to the Anglo-Norman World* (Woodbridge, 2003).

Haskins, C., *The Normans in European History* (Boston and New York, 1915).

Hattendorf, J. and R. Unger, eds, *War at Sea in the Middle Ages and the Renaissance* (Woodbridge, 2003).

Haywood, J., *Dark Age Naval Power: A Re-Assessment of Frankish and Anglo-Saxon Seafaring Activity* (London, 1991).

Heyd, W., *Histoire du commerce du Levant au moyen-âge*, trans. F. Raynaud (Leipzig, 1885–6).

Heywood, W., *A History of Pisa, Eleventh and Twelfth Centuries* (Cambridge, 1921).

Hocker, F., 'Late Roman, Byzantine, and Islamic Galleys and Fleets', in *The Age of the Galley, Mediterranean Oared Vessels since Pre-Classical Times*, eds R. Gardiner and J. Morrison (London, 1995), 86–100.

Hocker, F., 'A Ninth-century Shipwreck near Bozburun, Turkey', *Institute of Nautical Archeaology Quarterly*, 22.1 (1995), 12–14.

Hocker, F., 'Sampling a Byzantine Vintage: Bozburun, Turkey', in *Beneath the Seven Seas*, ed. G. Bass (New York, 2005), 100–105.

Hooper, N. and M. Bennett, *Cambridge Illustrated Atlas: Warfare – The Middle Ages, 768–1487* (Cambridge, 1996).

Horden, P. and N. Purcell, *The Corrupting Sea, A Study of Mediterranean History* (Oxford, 2000).

Houben, H., *Roger II of Sicily, A Ruler between East and West*, trans. G. Loud and D. Milburn (Cambridge, 2002).

Hutchinson, G., *Medieval Ships and Shipping* (London, 1994).

Idris, H., *La Berbérie Orientale sous les Zīrīdes, X–XII siècles* (2 vols, Paris, 1962).

Jamison, E., *Admiral Eugenius of Sicily, his life and work* (London, 1975).

Jamison, E., 'The Sicilian Norman Kingdom in the Mind of Anglo-Norman Contemporaries', *Proceedings of the British Academy*, XXIV (1938), 1–51. Reprinted in E. Jamison, *Studies on the History of Medieval Sicily and South Italy*, eds D. Clementi and T. Kolzer (Aalen, 1992), 159–207.

Jamison, E., *Studies on the History of Medieval Sicily and South Italy*, eds D. Clementi and T. Kolzer (Aalen, 1992).

Johns, J., *Arabic Administration in Norman Sicily, The Royal Dīwān* (Cambridge, 2002).

Johns, J., 'The Norman Kings of Sicily and the Fatimid Caliphate', *Anglo-Norman Studies*, XV (1992), 133–159.

Joranson, E., 'The Inception of the Career of the Normans in Italy – Legend and History', *Speculum*, XXIII (1948), 353–396.

Keen, M., ed., *Medieval Warfare, A History* (Oxford, 1999).

Kehr, K., *Urkunden der Normannisch-Sicilischen Könige* (Innsbruck, 1902).

Kehr, P., *Die Belehnungen der süditalienischen Normannenfürsten durch die Päpste, 1059–1192* (Berlin, 1934).

Khalilieh, H., *Admiralty and Maritime Laws in the Mediterranean Sea (ca. 800–1050): The Kitāb Akriyat al-Sufun vis-à-vis the Nomos Rhodion Nautikos* (Leiden, 2006).

Kocabaş, U., ed., *The 'Old Ships' of the 'New Gate', Yenikapi Shipwrecks, Vol. I* (Istanbul, 2008).

Kolias, T., 'The *Taktika* of Leo VI the Wise and the Arabs', *Graeco-Arabica*, III (1984), 129–136.

Kreutz, B., *Before the Normans, Southern Italy in the Ninth and Tenth Centuries* (Philadelphia, 1991).

Kreutz, B., 'Ships, Shipping and the Implications of Change in the Early Medieval Mediterranean', *Viator*, VII (1976), 79–109.

Krueger, H., 'The Wares of Exchange in the Genoese–African Traffic of the Twelfth Century', *Speculum*, XII (1937), 57–71.

Lane, F., *Venetian Ships and Shipbuilders of the Renaissance* (Baltimore, 1934).

Lane, F., *Venice, A Maritime Republic* (Baltimore, 1973).

Lev, Y., 'The Fatimid navy; Byzantium and the Mediterranean Sea 909–1036CE, 297–427AH', *Byzantion*, LIV (1984), 220–252.

Lewis, A., *Naval power and trade in the Mediterranean, A.D. 500–1100* (Princeton, 1951).

Lewis, A. and T. Runyan, *European Naval and Maritime History, 300–1500* (Bloomington, 1985).

Lopez, R., 'Market Expansion: The Case of Genoa', *Journal of Economic History*, XXIV (1964), 445–464.

Lopez, R. and I. Raymond, eds and trans., *Medieval Trade in the Mediterranean World, Illustrative Documents* (New York, 1955).

Loud, G. A., 'Anna Komnena and her Sources for the Normans of Southern Italy', in *Church and Chronicle in the Middle Ages. Essays presented to John Taylor*, ed. I. Wood and G. Loud (London, 1991), 41–57. Reprinted in G. Loud, *Conquerors and Churchmen in Norman Italy* (Aldershot, 1999), essay no. XIII.

Loud, G. A., *The Age of Robert Guiscard: Southern Italy and the Norman Conquest* (Harlow, 2000).

Loud, G. A., 'Byzantine Italy and the Normans', in *Proceedings of the XVII Spring Symposium of Byzantine Studies*, ed. J. Howard Johnson (Amsterdam, 1984), 215–233. Reprinted in G. A. Loud, *Conquerors and Churchmen in Norman Italy* (Aldershot, 1999), essay no. III.

Loud, G. A., *Church and Society in the Norman Principality of Capua 1058–1197* (Oxford, 1985).

Loud, G. A., 'Church, Warfare and Military Obligation in Norman Italy', *Studies in Church History*, XX (1983), 31–45. Reprinted in G. Loud, *Conquerors and Churchmen in Norman Italy* (Aldershot, 1999), essay no. XI.

Loud, G. A., *Conquerors and Churchmen in Norman Italy* (Aldershot, 1999).

Loud, G. A., 'The Genesis and Context of the Chronicle of Falco of Benevento', *Anglo-Norman Studies*, XV (1991), 177–198.

Loud, G. A., 'The *Gens Normannorum* – Myth or Reality?', *Anglo-Norman Studies*, IV (1982), 104–116. Reprinted in G. A. Loud, *Conquerors and Churchmen in Norman Italy* (Aldershot, 1999), essay no. I.

Loud, G. A., 'How Norman was the Norman Conquest of Southern Italy?', *Nottingham Medieval Studies*, XXV (1981), 13–34. Reprinted in G. A. Loud, *Conquerors and Churchmen in Norman Italy* (Aldershot, 1999), essay no. II.

Loud, G. A., *The Latin Church in Norman Italy* (Cambridge, 2007).

Loud, G. A., *Montecassino and Benevento in the Middle Ages* (Aldershot, 2000).

Loud, G. A., 'Norman Sicily in the twelfth century', in *New Cambridge Medieval History*, IV, *c.1024–c.1198*, Part II, eds D. Luscombe and J. Riley-Smith (Cambridge, 2004), 442–474.

Loud, G. A., 'Southern Italy in the tenth century', in *New Cambridge Medieval History*, III, *c.900–c.1024*, ed. T. Reuter (Cambridge, 1999), 624–645.

Loud, G. A., 'Southern Italy in the eleventh century', in *New Cambridge Medieval History*, IV, *c.1024–c.1198*, Part II, eds D. Luscombe and J. Riley-Smith (Cambridge, 2004), 94–119.

Loud, G. A. and A. Metcalfe, eds, *The Society of Norman Italy* (Leiden, 2002).

Luscombe, D. and J. Riley-Smith, eds, *New Cambridge Medieval History*, IV, *c.1024–c.1198*, Parts I and II (Cambridge, 2004).

Maalouf, A., *The Crusades through Arab Eyes* (London, 1984).

Mack Smith, D., *A History of Medieval Sicily, 800–1713* (London, 1969).

Mahan, A., *The Influence of Sea Power upon History, 1660–1783* (London, 1890).

Makrypoulias, C., 'Byzantine expeditions against the emirate of Crete c. 825–949', *Graeco-Arabica*, 7–8 (1999–2000), 347–362.

Makrypoulias, C., 'Muslim Ships through Byzantine Eyes', in *Aspects of Arab Seafaring: An Attempt to Fill in the Gaps of Maritime History*, eds Y. Al-Hijji, V. Christides, P. Moschona and C. Makrypoulias (Athens, 2002), 179–189.

Makrypoulias, C., 'The Navy in the Works of Constantine Porphyrogenitus', *Graeco-Arabica*, VI (1995), 152–171.

Manfroni, C., *Storia della Marina italiana dalle invasioni barbariche al trattato di Ninfeo, anni di C. 400–1261*, I (Livorno, 1899).

Martin, J., *Italies Normandes XIe–XIIe siècles* (Paris, 1994).

Matthew, D., *Norman Kingdom of Sicily* (Cambridge, 1992).

McGeer, E., *Sowing the Dragon's Teeth: Byzantine Warfare in the Tenth Century* (Washington, DC, 1995).

McQueen, W., 'Relations between the Normans and Byzantium, 1071–1112', *Byzantion*, LVI (1986), 427–476.

Ménager, L.-R., *Amiratus-Ἀμηρᾶς, L'Emirat et les origines de l'amirauté (XI–XIII siècle)* (Paris, 1960).

Ménager, L.-R., 'Inventaire des familles normandes et franques emigrées en Italie méridionale et en Sicile (XIe–XIIe siècles)', *Roberto il Guiscardo e il suo tempo: relazioni e communicazioni nelle prime giornate normanno-sveve* (Bari, 1975), 261–390.

Metcalfe, A., *Muslims and Christians in 'Norman' Sicily: Arab Speakers and the End of Islam* (London, 2002).

Moretti, U., *La Prima Repubblica Marinara d'Italia: Amalfi* (Ravenna, 1904).

Morrison, J., J. Coates and N. Rankov, *The Athenian Trireme: The History and Reconstruction of an Ancient Greek Warship* (2nd edn, Cambridge, 2000).

Mott, L., *Sea Power in the Medieval Mediterranean: The Catalan–Aragonese Fleet in the War of the Sicilian Vespers* (Gainesville, 2003).

Musca, G., *L'emirato di Bari, 847–871* (Bari, 1964).

Musset, L., *La Tapisserie de Bayeux* (Paris, 2002).

Nebbia, U., *Arte navale Italiana, Pagine di storia e d'estetica marina* (Bergamo, 1930).

Neumann, C., 'Die Byzantinische Marine', *Historiche Zeitschrift*, XLV (1898), 1–23.

Nicholson, H., *Medieval Warfare: Theory and Practice of War in Europe, 300–1500* (New York, 2004).

Norwich, J., *Byzantium, The Apogee* (New York, 1991).

Norwich, J., *A History of Venice* (New York, 1982).

Norwich, J., *The Normans in the South, 1016–1130* (London, 1967).

Norwich, J., *The Kingdom in the Sun, 1130–1194* (London, 1970).

Oman, C., *The Art of War in the Middle Ages* (2 vols, London, 1924).

Pace, B., *I Mosaici di Piazza Armerina* (Rome, 1955).

Partington, J., *A History of Greek Fire and Gunpowder* (Cambridge, 1960).

Pennington, K., 'The Normans in Palermo: King Roger II's Legislation', *Haskins Society Journal*, 18 (2006), 140–167.

Peters, E., ed., *The First Crusade: The Chronicle of Fulcher of Chartres and Other Source Materials* (Philadelphia, 1971).

Picard, C., *La mer et les musulmans d'Occident au Moyen Age: VIIIe–XIIIe siècle* (Paris, 1997).

Pirenne, H., *Medieval Cities: Their Origins and the Revival of Trade*, trans. F. Halsey (Princeton, 1952).

Pirenne, H., *Mohammed and Charlemagne*, trans. B. Miall (New York, 1992; original publication Paris, 1937).

Prawer, J., *The Crusaders' Kingdom: European Colonialism in the Middle Ages* (New York, 1972).

Pryor, J., 'Byzantium and the Sea: Byzantine Fleets and the History of the Empire in the Age of the Macedonian Emperors, C.900–1024 CE', in *War at Sea in the Middle Ages and the Renaissance*, eds J. Hattendorf and R. Unger (Woodbridge, 2003), 83–104.

Pryor, J., *Commerce, Shipping and Naval Warfare in the Medieval Mediterranean* (London, 1987).

Pryor, J., 'The Crusade of Frederick II: The Implication of the Maritime Evidence', *American Neptune*, 52 (1992), 113–132.

Pryor, J., 'From Dromōn to Galea: Mediterranean bireme galleys AD 500–1300', in *The Age of the Galley, Mediterranean Oared Vessels since Pre-Classical Times*, eds R. Gardiner and J. Morrison (London, 1995), 101–116.

Pryor, J., 'The Galleys of Charles I of Anjou, King of Sicily: ca. 1269–84', *Studies in Medieval and Renaissance History*, XIV (1993), 34–103.

Pryor, J., 'The Geographic Conditions of Galley Navigation in the Mediterranean', in *The Age of the Galley, Mediterranean Oared Vessels since Pre-Classical Times*, eds R. Gardiner and J. Morrison (London, 1995), 206–216.

Pryor, J., *Geography, Technology, and War: Studies in the maritime history of the Mediterranean, 649–1571* (Cambridge, 1988).

Pryor, J., ed., *Logistics of Warfare in the Age of the Crusades* (Aldershot, 2006).

Pryor, J., 'The Mediterranean Round Ship', in *Cogs, Caravels and Galleons: The Sailing Ship, 1000–1650*, ed. R. Gardiner (London, 1994), 59–76.

Pryor, J., 'Modelling Bohemond's march to Thessalonikē', in *Logistics of Warfare in the Age of the Crusades*, ed. J. Pryor (Aldershot, 2006), 1–24.

Pryor, J., 'The naval Architecture of Crusader Transport Ships: a Reconstruction of some Archetypes for Round-hulled Sailing Ships', *The Mariner's Mirror*, LXX (1984), 171–219, 275–292, 363–386.

Pryor, J., 'The Naval Battles of Roger of Lauria', *Journal of Medieval History*, IX (1983), 179–216.

Pryor, J., 'Transportation of horses by sea during the era of the Crusades: eighth century to 1285 AD', *The Mariner's Mirror*, LXVIII (1982), 9–27, 103–125.

Pryor, J., 'Types of ships and their performance capabilities', in *Travel in the Byzantine World: Papers from the Thirty-fourth Spring Symposium of Byzantine Studies, Birmingham, April 2000*, ed. R. Macrides (Aldershot, 2002), 33–58.

Pryor, J., 'A view from a masthead: the First Crusade from the sea', *Crusades*, VII (2008), 87–152.

Pryor, J., '"Water, water everywhere, Nor any drop to drink." Water Supplies for the Fleets of the First Crusade', in *Dei Gesta per Francos: études sur les dédiés à Jean Richard*, eds M. Balard, B. Kedar and J. Riley-Smith (Aldershot, 2001), 21–28.

Pryor, J., 'The Σταδιδρομικό (*Stadiodromikon*) of the *De Cerimoniis* of Constantine VII, Byzantine warships, and the Cretan expedition of 949', in *The Greek islands and the sea: Proceedings of the First International Colloquium held at the Hellenic Institute, Royal Holloway, University of London, 21–22 September 2001*, eds J. Chrysostimides, C. Dendrinos and J. Harris (Camberley, 2004), 77–109.

Pryor, J. and E. Jeffreys, *The Age of ΔΡΟΜΩΝ (Dromōn)*, The Byzantine Navy ca 500–1204 (Leiden, 2006).

Purpura, G., 'Un relitto di età normanna a Marsala', *Bolletino d'arte*, ser. VI, XXIX (1985), 129–136.

Reuter, T., ed., *New Cambridge Medieval History*, III, *c. 900–c.1024* (Cambridge, 1999).

Riley-Smith, J., *The Crusades, A Short History* (London, 1987).

Riley-Smith, J., *The Atlas of the Crusades* (New York, 1990).

Riley-Smith, J., *The First Crusaders, 1095–1131* (Cambridge, 1997).

Riley-Smith, J., 'Government in Latin Syria and the commercial privileges of foreign merchants', in *Relations between East and West in the Middle Ages*, ed. D. Baker (Edinburgh, 1973), 109–132.

Rogers, W., *Naval Warfare under Oars, 4th to 16th Centuries: A Study of Strategy, Tactics and Ship Design* (Annapolis, 1940).

Rose, S., 'Islam versus Christendom: The Naval Dimension, 1000–1600', *The Journal of Military History*, LXIII (1999), 561–578.

Rose, S., *Medieval Naval Warfare, 1000–1500* (London, 2002).

Rowley, T., *The Normans* (Stroud, 1999).

Rudt de Collenberg, W., 'L'Empereur Isaac de Chypre et sa fille (1155–1207)', *Byzantion*, XXXVIII (1968), 123–179.

Runciman, S., *A History of the Crusades* (3 vols, Cambridge, 1951).

Schwarz, U., *Amalfi im frühen Mittelalter (9.–11. Jahrhundert)* (Tübingen, 1978).

Shepard, J., 'The Uses of the Franks in Eleventh-Century Byzantium', *Anglo-Norman Studies*, XV (1993), 275–305.

Siragusa, G., *Il Regno di Guglielmo I in Sicilia* (Palermo, 1886).

Sismondi, J., *A History of the Italian Republics* (London, 1832).

Skinner, P., *Family Power in Southern Italy: The Duchy of Gaeta and its neighbours, 860–1139* (Cambridge, 1995).

Smail, R., *Crusading Warfare, 1097–1193* (Cambridge, 1956).

Steffy, J., 'The reconstruction of the 11th century Serçe Liman vessel: A Preliminary Report', *The International Journal of Nautical Archaeology and Underwater Exploration*, 11.1 (1982), 13–34.

Steffy, J., *Wooden Ship Building and the Interpretation of Shipwrecks* (College Station, 1994).

Takayama, H., *The Administration of the Norman Kingdom of Sicily* (Leiden, 1993).

Takayama, H., 'Law and monarchy in the south', in *Italy in the Central Middle Ages*, ed. D. Abulafia (Oxford, 2004), 58–81.

Taviani-Carozzi, H., *La Terreur du Monde. Robert Guiscard et la Conquête Normande en Italie* (Paris, 1996).

Toeche, T., *Kaiser Heinrich VI* (Liepzig, 1867).

Toynbee, A., *Constantine Porphyrogenitus and his world* (London, 1973).

Tramontana, S., 'Populazione, distribuzione della terra e classi sociali nella Sicilia di Ruggero Il Gran Conte', *Ruggero il Gran Conte e l'inizio dello stato normanno: relazioni e communicazioni nelle seconde giornate normanno-sveve* (Bari, 1977), 213–270.

Treadgold, W., *Byzantium and its Army 284–1081* (Stanford, 1995).

Tsamakda, V., *The Illustrated Chronicle of Ioannes Skylitzes in Madrid* (Leiden, 2002).

Unger, R., *The Ship in the Medieval Economy, 600–1600* (London, 1980).

Van Doorninck, F., 'The Byzantine ship at Serçe Limani: an example of small-scale maritime commerce with Fatimid Syria in the early eleventh century', in *Travel in the Byzantine World: Papers from the Thirty-fourth Spring Symposium of Byzantine Studies, Birmingham, April 2000*, ed. R. Macrides (Aldershot, 2002), 137–148.

Van Doorninck, F., 'Did tenth-century dromons have a waterline ram? Another look at Leo, *Tactica*, XIX, 69', *The Mariner's Mirror*, 79 (1993), 387–392.

Van Houts, E., ed. and trans., *The Normans in Europe* (Manchester, 2000).

Van Houts, E., 'The Ship List of William the Conqueror', *Anglo-Norman Studies*, X (1988), 159–183.

Vasiliev, A., *Byzance et les Arabes* (3 vols, Brussels, 1935–68).

Vasiliev, A., *History of the Byzantine Empire* (2 vols, Madison, 1952).

Verbruggen, J., *The Art of Warfare in Western Europe during the Middle Ages* (Amsterdam, 1977).

Waley, D., '"Combined Operations" in Sicily, A.D. 1060–78', *Papers of the British School at Rome*, XXII (1954), 118–125.

Weitzmann, K., *The miniatures of the Sacra parallela, Parisinus Graecus 923* (Princeton, 1979).

White, L., *Latin Monasticism in Norman Sicily* (Cambridge, MA, 1938).

Wilson, D., *The Bayeux Tapestry* (London, 2004).

Wolf, K., *Making History: The Normans and their Historians in Eleventh-Century Italy* (Philadelphia, 1995).

Woody, K., 'Sagena piscatoris: Peter Damiani and the papal election decree of 1059', *Viator*, I (1970), 33–54.

Wright, D., *The Roman Vergil and the Origins of Medieval Book Design* (London, 2001).

Yewdale, R., *Bohemond I, Prince of Antioch* (Princeton, 1924).

Index

Warfare in History

The Battle of Hastings: Sources and Interpretations, *edited and introduced by Stephen Morillo*

Infantry Warfare in the Early Fourteenth Century: Discipline, Tactics, and Technology, *Kelly DeVries*

The Art of Warfare in Western Europe during the Middle Ages, from the Eighth Century to 1340 (second edition), *J.F. Verbruggen*

Knights and Peasants: The Hundred Years War in the French Countryside, *Nicholas Wright*

Society at War: The Experience of England and France during the Hundred Years War, *edited by Christopher Allmand*

The Circle of War in the Middle Ages: Essays on Medieval Military and Naval History, *edited by Donald J. Kagay and L.J. Andrew Villalon*

The Anglo-Scots Wars, 1513–1550: A Military History, *Gervase Phillips*

The Norwegian Invasion of England in 1066, *Kelly DeVries*

The Wars of Edward III: Sources and Interpretations, *edited by Clifford J. Rogers*

The Battle of Agincourt: Sources and Interpretations, *Anne Curry*

War Cruel and Sharp: English Strategy under Edward III, 1327–1360, *Clifford J. Rogers*

The Normans and their Adversaries at War: Essays in Memory of C. Warren Hollister, *edited by Richard P. Abels and Bernard S. Bachrach*

The Battle of the Golden Spurs (Courtrai, 11 July 1302): A Contribution to the History of Flanders' War of Liberation, 1297–1305, *J.F. Verbruggen*

War at Sea in the Middle Ages and the Renaissance, *edited by John B. Hattendorf and Richard W. Unger*

Swein Forkbeard's Invasions and the Danish Conquest of England, 991–1017, *Ian Howard*

Religion and the conduct of war, c.300–1215, *David S. Bachrach*

Warfare in Medieval Brabant, 1356–1406, *Sergio Boffa*

Renaissance Military Memoirs: War, History and Identity, 1450–1600, *Yuval Harari*

The Place of War in English History, 1066–1214, *J.O. Prestwich, edited by Michael Prestwich*

War and the Soldier in the Fourteenth Century, *Adrian R. Bell*

German War Planning, 1891–1914: Sources and Interpretations, *Terence Zuber*

The Battle of Crécy, 1346, *Andrew Ayton and Sir Philip Preston*

The Battle of Yorktown, 1781: A Reassessment, *John D. Grainger*

Special Operations in the Age of Chivalry, 1100–1550, *Yuval Noah Harari*

Women, Crusading and the Holy Land in Historical Narrative, *Natasha R. Hodgson*

The English Aristocracy at War: From the Welsh Wars of Edward I to the Battle of Bannockburn, *David Simpkin*

The Calais Garrison: War and Military Service in England, 1436–1558, *David Grummitt*

Renaissance France at War: Armies, Culture and Society, *c.* 1480–1560, *David Potter*

Bloodied Banners: Martial Display on the Medieval Battlefield, *Robert W. Jones*

Alfred's Wars: Sources and Interpretations of Anglo-Saxon Warfare in the Viking Age, *Ryan Lavelle*

The Dutch Army and the Military Revolutions, 1588–1688, *Olaf van Nimwegen*

In the Steps of the Black Prince: The Road to Poitiers, 1355–1356, *Peter Hoskins*

Norman Naval Operations in the Mediterranean, *Charles D. Stanton*

Shipping the Medieval Military: English Maritime Logistics in the Fourteenth Century, *Craig L. Lambert*

Edward III and the War at Sea: The English Navy, 1327–1377, *Graham Cushway*

The Soldier Experience in the Fourteenth Century, *edited by Adrian R. Bell and Anne Curry*

Warfare in Tenth-Century Germany, *David S. Bachrach*

Chivalry, Kingship and Crusade: The English Experience in the Fourteenth Century, *Timothy Guard*

The Norman Campaigns in the Balkans, 1081–1108, *Georgios Theotokis*

Welsh Soldiers in the Later Middle Ages, 1282–1422, *Adam Chapman*

Merchant Crusaders in the Aegean, 1291–1352, *Mike Carr*

Henry of Lancaster's Expedition to Aquitaine, 1345-1346: Military Service and Professionalism in the Hundred Years War, *Nicholas A. Gribit*

Printed and bound by CPI Group (UK) Ltd, Croydon, CR0 4YY

13/04/2025

14656515-0005